W9-ARK-723

# Civilization

Volume I / The Emergence of Man in Society

# Writers & Advisors

**John Roberts**
Chief Academic Advisor

**Book 1**

**Helena Curtis**

**C. C. Lamberg-Karlovsky**
Harvard University

**Norman Hammond**
Cambridge University

**Liam De Paor**
University College, Dublin

**Book 2**

**John Boardman**
Ashmolean Museum, Oxford

**W. H. C. Frend**
Glasgow University

**J. M. Wallace-Hadrill**
Oxford University

**Book 3**

**R. H. C. Davis**
Birmingham University

**R. R. Davies**
London University

**Kenneth Fowler**
Edinburgh University

**Colin Morris**
Southampton University

**Book 4**

**A. L. Basham**
The Australian National University, Canberra

**Ira Lapidus**
University of California, Berkeley

**Andrew Roberts**
London University

**Charles Sheldon**
Cambridge University

**E. P. Wilkinson**
London University

# Civilization

## Volume I / The Emergence of Man in Society

**Book 1**
The Earliest Civilizations

**Book 2**
Civilizations of the Mediterranean Lands

**Book 3**
Medieval Christendom

**Book 4**
Civilizations of Asia and Africa

Library of Congress Catalog Card Number: 72-93821

Standard Book No. 87665—156—2

Manufactured in the United States of America

9 8 7 6 5 4 3 2 1

# Preface

"Whether we consider the position of the rock layers that envelop the earth, the arrangement of the forms of life that inhabit it, the variety of civilizations to which it has given birth, or the structure of languages spoken upon it, we are forced to the same conclusion: that everything is the sum of the past, and that nothing is comprehensible except through its history," wrote Pierre Teilhard de Chardin.

Many of us, preoccupied by the turmoil of rapid change through which we are living, are impatient with the past. What "relevance" has the past to our present world, let alone the world-yet-to-be that our imaginations dwell upon? But man's life on earth has been a continuous process, of which we are a small part, and if the future is ours, then our present was shaped by those who went before us.

This work, *Civilization*, is meant to illuminate the forces that have shaped our world, and in the process, tell the most compelling story of all, the story of man.

We also wanted to do something entirely new. It was to bring together historians and scholars from all over the world, not simply from the United States. This was intended to provide a universal perspective on the development of civilization, rather than a narrow American- or Euro-centered version. We hope and believe that we have succeeded in this ambitious aim.

Richard Holme

Richard Holme
*President and Publisher, CRM BOOKS*

# Introduction

The Greek word from which we have derived our word "history" meant something like "enquiry" or "investigation." That sense has now been lost, but something has been added to it; to us, history means finding out *about the past*, about what has happened rather than about what is. People have not always had a taste for this. They have, on the other hand, often had an interest of a vague sort in the past without wanting to investigate it very specifically. Nonetheless, some sort of importance the past has always had. Even in remote times, the experience of, say, good hunting-grounds, stored in the memory banks of tribal elders had real practical importance. Even totally nonsensical versions of the past mattered; the claim that they were god-descended sustained the morale of aristocracies in many different times and places. Modern men, too, have been known to feel that the technical success in the past of their own societies gave them indisputable rights to tell other peoples how to run theirs.

Such an interest in the past is not a historical interest until it wants to take account of the grounds of belief and to weigh them critically. This is what historians do. If today they have to justify this, it is only because there are other claimants on our time and attention. Someone living in a run-down urban ghetto or a poor country dependent on one main product for its income may justifiably feel that an economist or an agricultural scientist may be a better person to interrogate than a historian if he wants to solve his problems. But this is not always true. There are sound utilitarian reasons for finding out about the past, as the peacemakers of 1919 (among them none more conspicuous than Woodrow Wilson) found out to their cost when they tried to redraw the map of Europe on more satisfactory lines. The past kept breaking in and complicating things.

The truth must be that there are many reasons for trying to understand the past, and the practical benefits are by no means the most important. It is very odd, in any case, that interest in the past should be thought wasted effort in a century so devoted to congressional investigation of What Went Wrong, psychoanalytical resurrection of long-since buried experience and the study of curves of population, production and many other things whose major dimension is time. The best reason for history is that it is limitlessly interesting because it is the investigation of humanity's experience. Knowing about that may or may not in individual cases offer a simple payoff in practical deductions about what we ought to do now, but it can hardly be thought to be positively harmful.

Like any intellectual activity, too, it is demanding, and that is a good thing. To find out what happened is hard work. Try a simple test: write down a full explanation of why you have spent the last twenty-four hours in the way that you have spent them. Memory is the first prop that proves unreliable: a receipt from a store or a railroad ticket will jog it, and perhaps correct it. Such documents are sources. Basically historians scrutinize sources to answer questions about what happened. Sources vary greatly in size and quality. For different purposes the following are all sources: a medieval will, the constitution of the United States, a Roman soldier's gravestone, the collected works of Shakespeare, a photograph of Abraham Lincoln, a shoulder blade of a sheep with ancient Chinese characters on it, the Dead Sea Scrolls. Nothing that survives from the past cannot be used to tell us something. But working out what it tells us is not easy.

Hence scholarship and scholarly method. But scholars are not machines. They approach their subject with certain preconceptions. If one of them simply dislikes Jews (or for that matter non-Jews), women, or any other group, then his preconceptions are called prejudices. If he takes rather more trouble to think out why he should interest himself in one topic rather than another, disapprove of one thing rather than another, accept one kind of evidence rather than another, then we dignify his preconceptions by calling them "critical assumptions" or even "philosophies of history." In any case, it is impossible entirely to evaporate the personal element. This matters less than it might appear. We read history not to get the authoritative view, but to make up our own minds.

There is ample scope for doing so over a field as wide as is contained in these two volumes. They represent certain points of view and cannot by themselves exhaust the topics that they deal with. Other books will have to be read to supplement them—and perhaps disagree with them. Their basic organizing assumption is that there is a rough-and-ready division in human history somewhere around the sixteenth century. Since that time, though colossal variety and startling differences of experience still exist, more and more of mankind has shared in a movement toward the generalization of certain patterns of life on a worldwide scale. A vigorous and dominant—some would say predatory—civilization originating in Europe has increasingly corroded the institutions and attitudes of older societies.

Some of the societies that were destroyed were in their foundations very ancient. In the earlier part of history, which comes before the division suggested above, and is the subject of this volume, many societies existed and flourished as powerful, self-confident entities. Islam held Europe in check for centuries, and it used to be a common belief among historians that if Charles Martel had not won the battle of Tours in the ninth century, modern Europe—to say nothing of the United States—might be Muslim. Sometimes no such dramatic threat was involved, but the contrasts were still violent. A visitor from Europe to Mogul Delhi, like the amazed conquistadors who followed Cortes to Mexico, would be vividly aware of spectacular alternatives to the Christian culture in which he had been raised.

Yet the future belonged to that culture and much of this volume had to be about its evolution before its era of dominance. This is why medieval Europe and the classical world from which it emerged are both treated at length. Their own background is set against a wider world, that of the beginning of organized society itself, and it is in that remote world that the first steps in the story of civilization are to be traced. When this has been done, the elements of the story told in the second volume are made clear. From about A.D. 1500 we move forward into a future whose termination is the world in which we live. Of this recent history, when different parts of the world increasingly move to the same rhythms and reflect the same forces at work, the best test is the extent to which we can interpret it through our own experience. Whether we like it or not, in the end it is ourselves that we seek to explain through history.

# Contents
# Volume I

# Book 1
# The Earliest Civilizations

# Book 2
# Civilizations of the Mediterranean Lands

# Book 3 Medieval Christendom

# Book 4 Civilizations of Asia and Africa

# Maps

# Civilization

Volume I / The Emergence of Man in Society

# The Earliest Civilizations

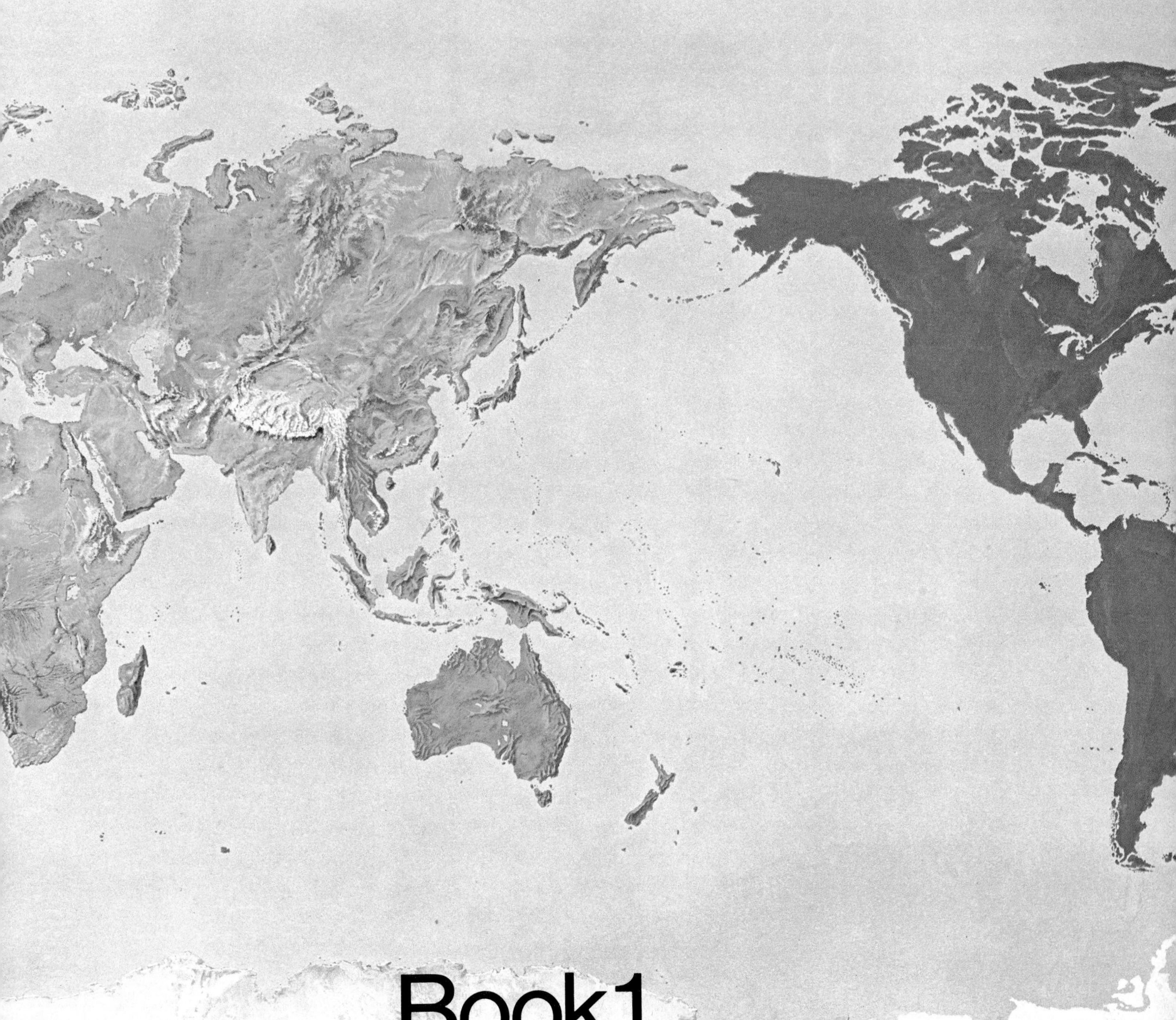

# Book 1

# Introduction

When does the history of the world begin? The first words of the Bible are the obvious answers to the question: "In the beginning." Unfortunately, it is not as easy as that. History is a curious subject, a great Swiss historian once pointed out, for it is the one field of study in which one *cannot* begin at the beginning.

A decision has therefore to be made about a starting point. Guidance can be found in another reflexion about history: only Man has one. Narrating the development of rock formations certainly requires a study of development in time, but it is geology or petrology, not history. The passage of animal life from invertebrate to vertebrate forms and the elaborations of simple rodents into primates is evolutionary biology, or comparative physiology; it is not history. History is the story of man.

It will appear at once, therefore, that there is a fair amount of non-history in what immediately follows. It does not take up many pages but it covers a lot of time—approximately nine hundred thousand times as much as the story of man in civilization which occupies well over ninety-five per cent of this book. There is a point in this brief survey of the vast stretches of prehistory. Man, when he does appear and starts to use his physical and mental equipment does so within restrictions and possibilities set not only by his environment but by his own genetic inheritance and the line which connects that to the first mammals—or even the first photosynthetic cell—is, though unimaginably long, continuous.

Somewhere along it man appears. It is another problem to decide where, but whenever he does, he has still a long way to go before he has any of the consciousness of an intelligible part which is the essence of a sense of history such as we today take for granted. He probably first had this 5,000 years ago at the most, for it is a product of civilization and the literacy which, in most early civilizations though not all, came with it.

The earlier civilizations are, after the emergence of Man, the second topic discussed in this book. The weight they exercized in the development of human society was enormous. In Egypt and Mesopotamia ideas and forces that were to shape the Near East until the days of Greece and Rome were cradled. The Near East was also the crucible from which the classical world would emerge. In Crete a fascinating and vigorous culture was also to contribute to Greek culture. Meanwhile, in the Indus valley of northwest India a civilization appeared in which some scholars have seen the first outlines of characteristic features of later Hindu society. A little later, China moved into literacy with the invention of the pictographic script that was to do so much to hold that great country together right down to modern times.

Long perspectives are therefore desirable at the start of a history of the world. Even if only remotely, all these great civilizations still to some extent shape men's lives today. The only exceptions were the civilizations that evolved in the Americas, of whose life we learn more and more from archaeologists but whose reality was destroyed forever by the coming of the European. That is another story and is dealt with in Book 4 of this History. In what immediately follows is a description of some of these achievements in civilization in their great creative ages. These were all the more amazing in retrospect because of the seeming lack of any fertilization from other centers of civilization—a fertilization that the other societies considered in this book came to enjoy.

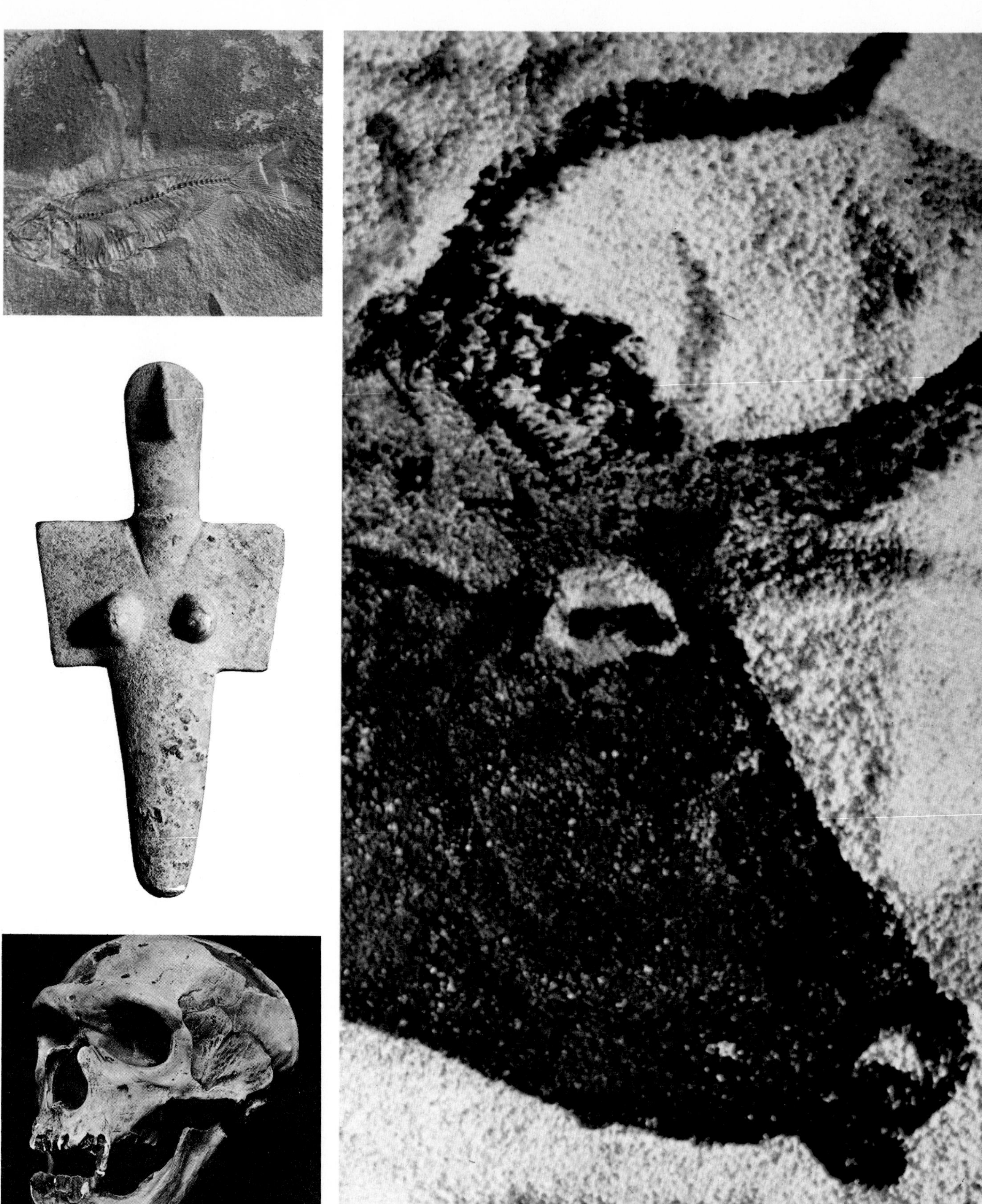

# Part I
# The World Before Civilization

Chapter 1

# THE DEVELOPMENT OF LIFE ON EARTH

The solar system came into being some 4.5 billion years ago. At the time of its formation, the planet Earth was endowed with certain physical characteristics that made it especially favored for the appearance of life on its surface.

Life as we know it can exist within only a relatively narrow range of temperature. At very low temperatures, the chemical reactions on which life depends—even the simplest forms of life—must virtually cease. At high temperatures, compounds become too unstable for life to maintain itself. The planets distant from the sun, such as Jupiter, are too cold. Mercury, the closest to the sun, is too hot.

Moreover, because of their low mass planets much smaller than Earth have a gravitational pull insufficient to hold an adequate atmosphere, which is the reservoir for water vapor and other gases containing the lighter elements of which life is composed. On a planet much larger than Earth, the atmosphere might be so dense that radiations from the sun could not reach its surface.

Of the nine planets in this solar system, life can theoretically exist only on three: Mars, Earth and Venus. Exobiologists—scientists concerned with life on other planets—have no evidence of even simple living things on Mars or Venus. However, astronomers estimate that in our own galaxy, the Milky Way (which contains about 100 billion stars), are a billion planets capable of supporting life, and within the range of our telescopes are about 100 million more such galaxies. So, at this very moment, other creatures, probably not much like ourselves, may be pondering their own histories of world civilization.

The Earth rotates on its own axis and, at the same time, moves in orbit around the sun. Its rotation causes the daily cycles of light and dark and also sets up currents of wind and water. These currents determine, to a large extent, the temperature and rainfall in various parts of the world and thus the varying patterns of life on earth. As we shall see, they also fixed the routes of the early migrants and explorers, who depended on these winds and waters to carry their vessels. The modern trade routes of the world still follow these ancient patterns. The Earth's axis is tilted (about 23°) in relation to its orbit, causing one hemisphere to point toward the sun for six months (half the orbit) and away from it for six months. As a result, the amount of sunlight reaching various parts of the earth's surface changes from season to season, and the areas around each of the poles spend part of the year in perpetual darkness.

*Above:* A relic of the first vertebrates: fossil fish discovered in North America. *Left:* The galaxy known as M31, as photographed through a 200-inch telescope. This galaxy, in the nearby constellation of Andromeda, is a huge assembly like our own Milky Way. Scientists now know that there are thousands of millions of such galaxies. One hypothesis currently offered for their origins is known as the "Big Bang" theory. It suggests that 10,000 million years ago all the matter of the universe was gathered in one place and then blasted into an expanding cloud. Another theory argues that this cloud will again coalesce within 70-billion years, restarting the same sequence.

## THE BEGINNING OF LIFE

Sometime between the time earth formed and the date of the earliest fossils found so far—an interval of less than 1½ billion years—life began. The chemical elements of which life is composed were present in a thin film of gases on the Earth's surface. This primitive atmosphere, as scientists reconstruct it, consisted mainly of water vapor, carbon dioxide, nitrogen, and some hydrogen-containing compounds such as ammonia and methane (but no free oxygen). In order to break apart the simple gases of the atmosphere and re-form them into organic molecules, energy was required. And energy abounded on the young planet. First there was heat, both boiling (moist) heat and baking (dry) heat. Water vapor spewed out of the primitive seas, cooled in the upper atmosphere, collected into clouds, fell back on the crust of the earth, and steamed up again. Violent rainstorms were accompanied by lightning, which provided electrical energy in addition to the radiant energy on which life now depends. The sun bombarded the earth's surface through its thin atmosphere with high-energy particles and ultraviolet rays. Radioactive elements in the earth's crust released particles into the atmosphere. These conditions can be simulated in the laboratory, and scientists have shown that under such conditions, complex molecules of the kinds found in living things are formed.

The steps by which these molecules aggregated in stable patterns and, most important, came to reproduce themselves are buried in the past. The first cell-like organisms, it is believed, lived by consuming the molecules formed, by the processes just described, in the thin soup of the primitive seas and, most probably, also by consuming each other.

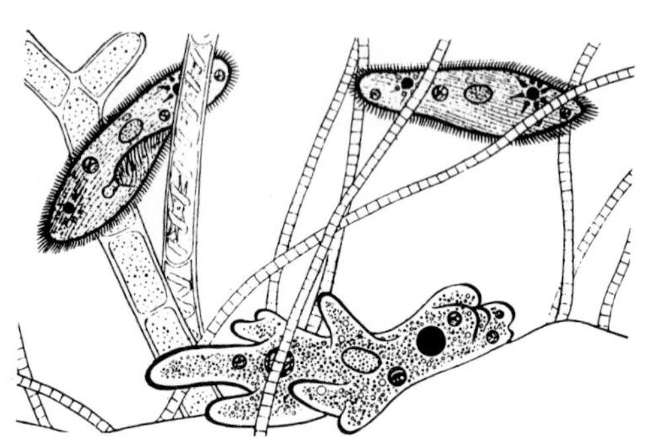

As these organisms multiplied and used up the accumulated resources, a new type of cell evolved that was photosynthetic—that is, able to convert the light energy of the sun into the chemical energy that living things require. Only very recently scientists have discovered fossils of primitive cells fixed in rocks that solidified 3.2 billion years ago, so even by that ancient date life had, indeed, begun. Some of these fossils were apparently photosynthetic cells, related to modern blue-green algae.

Photosynthetic cells, with their remarkable property of being able to live off the abundant energy of the sun, began to prosper and multiply, and as they did so,

*Above:* Sketch of microscopic views of a paramecium and an amoeba, living examples of the simple organisms that flourished in the primitive seas.
*Right:* Restored skeleton of a pareiasaurus, one of the first plant-eating quadrupeds, found in South Africa. The fossilized remains of this giant reptile, which measured ten feet in length, date from between 250 and 230 million years ago. Reptiles became the dominant form of terrestrial life during this period. The pareiasaurus had leaf- or peg-shaped teeth for chewing plants, and limbs flexed at ninety-degree angles.

they initiated a new stage in life on earth. This stage, characterized by the capacity of living things to change the natural environment, has extended and accelerated to the present time.

Photosynthesis, although complex in detail, is simple in its effects: carbon dioxide and water are combined to form sugar, and in the process, oxygen is released. The release of oxygen by the early photosynthetic cells changed the atmosphere, and as the atmosphere changed, other kinds of cells were able to evolve, which, like almost all modern cells, were aerobic—dependent on oxygen for their energy-supplying reactions. These aerobic reactions were much more efficient than the more primitive anaerobic ones. If our atmosphere had not come to contain oxygen, it seems almost certain that higher, complex forms of life could not have evolved.

Also, as oxygen collected in the upper atmosphere, it formed a shield against the more harmful wavelengths of radiant energy from the sun. The earliest cells probably escaped the destructive effects of ultraviolet light by remaining below the surface of the water. As the oxygen shield accumulated, cells were gradually able to rise to the surface. Eventually, forms evolved that could live on the shore and, finally, on land, which until then had lain barren. As the plants slowly took over the surface of the earth, the animals followed, for the animals were then, as now, totally dependent on plant life. Through photosynthesis plant life was the only channel by which the sun's radiant energy could reach animals.

## THE PATH TO THE MAMMALS

According to the fossil record, invertebrates abounded in the warm seas that existed 600,000,000 years ago. One small group of these gave rise to the first vertebrates, animals with an internal skeleton that grows as the animal grows and with a protective flexible covering enclosing the central nervous system. The first verte-

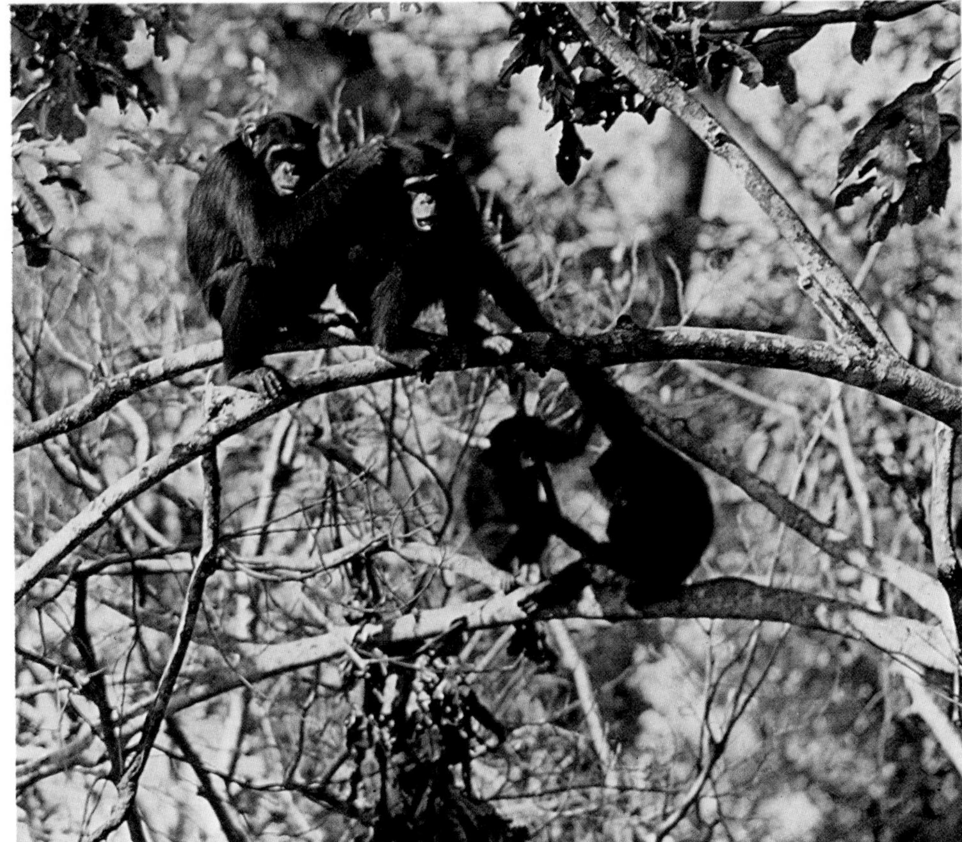

A chimpanzee family in its natural habitat. Darwin's theory of evolution is frequently misunderstood by the layman. He did not argue that man descended from modern primates like these, but rather that we share a common ancestral form with them. About 14 million years ago, a fork occurred in the primate evolutionary pathway. One road led to the chimpanzees and gorillas, another ultimately to modern man.

brates, the fish, evolved for 150 million years before giving rise to any land forms. Among the many lines of fish evolution, several small groups developed simple lungs. In some of these groups of lungfish, strongly developed pectoral fins evolved with which the fish could lumber from one body of water to another. Eventually, a fully terrestrial lung appeared.

The amphibians, of which the modern representatives are frogs, toads, newts, and salamanders, evolved directly from a line of lungfish. Like its modern counterpart, the primitive amphibian spent some of its life in the water and some on land, thus exploiting both environments but never truly adapting to the land. The great contribution of the reptiles, which arose from a group of primitive amphibians almost 300 million years ago, was the terrestrial egg, fertilized internally and able to maintain itself on land. With the egg, vertebrates became truly terrestrial.

For 200 million years, the reptiles were the dominant animal form on the planet. During this period of earth's history much of the surface of the continents was covered by marshes and inland seas. The temperature was mild, with little fluctuation. Plant life flourished. The great deposits of fossil fuels, on which our industrial revolution was later to depend, were formed during this period. Dinosaurs, with their enormous bodies and tiny heads, roamed the surface of the earth. For far longer than man has maintained his tenuous foothold on the planet, these reptiles flourished, reaching their zenith about 130 million years ago. Then, quite suddenly as geologic time goes, they disappeared for reasons that are unclear.

At just about the time the dinosaurs reached their peak, a new form of life appeared, the first primitive mammal. According to its fossil remnants, the earliest known mammal was only a few inches long (including its tail) and resembled the modern European shrew. It was a carnivore (meat eater), but since it was so small, it probably ate mostly insects and worms, supplemented perhaps by tender buds, fruits, and reptile eggs. It was probably, like the European shrew, nocturnal, feeding only at night, and also active, nervous, perpetually hungry, and poor of vision. At first glance, this earliest primate would not seem much of a match for the giant carnivorous dinosaur *Tyrannosaurus rex*. But the little protomammals had one extremely important advantage over the dinosaurs: like all subsequent mammals, they were warm-blooded. Because of this capacity to maintain a high and constant internal temperature (found also in the birds, which evolved about this same time), they were able to roam at night, when dinosaurs were immobilized by the lower temperatures. More important to subsequent developments, warm-bloodedness made possible not only a high degree of constant physical activity but also a level of mental alertness and intelligence that had never existed before on earth.

For about 80 million years, these animals coexisted with the giant reptiles. Then, once the dinosaurs had disappeared, an explosive radiation of the mammals began. By about 50 million years ago, the present orders of mammals were all established, including the primates, the group to which we belong. The stage was set for the evolution of man.

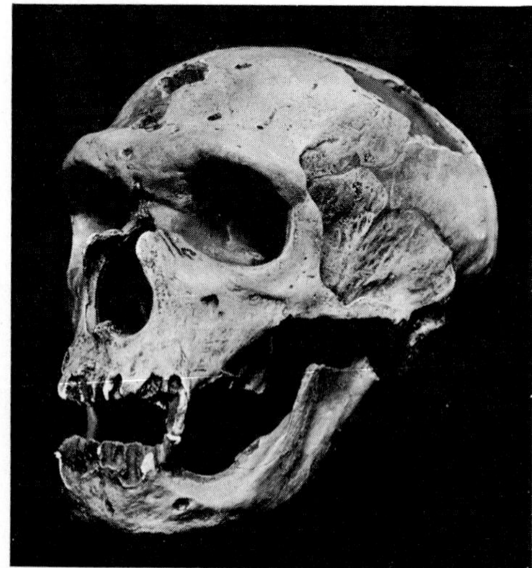

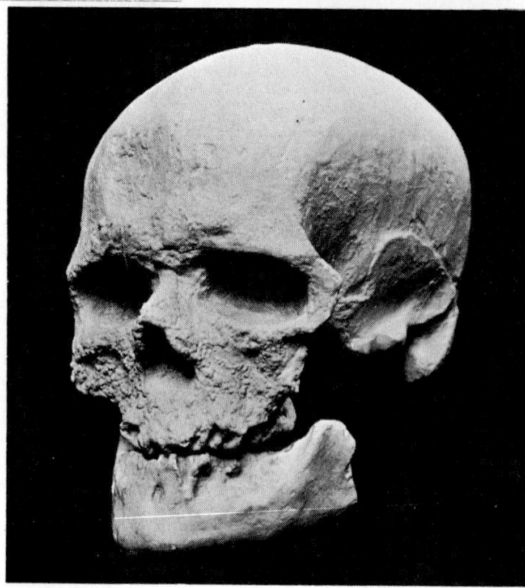

*Top:* Reconstructed fossil skull of *Homo erectus*. This species dates from at least one million to about 350,000 years ago. *Homo erectus* had a body skeleton similar to that of modern man; remains of leg bones indicate a similar stride as well. However, the *Homo erectus* skull had a low forehead and a brain capacity reaching the lower levels of modern man. *Above:* Reconstructed fossil skull of *Homo sapiens sapiens*, or modern man. Between 40,000 and 30,000 years ago, modern man appeared in southern Europe, at about the same time as Neanderthal man disappeared.

## THE EVOLUTION OF MAN

When Darwin wrote *The Descent of Man*, a little more than a hundred years ago, he was well aware that man was not the evolutionary descendant of modern primates but rather that man and the other primates had an ancestral form in common. Apparently, there was a division in the primate evolutionary pathway about fourteen million years ago. One road led to the chimpanzees and the gorillas, whose routes were to split again about twelve million years later. The other, according to the fossil evidence, led ultimately to modern man. The creatures found along this road are called hominids.

## Ramapithecus

Since the hominids first began their separate evolutionary course, they have passed through several distinct stages. The first, which has been called *Ramapithecus*, is known only from two fossil fragments, one found in northwestern India and one in Kenya, in eastern Africa, and both dated about 14 million years ago. Each fossil consists only of a few teeth and some fragments of jaw bone. When the bits of jaw bone are pieced together, it is clear that *Ramapithecus* had a smaller and broader dental arch than other large contemporary primates or, indeed, than the modern apes. The jaw fragments also indicate that *Ramapithecus* was comparatively small, about the size of a modern gibbon. Most important, the teeth and their condition indicate that tasks such as biting off and tearing up vegetation for which apes use their front teeth, were not carried out to the same extent by the teeth of *Ramapithecus*. So we assume that he used his forelimbs for these purposes, and on the basis of this assumption, we further assume a trend toward bipedalism. And then the curtain falls for another eleven to twelve million years.

An early photograph of a Canadian Woods Indian, taken in 1910. Men began to hunt large game for food in the final stages of evolution, that of *Homo sapiens sapiens*. Yet this method of securing a livelihood persisted until the twentieth century in many parts of the world. It was certainly practiced by this Canadian Indian at the beginning of the century, despite the advances made by other cultures. Some hunting-and-gathering communities still exist today.

## Australopithecus, "Leakey Man," and *Homo erectus*

Hominids next appear in a form generally known as *Australopithecus* (southern ape). The australopithecines are represented by more than 300 fossil fragments found in sites in eastern and southern Africa. The oldest, according to radioisotope dating methods, are the specimens found near Lake Omo in East Africa, representing remains of creatures that lived about 4 million years ago.

Australopithecines had cranial capacities ranging from 450 to 700 cubic centimeters (modern man's ranges from 1,200 to 1,800 cubic centimeters). Their hands had a broad flat thumb and the beginnings of a human-style grip. The teeth were very much like our own, although the molars were larger. Australopithecines walked upright, probably covering the ground with quick short steps in a sort of jog trot, rather than the far more efficient heel-and-toe walking of modern man. They were generally small, perhaps not more than five feet tall.

Until recently, Australopithecus, who continued until about a million years ago, was the presumed antecedent of modern man. In late 1972 the British anthropologist Richard Leakey discovered a contemporary, but seemingly more modern hominid, at Lake Rudolph. This hominid has a brain case shaped like that of modern man, with a capacity of 800 cubic centimeters. It lacks the heavy, protruding eyebrow ridges of even later hominids. Leg bones found near the skull are also shaped like those of modern man. Scientific dating shows these fragments to be at least 2·6 million years old. Leakey's discovery is not yet fully accepted by authorities but similar discoveries could mean the backwards revision of evolutionary theory.

*Homo erectus* made a first appearance at least a million years ago. The first fossil specimen of *Homo erectus* was discovered in 1891 on the bank of the Solo River in central Java and so became known as Java man. Fossils similar to Java man have been found not only along the Solo, which yielded a number of other specimens, but in China (Peking man), where nearly forty have been found, in eastern and northern Africa, and in Europe.

Members of the species *Homo erectus* had body skeletons much like our own and were about the same size as modern man. The bones of their legs indicate that they had a stride similar to our own. However, they had thick and massive skulls, with low foreheads. Brain capacities range from 775 to 1,200 cubic centimeters, reaching into the lower levels of the capacity of modern man, and there appears to be some correlation between larger brain size and changes in appearance. *Homo erectus* was in existence for at least 650,000 years. The most recent fossils clearly belonging to this group have been dated at about 350,000 B.C.

### Homo sapiens Neanderthalensis

The problem of where our immediate ancestors came from remains to be resolved. The earliest fossils that are classified as members of our own species (*Homo sapiens,* knowing man) come from Swanscombe in England and Steinheim in Germany. They consist only of some skull fragments, which demonstrate that the brains of these men were larger than those of *Homo erectus* although the skulls were less massive. They are dated at about 200,000 to 150,000 years ago, an interglacial period when Europe was warm, perhaps warmer than today.

Then we have another of those large and frustrating gaps in the fossil record. The next specimens that are known to us date from around 80,000 years ago to about 40,000 years ago, during the period of the last glaciation. This period abounds with specimens of what we have come to call Neanderthal man.

The first Neanderthal specimen to be recognized as a primitive man, was discovered in the Neander Valley near Dusseldorf in 1856. He had apparently been heavy and muscular, but had stood as erect as modern man. He had a thick skull, a prognathous (protruding) muzzle, a low forehead, and heavy brow ridges. This Neanderthal variety has been found in many sites throughout Europe and, more recently, in Palestine and Morocco.

Between about 40,000 and 30,000 years ago, Neanderthal man abruptly disappeared. Modern man, *Homo sapiens sapiens* (also known as Cro-Magnon man), appeared at about this same time.

### Homo sapiens sapiens

Where did modern man come from? He clearly did not arise from the Neanderthal variety of *Homo sapiens* previously present in Europe. He had a light skull, a high forehead, and a well-defined chin; suitably attired, he would look like a modern man.

The best guess that it is possible to make at present is that Steinheim and Swanscombe man, then Neanderthal, then *Homo sapiens sapiens* all came into Europe from the south or southeast (perhaps from southern France where some suggestive fossil evidence has been found) and had common ancestors. The classic Neanderthalers, perhaps because they were isolated by the return of the glaciers, represent an extreme variation. Modern men are the more generalized form.

Perhaps the Neanderthalers disappeared because they were exterminated in warfare—although there is no evidence of this. It is even possible that modern men brought with them some disease to which they were resistant and the Neanderthalers were not. In any case, soon after the appearance of *Homo sapiens sapiens*, there were no other hominids on the earth, and within the course of 10,000 to 20,000 years, this new variety of primate was spread over the face of the Earth.

## Man's Brain

Since the australopithecines, human brain capacity has almost tripled, but we do not know the precise correlation between this great increase in brain size and increasing intelligence. There is no clear correlation between brain size and the intelligence of its possessor. Moreover, organization of the brain plays an important part in its functional capacity, but we know nothing about the organization of the brain of fossil men and, indeed, not a great deal about the organization of our own brain. However, when we compare the intellectual capacities of animals of different species that have brains of different sizes in proportion to their weights, those with larger brains appear to be more intelligent. Therefore, we assume that this tremendous change in brain size reflects a change in intelligence and that, during a relatively brief period in man's history, powerful evolutionary pressures were at work selecting individuals of slightly greater mental capacity over those of slightly less.

Before so much fossil evidence was available, it was popular to suppose that tool use progressed concurrently with the increase in brain size and that each stimulated the other. This may be true, but during the period of the most rapid change in brain size, the tools being used were still very simple. No really elaborate tools came into existence, according to the fossil evidence, until the appearance of *Homo sapiens sapiens*, sometime well after brain size had reached its peak. It has been suggested that brain size increased rapidly at the time man was beginning to speak (see chapter 2). Another suggestion takes note of the fact that hunting of large game began to occur during this period of brain increase. Such hunting activities would have required new skills and also, in particular, greatly increased social cooperation among the hunters, and this may have been the selection force for intelligence. In any case, modern man as he evolved is neither strong nor swift nor highly specialized for any ecological niche. He differs from all other animals chiefly by reason of his mind, the contents of his skull. And it is this difference that is responsible for most of the events that have taken place on the face of the planet in the brief period that he has inhabited it.

### Geological Time Chart

| Millions of years Ago | | | |
|---|---|---|---|
| | Man Apes appear | Mountain building | CENOZOIC |
| 30 | 2 million years ago | Rise of Alps & Himalayas | |
| 60 | First primates | Seas disappear | |
| | Extinction of dinosaurs | | MESOZOIC |
| 90 | Age of reptiles | Last widespread oceans | |
| 120 | | | |
| | First birds | Continents low; Mts rise | |
| 150 | Dinosaurs zenith | from Alaska to Mexico | |
| 180 | | Appalachians uplifted & | |
| | Primitive mammals | broken into basins | |
| 210 | First mammals | | |
| | | Glaciation in the southern hemisphere | PALEOZOIC |
| 240 | Reptiles evolve | | |
| 270 | | Appalachians formed | |
| 300 | First reptiles | Coal swamps formed | |
| | Age of amphibians | Mountain building in eastern U.S.A. | |
| 330 | | | |
| 360 | Amphibians appear | Mountains & volcanoes in eastern U.S.A. | |
| 390 | Age of fish | | |
| 420 | | | |
| | Rise of fish | Continents generally flat | |
| 450 | | | |
| | First fish | Sea covers U.S.A. | |
| 480 | | | |
| 510 | | | |
| | | Seas spill over continents | |
| 540 | Age of shell animals and marine invertebrates | | |
| 570 | | | |
| 600 | | | |

Mammals non-existent or insignificant—

Mammals dominant

# Dating the Past

*Right:* The south rim of the Grand Canyon, Arizona. This shows the different rock formations caused by erosion.

Modern archaeologists and paleontologists date the past by two methods. One, relative dating, depends on the fact that, as changes take place on the earth's surface, as they do constantly, older layers (technically called strata) of earth and rock, together with the traces of any living organisms or their activities, will be buried beneath the more recent ones. Because portions of the surface heave, fold or are swept away, no single area will contain all the strata, but by comparing strata from different parts of the world, the geologist can piece together a general sequence of events. For example, the appearance of certain types of marine fossils, no matter where they are found, set a relative chronology for the adjacent strata; the trilobite preceded the dinosaur and the wooly mammoth, to put it in a very general way. Until quite recently, most of our reconstruction of past events has depended on this skillfully and laboriously constructed system. Although it is slowly giving way to absolute dating, it leaves many legacies in our language, such as Devonian and Pennsylvanian, which refer to localities where particular strata were identified, or Stone Age and Bronze Age, which are characterized by particular artifacts. The limits of the method are indicated by the fact that although the Stone Age—for better or worse—is over for most of us, a small portion of mankind would still be identified by archaeologists as belonging to this period.

Absolute dating attempts to fix a definite chronology—"years ago"—expressed either as B.C. (before Christ) or, more widely applicable though less generally used, B.P. (before present) for past object or events. It depends largely on the use of atomic isotopes. Isotopes are simple atoms of carbon, or nitrogen, or lead or any other element which differ from each other by reason of having more or fewer neutrons in their nuclei. Some isotopes have unstable nuclei and therefore tend to break down, or disintegrate, giving off energy as they do so, and stop only when they reach a stable state. Such atoms are known as radioactive isotopes. Radioactive isotopes have a property which makes them extraordinarily useful in dating the past: they decay at a fixed rate. This fixed rate is measured in terms of half-life. The half-life of a radioactive element is defined as the time in which half the atoms in a sample lose their radioactivity and reach a stable form. Radioactive nitrogen (13N) has a half-life of ten minutes; radioactive carbon (14C) has a half-life of 5,730 years; radioactive potassium (40 KO), 1.3 billion years.

Radioactive dating had its origins in 1905 when a geologist pointed out that whenever uranium was present in rock, lead was, too. Moreover, he noted that the ratio between lead and uranium was surprisingly constant in samples of rock from the same period. Subsequent investigation showed that by comparing the relative amounts of uranium 238 and lead 206 (the stable form to which the uranium decayed), it is possible to tell when a particular rock was formed. Fortunately for the daters, the lead formed from uranium decay is different from the lead naturally present, so the two can be distinguished. A variety of isotopes are used in radioactive dating—depending both on the type of material and its age—but the principle is the same for all of them. The use of more modern methods of dating the past has resulted in extensions both of the age of the earth and also of phases of its evolutionary history. Within the last decade it has been discovered that the Pleistocene—the period during which *Australopithecus* gave way, by successive stages to modern man—thought little more than a decade ago to have a duration of about 600,000 years, actually began at least 1.5 million years ago. Although not all of us would like to age at the rate of 900,000 years per decade, this information has of course been invaluable to students of evolution.

**Chapter 2**

# THE SOCIAL LIFE OF EARLY MAN

What we know about how early man lived is largely pieced together from three sources of information, each with its own limitations. One of these sources is the other modern primates, which are now being studied intensively, almost for the first time, by scientists living near the animals in their own natural environments. The second source comprises the few groups of present-day people—such as the Bushmen and the pygmies of Africa, the Eskimos, the Australian aborigines, and some North-American Indians—who are still, or were until very recently, hunter-gatherers, using primitive tools. The third source, and the only direct one, consists of the traces that early man has left behind him—tools, food debris, hearths, home-sites, works of art, and his own bones. In addition, we know something about the countryside in which early man lived from such ecological evidence as pollen grains and fruit seeds preserved in the soil and at campsites.

The most important influence in man's cultural and evolutionary history was his long existence as a hunter of wild animals. About 1.5 million years ago, his mode of existence began to develop gradually from a much simpler pattern of subsistence. Other large primates "make a living" by moving from place to place over a fairly large range of territory, gathering fruits, tender buds, shoots, insects and so forth, which they eat as they find them; there is no division of labor between the sexes. Infants are nursed for several years by species such as the chimpanzee, but they forage for themselves as soon as they are old enough. We have no reason to believe that the primates that were the early ancestors of man did not follow this general primate pattern. At any rate, there is evidence of organized hunting of large animals by about 1 million years ago.

It used to be thought that one of the big differences between man and his fellow primates was man's desire for meat. Recently, however, field studies have shown that chimpanzees and baboons (and probably other anthropoids as well) eat meat whenever they can get it—which is usually in the form of some small or immature mammal they come across in the forest—and that it is clearly a highly prized dietary item, although not a staple food. So the transition to the meat-eating, omnivorous way of life characteristic of modern man was apparently not the result of some abrupt change in pre-man's nature. The reason that australopithecines ate more meat than other primates was probably simply that they were able to catch it more efficiently. At various australopithecine sites, fossil remains of early man have been found along with broken bones of small animals—frogs, lizards, rats, and mice—and the young of larger animals, such as antelopes, all of which are regarded as food debris. The transition to a diet higher in proteins was important in human evolution because it reduced the amount of time spent in eating and so made other activities possible. Large herbivores—cows and horses, for instance—spend much of their waking hours feeding.

*Above:* An aborigine in contemporary Australia carrying a hunting spear.
*Left:* Painted head of a bull from the Lascaux caves in Dordogne, France, Upper Paleolithic period, c. 15,500–12,500 B.C. The first known art appeared in Upper Paleolithic times. The Lascaux caves contain perhaps the finest known examples of this early art. Very few human figures are shown, and those that are lack the vivid naturalism of animal figures like the one here. Instead some 170 figures of game animals adorn the walls.

Members of the species we call *Homo erectus* became hunters on a different scale. In the Miocene, during which man was evolving, not only were all the present orders of mammals present but there were species that today are extinct. Many of these species were larger than the modern forms; for example the biggest of all was a kind of rhinoceros eighteen feet high at the shoulder and twenty-five feet long.

During various stages of the Pleistocene epoch, the period marked by the glaciations, there seem to have been far more grasslands than now exist. Some areas that are now deserts were tropical grasslands, savannahs, and to the north, much land that is now forest was prairie or steppe, which were abundantly able to support large numbers of grazing and browsing animals. Man, one of the smaller, rarer species, would have had little difficulty locating game. And indeed, from sites as far apart as eastern Africa (Olduvai and Olorgesailie) and China (the Choukoutien caves, near Peking) and dating back from a million to half a million years ago, the bones of very large animals—elephants, rhinoceros, antelopes, bears, hippopotomuses—are found in the debris of human campsites. At Olorgesailie, the remains of sixty-five giant baboons of a type now extinct were accumulated, representing either a preference for baboon meat expressed over a long period of time or a single slaughter by a skilled and successful hunting party. We do not know how these early hunters killed animals so much larger and more ferocious than themselves. Stone implements found at the sites were, apparently, made to be held in the hand and used for chopping, cutting, or pounding—in other words for butchering or preparing food rather than for killing game. There is some evidence that early man killed animals by stampeding them into marshes or over cliffs, perhaps with the help of fire to frighten them. The American Indians continued this practice until very recent times. Certainly hundreds of thousands of years passed before men developed weapons as sophisticated as spears with stone or metal tips or bows and arrows. Anthropologists who have studied primitive tribes have been impressed by the fact that their weapons are not always efficient and that some hunting groups take little interest in perfecting them. Like prehistoric men perhaps, these modern hunters emphasize patience, endurance, skill in stalking, and specialized knowledge of animals and terrain.

Cave-drawings of a mammoth, Upper Paleolithic period. Large game was probably hunted during the Ice Age by being driven over pit-traps and cliffs. Hunting involved social organization of a kind that distinguishes man from other primates. The artists who drew such figures used a wide range of tools: flint chisels, awls, knives, scrapers, a form of crayon, and brushes made by chewing the ends of sticks. Animal shoulder-blades served as palettes, and pads of fur or moss were employed to spread large areas of color wash. To see in the darkness, these cave-artists used the first lamps, which were fueled by fat or blubber.

## THE SOCIAL GROUP

Early man lived in groups. In this, he resembled almost all other higher primates. Tribal behavior appears to be a strong primate characteristic; the only known exceptions are gibbons and orang-utans, both of which live high in treetops and so have less need of the protection a group affords. The chief functions of grouping among primates—the reasons apparently that evolution selected for group behavior—seem to be the social interdependence of the group; cooperation in obtaining food; and protection against predators. With regard to protection, secondary sexual characteristics figure importantly. Male primates are characteristically considerably larger than the females, and they often have ferocious canine teeth that are lacking in the females. When a baboon tribe moves across open country, for example, the females and juveniles keep to the center of the pack and are surrounded by adult males to guard them from attack.

Primate groups typically number between twenty and forty individuals, including infants. They seem to be organized by clear-cut social hierarchies ("pecking orders"), which, once established, serve to reduce intragroup fighting. Individuals recognize members of their own group and are suspicious and hostile toward other groups of the same species. Fighting does not appear to be frequent between groups, however, probably because each tends to stay within its home range or to retreat to it when confronted.

Based on the size of a single campsite (at Olduvai Gorge in East Africa), it appears that bands of australopithecines contained three or four families. Living areas of *Homo erectus* seem to have been somewhat larger, perhaps big enough to accommodate twenty to thirty adults, which is about the size of some present-day hunting tribes. The little bands probably lived at relatively great distances from one another, at least where food sources were sparse. Judging from contemporary hunting societies, several hundred square miles were needed to support a single hunting group in desert or marginal areas.

At some distance from camps, other sites have been discovered at which game was butchered and presumably divided up among members of the hunting party. In other words, these early men not only hunted as a cooperative group but also shared their food, a practice that does not really occur among other primates. Clearly, a capacity to get along equably with one's fellow man was very important for the survival both of the individual and the group during this long period of man's history, and the ties that held the group together must have been strong.

We have one fossil record of such ties, dating not from *Homo erectus*, however, but from Neanderthal times. In Shanidar, a cave 2,500 feet high in the Zagros mountains in Iraq that had once sheltered a band of Neanderthalers, archaeologists found a skeleton of a man who, because of a deformity obviously present since birth, had had a withered right arm. The arm had been amputated below the elbow some years before the man's death. The teeth showed signs of unusual wear, suggesting that they had been used to compensate in some way for the lack of a right hand. And yet the man had lived to be about forty years old. Although he must have been an almost totally nonproductive member of the hunting group and completely dependent on it for his survival, he was obviously cared for throughout his lifetime, some 50,000 years ago.

*Above:* Among most primate species, the primary responsibility for child care lies with the mother, who may receive help from other members of the group. Human beings, however, tend to organize into nuclear family units, in which both sexes cooperate to some degree in caring for, or at least providing for, the young.

*Left:* A group of olive baboons. Primate groups typically number between twenty and forty, including infants. Like almost all other primates, except the tree-dwelling orang-utans and gibbons, early man lived in groups.

## THE FAMILY

Although man resembles other primates in his group behavior, he differs from most other primates in his formation of permanent male-female bonds. Among other primates, and indeed, all other mammals, females have periods of "heat" or estrus, during which time they can become pregnant. Only females in heat are sexually receptive. Among most primate species, when a female is in heat she presents herself to all of the males in the group and all or nearly all will mate with her during estrus, which usually last a few days to a week, depending on the species. Because estrus does not occur in immature females, and mature females are usually either pregnant or nursing (which suppresses estrus), sexual activity is relatively rare in these primate groups, although sex play occurs among the younger members of the tribe. (Apparently sexual behavior is learned, not innate, among higher primates; apes and monkeys raised in laboratories or zoos in isolation usually cannot be bred). The primary responsibility for child care devolves on the mother, who may receive help from other members of the group.

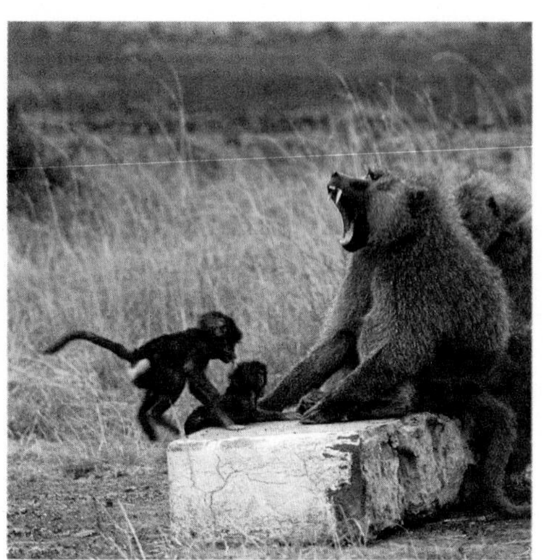

A male baboon displaying the canine teeth which distinguish him from the female. Some secondary sex characteristics, such as differing size, are evident in non-human primates.

Most human societies, however, are based on some version of the nuclear family in which a single male has exclusive sexual rights to one or more females and in which both sexes cooperate in caring and providing for the young. We do not know whether pre-men grouped themselves first in family units and then the family units eventually banded together, or whether the group became subdivided into families. In either case, it is interesting to reflect upon what the effects of large-game hunting must have been on the relationship between the sexes. To the extent that the tribe depended on elephant, antelope, and rhinoceros as its staple diet, the women and children were totally dependent on the men. However, recent studies have tended to minimize the large-game element of the daily diet. Sexual dependency may have been less important to people who fed on plants and small game.

The problem of dependency also would have increased during this period because of the increase that was taking place in the size of the skull. The size of the brain at birth of a human infant today is only about one-fourth of its adult size; in other words, human beings are born at a very immature stage in their development. Delaying birth longer increases its difficulties; delivery of the head is much the most hazardous stage of human birth for both mother and child. Judging from the age at which eruption of the permanent teeth occurred, the young of *Homo erectus* matured at about the same rate as those of modern *Homo sapiens*. We guess that, on the basis of studies of today's hunter-gatherers, children in prehistoric families were spaced further apart than modern children. This was due to prolonged nursing, which depresses fertility, high infant mortality, and very likely, infanticide. Nevertheless, a female member of the tribe probably had immature children to take care of from the time she reached puberty until her death (which would probably have occurred by the age of thirty).

Women played a very important role in the life of the group. Not only did they undoubtedly supervise the raising of the children but they also were probably responsible, as is the case in today's tribes, for the gathering of vegetable products and perhaps also of small game. These items probably made up most of the day-to-day menu, because there was no way of storing meat that we know of. Woman's role must have been a completely different one from the man's, and it has remained so until very recently, although now it is chiefly an anachronism from our hunter-gatherer past.

## SECONDARY SEXUAL CHARACTERISTICS

One of the reasons we can be reasonably sure that pair-bonding has been in existence for a long time is that there are physical changes in the human female which must have occurred as a result of, or concomitant with, the evolution of bonding behavior. One of these changes is the suppression of estrus. The human female is the only female animal continuously sexually receptive throughout her adult life. Although not the only tie, this behavioral adaptation is clearly a strong bond holding the nuclear family together. Although we often speak of our sexuality as "an animal instinct," and it clearly is, it is noteworthy that human males and females have a far more active sex life than most other animals.

Other physical changes related to the continuous sexual receptivity of the human female involve the secondary sex characteristics. Among primate groups, the chief visible differences between males and females involve the larger size of the males and other male characteristics, such as large canines, associated with social dominance and defense. When the female is in estrus, her sexual availability is signaled in most species by swelling of the genital area and bright coloring of the skin surrounding the anus and the genitalia. Human females signal their continuous sexual receptivity by permanent signs, such as their enlarged mammae (other female primates provide adequate milk for their offspring but do not have breasts), their distinctive distribution of hair and body fat, and their more delicate facial features, all of which are sexually attractive to the human male.

Artist's rendering of the Choukoutien caves, near Peking, inhabited 500,000 years ago. These early cave dwellers had fires, which made the caves safe from large predators. Their food included venison and berries.

## INCEST TABOOS AND EXOGAMY

Because almost all primitive peoples have laws or taboos against incest, it is believed that these developed early in human culture. There are sound biological reasons for discouraging inbreeding, which tends to bring out genetic defects which would otherwise probably remain latent. It is unlikely, however, that prehistoric groups would have been aware of these effects. Incest taboos probably arose because intermarriage among family members would have been disruptive to the formation of nuclear families. There may also be some instinctive avoidance of inbreeding among primates; young male chimpanzees, for example, will mate with other adult females in estrus but seem to avoid mating with their mothers, so perhaps there are more strictly biological factors as well. Lower animals and plants have many devices to discourage self-fertilization and encourage outbreeding, and an outbreeding instinct among higher animals may be an extension of this.

Seemingly related to incest taboos but perhaps of quite separate origin are social rules promoting exogamy—marrying outside the group. Such rules would appear to have a highly practical basis. In the first place, a small band comprising only, for example, eight or ten families might well not be able to provide a suitable mate for the right young man or woman at the right time; exogamy probably started for just this reason. Second, intermarriage to neighboring groups promotes friendly relations on one's borders and also opens the possibilities for cooperative activities when these would be useful—as in a large hunting expedition.

Among hunting people, the women usually leave their own group and go to live with the husbands' groups. This is a logical arrangement since much of a boy's preparation for manhood is gaining knowledge of the territory which will be his future hunting ground. Exogamy is important in man's cultural development because it clearly serves as a deliberate device for eliminating inter-specific fighting. In an analogous way, marriages were arranged among the children of various royal households until very close to the present time.

## SPEECH AND COMMUNICATION

By speech, we mean the formulation and articulation of abstract ideas. Most higher animals can communicate the concept "I am hungry now." Only man can express "I was hungry yesterday." Yesterday is an abstraction.

Man was clearly preadapted to speech simply by being a primate. No order of animals is noisier. Social monkeys and apes hoot and chatter and bellow continuously, crying out with pleasure and alarm, threatening, calling, and just generally keeping in touch. The ability to communicate would have been a tremendous advantage to men hunting in groups ("Head off that hippopotamus!"), but we have no way of knowing whether or not they were able to speak. Wolves, for example, certainly hunt efficiently in packs without complex communication.

Some experts believe that Cro-Magnon—modern man—was the first really to master speech and that it was his power of speech that enabled him to supplant the Neanderthalers with such ease and also to develop the first complex culture. On the other hand, Neanderthal man buried his dead, sometimes with gifts of food and tools. Formal burials such as this seem to suggest strongly a concept of life after death, and it is difficult to understand how a society could hold such beliefs without some fairly sophisticated means of exchanging ideas between its members. Also, the precise repetition of tool forms over long periods in pre-Neanderthal times suggests a learning process that may have involved speech.

Flint handax from the Lower Paleolithic period, found in Maidenhead, England. The handax was worked to provide a gripping surface and various combinations of cutting edges. The actual size of this one is about ten inches long.

## HABITATIONS

All higher primates apart from man are continuously on the move, and though they range back and forth over the same territory, they sleep in a different place every night. Members of the group who cannot keep up are left behind, as a rule, although the young are often aided.

Early men were also nomads (as are most modern hunters), but there is evidence that they maintained base camps, some of which appear to have been fairly permanent, in the sense that they were returned to year after year. Hunting parties operated from these sites, leaving children and other members of the group behind and bringing game back with them. Sometimes, apparently, if a very large animal was killed, the entire group would move to the butchering site for several days, consuming part of the kill on the spot and preparing the rest for carrying back to the base.

The australopithecines and the earliest men probably lived mostly in the open, although one australopithecine site is in the natural shelter of overhanging rocks. The campsites found in southeast Africa are near streams or lakes, which would not only have provided water for the camper but would also have attracted animals.

The Choukoutien caves, near Peking, inhabited 500,000 years ago, are among the earliest caves known to be used for human habitation. It is probably no coincidence that within these same caves is also one of the first traces of the human use of fire. Before men had fires, caves, which are also the homes of bears and other large carnivores, would have been too dangerous for habitation, but since fire made them available for human occupation, they have been used up to modern times. The caves near Shanidar, for example, are occupied by the mountain people of today.

Prehistoric cave dwellers usually remained near the mouth of the cave, where there was light and where the smoke of the fire could escape. Often the caves had terraces outside them. Here, one would imagine, much of the toolmaking and other activities were carried on in good weather.

On the shores of the Mediterranean, near what is now Nice, are the remains of crude huts built some 300,000 years ago. The huts were oval-shaped, from twenty-six to forty-nine feet long and from thirteen to twenty feet wide; their outlines can be traced both from postholes and from lines of stones which apparently served to brace the walls. It appears that each year a hunting group would arrive at this area in the late spring (the time of year has been fixed by analysis of pollen in fossilized human feces), erect huts and hearths and windscreens, and move on in the course of the summer. After the departure of the group, the simple structures would collapse. Wind would cover the living floor with sand, and rain would pack it down. When the hunters returned the following spring, they would construct the temporary dwelling again, often in exactly the same place. In one dune, there are eleven living floors, each constructed over the previous one; it is believed that these represent consecutive yearly visits, probably by the same group of people.

Man-made dwellings of far more recent times (about 20,000 years ago) have been found in Czechoslovakia, southern Russia, and Siberia, in vast caveless areas. Massive accumulations of mammoth bones and ivory have been discovered at these sites; the men who lived there were apparently primarily mammoth hunters and are likely to have followed the great herds on their long seasonal migrations. Judging from the size of the living floors, some of these dwelling places were inhabited by as many as ninety or a hundred people at a time. Perhaps a number of smaller groups would converge at such places at specific times of the year for hunting parties.

These dwellings were made of more substantial materials than the flimsy shelters found near Nice. Some, apparently winter dwellings, were made of earth and sunk slightly below ground; others, which resemble the summer homes of the Eskimos, were tentlike constructions of animal skins that presumably could be carried to new sites. However, like the shelters at Nice, most were just stopping-off places, way stations on the perpetual journey that was characteristic of hunting men.

## FIRE

Man probably "stole" his first fires. Fires occur naturally as a consequence of lightning, in smoldering volcanoes, and, in some areas, from spontaneous combustion of gases. A fire, once captured, was probably tended carefully and carried from place to place, still a practice among some primitive tribes. Although cooking undoubtedly made meat more palatable and certainly easier to chew, its biggest influence on man's diet was probably in making it possible for him to eat certain vegetable products—in particular, seeds and grains—which otherwise cannot be digested by the human alimentary equipment.

The first known use of fire occurred about 500,000 years ago; hearths have been found both in China and in Hungary dating from that period. We do not know when man first learned to make fire, but it could have come about as a by-product of his stone toolmaking, which must, from time to time, have produced sparks. The first object interpreted as a firemaking tool dates from Upper Paleolithic times, about 30,000 years ago. It is a stone disk with a central hole in it, found with other objects in a grave.

## TOOLS

The earliest tools of which we have any record are found in association with the remains of an advanced form of australopithecine at Olduvai Gorge and near Lake Rudolf, both in East Africa. These stone tools are of the sort known as pebble tools, which typically have flakes split off at one end to provide a chopping, cutting, or scraping edge. Both the pebbles and the flakes were used as tools. Similar simple stone chopper tools and flakes were also used by early *Homo erectus* in China and Southeast Asia.

By slow stages, presumably in the hands of *Homo erectus* in Africa (but not in the Far East), the pebble tool became a new and highly distinctive implement, the so-called handax. The handax is a stone that has been worked on all its surfaces to provide what appears to be a gripping surface and various combinations of cutting edges, sometimes with a more or less sharp point. Making such an implement requires both skill and time—an impression confirmed by anthropologists who have tried. Handaxes, therefore, were not always manufactured on the spot at the time they were needed but were often conscientiously stockpiled for future use. In one of the butchering sites in East Africa, among all the previously mentioned baboon bones, 459 handaxes were found, apparently having been discarded as they became dull through use.

Handaxes were used extensively throughout Africa, India and much of the Near East, and tens of thousands have been found in the valleys of the Somme and Thames alone. In Asia, they were used only in the south and west; further east, in China and southeast Asia, men continued to use the pebble tools until a late date. In other words, the type of tool being used was not a reflection of the stage of physical evolution of the species but a consequence of cultural spread. This concept is confirmed by the close resemblance of the handaxes to one another. Unlike the pebble tools, they were clearly fashioned according to a formal pattern, which indicates communication and exchange among the groups of men roaming over these vast territories at that time.

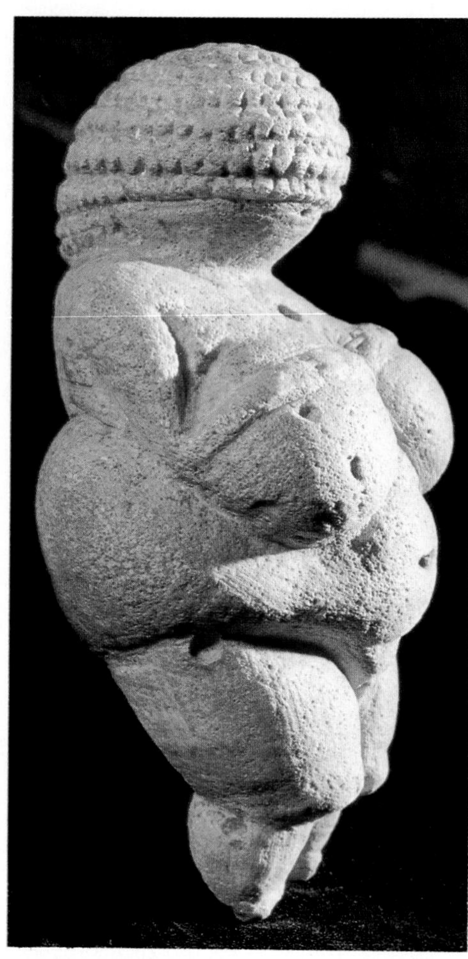

Limestone carving of a woman, known as the "Willendorf Venus" after the place of its discovery, in Austria; c. 23,000 B.C. Stylized figures like these have been discovered across Europe and Asia. Like the Lascaux cave paintings they may have been executed in the belief that art had certain magical powers. These statues, and certain prehistoric drawings of subjects like mating horses, may have been attempts to gain power over the sources of fertility.

Neanderthal man continued occasionally to use the handax but also developed a new type of tool, based on a new method of toolmaking. A basic core, shaped somewhat like a disk, was first prepared and then multiple flakes were struck off its upper surface. This technique and the type of sharp, lightweight, versatile flakes it produces are so typical of the Neanderthal culture (often referred to as the Mousterain, from Le Moustier, a cave in Southern France where many traces of Neanderthal man have been found) that wherever these cores and blades are found, it is now possible to say with certainty that Neanderthal men had been present. The form of many of the flints is such that they would have been useful for scraping animal hides, suggesting the use of crude clothing, which is certainly in keeping with the cooler environment into which man had now spread more thickly.

The changes that took place in the stone tools during most of man's prehistory were very minor. Large improvements did not take place until modern man, *Homo sapiens sapiens*, appeared—at least 40,000 years ago.

*Homo sapiens sapiens*, when he first appeared in Europe, came bearing a new, quite different, and far better tool kit. His stone tools were essentially flakes—which, of course, had been in use for more than 2.5 million years—but they were struck from a carefully prepared core with the aid of a punch, which is a tool made to make another tool. These flakes, usually referred to as blades, were smaller, flatter, and narrower, and, most important, they could be and were shaped in a large variety of ways. They included, from the beginning, various scraping and piercing tools, flat-backed knives, awls, chisels, and a number of different engraving tools (burins). Using these tools to work other materials, especially bone and ivory, Upper Paleolithic man made a variety of projectile points, barbed points for spears, harpoons, spear throwers, fishing hooks, and—a remarkable and useful invention—needles. Thus, although Upper Paleolithic man lived much the same sort of existence as that of his forebears, he lived it with more possessions, more comfort, and more style.

### Burials

Neanderthal man was, apparently, the first creature on earth to bury its dead. Because burials often took place in the inhabited caves, a number of Neanderthal graves have been found. Often the bodies are gently flexed, as in natural sleep, but in some of them the limbs are pulled tightly to the body, so that they may have been bound before being buried. Such binding, when practiced by primitive tribes, is done to keep the dead from rising to disturb the living. Some Neanderthal bodies were daubed with red ochre before burial, a custom also found among other primitive peoples. Many examples of burials with food and weapons—and one with spring flowers—have been uncovered. At es Skhul in Palestine, for example, where ten bodies have been found in separate graves, one man was buried holding a joint of meat. In the Russian cave of Teskik Tash, the body of a Neanderthal boy was surrounded by the horns of a Siberian mountain goat, their points stuck into the ground. Over another grave, also of a child, a large stone was placed, and on its undersurface are arrays of rough pits—cup-shaped marks—arranged in pairs. Their meaning is unknown.

Burials of Upper Paleolithic peoples, while generally similar to those of the Neanderthalers, were often much more elaborate. Some of the skeletons are richly decorated with headdresses and necklaces, and some are overlaid with shells, which appear to have been attached to garments.

One unusual and particularly interesting grave, about 20,000 years old, has been found at Vestonice in Czechoslovakia. The body is that of a slightly built woman, five feet three inches tall, about forty years of age (old for that time). It was covered with red ochre and protected by two shoulderblades of a mammoth, one of which had a network of irregular lines scratched on its surface. Buried with her were stone tools. On one hand had been placed the paws and tail of an Arctic fox (the swiftest and wiliest of animals), and in her other hand, its teeth. Clearly, she had been an important personage, the possessor of some special skill or wisdom or, most likely, considered to have magic powers.

## Art

Unless we count the gravestone with its cup-marks or the circle of stones at Mt Circeo, the first known art appeared in Upper Paleolithic times, very late on the scale on which we have been viewing human history. During this period, art suddenly began to appear everywhere and in all its forms—sculpture, modeling, relief, engravings, drawings, and paintings. There are delicately worked tools and weapons made of bone and mammoth ivory and often decorated with fine engravings, usually of game animals. There are small carved and modeled figures, some of animals, particularly game animals, and some of human beings, nearly all of which are women.

The most famous of these figurines is a small statue of a female form, discovered near the beginning of this century, which has come to be known as the Willendorf Venus. It was carved of limestone about 25,000 years ago. The figure is deliberately faceless; fat and fecund, with huge full sagging breasts, it is also probably pregnant. Numerous other "Venuses" have been found at sites from France to Siberia. (Upper Paleolithic art, or at least what remains of it, was confined almost exclusively to Europe.) There are variations among these "Venus" figures. Some are modeled of clay, and some are carved in relief on stone surfaces. Some are abbreviated, with two breasts hanging on a sticklike figure or sometimes just the breasts all by themselves, like a pair of discarded water wings. They are often found in the remains of human habitations, and they apparently performed some function related to fertility, childbirth, or nourishment. Or perhaps they were simply the guardians of health and household, the realm of the female principle.

The art of Upper Paleolithic man reached its height with the cave drawings and paintings of southern France and western Spain. The examples which remain to us, many surprisingly untouched by time, clearly form a part of a rich and highly respected artistic tradition, integrated in its concepts and its vision, and enduring for a remarkably long time—at least 10,000 years.

What one usually notices first about the cave drawings is that they are almost entirely of animals. A census of the figures in the caves at Lascaux, France, reveals, for example, more than 100 horses, some 30 bovids (oxlike animals), 20 deer, 10 ibexes, 7 bison, 1 musk ox, 1 reindeer, and 1 rhinoceros, all game animals, although not represented in proportion to their use as game, judging from other evidence. In addition, there are six felines and one bear. There are no plants, unless one interprets a few scratchings as grasses. In Lascaux, as in the other caves, there are very few drawings of people and those that do exist are often shown as simple stick figures, often wearing animal heads or masks.

Paints were prepared from deposits found in the soil of iron and manganese oxides or from carbon blacks. These pigments were ground to a fine powder (special pestles and mortars have been found that were used for this purpose) and mixed with water. They were applied with fingers, with pointed instruments (perhaps quills), and with pads of moss or fur. It is thought that some of the colors were applied as a kind of spray, perhaps by blowing dry powder through a tube onto a wetted surface. Engraving is combined with drawing and painting to produce three-dimensional effects. The colors—reds, yellows, browns, and blacks—are shaded to suggest muscular contours.

In all cave art, the cave itself plays an important role. The placement of some of the drawings indicates that their form was suggested by the contours of the rock surface—which is incorporated as the swelling of a rump, for example—or by a natural marking, which becomes an eye or some other feature of the animal. More strikingly, the animals often appear to be moving into or out of tunnels, emerging from behind ledges, guarding entrances, or tumbling off precipices.

Cave art is almost never found near the mouths of caves, where daylight penetrates; it is almost always deep, and sometimes very deep, in the interior. In fact, many of the paintings are in almost inaccessible places, even at the ends of tunnels, or on ceilings, where it is very difficult to see them and must have been even more difficult to execute them. Some available surfaces are not used at all, while others nearby have been used over and over again. They must all have been painted and also viewed by the light of crude lamps or torches.

The meaning of these drawings and paintings has long been a matter of debate. Some of the animals are clearly marked with darts or wounds (although very few appear to be seriously injured or dying). Such markings have led to the suggestion that the figures are examples of sympathetic magic, in which there is the notion that one can do harm to one's enemy by striking needles in a small image of him. The fact that many of the animals appear to be pregnant suggests that they may represent fertility, perhaps in some way related to the "Venuses." Many appear also to be in movement. Perhaps these animals, so vital to the hunters' welfare, were migratory in these areas, and they may have seemed to vanish at certain times in the year, mysteriously returning, heavy with young, in the springtime. This return of the animals might have been an event to be solicited or celebrated in much the same spirit as the rites of spring of more recent people or our own Easter.

Cave art came to an end perhaps 8,000 or 10,000 years ago. Not only were the tools and pigments laid aside, but the sacred places—for such they seem to have been—were no longer visited. New forces were at work to mold the course of men's existences, and the end of this first great era in human art is our clearest line of demarcation between the old life of man the hunter and the new life that was to come.

# Climate and Evolution

As we have seen, one of the principal forces of evolution is the changing climate of the earth. During most of the planet's history, the climate has been warmer than at the present time. However, these long periods of mild climate have been interrupted briefly by Ice Ages—so-called because they are characterized by glaciations, persistent accumulations of ice and snow which occur whenever summers are not hot enough to melt as much water as may have frozen during the previous winter. (For many parts of the world, such conditions can be met by not very large changes in temperature.) One such Ice Age appears to have occurred at the beginning of the Paleozoic (Old Life) Era, some 600 million years ago. Another, marked by extensive glaciations in the southern hemisphere, left its traces about 250 million years ago. A more recent but less drastic drop in temperature began at the end of the Mesozoic (Middle Life) Era and, about 35 million years ago as we noted, appeared to hasten the end of the dinosaur dynasty. The most recent Ice Age, which began about 1.5 to 2 million years ago, has been marked by a number of extensive glaciations, the last four being particularly important, which have covered large parts of North America, England, and Northern Europe. The last glaciation began about 70,000 years ago and, after some fluctuations, finally began to subside about 12,000 years ago. Earlier glaciations are somewhat more difficult to date because each subsequent one tends to scrape away the traces of its predecessors. Between the glaciations, there have been intervals—interglacials during which the climate has become warmer although not, on the average, nearly as warm as during the preceding period of the earth's history. These periods of glaciation in the North were accompanied, according to the results of examination of fossil plants and pollen, by periods of cooler temperature and increased rainfall in the south. Thus parts of Africa which are now desert were, at that time, savannah (tropical grassland) and wood-land. Thus although no single generation of men would have been aware that changes in climate were taking place during much of his early history, man and his fellow animals have lived in a period of extreme environmental pressures.

The reason for these large changes in temperature is one of the most hotly (or coldly) debated issues in modern science. They have been variously ascribed to changes in the earth's orbit, variations in the earth's angle of inclination toward the sun, migration of the magnetic poles, fluctuations in solar energy, and combinations of these and other causes. Are the glaciations over—perhaps for another 200 million years—or are we merely enjoying a brief interglacial before the ice begins to *move southwards* once more, perhaps in 10,000 years or so? This is one of the several questions climatologists would very much like to answer.

**The Evolution of Man**

| Years BC | | Climate of northern Europe |
|---|---|---|
| | Homo Sapiens | End of Ice Age |
| 30,000 | | Cold Glacial Period |
| 60,000 | | |
| 90,000 | Homo Neanderthalensis | |
| 120,000 | | Warm Interglacial Period |
| 150,000 | | Cold Glacial Period (Glacial Maximum) |
| 180,000 | | |
| 210,000 | | |
| 240,000 | | Warm Interglacial Period |
| 270,000 | Homo Erectus | |
| 300,000 | | |
| 330,000 | | |
| 360,000 | | Cold Glacial Period |
| 390,000 | | |
| 420,000 | | |
| 450,000 | | |
| 480,000 | | |
| 510,000 | Australopithecines | Warm Interglacial Period |
| 540,000 | | |
| 570,000 | | Cold Glacial Period |
| 600,000 | | |
| | The earliest hominoids occurred about 2 million years ago | Within each cold glacial period were a number of warmer phases known as interstadials |

Chapter 3

# THE AGRICULTURAL REVOLUTION

Earlier in this century prehistorians applied the term "Neolithic revolution," sometimes modified to "agricultural revolution," to a series of important changes that they viewed as one of the major developments in human history. As these writers saw it, after the great time-span of the Stone Age there occurred quite suddenly (relatively speaking) a sharp change in the human condition. Men moved from a hunting-and-gathering economy to one of husbandry: to the domestication of animals and the cultivation of crops.

As researchers have continued to work on the origins of agriculture, however, and as more and more information has accumulated from radiocarbon dates, our view of this change has altered somewhat. It now seems that the process of change was slow, diverse, and prolonged. Stone age man, we now know, was not *primarily* a big game hunter but an able scavenger who fed on vegetables, small animals, and shellfish as well as large game. And, far from being a single event (which ultimately affected most of the world through cultural diffusion) the later "invention" of husbandry was a complex and widely dispersed process. Nowadays, some would prefer to apply to it the term "evolution." This is not altogether satisfactory and the word "revolution" can be justified on the grounds that a new kind of economy, with far-reaching cultural effects, emerged in a number of parts of the world during the millennia after the last major glaciation.

There are two contradictory theories as to the origin of agriculture. The first is based on the large territory that hunters and gatherers generally need to support a small population. They must often devote an undue proportion of their time and energy to the primary task of winning food. It is then difficult for them to provide a surplus that will feed members of the community who are engaged in secondary tasks. This is not always so, however. In some favorable circumstances, game is plentiful: there is a surplus. When there is, the hunting territory can be relatively small, and the community does not have to move about so much, in pursuit of the food-animals. Settled or semi-permanent occupation of dwelling-sites becomes easier, and there is more scope for people to make use of the local vegetation for food, and perhaps even to make some experiments. If conditions remain favorable in this way, the community is very close to the significant changeover from dependence on the environment to the beginnings of control over it.

Conversely, some archaeologists argue that *un*favorable conditions may stimulate bold human experiments like the first agriculture. According to this hypothesis, people living in areas where the hunting is bad, or where the population has grown in excess of the available wild resources, resort to cultivation in a desperate attempt to improve their circumstances. Perhaps, at least in some cases, high population was the cause—rather than the result—of changeovers to agriculture.

A fine example of Neolithic Chinese pottery. Lung-Shan culture. The changeover from a hunting to an agrarian economy made a vast difference to human culture. Men did not make pottery until they planted crops and lived in villages. Fragile and time-consuming in its workmanship, this pot is unsuited to the mobile existence of the hunter. Nor could many early hunting societies spare the labor for this kind of specialized endeavor. Finally, the pot is a container. With the initiation of a sedentary lifestyle, man began to lay claim to the ground and its fruits, to fence in and to store, as well as to consume.

Such changeovers took place widely in the period after the slow withdrawal of the great ice sheets which, in the last major glaciation, had extended far from the polar regions and had blanketed the principal continental highlands. At that time recognizably human societies had already existed for a million years or so. As the world climate began slowly to improve, say 20,000 years ago, the Upper Paleolithic hunters who lived on a variety of plants and game had, by comparison with their Lower Paleolithic predecessors, quite a sophisticated range of equipment. This was the product of hundreds of thousands of years of experience and innovation. They were, in hunting-and-gathering terms, versatile, or at least capable of versatility.

This is important, because, as the climate changed, so did the natural environment. Tundra in many parts of the world gave way to forest, forest to desert, and so on. The game on which men had subsisted died out or moved away. Mankind was put to the test of adapting to greatly changed conditions. Such changes had occurred before, at long intervals, and mankind had survived, apparently without any profound change in the basic way of life. Now, parts of the human race rose magnificently to the challenge. Others, unlucky or unfit, failed to meet it, and disappeared just as the Neanderthalers had done 25,000 years before. *Homo sapiens* survived in a number of varieties which show the signs of physical adaptation to different environments—the major racial groupings of our species, with their variations in pigmentation, blood-groups, and superficial anatomy.

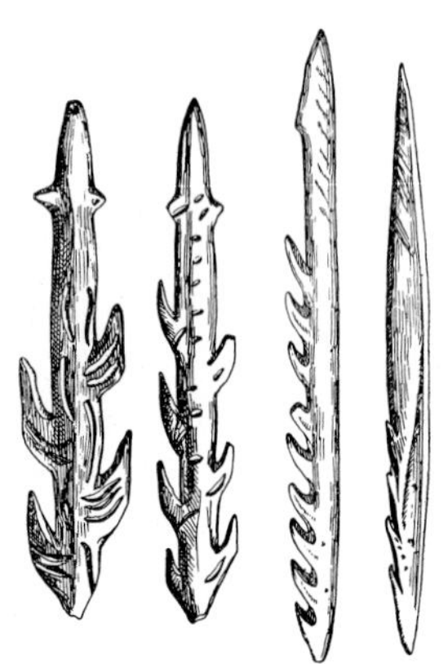

Barbed harpoons carved from reindeer antlers, dating from the end of the Upper Paleolithic period. The European hunters who made these tools were well adapted to the cold temperatures of the last glaciation. Reindeer were an important source of food and tools. Their extreme dependence on reindeer may have spurred a changeover from simple hunting to domestication. Tools of the period are also notable for their decorative, as well as utilitarian qualities.

In many parts of the world the transition was marked by the appearance of cultures which are often grouped under the broad heading of Mesolithic. In what are now temperate regions, the peoples of these cultures had adapted to forest. They designed implements to cope with timber, and hunting gear which was intended for the pursuit of game, including small game, quite different from that of the tundra.

What is most striking about the human communities of the centuries and millennia after, say, 10,000 B.C. was their adaptability in general. Generalization can be misleading. Local groups everywhere made their own adjustment to their circumstances, often, no doubt, enriching their experience by contact with other groups. The archaeological record indicates a considerable variety of cultures. Many of these were already beginning to make the transition from hunting and gathering, even as the Ice Age drew to a close.

## THE DOMESTICATION OF ANIMALS

Zoologists use the word "symbiosis" to describe a relationship between two animal species from which both benefit, and the term is applied by extension to the domestication of animals by man. The distinction between the close relationship which hunters may establish with the herds which supply their food and the relationship between men and animals in the earliest stages of domestication is a fine one. It is an important part of the hunter's skill to study and be familiar with his prey and its habits. Indeed, in the rituals of many societies, the hunter pretends to *be* the animal he hunts: in the most strictly literal sense he "gets inside its skin." Once he begins to exercise selection and control in his killing of the animals, choosing the young or the fat, the weak or the large, and once he begins to interfere sufficiently, for his own purposes, with the animal's habits, he has entered on a process that is difficult to distinguish from domestication. For example, in modern times, the Eskimos of North America hunted reindeer; the Chukchi of Siberia, just across the Bering Strait, herded them. It would be difficult to make this distinction on the archaeological evidence alone. In the concept of "domestication," the essential point appears to be the exercise of control over the breeding habits of the animals.

In particular, once a herd is prevented from breeding with "wild" animals of the same species, it is said to be domesticated.

Why this should happen so widely now, and not in earlier inter-glacial periods, requires some explanation. Indeed, it is not certain that it did not happen earlier, but if it did it was without immediate major economic and cultural consequences. The answer probably lies in the elaboration of human culture that had taken place in the immensely long Stone Age, and may be closely connected with the development of language. What is important in the origins of husbandry is not that this or that technique was applied to the provision of food, but that a whole new economy, combined with cultural complexity and systems of communication, provided the basis for the growth of specialization and urban civilization.

We can perhaps discern the beginning of the process in the cultures of hunters of late-glacial times. For example, there were, in the closing stages of the glaciation, bands of reindeer-hunters who moved across the North European plain. Their origins probably lay to the south-east. They produced elaborate antler- and flint-work, and were well advanced in efficient accommodation to their environment. The people of Moldavia, on the Dniestr River ate almost no meat apart from reindeer. They may possibly have been herders rather than hunters.

The earliest generally accepted evidence for domestication of animals, however, concerns sheep and goats. The skeletal remains of the two are notoriously difficult to distinguish. There appears to be no clear evidence that men hunted wild sheep before they domesticated them. Indeed there is a possibility that there *were* no wild sheep; that the sheep has been produced by domestication from a common wild sheep-goat stock. Undomesticated species of sheep exist today, in.parts of western Asia, but they could be wild descendants of domesticated ancestors.

Modern Navaho Indians shearing sheep. The wool will be exchanged for groceries or woven into blankets. Prehistoric lifestyles persist even in the modern world. These Indians of the American Southwest retain many aspects of the ancient pastoral and agricultural economy first developed by Neolithic cultures.

Shanidar, in northern Iraq, appears to have been a site where wild game was so plentiful that semi-permanent settlement was feasible, and the people in an early village there are believed to have kept domesticated sheep by 8,900 B.C. It seems certain that by 6,000 B.C. both sheep and goats were being kept for their meat at similar game-rich sites such as Ali Kosh. Bones of apparently domesticated goats were found in pre-pottery levels at Jericho and Jarmo. It would seem that about the same time cattle were already being domesticated in Greece, Crete and Anatolia (where there is somewhat ambiguous evidence from Catal Hüyük). These were derived from the primitive wild ox, a large animal with a wide Pleistocene distribution in the Old World. The much smaller shorthorn species appears not to have been domesticated until much later. Different varieties of domestic cattle are known from a very early date in Egypt and India, and it is very probable that domestication took place independently in different areas. Dogs were probably domesticated early; indeed it has more than once been suggested that the dog may have been the first animal to be so kept by hunters. This was not to help them in their task, since there is no evidence for this, and much contrary evidence to suggest that the use of hunting-dogs is, comparatively, a very late development. Like other animals dogs were domesticated in the first instance as sources of meat. They are animals easily domesticated, and as pack-hunters themselves they would have come much to the notice of late-glacial man. In the early stages of domestication the bones of dog are difficult to distinguish from those of wolf, and there is therefore some doubt about the dog-bones from the important Mesolithic site of Star Carr, in northern England, dated to about 7,500 B.C., just as there is a good deal of doubt about reputed dog remains from Idaho about a millennium earlier. However it is certain that the forest-adapted hunting-and-gathering cultures of northern Europe had domesticated dogs early in post-glacial times. The domestication of the pig in the Old World appears to have taken place later than that of some of the other animals mentioned, but by the time pottery was being made in the Neolithic villages of the Near East, pigs were being kept.

## THE BEGINNINGS OF CULTIVATION

The process of the domestication of animals has been discussed first because it seems to stem directly from the close contacts hunters, of necessity, maintained with the animal world. But hunting communities, of course, were not exclusively carnivorous. They exploited the food-resources of vegetation as well as animals and fish. They gathered berries, fruits, seeds, fungi, leaves, and whatever was found to be edible and sustaining. Men may have begun some cultivation of certain plants even earlier than they began domesticating animals. The priority is not known, nor is it in itself of great importance. What is important is the emergence of the new economy which combined domestication and cultivation. In looking at the origins of agriculture then, we are concerned with a process that is broadly contemporary in its development with animal husbandry.

A Neolithic spearhead dating from 2,500 B.C.

The process occurred independently in a number of areas. What they mostly have in common is a certain favorable combination of circumstances. The essential conditions that enabled men to develop the new economy appear to have been twofold: a comparative variety of environment, and its existence within a small area. Grassy uplands and hill-slopes, with a light and variable rainfall, provided such conditions in various parts of the Near and Middle East, in parts of Mesoamerica, in southeast Asia, north China, and Japan. Hill-slopes provide, within a short space measured horizontally, a range of mini-climates staged by altitude, so that a wide variety of plant and animal species is produced. If to this qualitative enrichment of the environment, quantitative enrichment is added by overall favorable circumstances of soil and climate, then it becomes possible even for hunting communities to settle down in fixed habitations and glean a surplus of subsistence from what nature provides. Such pre-cultivation villages are known from most of the areas mentioned, the earliest probably being villages on the slopes of the Jordan valley and scattered among the foothills to the north of the Tigris-Euphrates river system.

Men were almost certainly harvesting wild crops before they began to collect and sow seeds. Wild grasses suitable for harvesting because of the size and quality of their grains grew on the grassy upland slopes along the present southern borders of Turkey and Iran. Here settled, but still preagricultural, people began to gather these wild crops, using sickles studded with flint blades. They stored the grain they gathered, and they could reap enough in the short harvest season to last a small community until harvest time again. The most suitable wild crops in this area were einkorn (a form of wheat) and wild barley. Farther south, along the Jordan valley, another form of wild wheat, emmer, grew. These crops were of high nutritional value.

So settled communities were established in these and some similar areas. They had enough grain to see them through the year, they had fish and game, and, in Sir Mortimer Wheeler's words, they had leisure to "think between meals." This leisure, in due course, they learned to apply to the consolidation and elaboration of their economy. Some of the stored grain was kept for replanting, and by selection and control, these earliest "farmers" soon produced new strains of wheat and barley which gave bigger grains and greater yields of food. The process by which the cultivated grains were produced took several thousand years, since there are considerable differences between the wild and cultivated types. It was done along the Tigris and Euphrates, in Jordan, and very early too in Egypt. As early as 6,000 B.C., cereals were cultivated by villagers, who also domesticated sheep and goats in the hills to the north and east of the Tigris and Euphrates.

On the basis of this economy, culture was further elaborated. One of the widespread features of early Neolithic industries is the development of flint and stone implements which show a shift from hunting-gear, scrapers for skins, and all-purpose tools. Pottery is an element in most Neolithic cultures, very often showing an origin in woven or plaited vessels, grass baskets and so on, which were plastered with clay to render them suitable for containing liquids, the clay baked on the cooking fire. Other early pottery vessels, however, with a smooth finish, appear to reproduce the form of leather containers, skin bags formed round a withy hoop and the like.

It is possible that the shift from hunting and gathering to early cereal agriculture may have taken place in the Far East independently as early as in the Near East, or earlier. There the post-glacial climatic improvement began to set in by about 12,000 to 10,000 B.C., and was accompanied by the widespread appearance of new evidences of material culture, marked first by ground or edge-ground stone implements, and later by cord-marked pottery. The post-glacial Jomon culture of Japan, from about 8,000 B.C., had such cord-marked pottery—probably the oldest pottery in the world. Early developments in pottery and ground stone implements also accompanied transitions to early agriculture in north China, on the lower Weishui and Yellow rivers. The cereal crops associated with these cultures are millet, and to a much lesser degree rice, derived probably from a grass that grew wild in swampy areas of southeast Asia. It is probable, although not certain, that this southeastern zone was the earliest to be cultivated in the Far East, and perhaps the world. In 1965–1966 a cave in northeastern Thailand yielded the remains of several edible plants, including nuts, water chestnuts, a species of cucumber, and two kinds of beans. Some of this material is 12,000 years old. If cultivated, southeastern Asia may replace southwestern Asia as the site of man's earliest farming endeavor.

Artist's reconstruction of Neolithic lake dwellings in Switzerland. The change to an agrarian economy and sedentary habitation encouraged important developments in environmental adaptation. This Swiss village was built on stilts to profit from marine resources while at the same time escaping floods.

In the New World, the picture is somewhat different, partly because of the greater variety of crops domesticated by the American Indians, partly because of the very different fauna of the American continents. There is abundant evidence from the Americas for early symbiosis of men and animals, and some of this may have occurred not much later, if at all, than in the Old World. The focal areas of development are in coastal Peru, the American Southwest, south-central Mexico, and northeastern Mexico. Maize is one of the important domesticated plants, but there were many others including squash, lima beans, gourds, and avocado pears. The domestication of the llama and the alpaca has been compared to that of the reindeer, in that the animals live in conditions close to those of their wild ancestors.

These complex processes by which in different parts of the world people changed the basic terms of their physical relationship with the natural world, demonstrate, in their independent and more or less simultaneous development, that something more than a mere environmental determinism was at work. Similar conditions must often have obtained before, during man's long history as man. What had changed, in the time after the last great glaciation, was man himself, not physically but through his elaboration of what anthropologists mean by the word "culture." He was by now equipped to make use of favorable environmental conditions and to go on to control and manipulate the environment. The "agricultural revolution" comes from within mankind, not from the accident of the occurrence of edible grasses or amenable meat-producing animals. It was a long-drawn-out, significant change in economic subsistence and cultural patterns.

Settled villages demand a very different system of relationships between people from the relationships of moving hunting-bands. Easing of the constant pressure of the need to find food provided leisure for thought, experimentation, and diversification of activity.

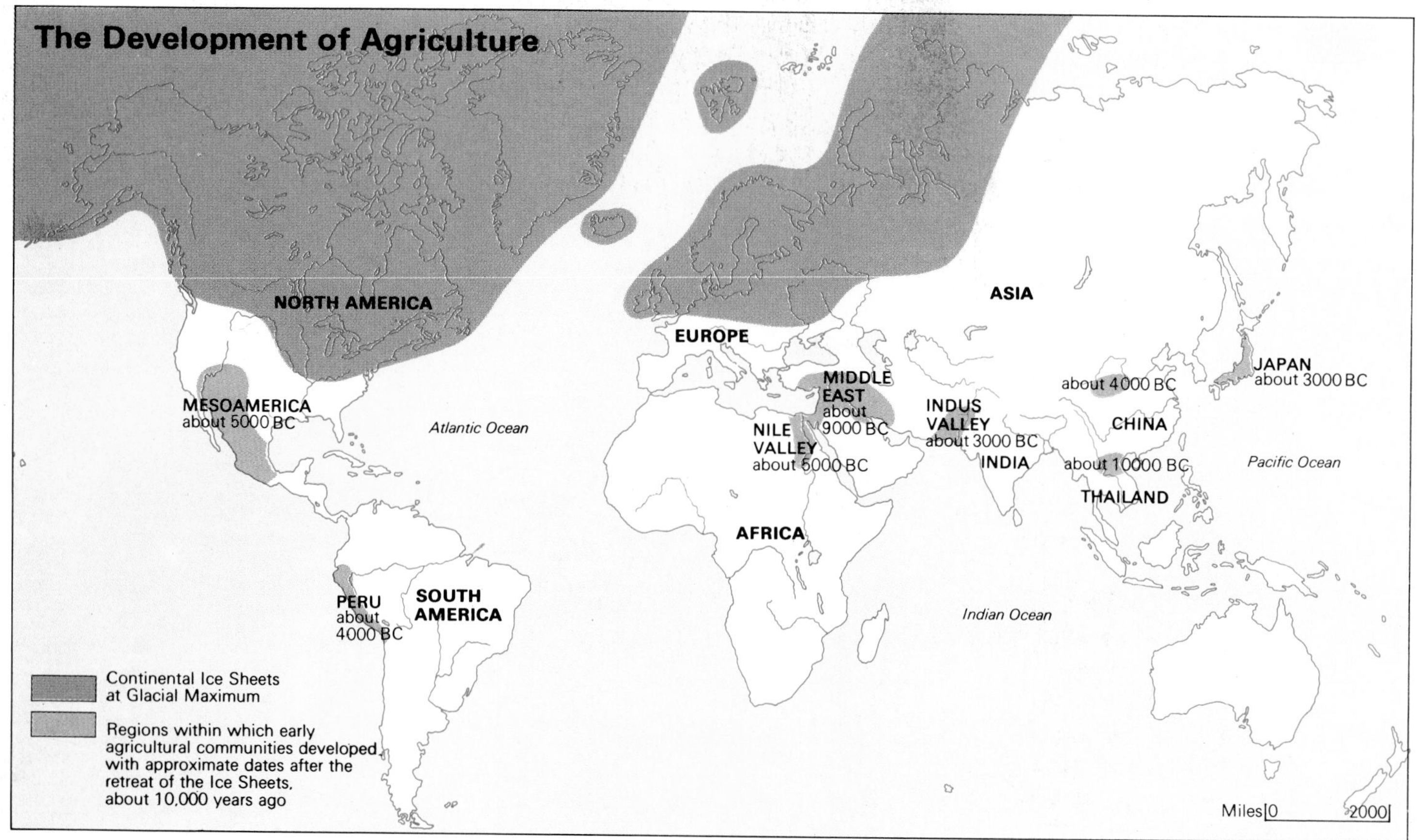

## THE CONSEQUENCES OF THE AGRICULTURAL REVOLUTION

Once families became sedentary, there was no longer the same urgent need to limit the number of births, and probably, also, there was a decrease in natural mortality. The tendency of human populations to expand to the limits of the food resources immediately available is a trend continued into our own time. (Pre-agricultural groups were ultimately limited, of course, by the food available to them, but because of behavioral adaptions they generally stayed well within the carrying capacity of their land.) Moreover, land used for agriculture can provide food for far more people than the same acreage used for hunting. Thus, agricultural populations could increase not only in size but also in density.

With the advent of a sedentary way of life communities came to be stratified. In the earliest villages, such as Jarmo, the fields may have been shared and worked communally. However, within a few thousand years a very small percentage of the population came to own a very large percentage of the productive land and of the domesticated herd animals, a situation that still obtains today. The possession and inheritance of land and, by extension, of other material wealth, impossible for the nomadic hunter, divided the human population into semipermanent categories of the haves and have-nots.

Also, because agriculture produced so much more food with so much less effort, communities became diversified. The work of a comparative few was sufficient to provide food for the entire group, and so other members of the group could develop special skills or trades or interests—tinkers, tailors, tradesmen, bankers, poets, scholars, all the rich mixture of which a modern community is composed.

The change to permanent settlement had profound consequences. An immediate and direct effect was an increase in population. One of the most striking characteristics of hunting groups is that they limit their numbers vigorously. A woman on the move cannot carry more than one infant along with her household baggage, minimal though that may be. When simple means of birth control—often just abstention—are not effective, she resorts to abortion or, more probably, infanticide. In addition, there is a high natural mortality, particularly among the very young, the very old, the ill, the disabled, and women at childbirth. As a result, populations dependent on hunting tend to remain small.

A Neolithic figurine carved in limestone from Senorbi. With the advent of sedentary agriculture, a new artistic style began to emerge, for reasons that scholars have yet to ascertain. Compare this stylized geometric figure with the brilliant realism of the Lascaux painting in the previous chapter.

Finally the observation of the rhythm of the seasons in agricultural villages was different from that of nomad camps following the yearly movements of the game. The change reveals itself in various ways, many of which in the absence of verbal records we can hardly begin to understand. For example, the brilliant impressionistic realism in art, which reflects the hunter's acute and fleeting observation of his prey, gives way in most areas to a linear, often non-representational ornamentation. We get many glimpses of considerable changes in religious and magical beliefs and practices, the slow rhythm of sowing, growth, harvest and decay replacing in men's imaginations the more fluid movement of the game. Little local gods of the fields appear to dominate the Neolithic religious landscape, and everywhere there appear to develop elaborate cults of the dead, reflecting perhaps a new consciousness of the earth which gives and receives.

But most important, having broken the earth with his stone hoes, having intervened successfully in the life of the animals with whom he shared his world, man went on, almost without a break to probe deeper into nature, studying the chemistry of its constituents to "domesticate" the earth itself; producing pottery, and not long afterwards, metals; studying the seasons, the stars which appeared to govern them, time, and space. The "agricultural revolution" was mankind's apprenticeship for civilization.

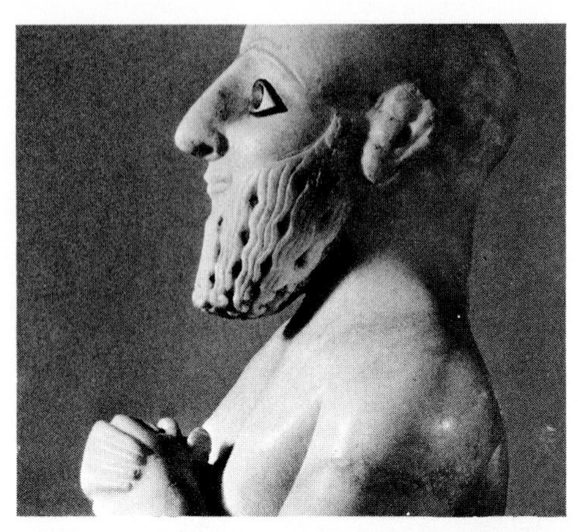

ΑΡΑΔΙΩΝ
ΙΝ
ΠC

# Part II Man's Emergence into Society

Chapter 4

# SUMER AND MESOPOTAMIA

## GEOGRAPHY

The modern nation of Iraq includes a broad plain watered by the Tigris and Euphrates rivers, known in ancient days as Mesopotamia (Greek for "between the rivers"). The names for these regions changed many times throughout their history, even in the epoch of the first civilizations. For purposes of clarity, the lower reaches of the plain, beginning near the point where the two rivers nearly converge, can be labeled Babylonia. Babylonia in turn encompasses two geographical areas—the delta of this river system in the south (which is known as Sumer) and the north (which later came to be known as Akkad). It was within this delta that the first civilization appeared.

## EARLY SETTLEMENT

As we saw in part I chapter 3, agriculture was practiced by 6000 B.C. in the regions to the north and east of the Tigris-Euphrates plain. A look at the map reveals 300 miles between the sites of these first farming villages in the Zagros foothills and the Tigris-Euphrates delta; yet it was here that the first civilization was founded. It is not known when the delta was originally settled because geological changes may have buried its first villages under tons of silt. The earliest remains excavated so far (dated about 5000 B.C.) show sufficient development to suggest that it may have been inhabited from the sixth millennium B.C.

Where these first settlers came from is equally unknown, but the population was rapidly enlarging in the agricultural northeast and may have encouraged migration. Working from known to unknown, archaeologists have labeled these people "Sumerians," a name referring not to a nationality, nor even to a specific migratory group, but to the speakers of a common language. The Sumerians may have been preceded to the delta by another people, or they may have coexisted there from the beginning of the settlement and later grown in number and influence. Certainly theirs was not the only language spoken in the area. Semitic-speakers are known to have lived in southern Mesopotamia from an early date, and there is evidence of a third, unknown language in some of the earliest place-names. But, whatever their origins, Sumerian-speakers were most numerous in the world's first fully developed cities, and the oldest writing so far discovered was made in their tongue.

| 4500 BC | 4000 | 3500 | 3000 | 2500 | 2000 | 1500 |
|---|---|---|---|---|---|---|
| | RISE OF SUMERIAN CITIES | | GREAT PERIOD OF SUMERIAN CITIES | | | |
| Irrigation farming<br>Towns and simple temples | Development of trade | Bronze produced<br>Writing introduced | Political disunity, cultural zenith | Sargon of Akkad (2371–2316)<br>Attacks by neighbors and barbarians | | Fall of Babylon (1531) |

Browsing goat, from the royal graves of Ur, c. 2750 B.C. This statuette, which stands about twenty inches tall, is elaborately crafted in gold, lapis lazuli, silver and shell—all inlaid upon an asphalt adhesive. All of these precious materials are imports, attesting to a range of Mesopotamian trade from India to Asia Minor. The original use or symbolic meaning of the figure is unknown. The motif of a goat climbing in a tree does, however, occur frequently in Mesopotamian art.

## AGRICULTURE: THE BASIS OF CITY LIFE (6000–3500 B.C.)

For the burgeoning population of the Fertile Crescent, the Tigris-Euphrates delta had its advantages: abundant wildlife, soft, fertile soil, and the rich fruit of the date palm. But there were also important drawbacks: the delta was a patch-work of swamps and sandbanks, with a water level that varied greatly with the seasons; it had very little rain. Seed could be sown in the mud left by the spring floods; but summer killed the growing shoots. The only solution was an artificial water supply. By 5000 B.C. the farmers of the southern valleys had learned to irrigate their crops, an innovation with crucial implications for their developing society.

These early settlers concentrated along the narrow strip of land adjacent to the rivers, where irrigation was a simple matter of cutting through embankments to water the lower surrounds. But the resulting density of population meant competition for the available game, grazing land, and fields. The pattern of the Zagros foothill settlements—similar self-sufficient villages located at some distance from each other—gave way to a closer society, where cooperation was essential to survival. Individuals with authority, a managerial class, were needed to create and maintain the irrigation systems and to reconcile divergent interests. The agricultural surplus produced in the easily plowed soil could support this non-farming class.

Geography contributed to social cohesion in another way: annual flooding renewed the fertility of the soil, making migratory cultivation unnecessary. Thus social units based on shared territory could supplant smaller groups based on kinship. The shared climate of a single locality may have influenced this transfer of authority. Local inhabitants could come to feel more bound to the gods controlling sun and storm, and to their priestly deputies, than to the ties of kinship.

Planned cooperation was also essential to the developing complexities of irrigation. Larger crop yields could feed bigger populations, which in turn could be

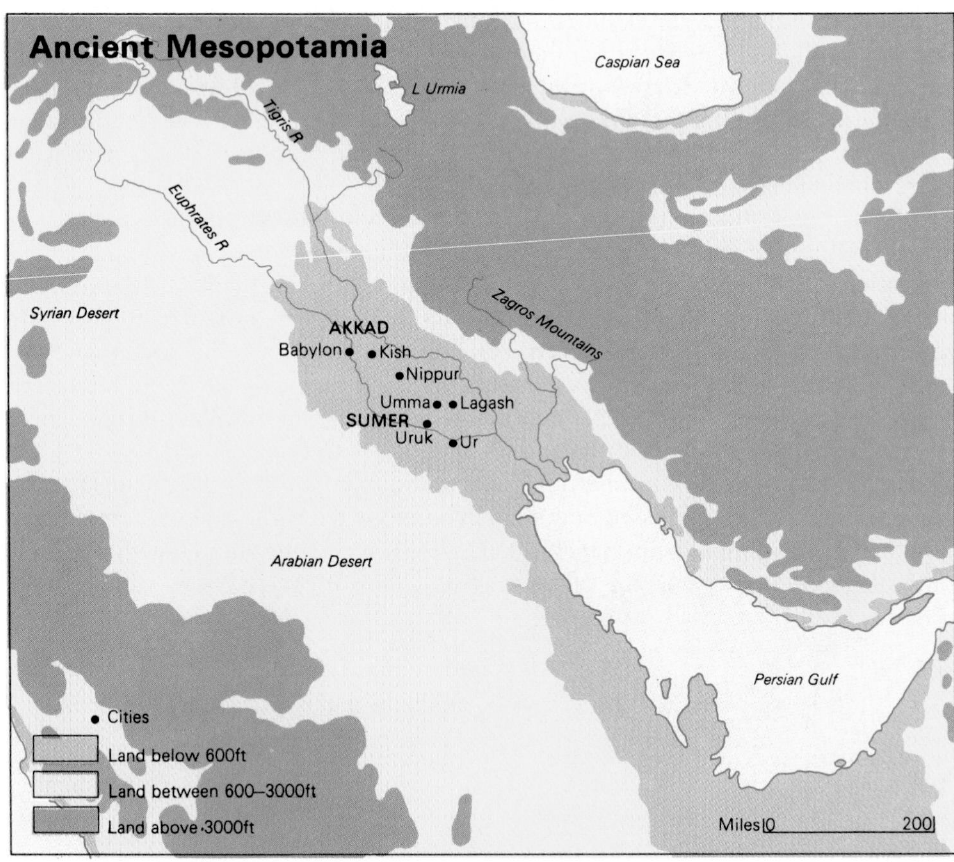

organized into large-scale projects extending the system of dikes and canals to cultivate still more land.

Other mixed blessings peculiar to the area contributed to its rise in importance. The plains lacked stone, timber, and metals, necessitating trading expeditions; but travel was facilitated by the region's waterways and unobstructed routes overland. Trade flourished, and the enlarging towns became centers of communication and stimulus for the whole surrounding region. Again, agricultural success provided a surplus for trading purposes.

The expansion of this river-valley settlement was not unlimited. Rising slopes could not be watered, nor could low-lying swamps be drained. The flat plain of the Tigris-Euphrates allows water to flow with gravity for several miles, but it also allows flood waters to roll along the same route. If drought dried up the canals, or flood caused the rivers to change course, immediate re-channeling was the only alternative to drought. As twentieth-century life continually demonstrates, reliance on technical innovation means vulnerability to technical failure.

A further check on Mesopotamian expansion was provided by the human environment. River-dependent societies are vulnerable to whoever controls the land upstream, a point of strategy crucial to the entire history of Mesopotamian politics and war. In spite of these constraints, a wholly new society emerged in these valleys, the first on this planet to deserve the title "civilization."

Marshlands in southern Iraq, site of the Sumerian civilization. The advantages and drawbacks of the region's geography are apparent here. The fertile soil, the nutritious date palm, and the land and marine animals which thrive in such conditions greatly benefited early inhabitants. These low-lying areas are, however, vulnerable to floods. It was necessary to drain and fill in large tracts in order to make them cultivable. Conversely, the Sumerian plain also includes larger areas of desert, which demand extensive irrigation for farming.

As early as 5000 B.C. the Sumerians lived in towns and constructed simple temples. In the next millennium and a half these towns would become cities and the temples monumental complexes. The years 3700–3200 B.C. saw a sharp rise in population, undoubtedly influenced by community cooperation, improved agriculture, and the technical innovations, such as the animal-drawn plow. As cities emerged during these years, bigger food surpluses freed many for specialized vocations. Trading contacts with surrounding areas and further regions, such as the Iranian highlands and even Afghanistan, developed in tandem with agricultural growth. As early as 4000 B.C. alabaster, obsidian, turquoise, cornelian, and lapis lazuli were imported into the region. Some idea of intervening obstacles and distances can be derived from an early myth, which tells of how one ruler of the Sumerian city of Uruk desired to import precious stones to decorate a temple. The necessary lapis and cornelian could be obtained from a city in eastern Iran—separated from Uruk by seven mountain ranges and at least one kingdom. Such trade was encouraged by the desire of emerging social classes to secure precious, status-differentiating objects. In turn, large-scale trade encouraged pictorial record-keeping which developed into the first writing by about 4000 B.C.

Excavations of Uruk dating from 3500 B.C. reveal a seventy yards by thirty yards temple, the lower walls of which are built of imported limestone. These remains also included a large terrace, on which stood other large buildings with elaborately embellished pillars, panelled and recessed walls, and a unique type of decoration called stone-cone mosaics. Uruk's citizens were literate, socially stratified, and technically innovative. Only a highly organized society could have constructed and decorated these buildings. By the time of this city, 3500 B.C., that collection of developments we call "civilization" had happened in Sumer.

## SUMERIAN CITY LIFE (3500–3000 B.C.)

Sumer was an urban society. Yet, like the Neolithic villagers, Sumerian city-dwellers were mostly farmers. Barley was the main crop, but wheat, emmer, millet, sesame, and other fruits and vegetables were grown, and cattle and sheep domesticated. But where the early villagers cultivated small family-sized plots, the irrigation necessary to Sumer demanded large-scale agriculture worked by community effort. Such cooperation, as we have seen, helped to furnish the political stability and food surpluses necessary for large, dense populations. Estimates for the population of Sumerian cities at their height (c.3000–2000 B.C.) range from 10,000 for several cities to half a million for the metropolitan district of Ur.

Besides farmers, such populations included a great many specialists: herdsmen, fishermen, merchants, craftsmen, doctors, architects, scribes, soldiers, and priests. Most of these people lived within the city walls in one-story brick houses consisting of several rooms grouped around an open court. The wealthy had houses of two stories, with servants' rooms and sometimes even a private chapel.

### The Temple Economy

Dominating the city, both physically and politically, was the local temple. Often the temple was constructed in the form of a *ziggurat*—a staged tower built like an artificial mountain with staircases winding around the outside. The biblical legend of the Tower of Babel may derive from such constructions. Each temple was considered the house of the local god, and suitably adorned with rich mosaics. Much of the city was deemed to be the god's property, the priests and temple community his personal household. Theology combined with large-scale agriculture to produce a temple-economy, with temple administration of as much as a third of the city's land and much greater indirect influence.

The arid Sumerian plain, as we have seen, could only be irrigated by large groups organized into work gangs. In addition to promoting social cohesion, such a system stimulated the rise of a managerial class—the local priests. When we remember how absolutely Sumerian agriculture depended on the weather, it is not surprising to learn that its forces were deified: Enki (the god of water), Ki (earth), Enlil (wind), Inanna (war and love), and An (heaven). Nor is it surprising that their

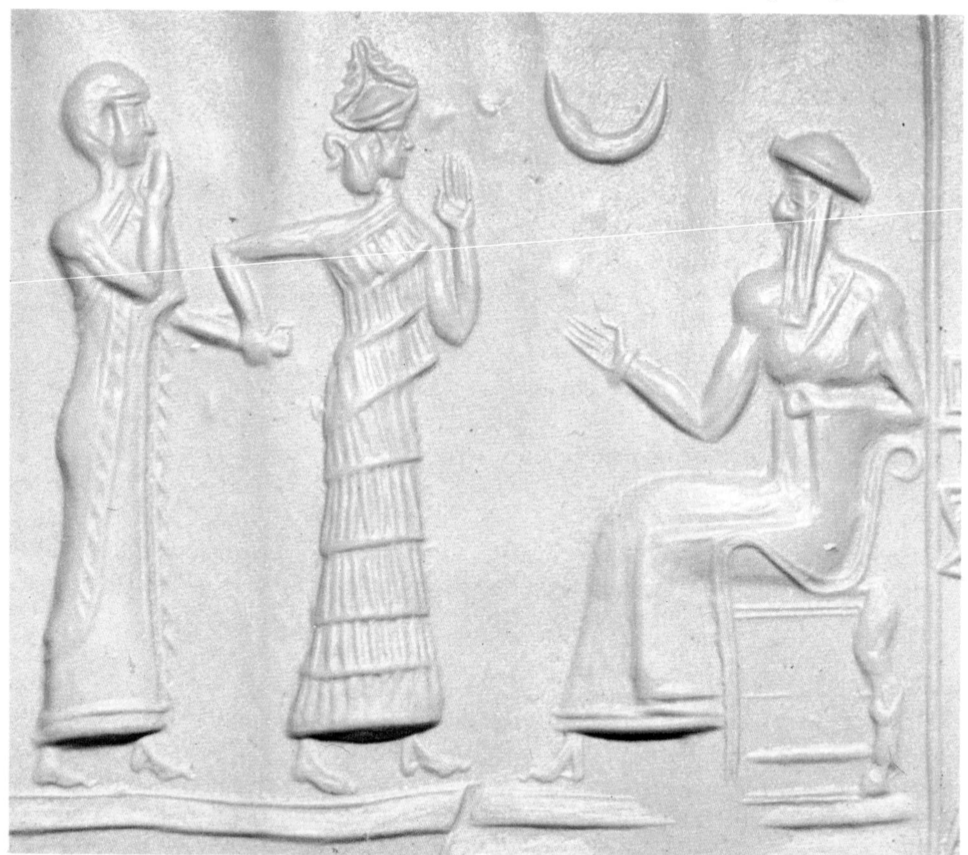

Sumerian cylinder seal impression, c. 2100 B.C., showing Ur-Nammu, the King of Ur, receiving an official. After the dissolution of the Akkadian empire, Sumer experienced a renaissance under the leadership of the city of Ur.

human agents, the priests, came to have supreme earthly authority over crop production and thus much of Sumerian life. As the steward of the local god, the priest not only supervised the temple and the ceremonies of religious worship, he saw to it that the crops were sown, irrigated and harvested. The technical skills appropriated to such functions—mathematics for surveying and book-keeping, astronomy for seasonal calculation—were a priestly monopoly. So, naturally enough, were the educational facilities by which these skills were transferred.

In addition to their supervision of agriculture and education, Sumerian priests had a third basis for their power—control of the grain surplus. Such a surplus, for all the security and development it provided, was rarely accumulated by Neolithic subsistence farmers. The Sumerians may have been persuaded to exert themselves to feed others by their fear of the unpredictable gods: a propitiatory share of the harvest might persuade them to continue their blessings. More practically, the grain hoarded in years of plenty could be redistributed during famines. Again innovation had its drawbacks, for whoever controlled the surplus could control the city-state. In early Mesopotamia, the priests were in control. Some idea of the extent and complexity of temple government can be gathered from the numbers employed by one Sumerian temple: 1,500 out of a probable urban population of 5,000. The priests, however, were not the sole authorities in the Sumerian cities. Assemblies of elders also played an important role in Sumerian city government.

Elaborate statue of Ebikil, superintendent of the palace in the Sumerian city of Mari, c. 2500 B.C. The clasped hands and large staring eyes suggest an anxious reverence. Ebikil's obedient pose is verbally expressed in a later Mesopotamian poem:
*My affliction grows, I cannot find justice . . . But I think only of prayer and supplication, Invocation was my care, sacrifice my rule. The day of the worship of the gods was my delight.*

### Religious Beliefs

The dependence upon natural forces which led the Sumerians to rely on their priests is further shown in their theology. These early city-dwellers believed that the universe and their personal lives were ruled both by formal gods and deified natural forces. The Sumerian story of creation, which comes to us on a tablet from much later times (early sixth century B.C.), is strikingly like that of the Bible, and forms part of the tradition from which Genesis derived:

*All lands were sea*
*Then there was a movement in the midst.*
*At that time Eridu was made. . . .*
*Marduk laid reeds on the face of the waters,*
*He formed dust and poured it out beside the reeds*
*That he might cause the gods to dwell in the dwelling of their hearts' desire.*
*He formed mankind*
*With him the goddess Aruru created the seeds of mankind*
*The beasts of the field and living things in the fields he formed*
*The Tigris and Euphrates he created and established them in their place:*
*The grass, the rush of the marsh, the reed and the forest he created . . .*
*The Lord Marduk built a dam beside the sea . . .*
*Reeds he formed, trees he created;*
*Bricks he laid, buildings he erected;*
*Houses he made, cities he built. . . .*

Of course, the Sumerians themselves brought civilization out of the deserts and watery wastes, but they attributed that achievement to the gods. Similarly, they saw their continued welfare at the mercy of the impersonal forces of these deities. To please them they practiced regular public devotions, employing priests, anointers, musicians, and eunuchs. Libations and animal sacrifices were offered daily; and the revival of the vegetation god who brought the spring was celebrated annually by a ceremonial marriage between a man representing the risen god and a priestess representing the goddess of the morning star.

### Social Conditions

The great majority of Sumerians were free citizens, and even the poorest owned a farm and livestock or a house and garden. Slavery existed, but as a system of purchased labor. A man might sell his family to pay off his debts, but once enslaved, these people could engage in business, borrow money, and buy their freedom —at an average price of ten shekels, less than that of an ass. Children were under the absolute authority of their parents, who could disinherit them, sell them into slavery, and arrange their marriages. Women, however, had some legal rights, including the right to hold property and engage in business. Marriage rights resided primarily in the husband, who could divorce his wife on slender grounds or take a second if the first proved unable to conceive.

### Recreation

Music was a well-developed art in Sumer, as evidenced by references to drums, tambourines, reed and metal pipes, and by the beautifully wrought lyres found in the royal tomb at Ur. Sumerian men enjoyed wrestling and boxing; they hunted; and they raced in light chariots pulled by four onagers, or wild asses. (The horse was a much later import.) At banquets they sat in groups and enjoyed a communal jar of beer sipped through long metal tubes.

### Trade

Lacking timber, metals, and stone, the Sumerians were compelled to barter their surplus or simply seize the resources of neighboring lands. Relative ease in overland and river travel facilitated this trade, but the distances covered are still striking. The Sumerians got tin from eastern Iran, from Asia Minor and Syria, and in the second millennium B.C., from Europe. Copper was imported from Oman in the

*Right:* Reconstructed bull's head decoration, found in a lyre taken from the queen or priestess Shub-ad's tomb at Ur, c. 2800 B.C. Modern understanding of Sumerian civilization was greatly advanced by Sir Leonard Woolley's excavation of these royal tombs in the 1920s. The treasures found in Shub-ad's tomb include some of the finest museum pieces ever to have been taken from the soil of Mesopotamia.

*Above:* Lyres like the one that it decorated are shown being played in a figured panel—the Standard of Ur—from the same royal graves.

south of the Persian Gulf (also a source of stone) and perhaps from the Caucasus as well. Afghanistan furnished lapis lazuli, India sent shells, and the mountains of Syria and Iran were sources of cedar and pine. Trade was carried out by direct expedition, by exchange of products with middle-men in neighboring communities, and by the establishment of trading centers abroad. Thus Sumerian influence reached far beyond their actual homeland, from Asia Minor to India, and this influence was reciprocal. Importation of metal tools and techniques improved Sumerian agriculture (animal-drawn metal plows are one example); larger monumental structures could be built with metal tools; and Sumerian warfare became more lethal as harder, more durable weapons were introduced.

### Technology

Agricultural improvements, long-range trade, and vocational specialization were the products of Sumerian ingenuity. And, as we have seen, these innovations stimulated further technical development. The potter's wheel, and then the wagon wheel, the plow, and the sailboat were Sumerian inventions. Measuring and surveying instruments and a sexagesimal number system developed from the needs of hydraulic engineering. By 3500 B.C. Sumerian smiths knew how to alloy copper and tin to produce bronze. They also worked in silver, gold, and lead. The first metal-casting is attributed to these smiths, as is the first riveting, soldering and engraving. This civilization can also be credited with the sophisticated work in textiles, including bleaching and dyeing. Prescriptions on Sumerian tablets show that physicians derived many drugs from plant, animal, and inorganic sources.

### Writing

But the outstanding achievement of this society was the invention of writing, a

*Above:* Sumerian tablet in early pictographic signs, c. 2800 B.C. The Sumerians, who invented writing about 4000 B.C., did not realize the possibility of analyzing a language into letters. When they meant to convey the idea of a hand they actually drew a hand. Abstractions were denoted by symbols or by the combination of two signs, for example, "mouth" and "water" meant "to drink". *Left:* Detail from the Royal Standard of Ur (c. 2800 B.C.). One side of this mosaic panel shows scenes of war, the other scenes of peace. Here men bring cattle and other gifts to the king.

development dating back to 4000 B.C. (See chapter 11). This early writing is pictorial, representing numbers and objects like sheep, cows, temples, and agricultural implements. This writing looks like inventories and receipts, and could have arisen from the need to record agricultural practices (such as grain storage and distribution) and the exchange of traded goods. At first the Sumerians wrote by scratching wet clay with the pointed end of a reed. Over the centuries a faster process was developed in which symbols were stamped into the clay with the wedge-shaped end of the reed—thus their name "cuneiform" or wedge-shaped writing. The cuneiform system served as the main form of writing in western Asia for 2,000 years—long after the civilization that invented it had disappeared. Transmission of this new technique from generation to generation meant schools. Originally vocational training centers for scribes, they gradually developed into cultural centers for scholars, scientists and poets. School discipline was severe, with one member of the faculty titled "the man in charge of the whip." The curriculum consisted of spelling, literature and composition, and mathematics.

Detail from a Sumerian relief c. 2560 B.C. showing soldiers from the city of Lagash, marching against the neighboring town of Umma. They are armed with spears and battle-axes, and protected by leather helmets, leather strips across their chests, and long wool skirts. War in Sumer was construed as a religious conflict between the patron gods of the contending cities. The king was seen simply as the agent of the city-god. His victories were the god's victories, his defeats the voluntary surrender of power from one god to another.

### Politics and War

Each Sumerian city was the center of a small city-state. Between fifteen and twenty city-states coexisted on the Sumerian plain. Though politically autonomous, these cities were bound by trading ties, shared language, and religious beliefs. The city of Nippur, home of the God of Wind and Storm, Enlil, may even have functioned as the religious capital of early Sumer.

As, however, all irrigable land came under cultivation, the city-states were brought into direct proximity. No authority existed to arbitrate disputes over boundaries and water rights, and the results were inter-city friction and chronic war. Barbarian raiders provided another threat to peace. As the cities gained in wealth, they attracted the interest of these plunderers; and their temple-centered social discipline was no match for the military lifestyle of the nomadic raiders. By the end of the fourth millennium, urban defense demanded a new political structure in the Sumerian city, one geared to war.

Later tradition held that after a flood ravished the land (another Biblical prototype) "the throne of kingship had been lowered from heaven" upon the rulers of Kish, a city near the northern border. Some archaeologists speculate that permanent kingship developed from the institution of the temporary war leader. Others observe that a considerable part of a city's territory consisted of collectively owned clan lands, which in time became the property of *lugals* (great landowners). Lugal later became a royal title, suggesting an economic basis for the rise to secular rule. Whatever its origin, kingship provided the concentration of power and the military discipline necessary to the troubled times. The temple bureaucracy declined in power, and by c.2900 B.C. kings, with supreme military and judicial authority, were the rule in Sumerian cities.

## CONFLICT (2900–1792)

Sumerian history after 2900 B.C. can be seen as a pattern of alternating political consolidation and division. Local quarrels between adjacent communities provoked larger systems of rival alliances, which from 2500 centered around the cities of Lagash and Umma. Royal authority was increased by alliances between local kings and priests. Religious control of agriculture was reduced and temple land redistributed, sharpening class distinctions. In response to the exploitation of the poor, Urukagina, king of Lagash, attempted reform. Inscriptions from the period state that he "removed from the inhabitants of Lagash usury, forestalling, famine, robbery, attacks; he established their freedom . . . (and) protected the widow and orphan from the powerful man." Before these reforms could bear fruit, Lagash was conquered by Lugalzaggisi of Umma, the first ruler known to have united most of the cities of Sumer under one lordship (c.2400).

But where political history reflects near total discord, the religious, cultural, and artistic achievements of this period laid the foundations for the entire Mesopotamian tradition. The great Sumerian pantheon gave a sense of identity to these quarreling states. The tradition of the scribal school, which would become the chief vehicle for the transmission of Mesopotamian culture for nearly three millennia, was established during these years. Finally, Sumerian statuary became a dominant art form and personal ornaments exquisitely shaped from precious metals, like gold, and exotic stones, like lapis lazuli, adorned the royal graves of Ur and Kish. Objects like the golden helmet of Prince Meskalamdug, a golden ceremonial dagger with a lapis lazuli handle, and bull-headed lyres which were discovered at the Royal Cemetery of Ur provide incontrovertible evidence for an affluent, highly stratified society structured around organized trade and specialized craftsmen. The years 2900–2350 B.C. were an age of great cultural achievement, marred only by the lack of internal political unity.

A generation later (c.2350) Semitic-speaking Akkadians, under Sargon whose land lay to the north of Sumer, united with their southern neighbors by conquest. Strategically located between the high civilization to the south and the barbarism of outlying regions, the Akkadians could draw on both barbarian military skill and civilized technology. Potential emperors have frequently exploited such positions.

Ironically, Sargon's conquest made very little difference to the daily existence of the average Sumerian, but it greatly influenced the life-style of the victors. Southern temple communities and local kingdoms continued as tributaries of Akkad, while the north imported the irrigation techniques, cuneiform writing, and cultural traditions of their enemies. Sumerian political systems, however, did not transfer. The Akkadians had preserved certain native traditions with the nomadic way of life which prompted them; for instance, secular officials, rather than priests, supervised their irrigation projects. This change had an important effect on Mesopotamia: it encouraged the transfer of hydraulic technology to secular administration which had begun before the Akkadian conquest. Now the knowledge of irrigation could spread without alien religious traditions or the jealous supervision of the priests. Large-scale agriculture, and resulting developments in civilization, could now expand more rapidly.

For 150 years the Akkadian empire brought unity to Sumer and trained contacts that reached, as Sargon boasted, "from the lower sea to the upper sea" (the Persian Gulf to the Mediterranean). Then it too succumbed to attacks by tribes from the Zagros mountains and the upper Tigris. A dark age of a century ensued. However, in 2111 B.C., Ur-Nanshe revived the southern city of Ur, united Sumer and Akkad, and established a period of Sumerian renaissance for another century. The administration of conquered territories was improved, with the foundation of the first known bureaucracy, controlling a professional colonial administration. Sumerian culture thrived, with new refinements in sculpture and the first recordings of many oral traditions and myths.

Weakened by successive conflicts with the semi-civilized Elamites to the east and barbarous Amorites to the west, the power of Ur was overthrown about 1950. Two and a half centuries of disunity followed in Mesopotamia, while events of great importance occurred elsewhere. Civilized social organization had, by this time, spread widely beyond the Tigris-Euphrates delta, so that powerful kingdoms bordered upon the old centers from which Mesopotamian civilization had sprung. To the north, the Assyrians conducted a large-scale trade in metals in the nineteenth century. On the Mediterranean, coastal kingdoms flourished, taking advantage of their relations with Egypt and Mesopotamia. Nearer to the Tigris-Euphrates plain, barbarians to the east and west, like the rising Amorites, grew in strength. Thus the balance of Mesopotamian power was no longer a matter of internal alignment between north and south, Akkad and Sumer. About 1792 B.C. this balance of power was overturned by an Amorite ruler, Hammurabi of Babylon.

## THE SOCIETY OF HAMMURABI (1792–1750)

Hammurabi is best known for his code of laws, engraved on a pillar of black basalt eight feet high still in existence. In fact, this code, though in part modeled on its Sumerian predecessors, exhibits a much harsher spirit in its punishments. Examination of it reveals important changes in Mesopotamian society:

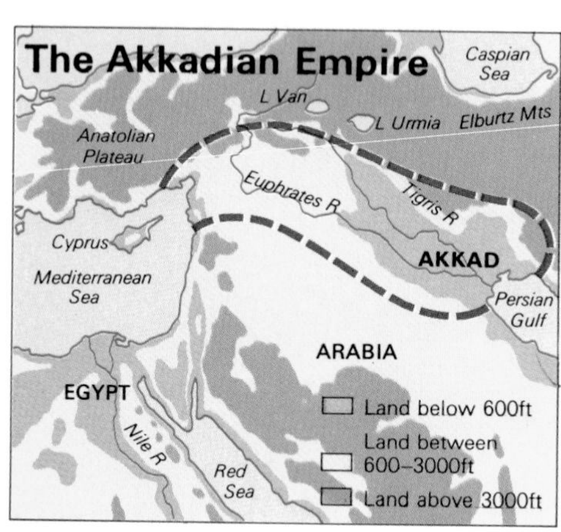


196. *If a man destroy the eye of another man, they shall destroy his eye.*
197. *If he breaks a man's bone, they shall break his bone.*
198. *If he destroys the eye of a common man or break a bone of a common man, he shall pay one mina of silver. . . .*
200. *If a man knock out a tooth of a man of his own rank, they shall knock out his tooth.*
201. *If he knock out a tooth of a common man, he shall pay one-third mina of silver.*

This was a stratified society, one which included the ruling elite and merchant classes appropriate to empire. It was also a highly organized one. The epilogue to the code styles Hammurabi "the efficient king," and his correspondence reveals amazing attention to detail. In one letter he orders the channel cleared to release a long string of boats held up in the lower Euphrates. In others he invites officials to a sheep-shearing festival, reforms the calendar, punishes an official for bribery, and postpones a lawsuit so that the temple baker can look after a religious feast at Ur. Royal responsibilities, and royal power, had grown since the early centuries of Sumerian civilization. Some of the Mesopotamian kings had even claimed divinity, although—unlike in Egypt—the idea did not take permanent hold. Heightened political authority, however, went hand-in-hand with territorial expansion. So did an enlarged officialdom and a well-organized army. To serve this administration, the Mesopotamians apparently adapted their invention of writing from its earlier uses in accountancy to that of transcribing ordinary speech. Again the eight-foot pillar commemorates an important historical step. By the time of Hammurabi, the oral conduct of government had long since yielded to a system of written records, written government instructions, and the uniform justice of a written code.

Hammurabi's conquests continued the northern drift of Mesopotamian power which had begun with the Akkadians. Under the Amorites, Babylon, formerly an obscure village on the Euphrates rose to important heights. Great temples were erected there, fine statues sculpted, and important discoveries made in mathematics and astronomy. Yet the old Sumerian fatalism—the sense of man's impotence against the inscrutable will of the gods—remained:

*Who can comprehend the counsel of the gods in heaven,*
*The plan of a god is deep waters, who can fathom it?*

Two centuries later (c.1540 B.C.) barbarous onslaughts from the north and east led to the fall of Babylon and brought Hammurabi's dynasty to an end.

Pillar engraved with the Code of Hammurabi, eighteenth century B.C. The relief shows Hammurabi raising his right hand respectfully to the god of justice. Hammurabi's personal concern for justice in his kingdom is evident in one of his letters: "The official, Lalum, has informed me as follows: 'the judge Ali-elatti has laid claim to ground which I have long possessed.' . . . Thirty acres are registered there in Lalum's name . . . investigate this matter. If Ali-elatti has done Lalum wrong, repair the damage he has suffered. Then punish Ali-elatti for the harm he has done him."

Chapter 5

# EGYPT

## THE NILE

"The Egyptians," wrote the Greek historian Herodotus, "live in a peculiar climate, on the banks of a river which is unlike every other river, and they adopted customs and manners different in nearly every respect from those of other men." This river is the Nile, and it greatly influenced the civilization that arose along its banks.

Four thousand miles from the Mediterranean, the Nile rises in the tropical lakes of present-day Uganda. From there it winds its way north, joined by its Blue tributary flowing down from the Ethiopian highlands. Next, the river rolls over a series of rock barriers, until at Aswan the last hurdle is cleared. The last 675 miles from Aswan to the sea constitute the land of ancient Egypt, for, as J. E. Manchip White reminds us, "Egypt *is* the River Nile." The only cultivable land lies in the narrow trench (never wider than twelve miles) that the river cuts through the desert. On both sides high limestone and sandstone bluffs guard a thin strip of fertile black soil, until—ten miles below the ancient city of Memphis—this strip fans into a delta that flows to the Mediterranean. The uplands (though south on the map) were known as the Upper Kingdom, the delta as the Lower Kingdom.

Each spring the rains pour down on the Ethiopian plateau, gorging the Nile until in June it begins to flood. First comes a green wave of vegetable matter, then a red one of soil rich with minerals and potash. The life-giving waters continue until October and then recede leaving behind some of the most fertile soil in the world, able to yield two or three crops annually. Recently, however, construction of the Aswan dams has reduced this fertility by keeping back much of the silt above the dams. In November seeds can be sown to ripen through the warm winter and be reaped in the spring. Within this oasis, rain is almost unknown in the south, though it is more frequent further north. Natural resources (except for large timber) abound. Beneath its golden skies, the Egyptians sang, "Praise to thee, O Nile, that issueth from the earth, and cometh to nourish Egypt. Thou art verdant, O Nile, thou art verdant. He that maketh man to live on his cattle, and his cattle on the meadow! Thou art verdant, thou art verdant; O Nile, thou art verdant."

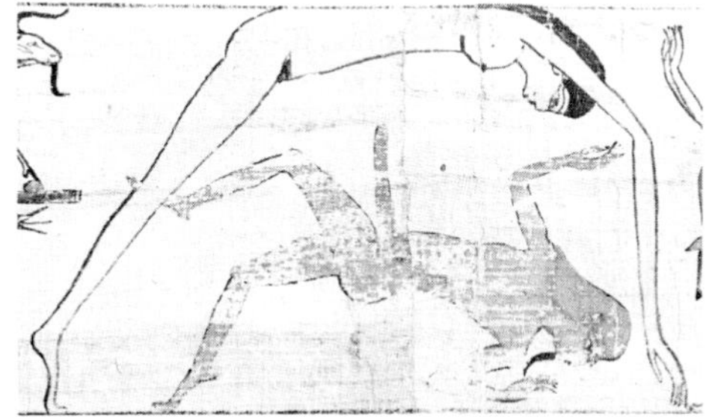

*Left:* Detail from a wall-painting on a tomb at Thebes, New Kingdom, 1400 B.C. The Egyptians delighted in the pleasure afforded by the natural abundance of the Nile Valley. Over the centuries, Egyptian artists painted magnificent scenes of natural life like the one here, which shows a nobleman hunting birds with a wooden throw-stick.
*Above:* Painting on papyrus showing Nut, the goddess of the Sky with Geb, the god of Earth. Egyptian mythology abounds with contradictory explanations for the origins of the universe. One legend held that the union of Nut and Geb produced a son, Re, the god of the Sun.

## EGYPT BEFORE THE PHARAOHS

The Nile had been a vast lake during the ice ages but as the retreat of the ice-cap dried the land of North Africa, it shrank toward its present bed. Gradually, the

| 4500 BC | 4000 | 3500 | 3000 | 2500 | 2000 | 1500 |
|---|---|---|---|---|---|---|
| Farming villages being united into provinces | | Unification of Upper and Lower Egypt (3100) | | OLD KINGDOM (2686–2181) | MIDDLE KINGDOM (2040–1786) | |
| | Chambered tombs<br>Flintwork art<br>Copper tools<br>Jewelry<br>Gold ornaments | | Magnificent tombs<br>Pottery exports<br>Plow introduced | First Intermediate Period (2181–2040) | Hyksos invade Lower Egypt (1786) | |
| | | | | Building of the pyramids | | |

inhabitants of the region were forced into greater concentration along its banks in their search for water. These early settlers found a rich valley teeming with fish and fowl, and bigger animals in the form of lions, hippopotamuses, elephants, and wild asses. Originally, however, this region probably lacked most domesticable varieties of plants and animals. Neither wheat nor barley, nor sheep nor goats are native to Egypt. (Efforts were later made in the third millennium to domesticate hyenas, gazelles, and cranes, but after centuries even Egyptian ingenuity was defeated.) As early as the fifth millennium, however, farming had made its appearance in Egypt, perhaps with the influx of new techniques and species from Palestine. When we observe that a walled town had been built in Jericho in 6500 B.C., and that fifth-millennium Sumerians were already constructing early temples, a time-lag in Egyptian development is evident. In the next millennium, when their Sumerian contemporaries were building cities, Egyptians were still living in farming villages ruled by local chiefs.

*Top:* The Nile near Aswan. The easily navigated section of the river which marked the southern boundary of ancient Egypt begins at Aswan.
*Above:* Painted relief of the gods of the Nile, from the Temple of Rameses II at Abydos, New Kingdom, c. 1250 B.C. On the left is Hapy, the personification of the Nile. He is shown bearing gifts, including jars of water, seven plants, fowl, and fish. A hymn to Hapy describes him as "The father of the Gods, Abundance . . . the Food of Egypt. Everyone rejoices on the day you come forth from your cavern," a reference to the annual inundation of the Nile.

The picture brightens however, when we examine the remains of this late Neolithic culture. Like their successors, these prehistoric Egyptians buried their dead with personal ornaments, food, and figurines—suggesting belief in some kind of after-life. By the second half of the fourth millennium the simple earthen graves of earlier times developed into chambered tombs. The varied wealth of these grave sites argues for a new stratification in Egyptian society—a development that generally encourages wider trade in the search for rare, status-differentiating objects. The technology of this period shows a greater refinement and widening range of materials. Not only had these people developed flint-working into an art (already revealing the superb skill with stone which distinguishes their civilization), they produced jewelry from precious stones like cornelian, turquoise, and lapis lazuli, and were able to cast tools in copper and ornaments in gold.

The existence of imported materials (lapis lazuli originates in Afghanistan) and imported techniques (metallurgy had developed in Western Asia by 4500 B.C.) has led archaeologists to wonder if Egyptian civilization itself was a foreign import. The answer is a qualified "No." Certainly trading contacts were extensive in the Eastern Mediterranean of the late fourth millennium. Excavations from Egyptian sites of this period have unearthed Mesopotamian cylinder seals, and art with Mesopotamian motifs—hunting scenes, beasts with intertwined necks, interlaced snakes, and Mesopotamian-type heroes subduing lions. The rapid adoption of Sumerian niched-brick architecture and the speedily developed hieroglyphic writing of a few centuries later suggests the possibility of Asiatic migration or conquest. But the unique character of the civilization that arose in Egypt militates against such conclusions. The hieroglyphs, for instance, retained pictorial characteristics for far longer than cuneiform, suggesting a special significance for the picture-signs themselves. A better explanation can be found by examining the steps by which the Egyptians changed from isolated village farmers to citizens of a civilized nation.

Early Egyptian farmers had only to tread their seed into ground that had already been plowed, manured, and watered by the Nile inundation. This ground would yield enough for a surplus, easily stored in the dry desert air of the region. This meant to Egypt, as it did to Sumer, that leisure time could increase, vocational specialties develop, and population expand. By the late fourth millennium, Egypt supported a class-stratified population welded into a nation by the Nile.

The river functioned as a spinal column, permitting easy travel and communication up and down the country. Whoever controlled river trade and travel (as did the Pharaohs) controlled the nation—a unity which the Mesopotamians had to forge gradually by developing law and bureaucratic administration. The narrow zone of intense fertility forced the scattered village communities to coalesce as they enlarged. These communities developed from isolated villages into the component provinces—or *nomes*—of civilized Egypt. Also the Nile flood, while relatively regular, varied sufficiently to encourage developments in mathematics and astronomy for forecasting its annual rise and volume. Flooding often swept away old landmarks, stimulating methods of surveying. Finally, the desert wastes bordering the Nile could be traversed by trading parties, but the area was remote enough to escape the frequent invasions that plagued Mesopotamia.

With all these natural advantages, and the example of Asiatic civilizations as a possible catalyst in the fourth millennium, the Egyptian civilization could rise very rapidly. One major development remained, the political unification of the region by a single ruler. Unlike the Sumerians, early settlers along the Nile did not group themselves into temple communities under priestly authority. Local rule included agricultural responsibilities, but might, rather than technical expertise, was the mainstay of the chieftain in a land that watered itself. And the strength which created local power could be multiplied over larger areas. The fifth and fourth millennia saw chieftains gradually unite villages into provincial nomes, and these nomes coalesce into the two distinct kingdoms of Upper and Lower Egypt before 3300 B.C.

Traditional history, as compiled by the third-century Egyptian priest Manetho, tells us that the two kingdoms were finally united by the Upper Egyptian Menes (real name probably King Narmer) about 3100 B.C. In reality, the process most certainly took at least two or three generations and a good deal of fighting, as evidenced by scenes of royal conquest from the royal city of Hierkonpolis. Still, 700 years before the Sumerian cities were united under the Akkadian yoke, Egypt became a nation. In this respect, at least, the Nile dwellers were precocious. Their nation was the world's first, and it would endure for the next three millennia.

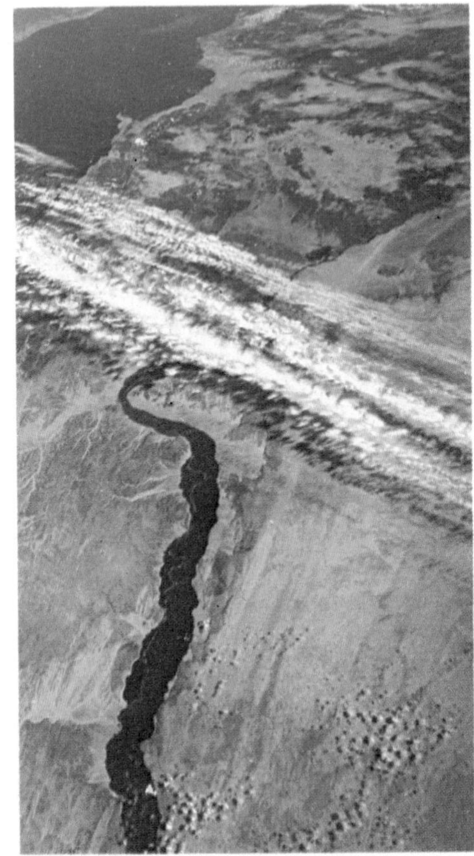

Egypt as seen from the Gemini XII Spacecraft during its thirty-fourth revolution of the earth on November 14, 1966. The view is to the southeast, with the Nile in the center and the Arabian Peninsula at lower left. The protection afforded by the intervening desert area is clearly visible. This hot and arid "Red Land" made military invasions difficult. The Egyptians, relatively secure in their fertile "Black Land," developed a serenity of outlook very different from that of strife-torn Mesopotamians.

## ARCHAIC EGYPT

Political unity coincided with the rise of Egyptian writing. Like that of Mesopotamia, this system of hieroglyphs ("sacred signs") began with pictures; but little of it survives for the years 3100–2686, so the literature and politics of Egypt's archaic age is scarcely known to us. Excavations, however, reveal a new magificence in the tombs of these first kings, and Egyptian pottery remains in Western Asia indicate a wide range of trade. The introduction of the plow at about this time (contemporaneous with, and probably independent of the same innovation in Sumer) greatly facilitated agriculture.

## THE OLD KINGDOM

The rulers of the period 2686–2181—known as the Old Kingdom—firmly established order and stability and the essential elements of Egyptian civilization. We have seen that Mesopotamian society developed and kept developing, meeting and adapting to new challenges over hundreds—even thousands—of years. By contrast the political unity of the Upper and Lower Kingdoms brought Egyptian civilization to sudden maturity. The Egyptians saw themselves as the chosen inhabitants of a paradise on earth, the fertile "Black Land." Outsiders, in their opinion, were scarcely human, condemned to the arid desert, the "Red Land." Compared to the anxious outlook of the Mesopotamians, their serenity is enviable, but it led to an extreme conservatism. Once established Egyptian culture underwent few radical changes in the whole of its history.

With the Old Kingdom local rulers lost their independence and all power was centered in the pharaoh (*Per-ao*, great house). Like the Mesopotamian states,

Egypt was a theocracy—that is, its ruler combined religious and political functions. But in Egypt the pharaoh was considered a god who returned to the heavens after death rather than the human agent of a god, as in Mesopotamia. Popular welfare was thought to rest in absolute fidelity to the god-king. "If you want to know what to do in life," one Egyptian writer advised, "cling to the pharaoh and be loyal. . . ." The basis for such power goes back to preagricultural Africa, when nomadic tribes depended on the rain-making abilities ascribed to their chieftains. These prehistoric rulers were killed when their powers began to wane, a rite replaced in historic times by ceremonies of royal rejuvenation or substitute sacrifice. But the tradition of royal responsibility did not die. Old Kingdom reliefs show an early pharaoh clearing the irrigation channels and spreading silt on the fields. The prehistoric rain-maker was transformed into the divine pharaoh, able to sustain the entire nation by his control over the Nile flood. The inauguration of centralized irrigation and land-reclamation projects at about this time undoubtedly strengthened this belief.

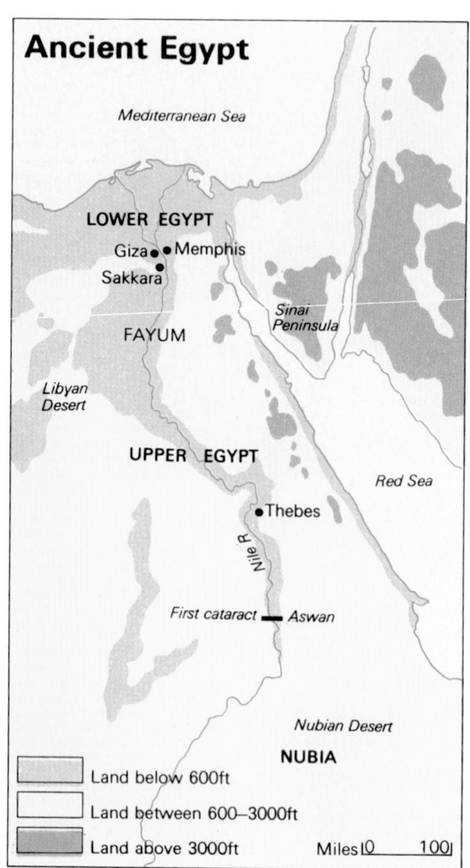


As the guarantor of national unity and prosperity, the pharaoh maintained *Ma'at* "the established order of the universe." Since he ruled as a god, all things and persons were his, and the law was his pronouncement. Rule by whim was offset by the heavy weight of precedent in conservative Egyptian society. With total authority and perfect knowledge of heavenly and earthly truth, the pharaoh (at least until New Kingdom times) issued no code of law; his word, based on his omniscience, was law. Beneath this god, Egyptian society can be divided into three main groups: the aristocracy, including the priest, the court nobility and the landed class; the middle class, made up of merchants and craftsmen; and the lower class, composed of peasants, laborers, and slaves. Stratification was not rigid; and records show, for instance, a keeper of a government storehouse who became successively caretaker of a royal pyramid, judge at a trial involving the pharaoh's harem, commander of an Asiatic campaign, governor of Upper Egypt, courtier, royal tutor, and companion of the bed chamber.

The one-man rule of the pharaoh existed only in theory. In fact, he ruled through an extensive bureaucracy. His chief deputy was the vizier, who acted as chief advisor, deputy chief justice, supervisor of all the departments, and overseer of the nomes. These responsibilities were later expressed on the walls of the tomb of Rekh-mi-re, a vizier of the fifteenth century: "I was the heart of the Lord, the ears and eyes of the Sovereign. Yea, I was his own skipper, and knew not slumber night or day. . . ." The pharaoh also had a treasurer, a minister of public works, a commander-in-chief, and a supply corps. The provinces were ruled by local governors, or monarchs, who came to form the nobility, with the nomes as their hereditary estates. As inheritance replaced appointment as the basis of power, these nobles and their private armies posed periodic threats to national unity.

The priesthood was an extremely important section of Egyptian society. In addition to the observance of daily rites and the annual festival of the temple god, the priest gave oracles and interceded with the gods in exchange for suitable fees. Temple complexes were large, with functionaries like deputy prophets, priestesses, musicians, and sacred concubines. Although the Egyptian temple, unlike the Mesopotamian, was primarily a religious institution, its priests occasionally claimed special privileges that challenged royal power.

On the border between the middle and upper classes were the scribes. Mastery of the elaborate hieroglyphs was essential to any professional career. As in medieval Europe, such education was a religious function, centered in the temple. In addition to literary instruction, these temple schools provided preliminary training in mathematics, architecture, medicine, and law, from which a man might rise in social status. Indeed, outstanding scribes mastered several disciplines and performed for their pharaoh the functions of an Egyptian Leonardo da Vinci.

Scribal training was not always necessary for artistic professions, but the Egyptian artist was a valued member of so artistic a nation, and several court artists were given handsome tombs by their grateful sovereigns.

A great gap existed between the upper and middle classes and the lowly laborers. The Biblical depiction of the Hebrews in bondage and Herodotus' account of the slavery necessary for the pyramids overstate the case, but agricultural workers and town laborers were uneducated, and at the mercy of their betters. They could be conscripted to work at the dikes or on remote quarrying expeditions, or for hauling stone for the pyramids. Fortunately, however, the Egyptian ideal included consideration for the weak and the defenseless, and the warm fertile valley made work a matter of short bursts of effort, with intervals of relative ease at the height of the flood. The Egyptians also employed slave-labor, using captives of war, but this custom was not extensive until New Kingdom expansion brought foreign prisoners into the Nile Valley.

*Top:* Palette of King Narmer or Menes (2950 B.C.). A distinctively Egyptian style is evident in this relief, which celebrates King Menes' unification of the Upper and Lower Kingdoms about 3100 B.C. Note the falcon on the right (a prototype of the later hieroglyphic figure).
*Above:* Detail of Battlefield Palette, c. 3000 B.C. The figures in this relief are carved in Mesopotamian style which has led some authorities to argue that outsiders were responsible for the final unification of Egypt. The lion who plays havoc with the fallen dead may symbolize an early Egyptian ruler.

## Religion

If you asked an ancient Egyptian, writes historian J. A. Wilson, "whether the sky was supported by posts or held up by a god, the Egyptian would answer: 'Yes, it is supported by posts or held up by a god—or it rests on walls, or it is a cow, or it is a goddess whose arms and feet touch the earth.' " Religion was the animating force of Egyptian life, and the Egyptians were not unwilling to assimilate another deity, another cult, into their extraordinary patchwork. Scholars have counted over 2,000 Egyptian gods, lesser gods, spirits, or demons—including three main sun gods—originating in the local cults of pre-dynastic Egypt. These cults included animals, both real ones (sheep, crocodiles, bulls, and cats can be still found carefully buried in their own cemeteries), and imaginary beasts. As time passed, Egyptian gods came to be seen as humans, but often they retained some animal feature.

A complex mythology developed around these deities, adding variations to original themes through the centuries. Osiris, for instance, began as a local god of the Nile Delta who taught man agriculture; Isis was his wife, and Set (the God of War) his brother and rival. Set killed Osiris (which did not rule out his worship, since the Egyptians did not view the behavior of the gods from an ethical standpoint.) Isis persuaded the gods to bring him back to life, but thereafter he ruled the underworld. Here we see a parallel to Mesopotamian beliefs in the vegetation-cycle. Gradually, Osiris came to be identified with the life-giving Nile, and Isis with the earth.

Old Kingdom Egyptians believed that the afterlife was reserved for the pharaoh, his family and the nobility, with popular welfare dependent upon his heavenly intercession after death. If his body was seriously damaged, the pharaoh's *ka*, or soul, would perish, leaving the people without a divine advocate among the gods. Hence the practice of mummification and the custom of placing in the tomb an image of the deceased which the *ka* could occupy if the corpse was destroyed. Massive funerary monuments were erected to protect the deceased pharaoh, and to perpetuate his honor by providing facilities for a large mortuary cult. (A town possibly constructed for this purpose is now being excavated east of the Third Pyramid at Giza.) The pyramids were the triumph of the Old Kingdom, and, like other elements of Egyptian culture, the art of their building was mastered with amazing speed. Less than 200 years after the Step Pyramid at Sakkara (built c.2600), the first Egyptian attempt at any sort of large stone construction, the Great Pyramids of Giza were begun. For one of these, the Pyramid of Cheops, 2 million large blocks of limestone were used, weighing up to fifteen tons. The organization necessary for such a project must have been extraordinary, especially at a time when only the simplest tools were available: ramps, rollers, and levers. Even the pulley was unknown.

Paradoxically, monumental building also weakened the nation, straining its financial resources. Tax exemptions were granted to local temples and cult institutions, the nomes became increasingly independent, with local nobles claiming the pharaoh's prerogative of immortality. Droughts, the incursion of Asiatic invaders from the northeast, and even the stagnation of the ninety-four years reign of a single king, Pepys II, may also have contributed to the Old Kingdom's decline. Gradually, central government fell apart.

*Top:* Funerary mask of Tutankhamun, New Kingdom c. 1340 B.C. The glory of the god-king is splendidly displayed on this mask of solid gold, beaten and burnished. The treasure of Tutankhamun is a magnificent collection of artefacts. *Above:* Model of a group of servants preparing a meal. New Kingdom c. 1400 B.C. Models like these were placed in the tombs of noblemen, so that when the dead were called to labor in the afterlife, the "answerers" would work on their behalf. *Right:* The Great Pyramids at Giza (c. 2250–2500 B.C.).

## THE FIRST INTERMEDIATE PERIOD (2181–2040)

With the collapse of the Old Kingdom, a period of anarchy and civil war ensued, most graphically illustrated by the fifteen kings who pretended to rule in the twenty-one years from 2181–2160. Ma'at, the Egyptians said, had disappeared from the world, and the land spun "around like a potter's wheel." The literature of the period portrays the self-rule and plunder which prevailed:

> *The bowman is ready. The wrong-doer is everywhere. There is no man of yesterday. The man goes out to plow with his shield. A man smites his brother, his mother's son. Men sit in the bushes until the benighted comes, in order to plunder his land. The robber is a possessor of riches.*

Not surprisingly, the infallibility of the pharaoh was now widely questioned, and one document of the period has the pharaoh apologize for his lack of foresight.

## THE MIDDLE KINGDOM (2040–1786)

As in the years before the Old Kingdom, rival factions based in the delta warred with those of the uplands. Eventually, Nebhepetre Mentuhotep of Thebes managed to re-unify the country and assumed the name *Sematowy* (He Who United the Two Lands). Centralized authority was regained, but the Egyptian view of that authority had permanently changed. The pharaoh was still considered a god destined for the heavens, but the afterlife was no longer reserved for royalty and nobility. Private individuals looked to the popular deity Osiris for admission to the underworld (the heavens remaining reserved for gods) and embalming became a general practice. The pharaohs stressed their role as shepherds of the people, expending their wealth on public works, like a drainage project which reclaimed 27,000 acres in the marshy Fayum district south of Memphis. The nome structure was reorganized, and the right of succession ensured by a co-regency system in which the king ruled jointly with his son. These changes led to prosperity. Egypt controlled trade with Nubia and wielded immense prestige in the cities of Syria and Palestine.

## SECOND INTERMEDIATE PERIOD (1786–1558)

Successive kings, however, could not maintain control. The country was easy prey to outsiders, and invading forces of Asiatics dealt the deathblow to the Middle Kingdom in the early eighteenth century. The area of the Nile Delta came under their rule, leaving Thebes and Upper Egypt in the hands of native Egyptian princes. Ancient historians called these people Hyksos (literally "Rulers of Foreign Countries") and they were probably a mixed group of Asiatic origin, mainly Semitic. Their influx greatly humiliated the patriotic Egyptians, one prince declaring, "No man can settle down when despoiled by the taxes of the Asiatics. I will grapple with him, that I may rip open his belly! My wish is to save Egypt and to smite the Asiatics!"

Chapter 6

# INDIA

The Indian subcontinent lies to the south of the greatest mountain chain in the world. This is important, partly because the Himalayas and their extensions to west and east have acted as something of a barrier to migration, but mainly because the wall of mountains intercepts the moist air blown over the Indian Ocean from the south and southeast from mid-June onwards, and causes heavy rain to fall for three months of the year in most parts of India. Without this regular annual rainfall, called the monsoon, most of India would be virtually a desert.

From the Himalayas flow the two greatest rivers of the subcontinent—the Ganges and the Indus, together with their many tributaries. They have over the centuries carried millions of tons of silt down their streams to form wide, fertile, thickly populated plains. In prehistoric times the Ganges valley was a shallow inland sea, and though India has a reputation for immemorial antiquity this part of it is one of the newest areas of the world's surface.

The Deccan, the southern region of India, on the other hand, is very ancient, and, long before man appeared on earth, was part of a great southern continent linked with Indonesia and Australia. Divided from the north by the Vindhya Mountains covered by thick jungle, the Deccan has always been rather different in culture from the Ganges plain. The coastal areas of India, with the exception of the southern seaboard of Pakistan, have heavier rainfall than the inland areas, and have been more closely in touch with the outside world by way of the sea.

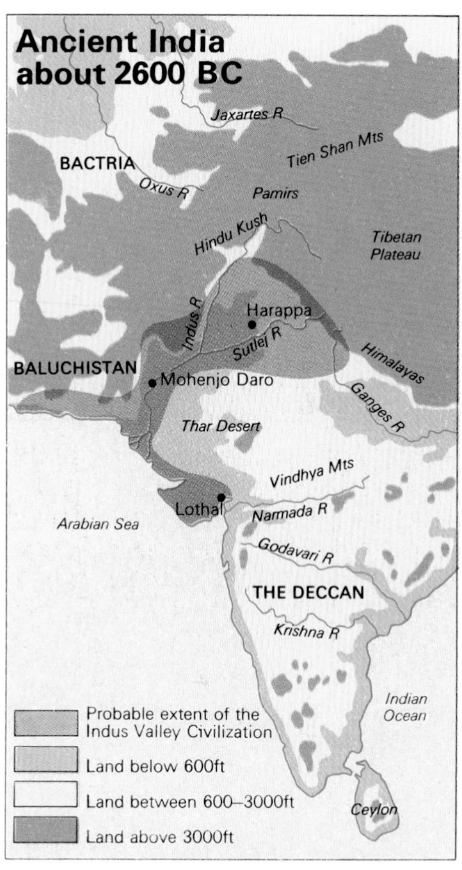


## EARLY MAN IN INDIA

Two important Paleolithic cultures have been identified in the Indian subcontinent. One of these was the work of men centered in the upper reaches of the Indus valley, while the other was the culture of the peninsula. Between the two cultures there lay the hills of Rajasthan and the swamps and lakes of the Ganges valley. The men of the northern culture of the Punjab were different from those of the South. The latter may have been of the proto-australoid type, which can be traced in many parts of India today as a substratum of the population, and is linked with the most primitive types of southeast Asia and the Australian aborigines. But we know very little about these people, because the only remains that they have left us are their stone tools.

Exactly how and why the inhabitants of the northeast turned to food production

| 3000 BC | 2500 | 2000 | 1500 |
|---|---|---|---|
| Pre-Indus cultures: early agriculture<br>Working in copper and bronze<br>Trade with Mesopotamia | HARAPPA CULTURE (Indus Valley)<br>Great cities at Harappa and Mohenjo-daro<br>Advanced architecture and brick buildings<br>Pottery and weaving. Internal trading | Aryans move into Afghanistan | Aryans invade India<br>Fortified village living replaces cities |

A rare example of stone sculpture from the Indus civilization, 2600–1700 B.C. This figure, found at the city of Mohenjo-daro may represent a priest-king or a deity. Although the writing of the Indus civilization has not yet been deciphered, evidence such as this sculpture suggests a very sophisticated society. The costume detail has been elaborately indicated, with trefoil decorations on the cloak, and an armband with a center-ring matching that of the headband. Moreover, the face has been given a great deal of character. The narrow slit eyes and receding forehead convey not a type, but an individual.

is not known. But from at least 4000 B.C. evidence of agriculture appears in the subcontinent, first in upland villages of Baluchistan in the northeast and then gradually spreading eastwards and southwards. With agriculture came many other arts and crafts, such as knowledge of making smooth stone (Neolithic) tools, weaving and pottery-making. The people who brought these innovations may have come from Iran, and have been in touch with the emerging civilizations of western Asia. Certainly our perspective on the spread of Neolithic agriculture in Asia should be enlarged to include Baluchistan and the Indus Valley, separated from Mesopotamia by the Iranian plateau.

Female figurine sculpted in terracotta, from Mohenjo-daro. Many of these figurines have been discovered on Indus River sites, suggesting that the modern Indian veneration of the mother-goddess (worshiped by various names all over the country) may date back to these times. Other possible ancestors of the great Indian pantheon found in the ruins of this civilization include several phallic-symbols associated with the god Shiva. The figure seated in a yogic position may be the prototype of Shiva himself.

In the area now called Pakistan, especially in the hills west of the Indus, the little agricultural settlements, no doubt picking up ideas that trickled over to them from further west, began to make advances towards civilization. A distinctive culture, which contained several features of the later mature Indus civilization, emerged c.3000 B.C. These people used objects of copper and bronze, though for a long time they also continued to make tools out of stone. Many of them seem to have worshiped a mother goddess, and there is also evidence that the bull was looked on as a sacred animal.

## THE EARLIEST CIVILIZATION

By 2600 B.C.—the era of the Old Kingdom in Egypt—a fully fledged civilization had appeared in the Indus Valley. Though two cities and several smaller sites of this culture have been excavated there is still much that we do not know about it, for the only written material that has survived is in the form of short inscriptions on seals, and these cannot be read with certainty. But difficulty in "cracking" these inscriptions has not led archaeologists to underrate this civilization. Archaeologist Grahame Clark points out that despite our lack of written data, the Indus Valley culture "is already recognized as one of the great historic achievements of the human race." Our chief knowledge of the civilization is derived from the excavations of Harappa and Mohenjo-daro, two large cities 400 miles apart, whose amazingly similar plan and features have compelled some archaeologists to regard them as twin capitals of the civilization. Both cities were carefully planned, with streets intersecting at right angles, and were built largely of baked bricks—some of the earliest baked bricks in the world's history. At the heart of each city was a citadel, a high platform of mud-brick on which important public buildings were erected. The purpose of the citadel was not so much defense against invaders as protection against flooding, which occurred frequently.

The inhabitants of the Indus cities had a strong feeling for cleanliness. Almost every house had a bathroom, where the occupants bathed by the traditional Indian method of pouring pitchers of water over their bodies. The bathrooms had outlets for the waste water, which flowed into a system of large brick-lined drains which must have been maintained and kept clean by the city authorities. In Mohenjo-daro there are the remains of a large bathing pool. A marked emphasis on washing and personal cleanliness is notable among modern Hindus, and the motive behind it is religion and ritual purity rather than hygiene.

Our knowledge of the religion of these people is derived entirely from material remains, chiefly in the form of the designs on the numerous seals found in the cities, together with statuettes, terracotta figurines and other objects which seem to have religious significance. The people probably worshiped a mother goddess; they held the bull sacred, and may have had other sacred animals; they revered the pipal tree as the abode of a goddess; they had a god who wore a pair of buffalo horns and was depicted seated in a posture similar to that of later *yogis*; they appear to have worshiped phallic emblems. All these features are characteristic of later Hinduism but are not found in the next phase of Indian history, that of the Aryans. Thus it seems that religious ideas and practices of the old culture survived its downfall and were revived after many centuries in a new form, when they blended with elements of Aryan religion to form Hinduism.

The culture of Harappa has been traced as far east as the neighborhood of Delhi; settlements have been found along the coast of the Arabian sea near the frontier of Pakistan and Iran. In the south there was an important Harappan seaport at a place now called Lothal in Gujarat, while a Harappan site has recently been found in the northwest of Pakistan, in the Gomal Valley, one of the main passes into the Indus Plain. Thus it was more widely spread than the civilizations of Mesopotamia and Egypt.

What united and held together this vast civilization? Metal weapons are rare, and evidence for conquest and internecine warfare—other than the silent witness of defensive fortifications—is slight. Communication and transport along the Indus must have been well-developed in order to account for the uniformity in material culture. Trade and the exchange of raw materials within the civilization appears to have been extensive, but that with foreign areas, even with the partial remains archaeology provides, seems surprisingly slight. Direct trade with Mesopotamia existed infrequently, if at all; most exchange appears to have taken place through intermediaries on the Persian Gulf or in Iran.

The more developed culture of the Indus people was not without effect on the less civilized people beyond them, and by the middle of the second millennium knowledge of bronze-casting, pottery and weaving had spread over much of India. In recent years, with further excavation and with the help of modern techniques such as carbon dating, our knowledge of India in this period has become more precise, though there is still room for speculation and theory, and much is yet to be

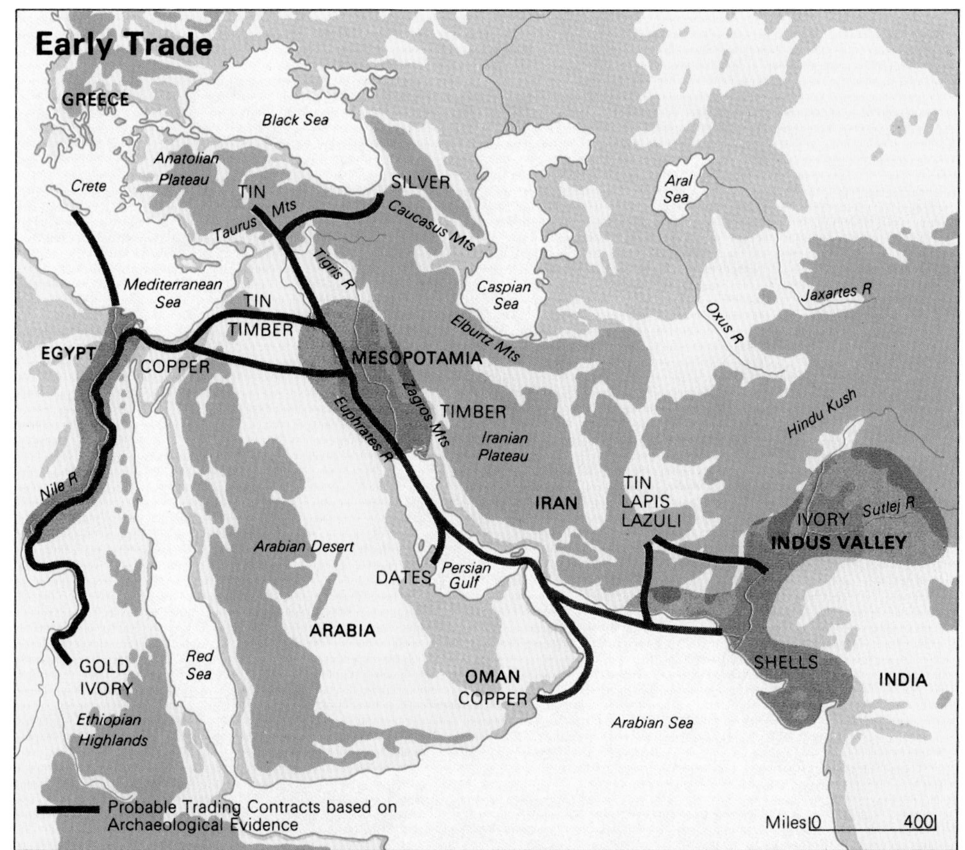

Seal impressions from Mohenjo-daro, 2400–2000 B.C. These impressions are taken from carved cylinder seals, of which more than 1,200 have been found. Although the inscriptions have not been translated, some authorities think they represent the writer's name, and the animal or god whose favor he hoped for. These seals include a number of very fine animal carvings, of real and also apparently mythical beasts. Seen here are an Indian humped bull, a rhinoceros, and what seems to be a unicorn standing before an altar.

discovered. Meanwhile we must note that modern archaeology is making short work of the more extreme form of the theory known as diffusionism, that all or nearly all elements of civilization were descended from a single source. The evidence of carbon dating tends to show that knowledge of bronze-casting, for instance, appeared independently in Mesopotamia, southeast Asia and China. As is shown in chapter 3, the first agriculture may have been practiced in southeast Asia as early as 13,000 B.C., 4,000 years before the earliest estimates of farming in the Fertile Crescent. Recent excavation shows that bronze tools were made in Thailand over 2,000 years before Christ. There is growing evidence of prehistoric cultural influence coming to India from southeast Asia, as well as from the west.

Prehistoric India probably made important contributions to the material culture of the world. One of these was rice, which appears first in prehistoric Ganges Valley settlements, but was not cultivated by the Harappa people. A second was the domestic water buffalo, which was known in the Indus Valley even before the first great cities were built there, and which appears to have been introduced from the East. A third was the domestic fowl. The Sumerians and Egyptians had domesticated ducks and geese, but it seems that every rooster in the world is ultimately descended from the wild Indian jungle fowl, bred in captivity by the Harappans. Moreover the earliest evidence of cotton textiles in the Old World comes from the Harappan culture, though cotton appears to have been discovered independently and used even earlier in Mexico.

## THE ARRIVAL OF THE ARYANS

From about 2000 B.C. onwards the ancient world was shaken by the appearance of hordes of people from the steppes of southeast Russia and Central Asia. The invaders brought with them an important new means of transport, which gave them a great

The drainage system at Mohenjo-daro, showing the high standard of engineering and sanitation achieved by the Indus Valley civilization. The citizens of Mohenjo-daro were highly concerned with personal cleanliness. They may have practiced river washing in their large (thirty feet by twenty-four feet, with a depth of eight feet) municipal bath. Many private houses included a bathroom with a brick-paved floor with a drain at one corner. The bathers would pour water over themselves from a large jar, and the water then would run through the drain into a main sewer under the street.

military advantage. This was the horse, hardly known in the civilized world in 2000. The invaders had no saddles or stirrups and preferred to harness their horses to chariots rather than ride on their backs. They were skilled in the construction of light chariots, which they fitted with spoked wheels, making a vehicle much faster than the ox and ass-carts of the older civilizations, whose wheels were solid and therefore heavy and unwieldy.

The most important of these nomads spoke related languages, which are the ancestors of most of the modern languages of Europe and northern India, as well as of Persian and one or two extinct languages of Western Asia. This great group of languages is known as the Indo-European family. In India these people called themselves *Aryans*, a word which appears in Persian as *Iran*.

The route taken by the Aryans and the chronology of their migrations to India are still not wholly clear, but the best theory is that many hordes of Aryans settled in the region later known as Bactria, on the banks of the Oxus River in north Afghanistan and Soviet Central Asia. After some time, perhaps around 1700 B.C., some of them started out across the Hindu Kush mountains and in a series of waves descended on the Subcontinent. Some centuries later others moved southwest and settled in Iran, to which they gave its name.

It is not certain that the Aryans were all of the same racial type—for Aryan is a linguistic term—but many of them were tall, long-headed and fair by comparison with the people whom they conquered. They were nomads or semi-nomads, more interested in breeding cattle and horses than in agriculture. Their society was patriarchal, and they worshiped gods, mainly associated with the sky, by means of sacrifices. They appear first to have occupied some of the frontier settlements of the Harappa culture, near the western border of modern Pakistan, and then to have moved down to the Punjab. There is evidence that horsemen, probably connected with the Aryans, occupied Harappa, but the fate of Mohenjo-daro is less clear, and it may have been abandoned by its inhabitants on account of heavy flooding well before the arrival of the nomads. Some archaeologists have argued that a series of ecological catastrophies broke the spirit of the Indus civilization. In addition to floods, the need for fuel to bake the countless bricks of the cities may have led to deforestation and soil deterioration, culminating in economic breakdown. In fact the Harappa civilization had much declined by 1900 B.C., well before the Aryans arrived. Afterwards the great cities of the Indus Valley were wholly abandoned, for the Aryans at this time were not interested in city life, but lived in small fortified villages in which most of the inhabitants were kinsmen. In Gujarat there is no evidence of the violent overthrow or sudden disappearance of the Harappa culture. It changed slowly and, gradually absorbing new elements, Aryan and otherwise, became part of classical Hindu culture.

## Chapter 7

# CIVILIZATION IN THE AEGEAN

The geography of Crete is particularly important to its development as the first European seat of civilization. The largest and southernmost island of the Aegean, Crete was fertile and well-watered enough to support a village population, and when prosperity brought a larger birthrate, abundant forests provided the timber for a large merchant fleet. In respect to trade, Crete again seems a beneficiary of nature. Its shores lie 60 miles from Greece, 120 from Asia, and 200 from Africa. A glance at the map shows that Crete was a natural stepping stone between the civilizations of the Near East and the European continent. This crossroad became the home of the first maritime civilization.

For the student of early cultures, Crete is a fascinating anomaly. Unlike the early river-valley settlements, with their concentration of cities, the island was the site of a sea-oriented civilization, whose small population dwelt in towns. This society came to prominence about 2000 B.C., thrived for a short time, and then disappeared, some fifteen centuries before Christ. Its memory was preserved only in Greek myth until the beginning of this century, when the English archaeologist Sir Arthur Evans unearthed the ruins of a great palace at Knossos. His excavations revealed an edifice which once stood at least three stories high and spread over nearly six acres. Evans called it "the Palace of Minos," and its culture "Minoan," after the legendary Cretan king, Minos. Now dated c. 1700 B.C., this palace was part of a complex of smaller palaces, villas, royal apartments, reception and storage, and open courtyard which stretched over the area of a small city. Its walls were painted with elaborate frescoes; its living quarters were plumbed with baths and toilets by an intricate system of stone drains. Only in the past 150 years has European plumbing surpassed that of Crete and Rome. The palace was linked to other parts of the island by well-paved roads. No record of Paleolithic man in Crete has been discovered. The first known occupants were farmers who migrated from Anatolia in Western Asia. Just when they appeared is not clear, but material from a Neolithic occupation at Knossos yields a carbon-dating of 6100 B.C. From this time obsidian was traded across the Aegean from the island of Melos to Crete, the Cyclades and mainland Greece, and ceramics often bore ship designs, suggesting a marine mobility for even these earliest settlers. People and ideas probably traveled to Crete by the same sea routes in the last half of the third millennium.

*Above:* The excavated part of Amnisos, Crete, one of three seaports which served Knossos. The sandy beaches allowed small single-masted Minoan vessels to be hauled ashore.
*Left:* Aerial view of the Minoan palace at Knossos, c. 1700 B.C. The palace (reconstructed in this century by Sir Arthur Evans) exemplifies the fluidity of Minoan art. The maze-like building forms the basis of the Greek myth of the labyrinth, in which a tyrannical Minoan king challenged Greek hostages to escape. In fact, the palace was an elaborate residential and commercial center.

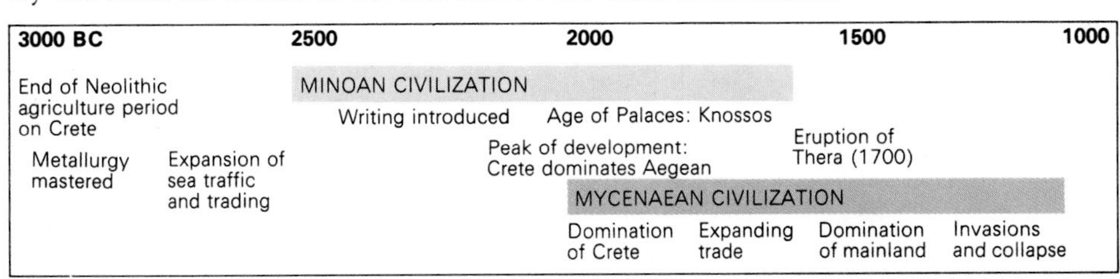

Unfortunately, even later Cretan prehistory is obscured by our inability to translate either their early hieroglyphs or the later syllabic script known as Linear A. Why their culture suddenly advanced from a Neolithic agricultural life (concluded between 3000 and 2500 B.C.) to its height, the Age of Palaces (2000–1500), can only be surmised, but archaeologists suggest an acceleration of sea traffic prompted by the acquisition of metallurgical knowledge on the Greek mainland (3000). Trade contacts increase when there is a commodity worth having, and some authorities argue that bronze weapons became crucial to the defense and extension of trading interests in the area. Whatever the cause, by 2600 there was a flourishing Aegean market in bronze tools and weapons, and also in ceramic mirrors, marble figurines, and ornaments of gold and silver.

The cultural cross-fertilization provided by this sea traffic included another factor: Egypt. The extent of Egyptian influence on Cretan culture is a matter of debate, but objects of Egyptian origin have been found in Cretan excavations dating from 2500–2000. By the fifteenth century, Cretan traders were notable enough in Egypt to be represented among foreigners bearing gifts on the wall of a high priest's tomb.

The palatial town excavated by Evans was not the only Minoan settlement, nor was it necessarily the capital. Earlier towns have been discovered on the island's Eastern coast, and there were at least three seaports on the Aegean coast near Knossos. A second great royal residence, the Palace of Phaestos, was located near the Southern coast, and—with a nearby town—controlled commerce with Egypt. The political organization of these towns is uncertain. Tradition ascribes power to a series of deified kings called "Minos" (a generic term like "pharaoh") who dwelled at Knossos. Whoever these rulers were, they were probably aided in their administration by the introduction of a hieroglyphic form of writing in about 2000 B.C.

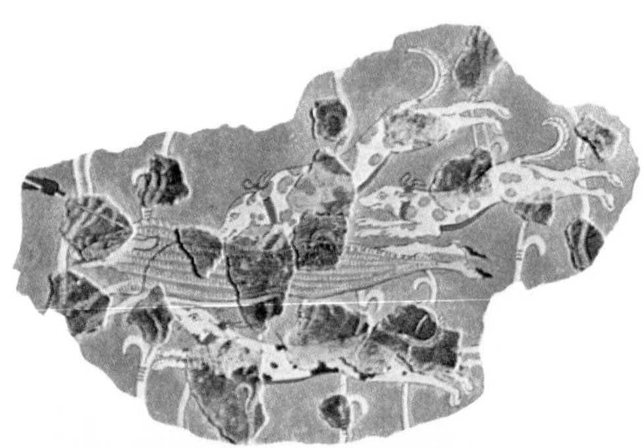

*Top:* Mycenaean fresco of a boar hunt, Tiryns. The boar was a much-prized quarry, whose teeth were often used as armor on Mycenaean helmets.
*Above:* One of the finest Minoan frescoes, known as the "Ladies in Blue."

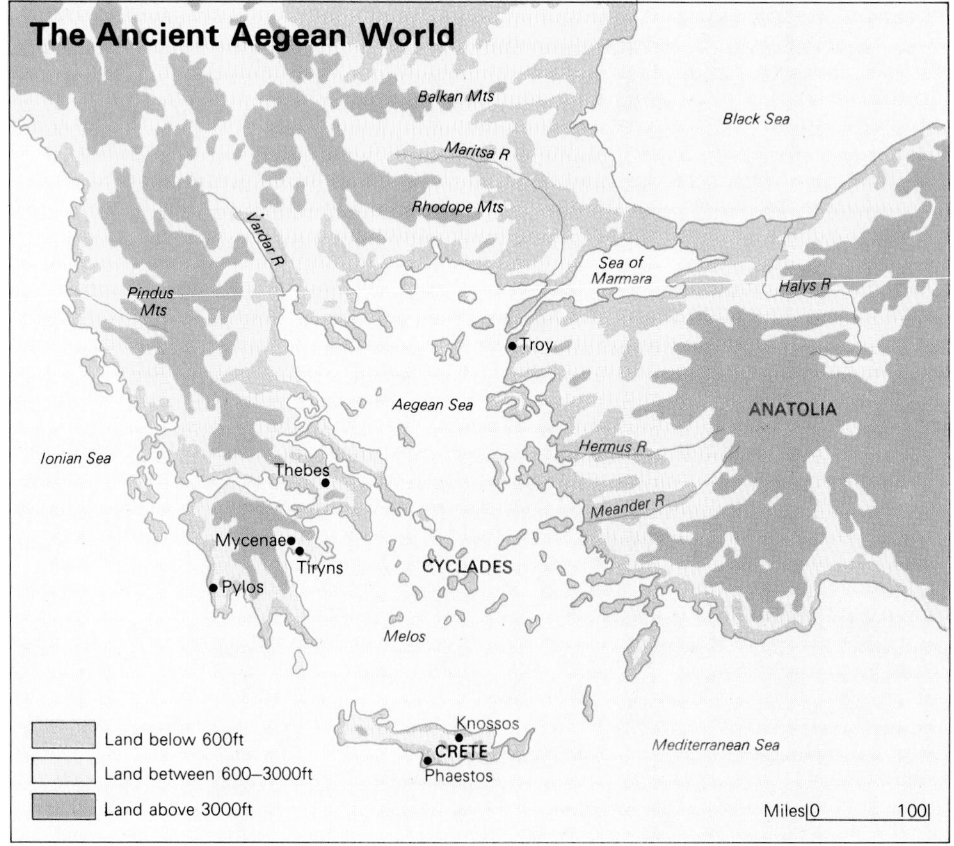

In comparison with other ancient societies, the Minoan civilization may have been relatively peaceful. Weapons have been excavated from Cretan sites, but the towns and palaces were not fortified. (However, the road into Knossos does have a final right-angled turn at the entry portico to enable the scrutiny of new arrivals.) Appropriately for such a commercial civilization royal power seems to have been essentially economic.

At its height, Minoan trade extended all over the Aegean basin and to Egypt, and the goods for export (pottery, textiles, metal products, olive oil in decorated jars) were produced and packaged by a highly efficient factory-system. The king was the chief capitalist, with factories connected to his palace. Despite this royal dominance of trade, private enterprise was not forbidden, and private agriculture and trade thrived. The factory system, although unmechanized, was modern in its scale, division of labor, and centralized control and supervision—but its material benefits seem to have extended to all classes of the civilization. Subsidiary palaces and villas, for instance, suggest a ruler who was first among equals, and houses in even the poorest quarters of industrial towns like Gournia were sturdy and large. Slavery seems to have been non-existent, and the number of inscriptions on the walls of lower-class houses suggest nearly universal literacy. Evidence from Minoan painting and sculpture suggests that Cretan women enjoyed a social equality unparalleled in the ancient (and perhaps even the modern) world. While later Athenian women were forbidden even to *attend* the Olympics, Minoan frescoes show female pugilists and young girls participating in the dangerous sport of bull-leaping. Indeed, there seems to have been no activity from which these women (who dressed in an oddly modern garb of ruffled skirts and short vests) were debarred, regardless of class. The liberty accorded their sex may have derived from the local religion, the Mediterranean worship of the earth-mother who ruled the cosmos—sea, earth, and sky.

Priestess with snakes, from the Temple Repositories of Knossos, c. 1600 B.C. Among the arts of Crete was the making of figurines like the one shown here in faience. This is a substance composed of a sand and clay mixture baked in a temperature at which the surface begins to lose its gloss. This figure probably represents a priestess or goddess, but her flowered skirt, broad belt and bared breasts are typical of the court fashion of the period. The Minoans did not worship such statues, but probably presented them to their gods as gifts.

The Minoans delighted in sport, dancing, and festivals, and the Knossos remains include a staged stone area which may have been used as a public arena. Their art conveys an unmistakable vitality in both its choice of subject and style. Before the end of the third millennium, Cretan painters showed fascinating glimpses of Mediterranean animal life: a wild goat, a deer resting in a grotto, a dog hunting in a wood, an octopus swimming among coral reefs. Their masters in this naturalism were Egyptian, but where the Egyptians strove for structural accuracy and framed permanence, the Minoans took an impressionist's pleasure in motion, fluidity, and color. The historian Michael Grant writes, "Cretan polypods and dolphins are less photographically accurate than Egyptian fishes, but they are more alive; and a Cretan cat, although less exactly represented than its Egyptian counterpart, gives a better impression of stealthy cruelty." The ruins of the palace of Knossos—despite its apparent luxuries and conveniences—show little regard for the principles of unifying form or architectural logic. With its several stories, and hundreds of compartments illuminated by narrow light wells, it may well have seemed like a maze or labyrinth. The actual palace or its later ruins may have provoked stories about such a labyrinth and its master-architect, Daedalus. These stories were preserved in Greek legend.

From 2000 to 1800, Minoan civilization reached a peak of development, only to have its towns and palaces destroyed in 1700 B.C. in unexplained circumstances, perhaps earthquakes, invasions, or local trade wars. At any rate, reconstruction took place on an even grander scale, Knossos achieved special prominence, and Minoan culture spread across the Aegean, suggesting political or at least commercial hegemony. Then, catastrophe struck. In 1500, the nearby volcanic island of Thera suffered an eruption of incredible strength; fifty square miles of the original island were blown away, and the resultant tremors and volcanic ash caused disaster seventy miles away in Crete. The Minoan towns were reduced to rubble, and a brief attempt at recovery ended in another series of destructions and abandonments about 1450. Local seismic instability may again have taken its toll, or perhaps the much-battered society succumbed to civil disturbance.

### Mycenae

But a most important third factor was also at work, the ever-growing power of a civilization on the Greek mainland. This warrior-dominated society, which provided the historical foundation for the poems of Homer, made important cultural advances in Greece between 2100 and 1900 B.C. Gradually (possibly for some millennia) a forerunner of the Greek language had developed; and in towns like Tiryns, Pylos, and Thebes there developed an imposing civilization, which takes its name from the citadel of Mycenae.

In A.D. 1876, Heinrich Schliemann, a retired German businessman, unearthed at Mycenae the greatest single collection of precious objects found anywhere before the discovery of Tutankhamun's tomb. Schliemann, who was searching for remains of the civilization described in Homer's *Iliad*, came upon the graves of a society which antedated that of Homer's poem by 400 years (1650–1510 B.C.)

The Minoans may have been relatively peaceful, but the Mycenaeans were certainly militarists. Their rulers were chieftains living in heavily fortified citadels, and their society was more united by shared language and religion than by a central political authority. By 1500 however, they were also extensive traders, and their citadels began to develop into commercial centers similar to those in Crete.

The Mycenaeans borrowed heavily from Minoan culture. They adopted the Minoan script for their language, employed Minoan artisans, and assimilated Minoan religious practices into their native beliefs. Mycenaean design, however, was geometric and formal compared to Cretan naturalism, and it is hard to imagine a sophisticated Cretan gentleman wearing a Mycenaean leather helmet covered with boar's tusks. Still, much of the mythology of later Greece must have been composed and perpetuated for a favorite pastime of the Mycenaean nobility—listening to poets recite the legends of Greek heroes and their gods. And Mycenaean expansion provided great opportunities for cultural acquisition and cross-fertilization. The graves which Schliemann excavated reveal a cosmopolitan variety of artistic styles, ranging from exquisite metal work of Asiatic inspiration to trinkets of tawdry vulgarity.

*Top:* Early Mycenaean grave circle, sixteenth century B.C. The Mycenaeans buried their noble dead in these graves. *Above:* Golden mask from the graves at Mycenae, sixteenth century B.C. Heinrich Schliemann, a retired German businessman, had loved Homer's *Iliad* in his youth. The poem describes how the king of Mycenae, Agamemnon, led the Greeks in the siege of Troy. When Schliemann discovered the masks shown here he telegraphed home, "I have looked upon the face of Agamemnon". In fact, the mask was later discovered to date from at least three centuries earlier.

Like the Minoans, the Mycenaeans traded extensively, and by the sixteenth century they seem to have achieved some measure of dominance, although not positive empire, over the Greek-speaking world. Commercial expansion led to the establishment of colonies in the Aegean and Asia Minor, depriving the Minoans of valuable markets. Gradually Crete too succumbed to the Mycenaeans. The Greek-based characters of the late Minoan alphabet, Linear B (successfully translated in 1953), and the stiffer and more formal late Minoan pottery and architecture indicate their control of Knossos by the last half of the fifteenth century. Whether this control was effected by force, political infiltration through Cretan use of Mycenaean mercenaries, or the opportunity afforded by natural disaster, is not known. Excavated armories of Mycenaean weapons near Knossos suggest rule by military command.

Sharp cultural changes in mainland Mycenaean remains suggest internal upheaval or external influences about 1350 B.C. Whatever the cause, burial practices changed. Instead of graves monumental tombs—half-underground chambers approached by entrance passages cut into the hill and surrounded by "bee-hive" domes—were erected. Growing skill in masonry made tombs like the Treasury of Atreus possible: fifty feet wide, forty-three feet high, with a lintel-block weighing 120 tons. Between 1350 and 1250 a citadel wall, 1000 yards in circumference and 20 feet wide, was built around Mycenae. Its Lion Gate entrance was the oldest monumental sculpture on the Greek mainland. Royal palaces of this period were more comfortable than the early citadels, with audience rooms, apartments, fresco-lined walls, and painted floors.

In the late thirteenth century Mycenae's commercial expansion may have lead to wars with the city of Troy, strategically located on the Hellespont between Asian and European markets. Schliemann's excavations revealed that the city whose siege is the subject of the *Iliad* actually existed, and later studies show that it was destroyed by fire of unknown origin in the late twelfth century, the traditional date of the Homeric victory.

Perhaps this conflict, as Homer suggested, weakened Mycenaean society at home. At any rate, these people fought so much among themselves and for the expansion of their trading empire that they seem to have been incapable of checking invasions into their own territory. Around 1200 B.C. the Mycenaean civilization declined in wealth, commercial influences, and artistic production. The responsibility may rest with invaders, although we have no evidence of them, or with internal social unrest or disease. At any rate, by 1120 Mycenae had fallen, and with it cultural unity, wide-ranging commerce, and writing. Four centuries of cultural darkness ensued, but from this chaos an even greater civilization—and a uniquely European one—would emerge.

The Phaestos Disk, c. 1900 B.C. This clay disk, which measures six inches in diameter, is unique among the remnants of early Cretan writing. It has nothing to do with the early cursive form Linear A, which was used for accounts. The archaeologist Sir Arthur Evans argued that the characters reveal Anatolian origins, but there is no evidence for this. It has forty-five different signs stamped with a forerunner of movable type. Nobody would produce such a complete set of these stamps for printing on a small scale, yet nothing comparable to this inscription has ever been found.

### The Minoan-Mycenaean heritage

A dark age descended on the Aegean world c.1100 B.C. and lasted over 200 years. But when the ancient Greeks began to develop their own civilization and established colonies throughout the Mediterranean and Black Sea regions c.750–550, they were following a pattern originally formulated millennia earlier and elaborated by the Minoans and Mycenaeans. Everyone knows that the Greeks were a sports-minded people, who initiated the Olympic Games in 776, but this pastime also can be traced back to Minoan times. Athletes, particularly boxers, are often depicted on Minoan frescoes. Finally, several classical deities including Zeus, Hera, and Athena have been identified in the Linear B texts. Greek religion developed from the synthesis of the Minoan-Mycenaean beliefs. A Minoan sarcophagus from a villa near Phaestos which may have been built under Mycenaean influence, shows a scene of bull sacrifice, features similar to those frequently depicted on Greek vases of the sixth and fifth centuries B.C. Greek civilization, like other civilizations, cannot be understood divorced from the historical developments which preceded it.

Chapter 8

# CIVILIZATION IN NORTH CHINA

## EARLY SOCIETY

More than 3,500 miles separate the region of the first Chinese civilization from that of its western Asian predecessors. Cut off from other advanced cultures by mountains, deserts, and oceans, China produced a unique civilization with its own calendar of development. As we saw in part 1, chapter 3, agriculture may have been practiced in southeast Asia as early as 12000 B.C. It is known for certain that regions in Japan, Taiwan, and northeastern Thailand cultivated two kinds of beans and a pea by at least 8000 B.C. and also produced a cord-marked pottery. In 1968 the oldest socketed tool ever discovered was unearthed at a site in northern Thailand. It dates from the fourth millennium B.C. Clearly, eastern Asia made significant cultural progress independently of its western counterparts, although their influence may have reached China in Neolithic times.

Little as yet is known about China before the fourth millennium. Remains which may date from 4000 B.C. have been found in Yang-Shao and other sites near the Huangho or Yellow River. Traditionally known as China's Sorrow because of its disastrous floods, this river traverses the great North China Plain. Here was the original center of Chinese culture.

The Yang-Shao people probably practiced slash-and-burn agriculture, a system by which a piece of land is cleared, cultivated for a few years, then left wild for ten or more years. If enough land is available for cultivation, this sort of agriculture can be practiced without necessitating a change in dwelling place. The Yang-Shao people settled in villages which they built just above the flood plain to escape seasonal flooding. The soft, fertile soil that they farmed was composed largely of loess, fine particles of loam and dust carried by winds from the central plateau and deposited in the river valley and along the northeastern coast. Its color has given rise to the name of the Yellow River. Early villagers found that it could be compressed solidly enough to make durable walls for dwellings hollowed out of the earth. Excavations from this period have also revealed houses built with thatched roofs and interior wooden pillars, a type of dwelling closer in design to modern houses than were the mud-brick homes of the Egyptians and Mesopotamians.

Already these early settlements displayed some typically Chinese characteristics. Rice was cultivated, although millet was China's chief source of carbohydrates until about A.D. 1000. The most important domesticated animals were

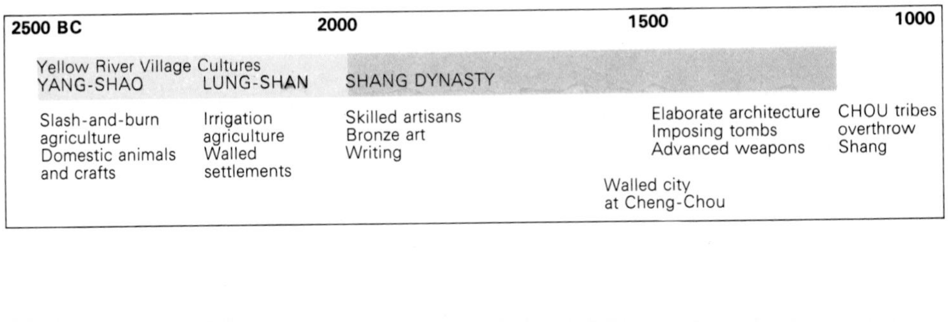

| 2500 BC | | 2000 | 1500 | 1000 |
|---|---|---|---|---|
| Yellow River Village Cultures YANG-SHAO | LUNG-SHAN | SHANG DYNASTY | | |
| Slash-and-burn agriculture Domestic animals and crafts | Irrigation agriculture Walled settlements | Skilled artisans Bronze art Writing | Elaborate architecture Imposing tombs Advanced weapons<br>Walled city at Cheng-Chou | CHOU tribes overthrow Shang |

Ritual vessel from the Shang period (eleventh century B.C.). The Shang civilization made extensive use of bronze, employing it for tableware, cooking utensils, tools, weapons, harness fittings and ornaments. But the outstanding achievements in metalworking were ritual vessels like the one shown here. These containers, filled with water, wine, grain or meat, were employed in ceremonies of religious sacrifice. The sophisticated techniques of ancient Chinese bronze-casting permitted extremely elaborate design and fine engraving.

pigs and dogs—but cattle, sheep, and goats were also kept. The Yang-Shao farmers raised silkworms for their fine textiles and sisal for their rougher clothes, a pattern which has lasted until modern times, except that now cotton has taken the place of sisal. The red-and-black pottery of these people was made by hand, rather than on a wheel. Similar pottery found in Central Asia is considered by some authorities to indicate western influence; alternatively, the pottery may have spread from east to west rather than vice-versa.

Physically, the Yang-Shao people were closely akin to the modern Chinese, although they were more like the southerners than the northerners of today, in whose veins runs the blood of many invaders and immigrants from the northern steppes.

The successors to the Yang-Shao have been discovered on another Yellow River site, Lung-Shan. Archaeologists have now established that this advanced farming culture developed from its simpler predecessors incorporating many new elements. These people no longer practiced slash-and-burn cultivation alone, but lived in settlements probably supported by irrigation agriculture. These settlements were surrounded by walls, remains of which measure anything up to thirty feet thick and a mile long. The walls resemble the town walls of later China. As in other late Neolithic cultures, improved agriculture brought larger food supplies and freed people for specialized occupations. The Lung-Shan period saw the emergence of specialists, such as the master potters who produced a lustrous, eggshell-thin black pottery; and the relative economic equality of the earlier period was succeeded by the rise of a stratified society.

Lung-Shan influences expanded widely into Manchuria, the eastern plains, and the primitive rice-growing areas of central and southern China—distances sufficient to promote regional variations in culture. Again, scholars have suggested

*Above:* Drawing of a Chinese hut of the Yang Shao period (c. 4000 B.C.). Open settlements of a dozen or so of these houses were built along the terraces bordering the Yellow River. Their inhabitants raised millet and domesticated pigs, cattle, sheep, dogs and chickens for food, used flaked and polished tools and buried their dead in simple trench graves. The most impressive remainder of this culture is their delicate hand-made pottery. *Right:* Aerial view of the Yellow River Valley. The yellow soil of this valley, which gives the river its name, is periodically enriched by flooding.

that the west may have contributed to this early Chinese culture. Jade appears at this time and may have been imported from Central Asia; and west Asian agricultural practices may have stimulated the increased use of certain kinds of livestock. Alternatively, agricultural changes may have arisen internally, as the result of population growth or sheer environmental potential.

## THE SHANG DYNASTY (1850–1100)

With the appearance of the Lung-Shan culture and its expansion, China was on the threshold of civilization. By the next period for which evidence exists, the Chinese had advanced to writing, bronze-working, and the use of the horse chariot. Such rapid cultural change again opens the question of foreign influence, certainly as far as the chariot is concerned. In most respects, however, Shang culture was a continuation of indigenous traditions.

At some time between 1850 and 1700 B.C., one Chinese tribe, the Shang, imposed themselves on their neighbors, overthrowing previous high chiefs and establishing their own royal line. For the next seven centuries, the Shang dynasty reigned over much of the Lung-Shan culture zone. We must remember, however, that this kingdom occupied only a small part of modern China. The area under effective Shang control may have been 40,000 square miles, about the size of the state of Ohio, though the high culture of the Shang left traces over a far wider area.

As in the Lung-Shan era, farming was the main source of Shang livelihood. Remains from the first two centuries of this dynasty (1850–1650) indicate that these people had developed bronze metallurgy sufficiently to cast knives, awls, and fish-hooks. There is also evidence for a system of writing in complex markings on pottery and on fascinating artifacts known as "oracle bones." These were fragments of the shoulder-blades of sheep and oxen, used in prophesying the future by the oracles who served the Shang kings. Heat was applied to the bones, and the lengths and angles of the resultant cracks were interpreted to predict the success or failure of crops, the likelihood of rain, or victory or defeat in a military encounter. Some bones contained inscriptions relating the prediction, and important ones were stored like state archives. If this writing arose as the result of Western stimulus, it was the *idea* of written communication—not the actual pictographic script—that was diffused. First used by oracles and astronomers to record past events and to make predictions, these ancient relics are inscribed with basically the same writing used today in China. From its beginnings it has always been closely supervised and regulated by China's rulers. A knowledge of writing has always been a closely guarded monopoly, at first of the oracles, and later of the scholar-officials. Today, with mass-education campaigns, most of the mystery surrounding the characters has gone, but calligraphy still remains the highest of Chinese arts.

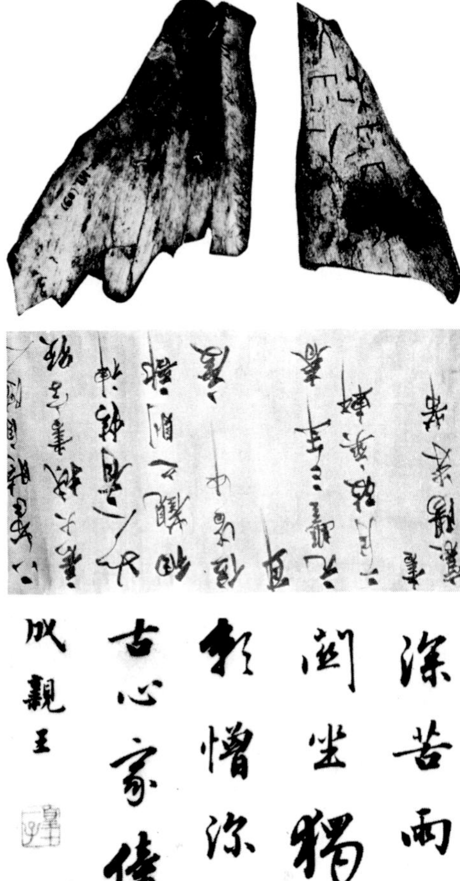

Three specimens of script showing the continuity of Chinese writing. *Top:* a Shang oracle bone on which questions to be divined have been inscribed. These inscriptions, together with markings on early Shang pottery, are the earliest known examples of Chinese Writing. *Middle:* the pictographs engraved on oracle bones later evolved into a more schematic script painted with five brushes on silk. *Bottom:* unlike other cultures, the modern Chinese have retained a non-alphabetic script which is a direct descendant of their ancient writing.

What was unusual about the Chinese script was not its partially pictographic nature, but the fact that it persisted so long after the rest of Eurasia had adopted phonetic scripts. The explanation for this probably lies in the mutually reinforcing factors of respect for the written character, as something on a higher plane than speech, and the bureaucratic advantage of a standardized written language which—because it was not phonetic—did not vary with local dialects. Thus an awkward way of writing probably did more to give China a unified high culture and national identity than any political measure could have done. It is only today, with the spread of a standard spoken language through all parts of the country by means of radio, films and mass education, that it becomes possible to consider introducing an alphabetic script without risking a cultural disintegration of the country.

Subsequent Shang developments continued the progress toward civilization. Excavations at the site of Cheng-Chou reveal a city which may have been the capital of Ao, founded, according to legend, in 1557 B.C. Differences in the size of houses, ranging up to palatial dwellings, indicate that these city-dwellers had a class system. They also had artisans of great talent. The bronze vessels produced for religious uses during this period appear only a few centuries after the first known Chinese use of the metal. Consequently it has been assumed that the technique was the result of western influence, but recent discoveries of copper implements from pre-Shang times in southeast Asia have suggested other origins. Yet the forms these vessels took were distinctly Chinese. More importantly, the technology of casting itself differed from that used in the west. There the most common process for making metal vessels was the lost-wax method, employing a clay core, wax modeled around the core in the desired shape, and an outer clay mold. The molten bronze would be poured onto the wax, melting it away as it flowed between the clay molds. The Chinese employed a much more complicated method: an original clay model of the desired vessel, often decorated in relief, would be transferred to a negative made of several pieces. Once the imprint was received, this mold would be disassembled and rebuilt around a core. Then molten bronze would be poured into the gap between core and mold, receiving a positive impression. Such a technique could produce much more elaborate bronzes than the simpler western method. The mature art of Shang bronzework has been described as "one of the outstanding arts of the ancient world."

Chinese ritual vessel of the Shang period (fourteenth–twelfth century B.C.). This bronze vessel is cast in the form of a tiger protecting a man. The animal motifs which cover both figures may relate to an indigenous fertility cult. It is unknown whether the techniques of bronze-casting were independently invented in China or were borrowed from western Asia, but the question seems irrelevant in the case of this highly individualized result. However the Shang craftsmen learned about metalworking, they soon made the art entirely their own.

It was during the era of these early bronzes (1650–1400 B.C.) that the huge city wall of Cheng-Chou, enclosing four square miles, was built. It has been estimated that the wall, which stood thirty feet high and had an average width of sixty feet, would have taken 10,000 workers 18 years to build. Needless to say, considerable political and social organization was required to direct this expenditure of human labor. Civilization had emerged.

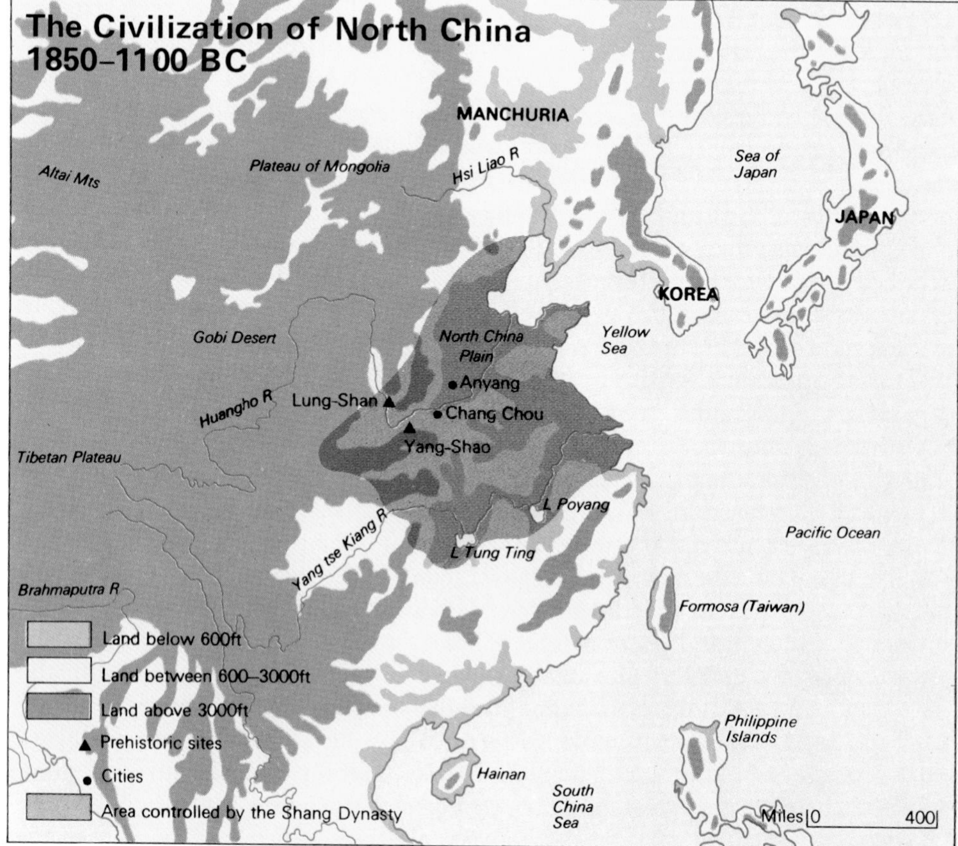

The three centuries from 1400 to 1100 saw an even more profound transformation in Chinese civilization. A city from this period located near Anyang included large buildings with stamped-earth foundations and stone pillars supporting the roofs. Here, surrounded by a ceremonial quarter which included bronze foundries, stone and bone workshops, and pottery kilns, lived the royal Shang aristocracy. Their burial places were similarly elaborate. One tomb consists of a pit thirty feet deep, with ramps leading from the ground to the bottom. In the pit's center, a wooden chamber was built to contain the king's coffin. Humans (most likely prisoners-of-war or slaves) and animals sacrificed to accompany the king into the next world were placed within the tomb—as were magnificent bronzes and fantastic animal sculptures.

Shang society was composed of three major groups: the aristocracy, craftsmen, and farmers, including slaves. The Shang rulers were essentially soldiers. The dynasty was inaugurated by military conquest, and it continued to defend itself against barbaric and nomadic tribes from the north and west. Their key weapon was the light, horse-drawn chariot of a type found right across Asia at the time. In the open country of the north China plain, the noble warrior used the chariot as a fast-moving platform from which he would fire bronze-tipped bamboo arrows from a compound bow at enemies armed only with wood and stone. (These compound bows were formed of two separate arcs of wood held together with horn, and are said to have been almost twice as powerful as the famous English long-bow.) On closing in for the kill, he would step down from the chariot to wield his bronze sword.

Shang burial of an aristocratic warrior with remains of his chariot and sacrificed horses, Anyang, fourteenth century B.C. The wooden chariot itself has long since decayed, but the recesses which once contained the shaft, axle, and wheels are still visible. The use of the chariot in Chinese warfare at this time may have been related to the rapid development in the West c. 1500 B.C. Later silk trade routes west from China show that distance and geographical obstacles were not insurmountable.

In addition to military power, the royal lineage maintained religious supremacy as well. It is not known whether or not the king was considered a god, but the spirits of his ancestors, the mythical founders of the Shang dynasty, were deeply revered and worshiped. The supreme god of the Shang pantheon, Shang Ti, presided over a divine court of five ministers. The use of oracle bones was the means by which the living communicated with royal ancestors, who in turn had direct access to Shang Ti's ear.

Craftsmen—smiths, carpenters, stone workers and the like—occupied intermediate rank in the social scale. The farmers, who comprised the vast majority of the population, shared the lowest position in Shang society with the slaves. They kept pigs, cultivated millet, rice, and wheat, and domesticated silkworms. Their way of life was still essentially Neolithic; bronze was too valuable to be used for farm tools.

The basic social institution in Shang China was the family. The king or a high noble might have several wives, but monogamy was the general practice.

### The End of the Shang Dynasty

The area to the west of the central Shang territory was probably under some form of Shang control before c. 1100 B.C. This area was occupied by a semi-barbarous people known as Chou, who rebelled in the late twelfth or eleventh century against their monarchs, using the same light chariots that brought the Shang to power. By 1100 China's first dynasty had come to an end, but the cultural patterns set during its 750 years of rule would persist to modern times.

Chapter 9

# MAN IN THE AMERICAS

The native civilizations of Pre-Columbian America developed in a manner similar to—but essentially separate from—those of the Old World. The developments which we may characterize by the term civilization—urban populations, highly productive economies, complex socio-political and religious organizations, monumental architecture, and great art styles and ideologies—arose from an earlier base of simple farming societies and cultures. Those, in turn, had their origins in still earlier hunting and gathering societies; and beyond those were the Pleistocene hunters who first peopled the New World from Asia.

## The Early Background

The first men to come to the Americas were the Mongoloid ancestors of the American Indian who arrived in the New World about 25,000 years ago. Although geological dating estimates vary, a Bering land bridge, between north Asia and Alaska was exposed by the low sea levels of the Pleistocene glaciers at this time, and for several thousands of years after this a passage through northwestern Canada was sufficiently free from ice so that entry from Alaska southward into mid-continental North America was possible. Several archaeological findings support such an early entry of man to the New World. In Peru, the lowest levels of human occupation in a cave in the central Andes are dated by radiocarbon to 18000 B.C. These early strata contain man-made stone stools and the bones of extinct Pleistocene animals. At two sites in central Mexico, human artifacts and extinct game animals are dated by similar means to 22000 or earlier.

The first distinctive American cultural tradition is usually referred to as the "Paleo-Indian" or "Big-Game Hunter," and artifacts pertaining to it have been found all the way from the North American High Plains south to the southern tip of South America. The sites in which these artifacts are found date as early as the tenth millennium, with occupation continuing in some of them until about 8000. These centuries span the closing phase of the Pleistocene, during which the North American glaciers made their final advance. The entire era was one of a colder, moister climate than that of today, with regions now semiarid then in grasslands, lakes, and swamps. Animals, now extinct, included the mastodon, mammoth, ground sloth, and small native horse. The most characteristic artifact of these

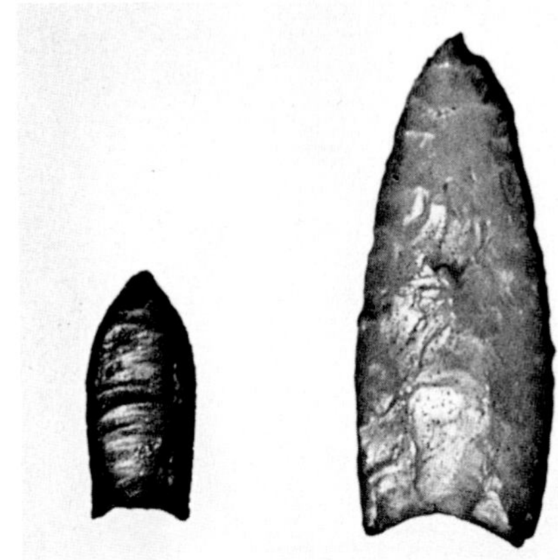

*Above:* Folsom Points, c. 9000 B.C. Named after the site of its discovery, Folsom, New Mexico, this type of spearhead has also been found in Wyoming, Texas, and Colorado.
*Left:* Colossal Olmec head, San Lorenzo, Mexico. Hundreds of years before Christ, and two millennia before the conquistadors, the oldest civilization of Mexico flourished in a small area in the Gulf Coast plain. These people were magnificent stoneworkers, carving enormous heads like the one opposite, which stands over nine feet high.

| 10,000 BC 9000 | 8000 7000 6000 | 5000 4000 3000 | 2000 | 1000 500 |
|---|---|---|---|---|
| PALEO-INDIAN STAGE | MESO-INDIAN STAGE | | | TEOTI-HUACAN |
| Nomadic big-game hunters<br>Flint artifacts | Coast settlements<br>Forest hunting<br>Plant collecting<br>Polished stone artifacts | Plant cultivation (Meso-America and Peru) | Growth of villages<br>Pottery<br>Weaving | OLMEC CULTURE (Mexico)<br>Hieroglyphics<br>Calendar |

"Big-Game Hunters" was a finely chipped flint projectile point. Used as a spear tip, it was a highly effective hunting instrument. Other tools from this period include knives and scrapers for butchering game animals and for preparing hides. Little else is known about these people. Presumably, they followed large herd animals and established their campsites near the watering places of such beasts. Many of the sites appear to be no more than "kill" spots, locations where the rib cage of a mammoth or other large animal has been found in Pleistocene strata in association with the distinctive flint points.

With the environmental changes that came about at the close of the Pleistocene, including the disappearance of many of the large-game animals, these "Big-Game Hunters" adopted other modes of subsistence and life. With the rising sea level, many of them settled along the sea coasts or along major streams and became dependent upon shellfish and fish. These particular groups, especially those of the North American Pacific coast, the Atlantic coast of the United States, the coast of Brazil, and the Peruvian and Chilean coasts, had an assured food supply. Their lives became increasingly sedentary: population grew; crafts and arts began to flourish, with ground and polished stone implements and ornaments being added to the earlier chipped stone heritage. Other groups adapted to forest hunting, as in the eastern woodlands of the United States, to upland hunting, as in the Peruvian Andes, or, in some instances, as in parts of the North American Plains and on the Argentine Pampas, to a modified version of the earlier "Big-Game Hunter" patterns. Still others became desert or semiarid region seed-collectors. This general stage of native American cultural development which spanned the time period of, roughly, 8000 to 2000 B.C., is referred to as the "Archaic Stage" or the "Meso-Indian stage," in contrast to the earlier "Paleo-Indian stage." It was the time of a changeover from the more nomadic and widespread hunting patterns of the Pleistocene era to the semi-sedentary and more regionally varying hunting-fishing-collecting ways of life in the millennia after the Ice Age. This period is comparable to the Old World Mesolithic era, and, as in the Old World, it prepared the way for the sedentary village farming life that was to follow.

Olmec vase, showing half-human, half-jaguar features.

### The Rise and Spread of Agriculture

The New World transformation from hunting, fishing, and food-collecting economies to those of plant cultivation was a gradual one. In some American areas plants were under cultivation as early as 5000 B.C. and perhaps a millennium or so before that; but they played a relatively small role in the Archaic stage economies. Hunting, fishing, and wild plant collecting were still the principal subsistence pursuits, with the domesticated "crops" a minor supplement.

The archaeological record for such a condition of "incipient cultivation" has been discovered in the dry caves of the Tehuacan Valley, just south of Mexico City. Here the remains of cultivated squashes and chili peppers were found, along with Archaic stage flint and ground-stone tools, dating back to before 5000 B.C. Maize appeared in about 5000 B.C. and in the subsequent 2,000 years the red bean and other plants were also domesticated. At about 3000 B.C. genetic changes have been noted in some of these plants. Man's selection of seeds for planting and his transporting of seeds from their original natural habitats into other environmental niches were beginning to have their effects. By 2000 B.C. the maize cob, which had been less than an inch in length a few thousand years before, had become a maize ear.

At this time, cultivated food plants, and especially maize, which for several millennia had been a minor but increasingly important element in the economy of an Archaic stage society, suddenly took over that economy. The results of this change were reflected in rapid population growth and in sedentary, year-around village settlement. New World man, quite independently, had attained a "Neolithic threshold" comparable to that reached in the Old World Middle Eastern regions some 4,000 years earlier.

The other major origins of New World cultivated plants were in South America. Probably the most important of these was in the Orinoco or Amazon basin, with the principal plant being the starch root, manioc. The early beginnings of this lowland cultivation are still to be determined; however, large sedentary villages in the Amazonian headwaters of eastern Peru are estimated to be as early as 2000 B.C. so that it seems likely that a manioc-farming subsistence base had been established by this time. It may be that further research will push the dating further back into the past.

At about 2000 B.C. maize first appears on the Peruvian coast, the definite result of Mesoamerican contact. And from the Amazonian lowlands manioc and

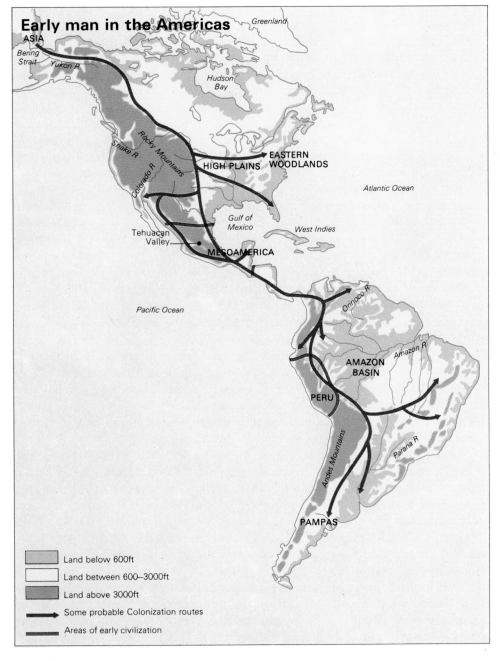

Seated figure in polished white pottery from the Olmec culture. Note the oblique eyes and infant features characteristic of Olmec sculpture.

the peanut were also added to the Peruvian coastal farming economy. These exchanges of food plants between American areas were vital to the development of New World agriculture. They were by no means all one way. South American plants, including manioc, were carried to Mesoamerica. By the middle of the second millennium B.C. a native American agriculture, of great plant diversity and high productivity, flourished in Mesoamerica, Peru, and the lands between these two areas. It was also beginning to spread outward to more northerly and southerly latitudes of the hemisphere. Within the heartlands, especially in Mesoamerica and Peru, New World man was starting to build upon this agricultural base the unique civilizations of these continents.

Standing jade figurine from Teotihuacan.

### Civilization: Mesoamerica

Settled village life based upon farming was established in southern Mesoamerica by about 2000 B.C. With this way of life came opportunities to develop arts and crafts such as pottery-making and weaving. About 1200 B.C. there appeared in at least one region a culture of much greater complexity than those of the village level. The developments of succeeding centuries (1200–400 B.C.) mark the first stirrings of civilization. They occur not in the uplands, where maize was first domesticated, but in the Gulf coastal lowlands of Mexico. They are identified with what is known as the Olmec culture. The great Olmec sites of San Lorenzo and La Venta are not simple villages but are marked by impressive mounds and other earthworks. La Venta was a ceremonial center which may have had a population of about 18,000; the main pyramid took some 800,000 man-days to construct. Little is known of the urban form of these sites, but it is likely that they were primarily religious or politico-religious precincts, with relatively small immediate populations but with "sustaining areas" of numerous outlying farm villages and hamlets.

However, the size of the construction in the Olmec centers is not the best clue to this nascent civilization but, rather, the Olmec art style. This style is essentially a sculptural one, and the outstanding examples of it are monumental ones. The basic themes of the style are human forms and the jaguar; but there is often a subtle blending of these two so that human faces, quite frequently those of infants, are given feline characteristics of a drooping, snarling mouth, an upturned, blunted snout, and markedly oblique eyes. The style results from Olmec religious belief, which maintained that in the past a woman and a jaguar were matched, bringing forth a species half-human, half-jaguar. Larger sculptures include colossal heads (one found at San Lorenzo is nine feet four inches high), altars carved with figures in relief, and columns with bas-relief representations. It seems probable that most of the adult human figures are meant as portrayals of distinguished personages, priests or rulers. Besides the monumental sculptures, Olmec art is also noted for its fine small figure carvings, many of which are jade.

Olmec art style influences have been excavated widely over the southern half of Mesoamerica in sites dating from 1200–400 B.C. These are readily recognizable in pottery and jade figurines; Olmec boulder carvings and cave paintings are known from as far south as El Salvador. The pervasiveness of the style, its occurrences across regional cultural boundaries, and its lack of any significant competitors are all strong arguments for seeing it as an important communication system among the peoples of Mesoamerica, and such a communication system is certainly one of the hallmarks of civilization.

One of the mysteries of the Olmec culture and art style is their sudden appearance. Olmec monumental sculpture, in its distinctly sophisticated style, is not foreshadowed by anything that has gone before. Nor are there any other specific clues to Olmec origins elsewhere in Mesoamerica. That the New World's earliest civilization should have arisen in the rainy tropical forests and swamps of the Olmec heartland has occasioned no little wonder and speculation among scholars. Unlike the environments of the river-valley civilizations of Egypt, Mesopotamia, India, and China, it seems a very unfavorable location. Two theories for the rise of civilization in this area have been suggested.

The first is that coastal-dwelling Olmecs greatly benefited by large supplies of marine foods and a strategic position on the diffusionary routes of manioc (along the coast from South America) and maize (from the Mexican highlands). Population swelled with the increased food supply, giving these people a head-start toward civilization.

The opposition argues that a large population alone cannot create civilization. An incentive for organization is also needed. In the case of the Olmecs, this incentive was provided by their lack of stone for grinding and cutting. Long-distance trade was necessary to obtain this stone, and such trade demanded complex organization. In response to this demand a group of merchant-managers came into existence. These merchants formed the nucleus of an upper class, providing the leadership for Olmec culture.

Neither theory has yet been proved, but the trading argument reminds us of the spur that a similar deficiency in metals and precious stones gave to Sumerian social organization 3,000 years earlier.

Whatever the causes of the Olmec achievement, it had a profound influence on Mesoamerican cultural development as a whole. In Olmec art the principal Mesoamerican deities, who continued to be represented in successively later cultures down to Aztec times, are represented: the Rain God, Tlaloc; the God of Spring, Xipe; the Death God; the Fire God; and the Wind God, Quetzalcoatl. It is also likely that the Mesoamerican calendar system including the 260-day ritual calendar,

The "Disk of Death," a sculpted figure from Teotihuacan.

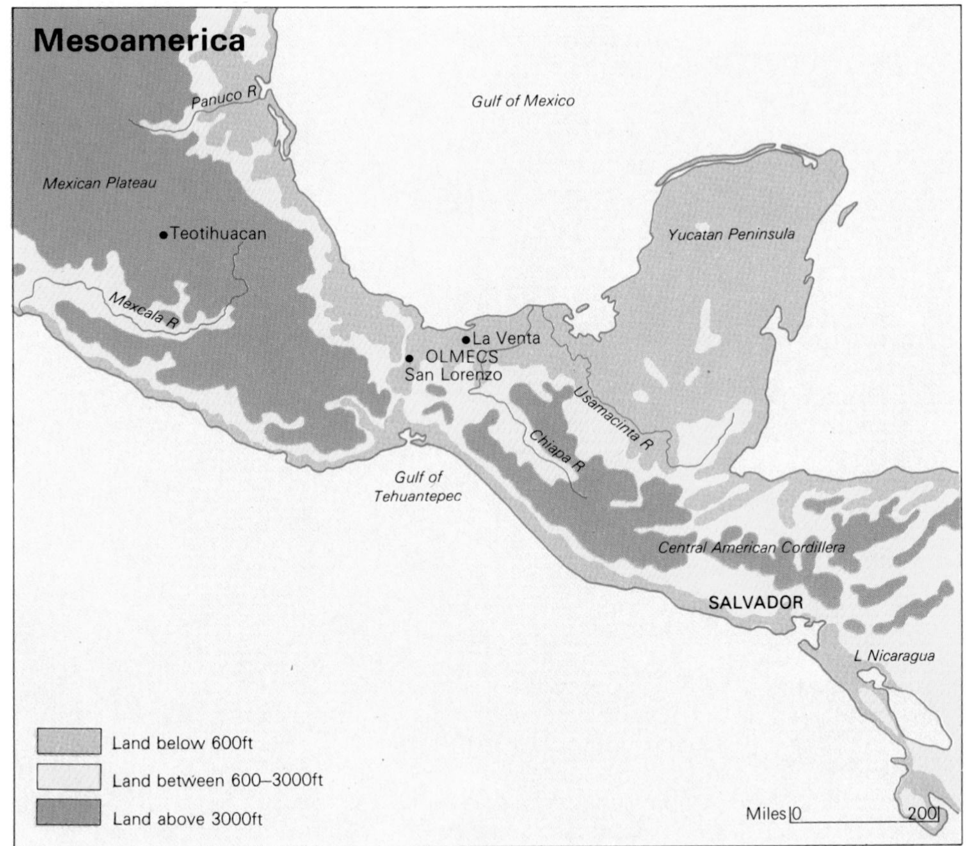

the solar 365-day calendar, and the Long Count system of reckoning time over periods of many years were perfected by the Olmecs and, thereafter, became a part of the Mesoamerican heritage.

After about 400 B.C. Olmec civilization waned and disappeared; in fact, its major centers in Tabasco and Veracruz were either greatly reduced or abandoned some centuries before this. In the years 400 B.C. to A.D. 200 the course of Mesoamerican civilization can be followed through successive cultural development in Central America. One of the principal advances of these centuries was the development of hieroglyphic systems. The origins of these are obscure, but it seems quite likely that they began in Olmec times, along with complex calendrical calculations. The earliest know glyphs, however, date from c. 300 B.C. The language spoken by the Olmec can only be speculated upon; very likely it pertained to one of the major language families known from Mesoamerica in later times, one branch of which, Zapotec, is still spoken in Southern Mexico.

## Teotihuacan

Another rising regional culture of the six centuries after 400 B.C. was that of the Valley of Mexico, as represented by the sites of Cuicuilco and early Teotihuacan. Earlier, the Valley of Mexico had come under Olmec influence, but the region did not assume the dominant role in Mesoamerican affairs until the early Christian era. This dominance was undoubtedly related to irrigation agriculture and the enormous productivity resulting from it in this semiarid upland basin. By the beginning of the Christian era Teotihuacan (the name means "place of the Gods") was fast becoming the greatest city in Mesoamerica. By A.D. 400, at the height of its influence, Teotihuacan covered an area of over three square miles of packed urban residences. At the heart of this urban zone was a huge political and religious

*Top:* Sculpture from the Chávin de Huántar culture (900–200 B.C.) in northern Peru.
*Above:* Gold mask adorning a mummy in the Inca region of southern Peru, c. 1500–1200 B.C.
*Right:* Aerial view of Teotihuacan. Here stood the greatest city of pre-Columbian America, a huge center of trade, religion, and government. It covered over three square miles and was laid out in a grid pattern still revealed by the field boundaries along old foundation walls. In the left foreground there is the Pyramid of the Moon, connected with the Pyramid of the Sun (center) by the Avenue of the Dead.

center of mammoth pyramids and palaces. A conservative population estimate for this first true great city of America is 80,000 persons; it may have been double this. From A.D. 200-600 Teotihuacan was the hub of a great trading network which extended to almost every part of Mesoamerica. This is evident in the distribution of Teotihuacan goods and in the spread of Teotihuacan influence in these other Mesoamerican regions as well as in the presence of foreign trading colonies within the Teotihuacan metropolis itself. How did the citizens of this city maintain their economic and cultural supremacy? Are we viewing the signs of political empire? There are some indications that the influence of Teotihuacan civilization on other parts of Mesoamerica was different from that of the Olmec. Whereas Olmec influences were largely in art motifs and religious symbols, the disseminations from Teotihuacan were often in manufactured objects, such as pottery, or in architectural design and the construction techniques of public buildings.

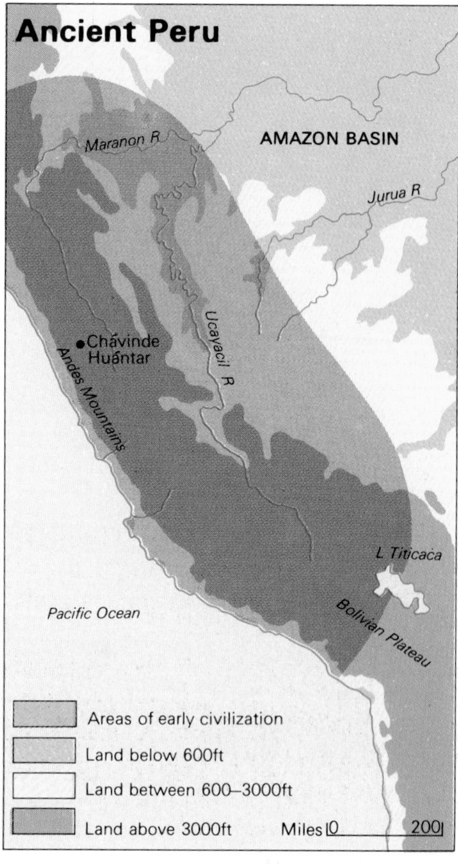


## Peru

The growth of civilization in Peru—that other area of Pre-Columbian high culture—followed a remarkably similar course to that of Mesoamerica.

In Peru, the centuries from 1800 to 900 B.C. are comparable to roughly the same era in Mesoamerica (2000–1200 B.C.) in that they mark the full establishment of a farming way of life. It should be noted, however, that on the Peruvian coast extensive settlement had been made possible in preceding centuries by fishing and shellfish collecting. The later combination of this fishing economy with agriculture is probably the reason why Peruvian sites of the 1800–900 period are larger than contemporary ones in Mesoamerica. Some of these were not only places of residence but also served as ceremonial or political centers, as indicated by huge flat-topped pyramidal mound structures.

The years 900–200 B.C. in Peru were the time of the Chávin culture. The site of Chávin de Huántar, in the north Peruvian highlands, is a mammoth ceremonial center of stone masonry platforms and courtyards. The platforms are distinguished by deep interior galleries which appear to have been shrines or places of worship. Surrounding this center are evidences of occupation indicating a sizable town or small city. The principal monuments of Chávin art are its unique stone sculptures. Some of these are grotesque human heads, others portray mythic monsters or deities. These embody and combine features of the cayman, the eagle, the jaguar, the serpent, and man. The various Peruvian regional cultures adopted the Chávin style much as the Mesoamerican cultures adopted the Olmec.

Because both are the first "great styles" of their respective areas, and because both embody certain thematic elements, such as the jaguar, it has been suggested by some authorities that Olmec and Chávin were related styles and that the style, and the religious ideology behind it, was carried from one area to the other. But such a specific connection seems unlikely. Any relationship between the two cultures must lie very far back in the past, in shared mythological beliefs involving animals commonly known to both Mesoamerican and Peruvian peoples. For the styles themselves are actually quite different, and there are no known styles from the intervening Lower Central America, Colombian, or Ecuadorian regions that can be considered as links between Olmec and Chávin.

Both styles, however, appear to signify a unification—whether religious, political, or something of both—of the several preceding regional cultures of its areas. And this unification seems to have been an extremely important step in the rise of native American civilization. For beginning with Olmec, and with Chávin, it is clear that civilization was on the march in Mesoamerica, and in Peru.

Chapter 10

# CHAOS AND CONSOLIDATION: MIDDLE-EASTERN CIVILIZATION, 1750-500 BC

During the sixteenth and fifteenth centuries the early civilizations went through a period of crisis. Barbarian threats to Hammurabi's empire culminated in the capture of Babylon about 1590 B.C. Those responsible, the Hittites, were one among several barbarian groups in motion at this time. Together with the Hurrians and the Kassites they threatened the civilized societies of the southwest Asian plains from their mountainous homelands. Egypt was under the power of another invading people, the Semitic Hyksos, who were expelled in the mid-sixteenth century B.C. Similarly, the Minoan civilization of Crete was undergoing a major crisis (though not necessarily one of invading forces) which led to its decline around 1450 B.C. From this vantage, Western Asian history by 500 B.C. seems a chaotic welter of invasions and counter-attacks. Certainly the earliest areas of Western civilization—Mesopotamia, Egypt, and Crete—declined in political independence and cultural achievement. "Yet," as William H. McNeill has observed, "for all their violence and rapine, fundamentally the barbarians sought not to destroy but to enjoy the sweets of civilization." A millennium earlier, Sargon I of Akkad (c. 2350 B.C.) had set a pattern of conquest which brought cohesion. In the wake of later barbarians we find not ruins but thriving cities, not geographic isolation but political and commercial connection. Gradually the original sites of civilization yielded to a larger, tumultuous, but cosmopolitan Western Asia.

## EGYPT: THE HYKSOS DOMINATION (1786–1548)

At their height, the Hyksos ruled Palestine and the Nile delta, but native Egyptian rulers survived upriver at Thebes. As Semites, the Hyksos were presumably favorable to Semitic immigrants, and many historians suggest this time for the Hebrews' entry into Egypt under the patriarch Joseph. Interestingly, Egyptians of this time used the term "Hebrew" (*Apiru*) to describe all aliens of nomadic habits.

Hyksos power was founded and maintained on the strength of an advanced arsenal. The horse-drawn chariot, the composite bow, and swords and daggers of bronze—all were introduced into Egypt by these invaders. The Egyptians chafed under this yoke, developing sentiments of outraged nationalism. Adopting the weapons of their enemies, the Theban rulers reasserted themselves against foreign incursion, finally expelling the Hyksos from the Delta in c. 1567 B.C. But the effect of foreign rule, like that of the anarchy of the First Intermediate Period, transformed Egyptian society. A novel spirit of aggression and imperial ambition arose in once-isolationist Egypt.

In combating the Hyksos, the Thebans may have been forced to recruit mercenaries from the Sudan, to their south. After Egypt was unified again, the Egyptian capital remained at Thebes, perhaps to maintain relations with the

*Left:* Mortuary temple of Queen Hatshepsut on the western bank of the Nile at Thebes, New Kingdom, c. 1480 B.C. The years 1500–500 B.C. were years of great turmoil in western Asia, but they also were a period of tremendous cultural achievement. This mortuary temple was built to sustain the cult of the dead queen and stands a mile from her tomb. The walls of the colonnades are decorated with scenes showing the queen's deeds such as the erection of great obelisks and a trading expedition to the spice-lands of Punt during her reign.

Sudanese. This was essential, for secure southern borders were vital to the new Egyptian expansion. The Hyksos were not only pushed out of the Delta, they were pursued into Palestine; and Palestine became the nucleus of an Egyptian empire in the late second millennium.

A prime example of this new Egyptian militarism was the pharaoh Thutmose III (1490-1436). Known as the Napoleon of Egypt, he conducted seventeen victorious campaigns in Western Asia. The first, for instance, resulted in the defeat of 330 petty princes, and the capture of 1,000 chariots and 450,000 bushels of wheat. Egyptian garrisons were set up in the conquered regions of Palestine, Phoenicia, and Syria, and Egyptian inspectors sent on constant rounds. Subject nations paid tribute to the Theban god Amon. Not surprisingly, Amon's temple (built at Karnak by Thutmose III's grandson, Amenhotep III) amassed incredible riches. Even in the Empire's decline, a twelfth-century inventory itemized temple property in towns and villages (seven of them in Asia), 433 gardens and orchards, 700,000 fertile acres, 81,000 servants, 420,000 head of cattle, and 46 factories. Rulers of defeated nations were left on their thrones, but their heirs were taken captive, educated in Egypt, and married to Egyptian noble-women. Thoroughly Egyptianized, they were returned to their native lands to rule as loyal vassals.

The late second millennium was also an age of great building activity. Amenhotep III (1417-1379) erected the magnificent temples of Luxor and Karnak, a vast palace, and a mortuary temple of which only the two giant statues called the Colossus of Memnon remains. This building program was continued by the next ruler, Amenhotep IV (1379-1362) but he is best known for his extraordinary reforms in religion. From his new rural capital at Amarna, Amenhotep and his beautiful wife Nefertiti led a revolution against the old Egyptian pantheon, encouraging instead the worship of one living creator, the god Aton—the sun's

*Top:* The Colossi of Memnon, Thebes, built during the reign of Amenhotep III (1417–1379 B.C.). The great constructions of this period convey the confident might of the Egyptian Empire. Because of Egypt's military success, the pharaoh Amenhotep was able to devote his forty year reign to the arts of peace. With him, statuary on an enormous scale makes its appearance—the most notable examples being the ones shown here. One of these statues was thought in classical times to sing at sunrise.
*Above:* Entrance to the tomb of Ramesses II at Abu Simbel, New Kingdom c. 1250 B.C.

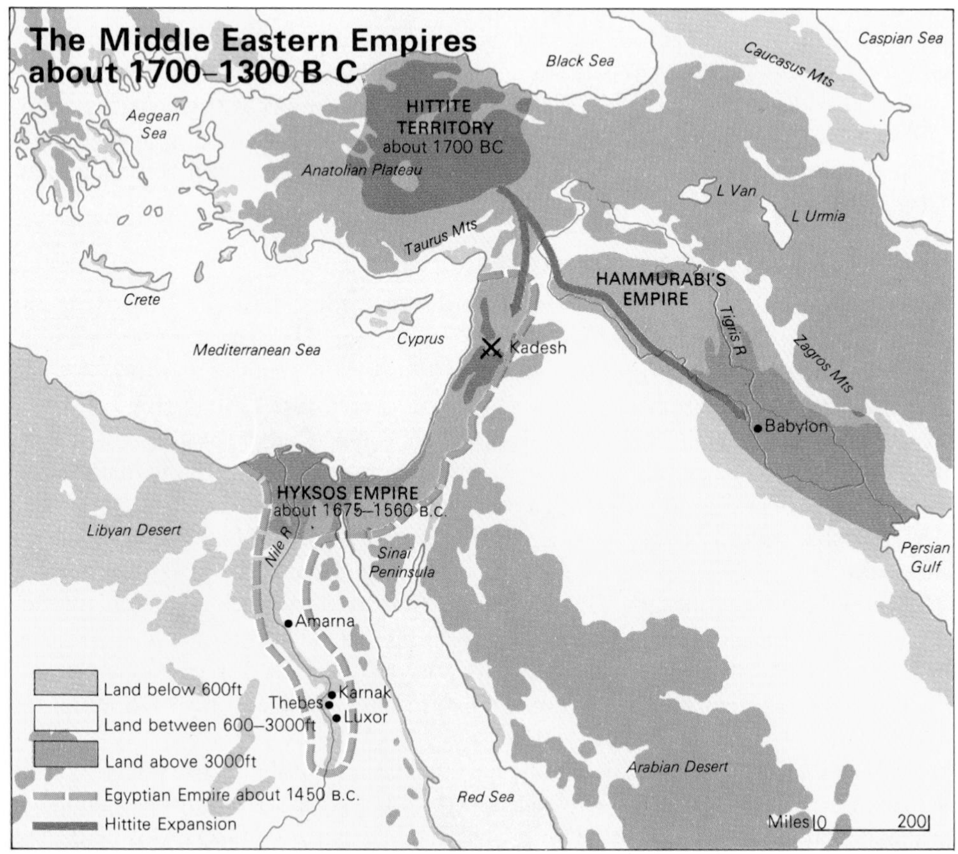

disc, who brought life to mankind with his warm rays. Such a practice cannot be equated with monotheism, as is commonly held. The other Egyptian deities may have been de-emphasized, but they were acknowledged. The worshipers of Aton prayed to him as "Thou sole god, there is no other like thee." But the earlier (and definitely polytheistic) worshipers of Amon had addressed their god as "Thou only sole one, who has no peer," suggesting that this expression was not taken literally. Instead of monotheism, the cult of Aton could be described as monolatry, the worship of one god when others are recognized as existing. The Pharaoh altered his name with his religion—from Amenhotep (Amon is satisfied) to Akhenaton (Glory of the Aton). We can only speculate on the motives for this theological development. Imperial expansion and intermarriage had brought Asiatic influences into Egypt, and Egyptian sun-worship may have been related to similar customs in Iran. Political incentive may have lead Akhenaton to oppose the powerful priesthood of Amon. At any rate, this internal dissent greatly undermined Egypt's empire. When Akhenaton failed to support his western Asian subjects against foreign invaders, the vassal princes defected. Despite these sacrifices, the cult of Aton died with its founder.

His successor Tutankhamun (1361–1352)—whose magnificent tomb was discovered in 1922—returned the capital to Thebes and the god Amon to his former prominence.

Succeeding years saw a brief resurge of imperial dominance but by the reign of Ramesses II (1287–1220) this power was again undermined. In his sixty-seven years of rule, Ramesses built monuments throughout Egypt, the most famous being the temples at Abu Simbel: these were rescued with modern engineering equipment in the 1960s before the Aswan Dam caused flooding in the region. But despite the architectural splendors and saber-rattling of his reign, Ramesses suffered a setback at the hands of the Hittites in Syria. A formal treaty, concluded sixteen years later with the Hittites, created an alliance between the two kingdoms and symbolized the end of Egyptian domination in North Syria.

Throughout the closing years of the New Kingdom, Egypt was on the defensive: first from invasions of Libyans from the West, then from the dreaded "Sea Peoples," a mixed band of invaders whose attacks upset the entire Eastern Mediterranean.

### The Late Period to 525 B.C.

The New Kingdom did not collapse totally like its Old and Middle Kingdom predecessors; it gradually broke down. At home, the pharaoh was forced to share power with his high priests and viceroys; abroad, the glory of the empire had passed. A pathetic tale from 1100 B.C., *The Journey of Wen-Amon to Phoenicia*, describes the contemptuous treatment accorded an Egyptian ambassador from the once-powerful Temple of Amon. Egypt entered into a period of decline, suffering a massive infiltration and takeover by African peoples from the west.

Later centuries brought no recovery, and Egypt fell successively to the Assyrians (in the seventh century B.C.), the Persians (525), Alexander the Great of Macedon (331), and Rome (30 B.C.)

## THE HITTITES

In the seventeenth century, the Hittites headed a strong tribal federation in the high plateau of north-central Anatolia. Starting about 1600, their King Mursilis took his army on annual forays south over the Caucasus. Conquests were effected as far as Aleppo in northern Syria, and in 1590 the Hittites swept down the Euphrates to sack Babylon. With Mursilis' death the first Hittite empire collapsed, but the

*Top:* Detail from a relief showing Akhenaton and his family offering sacrifices to Aton, god of the sun, c. 1379–1362 B.C. Akhenaton opposed the powerful priesthood of the god Amon with his devotion to a god who was seen as a loving creator. He also fostered important changes in Egyptian art. This style, known as "Amarna art" after Akhenaton's capital, has a delicate fluidity very different from the still earlier style. The change in styles seems to correspond to the change in religion. The little hands at the end of the sun's rays have a humanizing effect.
*Above:* Relief of a Hittite warrior from Tel Halaf, ninth century B.C.

blows it had dealt to the Babylonians enabled other tribesmen, such as the Kassites and the Hurrians, to take control of northeastern Mesopotamia. A century later, the Hittites shared a brief partnership with the new Egyptian Empire. But when Amenhotep II allied Egypt with rival Hurrians, the Hittite-Egyptian alliance came to an end.

Internal religious dissent, as we have seen, left Egypt heedless of threats on the Asian mainland. While Akhenaton challenged the priests of Amon, the Hittite king Suppiluliumas took over the northern part of the Egyptian Empire. His son, Mursilis II (c. 1339–1306) extended Hittite power over virtually every Asian state from the Black Sea to Cyprus. About 1300 B.C. a Hittite army of 25,000 stopped Ramesses II at the Battle of Kadesh.

Relief of a Phoenician Galley. The Phoenicians were the most adventurous mariners of the ancient world. They were also extremely sagacious traders, and these two talents gained for them almost total monopoly of international commerce. The shores of the Mediterranean were dotted with trading posts and warehouses which Phoenician fleets brought to the East in exchange for their own dyestuffs, glassware and jewelry and also for goods from further East. By the ninth century B.C. Phoenician trading centers were established in Cyprus, Sicily, Sardinia and Africa.

### Hittite Society

At the top of Hittite society, the king, although he was not deified, combined the function of ruler, general, priest and chief judge. The law he administered was unique among western Asian codes for its emphasis on unbiased discovery of the facts and compensation rather than "eye for an eye" retaliation. Hittite military expansion was aided by generals who were excellent strategists and also by the use of two-horse chariots—an innovation which also gave the Hyksos a great advantage over their enemies. Once conquered, the territories of the Hittite empire were allowed to retain many local customs and local deities. Indeed the Hittites themselves adopted a great many features of Babylonian culture, including cuneiform writing, legal codification, a number of Sumerian and Semitic gods, the Babylonian standard of weights and measures, and certain artistic conventions. Imperial government was administered by appointed officials, but the nobility were granted large estates by the king in return for providing weapons and troops. The Hittite economy was primarily agricultural but the mining and working of copper, silver and lead was also important. Most of the population worked in the fields, but the towns included a middle-class of craftsmen.

Tradition credits the Hittites with the first working of iron (c. 1400)—a fundamentally different process from that of bronze. The new metal could not be cast in molds like bronze, for the results were too brittle. Instead the molten ore had to be hardened by direct contact with carbon (charcoal), hammered, and cooled to produce a tempered blade. By the thirteenth century this process was used by the Hittites to produce hard, cheap weapons—a development with important implications for ancient warfare. From this time on the relatively abundant iron ores could arm and protect not only the nobility (for whom the more expensive bronze had been reserved) but the common soldier as well. Sheer numbers became correspondingly important and battles were no longer decided by the maneuvers of a few score chariots. Agriculturally, ironworking proved a great benefit to the West Asian peoples. The wider availability of strong metal plows made hitherto uncultivable land suitable for farming. Militarily, however, the new iron technology told against the aristocratic Hittite warriors. Reluctant to arm the general populace (whether from snobbery or fear) they were vulnerable to the iron-clad masses of the more homogeneous barbarian societies. Shortly after 1200, the Hittite empire was destroyed by such an influx of invaders (the Sea Peoples) who crossed the Hellespont from Europe.

## THE PHOENICIANS

The southwest Asian lands bordering the Mediterranean—a region now composed of the states of Syria, Lebanon, and Israel—is known to historians by its biblical name, "Canaan," "a land flowing with milk and honey." By the second millennium

B.C. this area was inhabited by a mixed population of native Semitic and non-Semitic speakers. It was never united into an imperial or national group, but instead organized in a series of independent city-states, such as Jericho, Hazor, Byblos, and Ugarit. Excavations of the latter city have revealed a thriving culture, with a palace covering 9,000 square yards and royal archives containing correspondence with the whole Near Eastern world. Later this city had connections with Mycenae. Agriculture was the bastion of the Canaanite economy, and trade and industry primarily local.

Better known to us is a later stage of Canaanite civilization, that of the Phoenicians as the Greeks christened those Canaanites who lived along the Mediterranean coast in the area of the modern Lebanon. During the second half of the second millennium this area was a protectorate of Egypt, and subject not only to its influence, but to that of the Hittites and later the Philistines, Hebrews, and Assyrians. When conflicts in the late second millennium destroyed the Hittites and the Mycenaeans and crippled Egypt, the coastal cities of Ardos, Beirut, Byblos, Tyre, and Sidon were able to safeguard their independence. Their inhabitants were ready to take advantage of the power vacuum in the Mediterranean during the twelfth century. Formerly Phoenician singlemasted ships had kept timidly to the coasts, trading mostly with Egypt by following the shoreline southwards. By 1000 B.C., however, Phoenician ships were plying the Mediterranean as far as the Pillars of Hercules (Gibraltar) and indeed beyond, into the Atlantic. Ivory, metalwork, glass, cedar, and much-prized linens dyed in purple (extracted from the murex, a shellfish found along the Lebanese coast) made for a rich Mediterranean trade. The Phoenicians founded mercantile colonies in such far-flung places as North Africa (Carthage, eighth century) and Spain (Gades, the modern Cadiz, sixth century). Carthage itself went on to found its own colonies in the Western Mediterranean (see book 2, chapter 8). Phoenician power was never transformed from this economic basis. Unlike other Western Asian peoples, the Phoenicians never formed a united state, or even a confederation although Tyre or Sidon occasionally dominated the region.

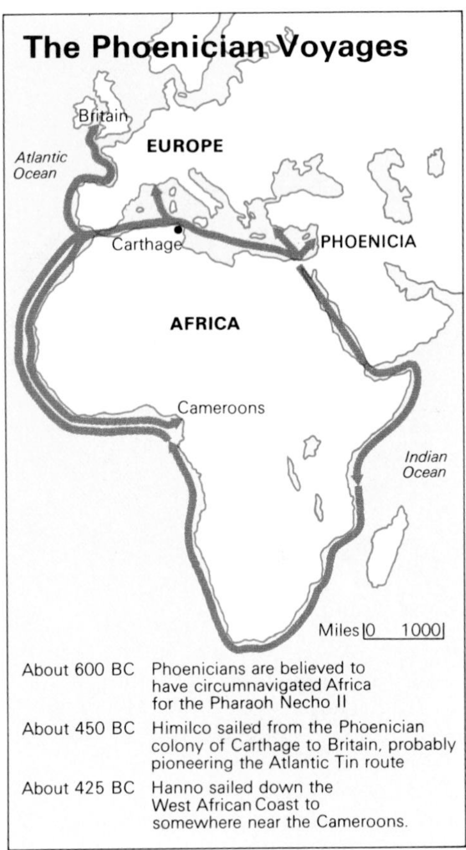


About 600 BC Phoenicians are believed to have circumnavigated Africa for the Pharaoh Necho II
About 450 BC Himilco sailed from the Phoenician colony of Carthage to Britain, probably pioneering the Atlantic Tin route
About 425 BC Hanno sailed down the West African Coast to somewhere near the Cameroons.

Their calligraphy was a gradual development, assuming final form in the ninth century B.C. Owing to cultural proximity and trading contacts with Mesopotamia, Babylonian cuneiform had become the accepted script of north coastal Palestine in the second millennium. Indeed, as international politics made a simplified form of communication imperative, cuneiform script was adopted as the diplomatic language of the Middle East. Even the Egyptian pharaoh had to abandon his native hieroglyphs to correspond with his Syrian satellites in cuneiform. But cuneiform signs were syllabic rather than alphabetical; that is, they stood for consonant-vowel combinations rather than single letters. Thus using them for non-Babylonian languages involved extensive and impractical efforts at transliteration. The business interests of traveling Phoenician merchants demanded a simpler script for rapid record-keeping. Some of these merchants were undoubtedly familiar with an Egyptian practice of abbreviating the hieroglyphs representing single syllables—a system that produced twenty-four sound-signs, unfortunately without dropping the multitude of other characters. This system of abbreviation was eventually attempted with cuneiform. Tablets found at the Phoenician city of Ugarit show a simplified cuneiform script with thirty signs: twenty-seven consonants and the vowels a, i, and u.

For reasons unknown, this system did not take hold, but another thirty-letter script, this one dating from the early fifteenth century B.C., has been discovered at Sinai. The signs are close copies of Egyptian hieroglyphs, but the sounds correspond to the Semitic names of the objects they represent. Here for the first time we find the sign of the ox-head (aleph) which persists today in our name for a script based on single letters, "alphabet." Gradually, this early ancestor of our own script was adopted by the Phoenicians, made less pictorial, and given a linear form. By the tenth century B.C., the Phoenicians had a consonantal alphabet of twenty-two symbols. The vowels were to be understood from the context, a system that still obtains in modern Arabic and Hebrew. Later the Greeks, in whose language vowels played a much more prominent part, completed the Phoenician alphabet. This simplified writing, with its easily memorized symbols set in a fixed order, brought literacy into the reach of less privileged classes. No longer were reading and writing necessarily the prerogative of priests and the educated few. The alphabet was to spread geographically (east to India, west to Europe) and also socially.

Canaanite god Baal brandishing a thunderbolt—second century B.C. Baal was the god of storms and fertility—the son of the supreme sun-god El and his wife Asherat, goddess of the sea. To the Hebrews, Baal was an attractive abomination. As a fertility figure, he was appropriate to their agricultural existence in the Promised Land, but alien to their belief in a supreme deity ruling over nature rather than through it. To the Canaanites, Baal was the essential rain-giver. If he failed, a Canaanite poem read, "No dew, no rain; no welling-up of the deep, no sweetness of Baal's voice."

## THE ASSYRIANS

The weakening of the Egyptian and Hittite grip on Western Asia provided opportunities for another people—the Assyrians. Strategically, their homeland in the foothills bordering the northern Tigris was extremely vulnerable. A broad southern plain welcomed invaders, while mountain ranges to the north and east made defense difficult. Thus early Assyrian history reads like a roll-call of great Asian powers, recording invasions by Sargon I of Akkad, the Third Dynasty of Ur, Hammurabi, the Kassites, the Hurrians, the Hittites, and even distant Egypt under Thutmose III. The Assyrians saw one method of protection: the military organization of their entire state. Gradually a defenseless people forged themselves into the most feared army of Western Asia. Every able-bodied Assyrian male was subject to military service, joining the largest fighting force of its time—the first army to be fully equipped with iron weapons. (Iron ores abounded in the mountains of northern Mesopotamia.) Sculptured battle scenes found in Assyrian palaces suggest a battle-order beginning with a stream of deadly iron-tipped arrows from the archers, followed by charging war chariots and cavalry, backed by pikemen for hand-to-hand encounters. Fortified cities were no problem for these battalions: the Assyrians devised siege artillery that could breach any city wall. Territories slated for conquest were softened up by espionage activities and the organization of fifth columns.

The use of force against enemy peoples did not end with conquest. New territories were bludgeoned into submission by mass murder, extraordinary acts of torture, widespread plunder and destruction, and the massive transplanting of subject peoples. Assyrian archives are graced with boasts like these:

> *Their booty and possessions, cattle, sheep, I carried away; I reared a column of the living and a column of heads. . . . Their boys and girls I burned up in flame. Pillars of skulls I erected before their town. . . . I dyed the mountains with their blood like red wool. . . . With their corpses I spanned the Orontes before there was a bridge.*

Whether or not Assyrian terrorism surpassed all records in Western Asia its use seems uniquely deliberate: The Assyrian war-god Ashur was represented as a divine archer, demanding the complete destruction of his enemies; and Assyrian art is unrivaled in its militarism. Terrorism, of course, was an effective device for subjugating conquered peoples—in the short run, anyway.

Eleven centuries before Christ, the Assyrian king Tiglath-pileser (c. 1115-1077) led a blitzkrieg through Western Asia that made Assyria a world power. While not achieving his boasted status of "King of the World, king of Assyria, king of all the four rims of the earth," he did lead his armies 400 miles from their homeland to the Mediterranean. Two centuries of conflict followed, marked by clashes with the Babylonians and the loss and reconquest of North Syria and the Phoenician coast. The Phoenician cities, accorded simple conquest rather than demolition, accepted Assyrian rule because it was good for business. Political stability and unrestricted trade over long distances were important to the commercial classes, and the Assyrian empire was strengthened by their support.

By 725, the Assyrians had conquered Babylon; it was then that the Assyrian policy of uprooting conquered populations was instituted. One king, Tiglath-pileser III (744–727), boasted of uprooting 30,300 people at a time. The cruelty and unpopularity of such a practice is obvious. Even Assyrian reliefs show the pathetic state of the victims, herded away from their demolished cities like so many head of cattle. The empire at large, however, probably benefited by the exchange of inventions and customs afforded by this misery.

Over the next century, Israel, the Egyptian delta, and the eastern state of Elam fell to the Assyrians. Their numerous subjects were governed by the most advanced system of its time, employing a council of scribal advisors and provincial governors empowered to collect taxes, raise armies by conscriptions, and settle legal disputes. A written legal code, empire-wide highways a postal system, the spread of Aramaic as a lingua franca, and the cultural interchange provided by the transplanting of native populations and the stationing of foreign soldiers in restive areas—all enabled the development of the first extensive cosmopolitan empire of Western Asia. As the archaeologist Thorkhild Jacobsen has observed, the Assyrians, "thus laid secure administrative foundations for central rule of the entire Near East from Mesopotamia to Egypt. It was these secure foundations . . . which made first the Persian, and later Alexander's, empire possible, and which are therefore a—perhaps the—major conditioning factor behind all of the following Hellenistic and Roman history. . . ."

But the factors that enabled the Assyrians to consolidate their holdings also hastened their decline. As the empire expanded increasing numbers of soldiers were necessary for its pacification, encouraging the use of foreign mercenaries. The Assyrians became over-extended and soon were unable to stem internal revolt and barbarian assaults. When recurring Babylonian uprisings coincided with attacks by the Medes of Iran and the Scythians from the northern steppes, the Empire could not summon the forces necessary for defense. The sixth century B.C. saw the rise in Babylon of a new Semitic people, the Chaldeans. In 612 after successfully rebelling against their Assyrian overlords, they joined the Medes in destroying Nineveh, the Assyrian capital. Such an event could hardly have been unpopular with the downtrodden subjects of the empire. Most probably they echoed the rejoicing of the Hebrew prophet Nahum:

"Nineveh is laid waste: who will bemoan her?"

*Top:* Horse-drawn chariot, detail from a relief of King Ashurnasirpal II's battles, ninth century B.C. To judge from the reliefs depicting this king, his forty-two year reign was a long succession of military campaigns, occasionally interrupted by lion hunts. In fact, he was also a patron of the arts, particularly of literature. Trained as scribe himself, he founded and maintained a giant library at Nineveh.

*Above:* Specimen of Assyrian script on stone, from Nimrud, 879 B.C. The writing is taken from an inscription of Ashurnasirpal II describing his conquests.

## THE HEBREWS

Politically, the Hebrews (or Israelites) made no lasting impact on the ancient world. They are credited with no special achievement in the fields of government, science, technology or the visual arts. For much of their early history, they were no more than a small group of nomadic tribesmen. Agriculture, elaborate social organization and literary activity reached them relatively late, despite their contact with such cradles of civilization as Mesopotamia and Egypt. Nonetheless, they are one of the most celebrated nations of antiquity. Out of their experience, a tradition of extraordinary importance emerged, providing the theological and ethical basis of three great living religions: Judaism, Christianity, and Islam.

The primary source for our knowledge of the Israelites is the Hebrew Bible or

Old Testament, a record in which elements of myth, legend and folklore are mixed with genuine history. According to the biblical account, the ancestors of the Hebrews, the Patriarchs, were nomads dwelling in the country of Haran, in Northern Mesopotamia. The book of Genesis claims that the family of Abraham originally migrated there from the city of Ur in Sumer. Archaeological evidence leaves this question open, but suggests that the Patriarchs belonged to the beginning of the second millennium B.C. Many Genesis stories (creation, Eden, the Flood, the Tower of Babel) are definitely associated with Mesopotamian traditions. The same book relates that Abraham, the traditional ancestor of the Hebrews, journeyed from Haran to Canaan and settled there, but that his grandson Jacob and his children were driven by famine to Egypt, where they were received by their brother Joseph. The presence in Egypt, from about 1700 B.C., of Semitic invaders, the Hyksos, may account for the welcome given to the Hebrews. The expulsion of the Hyksos by the Egyptians in 1570 may have been the cause of the Hebrews' bondage. An Israelite exodus from Egypt, led by Moses (who bears an Egyptian name), is likely to have occurred in the thirteenth century, possibly during the reign of Ramesses II (1290–24). It is with the departure from Egypt, and the heroic and legendary forty years in the Sinai wilderness, that Hebrew tradition as it is known today began to take shape.

*Top:* Relief of Assyrian archers in combat. Assyrian military strategy organized these archers into the first wave of attack. After a deadly stream of their arrows, the cavalry would charge the confused enemy. Then foot soldiers armed with pikes would finish off the opponent. *Above:* Relief of Assyrian warrior adding to a pile of decapitated enemy heads, from Sennacarib's Palace (seventh century B.C.). The Assyrians were infamous for their brutality to defeated peoples. Ashurnasirpal II's chronicles boast: "Of the soldiers I slew 600 with the sword, 3,000 prisoners I burned in the fire, I kept no one alive and no hostage . . . I piled their corpses as high as towers."

The passage from slavery to nomadic freedom resulted, it seems, in a rudimentary social structure. The book of Exodus relates how Moses went up to Mount Sinai to encounter Yahweh, the God of Israel, and brought down the Ten Commandments summarizing the essence of biblical religion and morality:

> *Thou shalt have no other gods before me.*
> *Thou shalt not take the name of the Lord thy God in vain.*
> *Honor thy father and thy mother.*

By agreeing to these laws and other precepts regulating individual and communal life, the Israelites made a pact, or Covenant, with Yahweh. They accepted him as their special master and received assurances of care and protection from him. They thus bound themselves to a "jealous" God who commanded exclusive worship and prohibited all figurative representation of himself (a prohibition later extended to representation of any living beings) and the misuse of his name. Unlike most other deities of the ancient Near East, the God of Israel was not identified with heavenly bodies or with the forces of nature, such as the sun, moon, wind, rain, vegetation, or fertility. He was celebrated, instead, as their creator, a benevolent, just, omnipotent God, invisible to the human eye, without a divine family and without geographical limitation.

It is not certain that the Hebrews in the time of Moses were strict monotheists, believers in only one god. They may have been monolatrous, like the Egyptian devotees of Aton, acknowledging, that is to say, the existence of the nature gods of the ancient Near East, while worshiping Yahweh alone. Nevertheless, after the settlement in Canaan and the adoption of a new agricultural life-style, many Israelites must have judged the cult of the local divinities of climate and fertility, Baal and Astarte, more immediately useful, and the Old Testament records numerous instances of idol-worship by the Hebrews.

The Israelites had to fight for the conquest of their "Promised Land." About 1200, under the command of Joshua, Moses' successor, they contended with the Canaanites, Semites who had occupied that country in the third millennium and had formed there a number of city-states. Then in the eleventh century they warred with the more formidable Philistines. While subduing the Canaanites, the Hebrews retained their original nomadic social structure, that of a confederacy of twelve tribes governed by elders and chiefs. From time to time, however, in periods of emergency, they were ruled by charismatic generals or liberators called judges. The Philistines (who gave their name to the land of Palestine) were a greater danger than the Canaanites. The Philistines were part of the second wave of invasion of the Eastern Mediterranean coast around 1200 by the "Sea Peoples," who had destroyed the empire of the Hittites and had traveled southward from Asia Minor towards Egypt. Repulsed by Pharaoh Ramesses III (c. 1190), they established themselves in the maritime plain of Canaan. Technologically more advanced than the Israelites—they were expert metal workers and used iron while their opponents still relied on weapons made of bronze—they exercised, by the middle of the eleventh century, a very powerful pressure on their neighbors. To resist them, all the Hebrew tribes joined together for the first time under a king, Saul (c. 1020–1000). The establishment of the monarchy strengthened the monotheistic tendencies of Israel, yet at the same time, kings, and especially foreign queens, often introduced the cult of pagan deities. However, the ultimate refuge to whom people themselves turned was always the God of their fathers.

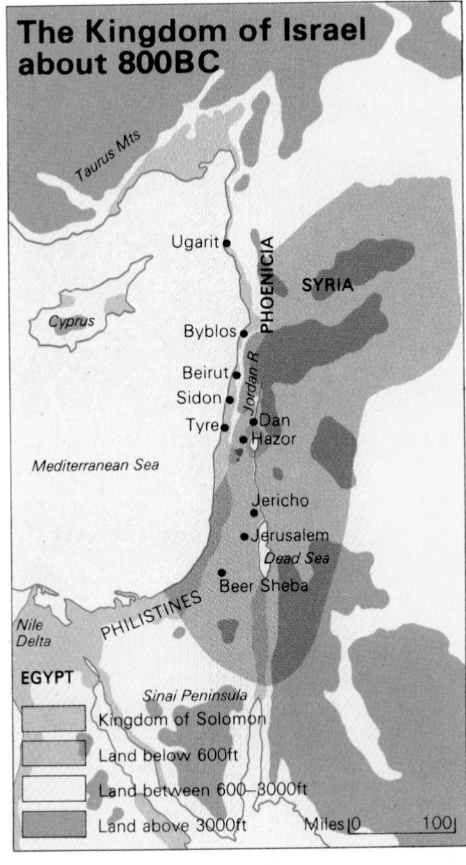


Saul fell on the battlefield fighting the Philistines, but they were defeated by his successor, David (1000–961) and ceased to be a threat to Israel. David occupied the old Canaanite stronghold, Jerusalem, and transformed it into his capital. He then went on to conquer all the surrounding countries from the Euphrates to the gulf of Aqaba. The Bible celebrates him as the ideal king of Israel. During the reign of David's son, Solomon (961–922), the Hebrew kingdom attained the height of its splendor.

Expensive building projects of this sort, and a standing army of 1,400 chariots and 12,000 horses, as well as an enormous harem of foreign and Israelite wives, were bound to be economically burdensome. High taxation and the loss of tribal independence led to internal conflicts, and on the death of Solomon in 922 his realm disintegrated into the rival kingdoms of Israel in the North and Judah in the South.

The Northern Kingdom lived under almost continuous Assyrian threat and in 722 its precarious independence came to an end, when Nebuchadnezzar destroyed the capital.

During the two previous centuries the Israelites had been warned of the coming of such calamities by a group of inspired teachers known as the prophets. They had fiercely preached against the worship by the Hebrews of Baal and Astarte, and the practices attached to their cult, including temple prostitution. In addition to defending the purity of the ancestral religion, strengthening monotheism, and criticizing kings and priests, the prophets were also the upholders of morality and social justice. Moreover, they argued that history in general, and the history of Israel in particular, was governed by their God. Even their oppressors, the Assyrians and the Babylonians, were seen by them as the "rod of Yahweh's anger," chastizing his erring sons.

In 539 Cyrus, king of Persia, described in the Bible as Yahweh's elect, triumphantly entered Babylon, and a year later authorized the captive Israelites to return to Judea. Their peaceful existence under Persian rule, during which most of the books of the Old Testament were finally edited, was followed by the more tumultuous Hellenistic era. This ended in a national uprising under the Maccabees in the early second century. However, the newly found independence that resulted from their victory was of short duration, for in 63 B.C. Judea came under the influence of Rome. Foreign domination reanimated the nationalistic sentiments of the Jews, which found expression in hopes of a God-sent savior or Messiah. The messianic ferment that developed inspired, on the political level, two unsuccessful armed rebellions against some in the first and second centuries A.D. In the religious field, it culminated in the birth of Christianity, a new faith centered on the person and teachings of Jesus, a holy man from Galilee.

## THE PERSIANS

As we saw in chapter 6, invading forces of Aryans began to move into what is now north Afghanistan and Soviet Central Asia about 2000 B.C. In later centuries, these people traveled southeast, into the Indian peninsula, and southwest, into the plateau to which they gave their name: Iran. The Caucasian origins of these tribesmen set the cultural tone of the much-later Persian civilizations: expert metalworking, and fine horsemanship. It was a group of these invaders, the Kassites, who brought the horse breed which superseded the primitive onagers of the Sumerians. The bronze artifacts of this civilization reveal its fascination with the horse: reinrings for guiding chariots, harness ornaments, and axeheads shaped like horses' heads. This passion for horsemanship and the possession of excellent breeding grounds in the high grassy valleys of the Zagros mountains and modern Kurdistan would prove a great advantage in later military campaigns.

A millennium later, a similar path south brought tribesmen to this region who spoke the languages which distinguish the Medes and Persians. With the earlier settlers, these people would develop an Empire of unprecedented organization and tolerance, while retaining the simple values of the tribesman: "To ride a horse, to draw a bow, and to speak the truth."

*Top:* The River Jordan. The Bible relates how Yahweh allowed the Hebrews to cross the Jordan upon their arrival in the Promised Land: "So . . . when those who bore the ark had come to the Jordan, and the feet of the priests bearing the ark were dipped in the brink of the water . . . the waters coming down from above stood and rose up in a heap far off . . . and the people passed over opposite Jericho. And while all Israel were passing over on dry ground, the priests who bore the ark of covenenat . . . stood on dry ground in the midst of the Jordan. *Above:* Mount Sinai.

The first written reference to the Medes and the Persians records their payment of tribute to Assyria in the ninth century B.C. At that time, the two tribes occupied the mountainous territory east of the Tigris, within striking distance of the Assyrian capital of Nineveh and the city of Babylon. The decline of the Assyrian Empire, furthered by both the rising Medes and the Babylonians, created political opportunities which the gradually uniting Iranian tribes used to great effect. Theirs was poor land for agriculture, and nomadic society encourages neither large living groups nor the concentration of authority, but by the eighth century B.C. a Median dynasty arose to challenge the Assyrians. For a century the Medes threatened the Empire's eastern borders, from the Caspian Sea to the Persian Gulf, while welding neighboring tribes (including the Persians) into unity.

In 626, the Median ruler Cyaxares II conquered the Persians and also laid siege to the Assyrian capital of Nineveh. As we have seen, the siege, supported by an alliance with the Babylonians, was successful in 612 B.C., and Cyaxares went on to dominate his ally and conquer upper Mesopotamia. The first Iranian empire was a reality.

This empire Cyaxares bequeathed to his son, Astyages, but it is not he who takes prominence in subsequent years. Among the Persian vassals of the Medes was a princely family—the Achaemenids—of northern Elam. Before the mid-sixth century B.C. they were no more than petty royalty, though they hailed their leader as "King of Kings, King of Anshan." A marriage between this house and the daughter of Astyages produced Cyrus, a leader who warranted the title.

The early life of Cyrus (reigned 559–530 B.C.) is shrouded in legend. We do know that he cultivated his power over surrounding areas by building the first Achaemenid royal city, Pasargadae, and then cast about for an ally against the Medes. He found one in Nabonidus of Babylon, usurper of Nebuchadnezzar's throne. Together, the two nations virtually rolled over the Medes: Nabonidus conquered almost all lands west to the seaboard of Syria, while the Persians plundered the Median city of Ecbatana and carried off its treasure to Pasargadae. Cyrus now had control of the crucial caravan route through the Median capital, but he treated the defeated king generously and retained the Median officials at their posts. This policy of generosity and respect for native government won him goodwill and a united kingdom.

The next target was the kingdom of Lydia in Asia Minor, determined to recover territories which it had lost earlier to the Medes. Its ruler, the legendary Croesus, had raised his kingdom to its greatest strength, conciliating Greek opinion by fabulous generosity towards their sanctuaries and admiration for their institutions. (Whether or not he actually *was* the richest man in the world, Croesus' use of the new invention of coinage, his generosity, and whatever wealth he had, certainly conveyed this impression. The historian Herodotus even constructed a fictional—but appropriate—account of a meeting between Croesus and the Athenian Solon: the richest man in the world and the wisest.) Croesus consulted the oracle at Delphi, and like so many others fell victim to equivocation: "If you make war upon the Persians you will destroy a mighty empire." That empire turned out to be his own. Cyrus took it and went on to subjugate the whole of Asia Minor by 540 B.C. Fifty years later the Persians would be turned away from the Greek mainland at Marathon and Salamis (see Book 2, part 1, chapter 3); but now they had ambitions in the East. Cyrus' conquests took the Persians as far as India, and by 539 B.C. Babylon and Syria had fallen in the west.

Again Cyrus was a model of clemency, demanding no more than the imprisonment of conquered kings, respecting local customs and beliefs, and releasing the Hebrews from their captivity in Babylon. Instead of decimating the populace and degrading their gods, Cyrus claimed (and received) the loyalty of his subjects by giving his kingship a constitutional basis and establishing himself, in Babylon for instance, as benefactor of Marduk, the chief local deity. In a chronicle of the period Cyrus claims that he "resettled" the Sumerian deities whom Nabonidus had brought into Babylon by restoring their images to their rightful places, "which made them happy."

The route to Egypt was now open, but not for Cyrus. He died in 530 B.C. and was buried at Pasargadae. In twenty years he had unified the world from the Indus to the Hellespont, creating what was certainly an autocracy—and a very severe one—but with an entirely new tolerance and charity towards the conquered.

Cyrus's son, the more autocratic Cambyses, succeeded in capturing the pharaoh and bringing him to Susa. But Cambyses' early death in 522 B.C. left the empire in a state of civil war. His brother-in-law, Darius of Parthia (ruled 521–486 B.C.) crushed the rebels mercilessly and went on to consolidate the empire in the form it maintained for 200 years. The conquered regions were divided into twenty satrapies, administered by Persian governors, but free to use their own languages, religions, and institutions. The governors themselves were not regional dictators, but responsible members of a graded imperial civil service, through which they were expected to govern. Although the satrapies paid great tribute to the Persian rulers, their native economies were not tampered with. Imperial protection fostered sea and land trade, and imperial coinage provided a standard of metal purity which made "the King's measure" acceptable everywhere. Royal inspectors were sent into the provinces, and efficient communications were maintained by 1,677 miles of Royal Road from Sardis to Susa. Its 111 post stations enabled couriers to travel the route in a week.

The enlightened rule of the Persians was greatly influenced by the ethical tenets of their religion—Zoroastrianism. Good men were to avoid heresy, be kind to domestic animals, practice justice, and never defile the sacred elements of earth, fire, and water. (Thus the statement of the Persian governor Arsites: "I will not stand by and see one farm burned of those which the King has committed to my hands.") But ambition would lead Darius' successor, Xerxes, to the fatal clash with the Greeks, which hastened Persia's decline. One hundred and fifty years after the death of Darius, the Persian empire would fall to Alexander the Great.

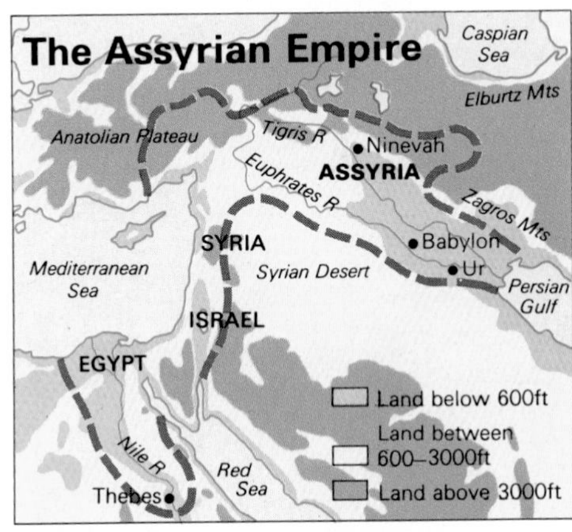


View of the city of Persepolis, sixth-fifth centuries B.C. Persepolis was founded by the Persian emperor Darius I after 518 B.C. to serve as the capital of the Achaemenid empire. It was destroyed by Alexander the Great in 331. The magnificent city consisted of a series of great palaces and apadana (columned reception halls) built on a terrace erected against a mountainside. Medes, Syrians, Anatolians, and Ionian Greeks were among the many imperial subjects employed in building the capital.

Chapter 11

# THE BEGINNINGS OF SCIENTIFIC THOUGHT

## CIVILIZATION OF THE VALLEY

"Civilization" is a word with many meanings. Basically, as its Latin derivation implies, it refers to the benefits enjoyed by the inhabitants of cities—to the goods and services which a civic community provides, the protection that it gives against the threats of a hostile environment and of the enemy at the gate, and the opportunities and incentives that it offers (to some men at least) to develop and communicate special skills and techniques. However even in Roman times the word meant more than this—it suggested enlightenment, refinement, a life enriched by the fine arts, music, literature, drama, a world in which one could cultivate the pleasures of the intellect, philosophy, speculative science. In this full sense, civilization began to develop on earth between the fourth and the first millennium B.C. in several fertile river valleys: in Mesopotamia, Egypt, India, China and Central America.

It is perhaps not suprising that this great human development began independently in several different parts of the world. It must have been obvious even in remote antiquity that a given amount of human effort yields greater rewards when directed cooperatively than when expended individually. One canal was worth more than many ditches; a few skilled craftsmen supported by the community—a baker, a weaver, a carpenter—could save all of its members hours of inefficient labor. Even small communities could reap some of these benefits: nevertheless there was a strong "snowball" effect; cooperative groups could be seen to enjoy a higher standard of living and so grew by accretion: as they grew, they could afford to increase the degree of specialization of their members, and hence enjoyed still greater benefits. The only essential condition for this virtuous circle was security—protection against the natural disasters of disease, fire and flood, and freedom from internal and external strife. One great advantage of a large cooperative community was that it could afford to allocate human resources to give itself this security; it could create a system of government which commanded defense forces and was responsible for anticipating and (if possible) preventing natural disasters. Inevitably, therefore, the earliest civilizations developed in regions that could support a relatively large community—where the soil was fertile and irrigation water was available and sunshine plentiful. In fact, the optimum environment proved to be one with a bright, sub-tropical sun, so water was a crucial element, and one can most easily understand the differences between the early civilizations by relating them to the rather different problems that they faced in harnessing the rivers to meet their agricultural needs, and in protecting themselves and their fragile dwellings and irrigation networks against the consequences of flood.

In Mesopotamia, the river bed was high above the cultivated plain, so water for irrigation was available throughout the dry season. This brought the advantage that it was possible (with good organization) to have two harvests a year: the snag was that the main canals had to be wide, and set at the same level as the river, in

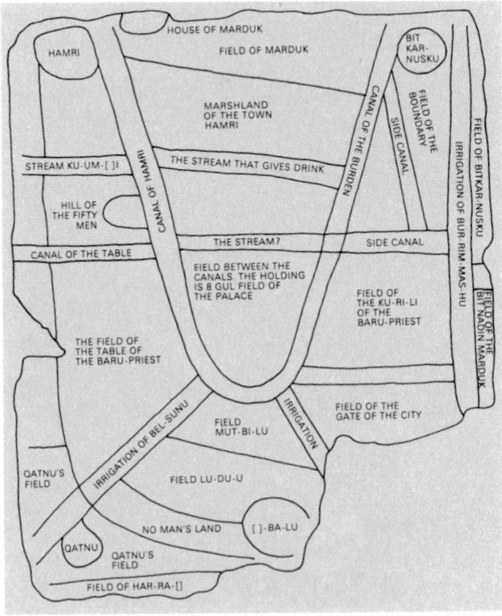

*Top:* Drawing based on a cuneiform map of irrigation canals on a royal estate near Nippur, Mesopotamia, c. 1300 B.C. Note how the villages (represented by circles) are linked with the waterways.
*Above:* Drawing of a shaduf, first devised by the Egyptians to transport water uphill. The hinged pole has a bucket at one end and a balance at the other.
*Left:* Detail of a fresco from the tomb of Menna, at Thebes, New Kingdom, c. 1422–1411 B.C. This colorful scene shows something of the immense range of technical skills practiced in ancient Egypt. Among these craftsmen are carpenters, smiths, cabinet-makers, and glassblowers.

order to prevent an excessive rate of flow, which would have eroded their banks. They consequently tended to silt up and needed constant maintenance. To minimize the vast amount of human labor involved in this system of irrigation, an organization evolved that was based on a relatively small number of independent canal networks, each with its own center of administration. This led to the emergence of the Sumerian city-states. The eventual consolidation of these warring states into one empire was perhaps partly a response to the ever-present danger of flooding (the Tigris and Euphrates being notoriously unpredictable): certainly a great organizational advance was made possible when (c.1792 B.C.) King Hammurabi conquered the entire Tigris valley (and much of the Euphrates) and imposed a strict central control. Some of his edicts survive: "Summon the people who hold fields on this side of the Damanu canal that they may scour it" he commands. Because of the countless thousands of man-years involved in canal-construction and maintenance, Sumerian mathematics advanced far in the computation of volumes enclosed by inclined planes—so much earth to remove or water made available! The outstanding technological achievement of this region was the great aqueduct built in 691 B.C. by King Sennacherib. It spanned the fifty miles from the Zab River to Nineveh, and was some twenty yards wide. It was lined with masonry blocks (about 2 million in all) each measuring 20 by 12 by 26 inches. These were transported on wheels down the dry channel itself, and a carved inscription proudly records that the entire construction was completed in one year and three months.

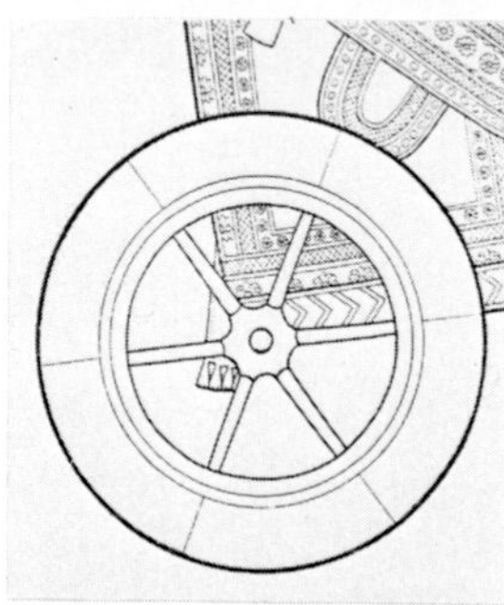

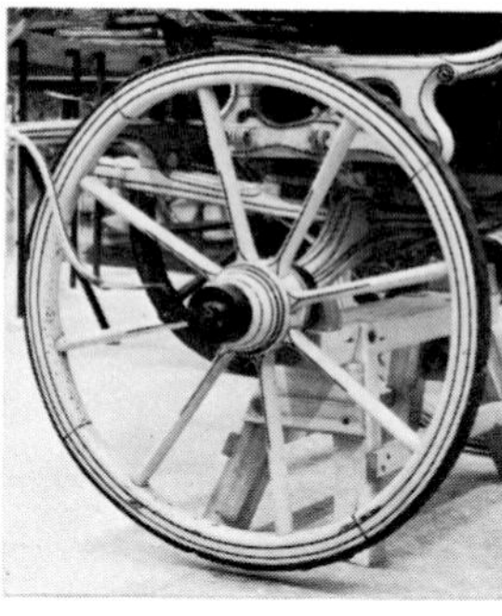

The development of the wheel. The basic but efficient design, dating back to at least 3500 B.C., has scarcely altered since. The main contribution of later centuries was to increase the speed and maneuverability of wheeled vehicles by reducing weight. The invention of spokes made the chariots of the Shang, the Aryans, and the Hyksos invincible in their time. *Top:* Sumerian solid wheel, made from three planks strapped together; detail from the Royal Standard of Ur. *Middle:* Assyrian spoked chariot wheel, c. 900 B.C. *Bottom:* An eighteenth-century English chariot wheel.

In Egypt, the problems were completely different. "Of all rivers, the Nile is the most gentlemanly." It rises and falls with almost calendrical precision, covering the arable land to a height of six feet every summer. Thus the Egyptian system of canals only had to control and spread out the flood waters. The canals were relatively short and had much less need of maintenance. In consequence the social structure was less centralized: the village was the basic unit. Central government, when it eventually came for other reasons, hardly affected the system. However, it provided a measuring service, based on "nilometers" at strategic points, so that precautions could be taken to avoid the consequences of flooding or drought. The readings of these nilometers were vital measures of their prosperity. Pliny said that in his day twelve ells meant hunger, thirteen suffering, fourteen happiness, fifteen security, sixteen abundance, but that if the depth exceeded eighteen ells, disaster followed. The predictability of the Nile focused the attention of the Egyptians on other related cyclical natural phenomena, and underlay their successes in time-reckoning and predictive astronomy.

The main limitation of basic Egyptian irrigation was that virtually all the arable land was inundated. For some purposes (for example to water the gardens of the rich) something more selective was required, which could involve transporting water uphill. The Egyptians were the first to develop an efficient means of doing so—the *shaduf*, a manually operated bucket pump. The seasonal behavior of the Nile also necessitated the storage of water, and the technology of cisterns and dams was already highly developed in Egypt by 1000 B.C.

## THE WHEEL

If water utilization was the original determinant of the location and social structure of the earliest civilizations, their subsequent development was influenced by the modes of transport which they adopted. As villages grew into towns, the traditional means of moving agricultural goods became inadequate. Women wearing head-straps, and loaded pack-asses gradually gave way to two-wheeled carts and papyrus canoes, and this new technology permitted a further growth of the centers of population. The crucial step was the invention of the wheel, which can be traced back to Sumer around 3500 B.C.—there is a pictograph of that date representing a wheel in the account tablets of a temple at Uruk. The wheels of this period were solid, and were constructed out of three planks strapped together. This rather odd feature is repeated elsewhere and suggests that the idea of the wheel spread by diffusion—east to Elam in 3000 B.C., to the Central Asian steppes and the Indus Valley in 2500, to Russia and Crete by 2000, to Egypt and Palestine around 1600, Greece 1500, China 1300, Italy 1000, and Britain in 500. However the wheel soon became more than just a means of bringing in the harvest. By the middle of the second millennium B.C. wheeled vehicles were transporting people over great distances. The wheel made its impact as a weapon of war, in the form of the chariot, which must have overwhelmed its feeble opposition very much as the tank did when it was introduced. The chariot revolutionized the practice of war, and was a vital factor in the rise of the Shang in China (c. 1850), the Aryans in India (c. 1700) and the Hyksos in Western Asia (c. 1786). It also abetted Middle-Eastern empire building by the Egyptians, Hittite and Assyrian war-lords.

Wheeled vehicles were also used as a means of travel for the privileged few at a very early stage—indeed the earliest surviving vehicles are those buried in the royal tombs of Kish and Ur. Nevertheless roads were few, and for long-range overland travel pack asses (and later camels and horses) remained the standard means of moving people and precious merchandize. As early as 2000 the deserts of Syria were regularly crossed by Assyrian merchant caravans.

In parallel with these developments in land transport came the evolution of the boat, starting with the scooped-out log or the papyrus raft, passing through small craft of reed and skin or papyrus canoes (which were certainly being constructed in Egypt around 2500), and reaching full fruition in the sail boat which was developed (again in Egypt) a few centuries later. The Nile positively invited this invention, since the prevailing wind is upstream. (However, there is less certain evidence for the independent invention of the sail boat by the Sumerians a millennium earlier.) During the second millennium B.C. the ship, like the wheel, became a machine of war, and as early as 1800 the Egyptians were building large wooden galleys—180 feet long with a crew of 120—which could venture out to sea. The use of boats for international trade also grew during this period, and became the basis for the Phoenician empire of the first millennium B.C.

These developments made it possible for the early civilizations to meet their most basic needs—a viable agricultural system and a means of trading goods and raw materials. However this does not mean that they were lacking in those refinements that (as we have seen) were certainly inherent in the Roman concept of a "civilization." During the second and third millennia B.C. mankind made three vital intellectual steps forward: he acquired a sense of time as a dimension, and he became numerate and literate. These steps were all closely related, and the precise sequence of events by which they occurred are obscure.

The indications are that primitive man endowed all the objects of the world around him with the qualities of a sentient being—will-power, unpredictability, even a tendency to anger. If the Nile failed to rise when he had hoped, it was because it had refused to do so; the sun every night struggles with (and hopefully defeats) the personal forces of darkness in its journey through the nether world. An eclipse occurs when a snake or a dragon swallows up the sun. In such a world of magic and superstition, it makes no sense to seek a pattern in one's experience: rather, primitive man sought a personal, placatory relationship with objects such as the sun and the river which affect life closely. So he treated the sun as a "thou" rather than as an "it." Only gradually did he begin to recognize patterns, and in

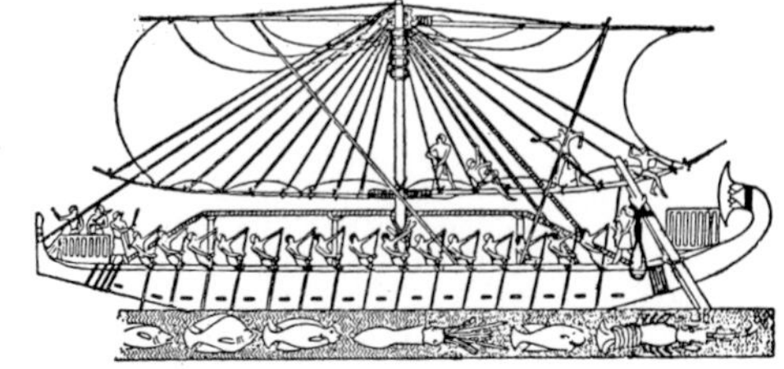

*Top:* Drawing from a relief in the tomb of Hatshepsut, queen of Egypt, c. 1400 B.C. The relief shows the triumphant expedition of discovery to the spice-lands of Punt on the coast of the Red Sea in 1493 B.C. The Egyptians were credited with the invention of the sail boat. By 1800 B.C. they were building seagoing galleys large enough to accommodate crews of 120.
*Above:* Cast of an Egyptian water-clock, 1415–1380 B.C. The water-clock is a cylindrical jar with gradated markings. Water drips through a small hole in the jar bottom at regular intervals, allowing the time to be calculated by the water-level.

particular, the pattern which we call "time." At first there was only a recognition of cycles and rhythms: the rhythm of day and night, the phases of the waxing and waning moon, the seasonal climatic and biological variations, the cycle of ovulation in woman, the yearly flooding of the banks of the Nile, the tidal motions of the sea. Then, building on these, came a primitive sense of history as a unique time sequence —the sequence of the storyteller "and it came to pass in those days. . . ." In parallel with this came questions about the beginnings of this sequence, and the earliest Creation myths appeared, some of them as early as the third millennium B.C.

## THE MEASUREMENT OF TIME

Aerial view of Stonehenge, considered to be the first major work of architecture in Great Britain. This monument, which dates from c. 2200 to 1220 B.C., was long thought to have been a religious monument of the Druids. The connection with the Druids has now been disproved, though many authorities still argue that the giant concentric rings had some religious function. Unlike similar monuments in Britain, these stones were carefully shaped and accurately jointed. The northeast–southwest axis of its construction gives Stonehenge sighting lines aligned to the setting and rising of the sun at the equinoxes and solstices, which recent authorities have cited as evidence for its use as a prehistoric observatory.

The next, and crucial, stage was to formulate the idea of a unique time sequence and of cycles, and to *measure* time by counting cycles. This worked best for long periods of time: it was a relatively simple matter to count years, say from the accession of a monarch. It was much more difficult to use the shorter cycles of the moon and the earth's rotation, because the periods of these cycles were incommensurable with each other and with the year itself. Thus the earth rotates not 365, nor 366, but 365.256366 times during one revolution about the sun. If the year is assumed, as at one stage it was by the Egyptians, to contain 365 days, the seasons will migrate forwards in the daily calendar (a difficulty which led to the term "wandering year"). Similarly the lunar month lasts a little longer than $29\frac{1}{2}$ days (the moon is full 223 times every 18 years, when it returns to the same position with respect to the sun and its orbit simultaneously). Thus a single year, as defined by the position of the earth in its orbit about the sun, contains between twelve and thirteen full moons.

The importance of a satisfactory means of reckoning days and months was the need to determine accurately the seasons of sowing and harvesting, and to predict such events as the annual flooding of the Nile. During the third millennium various calendrical schemes coexisted. They differed in their dependence on astronomical observations and in their consistency with the astronomical facts. At the most primitive, there were systems based on moon counts, starting with a suitable full moon for the ploughing festival, and counting up to ten moons (hence the Latin name December), and then restarting at the next plowing festival some two or three moons later. Day counts were never much favored, because of the uncomfortably large numbers involved, and because they led to a "wandering year." However the Egyptians are known to have established that the complete cycle of migration of the wandering year, the so-called Sothic Cycle, was 1461 years (since every four years one day was lacking, the calendar migrated one complete cycle in $4 \times 365.25$ years). They established this by observations of the heliacal rising of Sirius, that is, the time when Sirius, the brightest star in the Northern hemisphere, rose in the morning twilight, coincident with sunrise. This occurs at a fixed point in the earth's orbit round the sun, and thus defines a fixed, as opposed to a wandering year. This heliacal rise of Sirius always presaged the beginning of the Nile flood, and was the basis for a chronology almost exactly in phase with the seasonal year. An accurate subdivision of the day into hours was made possible by the sundial, introduced in Egypt around 1450. Prior to this, a number of imprecise measures had been in use, for example the Sumerian unit *danna*, originally a unit of length, and later a certain fraction of the day (perhaps the time taken for a man to walk that distance). The sundial raised a difficulty, in that no simple scheme of marking on the dial permits the daylight to be divided into a fixed number of hours. This apparently irritated the Egyptians, who were so attached to such "temporal hours" that the first water-clock, constructed in around 250 B.C. in Alexandria, was arranged to measure time in this unnatural unit.

## ASTRONOMY

In parallel with the developments in time-reckoning in the early eastern civilizations went an increasing interest in astronomy. The apparent movement of the sun and planets against the background of the fixed stars was well known to the Babylonians, who picked names for twelve constellations (such as the Crab, and the Scorpion) to match the region of the sky through which the sun passed in successive months. In some way that is by no means fully understood the belief developed that human destinies were tied up with the motions of the planets through these constellations, and so grew the passion for astrology. Strange as it may seem, this religious belief (if that is the right term) was the dominant motive for astronomical observation during this period because it led to a demand for accurate predictions of the sun's and the planets' motions.

By 747 the Babylonians had developed extremely successful rules for predicting many astronomical events. They traced the annual path of the sun against the background of the stars, known as the ecliptic, listing those constellations whose heliacal rise corresponded to the various months. Five of the planets were distinguished from the fixed stars and their courses traced and recorded. In the case of Venus, one tablet of cuneiform script calculates its apparent period to be 577.5 days (the accurate value is 584 days).

By exact chronological recording, the Babylonians noticed that lunar eclipses occur in sequences of five or six at equal time intervals separated by a long interval of seventeen lunar months. They were thus enabled to predict the possibility of lunar eclipses on the basis of this regular behavior. Perhaps the greatest achievement of the priests of the kings of Nineveh was to anticipate a lunar eclipse. "On the fourteenth day of the month an eclipse will take place; misfortune to Elam and Syria, but blessed be the King; let the King be set at ease. Venus will not be present, but I say to my lord there shall be an eclipse. Irassihe the elder, the King's servant."

In 606 Nineveh was destroyed, but Babylonian astronomy revived under the prosperous reign of Nebuchadnezzar, and by the second century B.C. the Babylonians were in a position to attempt the most difficult of astronomical predictions, an advance ephemerides determining the positions of the planets against the background of the stars of the zodiac. If the Babylonian astronomers were unable to see sufficiently beyond their measurements and their predictions based on the rhythmic behavior of the solar system to attempt a three-dimensional mental picture of the world and its relation to the universe, their brilliant astronomical successes were no less important for that.

The prehistoric inhabitants of Britain and France between about 2000 and 1000 developed some astronomical knowledge, reflected in their menhirs—vast stone and wood circles such as Stonehenge. These were constructed around sighting lines aligned to the setting and rising of the sun at the equinoxes and solstices, and to other important solar and lunar behavior. But their true astronomical and scientific skills were almost certainly inferior to contemporary Egyptian and Babylonian civilization.

Even before the advances made in Egypt and Mesopotamia, a highly developed knowledge of predictive astronomy had grown up separately in China. There is some evidence that Chinese astronomers were able to calculate lunar eclipses as early as 4000, and by 2317 the seasonal year was known to contain 365.25 days and the circle had been divided into the same number of degrees. However, many of the early records of Chinese science prior to the fifth century B.C. are lost.

That this was not so in Mesopotamia and Egypt is fortunate. All that we know of Babylonian astronomy comes from comparatively recent excavations, from fragile clay tablets in which the secrets of the heavens have been meticulously recorded. It is humbling to realize that at the turn of this century the most accurate calculation of the point at which the moon crosses the sun was determined with the help of records of eclipses made in 1062 B.C. and 762 B.C. by Babylonian astronomers pressing a reed stylus into blocks of soft, wet clay.

## MATHEMATICS

If the dominant motive for the Babylonian development of astronomy was religious or astrological, their familiarity with numbers, which alone made their astronomical achievements possible, was firmly based on the market place. Numeracy is essential in any civilization where many individuals have specialized functions: in a small village, it is perhaps possible to rely exclusively upon a system of barter, but in a town this soon becomes too complicated and counting and accounting become essential. There is a fundamental sense in which all systems of counting are the same, reflecting some innate characteristic of the human mind: to every number, there is just one successor, and every number is unique and needs a name. The snag is that one eventually loses track of the names, and a system that makes do with a finite set of names is devised. All the ancient civilizations adopted essentially the same approach: they started with the selection of some number as a base or scale. They then assigned names to the sequence, 1,2,... base b, and devised some role for naming numbers larger than b by using combinations of the names already in that sequence. Since early man probably counted with his fingers—a practice still reflected in our word of Latin origin, the "digit"—it is not surprising that the most common base was five or ten. Some South American tribes still use a quinary scale of the form "one, two, three, four, hand, hand and one, hand and two." The predominant scheme in the world now is of course the decimal system, to base ten. However the ancient Babylonians used a sexagesimal scale to base sixty, which is still reflected in our own division of the circle into angular measures of minutes and seconds, and in our units of time.

In addition to the spoken representation, a written scheme based on some form of grouping of numbers is necessary. The simplest of these is one in which symbols are adopted for the number 1, for the base b and its powers $b^2$, $b^3$, $b^4$, but not for the other "named" numbers 2, 3, 4 etc. below b. The Egyptian hieroglyphic scheme which was developed by about 3400 B.C. is an example of this type of simple grouping scheme. The first three symbols, for 1, the base 10, and its square, were:

| | | |
|---|---|---|
| *1* | ǀ | *A vertical staff* |
| *10* | ∩ | *A yoke* |
| *$10^2$* | ? | *A coiled rope* |

The Egyptians normally wrote from right to left, so the number 315 would be written ǀǀǀǀǀ∩???. The cuneiform tablets of the Babylonians dating from 2000 onwards, show that they used a similar simple group structure.

A more compact scheme, known as multiplicative grouping, was used by the Chinese, who gave symbols to all integers less than the base, as well as to the base and its powers, so that a number was written as a sum of products of named integers and powers of the base. The Hindu-Arabic system, now almost universal, has even greater compactness, since the position of the symbol signifies the power of the base. Once the concept of zero has been introduced, this "positional" scheme is unambiguous. The Babylonian sexagesimal system for numbers greater than sixty was written according to this positional principle, but their scheme was ambiguous because they lacked a symbol for zero (until after 300).

Once men had evolved a code of symbols to represent numbers, it became possible to do computations with them, and arithmetic was born. By 2000 the

Babylonians of the Sumerian period were recording all kinds of domestic and legal calculations. Several hundred mathematical texts of cuneiform writing are known, the majority in the form of mathematical tables—multiplication, reciprocal, squares and cubes—for use in business transactions. Some, however, deal with the solution of algebraic or geometrical problems of a practical, individual nature.

In the tablets of multiplication and reciprocal tables, one peculiar feature emerges. The two tables generally lack the sexagesimal equivalents of seven, eleven, thirteen, fourteen. Further examination of the reciprocal tables reveals why. For the reciprocal of seven in the sexagesimal system is a recurrent fraction (as it is also in our own decimal system). This is true for all prime numbers containing them as factors, excluding two, three and five, since the latter are factors of sixty. Indeed, some of the tables reflect the Babylonians' acceptance of this situation, with the remark "seven does not divide."

However we know that the reason for this exclusion was purely to provide a simple and flexible set of instructions for rapid computation. Other tables do exist where the recurrent reciprocals are included, approximated to three or four places. Indeed Babylonians are known to have determined very early a value of $\sqrt{2}$, or the square root of two, equal to 1.424213 . . . rather than the accurate value of 1.414214 . . . and moreover knew that this was equal to the hypotenuse of a right-angled triangle of base 1. They have also recorded numerous precise geometrical determinations of the area of rectangles, and right-angle and isosceles triangles, and of the volume of rectangular parallepipeds (six-sided prisms), and right prisms.

Babylonian geometry was in the main algebraic in character. Problems leading to quadratic (or even cubic or quartic) equations or systems of simultaneous equations are common, and they were solved by a skillful use of tables. Even though our knowledge of Babylonian mathematics is based on interpretation of only a few hundred tablets, the range and penetration of the problems that were tackled in their day-to-day life is steadily apparent.

Ancient Egyptian mathematical skill was never so highly developed, though it is true that our knowledge is based on only two papyri of a mathematical nature, discussing in total a little over 100 problems. The Egyptian additive numeral system lends itself naturally to a simple scheme of multiplication, namely repeated addition, similar to that used on an abacus. It was used in Europe as such until well after the fifteenth century A.D. Thus they never developed sets of tables similar to the Babylonians. However, the known papyri, dating from between 2000 and 1500 B.C., show that the Egyptians were able to solve simple linear equations by means of general rules. They also developed some degree of sophistication in the use of ideograms for mathematical symbols, such as equals and plus and minus signs. Several of their problems deal with land areas and grain storage volumes, that is, with geometric calculations. Though they were almost certainly ignorant of Pythagoras' theorem, they did know that the area of any triangle was half the base times its height.

The early mathematicians were straightforward men who taught a set of rules for getting the right answer to a practical problem. However, increasingly, as time passed, men became fascinated with the properties of numbers as an end in themselves. The Babylonian choice of sixty as a base was presumably made by men who recognized that it was a number with exceptionally many factors. The builders of the Egyptian pyramids gave concrete proof of their concern with pure geometry—the area of each triangular face is equal to the square of the vertical height—and they had an enthusiasm for theoretical problems with no practical applications.

This wealth of Egyptian geometrical and arithmetic results passed to the Greeks during the seventh century B.C., thanks to early traveling scholars such as

Thales of Miletus, and inspired the thinking of the Ionian school. Indeed Pythagoras, their outstanding genius, can more readily be understood as the last of the ancient mathematicians than as the first of the moderns. His attitude to numbers smacks of ancient superstition—one was identified with reason, two with wavering opinion, four with four-square justice, five suggested marriage (the union of the first even with the first genuine odd number), seven the maiden goddess Athene "because seven alone within the decade has neither factors nor product." The theorem for which he is famous today may seem modern enough, but, according to one tradition, when he discovered it he sacrificed an ox.

*Top:* Sumerian clay tablet showing the pictographic characters of the first writing, c. 3300–3100 B.C.
*Above:* Detail of a relief with a hieroglyphic inscription, from the tomb of Sesostris I, Middle Kingdom, 1971–1930 B.C. Egyptian hieroglyphs were a beautiful and revered form of writing which probably encouraged their retention even during the Greek and Roman conquests of Egypt. This panel shows two of the royal titles of Sesostris I carved in elegant and beautifully proportioned detail.

## WRITING

The earliest forms of pictorial representation of any sophistication date from Paleolithic times. The cave paintings of Lascaux tell us, across some 20,000 years, of the events of the Paleolithic hunter's life. These paintings might be described as the earliest forms of pictographs. By the Neolithic period the figures and objects had been reduced to simple diagrammatic forms of expression.

The development of an ideographic script, that is, a representational form in which pictures represent word sounds as well as the objects themselves, started in Sumer in about 4000 B.C. The pressure which brought about the invention of writing was, as with so many of the Sumerian discoveries, economic. For example, a means of levying dues by the temple priests on farmers was necessary, since state land was held to be owned by the god of the city.

Thus tablets containing pictures of a cow's head, or an ear of corn beside a sequence of numerals, are common. Some of these early Sumerian tablets already attempt to express verbal actions, with, for example, the combination of signs for a man's head with bread, to indicate the concept of eating. But obviously such a limited pictorial representation cannot alone fulfil the function of a complete system of writing. For inevitably it leads to ambiguities. The combinations of the symbols for man and house may mean "the owner of the house," "the keeper of the house," "the building of the house," "the man goes to the house," or one of several other meanings. Egyptians resolved this difficulty in their hieroglyphic system, used on inscriptions and stone memorials, by increasing the detail in each picture. This made it possible to represent the states or activities of the objects or people. The Sumerians introduced refinements to modify the original meaning of an ideogram. Thus a line beneath the chin of a man's head meant "mouth." However both systems are cumbrous owing to the welter of signs that are needed, and neither could hope to express subtleties of abstract intellectual thought.

The ultimate solution lay in the development of a scheme wherein picture-signs represent language sounds, instead of having pictorial meanings. The first use of such a process may have been with homonyms, that is words with the same vocal sound but different meaning. A cuneiform script dated c. 3000, found on the banks of the Tigris, has the word-sign *En-lil-ti*, which being translated means "The god Enlil gives life." The sign for the word *ti* is an ideogram of an arrow, but in Sumerian the sound *ti* meant both an arrow, and life.

At the same time, other changes were occurring in the written language. To avoid ambiguities, descriptive prefixes or suffixes, known as determinatives were introduced. By prefixing the Sumerian sign for man before that for plow, the concept of "plowman" was formed. If the sign for wood was prefixed then the meaning "plow" was itself unambiguously made. Similar determinatives meaning "god," "country" and "city" are commonly found before proper names.

The next stage came with the development of a set of syllables. Sumerian had some 300 signs which expressed the sounds of syllables, rather than the simple single sounds of a complete alphabet. These syllables enabled grammatical elements of speech that cannot be given pictorial expression to be represented. Parallel with these changes, the cuneiform script itself was evolving towards a simpler, more stylized form. The Sumerians later bounded their cuneiform signs within compartments, thus ordering the collection of inscribed symbols. However they never achieved a complete basic alphabet in which sounds were phonetically represented by symbols without any pictorial representation.

The Egyptian hieroglyphic system was almost certainly heavily dependent on the Sumerian script for its early genesis, although it did not develop in the same way. It always remained pictorial, but rapidly spawned an additional cursive, or continuous running form, called hieratic script, which was commonly used on papyrus records. The Babylonians, with their clay tablets, could only speed the writing process by simplification. But the Egyptians, with sheets of paper made by pressing and drying the pith of papyrus reed laid both vertically and horizontally, and then gummed into long strips or rolls, used a system that, in its purely mechanical nature, was far closer to our own.

The purposes of written language in Egypt were somewhat different from those of the Sumerians. One of the driving forces in the society of the Old Kingdom in Egypt was death and the relation of the living to the dead. In this context, the pictorial written word had a new significance, a magical or efficacious meaning, that never existed for the more down-to-earth Sumerians. Thus preserved in their tombs we find recordings of prayers and incantations for the dead which are as much a part of the ritual magic as the original funeral ceremony.

The growth of other script, for example amongst the Indus valley civilizations, and of Linear A and B amongst the Minoans, proceeded in parallel with these. But it is not until the Phoenicians that a fully developed phonetic alphabet came into being, first seen in the seventeenth century B.C., and reaching an almost perfect state, by the eighth century. It spread both eastward through Syria, Palestine, and Arabia, and westward along the maritime colonies of the Mediterranean. It is thus that the Phoenician alphabet gave birth to the earliest Greek alphabets and in time to all those of the West.

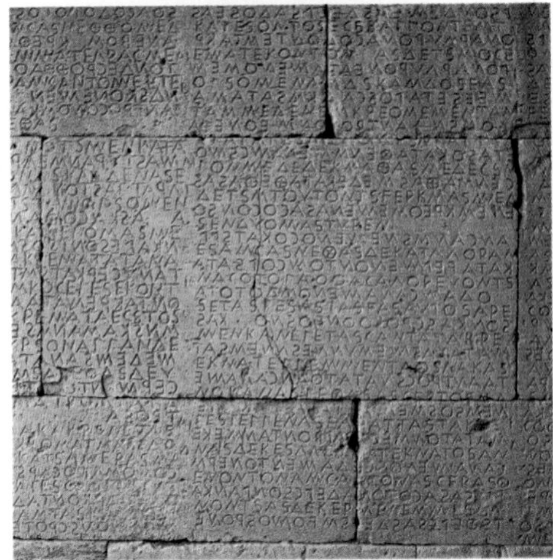

*Top:* Mesopotamian cuneiform inscriptions, c. 1980 B.C., showing dimensions of fields. The use of a stylus on clay encouraged the evolution of Mesopotamian pictographs into the more efficient, and more stylized, cuneiform.
*Above:* Greek legal code of the fifth century B.C., found in Gortyn, Crete. Here the culmination of the long development from Sumerian pictographs to classical Greek letters can be seen. The Phoenician-derived alphabet of the Greeks now influences the writing of the entire western world.

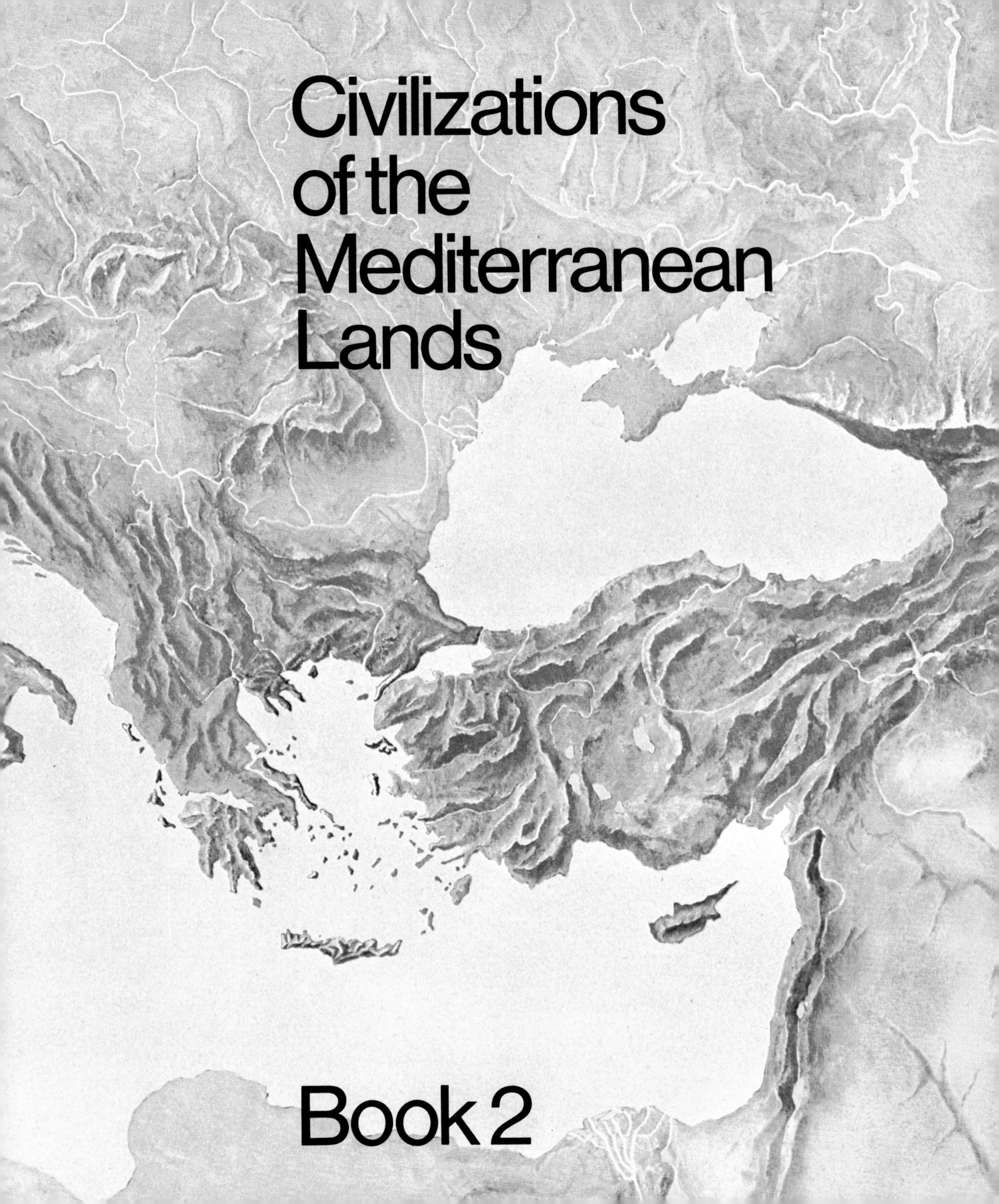
Civilizations of the Mediterranean Lands
Book 2

# Introduction

The subject-matter of this book is the most concentrated, both in its character and in place in this whole History. It is about a civilization that was the source of ideals, beliefs and principles that later Europeans came to think of as fundamental to their own lives. They thought of this part of their common past as a classical age which had set the standards by which they lived. The people who lived during this age and were part of its civilization did not, of course, think of themselves as doing anything so remarkable. Or, at least, only a very few of them did. Some of them thought of themselves as Romans or Greeks; others thought of themselves as Franks or Goths, though it is not likely that most thought this. Most of the people who lived in the period described in this book probably never thought in such terms at all, but only knew of themselves as the men of a certain village, the slaves of a certain lord, the members of a certain clan. It is the men of later times who, looking back, thought they saw something they could call the classical world to which they all belonged.

Looked at more closely, the unity they discovered turns out to be a group of cultures and civilizations developed between about 500 B.C. and A.D. 300, beginning in paganism and ending in Christianity, all of whose great literary relics were written in or turned into Greek or Latin. The literary unity of this world was supported also for a long time by a legal and political unity which rested on Roman domination. Furthermore, it all took place within a narrow theater that was little more than the lands which formed the shores of the Mediterranean sea, together with the hinterland of Asia Minor as far as Persia. Of course, there were other barbaric appendages, stretching as far north as Hadrian's Wall and as far east as the Rhine and Danube; these were formally part of Rome's dominion but the degree to which they underwent civilization in an enduring way was slight.

In time, this whole divides fairly naturally into something like a three-act drama. There is a first act which is Greek, when the very basis of classical civilization and the nature of its standards are being worked out. It is also then that the economic pattern of the classical world is broadly established, for there are few great changes in it subsequently and none of the magnitude of those brought by rapid industrialization or technological change in later times.

Act two is the dominance of Rome. People have often tried to express the difference between the Greek and Roman achievements. One essential feature of that difference is that the Roman achievement was secondary in form, though not in its importance. It starts, effectively, with the absorption of the Greek world, but, as the Latin poet Horace wrote "Captive Greece took prisoner her wild conqueror." He meant that the Romans eagerly absorbed Greek ideas and fashions, they thought in Greek categories and interests; Greek was to be the everyday language of the Roman Empire. That Empire demands lengthy consideration in this book because it was not only the transmitter of Greek civilization to posterity, but also the cradle of Christianity, the most successful of all world religions in its missionary power and one of the great, possibly the greatest, factors in the making of Europe. It embodied a curious blend of Jewish belief, Greek philosophy and the practical possibilities inherent in Roman administration and policy; these were to go on shaping history in countless ways down the centuries to our own day. World history without Christianity is unimaginable. World history without the Church (which is not the same thing) is almost as hard to envisage.

After this great creative period, something goes wrong. The third act of the drama brings a discernible flagging in the vitality of the classical world. What happened, and whether it should be called "decline" or something else is still much debated, but it is indisputable that there is a sense of ebb, and evidence of weakness. Politically and culturally, the Empire broke into two before crumbling still further. By the fifth century parts of the old traditional structures were already barbarized. In other places, barbarians were romanized. Some institutions atrophied, while others preserved much of their power though in changed forms. Here this book ends, with a new world coming to birth amid the ruins of an old.

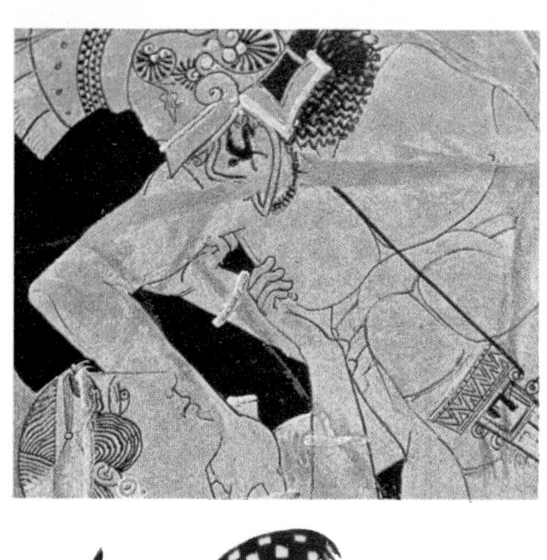

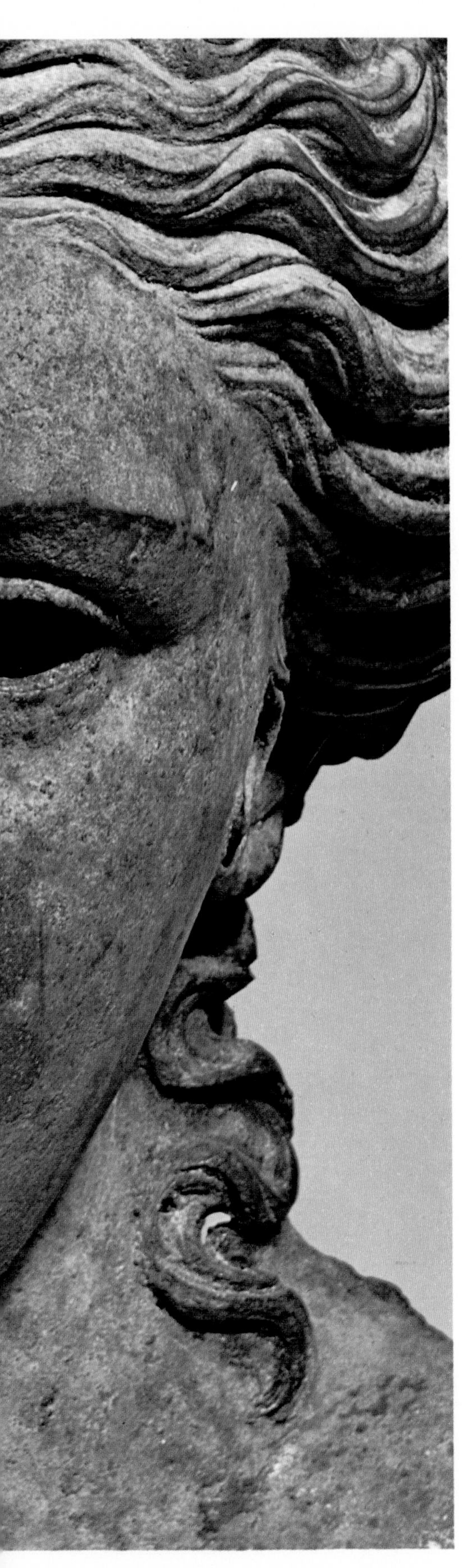

# Part I
# The Greeks

Chapter 1

# THE RISE OF THE GREEK PEOPLES

## THE LAND

In many respects it is the Aegean Sea that should be regarded as the focus of the Greek world, rather than the southern Balkan peninsula. Its coastline, to east and west, shared a common culture through much of antiquity, and the islands which stud the southern Aegean saw the rise of the earliest civilization in the area (Cycladic). Eastern Greece and the western coast of Asia Minor with a long coastline, a land mass split into innumerable minor valleys and plains, and with a host of offshore islands, offered no sort of geographical unity in which a single nation could easily develop. Independent development of separate small city-states was the logical outcome. What is remarkable is the strength and uniformity of the shared culture. The geographical explanation for this lies partly in the quality of the land which, however hard-worked, could not support a growing population nor provide the variety of resources which the metalworking societies of antiquity required (little copper and iron; no tin). Specialist farming in marketable commodities—wine, olive oil—naturally developed, and the importance of the seaways in an area where overland travel was slow and difficult led quickly enough to more ambitious prospecting for new markets, or new land to farm. It was economic need as well as dreams of empire which carried Greek culture so far.

*Above:* Hellenistic portrait bust of Homer. This follows long-established tradition by showing him to be blind. Homer's dates and birthplace are unknown. Smyrna and the island of Chios have the best rival claims to being his birthplace, and certainly the language of the poems points to an Ionian origin. He is now conventionally placed c.700 B.C. Scholars still dispute whether he was the actual author of the poems or whether he merely wrote down and edited epic poems with origins in the deep past of the second millennium B.C.
*Left:* Scene from an early clay shield, dating to about 700 B.C., showing Heracles in battle with the Amazons. The figures are rather crude and classical Greek art is here seen at the beginning of its development.

## THE PEOPLE

Commercial interests brought Greeks together, in competition or partnership, but commercial interests took time to develop. The common language was a stronger bond, so strong that Greeks came to regard all unintelligible foreigners, the "bar-bar" talkers, as barbarians, whether they were African slaves or Persian kings. There was no political unity to support this view of themselves and it was expressed most readily in their religion. The only occasion on which the Greeks behaved as a nation was in the national festivals at great sanctuaries, like that of Zeus at Olympia, where the rule of admission was "Greek-speakers only." But matters of greater importance to them as a nation, such as the military threat presented by the Persians, found them still divided.

A different quality, well expressed in their literature and art, and one which marks them off completely from their barbarian contemporaries, was their attitude to themselves: "man the measure of all things." The demonic played some part in Greek life but their myth-makers and poets gave their gods human attributes and weaknesses, while their artists expressed their feeling for pattern and composition in terms of the human body, attaining ultimately a stage at which accurate expression of mood meant as much as accurate expression of action. In the first man-centered society of antiquity, unhampered by a hierarchy of priests and god-kings, it was natural that the human rights of men and women came first to be recognized, and that democratic ideals were debated and, hesitatingly, practiced.

## THE HOMERIC WORLD

After the collapse of the Mycenaean civilization, which is covered in Book I, Greece withdrew into herself, and the sparse archaeological evidence that we have points to a period of great poverty, which has become known as the Dark Ages. Even the pottery of the period is dull and uninteresting. Gradually, however, peace and stability began to take effect and the people of Greece began to look outside once again. We enter what scholars call the Geometric period, because the pottery of this time is painted over with geometric patterns and circles, carefully executed. Athens is to the fore in this type of art, which accords well with the later tradition that she alone was not affected by the invasion of the Dorians, a peripheral Greek people from the north. Also, her land is to the east of Greece and all the new ideas which were soon to flood Greece were to be found in Asia.

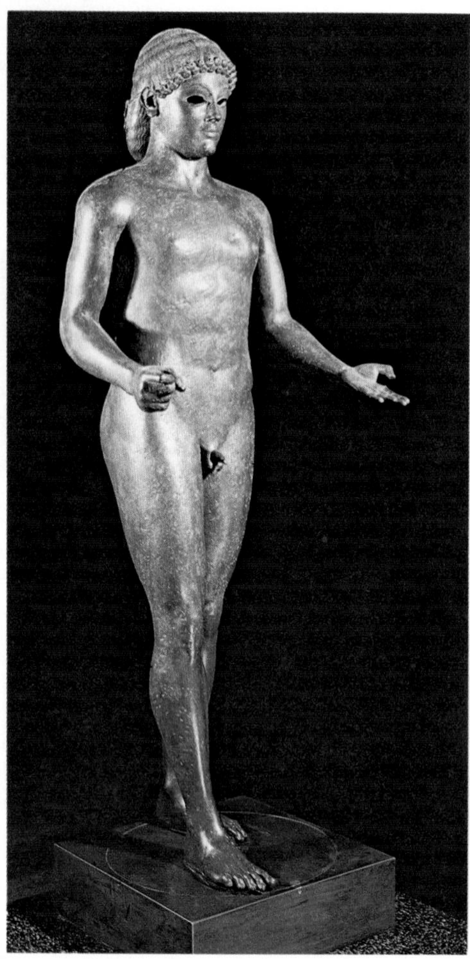

Statue of Apollo known as the "Piombino Apollo." This bronze is thought to be a copy of an earlier sixth century work, the "Philesios Apollo," which was removed by Darius I from Miletus after he sacked the city in 494 B.C. The Philesios was returned two centuries later by one of Alexander the Great's successors. However, this statue conveys well the frontal pose which the Greeks adopted, perhaps under Egyptian influence. The eyes would have been filled in just as they were painted in on marble statues.

The tenth to eighth centuries B.C. saw a steady growth in the population of Greece. New cities grew where before there had been villages. The areas controlled by minor kingdoms, to develop later into the classical city-states, became more clearly defined. Athens, Corinth, Argos, the cities of Euboea (Chalcis and Eretria) and later Sparta emerge as the dominant centers. In these years too, emigrations eastward across the Aegean, started by the pressure of invasion and continued by the pressure of population growth, settled the coastline of Asia Minor and its offshore islands, where other powerful new Greek foundations, notably in Ionia, soon rivaled those of the homeland. Iron was now known, though little used, and since Greek resources of copper and tin for making bronze were inadequate for the growing demand, distant shores were prospected for new material sources. At the end of the ninth century the Euboeans established a trading post at the mouth of the river Orontes (Al Mina) in North Syria, to tap the resources of the East. The renewed contacts with the old civilizations of the East revolutionized Greek life, and inspired their artists' first attempts at representational narrative art.

From the Phoenicians, who lived particularly in the area round Al Mina, they learned the art of writing once again and by the year 725 we find that art developed enough for lines of poetry to be painted on vases. It must have been not long after this date that those two great poems, the *Iliad* and the *Odyssey*, were committed to paper, to a large extent, if not completely by Homer. Besides being great works of literature, the two poems give us much information about life in those early days. It has been shown that the poems were composed orally over many centuries and that their evolution was only stopped when they were written down. They are set in the Mycenaean period and describe one of the rare occasions when the Greeks, as opposed to any single state, did something together. Although they describe the Mycenaean age, the greater part, and here especially the similes, must correspond far more nearly to the times in which the poems were written down. The poems prove that, despite the Dark Ages, memories of a more glorious time lingered on. The poems were written in Asia Minor, and the Greek settlements on the Aegean coast assumed great importance in the new awakening, both because they provided a channel for eastern art to make its way west and also because it was here that the Greeks could find the trade that was necessary to their economy.

If the East showed the Greeks tempting opportunities for trade, so it also offered land on which the Greek cities, becoming steadily more overcrowded, could settle their surplus populations. Italy and Sicily had similar potential and the eighth century saw a great era of colonization. First it was the Euboeans who explored the coasts of Italy and Sicily, sought metals from the Italians, and planted colonies there. They were followed by Greeks from Corinth and Achaea (in southern Greece). The process of disseminating the Greek way of life in the Mediterranean world was already under way.

*Above:* Theseus, the legendary king of Athens, wrestling with one of his enemies and with a bull, from a vase painting. It was painted by an Athenian, Euphronius, who lived in the late sixth and early fifth centuries. He was a potter and vase painter who is known from his signature on several of his works. Euphronius was contemporary with the emergence of the "red-figure" style of vases, but not all his work is of that style.
*Left:* Temple of Concord at Acragas, modern Agrigento, c.450. This is a very well preserved example of the Doric order of architecture, of which the most famous and refined example is the Parthenon on the Acropolis at Athens. This temple is earlier than the Parthenon, but illustrates well the unadorned simplicity of line and the lack of elaboration.

Trade Routes and Areas of Colonial Influence about 500 BC
North Sea
Baltic Sea
AMBER
TIN
Vistula R.
Oder R.
Seine R.
Atlantic Ocean
Carpathians
Dniester R.
GAUL
Alps
Rhone R.
Pyrenees
Massilia
Danube R.
Black Sea
IBERIA
ITALY
Corsica
Rome
Epidaurus
THRACE
Cumae
Sardinia
Balearics
Tartessus
Megara
Corinth
ASIA MINOR
LYDIA
Taurus Mts
Miletus
Sicily
Carthage
Athens
Sparta
Aegina
Crete
Cyprus
PHOENICIA
Atlas Mountains
Mediterranean Sea
Sidon
Tyre
TRIPOLITANIA
LIBYA
EGYPT
Nile R.
Greeks
Phoenicians
Etruscans
Sea Trade Routes
Land Trade Routes
Miles 0 500

Chapter 2

# THE GREEK WORLD OF THE CLASSICAL PERIOD

The Greek society depicted by Homer was governed by kings, but by the seventh century B.C., these had largely disappeared. Political control of the city-states had passed to the nobles, members of distinguished aristocratic families who also formed the cities' fighting forces, usually as cavalry. The nobles of Euboea and Thessaly were especially famous in this respect.

During the seventh century the nobles, in turn, began to lose their political monopoly. The greater material prosperity and the greater contact with the outside world brought about this change. Greater skill in metalwork enabled heavy armor to be made and a new type of fighting, phalanx warfare, emerged, created, according to legend, by Pheidon of Argos. This new, closely packed unit of troops quickly replaced the older and more gentlemanly cavalry forces. The members of the phalanx were called hoplites and they were drawn from all those who could afford their weapons. So money gradually assumed the importance that birth had previously. Some bemoaned the fact that the low-born could reach power and that wealth (*ploutos*) mingled with breeding (*genos*). The merchant class thus assumed great importance in the cities, being the class, after the aristocrats, who could afford weapons, and they soon wanted political power as well. For their leaders they sometimes chose an aristocrat, but sometimes preferred one of themselves who had grown wealthy through his trade. There followed revolutions, sometimes peaceful but often violent, from which the victorious leader, whether a merchant or an aristocrat, emerged as the ruler, or *tyrant* (the word at first had none of its modern sinister overtones).

The oldest known example of Greek hoplite armor. It dates to the eighth century B.C. There is no trace on the helmet of a protecting nose-piece. The body armor is made of solid bronze. All soldiers in a hoplite phalanx would have been similarly equipped and their concerted weight added to by that of their armor helped the principal tactic of out-pushing the enemy. Usually deployed in eight ranks, the hoplite phalanx advanced en masse and could build up a considerable speed-thrust ratio as the Thebans showed at the battle of Leuctra, 371.

Trade in mainland Greece had first affected the cities on the Corinthian Gulf (the main east-west trade route). Therefore wealth and the new ideas that circulate in busy trading ports had also reached them first; it is in cities such as Corinth, Sicyon, and Megara that tyrants first sprang up. The best of the tyrants were men of new ideas, encouraging trade and building, creating employment. The era of the tyrants, from 650 to 600 B.C., was one of rapid economic development in the Greek cities, a development which was powerfully aided by the maintenance of peace, for the relations among the tyrants of the different cities were friendly. Internally, it was a revolutionary age, which witnessed the breakup of the encrusted conservatism of the aristocracies. At the same time, it was a period of transition, allowing the peoples of the cities to gain sufficient political maturity for self-government. The rule of the tyrant rarely lasted more than two generations, for in the second generation tyrants were all too often corrupted by absolute power. So they were evicted, and full democracy ("rule by the people") was established, as in Athens; or a mercantile oligarchy ("rule by the few") replaced the aristocratic one, as in Corinth. Sparta, which never went through the stage of tyranny, was always a predominantly aristocratic state.

## A DEMOCRATIC CITY-STATE: ATHENS

The most extreme form of democracy was developed in Athens. Here all political decisions were taken by majority vote at mass meetings of the citizens (the *ecclesia*), where the magistrates, including the army generals, were chosen by open election of the whole people, voting in the ten tribes into which the citizens were divided. Members of the large standing political body, the *boule* of 500, were elected by popular vote, fifty from each of the ten tribes. The boule was responsible for day-to-day administration but was not empowered to make any political decisions; it simply prepared the agenda for the ecclesia.

The division of the citizens into ten tribes was the ingenious invention of the statesmen Cleisthenes (508 B.C.), after the expulsion of the tyrant Hippias. Each tribe consisted of three *trittyes*, and each trittyes was composed of ten or more *demes*. In their allocation to tribes, the trittyes were not adjacent; each tribe was assigned one trittyes in the city itself, one on the coast, and one in the inland countryside. The geographical diversity of the three trittyes admirably prevented the formation of power blocks within the urban mercantile class or among the farmers.

A Corinthian jug, date c.600 B.C. The geometric style of pottery started toward the end of the eighth century and was influenced by designs of an oriental character. During the seventh century the proto-Corinthian style of pottery was one of the most popular to emerge and retained some of these features. The proto-Corinthian style gradually gave way to the Corinthian style. The use of gryphons as a decorative motif was a feature imported from the Orient where Corinth had trade contacts.

Athenian participation in government was particularly time-consuming. The ecclesia met for whole days at a time during the Peloponnesian War, and it was invariably convened at least four times a month, often more frequently. In addition to participation in the ecclesia, any citizen might be named as a magistrate, a member of the boule, or a juror. Also, every citizen was obligated to attend assemblies of smaller kinship groups, that is, his deme and his tribe. Given these great demands on the citizens' time, it is not hard to understand why, on occasion, a little gentle persuasion was necessary to ensure that the business of government ran smoothly. Loungers at the Agora, or marketplace, had to be encouraged to reassemble at the Pnyx (the hill in Athens on which public business was transacted). The police used to barricade the roads leading to the Agora and use a rope smeared with red paint to herd the citizens in the right direction.

Despite their heavy reliance on individual involvement, Greek cities were always sovereign over their citizenry. They were often repressive—even, in some respects, totalitarian. Athenian liberty was only partial; freedom of expression in matters of religion was discouraged and even humorous sacrilege could result in severe punishment. When a clash of personalities occurred in politics, the issue was often resolved by a special meeting of the ecclesia. Each man wrote down on a potsherd (an *ostrakon*) the name of the person he disliked most and, after the votes had been counted, the man with the highest number of votes was ostracized, that is, sent into exile for ten years. Many of the great names in Athenian history were ostracized; it is difficult for us to appreciate fully the severity of this sentence.

## AN ARISTOCRATIC CITY-STATE: SPARTA

Sparta was in many ways unique among the Greek states. It lacked much that we customarily associate with classical Greece—art, literature, philosophy. Sparta even lacked public monuments. All these things were subordinated to the supremely important ideal of rigid military discipline. The Spartans revered self-discipline and taught it to their children by means that seem to us barbaric. In public whipping contests, young boys were said to have died rather than endure the ignominy of crying out in pain. Physical comforts were withheld as a matter of course; "womanly" softness was abhorred. Even trade and farming were turned over to the *perioeci* (free noncitizens) and *helots* (serfs).

The basic Spartan constitution was believed by Spartans to have been written by the legendary Lycurgus in the ninth century (about this remote Spartan lawgiver relatively little is known). At the head of the government were two kings, ruling jointly in succession from two royal houses. The kings together with twenty-eight statesmen constituted the *gerousia* (council of old men). For certain measures the people (the *Spartiates*, or true Spartans) were consulted in public assembly (the *apella*), but beyond voting for or against measures put before them, the people had little initiative.

In the early seventh century a new magistracy, the five annually elected *ephors* (overseers) came into existence. They could bring even kings to trial, so that much of Spartan history was a conflict between the ephors and the kings. The Spartans avoided tyranny and were always on the watch for a king who, like Cleomenes at the end of the sixth century, was suspected of unhealthy personal ambition.

### Helots

After a series of wars in the eighth and seventh centuries, Sparta annexed the rich plain of Messenia to the west, across the barrier of Mount Taygetus. The Messenians were reduced to serfdom and became helots, agricultural serfs without political rights.

The Spartiates kept the helots in harsh subjection. They were outnumbered by the helots and lived in constant fear of helot revolts, by which more than once the state was seriously endangered. Helots were not slaves (they were personally free), but they were bound for life to state-owned lands. Once, during the Peloponnesian War, enterprising and ambitious young helots were invited to volunteer for military service, with the promise of Spartan citizenship as a reward. Two thousand volunteered. Having thus identified themselves as dangerous men, they were quietly eliminated. The *crypteia*—a secret police force of young Spartans—was authorized once a year to organize a hunt for disobedient or potentially disruptive helots.

The life peculiar to Sparta has been attributed to this ever-present fear of helot uprising. Society was organized as if in imminent peril of attack.

An archaic bronze statuette, probably sixth century, from the Peloponnese. It represents a youth running. Although the work is early, animation is attempted for the running figure. The legs show developed calf muscles. Athletic contests were common and popular among the Greeks and eventually four major games, the Olympian, Isthmian, Nemean, and Pythian were established. Great honor was accorded to victors, particularly to those who won the prize at the Olympian Games. The prizes took the form of crowns, or wreaths.

### Spartan Society

Much of our knowledge of Spartan life comes from a biography of Lycurgus by the second-century Greek writer Plutarch. It was Lycurgus, according to Plutarch, who organized Spartan society as a military machine in the service of the state.

Regimentation of life began at an early age in Sparta. Children judged to be too weak to survive the Spartan system were exposed on Mount Taygetus to die. Those that were allowed to live were regarded as the property of the state. They were taken from their mothers at the age of seven to be trained by nursemaids who taught them to eat anything, not to fear the dark or being alone, and not to cry out. This training was not considered overly harsh by other Greeks; Athenians frequently tried to get Spartan nursemaids for their children. Meager meals promoted self-reliance and cunning. Stealing was honored when successful, but a thief who was caught was severely punished. The ideal Spartan youth honored and obeyed his elders. The Spartans (sometimes called Laconians, since Laconia was the area of which Sparta was the capital) were typically abrupt and curt in speech—hence the term "laconic"—and they had no use for wordy debate. Life was, in short, so austere that, ironically, war offered a respite from the disciplined military training of peace.

The position of Spartan women reflected the same regimentation. Trained physically alongside the men, Spartan girls participated in wrestling, discus throwing, and javelin throwing, as well as in processions and athletic contests, in the nude. This rigorous exercise was designed to ensure that the women would bear strong sons. Celibacy was condemned. From time to time, celibates were made to march about the city singing a humiliating song about their unworthiness, since they had failed to produce future soldiers for the state.

Spartan bridegrooms abducted their brides. In his life of Lycurgus, Plutarch, who is not always a reliable historian, tells how the bride was taken to a "bridesmaid," who cut her hair on a straw cot alone in a dark room. The bridegroom ate his dinner with his male companions as usual, after which he entered the room and spent a rather short time with his bride. He then returned to the barracks to spend the rest of the night with his soldier-companions. This continued to be the pattern of married life; a man might see the face of his child before he saw his wife's face by daylight. Spartan women appear to have adapted well to their role. To the foreign woman who remarked, "You Spartan women are the only ones who rule your men," Gorgo, the wife of Leonidas, replied, "We are the only ones who bear men." The Spartan mother's proverbial injunction that her son return "with his shield or upon it" was not unique. (A Spartan's name was not inscribed on his tomb unless he had fallen in battle).

Marble *kore* (statue of a maiden) in the archaic style, c.530–515. There are several conventional features to be noticed: the enigmatic smile, possibly influenced by Egyptian models, the idealized face, braided hair and drapery. This form is the female equivalent of the *kouros* (young male), which was usually naked. Several features both of the *kore* and the *kouros* passed into Etruscan art, probably as a result of contacts in southern Italy. Greek statues, both archaic and classical, were painted and not left in the original, unadorned stone, and traces of paint survive.

Spartans were brave and well-disciplined foot soldiers, the best in Greece. Yet the government was always reluctant to send a large army out of the country, partly because this weakened the city's internal defense against helot insurgence and partly because Spartan generals abroad fell easy victims to the temptations of wealth and luxury that existed outside Sparta. Following the Persian Wars, the Spartan Pausanias, who had distinguished himself as Greek commander on the battlefield, was executed because it was claimed that, when at Byzantium, he had succumbed to temptation and emulated the extravagance of a Persian satrap.

In order that Spartans would not be tempted by luxury at home, Lycurgus decreed that the national currency be made of iron; it would have taken an oxcart to carry several Spartan "dollars." Nor was there anything to buy if one did have money. The communal meals were provided by the helots, and all land was state-owned. There was no "business" in Sparta except soldiering. Abroad, of course, Spartan iron money was considered ridiculous and worthless, and this had the effect of curtailing the state's revenues and potential financial reserves. Sparta never had a state treasury. Long after other city-states had established thriving commercial networks through their daughter-cities in Italy and Asia Minor, Sparta still held only one colony. In keeping with Lycurgus' policy of discouraging the corruption of foreign influences, foreigners on no useful errand were frequently expelled from Sparta.

Sparta strove for an ideal in a hostile environment. Laws were not written down: one of Lycurgus' rules, or *rhetras*, specifically forbade the writing down of laws, believing that it was better to imprint the values of Sparta on the hearts and minds of its citizens through rigorous training than to compel them to obey a written code.

## EXPANSION OF THE GREEK WORLD

The founding of colonies helped to absorb surplus energies and ambitions in seventh-century Greece, a fact which may well have contributed to the stability of the city-states. Late in the period of aristocratic government there were, thanks to more settled conditions generally, a rise in the survival rate and, as a consequence, a population explosion in Greece. A few great cities—Corinth, Aegina, and Athens—were expanding their commerce and were able to support a population larger than the country itself could support by importing food and paying for it with exports (a policy that was to make Athens, like Britain in the two World Wars, exceedingly vulnerable to naval blockade in wartime). Other cities, however (Sparta excepted), had to unload a part of their population, often very much against the wishes of that population, by sending it under a founder-father (*oekist*) to find a fresh home in a new settlement overseas. Where should the colonists go in search of their new homes? They wanted a site as like home as possible—land with an easily defensible strongpoint, an acropolis, near the sea but not too near it, for fear of pirates; land which had an adequate water supply and which would grow grain, wine, and if possible, olives, supporting the same sort of economy to which they had been accustomed at home. If it was potentially a good trading site, so much the better.

In cities where commerce was already active, traders could supply information about promising sites; in other cases, the obvious course was to consult the oracle at Delphi, where, without doubt, good geographical knowledge was available. Certain areas were barred; these were the areas that were already controlled by the Phoenician and Carthaginian fleets—broadly, the coasts of southern Asia Minor, Syria, and North Africa, with the exception of Libya and Tripolitania. We know of the successful enterprises, but there must have been many attempts that failed because of the opposition of the natives at landing places or from other causes.

So, in the eighth and seventh centuries, the Greek world expanded, with cities in Greece and Asia Minor spreading their sphere of influence along the Black Sea, in Thrace, Libya, all around the southern coast of Italy and up the west coast, short of Etruscan territory, as far as Cumae; in Sicily, except along the extreme west coast, which was controlled by Carthage; and furthest of all, along the southern coast of Gaul. This last area was discovered and exploited by the enterprising little city of Phocaea on the west coast of Asia Minor, which even traded with Tartessus (Cadiz) in Spain. By the mid-sixth century, the Carthaginians and Etruscans combined to seal off the western Mediterranean from further Greek penetration, but the already existing colonies survived and flourished.

The colony retained a strong sentimental attachment to its mother city. When its founder died, he was buried, unlike other people, inside the walls in the main square. A shrine was erected, and sacrifices were made annually in his honor.

The vast enlargement of the Greek world which followed colonization resulted in a great increase in trade. Corinthian and (later) Athenian pottery flooded the Italian and Sicilian markets, iron came to Greece from the Etruscans through Cumae, silphium (to become a universal laxative) and wool came from Cyrene, and precious metals were shipped from the Balkan mines to Corinth.

Colonization spread the Greek dialects, culture, and government to large parts of the coasts of Asia Minor, the Black Sea, southern Italy and Sicily, and even Gaul and Iberia (modern France and Spain). The Aegean islands, too, were indissolubly linked to the Greek mainland. From the sixth century on, these areas were to share the political fate of the Greek city-states—sometimes with disastrous results.

The Greeks continued to found colonies in the fifth century. The Athenian ruler Pericles regularly sent out groups of colonists, mainly to areas within the Athenian empire; he sent 1,000 to the Chersonese, 500 to Naxos, and 1,000 to live among the barbarians in Thrace. "By these means," Plutarch wrote later, "he relieved the state of numerous agitators, assisted the needy, and overawed the allies of Athens by placing his colonies near them to watch their behavior."

But along with these benefits, colonization brought a new cause for interstate warfare. Trading jealousies and alliances set Corinth against Megara, Megara against Athens, Miletus against Samos. The seventh-century Lelantian War involved most of the Greek states in a general struggle for trading supremacy.

*Top:* Head of the god Dionysus, the Greek god of wine and revelry, on an early coin from Sicily. It was common for cities to put the head of their patron god or goddess or a design associated with the city on their coins. Athens, for example, had an owl, while Corinth had Pegasus, the winged horse.
*Above:* An Ionian coin showing a warrior with a bow and spear. Because of his weapons he is probably not a Greek. He may represent a Persian conqueror, or an oriental bodyguard for one of the pro-Persian tyrants who ruled the Ionian cities until c.492.

Chapter 3

# THE PERSIAN AND PELOPONNESIAN WARS

The states of Greece in the sixth century represented a political experiment unprecented in the ancient world. Economically interdependent, they were politically autonomous. Each could wage war or make peace unilaterally, and each was free to ally itself with other states at will. Each state chose its own form of government, and as we have seen, a variety of forms resulted. This autonomy, though highly valued, was not carefully guarded. In the aftermath of the struggle with Persia, the possibility of federation and of single-state control became apparent; after 400 B.C. Greek history was to be the story of successive states fighting to gain and maintain hegemony over the entire Hellenic world.

## THE PERSIAN EMPIRE

We have now seen how the Greeks established themselves along the shores of Asia Minor. This brought them into contact with the peoples who lived further inland. The interior of Asia came under the domination of one people, then another. In the sixth century it was the Lydian Empire, ruled by the famous Croesus. Croesus' treatment of the Ionian cities, that is the Greek cities on the Aegean coast, was generally very fair, but in 546 B.C. his Empire and his capital, Sardis, fell to Cyrus, the King of the Persians.

Most of the Greeks scorned the Persians. The idea of the Great King, whose subjects were all in name his slaves, prostrating themselves on the ground before him (as if, to Greek eyes, he was a god) and whipped into action in battle, was repulsive; this was despotism, in contrast to individual freedom (*eleutheria*), which the Greeks regarded as the first condition of civilized existence. At the same time, rich and prominent Greeks looked enviously at the great wealth of individual Persians, their retinues of servants, their hunting lodges and parks.

### Zoroastrianism

The Persians' religion—Zoroastrianism—was their unique contribution to the classical world. Adopted throughout western Asia, it had only recently been established by Zoroaster (the Greek form of the Persian Zarathustra), in the period before the wars with Greece. It was a dualistic religion, with a good deity (Ahura-Mazda) and an evil deity (Ahriman). Zoroaster taught the future coming of a messiah, the resurrection of the dead, an inevitable last judgment, and an eternal heavenly afterlife. All these beliefs influenced the religions that arose in the Roman Empire, among them Christianity.

An important minor figure in the Zoroastrian pantheon was Mithras, who aided Ahura-Mazda in his struggle with Ahriman. In time, Mithras became the object of a cult all of his own. His life and worship contain some parallels with those of Jesus.

*Left:* An Athenian oil-flask from the third quarter of the fifth century B.C. It has as its design a hoplite departing for battle with his spear. The device on the shield is interesting because, particularly in the Peloponnese, shields usually bore the initial letter of their city state. Thus Spartan shields bore the letter L for Lacedaimon, the more usual name for the area in which the city of Sparta stood. *Above:* A fifth-century Athenian cup showing the Athenians fighting the Amazons. The cup dates to the period when the common style of pottery was the Attic "red-figure". Red-figure ware was exported all over the Mediterranean, and drove most rival products from the market.

## WAR WITH PERSIA

In 498 the Ionian cities of Lydia, whose freedom had been restricted by the Persians, and small contingents sent to their assistance by Athens and Eretria joined in setting fire to Sardis, the capital of Lydia. This act of aggression invited reprisal, and when the revolt was put down in 494, the Persians turned toward mainland Greece. An invasion fleet was wrecked off Mount Athos in 492, but two years later a Persian (mainly Phoenician) fleet crossed the Aegean, sacked Eretria, and then landed an army at Marathon in Athenian territory. To the special glory of Athens, the Persian army was soundly defeated on the field of Marathon by the Athenians fighting, almost unaided, under Callimachus, and the general, Miltiades.

In 480 the Persians mounted a joint military and naval invasion of Greece by way of Thrace and the north. The Persian expeditionary force, which Greek imagination inflated to the size of several millions, was, in fact, a land army of about 80,000 men, accompanied by a fleet of 1,000 vessels—in any case, far larger than any force which the Greeks could gather to oppose it.

A miracle happened. Abandoning their separatist traditions and instincts, the Greek cities united in self-defense (except for Argos which had already sided with the Persians). The cities agreed to accept the leadership of Sparta by land and, despite Athenian naval strength, by sea.

Though outnumbered, the Greeks had certain advantages. They could choose the best defensive positions (narrow passes, narrow waters) to counter the numerical advantage of the invader. Their heavy infantrymen (hoplites) were better armed and better trained than the Persians. The mountainous Greek countryside was not well suited for cavalry, and it was in their cavalry that the Persian forces had their greatest advantage. They were fighting for survival against a barbarian despot whom they despised. Finally, the Persian fleet had been reduced by storms at sea.

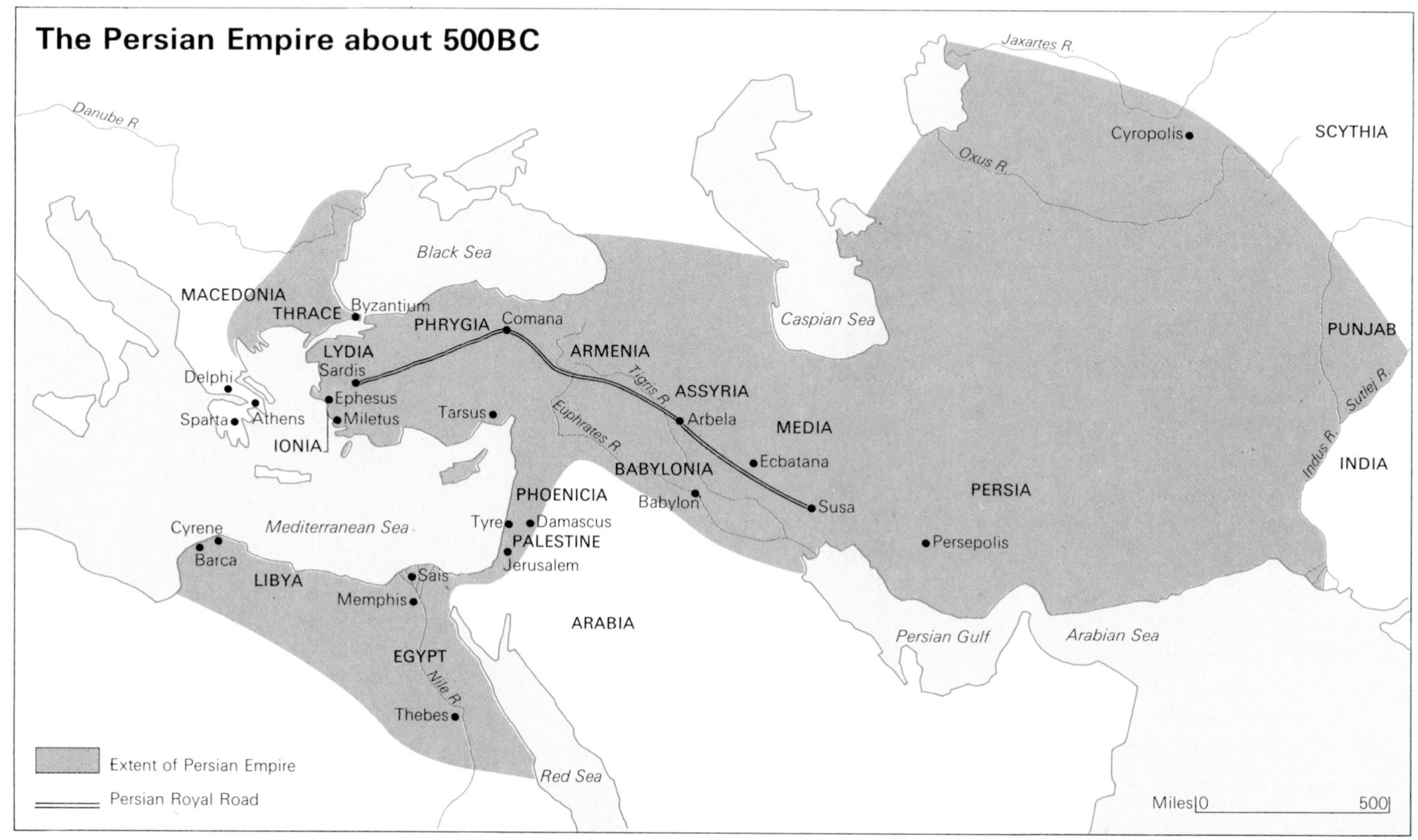

First, the Greeks held the communicating positions of Artemisium (the strait north of Euboea) and the narrow defile of Thermopylae, "where the mountains look on Marathon and Marathon looks on the sea." The Greek position at Thermopylae was attacked and the Spartan king, Leonidas, and his 300 Spartans fought to the death. The way south was now open to the Persians. The Greek army took up its position on the Isthmus of Corinth and the navy lay in the bay of Salamis, near Athens. The Athenians made the supreme sacrifice of abandoning their country to the Persians, after evacuating the population to the islands of Aegina and Salamis. By now it was late in September.

The Persians had neither the clothes nor the supplies to face a hard Greek winter, and King Xerxes rashly determined to engage the Greek fleet in the narrow bay of Salamis. Unable to maneuver, the Persians lost the advantage of numerical superiority, and the Persian fleet was disastrously defeated. Xerxes made an ignominious retreat overland to Persia. An army that he left behind was defeated by the Greeks under Pausanias at Plataea in 479; in the same year, a Greek fleet crossed the Aegean and won a second great victory over the Persians at Mycale.

Greek states had never united so wholeheartedly before and they never united in this way again, against the Macedonians or against the Romans. A number of states won immortal glory—in particular, Sparta and Athens (which also had the credit of an unaided victory at Marathon). Greek freedom had been preserved.

Early-fifth-century bas relief from Persepolis showing Persian guard. Persepolis was begun by Darius I (c.522–487), and completed by his son and successor, Xerxes. However, additions were made by Xerxes' successor, Artaxerxes I. The reliefs contain some of the finest examples of Persian art. Architecturally there are traces of Greek influence. This guard may well represent one of the 10,000 "Immortals" who were the elite of the Persian army.

### The Delian Confederacy

After the naval victory at Mycale, many of the Greek cities of Thrace and Asia Minor threw out their Persian governors and declared their independence. Others were eager to follow suit. However, this new independence could only be ensured if the Greek war fleet, together with contingents from the newly freed cities, remained in existence to guard against a Persian counteroffensive. The Greek fleet was still under Spartan command but Pausanias, the Spartan commander, was so unpopular that he was recalled to Sparta in 478. Meanwhile the Ionians, Thucydides tells us, asked the Athenians to become their leader because of their blood tie with them. When the Spartans sent out a commander to succeed Pausanias, it was the allies who refused to accept him. The Spartans accordingly left without fuss and sent out no one else, fearing lest future commanders might become corrupt like Pausanias and also thinking that the Athenians were capable of doing the job. In this way Sparta turned in on herself once more and allowed the Athenians not without debate a great opportunity for increased wealth and prestige. The partnership between the two states, despite moments of tension, continued another sixteen years.

Thus was formed the Confederacy of Delos. Delos was a fairly central island in the Aegean and was one of the great religious centers of the Greek world. It therefore seemed an ideal seat for the federal council which was formed from the Aegean islands and the newly liberated cities. All the members of the Confederacy or League contributed money or ships towards a fleet, whose task was to free the remaining cities from Persian rule, to guard the seas against the Persian fleet, and to police the seas against piracy. Athens assumed chairmanship (*hegemonia*) of the council and an Athenian admiral commanded the fleet.

It was not long before the actual position of individual members of the League came into question. Athens was no more than the leading member of the League but when the islands of Carystos, Naxos, and Thasos chose not to continue their contributions she used force to bring them back to heel. Thucydides uses his vocabulary carefully as he narrates these events—Carystos agreed to return to normal, Naxos had to be forced and was, therefore, the first of the allied communities to be enslaved contrary to the original arrangement.

The question how the Delian League gradually changed in character so that it eventually became the Athenian Empire is one that has occupied many scholars since Thucydides. But his own reasons (set out in Book I, chapter 99) are well worth reading. Many of the allies disliked the military service involved in keeping up their obligations to the League and preferred to supply money rather than a contribution of ships. Gradually the Athenians built up a large fleet of their own with this money, whilst the allies became dependent on them for protection. It was a logical step for the allies to become more like subjects than allies. "It became easy," says Thucydides, "for the Athenians to use force on those who revolted, and for this the allies had only themselves to blame." It seems clear from the course of events and from Thucydides' account that the Athenians did not have imperial motives when the League was formed, rather that time and circumstances effected the change. It is interesting to look at some of the inscriptions which we still possess on stone. These reflect various agreements and settlements between Athens and other cities of the League. In the early years, a reference is usually made to "the Athenians and their allies" but later it becomes "the Athenians and the cities over which they rule."

Commemorative tomb slab, of a hoplite, c.500. The *stele* (tomb slab) is found from Mycenaean times onwards, but became particularly popular at Athens from c.600. It usually portrays the dead person, or scenes of parting. There was a change in style during the fifth century at Athens, but stelai remained fairly standard elsewhere. They served the same purpose as tombstones and commemorative plaques.

One of the more significant stages of the transition was the moving of the treasury of the League from Delos to Athens in 454. The reason for this may perhaps have been fear of attack from Persia but the effect was to turn the League fund into an Athenian fund. During this period the revolts of members of the League, notably cities in Asia Minor, became more frequent. This may have been due to increasing Persian pressure, resulting from attacks by the League. There is some evidence that in the big cities like Miletus and Erythrae there were rich citizens with Persian sympathies who encouraged the Persians to help them effect an oligarchic revolution. The Athenians reacted violently and crushed the revolts with increasing

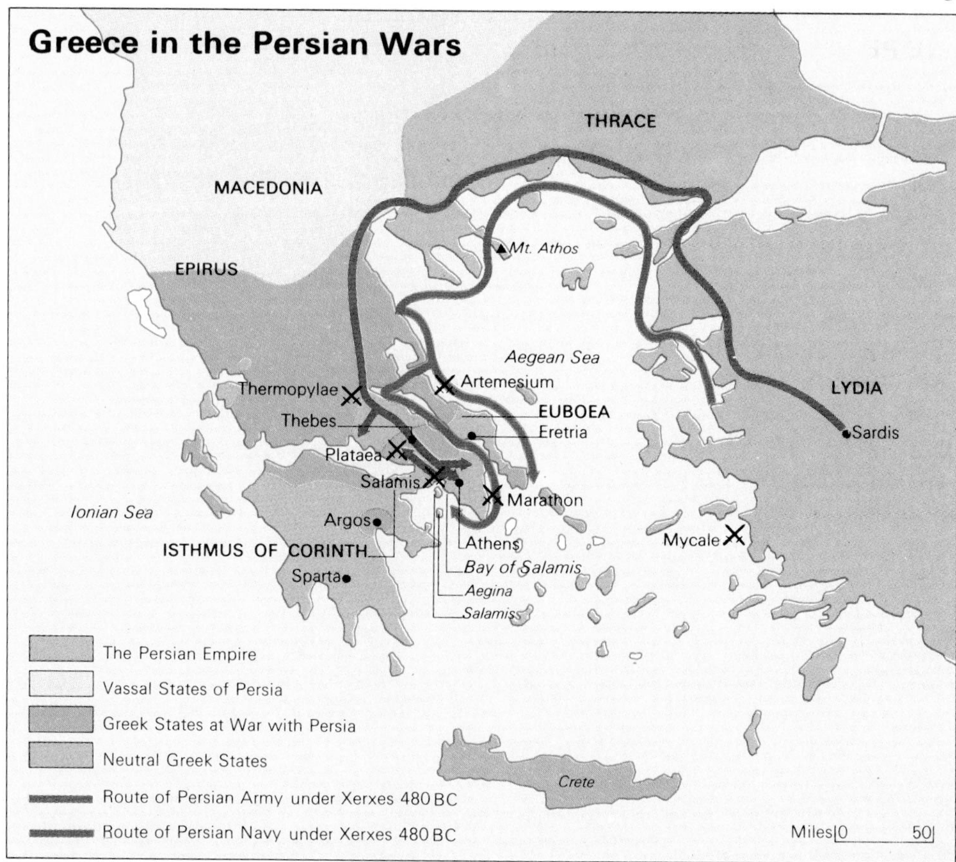

severity. They imposed democracies in the cities, installed garrisons and governors where necessary, sent officials out to see that all was in order, and in some cases even insisted that certain legal cases originating in member cities should be tried in Athens.

In 450 a formal peace may well have been negotiated by the Athenian Callias between the League and Persia. Strangely enough, Thucydides does not mention this peace and some scholars have claimed that it never happened. But the fact that in the following year the temple of Athene Nike (Victory) was commissioned to be built on the Acropolis would suggest that something had occurred worth celebrating. As our other sources tell us that by this peace Persia virtually guaranteed the freedom of the Greek states in her territory and agreed not to sail her ships in the Aegean, it was more of a victory than a peace. Now that peace had been made, it might well be argued that the League was no longer necessary and many of the cities apparently held this view and discontinued their tribute payments. Pericles, an imperialist, who had emerged as the leading figure in Athens, had no intention of disbanding the League, and despite opposition in Athens, began to use the tribute money for rebuilding the temples on the Acropolis which had been destroyed by the Persians. Athenian ships were sent to the cities and the system of collecting the tribute was tightened up. By 447 the tribute was being paid in full again and cities like Colophon and Miletus, which persisted in revolt, were summarily dealt with. By this time Athens was no longer the chosen leader of a confederacy, she was plainly the ruler of an empire and this was a situation that may not have troubled the ordinary citizens of the subject-cities but was certainly resented by the richer citizens, who had to foot the bills and whose attitudes are nicely voiced in a pamphlet written by someone known either as the Pseudo-Xenophon or the Old Oligarch. This pamphlet contrasts sharply with the funeral oration of Pericles in its attitude to the Athenian Empire.

A detail from a frieze from the Nereid monument of Xanthos in Lycia, depicting Greek hoplites in battle. The large shield used by the hoplites protected the soldiers from shoulder to knee. When lined up before battle the hoplite would link his shield with that of his neighbor so that he covered his neighbor's right side. The man at the extreme right had no such protection. This often caused the line to bend to the right as he sought some safety and others edged after him.

## THE PELOPONNESIAN WAR

Between 470 and 460 Sparta had great internal troubles when the helots revolted. During that revolt the uneasy friendship with Athens broke when the Spartans sent home the Athenian contingent that had come to help. This antagonized the Athenians and resulted in the ostracism of Cimon, one of the pro-Spartan Athenians, and the emergence of full democracy. In 459 Athens had actually taken the offensive and invaded the Argolid but only once in the following years did the Spartans retaliate, such was their insecurity. As the power of the Athenians grew and the trading members of the Peloponnesian League, notably Corinth, became more and more concerned, Sparta became more active. In 446 her army actually invaded Attica, but went home without even fighting and in the following year a thirty-year peace was signed by Athens and Sparta, with terms very much in favor of Sparta.

Gradually, however, relations became more and more strained as Athens clashed twice in rapid succession with Corinth, first over the island of Corcyra, modern Corfu, and then over Potideia, a town in Chalcidice, which was originally a Corinthian colony but had become a member of the League. These clashes, together with the question of the position of Megara, a city on the Athenian side of the isthmus of Corinth, were what Thucydides calls the causes of the full-scale war between Athens and Sparta which broke out in 431. But they were mere excuses rather than causes, for Thucydides himself says: "These were the reasons, openly referred to by each side, why they broke the thirty-year treaty and went to war, but I think that the truest reason is that the Athenians, by becoming great, had put fear into the Spartans and compelled them to fight." So it was that the Peloponnesian War began with Sparta, her Peloponnesian allies (but not Argos which, as in the

Persian wars, was cleverly neutral), Corinth and Boeotia on one side, and Athens and her empire on the other. The one side was overwhelmingly strong on land, the other on sea.

In Athens, on paper an extreme democracy, policy had, in fact, since 445 been under the influential control of Pericles. A member of the board of ten *strategoi* (generals), which was the chief executive magistracy, Pericles was also what was called *prostates tou demou* (chief popular orator) who overshadowed all other speakers in the ecclesia, where all decisions of state were taken. He was an unhesitating exponent of Athenian imperialism. He accepted, indeed welcomed, the war, which he expected to demonstrate that Athenian strength was invulnerable, and his war strategy was already worked out, but it was ruined by contingencies which he could not have foreseen. In the second year of the war, a devastating plague broke out, encouraged by overcrowding and unsanitary conditions inside the walls. A year later Pericles himself died, and there was no politician of his caliber to follow him.

An early Greek bronze of a hoplite c.600, showing the development of cheek pieces. The hoplite had to provide all his own equipment. At Athens this was not paid for or provided by the state. Anyone who could afford the armor could be a hoplite and it was obviously in a city's interests to have as many as possible. However, until the increase in wealth in the fifth century, numbers seem to have been fairly constant at Athens.

The war dragged on for ten years with no conclusive result, and in 421 peace was made, leaving both sides frustrated. In Athens the frustration, exploited by the dangerous genius of the brilliant young aristocrat Alcibiades, a pupil of Socrates, was fatal. Disregarding the danger from their still-dissatisfied enemies in Greece, the Athenians launched a vast naval expedition to Sicily in 415. They hoped to capture Syracuse and master the western Greek world, with all its vast resources. After three years, the expedition ended in disaster. The Athenian ships were captured or sunk in the harbor of Syracuse, and the troops were killed or taken prisoner. Athenian mastery of the sea, the guarantee of her empire, vanished overnight.

Her enemies pounced. Sparta resumed the war. To finance the fleet that was necessary to support the Athenian imperial subjects in revolt, they allied themselves

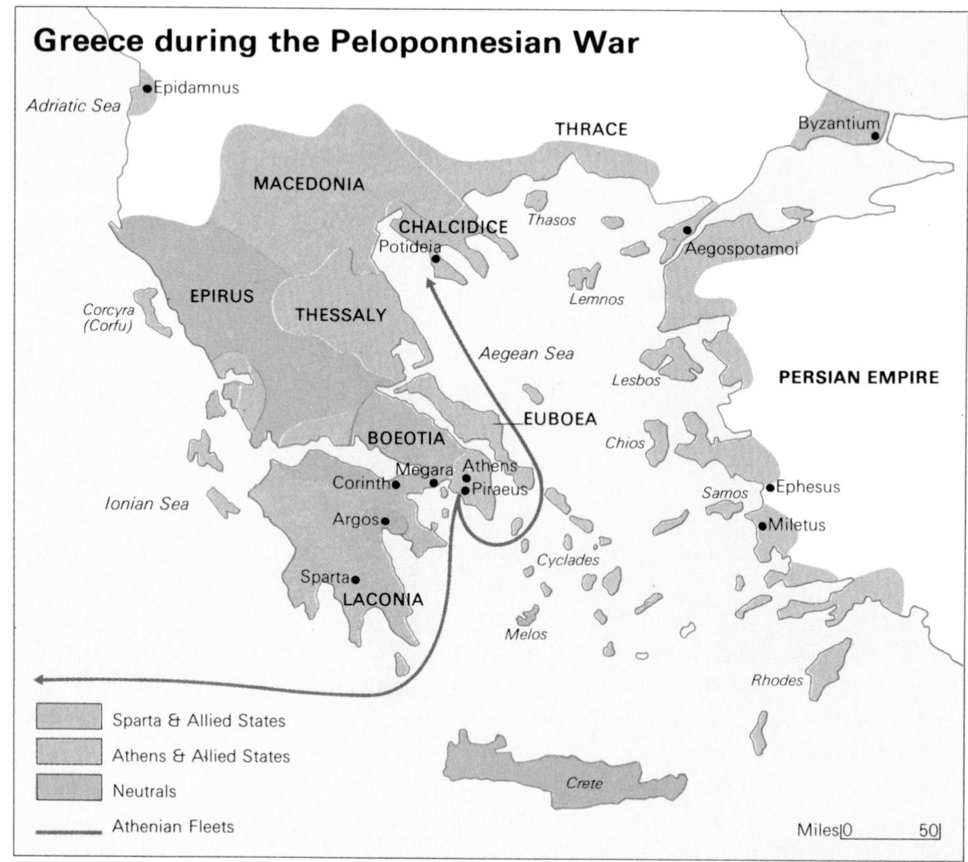

with Persia—a guarantee, as it seemed, of unlimited money. They occupied a permanent garrison in Attica (instead of making annual incursions and then retiring, as they had done in the first part of the war). Athens was also beset by internal problems: there were several coups d'etat.

With some suspicion of treachery, the whole Athenian fleet was captured at Aegospotamoi in the Hellespont in 405, and their enemies imposed a naval blockade. The city was starved into surrender. The great walls were breached. The empire was an empire no longer. The wealth on which the glory of fifth-century Athens was built had gone. There was another short and bloody period of oligarchy (the government of the Thirty), and then, once more, democracy was restored.

## THE END OF GREEK INDEPENDENCE

As the victor in the Peloponnesian War, Sparta so abused her power that she became the most hated state in Greece. Profiting by this unpopularity, Athens, which had made a remarkable economic recovery from the war, established a second League in 377. In mainland Greece, Thebes, the victim of unprincipled interference by Sparta, produced a military genius in Epaminondas. The Theban army defeated and practically annihilated the Spartan army at Leuctra in Boeotia in 371. It then entered the Peloponnese, which was at its mercy, intent on setting up rival powers to Sparta at Sparta's doorstep. Messenia regained its independence, and the Arcadian cities of the central Peloponnese were formed into a single state.

For the future of Greece, however, and indeed of the whole eastern Mediterranean world, the momentous event was the organization of Macedonia into a powerful kingdom by King Philip II. He organized and trained a new-style army, whose strength lay in a development of the phalanx. He strengthened the northern boundaries of his country and eventually secured the coastal cities, together with the

*Left:* Vase painting of hoplites arming. Here one can see the spear, about seven feet in length, the Greek sword, and the grips inside a shield. The helmets have now acquired large crests.
*Lower left:* Relief showing an Athenian warship. This is a detail from what is known as "The Lenormant Relief," c.400. The Athenian warship was known as a trireme. There has been a long debate over how the rowers sat but, a recent theory suggests that the benches on which the rowers sat sloped forwards and that three rowers sat on each bench, but each one pulled his own oar.

rich mines of Mount Pangaeus. This expansion was at the expense of Athens, which had intimate connections with Macedon and had been drawing great wealth from it.

In Athens the crisis was confronted by the forlorn genius of the greatest of Greek orators, Demosthenes, many of whose speeches survive. In a series of manful and spirited orations (the *Olynthiacs* and the *Philippics*), he tried to awaken the Athenians to the danger and to re-create, in the face of this new "barbarian," the spirit of patriotic self-sacrifice which had defeated the Persians in 490 and 480. But times had changed; many people agreed with the Athenian pamphleteer Isocrates, who had long advocated a united front against Persia and saw in Philip the ideal leader for that front, as he had seen in others previously, judging from his speeches. When Athens acted, she did too little and she did it too late. Philip moved south into Greece.

A corner of the fifth-century temple of the Dioscuri (Castor and Pollux), at Acragas. Castor and Pollux, the heavenly twins, were the semi-divine brothers of Helen of Troy, whose unfaithfulness caused the Trojan War. Acragas was founded by another Greek city in Sicily, Gela, in the early sixth century. It enjoyed prosperity during that and the following century and was able to afford to put up many temples of which many fine remains are still extant.

The two great religious sanctuaries in Greece, Olympia and Delphi, possessed great wealth, thanks to the gifts and dedications of centuries. At the beginning of the Peloponnesian War it had been suggested that the Peloponnesians should try to raise a loan from Olympia. In 355, the state of Phocis in central Greece did something more drastic: it took possession of Delphi and used the money to raise a large mercenary army. Phocis was supported in this act of sacrilege by Sparta and Athens, because of their enmity with Thebes, against whom Phocis was at war.

The activity of Phocis, while it ended Theban dominance in central Greece, opened the way south for Philip and exhausted Phocis itself. Finally in 346, after complicated negotiations, Athens made peace with Philip on the understanding—or misunderstanding—that her ally Phocis should not suffer. Instead, the peace treaty was hardly concluded when Philip came south and the surviving Phocian force surrendered to him at Thermopylae. He had established a position for himself in central Greece.

Athens and Philip were soon in conflict in the Propontis, the vital channel for Athenian grain-ships. After a fierce political struggle in Athens, Demosthenes succeeded in inciting the people to alliance with Thebes and war with Philip. Overwhelming defeat at Chaeronea in Boeotia (338) was the consequence.

Philip was merciless to Thebes, selling its prisoners as slaves. To Athens and the rest of Greece, he showed generosity. He created a league of all Greek states—the League of Corinth—by which the independence of each was guaranteed. Philip was its president and commander in war. The advertised purpose of the league was reminiscent of the original Delian Confederacy—to restore the independence of Greek cities in Asia Minor against Persia (which had been pumping money into Thebes in the hope of arresting Macedonian growth) and perhaps even to embark on the conquest of Persia.

The Peloponnesian War and Sparta's victory saw a greater limitation of individual autonomy than had ever been imposed by Athens. Sparta's established bias towards oligarchy, and the massacre of numerous democrats saw Athens alone retain for some time a full democratic constitution of the major mainland Greek city-states. Though we know of the existence of quite a strong democratic party, or perhaps we should say "feeling," at Corinth and at Argos, democratic ideas were not easily eradicated. However, Sparta firmly controlled her subjects with garrisons and military governors, and the end of her domination only gave way to Theban and then to Macedonian rule. The internal conditions of the individual states changed little, but the proud concept of being *autonomoi* (under one's own laws) was being gradually eroded until it finally vanished.

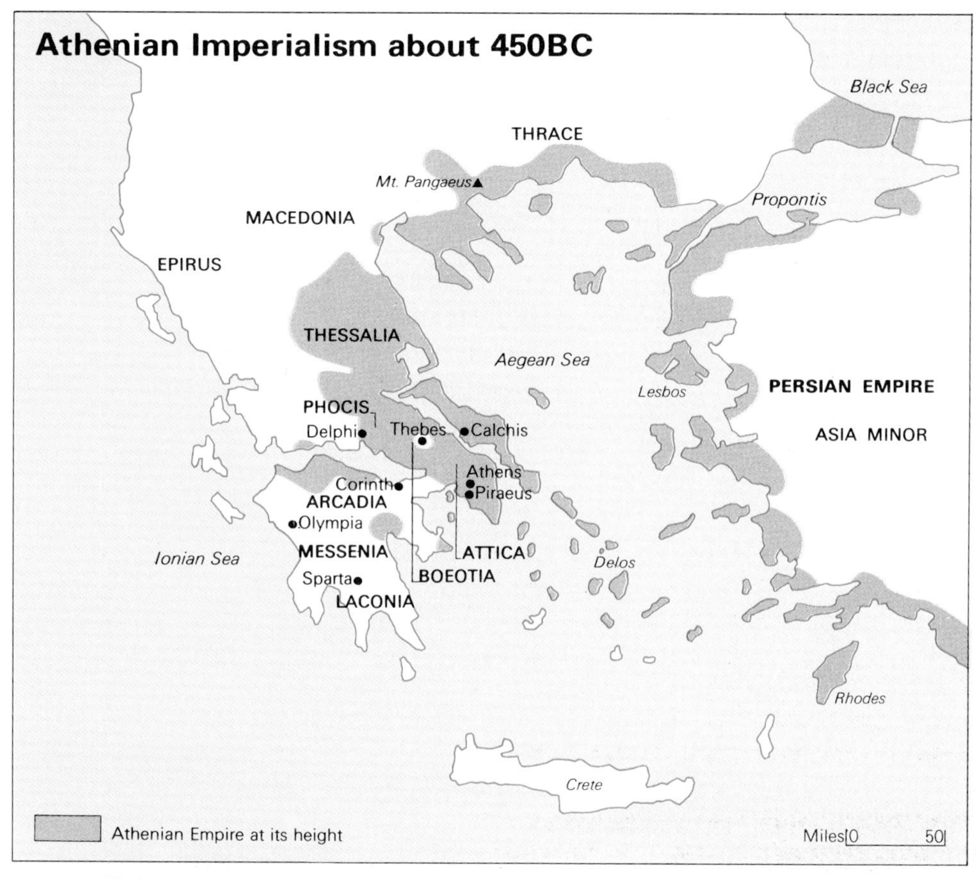


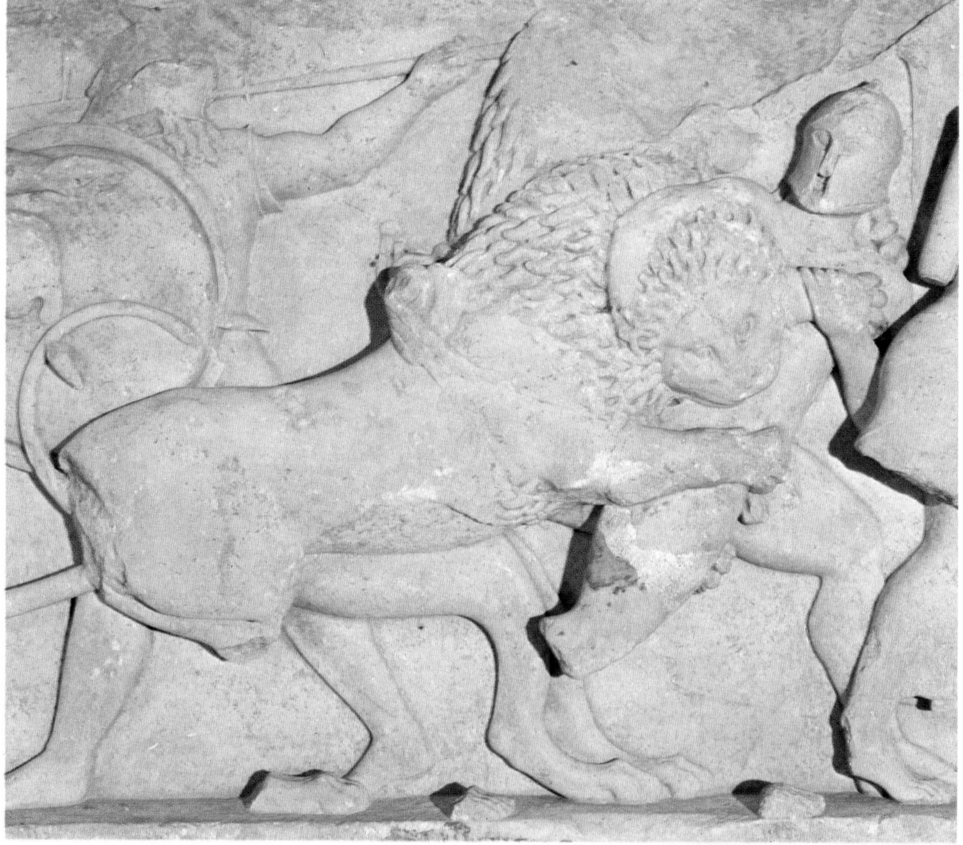

Detail of a lion attacking a giant, from the frieze of the Treasury of Siphnos at Delphi, c.530. Sudden wealth allowed the people of the otherwise small and obscure island of Siphnos to erect a Treasury at Delphi which normally only the wealthiest cities could afford. Delphi was one of the religious centers of the Greek world. Its world-famous oracle attracted donations which were stored in the appropriate Treasuries.

Chapter 4

# FIFTH-CENTURY ATHENS

Historians and students often tend to emphasize state relations in Greece, or city government, but the Greeks themselves did not think in these abstract terms; they spoke not of "Corinth" or "Athens" but of "the Corinthians" or "the city of the Athenians." Similarly, they referred to the entire cluster of Greek communities as the "land of the Hellenes" (rather than of the *Graeci*, which was the harsh-sounding term the Romans used). Emphasis was consistently laid on the "people." When Aristotle, for example, considered the relative merits of different forms of government in his *Politics*, he discussed the kind of people that should live in them. (Democracies, he concluded, were most successful if run by an agricultural population.)

Perhaps there was this emphasis on people because the population of Greece was so small compared with that of the modern world and because the particular forms of government in classical Greece demanded more of the individual citizen. In the fifth century Athens had approximately 40,000 citizens and some 20,000 *metics* (alien residents who paid a tax to remain in the area). The entire free population, including women and children, totaled about 200,000. In addition, there were at least 200,000, and perhaps over 300,000, slaves. Of the 40,000 Athenian citizens, many were Attic countrymen, who lived outside the city.

Those who did live in the cities in ancient times were not necessarily to be envied. Ancient cities were small, narrow, dirty, and crowded. Houses faced inward rather than toward the streets. There were no sewers, and garbage was not always removed at regular intervals. Greek cities, though, had this advantage: unlike Roman cities, they had no idle, pauperized proletariat. Although demagoguery was by no means unknown in Greece, the absence of such a proletariat, the exclusion of non-citizens from politics, and the relatively small number of citizens helped prevent it. There was no dole—too few needed it. Surplus population and many of the poor migrated to colonies, especially to southern Italy (*Magna Graeca*).

*Above:* Detail from a design on a mid-sixth-century Athenian black-figure vase, showing men gathering olives. Olives were one of the staple products of Attica and one of her few exportable crops.
*Left:* Bronze head of Aphrodite, the Greek goddess of love. This comes from a reproduction of a fourth-century work by Praxiteles, one of the supreme masters of that age.

The Greeks regarded manual labor as despicable and as a hindrance to effective political participation. Aristotle maintained that the ideal city had no need of citizens who did manual labor or who received salaries. In the *Politics* he wrote, "a state with an ideal constitution cannot have its citizens living the lives of mechanics or shopkeepers, which is ignoble and inimical to virtue." How could anyone have sufficient time to devote to politics if he had to practice a craft or work at the beck and call of an employer? At Thebes, Aristotle noted, no businessman was allowed to take part in the government unless he had been retired from business for at least ten years. Though Socrates claimed to have learned a good deal from the time he spent in artisans' workshops, his pupil Plato expressed a more common view when, in the *Phaedrus*, he classed only demagogues and tyrants lower than laborers and artisans in the scale of worthwhile occupations. This attitude to manual labor was, however, commoner among writers than others.

In reality, over two-thirds of the Athenians were craftsmen, farmers, shopkeepers, and the like. Probably less than one-third owned slaves. But the Athenians had a well-developed sense of what constituted an aristocratic life (the life of a civilized and sophisticated man), and this conception did not include manual labor. Nor did it include the desire for external, material luxury. "The people there (in Athens)," one observer wrote, "are in no way better dressed or better looking than the slaves and resident aliens."

A stele of c.400, showing an athlete with a *strygil* (an instrument used for scraping the body to remove dirt and perspiration), and a slave who appears to be holding his *chiton* (tunic).

## THE ROLE OF THE SLAVE

Slaves were often prisoners of war (except that, in time, the Greeks came to observe a convention by which they did not enslave fellow-Greeks whom they captured), people seized by highwaymen or pirates, or others bought by slave dealers. Slaves might secure freedom, but they never became citizens of the cities in which they were liberated. (In Rome, on the other hand, by a practice which astonished the Greeks, an emancipated slave was at once a Roman citizen.) Employed as servants in families, as craftsmen, or as workers in factories (which might have as many as 160 slaves), their condition was not one of great hardship. In the mines, on the other hand, or on heavy building work, they were treated like animals and did not survive long. In the fundamentally elitist societies of Greece, slaves existed to get their hands dirty, doing jobs which free men regarded with contempt.

Though the concept of slavery is abhorrent to us, no moral stigma was attached to it in ancient times. Fourth-century philosophers accepted slavery and even justified it. Plato advised that Greeks should not enslave other Greeks and that slaves should be treated well. Aristotle, on the other hand, wrote that certain members of the human species—men as inferior to the rest as the body is to the soul or the beast is to man—are capable of tasks no higher than routine physical labor. These individuals are destined by nature herself for slavery, he wrote. There is nothing better for them than to obey others.

Slavery was certainly based less on heredity and racial prejudice in ancient times than in, say, nineteenth-century America (though it should be noted that *Thratta*, meaning "female Thracian," was the Athenian slang equivalent of "slave"; slaves usually had no name and were called by their race). But slavery was arbitrary. Anyone might be on the losing side in a war or be captured by pirates or fall into debt. Anyone, in short, might be enslaved. Even Plato was once sold as a slave. Dionysius, tyrant of Syracuse, forced Plato to leave Syracuse on a Spartan ship and ordered the captain to sell him as a slave at Aegina. As it happened, a Cyrenean bought him and sent him back to Athens. Hermias, uncle or guardian of Aristotle's first wife, began life as a slave but died prince or *dynast*, of Assos and Altarneus. Such was the capricious nature of slavery.

The average Athenian slaveholder had about a dozen slaves: a doorkeeper, a cook, a teacher (*pedagogos*), and also water bringers, cleaning slaves, weavers, and spinners. Plato's will mentions five; Aristotle's, a good many more. Greek slaves could own property. In Athens, slaves could not be whipped. They were often buried with their master's family, in the family tomb, and were even allowed to participate in religious ceremonies.

There were also state slaves. Public sanctuaries had *hierodules*, who were dedicated to the service of a deity. State slaves ran the Athenian bureaucracy as clerks, made the coins, and often formed an important part of the police force. Public slaves lived where they liked, received salaries, engaged in business, and were allowed to marry. In short, they were a recognized part of the society and not simply outcasts. Small wonder that slaves figure prominently—and are flattered—in Athenian drama.

## WOMEN IN ATHENIAN SOCIETY

It is extremely difficult to assay the position of women in classical times. The evidence is slight and often contradictory. We do know that Athenian women lived in a separate part of the house and rarely appeared in public. Young, unmarried girls were not allowed even into the inner court of the house; they were kept from the view of men, including their own male relatives. On rare occasions they participated in religious festivals. Adultery was therefore almost comically hard to arrange: one unhappy husband confessed that if only his mother had not died, his wife would not have cuckolded him; it was at his mother's funeral that she first encountered her future lover. Once female infidelity was legally established, the husband was required to divorce his wife. Husbands, in fact, could divorce their wives for any reason, or none.

Marriage was frequently nothing more than a business proposition. In an imaginary dialogue by the soldier-writer, Xenophon, a wealthy Athenian named Ischomachus discusses with Socrates the training of his young wife, pointing out that his parents could easily have found another girl for his bed, as his wife surely realized. But after thinking about it, he continues—his parents considering their interests and her parents theirs—the families decided to choose her for Ischomachus, and him for her, from among the other candidates.

Athenian women of the fifth century had no political rights and very few legal ones. In the Homeric period they had been freer; they were, in fact, flatteringly portrayed in the Homeric epics as important persons. But in later centuries, misogyny was common. The Boeotian poet Hesiod hated women, seeing them as a source of evil. "Get first a house," he wrote, "and a woman and a plowing ox; and get a slave woman, not a wife."

Somonides of Armorgos drove home the ethic of misogyny:

> *For Zeus did make this greatest evil,*
> *The woman; for even if they seem to furnish usefulness,*
> *To him who weds them most they prove a bane,*
> *For never he with cheerful spirit passes through a day*
> *Complete, who with a woman is . . .*

A woman's real function was restricted to the production of offspring. Marriage ("a necessary evil" in the Athenian playright Menander's words) was instituted for this purpose. In Athens, childless men were viewed with public disfavor, though this was less true if they had elder brothers who had produced children. In Sparta, as we have seen, celibates were publicly humiliated. Children were important for both practical and religious reasons. Athenians needed children to look after them in their old age (in the absence of any form of welfare) and to bury them according to the prescribed religious rituals. Only a male heir could continue the family line and, more important, offer his father the cult worship necessary for his happiness in the afterlife.

But even with respect to childbearing, her recognized function, the Greek woman had little to say. Both abortion and exposure of newborn infants were acceptable means of avoiding overly large families in Athens (infants were not "people" until they had undergone certain rituals and received a name: therefore, exposure was not a crime against society). But a woman could not abort without her husband's consent, nor could a female slave without her master's consent. Fathers could sell their children, in many Greek cities, without the mother's consent.

Prostitution was a recognized part of Greek life. At the bottom of the hierarchy of prostitutes were the common brothel whores; their services were very inexpensive, though they were customarily given a small gift in addition. Streetwalkers

*Top:* Painting on a kylix, 490–480. This is in the red-figure style which gradually began to replace the black-figureware from c.530 onwards. It allowed greater freedom to the artist. In black-figure a design in dark paint was put on the red clay and glazed. In red-figure the scene was left in the ground color and the rest of the vessel was painted black. *Above:* Detail from a painting on an Athenian red-figure *krater*. The krater was a large mixing bowl in which wine would be diluted with water for serving at dinner.

*Top left:* Two Greek women in conversation; a terracotta figurine of the late fourth century B.C., from Tanagra.
*Top right:* Athenian oil-vessel showing mistress and maid, painted by the Achilles painter, 450–440 B.C.
*Bottom:* Two Greek ladies playing the game of knucklebones, terracotta, fifth century B.C.
*Opposite top:* Women washing, a vase painting, c.450 B.C. Although the extent of female seclusion in Athens is not known, Greek art commonly shows women in the company of their own sex or with children. Spartan women, by contrast, mixed freely with men. They dressed in tunics unsewn at the side from the waist down, and even competed with men in public athletic events—customs that the Athenian playwright Euripides found disgusting, "Wish as you might, a Spartan girl could never be virtuous. They gad abroad with young men with naked thighs, and with clothes discarded they race with 'em, wrestle with 'em. Intolerable . . . " But Plato, in his utopian *Republic* argued that this prudery would have to go, if women were to be trained for their rightful place in the government of the Athenian state: "If then we are to employ the women in the same duties as the men, we must give them the same instructions . . . giving them besides a military education, and treating them in the same way as man. . . . Perhaps many of the details of the question before us might appear unusually ridiculous, if carried out in the manner proposed. . . . Is it not obviously the notion of the women exercising naked in the schools with the men . . . ? We must not be afraid of the numerous jests which worthy men may make upon the notion of carrying out such a change in reference to the gymnasia and music and above all, in the wearing of armor and riding on horseback. . . . He is a fool who thinks anything ridiculous except that which is evil." Yet Athens failed to implement Plato's suggestions, and the city, although renowned for its democratic institutions, actually granted fewer rights to women than many other ancient societies.

*Opposite middle:* A hetaira reclining and drinking with an admirer, painted on a vase by Phintias, c.500 B.C. There were licensed brothels in Athens as far back as the early sixth century B.C. Later, street-walkers also plied their trade. But the position of the hetairai was very different from that of other prostitutes. The word itself means "companion" as well as "mistress" and the hetairai were very much that. They were the only women in Athens accepted into male society. Often foreigners from other Greek states, these women might earn a living from business or as artists' models. One of the most famous hetairai of the fourth century, Phryne, sat for the sculptor Praxiteles and the painter Apelles, posing as Aphrodite because of the perfection of her figure. Such women were frequently invited to parties at which wives did not appear. Attendance meant loss of respectability, but it also meant entry into a world forever closed to the vast majority of Athenian women.

*Below, this page* Painted wall relief of Nefertari, queen of Egypt and wife of Rameses II, Thebes, c. 1250 B.C. Unlike their Athenian counterparts, the women of ancient Egypt played an important role in public life. Female ownership of property was common in all social classes. The wife was as likely as her husband to hold the deed on the family fields or house. An Egyptian scribe warned, "Be not rude to a woman in her own house. . . . " Family property was frequently inherited from the mother, and a man who begot a child outside of marriage was legally responsible for his action. The royal heiress was exceptionally important, since her dowry was the land of Egypt itself—a situation which led to frequent royal marriages between the eldest son and daughter of the pharaoh. In ancient Egypt, a queen like Nefertari was the acknowledged equal of her husband, the pharaoh.

transacted their business in dark corners, at the bases of public monuments, or at the baths. Prostitutes who managed to reach the top of the hierarchy—the *hetairae*—were respected and often highly educated. Portrait statues were dedicated to them in temples and public buildings, alongside those of generals and statesmen. Occasionally they even had altars and temples built to them.

Pederasty—an intimate relationship between an older man and young boy that was both sexual and tutorial—was commonplace in Greece. It has often been noted that the Greek word for "passionate love" (*eros*) is only rarely used to refer to heterosexual affection in classical texts. Aeschylus never included a romantic relationship between a man and a woman in any of his plays. Athenian society, which shut women away even from their male relatives, was essentially a society of men.

*Top:* The Venus de Milo. The statue is so called because it was found on the island of Melos. It is not a classical Greek work, but a later copy of one dating to about 100 B.C.
*Above:* Detail of a terracotta figurine of Aphrodite from Myrina in Asia Minor. This is a Greek work dating to the Roman era, A.D. 20. It has much in common with other works of Aphrodite
*Right:* Detail from one of the Parthenon friezes. It shows heifers being led to sacrifice at the Panathenaea, the festival in honor of Athena, the patron goddess of Athens.

## RELIGION

If we define religion as broadly as possible, we may say it deals with what Gilbert Murray has called "the uncharted regions of human experience." In the ancient world, a great many unexpected aspects of life came under the aegis of religious law or custom; agriculture, most crimes, and governmental procedure were all fundamentally religious concerns.

The ancient Greeks sought the favors of the gods by prayer, and offering, and were careful not to antagonize them. States could not go to war without observing the proper religious formalities; otherwise, they were courting defeat. That is why every state, in going to war, was anxious to persuade itself and the world (and the gods) that it took up arms to repel aggression. Every war was, in Roman language, a *bellum iustum*, or "just war." More than this, there was the possibility of supernatural knowledge of what the future held. Before an army went into battle, sacrifice was offered and the entrails of the animals were scrutinized by priestly experts; if the result was satisfactory, it was safe to engage in the battle. If things then turned out badly, the fault was not with the gods but with the priest, who had evidently misread the signs.

In civilian life, there were oracles, some (by the standards of those days) world famous and greatly frequented—in particular, the oracle of Apollo at Delphi in Greece, the oracle of Apollo near Miletus in Asia Minor, and the oracle of Zeus Ammon in Labya. To these went the envoys of kings and cities, as well as private individuals. They put their questions. From the prophet or prophetess came sounds incomprehensible to the ordinary ear, which a "spokesman" interpreted. The question was answered, more often than not, in highly ambiguous language, which the questioner was unwise to accept at face value. There was no time in antiquity when people at large did not believe that it was possible to secure advance knowledge of the future.

Other superstitions were a part of everyday belief. The gods were jealous gods, and an individual or state was exposed to very great danger in the moment of success, for success was always liable to be balanced by disaster. This was an argument which, however forlornly, conquered states used to their conquerors in the hope of receiving generous treatment; the victors of today, they warned, were the victims of tomorrow. Particularly did this affect the successful individual who, mistaken into thinking himself a cut above the ordinary man, was in danger of some act of overweening arrogance (*hubris*), which the gods were sure to punish. People were always afraid of the gods, however much the intellectuals might affect to despise them.

The classic Greek gods were the Homeric gods; they came to Athens with the Homeric poems sometime in the middle of the sixth century. Homer and Hesiod,

*Above Right:* Vase painting of Apollo holding a lyre, his traditional instrument and pouring a libation from a bowl. Libations were common in the Greek and Roman world as parts of religious ceremonies.

*Right:* A detail from the altar in the *temenos* (precinct) of Dionysos Eleutheros. This shrine dates to the second century B.C., but worship of the god had been introduced to Athens in the sixth century, probably from Boeotia, her northern neighbor. Dionysos is widely connected with fertility rites, but also with the theme of sacrament and rebirth. Hence his worshipers' interest in the ritual death and eating of the god.

the Greek historian Herodotus wrote, "made the generations of the Gods for the Greeks and gave them their names and distinguished their offices and crafts and portrayed their 'shapes.'" Homer's poetry, recited at public festivals called *panegyrics*, constituted a kind of Greek bible.

Homer's Olympians eventually supplanted the many local cults of gods—folk deities rarely recognized for more than a few square miles of countryside. Nevertheless, throughout classical times, "obscene and cruel rites" lingered. Outside the cities, anthropologists have demonstrated, peasant culture retained its primitive superstitions. Peculiar rites survived that had once served lowly deities, powers of vegetation or of the underworld. Some of these were half-animal or even wholly animal. According to an old Greek proverb, "The city may do what it will; the old custom is best."

Homer's gods and goddesses were conceived of in human form, austerely beautiful, and the Romans, who at first did not think of gods in human form, came to accept this notion of them from the Greeks. Each was thought of as patron of some valuable branch of human activity: Artemis (Roman Diana), of hunting; Apollo of medicine; Athena (Roman Minerva), of education and craftsmanship; Poseidon (Roman Neptune), of the sea and of hunting. Zeus (Roman Jupiter) was their easygoing and amorous king, and Hera (Roman Juno) his jealous and resentful queen. Temples were built to them, containing lovely statues (like museums with attendants) and sacrifice was offered on altars in front of the temples. As long as this was done properly, what the Romans called *pax deorum* ("peace of the gods") was achieved.

But this anthropomorphism and image worship can be misleading. In reality, the nature of the gods was discussed among the Greeks in highly abstract terms, and the definitions of deity varied widely. The Pythagorean philosopher Parmenides wrote that God was coincident with the universe—like it, a sphere and immovable. To Heraclitus, God was "day night, summer winter, war peace, satiety hunger." Maximus of Tyre defended the worship of idols by comparing it to an earthly lover's worship of little objects or places that remind him of his beloved: " . . . we, being unable to apprehend His essence, use the help of sounds and names and pictures, of beaten gold and ivory and silver, of plants and rivers, mountain peaks and torrents . . ." If the Greeks, he wrote, are reminded of God by a statue, or the Egyptians by animals, or others by the elements, then all these things are useful.

Greek religion, although one of the most effective forces for unity in Greece, had no creed, no theology, no church. There were no ethical standards but those of the Homeric heroes and gods, and there was no ecclesiastical hierarchy. Nevertheless, religion was intimately bound up with politics. The ancient world did not distinguish between spiritual and temporal. Athens was a political entity, and the priests of Athens were, as a matter of course, considered a part of the city government. Even mystery cults—the mysteries of Eleusis, for example—were controlled by the state. This explains why sacrilege was a serious crime. It was a *political* crime: that is, it was treason as well as impiety. Socrates was caught in this trap; by teaching his students to question the gods, he undermined their political loyalties. For this reason, his conflict with the state, which has often been represented as a conflict between wisdom and ignorance, was, in fact, a conflict in which both sides were right. The Athenian government put Socrates to death in 399 B.C. as part of a larger struggle for self-preservation in the face of profound and disintegrating changes.

Bronze statue of Zeus or Poseidon, mid fifth-century. It is a splendid example of the striding figure. At first the Greeks had difficulty with this sort of figure, getting their creations too perpendicular and the torso out of proportion from the legs and with incorrect muscular detail. Here these faults have all been ironed out and the figure is excellent. The figure probably held a thunderbolt in its right hand originally. It is thought likely that it represents Zeus, the king of the Greek gods who regularly hurled thunderbolts at his enemies. But it may represent Poseidon, Zeus' brother, and lord of the sea.

*Top Right:* A general view of the Acropolis from the Agora.

*Top Left:* The Parthenon

The Parthenon was the crowning achievement of Athenian architecture, and was as much an expression of civic pride as of religious sentiment. Pheidias, the foremost sculptor of the day, was the overseer and Iktinus the architect, and the work was begun in c.448 B.C. Apart from being the public treasury it was the temple of Athena Parthenos, the patron deity of Athens, and contained her monumental statue in the *cella*. The plan was conditioned by the size of the statue and thus was constructed with eight columns at each end and seventeen columns on both sides. This was an innovation which became the canon for later classical temples. In this building, the severity and strength of the Doric order is combined with the grace and refinement of the Ionic, which was then coming into fashion.

*Center Right:* The Theater of Dionysus

The theater always had important religious connections, since the dramatic performances took place at the festivals of Lenaea and the Greater Dionysia, which were devoted to the god and presided over by his priest. This theater, as shown, is a second-century reconstruction.

*Bottom Left:* The Erectheum

The Erectheum was built between 421 and 409, and contained the old and revered wooden statue of Athena Polias. The plan of the Erectheum is complicated but basically consists of a rectangular temple with porches on three sides. The six caryatides (female figures), supporting the entablature of the south portico, are often mentioned as a classical example of the successful combination of function and beauty

*Bottom Right:* The Frieze on the Parthenon

The overall conception of this work is probably Pheidias', although he probably did not touch it. The continuous frieze, unusual in Doric, runs both sides of the "cella" (central chamber), representing the Great Panathenaea (a religous festival held every four years) and leads to the east front where the gods are waiting to receive it.

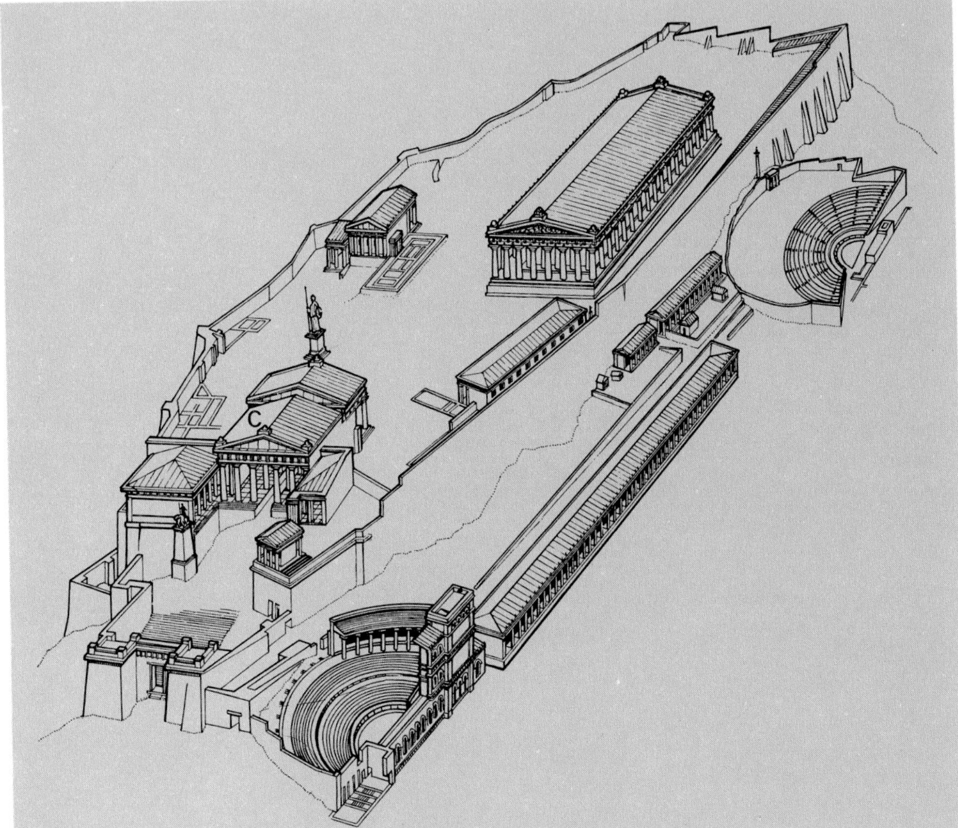

*Top left:* The Stoa of Attalus II

The *stoa* was the most versatile of Greek buildings, serving many functions —storehouse, shop-center and assembly place. The best known *stoas* are of the Pergamene type of which this is a fine example. It shows a mixture of Doric and Ionic, which is revealed by Doric columns on the lower level and Ionic on the upper level.

*Center Left:* The Acropolis

The Acropolis is basically a sanctuary site and marks the culmination of Greek temple building in the fifth century. Originally the fortified center of the city,

from the sixth century it became the sanctuary of the gods. A little more than thirty years after the destruction of the Acropolis by the Persians, Pericles took 5,000 talents from the Delian Confederacy (page 128) to pay for the building program. The Propylaea is the ornamental gateway, by which the Panathenaic procession would enter. To the left stands the Ionic Erectheum and to the right the Doric Parthenon for balance. In front stood the great altar on which cows were slaughtered at the Panathenaea to feed the city.

*Above:* The Classical orders

The Doric (left) is the oldest and the simplest of the classical orders, dating from the seventh century. The Ionic (center) developed in the eastern Aegean and is easily recognizable by the scroll at the top of the capital (see the capital from the Erectheum below left). The Corinthian (right) dates from the fifth century and is recognizable by its elaborate carving and its acanthus foliage.

*Bottom Right:* The Olympieum

This massive temple of Zeus was begun under the Peisistratids (the sixth century tyrants) but upon their expulsion in 510 was left unfinished for three centuries. Antiochus IV, in the mid-second century B.C., attempted to complete it, but it was left to the Roman emperor, Hadrian, to finish it in the second century A.D.

Chapter 5

# THE GREEK GENIUS

The Greeks set themselves apart from other Mediterranean peoples. They believed that they were radically different and that this difference was essentially intellectual. The Greeks, Herodotus wrote, have never been fools; exalted civilization emerged among the Greeks because "the Hellenic race was marked off from the barbarian, as more intelligent and more emancipated from silly nonsense."

Eager questioning was a trademark of Greek thinkers (Socrates being the outstanding example) and was regarded as an art and end in itself. Xenophon wrote, "Education is questioning." Similarly, a Greek proverb states, "Wonder is the mother of thought."

The Greeks were the first educators of the western world. They seriously pondered the question of what education is and how it is best accomplished. As with many societies that flourished before printed books were available, education in Greek society put a premium on memory. Because culture was acquired "by heart," it penetrated deeply and took permanent root. The Greeks truly loved the Homeric poems, for example, and paid public reciters to repeat the *Odyssey*, the *Iliad*, and other great poetry in the streets. High culture was not restricted to a tiny segment of the society. After the disastrous Sicilian expedition (see Chapter 3), some of the defeated Athenians—prisoners and fugitives—saved themselves by reciting all they knew of Euripides' poetry, which the Sicilians loved and were anxious to learn. Some were given food and water for singing these songs and permitted to make their way back to Athens. Where but in Greece could such a cultural ransom be envisioned?

*Above:* Coin of the second century A.D. showing Eshman the Phoenician god of healing. He is portrayed with twin serpents, a theme common to gods of healing throughout the Mediterranean area.

*Left:* The amphitheater at Delphi. Delphi established its influence by the middle of the seventh century, and became a center of the cult of Apollo. It established the Pythian Games in about 590 and included in them, unlike the Olympic and other games, music and poetry competitions as befitted a god of inspiration. The famous Oracle seems to have owed much of its success to good intelligence, but whatever the secret, it helped to establish Delphi's reputation.

## THE SOURCES OF GREEK CULTURE

A seafaring people themselves, the Greeks naturally came into contact with others who came to trade. Colonization quickly multiplied trading contacts and meant that large numbers of Greeks lived permanently alongside other peoples. Miletus alone was supposed to have founded sixty colonies. Vigorous and eager for opportunities, the Greeks first learned about other cultures by serving as mercenaries in the armies of the Near-Eastern empires. Later, they remained great travelers.

One source of influence were the Phoenicians. With colonies throughout the Mediterranean and large navies, the Phoenicians and Greeks often came into contact with one another. Greek and Phoenician settlements divided the island of Cyprus; Carthage, later Rome's determined enemy, was a Phoenician colony. Asian culture—in particular, the alphabet and the Babylonian system of weights and measures—was brought to the Greeks by the Phoenicians.

Egyptians and Greeks also learned from one another. Greeks first came as mercenaries to support a native revolt against Assyria. When the revolt was over, they remained in the Nile Valley as traders. The Ionian city Miletus built a factory on the lower reaches of the Nile; later, two camps of Greek mercenaries were permanently stationed in Egypt. There were so many Greeks in Egypt by the early-sixth century that a permanent township was accorded to them; nine Ionian cities joined to erect a sanctuary there. Throughout the sixth century, trade tied the two cultures together.

But while the Greeks were eclectic, they were also selective. They were cautious, at least in the sixth and fifth centuries, about most foreign religions. They seldom borrowed other forms of government, and their dislike of manual labor made them reject the technological advances of other countries, especially those of the Egyptians. Thus they took much from Chaldean astronomy and mathematics but ignored their technology and religion. Foreigners came to the Greek states in large numbers, mostly as traders. They were not given citizenship, but they mixed freely with the citizen population and frequently acquired wealth and influence. Others came as slaves or laborers. The Greek language adopted foreign words, and Greek art began to incorporate aspects of Egyptian and Near-Eastern art. Governmental forms changed, too. Older, kingship-centered institutions gave way to new groupings based on geography or party attachments. Sparta alone resisted any change in its way of life, maintaining a rigid and strict adherence to her archaic social and governmental institutions, and this was accomplished only by the exclusion of foreign influences.

Archaic statue of the *kouros* type made of bronze, bearing some relation to the Piombino Apollo in the positioning of the hands. There is quite a good sense of proportion and the enigmatic smile is fading from fashion. Because of the open right hand it may be an Apollo.

## THE FIRST HISTORIANS

Earlier and more widespread among the Greeks than an interest in their own history was an interest in the geography and anthropology of the distant parts of the earth: in the people who lived outside their own temperate climate, the Hyperboreans in the icy North on the one hand and the inhabitants of the tropics on the other; in what travelers had discovered on their journeys; in Egypt, above all, with its vast antiquity and legendary connections with early Greece; in the Nile flood, the biggest natural mystery of the ancient world. The earliest travel book of which we know (it does not survive) was written by Hecataeus of Miletus in Ionia. It was called *Ges Periodos* ("Around the World"), and in principle and arrangement it was very similar to a modern travel guide.

### Herodotus

A more important figure was Herodotus. After traveling through Asia Minor, Syria, Persia, Egypt, and southern Italy, he returned to Athens early in the Peloponnesian War and published a history in about 425 (*historie* is an Ionian word meaning "enquiry"—not what we call history). He is called the "father of history" because, taking the same kind of subject matter as Hecataeus used, he turned it from the horizontal into the vertical; that is to say, he gave it a single setting in time.

Herodotus wrote a chronological story of the growth of the Persian Empire, conquest by conquest, up to the Ionian revolt. After that, for the last five of his nine books, he described chronologically the Ionian revolt and the successive Persian invasions of Greece down to the final disaster of Mycale. But in the first four books he stopped and gave long Hecataeus-type sociological and geographical accounts of the Medes and Persians and, at the moment when the Persians made contact with them, of the Lydians, the Babylonians, the Egyptians, and the Scythians. The whole of the second book, for instance, is an account of Egypt. Though digressions are innumerable, the work has a firm structural plan. It is, even in translation, one of the most delightful and readable books ever written, remarkable for being utterly free from the normal Greek contempt for "barbarian" peoples. It is our most important source for the Persian invasions of Greece.

Apart from Hecataeus, from whom he may have pilfered, he based his account entirely on conversations with people whom he had met in Persia and Egypt (speaking through interpreters). And, accurate or not—how could he tell?—he wrote down everything he was told.

### Thucydides

Thucydides, a severe rationalist and a far cleverer man than Herodotus, although with none of Herodotus' cosmopolitan interests, was a product of the lively intellectual atmosphere of Periclean Athens. He was in his late twenties when the Peloponnesian War started (431), and he began to write an account of it from the conviction that it would be the greatest war in history, recording and analyzing every aspect of the war as it proceeded.

Strongly mistrustful of Herodotus' notion of history—in particular, his uncritical acceptance of everything he was told—Thucydides was convinced of the necessity of absolute truth in the reporting of facts. He knew that true history must be something more than a description of events; it must supply an explanation of them. Why, for a start, did the Peloponnesian War break out? The ultimate cause of the war, he concluded, was to be distinguished from the episodes which sparked it off. Why were particular strategic and political decisions taken—the fatal decision to invade Sicily, for instance? For this analysis, he made use of speeches to convey what, he thought, must have been the motives. In his book he attempted to explain the internal disintegration of political life in wartime, the civil war (*stasis*) between oligarchs and democrats, the factional fanaticism which put patriotism out of men's minds and perverted the accepted standard of peacetime life. His economic, logical, often difficult account got as far as the year 411, but he died before it was completed.

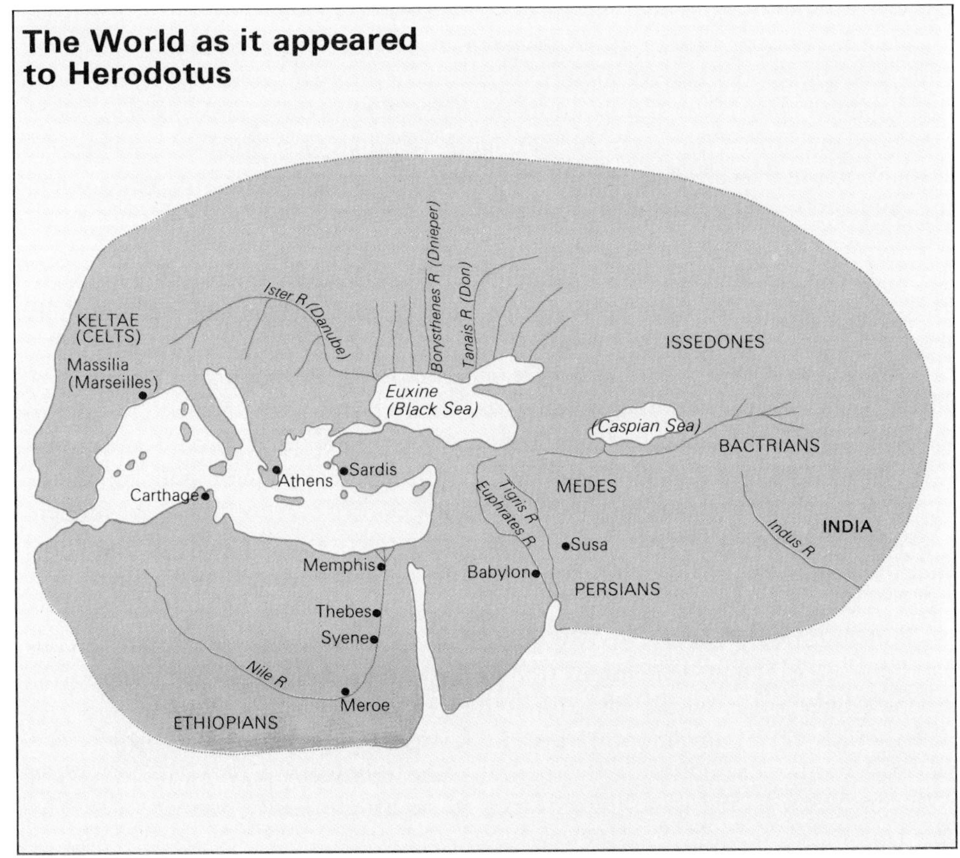

Thucydides was the first man to comprehend the true nature of history. He was the more conscious of the historian's moral duty to seek out the truth because he believed that the history of the past has a practical use for the statesman of the future—indeed, that it is the function of history to instruct rather than simply to interest and give pleasure.

## TRAGEDY AND COMEDY

Plays belong to festive occasions, and festivals in Greece, as later in Rome, were in honor of the gods. The drama, therefore, had deep religious significance from the start. Tragedy developed from the dithyramb, a chorus with one soloist, who was raised on a platform. From one, there came to be two "actors," then three, making entrances and exits. The chorus, which remained below the stage, nearer the spectators and detached from the actors, commented on the action, involved yet remote. The play consisted of "acts," that is, spoken dialogue on the stage between actors who wore masks, with intervals in which the chorus sang. Performances lasted through the day; three tragedies (constituting a trilogy) were performed in succession, followed by a satyr-play to relieve the tension. The subjects of the plays were stories from Greek mythology and legend, stories with which the audience was already familiar. Playwrights submitted scripts to be judged, and each of the three winners put on one-day performances. The production expenses were paid by a rich citizen. After the last performance the judges announced the winner.

Two fifth-century vase paintings: the top one shows students learning to play the lyre, and to recite; the lower picture shows a youth being taught how to play the *aulos* (double-flute), and how to write with a *stylos* (pen). Education was very important to the fifth-century Athenian. The arts figured prominently: for example the name of Pericles' music teacher, Damon, is known.

The outstanding dramatists of the fifth century were Aeschylus, Sophocles, and Euripides. One complete trilogy by Aeschylus survives; the *Agamemnon*, in which Agamemnon is murdered on his return from Troy by his wife Clytemnestra; the *Choephori* ("Libation Bearers"), in which Clytemnestra is murdered by her son Orestes, brother of Electra; and the *Eumenides* ("Gracious Goddesses"), in which Orestes is absolved of blood guilt. Aeschylus' tragedies depicted the relentless power of the gods and of destiny; those of Sophocles showed a deeper humanity. Euripides, with a sympathetic understanding of ordinary human psychology, produced characters who are recognizable human beings, the sport of gods who were sometimes cruel and often unprincipled. The appeal of Sophocles' *Antigone*, the dilemma of the individual faced with a conflict between the unwritten and the written law, and of Euripides' *Trojan Women*, depicting the horrifying impact of war on women, is timeless.

In Aristotle's view, the audience left the tragic theater the better for its experience. The function of tragedy, he wrote, is to cleanse the emotions through pity and fear.

The genius of fifth-century Athenian comedy was Aristophanes, a number of whose plays survive, named generally after their choruses: the *Knights*, the *Acharnians*, the *Clouds*, the *Birds*, the *Frogs*. They are outspoken, often obscene, and always very funny political attacks on leading politicians and current policies. In the *Lysistrata* (411), which is still from time to time presented successfully on the modern stage, the women of Greece decide to restore peace, remedying the disaster that their menfolk have made by reserving the one need that men have of them, their sex.

Fourth-century Greek comedy abandoned politics for private life. The conflict between different generations (the stern father and the gay, spendthrift son), the intriguing slaves whose sympathies are generally on the right side, and love affairs which never run smoothly became favorite comic subjects. Menander was the outstanding dramatist of the period. One complete play of his, *Dyskolos* ("Curmudgeon"), and large parts of five others have recently been recovered on papyrus.

## PHILOSOPHY

Greek speculative thinking was in part scientific (dealt with in Chapter 7), in part philosophic. Scientific hypotheses were rarely tested by practical experiments, so that there was no general advance in natural science. But because the Greeks were highly intelligent, some of their guesses were very good guesses indeed.

### The Ionian and Pythagorean Schools

In the sixth century, two schools of thought emerged: one in the Ionian cities of Asia Minor—particularly in Miletus, then the intellectual capital of the Greek world—and the other in the west, founded by Pythagoras at Croton, in southern Italy. From the discovery by Pythagoras of harmonics, the mathematical basis of musical intervals, down to Archimedes in third-century Sicily, the western school was interested primarily in mathematics. The Ionian school, on the other hand, was intent on discovering the physical nature of the universe: What was its material constitution? How had life begun?

The Ionian school started with the four elements—air, water, fire, earth (dry, wet, hot, cold)—and the first philosphers found the divine attribute of eternity in one or another of these primary substances. The whole direction of their thinking was to reduce all phenomena to the motion of dead matter. These speculations culminated, in the fifth century, in an atomic theory.

Votive relief from the Piraeus, c.400, showing the actors making an offering to Dionysos. Athenian dramatic competitions were held in honor of the god Dionysos at the winter Lenaea, the festival of the wine press, and at the Great Dionysia in late spring. The masks may originally have been connected with more primitive forms of Dionysos' worship, but became an essential part of the Greek and Roman theater. The design represented the character: god, king or slave.

To explain the creation of the universe, the Ionian school held that, from a primordial Unity, the One somehow became first Two and then Many—and yet, in a contradictory way, the One still remains One. Heraclitus (c. 500 B.C.), however, claimed that the world has always been as we know it: always both Many and One, ever-living fire and yet not undying. All is flux; change is constant. Instead of a system of stability and rest (that is, a balance of conflicting forces) the life process represents unceasing strife of opposite powers.

The culmination of the Pythagorean school (aside from pure mathematics) is represented by Parmenides in the early-fifth century. In Parmenides' view, the sense world, exhibiting plurality and change, cannot be wholly real. For this reason, the "evidence" of the senses is fallacious. The One Being is apart from the world of the senses and can be grasped only by thought. From this followed the scepticism regarding sense data that was to be basic in the speculations of Plato and the Academy.

### Socrates and Plato

It is a curious fact that Athens' greatest philosophers—Socrates, Plato, and Aristotle—flourished during and after the disastrous Peloponnesian War, in a period when Athens herself was in a state of political decline and social turmoil. But it is often the questioning atmosphere characteristic of a society in the process of transformation that provides the most fertile environment for speculative thought.

The fifth-century Sophists began the questioning process. They were something like modern business-school instructors. They taught the way to material success—in particular, how to argue both sides of a case with equal conviction and even how, at the worst, to exploit self-interest at the expense of conventional moral standards. For this teaching Sophists were paid by their pupils, and many became wealthy.

These were the men whose shallowness Socrates exposed. Socrates himself took no money, and he vaunted his own ignorance as ostentatiously as the Sophists paraded their supposed knowledge. He held that goodness (*arete*, or life in pursuit of a clearly considered aim) was knowledge, something to be discerned intuitively, which could not be taught—as carpentry and medicine, for example, could be taught—and that it was the cause of happiness. Wrongdoing proceeded from ignorance, for nobody could do wrong wittingly.

His attraction for clever young men was irresistible (as is evident from the caricature of him in Aristophanes' *Clouds*, produced in 423), and it was through the antidemocratic activities of some of his keenest followers (including Critias) that he became suspect and was condemned to death in 399. As a thinker and person, he is deeply alive to us in the records of two of his pupils, the *Memorabilia* of Xenophon and the dialogues of Plato, in which Socrates is the major questioner.

The teachings of Socrates, with his refutation of the Sophists, affected Plato's whole life, inducing him to abandon politics, his intended career, in favor of philosophy. In Athens Plato founded the Academy, a school of philosophy which continued through the centuries. Fundamental to Plato's philosophy is the doctrine of forms, or Ideas. In human life, he held, we are acquainted only with "images" of true forms, which themselves are remote heavenly things. When we speak or argue on the level of our experiences, we are in a world of opinion; only thought can penetrate to the Ideas, which are the goal of knowledge. The highest form of all is the Idea of the Good.

A double bust of Sophocles and Aristophanes of the early fourth century. Sophocles was one of the three great tragedians of fifth-century Athens. He is said to have composed over a hundred plays, although only seven survive, of which the most famous is probably the *Oedipus Rex*. Aristophanes lived from c.450 to 388. He wrote many trenchant comedies containing biting attacks on the politicians of his day. He was far from being the only comic playwright, but was certainly the grand master of the Old Comedy.

Plato was influenced by the Pythagorean belief in the transmigration of souls and by Pythagorean mathematics. Intuition of Ideas is possible only through recollection, because the soul is in contact with Ideas before birth. Thus, in seeking to comprehend the Idea of the Beautiful from the sight of beautiful things, men proceed by intuition and dialectic, just as mathematicians divine the premises and deduce the conclusions by demonstrative proof.

Man's character, Plato believed, consists of three elements: appetite, resolution, and reason. Temperance indicates a proper balance of the parts, with reason as guide and resolution as its servant in the control of appetite. In the ideal state depicted in the *Republic*, protection would be afforded by the warrior class, consisting of men without family or property, and government would be in the hands of philosophers. A strict censorship of literature would be imposed. Like most other Greek philosophers, Plato thought democracy one of the worst forms of government.

### Aristotle

Alexander the Great's tutor, Aristotle, had been a pupil of Plato, but after Plato's death he left the Academy and founded his own philosophical school, the Lyceum. The members of this school were called Peripatetics because it was Aristotle's custom to discuss philosophy with his pupils while taking walks (*peripatoi*).

Although Aristotle abandoned the Platonic theory of Ideas, he never really emancipated himself from Platonic thinking. Abstract ideas, he held, belong to the field of metaphysics and are detached from the material world. The components of the material world are Matter and Form, Potentiality and Actuality, and their relationship is that of a lump of bronze to the finished statue or of a seed to the grown tree, the cause of anything being its form. Soul and body are one; the soul and its activities are the actuality of the organic body, yet active reason, an element of the soul, is without matter (like the intelligences which rule the spheres and like God, the Prime Mover). The lower faculties in man are interpenetrated by his reason, and he is capable of pursuing the good life. Moral virtue is in every case a "mean" between two opposite vices. Of his rational part, man's two highest intellectual virtues are theoretical and practical wisdom—the possession and contemplation of truth on the one hand and statesmanship, which aims at the achievement of human happiness, on the other.

The son of a doctor, Aristotle was deeply interested in biology, and he did original scientific work of the first importance in observing and classifying the properties of minerals, plants, and animals. "It is in the works of nature above all," he wrote, "that design, in contrast to random chance, is manifest."

The same interest in classification attracted him to the historical field. Aristotle produced the first chronology of victors at the Pythian Games, and he wrote a history and analysis of the constitutions of 158 Greek city-states, forming the basis of his work on political science, the *Politics*.

On Alexander's death, Aristotle went into voluntary exile; there is some evidence that, as a former tutor of Alexander, he feared execution by the Athenians. In all, Aristotle probably wrote a million words on many subjects. Many of his works have been lost, but enough remained in the centuries that followed his death to form the foundations of scientific thought in the Roman world and on into the Middle Ages.

### Diogenes the Cynic

Plato, Socrates, and Aristotle have remained the most influential thinkers of Hellenic Greece. But it was Diogenes who caught the fancy of the fourth-century Hellenes themselves. Next to Alexander, Diogenes was probably the best-known man of his age, and his career and personality tell us much about fourth-century thought.

An irreverently Rabelaisian philosopher who delighted in insulting people—and the more famous they were, the greater was his delight—Diogenes adhered to strict empiricism and mocked all teachings, such as Plato's, which proposed the existence of unseen, abstract entities. Religion was anathema to him, as were doctrines which seemed to contradict common sense. (Once when a philosopher was lecturing on the non-existence of motion, Diogenes was seen to get up and start walking around the room.)

Everything was fodder for a joke or insult, even religion. When asked if he believed in the gods, Diogenes looked at his questioner and remarked, "How can I help believing in them when I see a godforsaken wretch like you?"

Of course, many of the sayings attributed to Diogenes by later biographers are apocryphal, but they do represent anecdotes that circulated about him probably while he was alive (he is said to have lived to be over ninety). In any case, what is important to us is not what he actually said or did but the way the Greeks *thought* he talked and behaved—the image they had of him, which had its basis in fact.

Drawing of Plato from an edition of his works published in 1578. Plato lived from 429–347 B.C. He was the pupil of Socrates who greatly influenced his philosophical thought. Many of his works are set in the form of dialogues between philosophers, usually Socrates and an opponent, and exhibit the Socratic dialectic method of investigation. Socrates' chief concerns seem to have lain in the theory that virtue is knowledge and that it is teachable. Plato developed Socrates' lines of thought and published in *The Republic* a superb discussion on the nature of justice.

We know less about Diogenes' philosophy than about his habits and character. Describing himself as "a Socrates gone mad," he denounced private property and advocated that men should hold all women in common. Good men, he said, he found nowhere, though he commented sarcastically that there were plenty of good boys in Sparta.

Diogenes was famous for his severe asceticism. He had no house of his own; when in Athens, he apparently camped out in a coffinlike stone monument—living, as he said, like a dog (the term *cynic* in Attic Greek means "doglike"). He took pleasure in shocking people by his lack of even the most basic proprieties; he ate, relieved himself, and made love in public. His uncouthness became proverbial. A later biographer recounted how, entering a magnificent house, Diogenes was warned by a companion against spitting indiscriminately. Clearing his throat, he spat in the man's face—"being unable," he said, "to find a meaner receptacle."

Diogenes appealed to the Athenian love of irreverent comedy, and at the same time he echoed the pervasive fatalistic tone of much of fourth-century thought, a tone which was not limited to philosophy.

The function of philosophy was changing: once devoted primarily to the abstract pursuit of truth and the good life, it was to become in the Hellenistic era a stopgap remedy for human wretchedness and despair. "Just as there is no profit in medicine if it does not expel the diseases of the body," Epicurus wrote, "so there is no profit in philosophy either, if it does not expel the suffering of the mind."

Chapter 6

# THE FOURTH CENTURY AND THE HELLENISTIC WORLD

## THE LEGACY OF THE PELOPONNESIAN WAR

The history of the fourth century often tends to be dominated by Alexander the Great's conquest of Persia. His achievements were a natural corollary of developments, economic and military, in Greece during the fifth and fourth centuries. What was spectacular was not that he defeated Persia, but the manner in which he did it, his subsequent additions to the Achaemenid empire and his attempt at organizing the unwieldy and heterogenous empire he had won.

If there was any swing from democracy to oligarchy or vice versa in fifth-century Greece, it had usually been effected by force and there was no more sign of "national unity," an end to inter-city rivalry, than there had previously been since the shaky and limited "pan-Hellenism" of 480–79. In the early-fourth century Sparta conducted a campaign in Ionia against Persia but was soon required to devote its attention to the more immediate and threatening problem of an alliance in Greece against Sparta. This alliance included not only Athens, but Sparta's ancient ally, Corinth. During the Peloponnesian War, 431–404, Athens and Sparta were the leading combatants at the head of their respective alliances.

The Peloponnesian War saw the commencement of a form of all-year-round campaigning. It also saw the emergence of the independent commander who chose his own troops and dealt with the problem of their pay himself. During the fourth century such commanders served their own and foreign states, becoming increasingly independent personally, often controlling a particular type of soldier. They were often wary of the home government. The professional mercenary soldier was rare in c.400. Dexippus, the Sicilian, was one of the few such, if not the only one, to join the expedition—immortalized in Xenophon's *Anabasis* ("The March Upcountry")—of Cyrus, younger son of Darius II, against his elder brother. Such men cast a long shadow forward, beyond the death of Alexander, to the heyday of the great mercenary commanders and their armies. This was but the small beginning.

Philip II of Macedon, Alexander's father, must have noted the military approach of the mercenary commanders and the type of forces they employed when he reorganized the Macedonian army.

The other legacy of the Peloponnesian War for the commercial states of mainland Greece, such as Athens and Corinth, was a diminished wealth. Economic

| 400 BC | 350 | 300 | 250 |
|---|---|---|---|
| Sparta defeats Athens (404)<br>Athens humbled but still independent | Philip of Macedon (359–336) subjugates Athens, unites Greek states except Sparta<br>Alexander the Great conquers Persia (336–323) | New Hellenistic kingdoms emerge: Pergamon, Macedonia, Syria (Seleucid), Egypt | Romans defeat Pyrrhus (275) |
| Plato (439–347) | | | |
| Aristotle (384–322) | | | |

Bronze relief possibly representing Alexander the Great on horseback. Many coins and statues representing Alexander exist, and there were in antiquity superb portraits. Alexander captured the imagination of the ancients, and of the medieval world, as no one else did. He was known in legend to the Celts and his memory survived in Afghanistan long after his death and the expulsion of Greek rulers from the eastern satrapies. He was regarded as the greatest military genius of all time, outshining Caesar, Hannibal and Scipio. His campaigns and tactics were studied by Napoleon.

problems grew as the century advanced, though in Ionia there was a "boom" period in the early-fourth century. The lack of wealth made the hiring of mercenaries, ever increasing in importance as the citizen militia took less interest in long campaigning, difficult. This poverty the Persians were not slow to exploit diplomatically. Persia's strength lay in her gold; by this means she could control the purse strings of any potential hirer of mercenaries and sow dissension between fellow Greeks to her own ends. States increasingly required mercenary troops, especially for the light-armed wing, far more than before because the citizen militia was ill-suited to long campaigns, particularly abroad.

The superiority of the Greek hoplite over his Persian counterpart had been demonstrated at Marathon, 490, and Plataea, 479, and was shown again at Cunaxa, 401. Moreover, in 396, a Greek cavalry force defeated Persian cavalry. Militarily Persia was vulnerable from that time on, when if ever the Greeks could find sufficient unity to launch a concerted attack without creating chaos at home in their rear.

## THE RISE OF MACEDONIA

The rise of Macedon under Philip II, son of Amyntas, was due to his skill as a diplomat, statesman, and general. He came to the throne in 359 at the age of twenty-two or twenty-three, as did his son, Alexander, and immediately set upon a course which was to lead to his election as hegemon of the League of Corinth, which he himself formed as a result of his victory at Chaeronea.

Not merely content with that, he developed tactical ideas and equipment, bringing to full effect the phalanx structure and an army with offensive and defensive wings.

By 346 Philip was in an imposing position. He was regarded by some as the leader of the anti-Persian crusade, by others as a despot to be defeated. Philip made

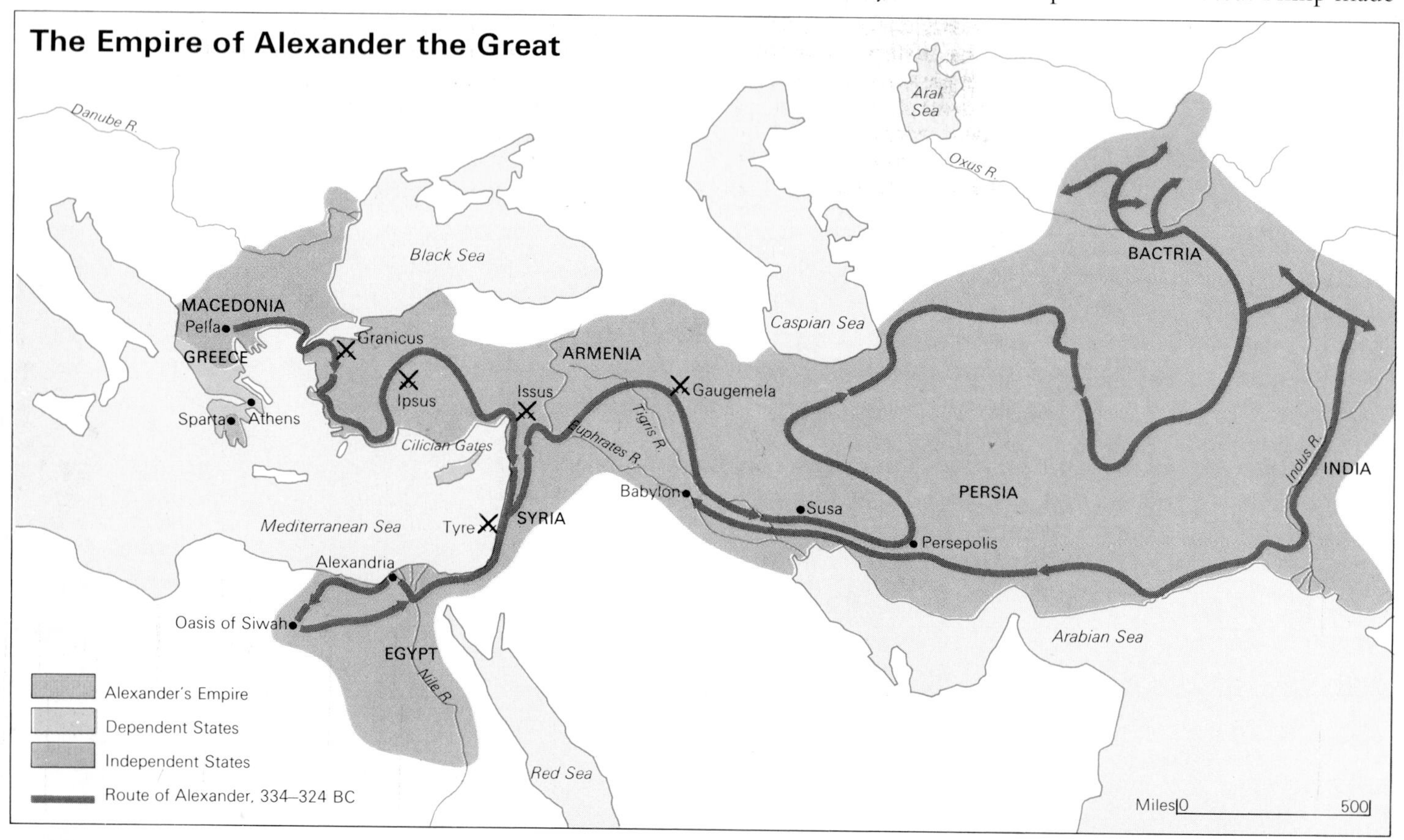

himself master of Greece by his victory at Chaeronea where he defeated Athens and Thebes, the only two mainland Greek states with large and effective citizen armies now left. Thereafter he began to plan for an invasion of the Persian Empire, but was assassinated in 336 before his plans were complete.

## ALEXANDER

Alexander developed his father's plan of limited conquest into one of total occupation of the Persian Empire. After destroying Thebes which must have impressed the Greeks as a warning, he set out in 334 and had broken Persian resistance by 331 in victories at the Granicus, 334; at Issus, 333; and at Gaugamela, or Arbela as it is sometimes known, in 331. He extended his dominion over the rest of the Persian Empire and beyond by hard fighting in Bactria, Sogdiana, and India until 325, when mutiny by his troops forced him to turn back.

Alexander was no blind pursuer of military glory. He did have concrete ideas about how to govern his empire, but whether his ideas would have proved a solution to the many problems he created is difficult to say. Despite his adoption of Persian dress and ceremonial and his marriage with an Iranian wife, he does not seem to have been very successful in placating the Persian nobility and he certainly deeply offended his Macedonians. They saw a very clear issue: they were the conquerors, the Persians the conquered. To see the conquered elevated to, or confirmed in, the satrapies; to have Persian wives foisted on them was more than they were prepared to accept. With a bad grace they had already accepted Alexander's divinity and the *proskynesis*, by which subjects were required to prostrate themselves before their king. Faced with this split over his "race relations" program and the threat of war looming in Greece, it is hard to know whether Alexander would have made his empire governable. The *diadochoi* (successors), such as Antipater, regent of Greece, Antigonus, satrap of Phrygia, Ptolemy, founder of the dynasty which ruled Egypt until 31 B.C., might have perished or have proved a very powerful influence on a man even of Alexander's stamp.

Coin of Alexander. One may see the ram's horn of Ammon behind the ear and faintly detect the *diadema* (royal headband) round the hair. Alexander's conquests released much gold onto the open market from the Persian treasury where it had been hoarded. This made the Greek world wealthy, but the wealth was far from evenly distributed. Alexander's coin types were adopted by his successors with few initial variations.

In the midst of whatever preparations and organization he had in mind, Alexander died in June 323, a military genius worn out by activity. His empire became the subject of dispute between his highly able generals.

## THE COLLAPSE OF ALEXANDER'S EMPIRE

Among these were, on the one hand, men such as Ptolemy, who carved out for himself a fief in Egypt and, on the other hand, men such as Antigonus I Monophthalmos (The One-eyed) who played for the higher stakes of the whole empire. From 323 to 301 Alexander's empire was split up between his generals in various combinations and alliances. If any had the intention of ever allowing his heir to rule, their goodwill was thwarted by the murder of the boy and his mother in 310 by Cassander who had made himself by this time ruler of Macedon. Meanwhile each sought some gain for himself. Many of Alexander's leading officers were killed in the ensuing struggles. The main activity came from Antigonus, who strove hard to reunite the empire under himself. He was opposed sometimes individually, sometimes in coalition, by Ptolemy from his Egyptian base; Cassander, in control of some of European Greece and Macedon; Lysimachus, in control of Thrace, the Hellespontine area, and some of Asia Minor; and Seleucus who was building up his power in the eastern satrapies of Alexander's empire. It is, however, impossible to draw firm boundary lines between rulers, as possession of territory fluctuated so often and so widely. Antigonus finally disclosed his intentions in 306 when he invited his army to hail himself and his son, Demetrius, by the royal title. This marked the formal end of Alexander's kingdom because, in the following year, all his major opponents assumed royal honors, very probably by mutual agreement, and banded together in face of the threat from Antigonus.

His first attempt to reunite the empire finally failed at the battle of Ipsus in 301. Here Antigonus died on the battlefield fighting against Lysimachus and Seleucus in a contest where tradition has it that 75,000 men fought on each side, the vast majority mercenaries who may well have seen service under several of the diadochoi before this engagement and might yet serve others.

However, Ipsus and the settlement did not resolve all hostilities, especially as Antigonus' son, Demetrius, was still alive, vigorous, and ambitious, and could always hope to find one supporter among his conquerors who would wish to discomfort another. Gradually this generation passed away with the kingdoms becoming more set in their boundaries, which at first had been very fluid. Cassander died in 298, Demetrius surrendered after an unsuccessful campaign in 285 and died a prisoner of Seleucus. Ptolemy died peacefully in 283 and his kingdom went without dispute to his son Ptolemy II Philadelphos. The last act was war between Lysimachus and Seleucus.

Lysimachus had not won popularity, especially with his Greek subjects, and in 282 Seleucus, prompted by refugees from Lysimachus, invaded his territory and was warmly welcomed. At the battle of Corypedium, 281, he decisively defeated Lysimachus, who perished on the battlefield, and went on to claim the crown of Macedon. However, before he could enjoy the fruits of victory he was stabbed.

We may possibly regard the "final date" by which the Hellenistic kingdoms received some form of set boundary as 275. In this year Antiochus I defeated invading Galatians in Asia Minor, and the son of Demetrius, Antigonus II Gonatas, established control over Macedon. His dynasty lasted until 168. However, he did not control all Greece. The city-states fell under various masters and enjoyed periods of autonomy as the dynasts warred and sought their friendship. "Freedom for the Greeks" had been coined as a watchword by Sparta in 431 and it remained a popular propaganda line during the next two centuries. The three main divisions of Alexander's empire which emerged were Macedon, Thessaly, and portions of Greece under the Antigonids; most of Asia Minor, northern Syria and the eastern provinces under the Seleucids, and Egypt and southern Syria and Phoenicia, referred to by the Greeks as Coele-Syria, under the Ptolemies. However, in time smaller kingdoms were created or carved out of the larger ones, most often at the expense of the Seleucids, the most famous being Pergamum ruled by the Attalids. Also, in Greece, two federations appeared. They were the Aetolian League in central and western Greece, north of the gulf of Corinth, and the Achaean League whose members were drawn from the city-states of the Peloponnese, though membership was rarely continuous.

The chief rivalries during the third century B.C. were between the Seleucids and Ptolemies over possession of Coele-Syria and between the Antigonids and Ptolemies over the control of the islands in the Aegean and the city-states of Greece. The Ptolemies started with the advantage of the richest kingdom, but the Antigonids had control of the finest manpower. All three dynasties used marriage alliance to try to cement claims or friendship, but on the whole there seems to have been more lasting accord between the Antigonids and Seleucids than between any other combination. The Ptolemies were the least adventurous militarily with the rare exception of Ptolemy II and a flurry of activity by his son in the Third Syrian War. The most continuously hard-pressed were the Seleucids who had the largest area to control and more opponents with whom to contend. They had to deal not merely with the Ptolemies in Syria, but with rivals and rebels in their eastern provinces, which they never held securely from c. 250 onwards, although Antiochus

III, 223–187, made a strong bid to reestablish Seleucid control. Between 279 and 200 there were no less than five "Syrian Wars" giving final control of Coele-Syria to Antiochus III after the battle of Panion in 200. However, by the time this victory was won, Rome was beginning to show a marked interest in the affairs of the Greek Mediterranean powers. This interest was to lead to war with the Antigonids, to the extinction of their line, and war with Antiochus III, which left Syria weak and, under careful Roman scrutiny, only capable of growing weaker. The once great empire of Seleucus I became a small, vulnerable area riven with civil war.

Though doubtless Pyrrhus had more than aroused her curiosity, Rome's formal interest in the Hellenistic kingdoms is first recorded in the form of an embassy to Alexandria in 273. Later, towards the end of the third century B.C. Egypt needed strong friends and Rome may have been the answer to her problems. Certainly Rome crushed her enemy Antiochus III at the battle of Magnesia in 190 and later humiliated his son or nephew, Antiochus IV, who had had the temerity to invade Egypt.

Alexander and the talking tree, which is foretelling his death. An illustration from the Duseley Manuscript in the Bodleian Library, Oxford.

Whatever the motives that first directed Rome's eyes eastward, a policy of deliberate intervention seems to have followed the alliance between Hannibal and Philip V of Macedon in 215. Thereafter, in a series of wars between 211 and 146, Rome reduced Macedon and Greece to the status of provinces, extinguished the Macedonian monarchy and dissolved the Achaean and Aetolian Leagues, both of which had been her allies at various times. With similar vigor she ensured that Seleucid Syria, despite Antiochus IV's solid attempt, would never be powerful enough to be a threat to her. The Seleucid royal line was allowed to linger on, but it produced no more men of the stamp to worry Rome. Egypt, under Rome's special favor and protection, seems to have eschewed intervention of her own after the reign of Ptolemy VI and VII.

The Hellenistic monarchies may have been no match for Roman arms and no equal to her vigor, but they did pass on to her something of their own developed culture and civilization amidst the debris. The Hellenized East, certainly for the first century of the Roman Empire, was the more secure and peaceful area and was more amenable to the necessities of empire such as emperor-worship, to which it was already accustomed. The literary legacy that Rome imitated or adopted was as much that of Alexandria and Menander as that of the great tragedians, if not more so. Roman portrait sculpture owed more to Hellenistic realism than to classical idealism, though it did, of course, have its strong native roots. The sons may not have been as great as the fathers, but they preserved and extended the Greek heritage over a wide area and it would be unfair to ascribe their decline and downfall to cultural decay.

## THE ORGANIZATION OF THE HELLENISTIC KINGDOMS

From the little that we know about Macedon it would appear that she enjoyed the least complicated governmental structure. Finances needed only a simple system and the rulers avoided flamboyance in their court ceremonial. The kings maintained the traditional partnership between themselves and the people and did not introduce a ruler cult. To control their Greek possessions they employed garrisons in key places such as Demetrias, Chalcis, and the Acrocorinth, but they tried to limit this method of control. By and large the Antigonids were tolerant and civilized.

The Seleucids by contrast had the largest area to govern and the most numerous threats to their power. Their control of their eastern satrapies was always tenuous and depended more on diplomacy than force of arms. They were prepared to recognize "vassals" in return for occasional military aid and even more occasional tribute. However, they were true to Alexander's policy in colonization, founding many cities in Syria and the nearer eastern satrapies. In several ways they anticipated the Roman administration of empire, or possibly Roman emperors consciously followed their example. Finance was taken away from the satraps, or *strategoi* as they now were, and regulated by the monarchs. In an effort to decentralize they made generous grants of autonomy to the cities.

With the exception of Antiochus IV, the Seleucids practiced religious toleration though they did impose set limits on the financial and even judicial rights which the Persians had allowed to some temple bodies. While at first she produced rulers of ability, the Seleucid Empire endured more civil wars and disputes than any of the others and this, plus Roman intervention, contributed as much to her decline as the loss of the eastern territories and the almost constant wars with Egypt in the third century.

The Ptolemies, like Alexander, were welcome successors to the Persians and inherited the old system of government dating back to the Pharaohs, but by then much run down because of Persian neglect. Ptolemy II was largely responsible for tightening up the system and producing a bureaucracy which became as self-perpetuating and hydra-like as that of the Chinese Empire. However, within the carefully, even rigidly, regulated system, the Ptolemies did look after the essential features: agriculture, the Nile, and revenue—the last with an almost Scrooge-like rapacity. The economy was directed through a ministry headed by an official entitled the *dioicetes*. Another official, the *architecton*, controlled the Nile and irrigation. The traditional division of the country into *nomes* (provinces) was accepted, but the peasants even had their crops regulated, though new stock and industries were introduced. Even in decline the wealth of Egypt tempted Caesar, Crassus, and Pompey to try to gain an Egyptian command in the middle of the first century B.C. As far as land went the system was simple: Ptolemy owned everything

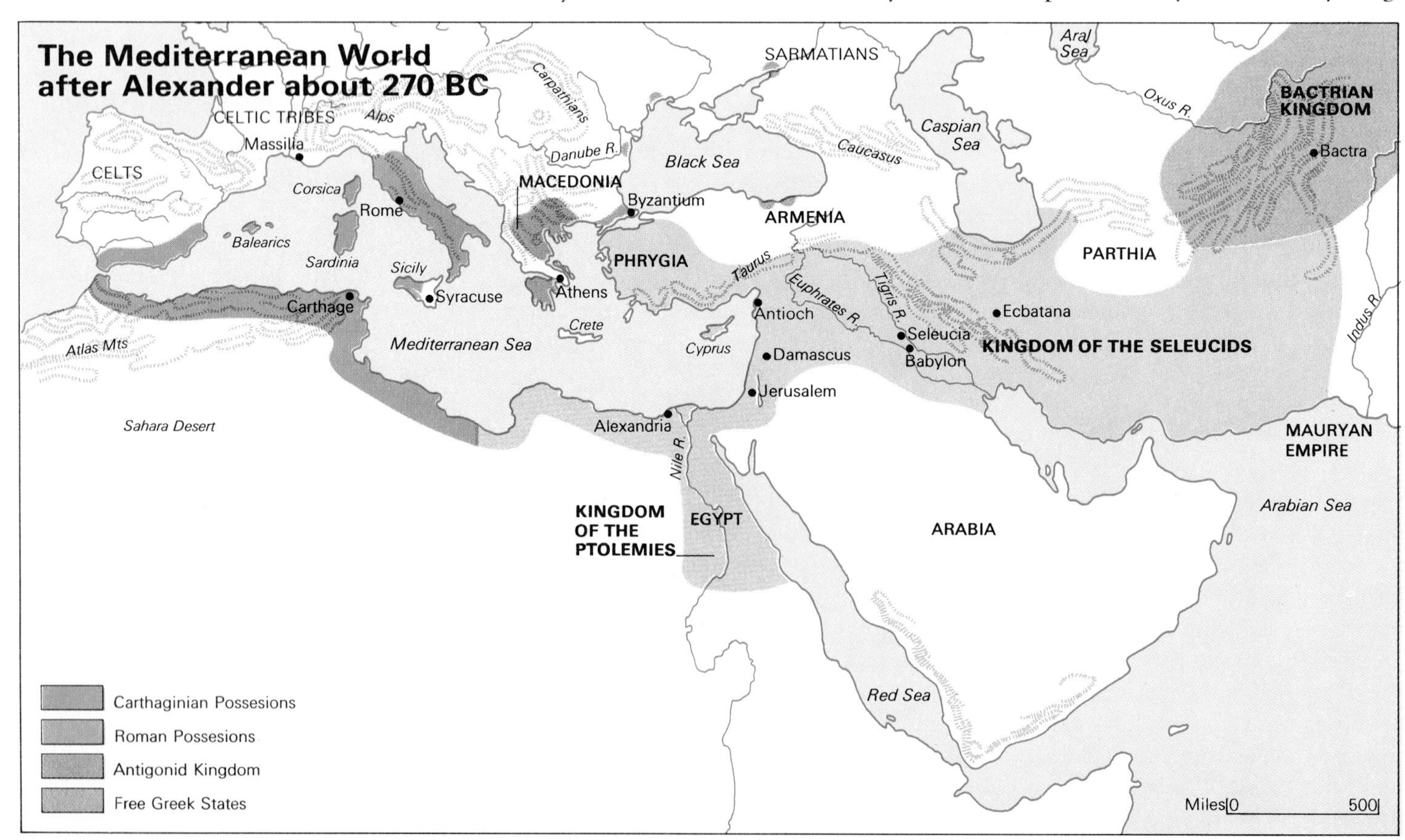

except that which he chose to award elsewhere. His revenues, direct and indirect, were carefully collected on a double-checking system. Egypt also had the population most amenable to its rulers and Alexandria became the showplace of the ancient world. To the Ptolemies their wealth was their power at home and abroad. There were periods of population disturbance, but they managed to surmount their difficulties and the system survived to be taken over by the Romans virtually *in toto*.

Though both the Ptolemies and Seleucids instituted ruler cults, this was by no means as offensive to their subjects, including the Greeks, as might be thought. The Egyptians, from time immemorial, had honored their Pharaoh as a god incarnate. If the god now spoke Greek, he was still Pharaoh. The Greeks too were accustomed to the idea of granting semi-divine honors to founders of colonies. True, Alexander and his successors went further than this, but they did not claim to be Zeus incarnate to their subjects. They were men, only more so. Thus two of the most popular *cognomina* of the kings became standard Greek terms for honoring a benefactor or ruler, those of *theos*, god, and *soter*, savior; so Julius Caesar is addressed on inscriptions raised by the Greeks. Perhaps they did convey more to the oriental mind, but to the Greek they were little more than epithets of gross flattery in origin.

In other respects the Seleucid and Ptolemaic courts remembered their Macedonian origins and eschewed an overindulgence in oriental ceremony. The Ptolemies remained solidly Macedonian in marriage and stock, as to a large degree, after Seleucus I, did the Seleucids. Both introduced ranks of honor at court, but both probably felt that distinctions had value. The lot of the common man may not have been easy, but at least these administrations brought some form of regularity and protection to it. Above all both disseminated and promoted the Greek heritage.

Hermaphroditus, son of Hermes and Aphrodite, who inherited the beauty of both parents. A Hellenistic legend, with an oriental origin, tells how, while he bathed in a fountain at Salmacis, a nymph prayed to the gods for perpetual union with him. The gods granted her request, but Hermaphroditus retained the characteristics of both sexes.

## LITERATURE, PHILOSOPHY, AND ART

All the Hellenistic rulers took an interest in the promotion of Greek culture in all its forms. The showpiece was the museum at Alexandria with its huge library, but Athens, Pergamum, Antioch and even Pella, the Macedonian capital, boasted their own libraries. At Athens the philosophical schools had flowered. Even if the doctrines were refined elsewhere, many were still drawn there to learn from the great masters. The new comedy of Menander and Philemon developed there and it was this style, the comedy of manners, which Plautus and Terence adopted as models at Rome.

Literary criticism, which had its foundations in Aristotle's *Poetics*, was refined by the Alexandrians and provoked an acrimonious argument between Callimachus and his pupil, Apollonius Rhodius, over the relative merits of the short, highly polished poem and the long, traditional epic form. "Mega biblion, mega kakon" (a great book is a great evil), remarked the poet Callimachus sourly. Apollonius, however, rose to be the director of the great library, and Callimachus produced his share of longer poems.

Much writing was produced on geography and history as well as poetical themes. It was an age of diaries and memoirs too. Ptolemy published his account of Alexander's campaigns. Later in Greece, Aratus of Sicyon, the founder of the Achaean League, wrote his memoirs. Authors were attracted to Alexandria by the largesse offered, but other courts competed for their favors. Callimachus is perhaps most typical of the Hellenistic poets and had as great an influence on Horace as the early lyricists. Theocritus too, the pastoral poet, was drawn to Alexandria to hymn Ptolemy II.

This was also the age for philosophy and the philosopher, but the philosopher might be a scientist, poet, mathematician or astronomer as well. The Hellenistic intellectual, like his classical forerunner, observed no petty restriction to one "field" and applied himself where he chose. However, as belief and interest in the old

Olympian deities waned, men turned to the new philosophical doctrines and their offshoots to satisfy their wants or their desire for some analysis of a "role in society." Many of these new doctrines had their origins in the teaching of Plato and Aristotle and were developments or refinements of them, but Stoic, Epicurean, Cynic, even the Cyreniac tried to justify the ways of man to man. Especially in the period 323–c. 270 men found themselves in a changed and changing world. The philosophers endeavored to bring man some appreciation of his existence. Zeno, Epicurus, Stilpon, and Pyrrhon were all active during this time and their influence on thought should not be underestimated. As the Hellenistic kingdoms became settled and organized so the schools crystallized and men began, as ever, to argue about the purity of the "party line" instead of the realities of existence and perception. Through many, under different names or phrases, ran the desire for what the Epicureans called *ataraxia* (freedom from disturbance), a tranquillity of mind. This object became coveted once more in the long civil wars at the end of the Roman Republic. The various doctrines lent themselves to eclecticism and syncretism, but their effects have been lasting. The *diatribai* of the cynics were subsumed into the Christian sermon. Aristotle's ethics made clear the way for men to see that morality is relative, that a man can act both above and below himself without being evil or good to the core. The Pyrrhonist distrust of the senses, developed from the cynics, remains a current point of philosophical argument under the heading of phenomenalism.

Hermes with the infant Dionysos, by the fourth-century Athenian sculptor Praxiteles. Hermes, a very popular deity, had many forms: messenger of the gods, conductor of souls to Hades and patron god of thieves and travellers. Here he is shown as a beardless, athletic youth: in archaic Greek art he is represented as a bearded man wearing a long chiton (tunic). This statue was probably painted by the artist, Nicias, whose work Praxiteles much admired.

In art the sublimity of the fifth century gradually mellowed through the influence of Praxiteles' and Lysippus' more human touch to a realistic expression of human emotions, as seen in the statue of the dying gladiator or the dying Gaul. The representation of the war between the gods and the giants, depicted on the frieze at Pergamum, perhaps echoes a little the monumental works of Pheidias, but here a common Hellenistic failing, overcrowding, may be discerned. Nevertheless, the sculpture has a powerful effect.

In architecture all three classical orders (Doric, Ionic, and Corinthian) were used side by side for the many buildings, but most important of all was the development of town planning. Both Alexandria and Pergamum are excellent examples of the rectangular road pattern and careful siting and laying out developed by Hippodamus and used by Alexander.

The transformation of the Greek world from a relatively small area to almost the whole coast of the Mediterranean and much of the hinterland, not to mention the vast reaches of Asia, did not dissipate the Greek genius. It further stimulated the natural investigative talent of a race already steeped in intellectual curiosity. True, the genius finds expression in different literary forms, but then no pale imitation of Homer, Pindar, or the great tragedians would have done justice to the originality of the Hellenistic mind. Their statuary and art may not appeal to the purist, their architecture may have a baroque character, but they epitomize their own civilization and culture. It was the Hellenistic Greeks who "civilized" the Romans, by adding something, however slight, to that dull, practical mind. So Horace could write:

> *Graecia capta ferum victorem cepit et artis*
> *intulit agresti Latio.*

(Captive Greece took prisoner her wild conqueror and instilled her arts into uncultured Latium.)

If the Hellenistic age had achieved that much as its sole legacy, it was a great deal. The cultural debt, and as has been noticed, possibly the administrative debt, that Rome owed to Greece was largely due to the natural vigor of the Greeks who preserved and enhanced the Greek tradition.

Chapter 7

# SCIENCE IN THE AGE OF GREECE AND ROME

This chapter covers the scientific achievement of Greece and of Rome. Greek mathematical achievement was the basis of developments in other fields. Hence the emphasis on mathematics in the next few pages. Whether or not the reader understands the mathematical formulas quoted in the first part of the chapter is unimportant. These formulas are included primarily in order to illustrate the extent and the significance of the Greek contribution to modern science. In this context it is felt they will be of interest even to the lay reader.

## GREEK AND HELLENISTIC MATHEMATICS

To the modern mathematician, looking back on the record of the mathematicians of Athens and Alexandria during the 800 years from Pythagoras to Diophantus, it is amazing to discover how much they achieved. Most modern arithmetic and geometry, and a substantial amount of algebra and trigonometry, was discovered or elaborated during this golden period. Indeed it is difficult to convey briefly a sense of the importance of this contribution to modern civilization, in which mathematical ideas play so dominant a role. One can only dip into each subject in turn and pick out a few outstanding gems.

The great Greek contribution to arithmetic was the discovery that there were "irrational" numbers—numbers which could not be represented as the ratio of two integers (or whole numbers). Characteristically, they made the discovery by way of geometry: as Pythagoras had shown, if the side of a square measured one unit, its diagonal measured the square root of two units, $\sqrt{2}$, and for all their ingenuity they were unable to represent $\sqrt{2}$ as a rational number. A similar difficulty was encountered with $\sqrt{3}$, $\sqrt{5}$, $\sqrt{6}$, $\sqrt{7}$, $\sqrt{8}$, $\sqrt{10}$, etc. and eventually a systematic proof was given by the Athenian Eudoxus (in the fourth century B.C.) that the task was in principle impossible.

Equally apparently irrational, and even more tormenting to the Greeks, was the number $\pi$, the ratio of the circumference to the diameter of a circle. The existence of this number was proved by Hippocrates (an Athenian of the mid-fifth century B.C.), who showed geometrically that the area of a circle was proportional to the area of the square based on its diameter, the constant of proportionality being $\frac{\pi}{4}$. An approximate value for $\pi$ could easily be obtained "experimentally" by measuring circles (and indeed had been by the practical-minded Egyptians). The Greeks despised so pragmatic an approach and brought the full force of their logical skill to bear on the problem. Archimedes, by purely geometric arguments, showed that $\pi$ lay within the limits

$$3\tfrac{1}{7} > \pi > 3\tfrac{10}{71}$$

Pythagoras' theorem from a mid-thirteenth-century manuscript. The manuscript is an English translation by Adelard of Bath. Pythagoras was born in the sixth century B.C. on the island of Samos, but later went to Croton in southern Italy. While he is now chiefly remembered for his work in geometry, he also founded a religious school with a belief in the reincarnation or transmigration of souls, known as metempsychosis. Pythagoras himself is said to have claimed to have fought at Troy in a previous incarnation. He had strong influence on Empedocles and Heraclitus.

However, by contrast with $\sqrt{2}$, they never succeeded in *proving* that $\pi$ was irrational in the full sense and this had to await the discovery of logarithms in the sixteenth century.

Academic though their arithmetical puzzles may appear, in fact they were of enormous importance for the future of mathematics. In the first place, they marked the breakaway of mathematics from studies which were of immediate practical significance, and this liberation coincided with the explosive growth of the subject. Secondly, they paved the way for a new conception of number. Hitherto, numbers had been intimately connected with counting (hence, if one had to have fractions, the importance of "rational" fractions): now it was realized that there were uncountably many numbers between any two numbers and the way was clear for "infinitesimal" calculus. However, before that crucially important branch of modern mathematics could be born, developments in algebra were required, and here the Greeks were less successful.

Picture of Archimedes' screw. Archimedes, a third-century mathematician, engineer and inventor, was born at Syracuse in Sicily. He is best known perhaps for his discovery of the principle of the displacement of water. However, he numbered among his inventions this device for raising water from a low level to a higher level.

Strange though it may seem to us, in a world where the phrase, "let x be the unknown quantity," becomes familiar at an early age, the principle barrier to the development of algebra in the classical world was the lack of an adequate notation—for example the ability to write "equations" such as $250\,x^2 - 5 = 0$. This deficiency itself stemmed from the inadequacy of their arithmetic notation, in which letters of the alphabet were used to represent numbers ($\alpha$, $\beta$, $\gamma$, for 1, 2, 3). Thus it was an outstanding triumph that the Alexandrian Diophantus (c. A.D. 300) succeeded nevertheless in devising a means of representing algebraic ideas. For example, the quantity which we write as $250\,x^2$, he represented as $\Delta\Upsilon\sigma\nu$: here the leter $\nu$ meant 50 and $\sigma$ 200 according to the ordinary Greek practice. The new idea lay in $\Delta\Upsilon$, short for the Greek work meaning "power", which symbolized "the square of the unknown number." Using such methods he found the solution of the general quadratic equation $ax^2 + bx + c = 0$. His work highlighted the unsatisfactoriness of the Greek arithmetic notation, and it is perhaps no accident that the modern decimal notation (250 instead of $\sigma\nu$) can be traced to a source in southern India shortly after the time of Diophantus.

If algebra was the weakest point in Greek mathematics, geometry was outstandingly its strongest. This was partly due to the influence of Pythagoras, and partly to the demand for new geometrical techniques created by Greek astronomy. Two stages can be distinguished in the Greek geometrical development. During the fourth and fifth centuries B.C., in which the Greek school of geometry flourished (including men such as Anaxagoras, Hippocrates, Menaechmus, Democritus, Plato, and Eudoxus), the emphasis was mainly on the borderline territory between geometry and arithmetic—such as the problems connected with $\sqrt{2}$ and $\pi$.

During the third century B.C., the era of the great expansion of Greek culture, Alexandria came to replace Athens as the focal point of classical mathematics. Here the influence of the systematic Greek philosophers and geometers dominated mathematical thinking. A branch of mathematics such as geometry now became a challenge to the systematizer. Given the innumerable snippets of geometrical insight gained in an earlier and more religious century, how could one now build these into one vast self-consistent edifice, resting on secure foundations and constructed by logically impeccable deductions? It was the achievement of Euclid to do this for geometry, and to do it so well that his *Elements* remained the basic textbook until the Renaissance and beyond. He began with careful definitions of things such as points and lines. Then he laid down his common assumptions or axioms, and then his postulates, before proceeding with the orderly arrangement of their consequences. The strength of his approach lay in the small number, and the apparently self-evident truth, of his postulates. Only one was widely attacked by his contemporaries, the so-called "parallel postulate"—"if a straight line meets two straight lines so as to make the two interior angles on the same side of it taken together less than two right angles, these two lines, being continually produced, shall at length meet. . . ." His critics were convinced that this postulate was unnecessary, and could be proved from other, and more obvious postulates, and hundreds of plausible but in fact erroneous proofs were constructed. Only in the nineteenth century was Euclid vindicated, with the discovery by Riemann and others of new non-Euclidean geometries for which this postulate alone is invalid.

One of Euclid's successors and probably one of his pupils, was Archimedes. Not surprisingly, in view of the practical achievements for which he is chiefly known, his mathematics was strongly practically motivated. He systematized what might almost be described as the "integral calculus"—the calculation of the areas, volumes, and centers of gravity of curves and surfaces, circles, spheres, conics, and spirals by summing small rectangles or discs. In doing so he devised some of the earliest algebraic and trigonometric formulae—for example (in modern notation)

$$\sum_{i=1}^{n} i^2 = \frac{n(n+1)(2n+1)}{6} \text{ and } \sum_{i=1}^{n-1} \sin(i\pi/2n) = \cot(\pi/4n).$$

The third great mathematician of this school, Apollonius of Perga in Pamphilia (c. 262–200 B.C.), was the founder of what is now called analytical geometry—the theory of conic sections, ellipses, and hyperbolae. From our own theory he could learn little except the notation. His other main contribution—the development of trigonometry, and its application to astronomy—is considered below.

With the death of Apollonius, the great era of Greek mathematics came to an end. From the time of Thales there had been an almost continuous chain of outstanding mathematicians. But until about A.D. 250, there seems to have been no mathematician of preeminence. During this interval of about half a millenium the pressure of Roman culture effectively discouraged Greek mathematics. The resurgence, when it came, was short-lived. The most important contribution, that of Diophantus, has already been mentioned. Those of Hero and Pappus were some less striking extensions of the earlier Hellenistic geometry. After the death of Pappus, Greek, and indeed European, mathematics lay dormant for about a thousand years.

Portrait of Archimedes. He produced many works on mathematical themes, some of which have been discovered comparatively recently. All his works are marked as the products of an outstanding mind, and he must rank as one of the ablest mathematicians the world has ever seen, considering the deficiencies of Greek mathematical knowledge. Among his many other investigations, he carried out work on square roots of large numbers. Archimedes died in 212.

## GREEK AND HELLENISTIC ASTRONOMY

There is a striking contrast between the mathematics and the astronomy of the Greeks. In mathematics they had a golden touch—even their failures, which were few, were interesting and important failures. In astronomy, for all their enthusiasm and imaginative spirit, they failed again and again—examining and rejecting the views which now prevail, and accepting instead a web of fantasy which was no less fantastic because it was founded on the best of Greek mathematics. To understand this failure it is necessary to appreciate the sources on which Greek astronomy drew, and the philosophical climate of opinion in which it was nurtured.

It has already been shown that the Greeks were not the first to take astronomy seriously—the Egyptian and Babylonian civilizations had attached crucial importance to the observation and predictions of the motions of the sun, moon, and planets against the backcloth of the fixed starry firmament, because of their astrological beliefs. They gathered and tabulated vast quantities of numerical data and sought (and found) systematic trends in the numbers which they wrote down. The Greeks continued this practice of observing the heavens but with different motives. For them the Babylonian numerical predictions were unsatisfying: they wanted a more fundamental understanding, and they sought this by attempting to reduce astronomy to geometry. Unfortunately they chose the wrong geometry, and their astronomy was fatally handicapped by its commitment to circles and spheres.

The evolution of Greek astronomical thought passed through several stages. In the earliest, Ionian period (sixth century B.C.), the primary concern of such speculative thinkers as Thales and Anaximander was the nature of the universe. What was it made of? Their answers were couched in essentially materialistic terms—Anaximander for example thought that the sun and moon were "hollow chariot-wheels full of fire, each with an opening like the nozzle of a pair of bellows." For all their crudity, such models of the universe prompted questions that the Babylonians had never asked—for example, how large were the wheels and the openings? Anaximander, who was a gifted geometer and a maker of scientific instruments, concluded that the sun's wheel was twenty-seven earth radii and the moon's eighteen.

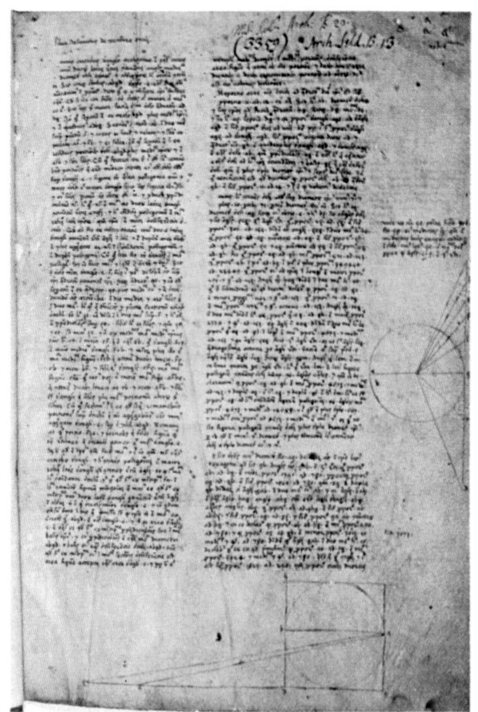

Archimedes' measurement of the circle, from a late-thirteenth-century English manuscript. Archimedes tried to measure the circle by using regular polygons with ninety-six sides. In the course of this investigation he came close to discovering the value of Pi.

It is tempting to speculate how Greek astronomy might have developed if it had not at this point become dominated by the personality of Pythagoras. He was the outstanding mathematician of his age, and his particular mathematical interest—the relationship of numbers and geometry—became an obsession which permeated all his other thinking. As Aristotle summed it up, "The Pythagoreans first applied themselves to mathematics, a science which they improved, and then, permeated with it, they fancied that the principles of mathematics were the principles of all things." "Heaven is harmony and number" they said, "all things exist by imitation of numbers." They transferred the numerical properties of the musical scale to the radii of the spheres on which the planets in their courses moved (in perfect circles, of course), and coined the phrase "the harmony of the spheres." They formed a brotherhood bound by a vow of secrecy, of which the symbol was the pentangle reminiscent of the five perfect ("Pythagorean") geometrical-solids that they discovered. It is not easy to recapture now the mystical, even religious frame of mind to which all this appealed: undoubtedly, however, it became a part of the mainstream of Greek thought, and many Pythagorean ideas were incorporated in the teachings of Plato and Aristotle, which mark the next stage in the evolution of astronomy.

Plato's *Timaeus* describes what became the canonical Greek view of the universe. The spherical earth is at rest in the middle of the cosmos. Surrounding it, like the skins of an onion, are a succession of transparent spheres which carry the moon, the planets, the sun, and finally the "fixed stars." All the spheres have a common daily rotation about the axis of the universe. In addition the planets have a "proper motion" along oblique circles lying on their spheres. Each sphere has a siren emitting one note and the eight sounds form one harmony. The trouble with this aesthetically pleasing (and basically Pythagorean) scheme was that it had to be admitted (though Plato was extremely reluctant to do so) that it was difficult to reconcile with the way in which the planets were actually observed to move. This difficulty became a major source of contention among the Greek astronomers. At one extreme was the view of the philosopher Zeno, that one should never sacrifice an elegant conceptual scheme simply because the "appearances" were against it. At the opposite extreme was the view of Aristotle and his successors—that if one undertook to explain the motion of the planets, one should do it thoroughly, by proposing a mechanical model which not only reproduced their observed motions, but also made mechanical sense. Plato appears to have adopted a compromise position—that although the inherent elegance and simplicity of the explanation was of primary importance, one should attempt to "save the appearances." Accordingly he recorded with evident pleasure near the end of his life that Eudoxus had succeeded (as he thought) in "saving the appearances" of the planetary motions by introducing some additional spheres which rolled (so to speak) on the crystal spheres, carrying the planets along in an "epicyclic" motion.

As the accuracy of observations increased, it became increasingly obvious that even Plato's modest task of "saving the appearances" was a major undertaking. This stage coincided with the great development of analytical geometry at the hands of Apollonius and he was the first of the three great Hellenistic astronomers to face this task. The immediate need was to revise the model of Eudoxus which, despite all Plato's enthusiasm, did not in fact save even those appearances which were known in his day. Eudoxus used a system of twenty-seven spheres (three each for the sun and moon and four each for the planets). Apollonius abstracted from this model the circles in space on which the centers of the various spheres moved, and built up his model from combinations of moving circles. There was first the "epicycle"—the circular orbit on which the planet itself moved; secondly the "deferrent"—a circle round which the center of the "epicycle" moved; and thirdly the "excentric"—a circle round which the center of the "deferrent" moved. While Eudoxus had contented himself with reproducing the qualitative characteristics of the planetary motions, Appolonius tried to fit the quantitative data, developing the necessary trigonometric techniques for the calculation of the radii of the various circles. He was only partially successful. It is tantalizing, in retrospect, that the man to whom we owe much of our knowledge of the properties of the ellipse, devoted so much of his life to the calculation of epicycles, and never realized that the secret which Kepler was to reveal 1800 years later—that the orbits of the planets really were ellipses—lay within his grasp. Apollonius' program was taken up 300 years later by the great Alexandrian observer-mathematician Hipparchus, who completed the task of "saving the appearances" of the sun and moon in this way. It was left to Ptolemy to finish the task—far more complex, as it turned out—of "saving" the remaining planets. The last few recalcitrant planets took no less than five circles apiece, making a grand total of forty circles to represent the cosmos. At least the new scheme worked: Ptolemy's Tables for calculating the motions of the planets were so reliable that they served, with some insignificant corrections, as navigational guides to Columbus and Vasco de Gama. Hipparchus' estimate of the distance of the moon ($30\frac{1}{4}$ earth diameters) has an error of 0.3 percent. But Aristotle's demand for a physically reliable model had become hopelessly lost, as Ptolemy himself admitted with regret. And few would disagree with the judgement of Alphonso the Wise, "If the Lord Almighty had consulted me before embarking upon The Creation, I should have recommended something simpler."

Bust of Hippocrates the father of medicine. Hippocrates was born on the island of Cos in 469 and died in 399, the same year as Socrates. In one sense he was the founder of scientific medicine, but it is unlikely that any of the works attributed to him are authentic. The great historian Thucydides, also a contemporary, was fascinated by medicine, as one may read in his description of the plague at Athens in 430. Perhaps it was the rigorous, investigative and rational approach that made Hippocrates famous and which Thucydides admired and followed.

Although this great system of spheres and epicycles, with the earth firmly at rest at the center, represented Greek orthodoxy, there were dissenting voices. One of Pythagoras' disciples (Philolaus or possibly Hicetas) allowed the earth to move in a circle, and Ecphantus and Heraclides claimed that it rotated about its own axis as well. In 280 B.C. Aristarchus of Samos completed the modern scheme, putting the sun at rest at the common center of the planetary circles. Alas for the historian of science, the only other Greek astronomer to accept this scheme seems to have been Seleucus. All the others rejected it, for reasons clearly stated by Aristotle and Ptolemy—the circular motion of the earth could not be reconciled with Aristotle's theory of "natural" motion: earth particles moved in straight lines!

Thus Greek civilization, in its decline, bequeathed an astronomical legacy which was the last thing that one might have expected—a system which was in excellent agreement with the experimental facts but was totally ill-conceived conceptually and was bolstered up by a web of plausible but fallacious arguments. The responsibility for this state of affairs lies at the door of the Greek physics, and to this we now turn.

## GREEK PHYSICS

If the Greek astronomers devoted too much of their time to "saving the appearances" of the world around them, their physicists did not spend nearly enough, partly because of lack of financial support, partly because of distrust of manual work. A typical example of their approach to physics was their theory of matter. By the time of Aristotle, the Greeks had reached a measure of consensus in favor of the unfruitful "four elements" theory of matter—that it was composed of earth, fire, air, and water in varying proportions. The sequence of ideas which led to this consensus is strange indeed. The early Ionian philosopher-mathematicians sought to find some unity underlying the diversity of experience: for Thales everything was water; for Anaximens, air; for Heraclitus, fire. By contrast the Pythagoreans, naturally, composed matter of "integral monads," which conformed to the laws of number and floated in the void. It was perhaps an attempt to reconcile these two conceptions that gave birth to the early atomic theories of Leucippus and Democritus. It is difficult to be certain, since our knowledge of their views comes from the works of later writers, such as the unsympathetic Aristotle. The key feature of their theory was that it provided a way of thinking about matter and its qualities as a whole: as Democritus put it, "According to convention there is a sweet and bitter, a hot and a cold, and according to convention there is color. In truth there are atoms and a void." The atoms of Democritus were without creator: they had existed from eternity and could never be split or annihilated; they were of many sizes and shapes but of one substance. The differences in the properties of material things were due to differences in the size, shape, position, and motion of the component atoms: in stone or iron the atoms could only throb or oscillate, in air or fire they rebounded at greater distances. This theory was 2,000 years before its time and, in spite of a spirited defense in later years by Epicurus and Lucretius, it was doomed under the onslaught of the Athenian establishment, especially Plato and Aristotle, who in essence resorted to the crude Ionian conception, but adopting four elements where the Ionians had taken one.

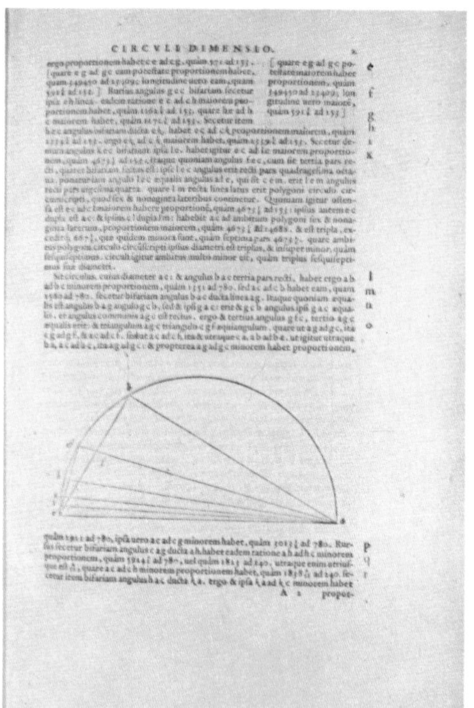
CIRCVLI DIMENSIO.

An illustration of Archimedes' work on the *Dimensions of the Circle*, from an edition of his works published in 1558.

It is impossible to summarize Aristotelian physics adequately within the present scope. Among the key elements in his philosophy were the ideas of "causes" and "motion." He distinguished "efficient causes" (the kind which we now regard as causing things to happen) from "final causes" (roughly, the end or goal towards which things strive). These final causes were ordained by the natural order, which he likened to the social order. In this world everything knew its place and, for the most part, kept to it. Natural motion occurred only when something was out of place and it tended to return to it again, for example, when a stone falls back to its place on earth. By invoking final causes in this way, he appeared to remove the need to discuss efficient causes, which alone admit of and require scientific investigation, and this philosophy cast a baleful shadow on science right up to the Renaissance. Fortunately for the reputation of Greek physics, in the Hellenistic period an independent school of physics emerged, more interested in efficient causes, perhaps because of the long overdue state patronage. The leading figures in this school were Archimedes and Hero. To Archimedes we owe the foundations of the science of hydrostatics: whether or not he actually jumped from his bath shouting "Eureka!," he certainly introduced the idea of determining the density of an object by measuring the volume of water displaced by it, and thereby detected a fraudulent craftsman who had debased the gold of the crown of King Hiero of Syracuse by alloying it with silver. Although he certainly did not invent the lever, which was familiar to the Egyptians 2,000 years earlier, he first systematized the laws of statics by relating them to geometry. He was a practical man, who has been compared to Leonardo da Vinci, and was famous for his design of war machinery (pulleys, burning mirrors, and the like) for the defense of Syracuse against the Romans. For the most part, his work was not followed up in classical times: the first edition of his works appeared only in 1543, the same year as the *De Revolutionibus* of Copernicus.

## GREEK MEDICINE

Medicine was the one other branch of science to which the Greek civilization made an important contribution. The Greeks inherited from the Egyptians a medical tradition which blended a considerable skill at diagnosis (the sick were after all always available and cases could be compared), a sensible reluctance to provide more than the minimum physical treatment (an Egyptian doctor who treated a patient's eyes unsuccessfully was liable to lose his own), and a considerable awareness of the importance of psychological factors, which however tended to degenerate into magic and sorcery. The earliest Greek doctors seem to have belonged to the cult or clan of Asclepius, the demi-god of medicine; they ran centers for treatment at Epidaurus, Athens, and elsewhere which relied heavily on psychological-magical techniques. The first outstanding personality to emerge is that of Hippocrates, who left a legacy of medical treatises with a strong clinical flavor. The Hippocratic oath, which bound the physician to act solely for the benefit of his patient, reflects the spirit of this period, as does the well-known Hippocratic dictum: "Life is short and the Art (of medicine) long, the opportunity fleeting, experiment dangerous, and judgement difficult." His emphasis was on diagnosis, on understanding the causes of disease, and on allowing the healing power of nature to carry out its good work. During this period, knowledge of anatomy and physiology was primitive: Alcmaeon practiced dissection, discovering the optic nerve and showing that the brain was the center of sensation and intellectual activity; Hippocrates did experiments in embryology by opening hen's eggs as incubation proceeded. Empedocles taught that blood flowed to and from the heart. Unfortunately for the development of medicine, he also introduced the doctrine of the humors—blood, bile, phlegm, and black bile—to match the four elements, and classified men as sanguine, choleric, phlegmatic, or melancholic according to which humor predominated.

The next stage in the development of biological science was the contribution of Aristotle which, by contrast with his work in physics, was based on first-hand observation. He began the classification of biological knowledge, undertook embryological research, and performed vivisection with a view to discovering the functions of organs. He was not infrequently mistaken, as in his conclusion that the object of respiration was to cool the blood, and that the heart rather than the brain was the seat of intelligence. His mistakes can in part be attributed to his espousal of the four humors theory and of his predilection for final rather than efficient causes.

The last, and by far the most important figure in classical medicine is Galen, who was born at Pergamum in A.D. 130, and after training there in Alexandria, settled in a lucrative practice in Rome. He systematized Greek anatomical and medical knowledge, and his writings remained the standard source of information about such matters until the Renaissance. Indeed, during the Middle Ages they came to be rated above independent observation in this respect. He dissected animals and a few human bodies, making many new discoveries in anatomy, physiology, and pathology. He also made experiments on live animals, examining the action of the heart and the spinal cord. His theory of the blood was that it was formed in the liver from food and then mixed with "nutritive spirits"; it moved in and out of the heart and along the veins in a tidal ebb and flow. In the brain the blood generated "animal spirits" which, pure and unmixed with blood, passed along the nerves to bring about movement and the higher functions of the body. By philosophy he was a theist and this attitude of mind appealed to both Christendom and Islam, which to some extent explains his great and lasting influence.

Bust of Apollonius of Tyana, a neo-Pythagorean of the first century A.D. He was an ascetic and seems to have been a sort of nomadic teacher and preacher who journeyed as far as India and was credited with miraculous powers. He is said to have foreseen the death of the emperor Domitian by clairvoyance. Parallels were drawn between him and Jesus, but no authentic works by him survive. He died in the reign of Nerva.

# Part II Roman Civilization

Chapter 8

# THE SUCCESS OF THE ROMANS

## Greece and Rome

Although we think of them together, ancient Greece and Rome were vastly dissimilar. In time, the Romans became acquainted with Greek culture and took over many of its elements, but it was in fact Hellenistic, not Hellenic, Greece they learned from—with its despotism, its *colossi*, and its reliance on astrology. Athenian rationalism and love of individualism were as foreign to the traditional, community-minded Rome of the fifth-century patriot Cincinnatus as they were to the orientalized Rome of Augustus. The speculative, city-loving nature of the Greeks was incomprehensible to the stolid Romans—countrymen at heart—who were forever talking of how they longed to escape to their quiet rural villas.

Greek society had its wealthy and its poor, but when the Athenians expropriated the Delian treasury, they spent it (military expansion apart) on the beautification of their city rather than on personal luxuries. As we have seen, the Greeks held relatively few slaves and, on the whole, lived simply. The Romans, on the other hand, built their social system squarely on wealth, and those who had wealth tended to display it. Privilege was openly allotted according to annual income. Political office-holding was limited to members of the wealthy equestrian ranks who were expected not only to spend lavishly on themselves but to finance public spectacles as well. Furthermore, the gap between the richest and the poorest was much wider in Rome than it had been in Greece. The Emperor Domitian (A.D. 81–96) had 20,000 slaves and a personal income that dwarfed that of even the wealthiest senator. At the same time, perhaps a quarter of Rome's citizens were living on public welfare.

Throughout their history, the Greeks tended to be particularistic and divided. The most striking capability of Rome's rulers was their ability to bind together diverse peoples. Unlike the Greeks, the Romans tended to agglomerate rather than assimilate, producing a civilization in which contrast and contradiction flourished.

It was this agglomerative ability and character that partly ensured Rome's political success. She could rule diverse nations and yet maintain harmony; she was only rarely threatened with uprisings from "subject populations." As her empire expanded, the distinguishable ethnic group called "Romans" disappeared entirely; there was, instead, a vast and constantly increasing number of citizens of various backgrounds and racial types. This meant that Rome was an almost exclusively

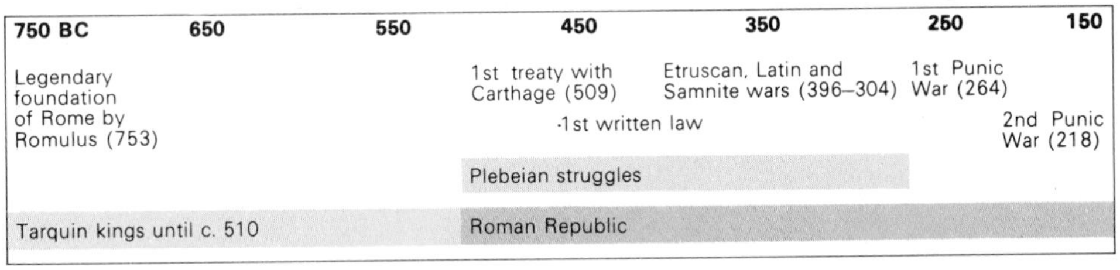

| 750 BC | 650 | 550 | 450 | 350 | 250 | 150 |
|---|---|---|---|---|---|---|
| Legendary foundation of Rome by Romulus (753) | | | 1st treaty with Carthage (509) | Etruscan, Latin and Samnite wars (396–304) | 1st Punic War (264) | |
| | | | ·1st written law | | | 2nd Punic War (218) |
| | | | Plebeian struggles | | | |
| Tarquin kings until c. 510 | | | Roman Republic | | | |

Bronze head of a wolf, one of the traditional symbols of Rome. This is an Etruscan work of the late sixth century B.C. dating to the expulsion of the kings from Rome. The wolf was the beast of Mars, the Roman god of war and father of Romulus and Remus, the founders of Rome. These twin brothers were said to have been suckled by a she-wolf. Speculation both in antiquity and the present day, however, has been aroused by the double meaning of the Latin word, *lupa*, which signified not only a "she-wolf," but also "prostitute".

*political* entity. Alexander's empire had been military and cultural, but it was also ephemeral and involved domination of the conquered by the conqueror. In the Roman Empire, few groups remained "conquered" for long. They became part of the conquering agency, subject to its law but also eligible for its privileges. Their loyalty was virtually ensured.

Rome's successful expansion would, of course, have been impossible without her armies and the genius of their commanders. But the continuity of her rule relied on other factors, and political participation may well have been the most important.

The most severe weakness of the Roman Empire was that it had to expand to remain economically healthy. Expansion continued throughout the Republic and early Empire, making Rome the political and geographical center of a far-reaching Mediterranean empire. But the limits of expansion were finite, and before A.D. 300 Rome had become a defensive rather than an aggressive power. Her economic system weakened, and economic and political fragmentation replaced the unity of the Augustan era and prepared the way for conquest by Germanic tribes and for the disunified Germanic states of the medievalWest.

## EARLY ROMAN HISTORY

According to legend, the founder of the Roman people was Aeneas, who came west to Italy after the fall of Troy (twelfth century B.C.); the founder of the city of Rome itself was Aeneas' descendant Romulus. With his twin brother Remus, Romulus had been exposed in infancy, but both had survived, suckled by a she-wolf. In 753 B.C., Romulus erected the foundations of Rome.

Legend is not history and our uncertainty about early Roman history results from our having almost no good evidence. Apart from scattered references in Greek writers, there was no Roman history until about 200 B.C. and none in Latin until fifty years later.

These first historians had only a few official records, such as lists of magistrates, and a tradition which consisted largely of the distorted versions current in the great families of the exploits of their ancestors. Today we possess, in addition, archaeological evidence, but there is much difference of opinion about its dating and significance. It is certain, however, that the Palatine hill in Rome was inhabited by a village community in the eighth century. Later, one by one, separate settlements on the seven hills amalgamated into a single city. Rome was at first ruled by kings but eventually threw them off, preferring to be a republic.

The early history of the Republic is one of continuous warfare against the surrounding Etruscans (culminating in the capture of Veii in 396) and against the other Latin cities and neighboring peoples. Finally, after confronting the Greek cities on the south coast, Rome became master of Italy.

As, in succession, Rome mastered the different peoples of Italy, she made treaties of alliance with them, by which they retained local government but were committed to follow Rome's foreign policy and to send contingents every year to fight with the Roman army. In the case of the Latin cities there was, in addition, reciprocity of citizenship; any Latin who took up domicile in Rome became a Roman citizen, and vice versa. This arrangement was ended in the early-second century at the request of the Latins, since migration was becoming a one-way traffic and the Latin cities, with reduction in manpower, found it hard to supply their quota of soldiers each year.

In addition, Rome created new civil settlements (colonies) as outposts on conquered territory in Italy. These were either small citizen colonies or larger Latin colonies. As in the Latin cities, a Roman citizen joining a Latin colony surrendered his Roman citizenship and assumed Latin citizenship.

Rome conquered two major powers early in her history: the Etruscans in the fifth century and the Carthaginians in the third and second centuries.

## THE ETRUSCANS

The Etruscans formed a loose federation of twelve cities, each under a king (*lucumo*), and they controlled the country north of Rome, reaching south into the Campania. Rome was at one time in their power; two, perhaps all three, of its last three kings were Etruscan. At the end of the sixth century, Rome broke free.

The piratical Etruscans were in prolonged contact with Greece and they imported from the Greeks much more than the vases found in such numbers in their tombs. Much of what they learned from the Greeks they passed on to the Romans, but what they passed on was overlaid with their own culture.

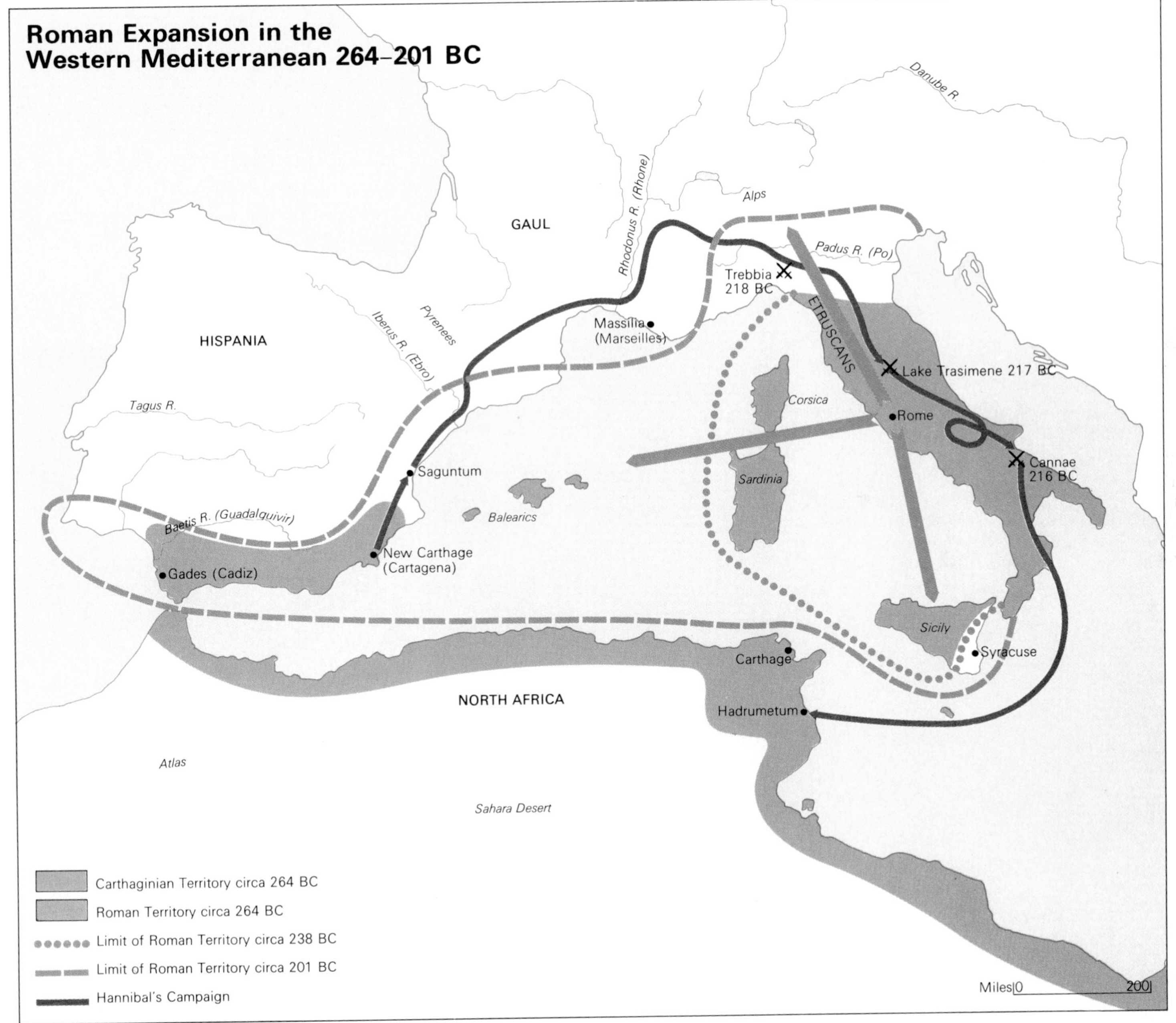

The Etruscan world was in many ways remote from the atmosphere of any Hellenic state. Government, religion, and even individual affairs were ruled by the *libri fatales* ("books of fate"), which revealed the future and the secrets of omens. Every Etruscan had to keep these omens constantly in mind, even in the most trivial circumstances. He had to stay away from certain trees that carried evil influences; bees, mice, and birds all had to be watched closely; the weather, too, contained hidden messages.

Vestiges of the material civilization of the Etruscans survive in towns such as Tarquinia, in sepulchral monuments in stone (with figures that are markedly obese), in bronzes (the famous she-wolf on the Campidoglio in Rome may be an Etruscan work), and, in particular, in the brilliantly colored and vivid paintings on the walls of the chamber-tombs of the rich. From these gay and lively illustrations we can glimpse details of their daily life.

## Etruscan Influences in the Roman World

In Rome the influence of the Etruscans persisted. A number of distinguished Roman families were of Etruscan origin and proud of the fact.

The paraphernalia of the triumphal ceremony of a general after a successful campaign owed much to Etruscan tradition, as did ceremonial dances of various kinds, including the Bacchic dances of stylized abduction. Etruscan brutality left its mark on Rome in the custom of murdering captives after a victory. Roman gladiatorial games originated in the games that were held over the tombs of Etruscan chiefs, in which men fought until mortally wounded, "to exorcise the omnipotence of death."

Most important, however, was the Roman acquisition of the Etruscan "science" of augury—divination by the flights of birds and by marks on the livers of sacrificed

Etruscan painting, part of a tomb fresco from the "Tomb of the Leopards" at Tarquinia, dating to the fifth century B.C. The Etruscans at one time dominated central Italy and had a marked influence on almost all facets of Roman life and conduct. Their origin is still a mystery. They may have come from Asia Minor or they may have been an indigenous tribe. Their language is indecipherable, but is certainly not Indo-European, the root of most European languages. They seem to have been influenced by the Greeks, especially in their art.

animals. Etruscan *haruspices* (readers of the auspices) continued to be employed throughout the Roman Republic and Empire to help determine favorable or unfavorable political or military conditions.

## CARTHAGE

Carthage, a Semitic city, was founded as a colony from Tyre around 800 B.C. Originally a trading post, it grew to be a powerful commercial city in its own right, establishing trading posts of its own in western Sicily, Corsica, and Sardinia and, eventually, along much of the Spanish coast. The Carthaginians were skillful sailors, with a very strong navy. They made common cause with the Etruscans to stop the extension of Greek colonization in the far west.

Carthage, instead of merging into the Roman world after Rome's final conquest, at the end of the Punic Wars, was obliterated. Consequently, the Carthaginians have left no literature and no art. In Europe there are vestiges of their civilization only in southern Sardinia and at Motya, their main trading depot in west Sicily, much of which remains to be excavated.

### The Punic Wars

The Punic Wars began in 264 B.C., when mercenaries who had seized Messana in Sicily were attacked by King Hieron of Syracuse. They appealed both to Carthage and to Rome for help, and Rome, fearing that the Carthaginians might establish themselves in Messana and use it as a jumping-off ground for the invasion of Italy, answered the appeal. War with Carthage resulted.

In engaging in such a war, the Romans, who had no warships of their own, were challenging the greatest naval power in the Mediterranean. Their first step, therefore, was to build a fleet. As they could scarcely hope to rival Carthaginian skill in

Etruscan sarcophagus of the fifth century B.C. from Cerveteri. The figures reclining on top probably represent husband and wife. The female hairstyle and the enigmatic smiles on the faces of the two figures show Greek influence. The Etruscans changed their funeral practice from cremation to burial, which led to a series of richly painted tombs and sarcophagus figures that have been discovered in central Italy.

# Why the Romans Nearly Always Won

"What man is so petty or lazy as to have no wish to know by what means and to what form of constitution almost the whole inhabited world fell beneath the sole rule of the Romans in the space of fifty-three years?" wrote the Greek historian Polybius in the second-century B.C.The question has continued to fascinate later historians.

The legions were the cornerstone of Rome's success. Discipline was savage: flogging was the punishment for minor offenses, decimation (the execution of every tenth man) for cowardice. There was a well organized chain of command. At the top was the general, usually a consul, who had beneath him a *legatus* for each legion. There were also junior officers, such as "the tribunes of the soldiers," who were often inexperienced. The key men below the legatus were the centurions, sixty in each legion. The senior centurion, the *primum pilus*, carried great authority, and could often save situations too difficult for the junior officers. But no centurion could save the army from an incompetent commander, as the disaster at the Allia (390 or 387 B.C.) showed. Rome produced few incompetent commanders, however, and many of outstanding ability, such as Scipio Africanus and Fabius in the Punic Wars, and Julius Caesar.

The Roman genius for the practical was at its best in military matters; training, logistics, the comisariat, and military engineering were all highly organized, and Rome was always ready to adopt new weapons. Equally important was the Roman's readiness to vary their tactical formation. Eventually the cohort of 600 men became the standard unit. There were ten cohorts in each legion.

The legionary himself was a highly mobile soldier who could turn to fight on any front, unlike the Greek hoplite, who had to act in mass formation. Yet a well deployed phalanx would have been a match for the legionary army. It was by good fortune that in the Macedonian wars Rome faced inferior generals.

A weakness that was only slowly remedied lay in the use of cavalry. In seapower Rome showed more flair, and the Mediterranean came to be regarded as *Mare Nostrum* (our sea).

What of the man who stood in the ranks? Originally he was the industrious small farmer, who was used to the vicissitudes of nature. He was disciplined in his way of life and was characterized by *officium* (sense of duty). It was not only Rome's manpower that displayed these qualities. The Latin and Italian allies were also good fighting men.

Diplomacy contributed to Rome's success. The policy of *divide et imperare* (divide and rule) was no accident. When, after her victory over Carthage, Rome had won the West, she employed the same tactics that had helped to win Italy. The policy was to fight necessary wars only. Threats and peace treaties could be as useful as wars.

Severe peace terms, confiscation of warships, and swinging financial demands all helped the Romans to ensure that even the most troublesome of conquered peoples could not threaten her. After the defeat of Hannibal no individual Mediterranean power had the resources to take on Rome. However, Rome also displayed tolerance toward local custom in the areas she ruled. So long as control was manifest, the populace might think and believe as they chose.

The legionary, the brilliant commander, organization, the weakness of her enemies, and luck, all contributed to Rome's success. It is significant that the Empire suffered more than the Republic because the "old stock" had vanished. The army had come to be made up of barbarians, rather than of Romans and Italians. In 410 the Visigothic king Alaric sacked Rome itself. As the Latin writer St Jerome lamented "Capta est urbs quae totum capit mundum" (the city that conquered the whole world has been captured).

naval maneuver, they fitted each ship with an original device: an erect gangway with a sharp spike attached. In battle, this dropped on to an enemy ship at close quarters; the Roman marines would then cross the gangway and hand-to-hand fighting, in which Romans excelled, would follow.

The Romans were successful and the First Punic War ended with Carthage deprived of Sicily and, shortly thereafter, Sardinia and Corsica as well. The Carthaginians turned to Spain, where Hamilcar Barca, his son-in-law Hasdrubal, and his son Hannibal, in succession, built up a position of great strength, to the alarm of Massilia (Marseilles), a Roman ally, who provoked Roman diplomatic protests to Carthage. In 218 Hannibal, then aged twenty-eight, marched through southern Gaul, crossed the Alps, and invaded Italy.

Hannibal lost half his army in the crossing of the Alps and entered Italy with only 20,000 infantry and 6,000 cavalry to face an enemy whose potential fighting manpower (Roman and allied) was 700,000 foot and 70,000 horse. But he was faced by Roman consuls whose incompetence in military command he cannot have anticipated, and he succeeded in the first three years in destroying one Roman army after another. Roman capitulation seemed inevitable. The question has often been asked: What would have happened if at that moment Hannibal had marched on the city? Instead, he went into winter quarters at Capua, and Rome's finest hour arrived. At last she found a strategist, Q. Fabius Maximus, who earned the title *Cunctator* (Delayer). Acknowledging the superiority of Hannibal in the field, he decided that pitched battles were to be avoided at all costs, for he saw that time was on Rome's side. The Latin allies of Rome had not abandoned her, as Hannibal had hoped. Unless he was reinforced, Hannibal's effective strength would diminish continuously, and as Rome held command of the sea, he was likely to be reinforced only overland from Spain.

The Romans, therefore, took the courageous and farsighted decision that, despite all disasters in Italy, they would keep a second front open in Spain. This was done effectively under two brothers, the Cornelii Scipiones. When both were killed in 211, Rome sent out the son of one of them, Publius Cornelius Scipio, later renamed Scipio Africanus, then only twenty-six years old. By 206, he had defeated the Carthaginians in Spain. Reinforcements for Hannibal, which had slipped through his fingers, were wiped out at the Metaurus in Italy in 207. The Second Punic War finally came to an end with the signing of a peace treaty in 202.

Carthage was as good as conquered; all that remained was to deliver the *coup de grace* by invading the city itself. After years of delay, Rome at last renewed the war in 149. At the end of this Third, and last, Punic War (146 B.C.), Carthage was destroyed. The inhabitants were massacred, the city was razed, and the site plowed over by the victorious Romans.

Coin bearing the head of Hannibal. Hannibal was the greatest of Rome's opponents in the Republican era, and the one who came nearest to destroying her. Such was the terror he inspired that even in imperial times parents would quieten their children with the phrase, "Hannibal ad portas" (Hannibal at the gates). He was a leader of genius who held together a mercenary army on alien territory for eighteen years. Despite the hostility of the sources, which are all Roman, he must rank as one of the world's truly great military commanders.

Chapter 9

# DID SUCCESS SPOIL ROME?

## GOVERNMENT IN THE REPUBLIC

In the period of nearly 500 years between the expulsion of Rome's last king, Tarquin the Proud, and the arrival to power of Rome's first emperor, Augustus, Rome was a republic.

The Latin words for republic, *res publica*, mean, "the common concern," and the government of the Republic was one in which the whole community shared. There is nothing in the concept of *res publica* which implies *rule* by the people, or democracy, and Rome never had a democracy such as existed at Athens. Democracy was not a practical form of government after Rome had expanded from being a compact city-state into being the head of a large confederacy. The Greek form of democracy worked only when it was easily possible for every citizen to attend the assembly. This was not possible at Rome.

Like Athens, Rome had a considerable number of magistrates but the similarity does not really stretch beyond the name. The Roman magistrates had varying powers and the system was designed to ensure that all of them could be kept in check. The most important magistrates were the two consuls, whose task was to lead the city in peace and war. On beginning their term of office, which lasted one year, they were given a grant of *imperium*, which included power of life and death, over their men in war. By far the most important feature of this power of *imperium* was that it was a discretionary power. Whereas the less important magistrates had restricted and well-defined powers, the consuls and the praetors were simply required at all times to act in the interests of the state. The word for general in Latin is *imperator*, which means "the man who gives the orders" or "the man with imperium." The word for emperor was also *imperator*, and the emperor was simply the man in the city with the supreme *imperium*, the widest powers.

The major part of the history of the Republic involves the decline of the *res publica*, a process which started during the second century B.C. The earlier years, however, were proud ones for Rome and ones in which those qualities which both Sallust and Cicero associated with the true Roman were established, qualities like *gravitas*, *pietas*, and *dignitas*, which summed up the way a well brought up Roman of good family ought to act in matters of family, state, and religion. The historian Sallust, himself an ex-politician, blamed increased wealth and idleness for the corruption that, in his opinion, ruined the Republic and constantly idealized those

| 150 BC | 125 | 100 | 75 | 50 | | 25 | 5 |
|---|---|---|---|---|---|---|---|
| Republic in decline | Internal strife develops (landless v. landed) | Breakdown of Senate's supremacy | | 1st Triumvirate (60) | 2nd Triumvirate (44) | Octavian sole ruler (30); Emperor (27) | |
| | Gracchi | Julius Caesar (102–44) conquers Gaul (51) | | | Pompey routed at Pharsala (48) | Province of Egypt (30) | |
| Provinces of Macedonia (148), Africa (146), Asia (133), Numidia (105) | | | | Provinces reorganized by Pompey (63) | | Mark Antony defeated at Actium (31) | |

The forum at Rome. The forum was the center of Roman legal and political life. Originally it was an open space, but it was eventually surrounded by temples, the senate house and various basilicas. At one end were the rostra, from which the people were addressed. Here the *comitia tributa* were held and meetings of the *concilium plebis* (the council of the people) as opposed to the senate. It served also as Rome's market place.

earlier years to make his own times appear blacker. Hard work and personal endeavor characterized the early Republic—typical was the great general Quinctius Cincinnatus, who was busy plowing his fields when a deputation arrived to ask him to save the state. In the Georgics, that glorification of country life by the poet Publius Vergilius Maro (Virgil), there is a plea for a new generation of hardworking Fabiuses.

## The Machinery of Government

The actual machinery of government was complicated, dominated by a desire to ensure that no one person could have the kind of powers which the dreaded kings had had. Other features were respect for age, experience, and tradition. The magistrates, who were the executive of the government, were elected by two assemblies, the *comitia centuriata* and the *comitia tributa*. The centuries and tribes were units of citizens, whose make-up goes back to the early days of the Republic. The *comitia centuriata* was the assembly that elected consuls and praetors and here the voting was by units and not a one-man, one-vote system. The units were heavily weighted in favor of the rich and the upper classes, so that it was possible for them to control the outcome of the elections. It was this assembly also that had to ratify all legislation and here again there was the same bias. In the early days, 80 of the 193 voting units (centuriae) were from the first property class and eighteen from the top of the second class. The units were not of uniform size—one unit of the lowest class contained more people than all the units of the top class, despite its relative weakness in voting power.

All the magistracies were generally held by members of the noble families and it was only rarely that a man such as Cicero was able to rise to the consulship from a yeoman country background. Such men, known as "new men," were rare

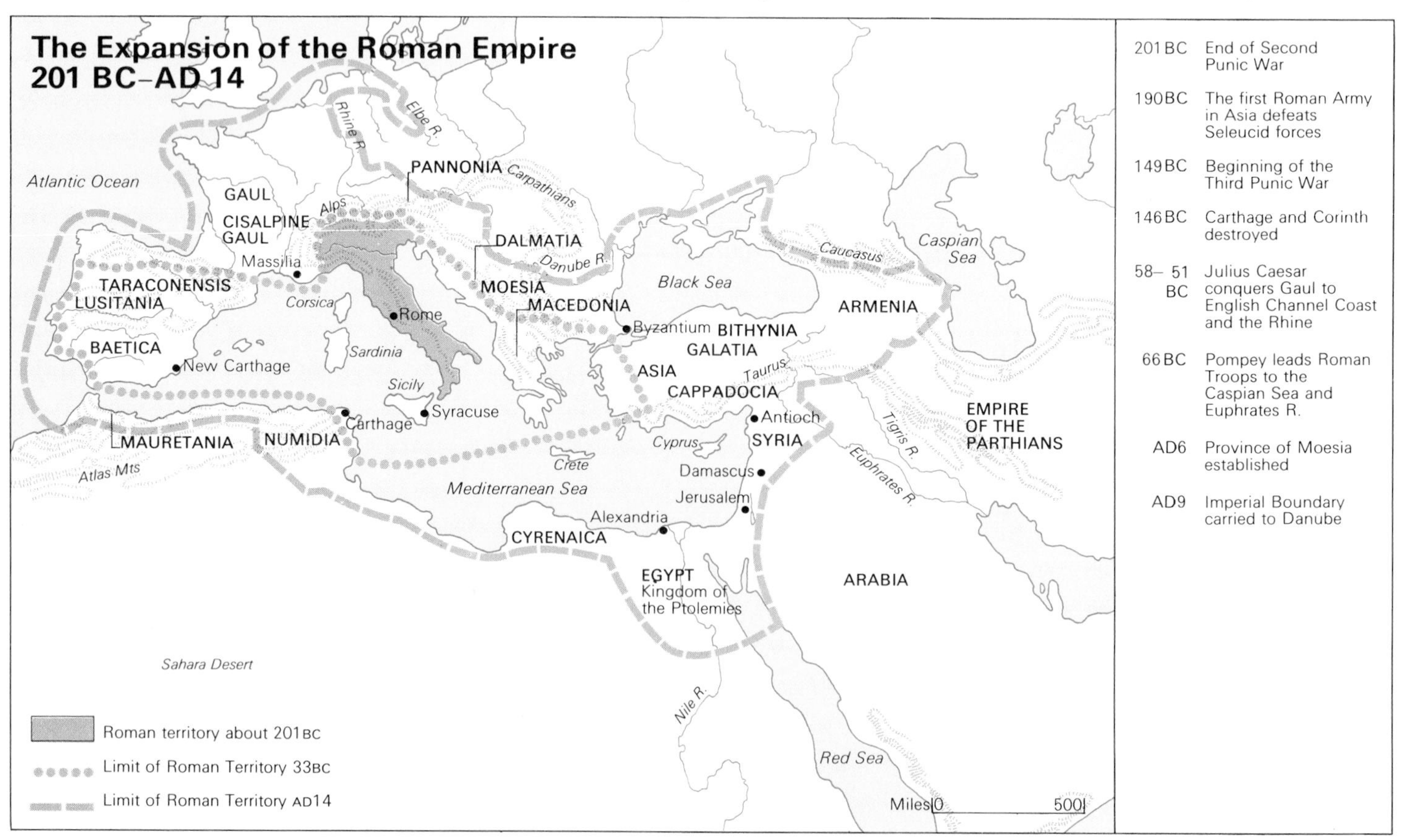

throughout the Republic and needed to cultivate links of political friendship with the established families, at least until they had got one foot on the ladder.

Apart from the consulate, one of the most powerful magistracies was the tribunate. The ten tribunes of the people had extensive powers. They were created in the days when the common people, the plebs, were oppressed by the patricians, and the tribunes were themselves plebeians. They had sacrosanctity, which meant that if they went to the assistance of an individual who was being arrested unfairly and intervened on his behalf, no one could touch them without committing a religious crime. They also had the power to veto any proposal and prevent it becoming law, no matter what support it had. This power, originally intended to be a safeguard of the people's interest, was to be a very dangerous weapon.

The legislative part of the government was in the hands of the popular assemblies. Membership of these assemblies was restricted to Roman citizens and, as Rome began to interfere more and more in the affairs of Italy, so the question of extending the franchise to the *socii*, or allies, of Rome became more hotly discussed. In fact the senate was more important than the assemblies. For the most part it consisted of ex-magistrates and, therefore, because of the electoral system, of members of a fairly restricted group of families. All legislation was discussed in the senate and, though the senate was only an advisory body, its agreement was almost essential for the success of any proposed legislation. As long as Rome was successful and prosperous, the senate maintained its position; it was only when her economic and military position changed that senatorial government lost respect and authority.

The machinery of government, with the senate and popular assemblies as the legislature, to whom the magistrates were ultimately responsible, remained much the same throughout the Republican era. It was a system that worked for four out of five centuries, so why did it not work for the last century? Was it simply that corruption set in, as Sallust claimed, or was the problem deeper?

## THE LAND PROBLEM

How Rome developed from being a small city-state into the leader of a large Italian confederacy and how the desire for land and greater influence brought her into headlong collision with Carthage was traced in chapter 1. The defeat of Carthage required the development of a navy, with the result that Rome was able to exercise her already-efficient military power abroad as well as at home, with her supply routes secure. By 167 B.C. she had acquired part of Spain, Tunisia, and Macedonia, leading Polybius, the Greek historian to say, "In fifty-three years the Romans succeeded in subjecting to their sole rule nearly the whole inhabited world —an achievement unprecedented in history."

The provinces brought a great deal of wealth to Rome and also a new source of manpower, slaves. The influx of slaves into Italy brought cheap labor to the richer landowners, who were increasing the size of their farms at the expense of the small landowners. Former small landowners were left searching desperately for some kind of employment in the cities. At the same time the provinces were by no means peaceful and Roman soldiers had to fight longer campaigns than they were used to. A small farmer could not possibly look after his land if he had to leave it for more than a few months, so that longer service was a further cause of the crisis in small farming that took place.

Conscription and the levy caused much bitterness in the second century and it can be said with justice that Rome's new provinces were a very mixed blessing. There was a grave economic crisis in Italy, which was never satisfactorily resolved. The resulting unemployment caused a shortage of available manpower for the army, as land-ownership was a necessary qualification for joining the army.

*For just as an excess of power in the hands of the aristocrats results in the overthrow of an aristocracy, so liberty itself reduces a people who possess it in too great degree to servitude. Thus everything which is in excess—when, for instance, either in the weather, or in the fields, or in men's bodies, conditions have been too favorable—is usually changed into its opposite; and this is especially true in States, where such excess of liberty either in nations or in individuals turns into an excess of servitude. This extreme liberty gives birth to a tyrant and the utterly unjust and cruel servitude of the tyranny. For out of such an ungoverned, or rather, untamed, populace someone is usually chosen as leader against those leading citizens who have already been subjected to persecution and cast down from their leadership—some bold and depraved man, who shamelessly harasses oftentimes even those who have deserved well of the State, and curries favor with the people by bestowing upon them the property of others as well as his own. If the better citizens overthrow such a tyrant, as often happens, then the State is re-established; but if it is the bolder sort who do so, then we have that oligarchy which is only a tyranny of another kind. This same form of government also arises from the excellent rule of an aristocracy, when some bad influence turns the leading citizens themselves from the right path. Thus the ruling power of the State, like a ball, is snatched from kings by tyrants, from tyrants by aristocrats or other people, and from them again by an oligarchical faction or tyrant, so that no single form of government ever maintains itself very long.*

*(Cicero* De Republica *book 1.68.) Loeb Translation*

In short, then, the second century saw an influx of wealth to Rome and greater prosperity for the large landowners and for the public contractors, but at the expense of the small farmer. Military service prevented him from looking after his lands, and if he lost his land, the property qualification prevented him from rejoining the army. This great problem is at the root of all the ensuing disorder. The breakdown of senatorial supremacy, the constant bloodshed and civil wars, can all be ascribed, in part, to the land problem. How did this come about?

### The Path to Destruction

In 133 B.C., Tiberius Gracchus, a tribune of the people, attempted a solution by bringing forward a proposal to distribute all the common land (land acquired in war) in small amounts to the unemployed citizens. This land had been acquired by rich landowners or by Italian allies who were not Roman citizens. Both these groups reacted violently to the proposal and the landowning faction of the senate persuaded another tribune to veto the bill. Tiberius, however, persuaded the people to depose the tribune from office, an unprecedented and illegal step, and got the bill passed despite the veto and the disapproval of the senate. When, after this, he tried to defy precedent by standing for a second term of office, there was a riot at the election and eventually the senate intervened using force. Tiberius was killed in the fracas, despite his sacrosanctity. Nevertheless a land commission had been formed to carry out the proposals and the census figures for the ensuing years suggest a certain improvement in the situation. Tiberius' brother, Gaius, continued the tradition, but was even more radical.

A Roman wreath of oak leaves made of gold, fourth century B.C. The oak leaf crown, the *corona civica*, was the reward for saving the life of a fellow soldier. Made of gold it represented a decoration open to the senior centurion rank, military tribunes, and senior officers. It was later revived in the Empire, by Septimius Severus, as a decoration for centurions. Most of the Roman higher decorations were in the form of a crown.

Against this background of unrest there comes into our story Gaius Marius, a new man who rose up through the ranks and offices in the traditional manner, until in 112 B.C. the revolt of Jugurtha, an African prince, gave him an opportunity to come to power. A succession of senatorial consuls suffered ignominious defeats, to the digust of the popular tribunes, and eventually Marius, who had been serving under one of these senatorial generals, returned home and stood for the consulship in his own right. He was easily elected and set about reorganizing the army.

His most important action was to allow the *Capite Censi* (those who in censuses were counted by head because they had no property) to serve in the army. It was an important step because these soldiers had nothing to fall back on after their discharge and depended, therefore, on their general to provide for them. This gave the general a possible power-base, in that his army found it more to its advantage to obey him than to obey the state.

After successfully defeating Jugurtha, Marius' popular support was such that the ancient convention that no one could be consul twice was ignored. Marius was elected consul seven times in just over twenty years. During this time the feud between the supporters and opponents of the senate got bloodier and, by the time of Marius' death in 86 B.C., Rome had in fifty years seen at least twenty men of consular status killed within her precincts in political struggles.

Later these struggles came to be thought of in terms of two groups: the *optimates*, who were generally from senatorial families and wished to maintain their existing position, and the *populares*, who wanted change and were prepared to by-pass the senate and use popular support to achieve that change. It is misleading to think of these two groups as parties; they were combinations of the interest of various families. Cicero, who was responsible chiefly for the introduction of this political terminology, regarded both Marius and Tiberius Gracchus as *populares*.

Land was the prime issue of conflict, but citizenship ran it a close second. The *socii* became more and more restless as the amount of fighting they had to do increased, while their own standing remained inferior and without the benefits of full citizenship. They lost their lands and, as non-citizens, were not entitled to benefit from the handouts of the land commission. Several times Roman politicians tried to get the franchise for the allies, but the senate objected, perhaps frightened by the potential size and importance of their vote in the assembly. Eventually the *socii* revolted in 90 B.C. and there followed what is misleadingly known as the Social War. After bloody fighting, in which Rome was threatened, citizenship was conceded to the *socii* by the senate.

Though beaten on this issue, the senate tried to regain some semblance of respect. The Social War, however, had engendered bitterness between the opposing groups in Rome and, as power swung from one group to another, the city became a virtual bloodbath. The senate won a temporary victory after Marius' death when Cornelius Sulla, one of the senatorial generals of the Social War, swept aside the Marian supporters who controlled Rome. Having had himself declared dictator, a position higher than that of consul and giving him supreme imperium, he attempted to restore to the senate all its former authority. He curtailed the powers, and especially the veto, of the tribunes so that they could no longer be so troublesome to authority. By mass confiscations, he obtained enough land to settle his veterans, but in the process he created even more bitterness, hardship and unemployment.

The newly dispossessed provided ideal support for any would-be agitators and when Sulla suddenly gave up his powers voluntarily in 79 B.C. there was no shortage of them. Many people were heavily in debt, as economic security had been almost impossible during the turmoil of the eighties.

## THE CATILINARIAN CONSPIRACY

Sallust claims that it was economic unrest that enabled Catiline in 63 B.C. to attempt a coup d'etat, "such was the strength of the virus that had infected the minds of the citizens." Catiline was of a rich family, but had got himself heavily into debt. His plan to redistribute land and to cancel debts was one that had much appeal for all those who had suffered from the Sullan settlement. Cicero's *De Lege Agraria* gives an idea of the extent of the discontent in the countryside. The conflict in the state had transcended the *optimate-populares* clash; it was between the men with financial stability and those who were desperate and in debt.

From Sulla's death up to the Catilinarian conspiracy, the political situation had reverted very much to its former state. The tribunes had regained their powers, and the struggles between factions and classes were as fierce as ever. Faced with the crisis of Catiline, the classes temporarily forgot their quarrels and united behind Cicero who, as a "new man" consul, dealt with the situation rapidly and efficiently. But as soon as the danger passed, the union of the classes began to disappear and Cicero was left to recall wistfully this unique occasion of harmony between citizens of all backgrounds. The security of the solid citizen was preserved for a little longer, but nothing was done for the hungry and the impoverished country-folk, whose plight remained as sad as ever.

### The First Triumvirate

In the meantime Rome's armies had remained active abroad and from the various campaigns there had emerged a great new general, Gnaeus Pompeius. His military successes gave him political power at Rome. His first consulship in 70 B.C. saw the end of the Sullan settlement, although later events were to turn him more towards the side of the senate. By the time of the Catilinarian Conspiracy he had held another extraordinary military command, cleared the seas of pirates and brought about a skillful settlement in the troubled provinces of the East. Cicero was hopeful

# Caesar in Britain

Head of Julius Caesar on a gold coin. Caesar is shown wreathed as is often the case, perhaps due to a wish to conceal baldness. Caesar was born in 100 B.C. and he was murdered on the Ides (15) of March, 44. The appearance of his head on coins was not a startling innovation, but it set the pattern for Augustus and later emperors who were very particular about the portraits they allowed their coins to bear. This coin profile does not give as good an impression of Caesar as some of the busts.

There had been close ties between Britain and Gaul long before Caesar invaded the former. Britain may well have been the training center for the Druidic religion to which the peoples on both sides of the Channel offered their devotion. Certainly this would help to explain the ferocity of the resistance on Anglesey—the heartland of druidism.

Both countries had Celtic populations. One tribe, the Belgae, had invaded Britain about 100 B.C. and thus had communities on both sides of the Channel. Moreover, in Caesar's time Cassivellaunus, king of the British Belgae was an important figure in the affairs of the southern half of the country.

In his history of the Gallic Wars, Caesar says that he wished to conquer Britain because reinforcements from Britain had been helping the Gauls. He also had a natural curiosity about the largely unknown island, and thought it was a wealthy country containing cattle, gold, iron and silver. But most important of all he wished to win a great, prestigious triumph by conquering this remote island. This conquest would have brought him more glory in Rome than his victories over the Gauls.

The first invasion, in 55 B.C., is generally accepted as a reconnaissance trip, but before he set out the Britons knew of Caesar's intentions. Envoys came to him in Gaul offering submission. Caesar sent Commius, king of the Gothic tribe of the Atrebates as his ambassador. King Commius was immediately imprisoned by the British. Caesar invaded the country, taking only two legions. He took some cavalry support also, but this was blown off course. Little was achieved bar some experience of fighting against chariots, new to the Romans, and damage to Caesar's fleet. Many hostages were demanded or guaranteed, but few actually appeared, although Commius was released to negotiate. After repairing his ships Caesar returned to Gaul with few casualties but even fewer gains.

In the following year an invasion on a much larger scale was planned. Six hundred special transports were built. Four legions and 800 cavalry were to be employed. The Gauls sent 4,000 horsemen as reinforcements. Caesar's departure was delayed by fear of a revolt in Gaul behind his back and by contrary winds, but eventually he set sail.

This time the Britons were better organized. After Caesar's initial landing and a foray, Cassivellaunus was appointed supreme commander of British forces. However, the hasty unity was dispelled by a victory of the legions and a march on the territory of Cassivellaunus. The Thames was forded against opposition and Cassivellaunus' stronghold, possibly the modern Wheathampstead or St Albans, stormed. Cassivellaunus himself conducted a desultory guerrilla campaign.

The most important tribe to submit to Caesar was the Trinovantes under their king, Mandubracius. Other lesser tribes followed suit. Cassivellaunus agreed to terms that the Trinovantes should be independent and that he should pay tribute and give hostages. The great booty which Rome had been led to expect was not forthcoming.

Though the two invasions caused a stir in Rome and even a thanksgiving in 55, they achieved little concrete for Rome as a power. It is doubtful if any tribute was ever paid and further intervention was rendered impossible first by a revolt of the Gauls and second by the Civil War. The invasions did perhaps reveal to the Romans something of British war tactics and of the difficulty of invading Britain. The British do not seem to have learned much about concerted resistance to the invader.

If Caesar himself hoped for vast success and wealth from his adventure, he was sadly disappointed, but recovered from his lack of success. The British remained a motley, disunited group of tribes. For a long time after Caesar's invasions, Rome resorted to peaceful penetration and to building up trading links. Augustus may have toyed with the idea of conquest, but other matters, or his natural caution, kept him from it. Claudius' general in A.D. 43 seems to have followed Caesar's ideas and conquered the southern portion of the country; the northern areas were conquered under the Flavians.

that Pompey might prove to be the champion and not the foe of the senate on his return to Rome. However, the senate did nothing to foster such a relationship. It was reluctant to ratify his Eastern settlement and blocked his attempt to find land for his discharged veterans.

In the circumstances Pompey turned elsewhere and made an official agreement with Marcus Crassus, whose great wealth had given him political influence in Rome, and Julius Caesar, who had had a successful pro-praetorship in Spain and was looking for the consulship. Politically he was considered a Marian and a popularist, and he was suspected of having encouraged Catiline in 63 B.C. These three created what is known as the first triumvirate and the bond was sealed by what proved to be a marriage of love and not of politics, that between Pompey and Caesar's daughter, Julia. This combination of interests was a very powerful one.

The year 59 B.C. brought Caesar his first consulship, and Cicero's correspondence reveals a fascinating conflict, as the *optimates* tried one device after another to thwart the plans of the triumvirate—to no avail. Pompey's veterans got their land, Crassus got a good deal for the business interests he represented, and Caesar himself obtained an exceptional five-year command in Gaul for his pro-consulship—later extended for a further five years. This year was, if any, the one which signaled death to the traditional *res publica*.

A Gallic bronze mask of the late second century B.C. from the Hautes Pyrenées. The Gauls were not lacking in skill as craftsmen or fashioners of jewelry. They had fought Rome throughout the centuries and their last major period of activity was at the end of the second century B.C. when Marius defeated the Germanic Cimbri. Caesar's conquest of Gaul brought him much wealth through his selling of prisoners. Disunity among the Gauls helped him to victory.

After Caesar's departure, the senate attempted to regain some semblance of control, which was made more difficult by the fact that during 59 B.C. Publius Clodius, an open supporter of the triumvirate, was elected tribune. One of his first acts was to legalize the *collegia*, or political clubs, which had been suppressed. This measure enabled him and other popular leaders to organize gangs of roughs, who increasingly dominated the political scene in Rome and disrupted order and security. Caesar kept a close eye on the situation and when his first command in Gaul was drawing to its close, he summoned his two partners to separate conferences: he met Crassus at Ravenna and Pompey at Lucca. At these meetings Caesar got his way—it was arranged that Pompey and Crassus should be consuls in 55, that Pompey should be given an extended command in Spain at the end of his consulship, and that Caesar's command should also be extended.

Caesar is probably the most fascinating figure of the Republican era, and Pompey, great general though he was, pales somewhat beside him. We can still read Caesar's own account of his campaigns and the short, matter-of-fact sentences, contrasting so strongly with the intricately composed rhetorical flourishes of Cicero's speeches, give us an insight into his direct and incisive approach to matters. Throughout his career he was ruthless and those who talk admiringly about his "mercy" completely misunderstood him. He only showed mercy if mercy would benefit him and he was capable of cruelty. His ten years in Gaul enabled him to train a superb army, absolutely devoted to him rather than to the state. If he had weaknesses, they were probably a love of display, learned during his time in the east and an inability to compromise. It was because he was not a great diplomat and not a subtle human psychologist that he failed where Augustus was to succeed.

After the conference of Lucca and the consulships of Pompey and Crassus, the triumvirate began to disintegrate. Crassus' death in 53 at the battle of Carrhae, during a disastrous expedition to Parthia, left Pompey and Caesar alone. They had never been close friends and, when Caesar demanded in 49 B.C. that he should be allowed to break precedent and stand for the consulship in absentia, Pompey did not support him. This whole issue has consumed more ink than most other Republican questions, but the main point is that, if Caesar had terminated his command in Gaul, and then stood for his consulship, he would have been a private citizen in the intervening period and thus liable to prosecution by his enemies for provincial misconduct. This was a risk he was not prepared to take and, when the senate continued to refuse his request and his enemies made it quite clear that they would prosecute him, he decided to march to Rome to get his way. Pompey was in Rome and decided this time to side with the senate. At last two great generals faced each other and Rome was plunged into civil war.

### Caesar's Dictatorship

The campaigns of the civil war covered most of the empire, but the decisive battle was fought out at Pharsalus where Caesar won a convincing victory. Pompey fled to Egypt, where he met a sordid end, stabbed to death on the beach where he landed on September 28, 46 B.C.

A first century A.D. cameo portrait of Julius Caesar. He is shown wearing a Roman version of the diadem, the headband of Alexander and the Hellenistic kings. The profile is much sterner and more arrogant than any coin portrait or bust.

Caesar returned to Rome in 47 B.C. but the war dragged on a further two years before the last Pompeian resistance at Thapsus in Africa and Munda in Spain was finally crushed. Caesar returned to Rome finally in October 45, and remained there until his assassination in March 44. It was his longest stay in Rome since 59. After each of his victories he was voted more and more extravagant honors by a now-servile senate; and in the end he was made dictator for life and perpetual censor. Plutarch interprets the situation accurately when he tells us, "This meant an undisguised tyranny; his power was not only absolute but perpetual. But the Romans gave way, because they thought they would obtain a respite from civil wars." Even Cicero, who hated the situation, cooperated to the extent of proposing some of these extraordinary powers.

In his six months at Rome Caesar initiated a number of plans and reforms. He started some colonies for the landless but had no real answer for the old problem. He followed Sulla's example by introducing a large number of new people into the senate. Most of these were drawn from non-senatorial families and from the country towns, which had often felt inadequately represented at Rome. On the practical front, Caesar initiated large and much needed drainage schemes and reformed the calendar. His period of rule brought no cure for the problems of the Republic, though perhaps it is unfair to judge him on the evidence of so short a time.

### The Death of Caesar

Caesar's absolutism ran counter to the whole political tradition of Rome and was resented by all conservative-minded men. The sanguine hoped that, with civil war at an end, Caesar would reconstruct the government on republican lines. When there was no sign of this and Caesar's interest was evidently focused on a great eastern campaign against Parthia, sixty bold spirits decided that, in Rome's interest, he must be killed before he left for that campaign. Their leader was Cassius who had fought for Pompey at Pharsalus and had been pardoned by Caesar, who had a great affection for him. On the Ides of March (March 15) in 44, at a meeting of the senate held in the portico of the new theater built by Pompey, under Pompey's statue, Caesar was stabbed to death.

Though many senators were jubilant over Caesar's death, no bouquets were thrown to the assassins. When the senate met on March 17, an amnesty was proclaimed, but the validity of all that Caesar had done as dictator was confirmed—including, of course, the right of the majority of senators to their places in the senate. When Caesar's wounded body was exposed to the people and his will, which included large bequests to the citizens of Rome, was read, there was pandemonium. His corpse was burned in the Forum. The appearance of an unanticipated comet at games given in honor of Caesar's victories in July convinced the superstitious that his soul was in heaven. In January 42 he was officially declared a god by the senate and a temple in his honor was later built where his body had been burned. The assassins were soon in danger and fled from Italy.

## ANTONY AND OCTAVIAN

With Caesar gone, there was left one big obstacle to the restoration of Republican government—Caesar's lieutenant, Mark Antony (Marcus Antonius). In his will Caesar had made his great-nephew, Octavian, his heir. Octavian became more than an ordinary heir by this action: it was as though Caesar had named his successor. Octavian obtained the allegiance and goodwill of Caesar's troops which was worth far more in terms of power than all Caesar's wealth. Cicero, who had enjoyed an Indian summer as elder statesman in the senate, hoped to win Octavian to the Republican side and to use his power to eliminate Antony; in a series of violent polemics he tried to rouse both the senate and Octavian against Antony. Unfortunately for Cicero, Octavian had no intention of restoring the old Republic. He joined Antony, and between them, in 43 B.C., they eliminated most of their opposition by proscriptions. Cicero's name was on the list and he met his death bravely, dying for the Republic, which perhaps he had loved too much.

Civil war and bloodshed continued through a second triumvirate of Octavian, Antony, and Lepidus (a name to be mentioned and then forgotten), culminating in a rift between Octavian and Antony, who had gone east and become enamored of the famous Egyptian Queen Cleopatra. For a time Antony ruled the East and Octavian the West but finally they quarreled. At the battle of Actium in 31 Octavian won emphatically and again Rome was at the mercy of one man.

Italy was by now on her last legs. She was sick of war and Octavian met with no opposition. Luckily for Rome, she had at last obtained a genius for a leader, a man who realized that an autocracy strong enough to bring about lasting peace was the only answer to Rome's problems, but who was also acute enough to realize that such an autocracy had to be disguised in a form acceptable to Republican traditionalists. So it was that the beginning of what we now call the Empire, that is when power lay ultimately not with the senate and people but with one man, was actually proclaimed by Octavian (or Augustus as he was called by that time) as the restoration of the Republic. In his autobiography, the *Res Gestae* ("My Achievements"), he was able to say that his constitutional position was no more than that of any leading figure in the Republic.

Head of the emperor Augustus. Augustus was Julius Caesar's great-nephew and later his adopted son. Originally he was called Caius Octavius hence he is often referred to by the adoptive name Octavian, which his own contemporaries did not use. Before 27 B.C. when he took the name Augustus and after Caesar's death he was referred to either as Caesar or Caius. He made great play of the *nomen Caesaris,* the name of Caesar, and the fact that he was the *heres Caesaris* (Caesar's heir), in his propaganda war with his opponents, especially Antony.

The Empire did not start with a great sound of trumpets but was the natural result of a process that we have seen throughout the period—more and more power being transferred from bodies to individuals. The restricted constitution of the Republic had not been designed for an area as vast as the empire and could not cope with the resulting problems of expansion. The result was a sad story of poverty and bloodshed, in which the insecure happiness of the few was always at the expense of the misery of others. Nowhere is this more poignantly illustrated than in Virgil's first *Eclogue*, entitled "The Dispossessed." Two rustic farmers are talking to each other. Melivoeus who has lost his farm tells Tityrus who is insecure in his:

> *Tityrus, whilst you lie there at ease under the awning of the spreading beech and practice country songs on a light shepherd's pipe, I have to bid good-bye to the home fields and the plowlands that I love. Is some blaspheming soldier to own these acres I have broken up and tilled so well—a foreigner to reap these splendid fields of corn? Look at the misery to which we have sunk since Romans took to fighting one another. To think that we have sown for men like that to reap.*

If there is any thread that continues through the Republican era, it is exactly this juxtaposition of happiness and misery.

Chapter 10

# THE AUGUSTAN AGE

## THE CAPITAL CITY

The civilization of Augustus' reign centered on Rome, now no longer capital of a provincial state but mistress of a world empire. By the late-first century B.C., Rome had grown in an unplanned sprawl into a complex site of seven hills and a river crossing. Much of it was a chaos of tall, rickety houses and winding narrow streets, and it was only at enormous cost that order was imposed upon the central political buildings to gratify Roman tastes for symmetry.

The largest streets in Rome were wide enough for only two carts; many were wide enough for only a single man to walk through or for one cart. Even the "highways" in and out of Rome—including the Appian Way—were only fifteen to twenty feet wide. Most Romanists disagree about the population of Augustan Rome, but probably nearly a million people clogged its streets. The city was not only crowded but chaotic, many streets were not named, and houses were unnumbered. First century Rome was extremely dangerous; the Roman poet Juvenal (c. A.D. 60–140) remarked that it was foolish to go out for dinner without having made your will.

From early times Rome had suffered from overcrowding and shortage of space and had had many areas of poor-class tenement houses. These largely timber structures were insecure and unsanitary and vermin flourished. The noise at night was terrible; collapses were frequent and fire a constant hazard. The solution to the painful administrative problem of spontaneous growth produced by a large urban proletariat was the building of *insulae*. These well-built blocks of several stories were not unlike modern apartment blocks, and they were, perhaps, Rome's chief contribution to urban living.

Overcrowding, of course, made rents very high. Under Trajan, the price of an apartment was equal to the price of a rural estate. Although Augustus fixed a maximum height for houses of seventy feet (later reduced by Trajan to sixty) and there were some attempts at rent control, his measures and others to the same purpose seemed to do little to curb the rapacities of speculative builders and landlords.

Successive rulers tried to offset the unsightly effects of Rome's cruel social extremes. Beginning with Augustus, the emperors took firm measures to limit Rome's sprawling growth and to improve conditions in the city. Fresh aqueducts were built, and public fountains multiplied. Stricter policing was instituted, and a fire brigade, armed with hand pumps and wet blankets, became a state charge.

As public amenities developed, the houses of the aristocracy grew larger; senators in Rome laid out huge gardens on the hilly outskirts of the city. Many had houses farther out as well, in the Alban Hills or (like the younger Pliny) by the sea. Veneers of brilliant, variegated marbles and other elaborate decorations soon became middle-class necessities, though in Sulla's time they had seemed an unnecessary, even scandalous extravagance.

*Above:* A view of a street and house in Ostia, second century A.D. Ostia developed first as a naval base during the Carthaginian Wars, and later as Rome's main port. Its facilities were improved under the Empire, the last major rebuilding being carried out in the time of Trajan and Hadrian. The city then became architecturally very presentable with little of the squalor of the Roman slums.

*Left:* An idealized portrayal of Augustus, who is perhaps posing as Apollo or Alexander the Great. The military dress may well be to emphasize Augustus' military achievements, though he himself was careful to make no reference to his victory over Antony and other Roman citizens.

## TOWN LIFE

Town and capital differed sharply in style and standard of living. Houses in the town of Pompeii, destroyed by an earthquake in A.D. 79, reflect the comfortable, middle-class conditions of a prosperous municipality, where some fifty leading families mingled on terms of tolerable amity with the rest of the population. There was no spectacular wealth. The walls were painted in flat primary colors to give the effect of light, since the windows were small and darkened by wooden shutters. The basic furniture is quite simple, though there is some elegance in the ornamental tables of wrought bronze. More typically Roman is the profusion of tableware: silver banqueting sets and many kinds of ornate cauldrons and casseroles of bronze.

Figurine of the Mithraic cult, second century. Mithras was in origin a deity in the Zoroastrian religion of Persia. He was the helper of the Power of Good and Light, Ahuramazda. In Roman imperial times Mithraism became a mystery religion in its own right and one popular with the army. There appear to have been seven stages or grades for initiates to pass through. Mithraic temples, which tend to be small in size, have been excavated. For several centuries Mithraism was more successful than Christianity, but Christianity eventually triumphed.

### Sanitation

Augustan Romans sought to improve sanitation. The Roman historian Livy (c. 59 B.C.–A.D. 17) stresses the difficulties in Rome, where uncontrolled building meant that "sewers originally laid down in public soil now everywhere run beneath private houses; it is like a city that has been created by squatting rather than properly apportioned." The new towns, however, were better planned. Under their streets, available for repair or inspection, lay a grid of drains. With aqueducts, there came a parallel system of lead water pipes, again under the streets, that served public fountains and—at a fee—private houses. There is hardly a site that fails to reveal Roman concern about sanitation—Pompeii, Ostia, even Mauretanian Volubilis show the care lavished on plumbing.

The typical Roman sewage system served the lower floors of buildings. The lavishly decorated public latrines were public in every sense of the word—people met there and conducted business. Expensive fountains, mosaics, and even statues adorned latrines. Such things were, of course, part of the Romans' wry image of themselves; as Livy put it, rather than the "useless though celebrated works of the Greeks," they preferred the great serviceable aqueducts, concerning themselves with "what the Greeks had neglected, paved highways, aqueducts, and sewers."

### A New Middle Class

With peace and prosperity, towns transformed themselves. Aristocratic residences gave way to middle-class activity. In Pompeii, for instance, from the time of Augustus, the old houses were converted into bakeries, fulleries, and wineshops; often they retained the faded ornaments of a nobler past. Houses were taken over, subdivided into shops and flats, and sublet. The fine old House of Pansa bore the following notice: "The Insula Arriana Polliana, property of Cn. Alleius Nigidius Maius. To let from July 1 next: shops with attached upper rooms, gentlemanly upstairs apartments, and the main house. Agreements to be made with Primus, slave of the above."

### Politics

These new towns also exhibited a certain political energy. The ordinary citizen had his vote and used it keenly at municipal elections, as the brisk painted propaganda of Pompeii shows: "Bruttius Balbus for duovir: he will maintain the town treasury"; "Helvius Sabinus for aedile: recommended by the united bakers, they and the neighbors want him." Elections tended to die out as they lost real political content, but they existed in the towns long after their suppression in Rome.

## RELIGION

When the Greek historian Polybius, living in Rome in the second century B.C., praised Roman officialdom, he noted above all their unique devotion to the gods.

Scrupulous fear of the gods, he wrote, is used "as a check upon the common people. . . . Seeing that every multitude is fickle, and full of unlawful desires, unreasoning anger, and violent passion, the only resource is to keep them in check by mysterious terrors and scenic effects."

Religion represented stability in both public and private affairs in the best days of the Republic. In public affairs the gods were regarded as saviors of the city in time of trouble. They were appealed to when danger threatened and thanked when danger was overcome. Family gods protected the spirit of the household.

The priests, who shouldered the responsibility for the well-being of the city, were not professional clergy; they were simply active and usually prominent citizens. In short, they were state functionaries, as were the six Vestal Virgins, who for thirty years (or longer, if they chose to remain) performed various religious tasks needed to preserve the health of the city. The importance of the Virgins' duties may be inferred from the severity of the punishment that followed neglect of those duties: if the fire went out in the Temple of Vesta, the Virgin responsible was thrashed by the Pontifex Maximus (Chief Priest). If a Virgin was found to be unchaste, she was buried alive in an underground chamber.

Statuette of a *Lar* (Roman household god). The Romans venerated within the home two sets of deities: the *Penates* (deities of the hearth) and the *Lares*, who in origin seem to have been agricultural deities, but later became associated with the house as well. As in all thoroughly Roman practices it is difficult to trace the exact origin and purpose of the worship of the *Lares*.

Until the middle of the second century B.C., the traditional Roman religion held firm. But the Greek civilization and ideas brought back from abroad by Roman armies persistently eroded the conservative power of traditional religion. The cult of the gods disintegrated. Religious faith (except, often, in the home) crumbled, as omens and portents were fabricated by politicians for personal gain.

When Augustus finally restored peace, ending the disastrous civil wars of the first century B.C., he attempted to revive religion. Augustus himself became Pontifex Maximus, beginning a practice later emperors were to imitate. Thus leadership in religion and state were merged in one man. Augustus' birthday and the day of his accession became annual occasions for celebration and sacrifice, and the *princeps* himself looked forward to becoming a god after his death.

Yet while ceremony and ritual could be easily revived, inward traditional piety had been permanently lost. Astrology, the new "scientific" approach to divination of the future, attracted increasing interest. Eastern cults such as those of Cybele (the Great Mother), Dionysus (Bacchus), and Mithras, the "Egyptian rites" of Isis, Osiris, and Serapis, as well as Judaism and Christianity all gained converts because they concentrated on the one aspect of religion which traditional Roman religion had always neglected: the question of redemption and survival after death. All also had some kind of initiation ceremony.

Cybele, the Great Mother, was a vegetation goddess. Romans were deeply shocked by the rites which accompanied her worship, during which frenzied initiates emasculated themselves. The Emperor Claudius sought to Romanize her cult, but it retained much of its ritual, partly because of its close connection with the powerful Julian family. The cult of Dionysus involved flagellation of initiates. The cult of Isis, the most widespread of all the mystery religions, held that initiates passed through the underworld during the conversion ceremony, and the goddess demanded periodic sexual abstinence from her believers. Isis was primarily a woman's goddess; many men, especially soldiers, preferred Mithraism, which had developed from Zoroastrianism, over all other mystery cults. In the beginning, ran the legend, were Mithras, the unconquerable ally of man in his fight against evil, and the bull. Mithras slew the bull, and from its blood came life and vegetation and the first human couple. Then Mithras was taken by the sun's chariot to heaven, where he remained, protecting his followers.

Not everyone, of course, favored the mystery religions with their dramatic, often bizarre, ceremonies. In the early second century, Juvenal berated a believer,

"Can't you see," he wrote, "how naive and comic a figure you cut these days, with your adamant belief that a man should stick to his word, that there's something in all this religious guff, the temples, the mess of blood?" On his deathbed, Vespasian wryly remarked, "I feel that I am beginning to become a god." But for all the cynicism and satire, religion had a permanent place in the Roman psyche. In the first century B.C., Cicero and Clodius, two very sophisticated men, haggled half in earnest over whose debaucheries had profaned the sanctuaries. It is precisely this sort of ambivalence that is typical. As Juvenal wrote, "there are others who believe in the gods, in retribution for evil, but still perjure themselves regardless. 'Let Isis,' they argue, 'Do what she likes with my body. . . . A penniless champion sprinter, if he wasn't plain crazy, a case for some smart Greek quack, would opt for wealth and the gout: where does athletic prestige get you in terms of cash? Can you eat an olive wreath? . . . If (the gods) make it their business to punish all wrongdoers, when will they get to me?' "

Statue of a vestal virgin, first century B.C. The vestal virgins tended the sacred and eternal fire of the goddess, Vesta (goddess of the hearth). The cult was said to have been founded by Numa, the second king of Rome and was ancient, though not the most ancient cult at Rome. There were six priestesses who tended a sacred fire for thirty years, and had to observe a vow of chastity during that time. They had many privileges, but were liable to be scourged if the fire went out, while a breach of the vow of chastity was met with burial alive.

## THE SOCIAL ORDER

The frankly admitted connection between political influence, privilege, and income is, to a twentieth-century observer, one of the most striking things about the social and political system of the Empire. The basic division between *honestiores* (men of noble birth) and *humiliores* (free men of humble birth) was absolute, and the distinctions due to each were apparent in every area of life. Intermarriage between the two groups was prohibited, and they did not mix at the games or theater, where the seating was strictly segregated. The *honestiores* were distinguished from the *humiliores* by their superior education, more expensive dress, and usually substantial retinue. In addition to clients—members of an influential man's political following, dependent on his generosity for their living—*honestiores* were dogged by flatterers and other parasites (literally called shadows, *umbrae*), and they often retained a bodyguard. *Honestiores* were expected to share their wealth with the populace. In return, they were accorded special treatment under the laws. *Honestiores* who committed crimes were punished more leniently than *humiliores* for the same offenses.

### Employment and Unemployment

The main source of income in Rome, as throughout the history of the ancient world, was agriculture. Both technology and trade were too inadequately developed to take over economic preeminence. Food was the one important commodity. Each community—indeed, each large estate—sought to produce its own. If the crops failed, there was no escape from famine. But the Romans did not see their agricultural economy as a weakness; tough, hardy peasants had traditionally been regarded as the strength and backbone of Rome. "It is from the farming class," wrote Cato in the second century B.C., "that the bravest men and sturdiest soldiers come; their calling is most highly respected, their livelihood is most assured . . . and those who are engaged in that pursuit are least inclined to be disaffected."

Farmers were indeed the backbone of the Empire. Almost certainly, the great majority of the populace lived on the land. It was a difficult existence; crop failure meant borrowing money, and if the debtor could not repay it, the creditor could reduce him to a form of bondage. Continuous conquests initially did much to improve the lot of the small man; confiscated lands were given to Rome's own citizens. But after the beginning of the second century B.C., wars spelled disaster for the plowman who served as a soldier sometimes for as long as six years while his farm lay neglected. For a variety of reasons, property began to be concentrated in the hands of a few rich men. The position of the yeomanry declined, and many of the displaced farmers resettled in the city of Rome.

The displaced could not easily find alternative employment in the towns, not only because large-scale industry was undeveloped but, more important, because they had to compete with slave labor. Thus the freeborn poor became dependent on the public grain doles and on the generosity of the rich. Casual labor, for which it was uneconomical to use slaves, and occasional employment in public building projects supplemented these sources of food and income. At times the poor freeman must have envied the security of the slave.

## Slavery

Plagued by perennial underemployment as the Roman economy was, slaveholding at first seems anomalous. The ethics of slaveholding largely remained a theoretical question in Roman times. One Roman jurist explained that although all men are born free under natural law, slavery exists under the law of nations. The influential Stoics taught that all men are brothers, but they added that since the essence of man is spiritual, his material condition is irrelevant. Christianity had much the same attitude toward slavery. The Apostle Paul in effect defended slavery, and when Christianity became the official religion of Rome in the fourth century, the Church soon acquired slaves of its own.

Most slaves came to Rome as the result of conquest and capture. One of Trajan's campaigns resulted in the capture of 50,000 prisoners, who were auctioned as slaves. Piracy by sea and brigandage by land also swelled the ranks. The children of slaves were also slaves. Perhaps one-third of Rome's population in the time of Augustus was made up of slaves. An average *honestior* household had eight or ten slaves, although some upper-middle-class Romans had "a battalion or more." Some wealthy Romans numbered their slaves in the thousands, and an emperor's household probably had some 20,000 in all.

*Above:* Bronze statuette of a negro slave cleaning a boot, possibly of Greek workmanship. Rome's huge slave population included people of many races. The slave was probably a houseboy. The boot is a *calceus*, a heavy boot worn only outdoors.
*Left:* Scene from a comic play, showing an irate owner beating his slave—a common scene from Roman comedy. Rome's two greatest comic writers, Plautus and Terence,relied heavily on themes drawn from the New Comedy of Greece. They did, however, insert a Roman element into their plays.

Slaves could be, and often were, freed. Once freed, however, they remained bound in some ways to their former masters, who now became their patrons (*patroni*). The new freedman had to pay his patron money or promise him services, and this was accompanied by the duty of *obsequium* (filial respect). But at least he was a citizen (though not until the third generation could his descendants have full citizen rights). Masters, especially if they had no natural heirs, frequently emancipated their slaves in their wills. In these ways, the slave population gained its freedom and gradually merged with the citizen population. One historian, by tracing name origins, has shown that at least eighty percent of the population of imperial Rome was descended from slaves.

Legally, Roman slaves belonged to the class of things, *res*, not persons. The Roman scholar Varro (c. 116–27 B.C.) classified a slave as a "tool that can speak." In practice, the law was not as harsh as its written form might indicate. Self-interest dictated that feeding and clothing a slave was economically profitable, while the free poor could go hungry without financial loss to anyone but themselves. Rather than punish his slaves, the intelligent master often rewarded them by paying them a wage or setting them up in business. With his savings a slave could buy his freedom. From the first century after Christ, to kill a slave without cause was murder and mistreated slaves could seek asylum with the state to be sold to another master. To be sure, the master who had been accused of cruelty to his slaves was judged by his peers and the verdict was not always just, but the prejudice was certainly against wanton mistreatment of slaves.

Statue of a comic actor. The actor is wearing a typical mask. The masks for both comedy and tragedy became stereotyped to depict a character rather than an individual. Different types prevailed in tragedy and comedy. Some masks for the large open-air theaters were fitted with megaphonic devices to assist voice projection.

One of the most persuasive arguments against mistreatment was the fear of slave uprisings. Mistreatment of slaves had been identified as the cause of the great revolt which swept through Sicily from 134 to 132 B.C. In another revolt, slaves led by Spartacus ranged over Italy and routed Roman armies in the seventies before Christ. Slaves were always running away, and the murder of masters was a constant fear. This led to a severe Augustan law requiring that when a master was murdered, all his slaves "under the same roof" were to be executed.

Despite its cost in human dignity, slavery was often not the worst fate for a man in Roman times. Many slaves were educated and skilled, and many were prized for the new inventions they brought to Italy. As in Athens, slaves occupied important positions in the Roman civil administration. Some slaves had slaves of their own. Until Claudius' time, the chief advisors of the emperor were invariably well-educated slaves or freed men. With the fatalism typical of Roman Stoicism, the younger Seneca, tutor of Nero, wrote:

> *The same prison surrounds all of us,*
> *and even those who have bound*
> *others are bound themselves; . . .*
> *Honors bind one man, wealth another;*
> *nobility oppresses some, humility*
> *others . . . All life is slavery.*

## LEISURE ACTIVITIES

All classes of free Romans had a good deal of leisure time. Not only did they work fewer hours each day than we are accustomed to, but no work was done on the many days devoted to festivals or to the games. By the first century after Christ public holidays, including festivals such as the *Lupercalia* (March 15) and *Saturnalia* (December 17–23) and local and regional celebrations of the emperor's birthday or accession day, totaled some 150 days each year.

### Public Baths

Much time was spent at the public baths. The bather stripped and proceeded through the temperate room to the hot bath or sweat chamber, where oiling and strigiling (scraping) did for him what soap does in a bath today. He then went to the cold bath, returning thence to the temperate room and the changing room, where he might receive a second light oiling to prevent him from catching a cold when he went out.

The great imperial baths in Rome contained art galleries of statuary, recreation halls, and reading rooms. These buildings are splendid even in their ruins. Other public baths varied in comfort and elegance, down to the lowest on the scale, which were thinly disguised brothels. There were 170 baths (most of them charging for admission and run by private enterprise) in the city of Rome at the time of Augustus, and more than 900 in the late period of the Empire. Snacks and drinks were available in the baths. We can well believe Seneca (c. 4 B.C.–A.D. 65), who lodged over one, when he wrote that they were often extremely noisy.

Women bathed in separate baths, often contiguous to the men's baths, so that the same hypocaust might be used to supply the heat. Sometimes they bathed in the men's baths at different hours. Mixed bathing probably flourished only in the lowest baths.

Bronze head of the first century A.D. This reveals admirably the Roman talent for lifelike and realistic portrait sculpture in both stone and bronze.

### Dining

The time was shouted aloud by street-criers, who were slaves. At the conclusion of the ninth hour (in the middle of the afternoon), it was time for dinner, the one substantial meal of the day.

In Rome, unlike earlier Greece, women and men dined together. Though in rich households of a certain kind the meal was often a gross orgy, most families dined alone or with a few guests, and the meal contained no more than three courses. The use of emetics, approved by doctors, was not always a mark of gluttony; Julius Caesar, who ate and drank very little, had recourse to emetics. Reading aloud by a slave with a good voice often supplemented conversation. At parties, there was sometimes prolonged drinking after dinner, and entertainment was often provided by professional acrobats or dancing girls.

### Games and Other Spectacles

Throughout the late Republic and during the Empire, games and gladiatorial exhibitions provided the most popular entertainments for Romans of all classes. The most important games were held in April and early May (twenty-two days in all), in July (nineteen days in all), in September (sixteen days), and in November (fourteen days). The first days of the games were devoted to theatrical performances and the last days to chariot racing. All these games and festivals, whether in Rome or in the municipalities, were a responsibility of the magistrates and a charge on their pockets.

Gladiatorial exhibitions were at first no part of the regular games. Of Etruscan origin, these exhibitions were first presented in Rome in 264 B.C. as funeral games, and throughout the Republic the pretense was observed that they were given for this purpose. Between combats, clowns dressed as the mythical figure Charon, ferryman of the dead, carried off the corpses. Julius Caesar's extravagant gladiatorial exhibition during his aedileship in 65 B.C. was ostensibly in memory of his father, who had died twenty years earlier, and his exhibition in 46 B.C. was in part given in memory of his daughter, who had been dead for eight years. The scale of these immensely popular exhibitions increased inside and outside Rome during the Empire. Ten thousand men fought in eight different games given by Augustus.

Neither comedy (after Plautus and Terence) nor tragedy had any important history at Rome. Audiences enjoyed only mime and pantomime and tolerated tragedy only if it was a spectacular riot. There were Greek-style games in Rome, but they were never popular; Romans found the nudity of the athletes "immoral." Yet these same spectators found nothing offensive in the sight of animals fighting one another (bulls fighting elephants, for example) or in the *venationes*, or wild-beast hunts. The immense interest taken in wild animals and in the vast business of their hunting, trapping, and transport is illustrated by sculptured reliefs and by mosaics from all over the Roman world. This, like the training and exhibitions of gladiators, was a business in which there was a lot of money to be made. Seneca describes the restless Romans' incessant search for the new and intriguing. When they tired of journeying from one resort to another, he wrote, they began to long for the applause and din of the games and remarked to one another that "It might be rather nice, too, to see somebody killed."

### THE VICTORY OF OCTAVIAN

*Now is the time to drain the flowing bowl, now with unfettered foot to beat the ground with dancing, now with Salian feast to deck the couches of the gods, my comrades! Before this day it had been wrong to bring our Caecuban forth from ancient bins, while yet a frenzied queen was plotting ruin 'gainst the Capitol and destruction to the empire, with her polluted crew of creatures foul with lust—a Woman mad enough to nurse the wildest hopes, and drunk with Fortune's favors. But the escape of scarce a single galley from the flames sobered her fury, and Caesar changed the wild delusions bred by Mareotic wine to the stern reality of terror, chasing her with his galleys, as she sped away from Italy, even as the hawk pursues the gentle dove, or the swift hunter follows the hare over the plains of snow-clad Thessaly, with purpose fixed to put in chains the accursed monster. Yet she, seeking to die a nobler death, showed for the dagger's point no woman's fear, nor sought to win with her swift fleet some secret shore; she even dared to gaze with face serene upon her fallen palace; courageous, too, to handle poisonous asps, that she might draw back venom to her heart, waxing bolder as she resolved to die; scorning, in sooth, the thought of being borne, a queen no longer, on hostile galleys to grace a glorious triumph—no craven woman she!*

(Horace Odes I no.37: Loeb Translation)

## LITERATURE

The Romans produced no original literary genius comparable with those of the Greeks, and until the late Republic and the time of Augustus, it was classical Greek literature on which the education of Roman schoolchildren was based. Later, however, Roman literature could stand on its own feet. There were the writings of Cicero, the deeply passionate love poems of Catallus (c.84–54 B.C.), and the no-less-passionate epic of Lucretius (c.97–54 B.C.), *De Rerum Natura* ("Concerning the Nature of Things"), an exposition of the Epicurean philosophy. In the time of Augustus, there was Virgil's superb epic of dutiful *(pius)* Aeneas, as well as his pastoral poems, the *Eclogues*, and the *Georgics*, a eulogy of the farmer's life and the glory of the Italian countryside. And at long last, in the books of Livy (59 B.C.–A.D. 17), there was a readable history of Rome.

Most writers of the Augustan age supported the state in their writings and were in many cases supported by it. Horace (65–8 B.C.) wrote his polished and witty odes under imperial patronage, and Livy underlined the qualities of heroism and integrity that Augustus aimed at restoring to contemporary life.

Rome became a literary center under Augustus. Provincials flocked to the city from distant parts of the Empire to make their literary fortunes and possibly to earn the favor of an influential political figure. Perhaps the most important of these patrons was Maecenas, a princely nobleman of Etruscan descent, whose immense fortune allowed him to indulge his exotic tastes. Third in the triumvirate of Augustus, Agrippa, and Maecenas, he was, at one time, called on to rule Rome when Augustus was away, and he was frequently employed on diplomatic missions. Politician, poet, and patron, he combined practical rule with the more refined and sensual pleasures of literature and Eastern luxury. Maecenas in many ways symbolized the changing cultural atmosphere of Augustan Rome.

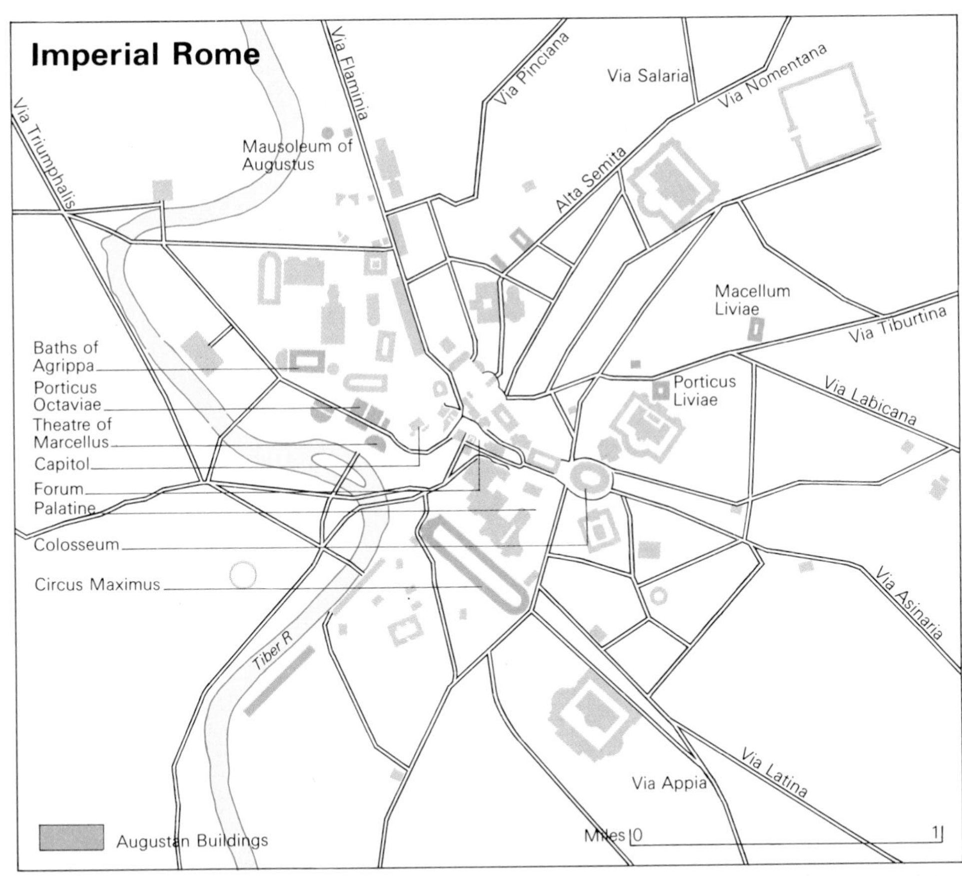

A Bacchanalian dance: the disciples of Bacchus were noted for their frenzied and drunken dancing, which often led to violence.

Chapter 11

# THE LIMITS OF EMPIRE

## AN EMPIRE ESTABLISHED: TIBERIUS

Before his death in A.D. 14 Augustus had already brought his successor, Tiberius, within the imperial decision-making machine. Indeed some have suggested that during the last few years of Augustus' life most policy was decided by Tiberius. Augustus had equipped him with the *tribunicia potestas* and the *imperium consulare*, both of which were essential to the office of princeps. Nevertheless, this acceptance of Tiberius had only come late and after the premature deaths of other "heirs." Though the problem of the transfer of power was accounted for, the fact remained that the recipient of that power was an embittered and elderly man of fifty-five.

In policy Tiberius was generally faithful to the ideas of Augustus, so faithful, particularly in foreign affairs, that he was often accused of over-caution. His military inactivity and general style contrasted badly with the flamboyance of his nephew, Germanicus, who has been represented by our sources as popular, able, and even a rival candidate for the purple. He came to be regarded as difficult and dangerous particularly after his visit to Egypt—an area strictly prohibited to all senators and members of the imperial family except with the emperor's express permission—and because of his quarrel with Piso, the governor of Syria. It is more than likely that Piso was specially appointed to keep an eye on Germanicus.

Germanicus died in Syria in mysterious circumstances in A.D. 19. Poison was rumored and his wife, Agrippina, seems to have held Tiberius as in some way implicated. Her opinion was almost certainly ill-founded, but the scandal brought the downfall and death of the luckless Piso. Agrippina and her family remained deeply suspect to the emperor.

One of Tiberius' most important attempted reforms was to try to put relations between himself and the senate on a better footing. He fastidiously refused honors for himself and granted the senate the right to elect magistrates from its own ranks, a right that had formerly belonged to the people, though it had been eroded under Augustus. However, his attempts to involve the senators in a genuine dialogue of government produced only bitterness and frustration. The senate suspected Tiberius of duplicity and hypocrisy; he suspected them as mere uncooperative and sycophantic toadies.

The failure of this attempt by Tiberius to give the senate greater responsibility and involvement in state affairs was probably a leading factor in his retirement to

| AD | 50 | 100 | 150 | 200 |
|---|---|---|---|---|
| Augustus dies (14) | Julian Emperors: Tiberius, Caligula, Claudius, Nero | Flavian Emperors: Vespasian, Titus, Domitan | Nerva, Trajan, Hadrian, Antoninus Pius | Marcus Aurelius, Commodus |
| | Province of Britain (44) | Rome burned (64) | Rhine-Danube frontier fortified | Growing barbarian threat; War in Germany (166–80); Parthian War (193–211) |

Scenes from the column of Trajan at Rome. The column was built to commemorate the Dacian campaign of the emperor Trajan, 101–106. At bottom the god of the Danube River is shown blessing the Roman army as it crosses the river on a bridge of boats.

Capri in A.D. 26, after which he conducted affairs by correspondence and never returned to Rome.

His chief agent in the capital became L. Aelius Sejanus, the Prefect of the Praetorian Guard. He gained influence over Tiberius before he left Rome, an influence that increased. He even dared to ask to marry the widow of Tiberius' son, Drusus, whom he was suspected of poisoning. Tiberius wisely refused, especially as an affair between the two was rumored. Sejanus played on Tiberius' morbid fear of assassination, finding plots involving the family of Germanicus against whom he seems to have conducted a personal feud. Rumored plots, real or unreal, were to remain fashionable throughout the Empire as a device for getting rid of unwanted opposition or rivals.

Apart from dangerous members of the imperial circle, many others of senatorial rank were charged with *maiestas* (high treason). Views on Tiberius' part in and attitude to this have been colored by the historian, Tacitus. He wrote with the reign of Domitian and the memory of the great *delatores*, informers, imprinted on his mind. He depicts these trials as deliberate anti-senatorial savagery on Tiberius' part. The truth may have been very different, but the precedent was set. Later in the century men such as the infamous Regulus made themselves enormously wealthy and feared by their informing activities. A successful prosecution brought a percentage of the victim's confiscated goods to the emperor's loyal and alert watchdog. Few were acquitted and rewarded zeal brought increased victims.

Apart from delating members of the imperial family Sejanus also concentrated the Praetorian Guard within the city, another precedent which was to have severe repercussions in future troubled times. Inevitably he fell suspect himself: possibly he aimed at the purple, possibly he was over-zealous in his feud against the emperor's relations, possibly he merely appeared too powerful. Warned by Antonia,

Stretch of a Roman road at Blackstone Edge on the Lancashire Moors in England. Rome's roadbuilding was mainly for military and administrative purposes. The quality of the roads that they built was only equaled in the nineteenth century after the invention of tarmac. Roman roads stayed in use for centuries after the end of the Roman Empire, and many roads in European countries still follow the routes of Roman roads.

Tiberius denounced him in a letter to the senate and he was executed, the Guard having previously been allotted a new Prefect, Macro.

In provincial matters Tiberius set yet another dangerous precedent which later emperors were to follow at their peril. He allowed provincial governors much increased length of tenure of office, preferring men established in office to frequent change. He was, however, prepared to stamp on the inefficient. Pontius Pilate was removed from Judea after a complaint of mismanagement by the governor of Syria. Other more important individuals paid for incompetence too. The danger created was that men in the provinces with large numbers of legions would become too powerful and ambitious. This danger became almost endemic.

Tiberius was also the first to experience mutiny by the legions at the start of his reign. Despite the activity of Drusus and Germanicus, provision of money was the major answer. This led inevitably to the open expectation of such gifts especially by the Praetorians at the start of each reign, and even to the open auction of the empire by them.

Despite the hostility of the sources to him, Tiberius' main achievements were stability, financial and governmental, and a strict—if remote—control. He built up the financial reserves and was sparing in expenditure so that at one point he could afford to lower the price of corn—an imperial monopoly. He left to Gaius, his successor, a large amount of money in the treasury and a peaceful empire.

The emperor Hadrian, from a coin issued during his reign, 117–38. Hadrian represented a strong Roman tradition of philhellenism (friendship toward Greek ideas), which led to great benefits for the city of Athens, on which he showered favors. But Hadrian traveled extensively elsewhere. Many remains, such as Hadrian's Wall in England, his villa at Rome, bear witness both to his culture and to his understanding of the military needs of the Empire. He attempted to wipe out injustice in the law courts.

The problematic legacies he left to all his successors were the power of the concentrated Praetorian Guard, the use of informers and the treason trial, the temptation to keep governors too long in office, and the difficulty of maintaining good relations with the senate. However, we should not regard any of these legacies as deliberate policy recommended to his successors as Tacitus sometimes implies, any more than we should believe with Suetonius that the retirement to Capri was merely intended to give Tiberius greater scope for the expression of his devotion to unnatural vice of every form and enormity. Tiberius left much that was good to his successors.

His chosen heir was not the best candidate for high office, let alone for emperor, and here Tiberius' reign signally marked one of the great problems which was to plague the history of the Empire: how to secure the best man for the job within a basically dynastic framework. This problem never really found a satisfactory solution, though often the Empire was sufficiently resilient to recover from one or more bad reigns in succession.

Whether from unconcern in retirement or as an act of deliberate policy, the more or less republican system which Tiberius inherited in A.D. 14, he left in 37 as an autocracy or monarchy. Consciously or unconsciously the role of the senate had been diminished. The career of Sejanus and his relations with the *princeps* had underlined how easily it could be ignored or manipulated. Though the empire was not yet a formal monarchy, after 37, people expected an heir and an heir they got. If the successors were not to their taste, the problem was answered by devising methods of elimination, but that was all to come. It is ironic that Tiberius, who has been credited with underlying republican sympathies and a genuine interest in decreasing the power in the hands of one man, should have done most by his administration to ensure that that possibility became increasingly remote.

## CALIGULA

Tiberius' successor, better known by his nickname of Caligula than by his official name, Gaius, was a welcome heir to the people and to the equestrian class. The former hoped for an increased lavishness by the man who controlled the purse strings, especially as his father's memory was still popular. The latter doubtless

hoped for increased advancement. Posts created by Augustus and maintained under Tiberius were still few in number for an ambitious non-senator and this group had claims which were eventually to be satisfied in the bureaucracy.

At first Caligula was associated in Tiberius' will with Tiberius Gemellus, his grandson. However, Caligula won the favor of the senate and Macro, the praetorian prefect. Gemellus was executed during the first year of his reign. Caligula was to some extent guided by his uncle, Claudius, and his grandmother, Antonia. The former was soon ignored and the latter forced to commit suicide.

After a serious illness Caligula seems to have suffered a personality disorder, though this is disputed by some scholars. The rest of Caligula's short reign was marked by the dissipation of the reserves carefully created by Tiberius, further treason trials and unsuccessful, and possibly unbalanced, attempts to enlarge the Empire which ended in a total fiasco when his soldiers refused to cross the English Channel to invade Britain.

To recoup the money he had squandered, Caligula turned to high taxation and this led to unpopularity. Taken with all the other resentment he had aroused this brought about his assassination by the Praetorian Guard.

His effect on the development of imperial administration was negligible, but his career should have suggested to the sober analyst of events the possibilities which could befall the Empire if it fell into the hands of an incompetent again. The delicate balances between city, provinces, client kingdoms, and wholly external powers could be too easily strained and the exchequer was seen to be a fragile creature, which needed to be carefully tended. That Caligula exhibited a high-handed style in his dealings with all was perhaps due to youth as much as illness, but it was indicative of things to come as the princeps emerged more and more as a monarch and the memory of Augustus receded.

## CLAUDIUS

Caligula died without leaving a successor. The Praetorian Guard decided upon Claudius, Caligula's uncle and partner in office. The senate accepted this suggestion without a murmur. Claudius' rule (41–54) came as a welcome surprise. A stuttering, lame scholar who had been the laughing stock of his family and who had had little administrative experience before middle age, he owed his survival of the purges to all these things and to the fact that although he had through his mother some Julian blood in him, he escaped the hatred connected with that name by belonging to the proud family of the Claudii. Caligula's taxes were abolished; the senators were treated with all the respect even they could hope for; no reprisals were taken against the assassins of Gaius. However, Claudius showed that he could be ruthless; in the course of his reign many senators and equestrians were executed. He decided to attempt to conquer Britain. This was one of the few conquests undertaken to convert the barbarians to a more civilized kind of life. Trade, however, was an important factor—the Cornish tin mines were important to Rome—and until Britain was in the control of Rome, continued trade was dependent on the friendliness of the country. Britain was conquered quite systematically. By the death of Claudius, Rome controlled all of southern and central England. Claudius extended the Empire on other frontiers as well, by absorbing client kingdoms in the East. Between the death of Augustus and the death of Claudius the population of Roman citizens had grown from 5 to 6 millions. This means that Claudius must have granted citizenship to many towns.

Claudius made several distinct advances in the organization of the government. He formally established as distinct posts, offices which had previously existed only informally. These offices were held by freedmen and included positions of great

Another scene of the Dacian campaign from Trajan's column. In all the scenes on the column the importance of the emperor's role in the campaign is emphasized. Under Trajan's energetic rule, the Roman Empire grew to its greatest extent, with the conquests of Dacia, Armenia, Mesopotamia, Assyria and Arabia. Armenia, Mesopotamia, and Assyria were quickly abandoned, but Dacia was held for over a century, and Arabia remained part of the Empire until the rise of Islam in the seventh century.

influence dealing with accounts, correspondence, and official records. These positions were later to be occupied by equestrians, but for the time, their association with the humble and despised freedmen made them unacceptable to those of higher class. To offset this, nevertheless, Claudius did increase the number of equestrian posts and set up what could have—and later did—become a method of promotion similar to that for senatorial governors of provinces. However, his ideas took a long time to come to fruition because of the vacillating policies of following reigns.

Another feature of his reign was the influence of his wives. Claudius was obsessed with his promiscuous, young wife Messalina. By astute maneuvering his last wife, the younger Agrippina, elevated her son to the purple. She was also suspected of poisoning Claudius himself. The pattern of strong-minded matrons manipulating weak, young men continued throughout the history of the Empire.

Claudius' other major achievement, in the face of strong opposition, was to broaden the membership of the senate by allowing more provincials to take seats in it. In his speech he made reference to the precedent of Julius Caesar, anathema to previous emperors because of the memory of his autocratic behavior. But times had now changed and those who laid claim to the *nomen Caesaris* could unlock the family cupboard. Such was the pace of reform that early in the second century Rome was ruled by an emperor of Spanish birth.

A bronze cavalry helmet of the late-first century A.D. The Roman infantry wore iron helmets from the third century B.C., as these were stronger than bronze, but cavalry helmets were often of bronze. Roman fighting methods, armor and weapons showed frequent changes. When a new design or tactic was found to be effective, it would be adopted. This adaptability was one of the reasons for Rome's long history of military successes.

## NERO

At first, Nero was very much under the influence of the famous philosopher Seneca. Seneca and the praetorian prefect together persuaded Nero that he should rule on his own, because they were afraid of Agrippina's influence on him. Eventually she was removed from the capital, and Nero was free to rule on his own. He could now wander the streets, consorting with Roman prostitutes, and enjoy himself with his favorite hobbies—singing, playing instruments, and painting. Meanwhile, government under a senatorial faction headed by Seneca was unimpeded. They passed laws that were intended to stop exploitation of provincials.

Nero devised a plot to murder his mother, but this was carefully interpreted by Seneca as an attempt by her to murder Nero. Nero's reputation escaped unscathed. But Nero wanted to be reprieved by no one: Seneca was murdered. Nero sang and played his way through these years, later even appearing in the much frowned upon theaters, becoming a slave to self-indulgence.

There is a story that Nero fiddled while Rome burned. In fact, although his alibi was suspiciously good, he is said to have invested all his efforts to provide help for the homeless when the great fire that broke out destroyed most of Rome's houses. Eventually the Christians were blamed for the fire. The persecution they suffered is described in chapter 11.

Nero was now in his element—to him fell the task of rebuilding Rome. From this period dates the famous Golden House of Nero, on whose walls some of the finest paintings and experimental ornamentation of Roman art are preserved. Their fine quality and clarity are unexpected. For this and other extravagances, Nero had to find money. The imperial supplies would soon be exhausted, so he took the inflationary measure of reducing the gold and silver content of his coins. Nero's thoughts were determined by essentially non-economic factors; the Roman populace had to be appeased, and any measure making money scarcer would bring hardship with it. Later emperors adopted Nero's solution, not realizing the disastrous effects that it would have by the middle of the third century (see chapter 12).

Nero's disregard for the army, even after the forced suicide of Corbulo, one of its major figures, was such as to extend the influence of the many able men such as Galba, Vitellius, and Vespasian who had begun their careers long before. This, coupled with the perennial problem of wasted money, and a lack of interest in matters political and diplomatic, led to his inevitable deposition.

In matters of organization Nero reversed some of Claudius' innovations. Others he allowed to hang fire. His own talents were not those of government, but he held power for fourteen years.

This was the end of the Julian dynasty. The result was civil war. The plotters feared that no emperor of any other name would be accepted by the whole empire, and it was only through lack of any alternative that Galba was made to accept imperial honors. He set about restoring the state to solvency. There were no shows, and no extra money for soldiers. But the German legions revolted. Galba was murdered by another general, Otho, who succeeded him. In his turn he went further than Galba, taking the name of Caesar to show that he considered himself to be ruling with the same right that the Julii had enjoyed. Because of his strange link with the house of the Julii via his wife Poppaea, who had been Nero's mistress, the Praetorian Guard actually did accept him as the rightful successor. Otho committed suicide.

A horned god found at Carvoran, by Hadrian's Wall in Northumberland, England.

## THE FLAVIANS

With the accession and the acceptance of Vespasian began a new era—that of good constitutional government with none of the court intrigues of the generations preceding these. In his nine-year reign (70–79), Vespasian stabilized the political situation. Vespasian began to recruit from the provinces for military and civil office. This threw careers open to men who previously had been unable to hope for them.

Vespasian granted his son Titus the highest powers of state during his lifetime. This system worked, for when Titus succeeded to the throne his abilities were well known. The only disasters were natural ones. The eruption of Vesuvius which buried Pompei in a night occurred at this time, and there was also another outbreak of fire at Rome. Titus behaved in a model fashion, repairing all the buildings with his own money. This time there was no hysteria. The temper of the age had changed. Titus built what is known as the Colosseum, the largest and finest amphitheater in Rome. Titus died young, leaving no heir.

His brother Domitian was recognized, saving the situation. Domitian wanted slavish service. There could be no question of senatorial rule any more. Senators were excluded from office because of their potential power which their influence and wealth gave them. As a result the position of the equestrian class improved.

In the sphere of provincial government, however, Domitian showed prudence. He saw that the best way to retain control in the provinces was to ensure fair government by delegating authority. Domitian's fears for his own safety turned his rule (81–96) into years of terror, in which no one could be safe from the lurking danger of denunciation for treason. He was finally murdered by members of his own household.

He was succeeded by yet another soldier, Vespasian, who had reluctantly allowed himself to be proclaimed emperor by his troops, and had the support of almost the whole East.

## NERVA, TRAJAN, AND HADRIAN

The senate nominated Nerva, a senator, as emperor. He was accepted by the army. Regular payments of money were promised and paid to the troops. Most of his reign was peaceful. He had no need to shut himself away in palaces with heavily armed guards to secure himself against assassination. There were few political murders. Nerva quickly made provision for his succession, and chose, instead of one of his relatives, Trajan, who had held senior civilian and military posts. This was a further milestone in the fair rule of the empire which was inaugurated at the end of the first century. Nerva dared to override the dynastic principle—the principle, that is, of succession from father to son. (This system held for a century, until Marcus Aurelius chose his son to succeed him).

Trajan (emperor 98–117) was the first emperor who was not an Italian. In his administration Trajan often paid scrupulous attention to detail, as his correspondence with the younger Pliny shows. He had a good staff of trained officials which suggests that he tried to pay attention to all provinces. Not unnaturally also the influx of non-Italians increased. The writer Juvenal in his *Satires* complains that honest, native-born Romans are excluded by provincials with influential friends. Juvenal is probably referring back to the reign of Domitian as much as to life under Trajan and possibly reflects a wider discontent on the part of Romans and Italians with the advancement of the provincials. In his external policies he broke away from his predecessors' policies of non-expansion. He moved into Dacia, the lands north of the Eastern Danube. A small piece was also added to the provinces of Arabia. Armenia, Mesopotamia, and Parthia were also added to the Empire as provinces. Lower Mesopotamia, however, refused to submit, and taking advantage of the situation, the Jews rose up and in all the countries of the East. There followed massacres which appear to have cost over a million lives. Trajan was not to return from the East. He died after a stroke, and it was only on his deathbed that he designated Hadrian, the governor of Syria, as his successor.

Hadrian (emperor 117–38) had the task, much as Tiberius had had, of taking over the Empire from a ruler who had administered it justly and well, under whom there were few wars.

Like Trajan, Hadrian's first assurance to the senate was that he would respect their position. He felt there was nothing to be gained from further expansion, and that the risk of further rebellions must not be taken. So he set himself to securing the Empire in its older boundaries. The three new provinces in the East were abandoned again to their client kings, and Dacia would have been abandoned too, had it not been for the already well-established Roman settlers there. He then set out to travel through the provinces. He was away from home, in fact, with short intervals, for about five years. Even when administrative problems called him back to the capital, he amused himself with his chief pastimes, architecture and music, sculpture and painting. He represents the most cultured of the emperors. The buildings he left include Hadrian's Wall in northern England and most of the *limes*, the frontier wall running along the upper Rhine and the Danube, linking Rome's furthest outposts against the barbarians. He founded many new cities in both East and West. But there were signs that city life was not flourishing as it had been. Hadrian had to help many cities out of their financial difficulties.

His interests in the Greek-speaking East did not extend to understanding the needs and wants of all his subject races. Under his rule, a further Jewish revolt occurred. Misgovernment by Roman procurators of Judea had caused the great rebellion under Nero, in which the real quest was for self-government. Vespasian, before he became emperor, was sent there and surrounded Jerusalem. The city was finally taken and totally destroyed by Titus. Hadrian, on his visit to the still-ruined city, decided to refound it, but as a city for gentiles; the Jews were to be able to enter it only once a year. A temple of Jupiter was built on the spot where the Temple had stood. For the Jews this could only be interpreted as the greatest insult. They rose in a revolt which lasted three years.

At home, Hadrian proceeded rather more tactfully. His financial arrangements were sound and showed foresight. Although its wider abuses seen under the Republic were largely curtailed by Augustus, it had remained an imperfect mecha-

*Top:* Golden bust of the emperor Marcus Aurelius. Marcus devoted much of his time to the material and spiritual wellbeing of the Empire. His actions largely sprang from his philosophy, a form of stoicism. This belief and the emphasis on man's duty that sprang from it are expressed in Marcus' *Meditations,* which although unoriginal in many of its ideas is a work of great sincerity. *Above:* Mummy portrait of a man, c. A.D. 150. Roman rule did not destroy ancient customs. Mummification continued to be common in Egypt well into the Roman period.

nism for its purposes. He abolished tax-farming almost entirely. In order to establish some sort of system in the legal world, he set about codifying new laws.

In the civil service Hadrian altered the system almost to that of a modern bureaucracy. Appointments were permanent and not filled by the emperor's personal staff. The heads of the great "ministries" were drawn from the equestrian class, as Claudius had possibly intended half a century earlier. There also remained the traditional offices in the Empire and the fleet which were the top appointments to which the equestrians could aspire.

## TROUBLES LOOM

Hadrian's choice of successor proved a good one: Antoninus Pius was respected by the senate. Because of his cautious treatment of the senate and his munificence to the people, his reign is always looked upon as one of the last reigns of deep peace. But in fact barbarian invasions were looming nearer. There was trouble in Britain and on the Rhine, and some Eastern provinces were being ravaged by brigands. Yet Antoninus died peacefully after a short illness.

Fresco showing a poet and an actor, c. A.D. 70. Although Roman cultural life lacked much of the vigor of that of Greece, poetry and drama were both popular arts, and many Latin writers such as Horace stand comparison with the best Greek writers.

Marcus Aurelius, his successor, was a philosopher. The pursuit of contemplation remained his mainstay throughout his reign, which lasted from 161 to 180. At first he ruled jointly with Verus, both men having the title of Augustus. There were two emperors with equal rights, for the first time in the history of the Roman Empire. It was a system which was to be adopted over and over again in the third century. Marcus' reign was marked by catastrophes: floods at Rome, earthquakes and famines and barbarian invasion. Roman Germany was invaded, Britain was in revolt, and in the East the Parthians invaded Syria. In the course of this large-scale war, troops were withdrawn from the northern frontier, and the barbarians took the opportunity to invade again, on a larger scale than before. The following years were spent in uninterrupted warfare at various points along the northern frontiers. Marcus then had to travel eastward to restore order there. To accustom his son Commodus to ruling of the Empire, Marcus ruled jointly with him, after Verus' death.

Toward the end of the second century a series of large and important barbarian invasions had begun. They were to last throughout most of the third century. The Empire's reaction to them is described in chapter 13. The story of imperial expansion and comparative peace ends with this philosopher emperor, Marcus. Significantly, his thoughts were not really tuned to the things of this world. His famous book, the *Meditations*, deals with his attempts to come to terms with his own soul. Yet the self-confidence of the Empire was not shaken until plague and wars shook the everyday security of life in the third century.

The Roman Empire of A.D. 180 was vastly different from the ad hoc but workable system of compromises which Tiberius had inherited from Augustus. There was a formal civil service and, in effect—despite pious utterances to the contrary—the senators merely formed its higher echelons. The army was no longer concealed as one of the chief sources of power. The principle of hereditary rule was practiced extensively, though families and dynasties changed. There was the ever-present and ever-increasing financial problem, which was to be greatly exacerbated by the barbarians and their demands. The Empire was now truly cosmopolitan in its approach; men of talent from any province might make a successful career. Altogether despite the stresses and strains put upon it by Caligula, Nero, and others, the imperial machine had survived and developed. The test was now to be whether it could last and deal with a new set of problems. Adaptability and flexibility were important weapons in the imperial armament. Their continuous employment was going to be necessary if new demands could be met.

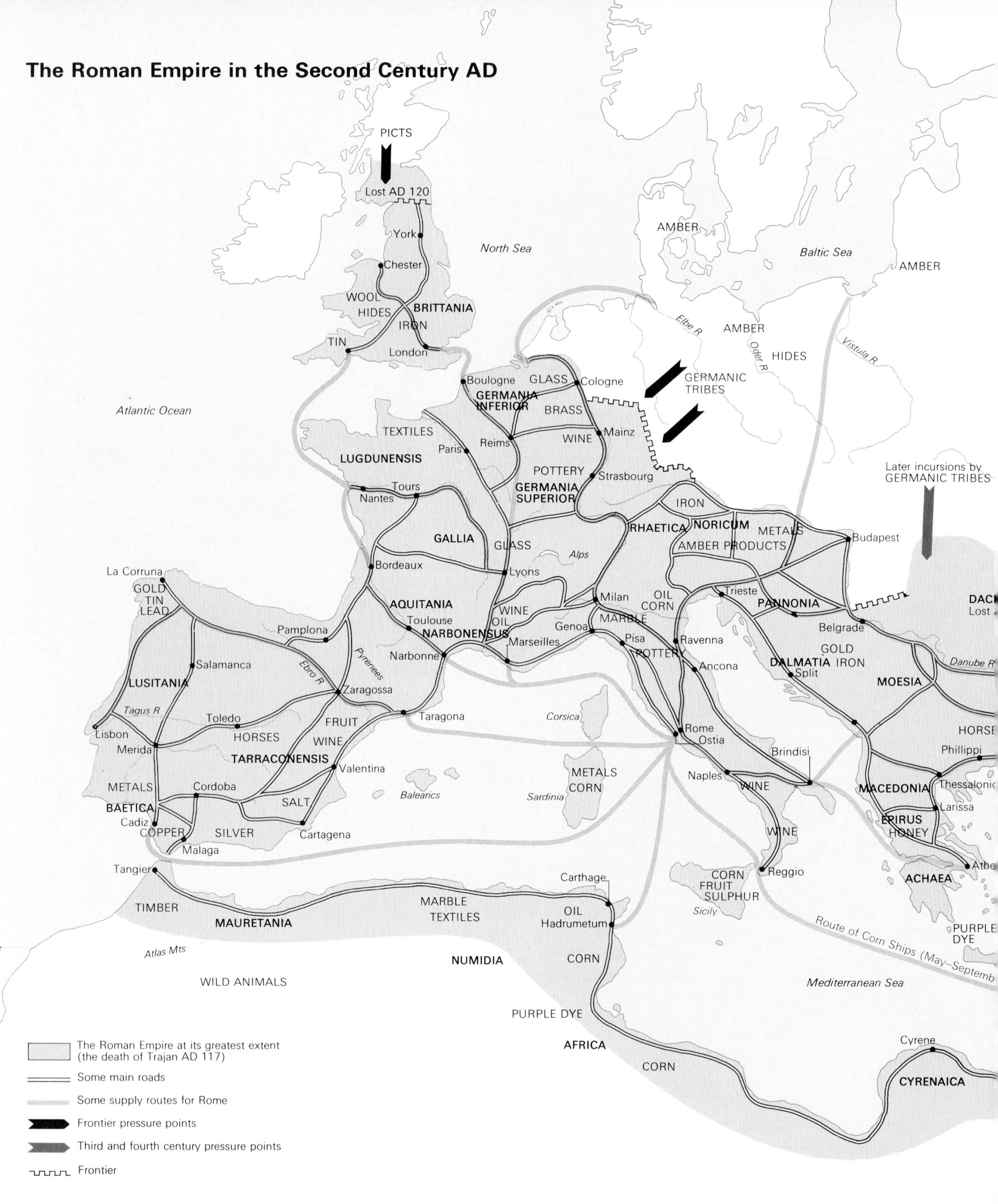
The Roman Empire in the Second Century AD
PICTS
Lost AD 120
York
Chester
WOOL
HIDES
BRITTANIA
IRON
TIN
London
North Sea
AMBER
Baltic Sea
AMBER
Elbe R
AMBER
Oder R
HIDES
Vistula R
Boulogne
GLASS
Cologne
GERMANIC TRIBES
GERMANIA INFERIOR
BRASS
Atlantic Ocean
TEXTILES
Reims
WINE
Mainz
Paris
LUGDUNENSIS
POTTERY
Strasbourg
Later incursions by GERMANIC TRIBES
Tours
Nantes
GERMANIA SUPERIOR
IRON
RHAETICA
NORICUM
METALS
GALLIA
GLASS
Alps
AMBER PRODUCTS
Budapest
Bordeaux
Lyons
La Corruna
GOLD
TIN
LEAD
AQUITANIA
Milan
OIL
CORN
Trieste
PANNONIA
DACIA
Toulouse
WINE
OIL
MARBLE
Genoa
NARBONENSUS
Pamplona
Belgrade
Marseilles
Pisa
Ravenna
Narbonne
POTTERY
GOLD
Salamanca
Ebro R
Pyrenees
Ancona
DALMATIA
IRON
Danube R
Split
MOESIA
LUSITANIA
Zaragossa
Tagus R
Taragona
Corsica
Toledo
FRUIT
Lisbon
Rome
HORSES
Merida
Ostia
HORSES
WINE
Phillippi
TARRACONENSIS
Brindisi
Valentina
METALS
CORN
Naples
Thessalonica
METALS
Cordoba
Balearics
Sardinia
WINE
MACEDONIA
BAETICA
SALT
Larissa
Cadiz
EPIRUS
COPPER
SILVER
Cartagena
WINE
HONEY
Malaga
Tangier
Reggio
Carthage
CORN
FRUIT
SULPHUR
ACHAEA
MARBLE
TIMBER
OIL
TEXTILES
Sicily
MAURETANIA
Hadrumetum
Route of Corn Ships (May–September)
PURPLE DYE
Atlas Mts
NUMIDIA
CORN
WILD ANIMALS
Mediterranean Sea
PURPLE DYE
AFRICA
Cyrene
CORN
CYRENAICA
The Roman Empire at its greatest extent (the death of Trajan AD 117)
Some main roads
Some supply routes for Rome
Frontier pressure points
Third and fourth century pressure points
Frontier

A manual for Roman farmers written by Cato the Censor shows that trade had already developed in Italy by the first half of the second century BC. "Tunics, togas, blankets smocks and shoes," he said, "should be bought at Rome; caps, iron tools, scythes, spades, mattocks, axes, harness, ornaments and small chains at Cales and Minturnae; spades at Venafrum, oil mills at Pompeii and at Rufrius's yard at Nola; nails and bars at Rome; pails, oil urns, water pitchers, wine urns, other copper vessels at Capua and at Nola; Campanian baskets, pulley ropes and all sorts of cordage at Capua, Roman baskets at Suessa and Casinum."

By imperial times Rome depended on imports, particularly of wheat to prevent famine. A million bushels of wheat a year was obtained from Sicily alone and even more from Egypt," the granary of the Mediterranean." Despite the importance of trade within the Mediterranean, the Romans left most of the seafaring to the Eastern Mediterranean peoples in the Empire, notably the Greeks and the Syrians.

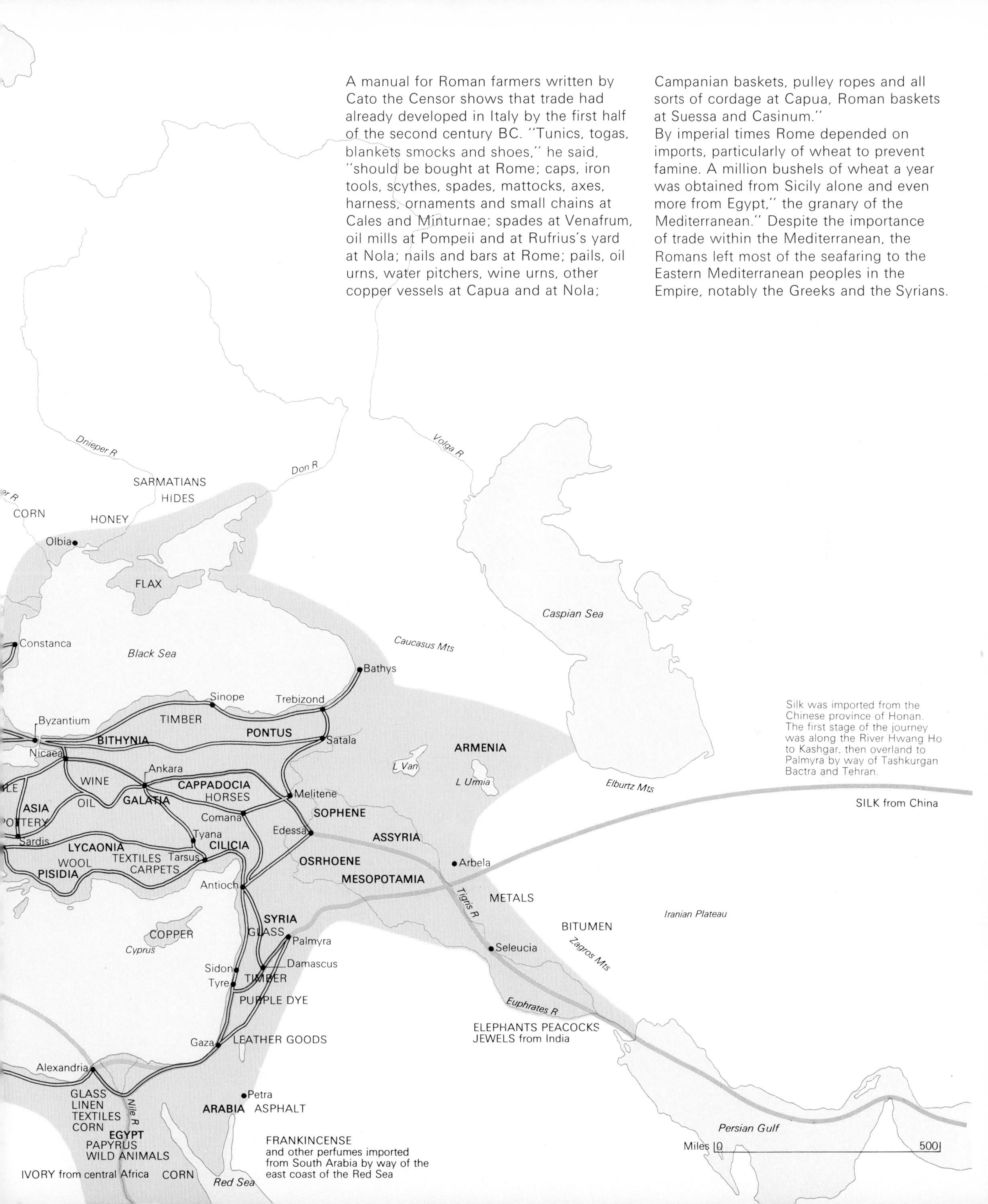

Chapter 12

# BIRTH OF CHRISTIANITY

## PALESTINE

The reign of the Roman Emperor Tiberius (A.D. 14–37) was reckoned to have been a quiet one in the province of Judea. Writing eighty years later, the historian Tacitus summed up the situation: "In Judea under Tiberius, all quiet." Both he and his contemporary, Suetonius, refer to minor matters in the province, such as taxation and friction between the Jews and the Samaritans, but of the events that have made the governorship of Pontius Pilate forever memorable, not a word. Jewish historians wrote about Pilate, but made no mention of Jesus of Nazareth.

Judea was the meeting point of three contrasting and conflicting civilizations. To the indigenous population of Jews and their Samaritan neighbors were added communities of Greek-Syrian settlers who, in the previous two centuries, had established themselves in the cities of the coastal plain and along the main lines of communication on both sides of the River Jordan. Then there were the Romans in increasing numbers, who governed Judea after A.D. 6 and had their headquarters at Caesarea on the coast. The Jews, only a bare majority in their own country, were confronted on all sides by idolatrous powers whom they regarded with deep-seated and scarcely concealed hostility. In A.D. 66 a Jewish rebellion was to break out, which almost drove the Romans from Palestine.

Christianity originated and developed its early mission within the framework of Palestinian Judaism. This framework was dominated by the Temple at Jerusalem and the high priesthood that served it. Associated with these were the Pharisees and the Sadducees, the custodians and interpreters of the law, who between them represented the traditional patriotic and intellectual outlook of Jewry. There were also many sects, some of whose ideals were absorbed by Christianity. Galilee, where Jesus grew up, was situated in the northern part of the province. It had been conquered and colonized by the Jews at the end of the second century B.C.

Jesus' background was connected with the local Jewish priestly class. In Jesus' family, piety was combined with an element of national feeling. Two of Jesus' brothers were called Juda and Simon, names associated with the heroes of the Maccabean wars of liberation against the Greek-Syrians in the second century B.C.

When Jesus was born at Bethlehem, a few miles south of Jerusalem, in about 6 B.C. the whole country from Galilee in the north to Idumaea in the south was ruled by King Herod. His reign was long, lasting for thirty-four years (37–4 B.C.), and

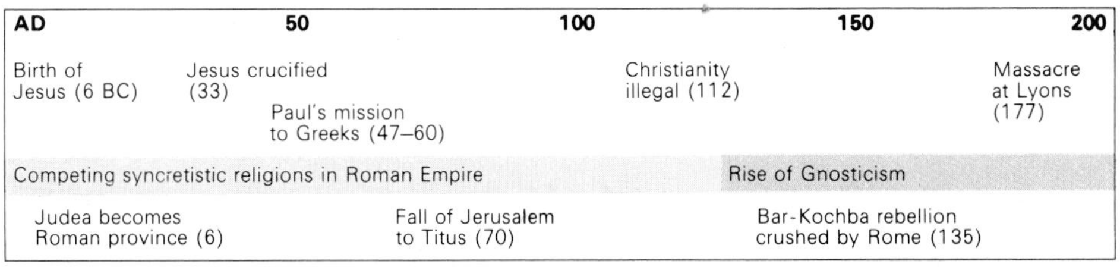

| AD | 50 | 100 | 150 | 200 |
|---|---|---|---|---|
| Birth of Jesus (6 BC); Jesus crucified (33) | Paul's mission to Greeks (47–60) | Christianity illegal (112) | | Massacre at Lyons (177) |
| Competing syncretistic religions in Roman Empire | | | Rise of Gnosticism | |
| Judea becomes Roman province (6) | Fall of Jerusalem to Titus (70) | | Bar-Kochba rebellion crushed by Rome (135) | |

The Sea of Galilee, background to many of the New Testament stories about Jesus. On the death of Herod the Great in 4 B.C. his kingdom was divided between his sons, Herod Antipas, Archelaus and Philip. Herod Antipas was ruler of Galilee and the Sea of Galilee formed part of the boundary between his territory and that of Philip. Hence in crossing the sea Jesus was moving from one judicial or political area to another. Pontius Pilate tried to pass the trial of Jesus over to Herod, the ruler of Galilee.

bloody. His friendship with Rome made him unpopular. Discontent was submerged but tended to be expressed through popular prophecies—for example, that the deliverance of the Jews would come through a new national ruler, descended from the warrior line of David—and in popular apocalyptic literature. This literature, circulated under the names of traditional Hebrew prophets, purported to reveal secrets of the future in cataclysmic terms. It was propagated vigorously and was probably produced by groups of sectarian Jews such as the Covenanters at Q'mran. Indeed, the discovery of the Dead Sea scrolls of Q'mran has added a new dimension to our knowledge of Jewish life and thought in Palestine in the era of Jesus. For the first time it has become possible to make valid comparisons between the teachings of the New Testament and those of contemporary Jewish sects. The Covenanters observed a strict discipline under a minutely organized hierarchy and regarded themselves as the elect of Israel, who were awaiting the coming of a deliverer.

An early-sixth-century mosaic. The theme of the baptism of Christ was one of the most popular in church decoration.

On the death of Herod, his kingdom was divided between his three sons. The Romans did not find this arrangement satisfactory, and in A.D. 6 they converted the three Jewish client kingdoms into the Roman province of Judea, governed by an imperial representative, a prefect. The reorganization was entrusted to the governor of Syria, P. Sulpicius Quirinus, and one of his first actions was to take a census of the whole area of Syria and Judea. This seems to have been the census referred to in the Gospel of Luke, though wrongly associated with Mary and Joseph's journey from Nazareth to Bethlehem. It was bitterly resented by the Jews who owed tribute only to Jahweh and his representative. (In the Gospels, the question put to Jesus about the tribute penny was framed deliberately to force him to declare hostility either to the Roman Empire or to the national aspirations of his fellow countrymen.)

## THE LIFE AND DEATH OF JESUS

The "hidden years" of Jesus' life, extending from the presentation in the temple to the baptism in the Jordan by his cousin, John the Baptist, are shrouded in mystery. Some contact with the Baptist's movement and call to national repentance in face of the approaching "Day of the Lord" may reasonably be assumed. Even so, some scholars have been tempted to discount the existence of the historical Jesus altogether. To Albert Schweitzer, for instance, "when all was said and done there remained only a shadowy figure walking by the Lake of Genaseret." To others, the personality of Jesus is unapproachable through the successive layers of transmission and edition of the gospels. To others, again, he is simply a figment of the imagination of the early Church. All this seems unduly pessimistic. The New Testament tells of people and events that would not be credible outside Palestine in the first half of the first century of the Christian era. The rival groups of Pharisees, Sadducees, and Herodians (supporters of Herod's dynasty) are accurately delineated, and so, too, is the underlying nationalist ferment that would make the ordinary people seize Jesus "to make him a king." That this was not impossible is indicated by the presence of a Zealot (Simon the Zealot) among Jesus' disciples.

Jesus' teaching comes across as that of an individual mind strongly imbued by the current prophetic and apocalyptic tradition, which yet deliberately shunned the role of conqueror and political leader that his contemporaries attributed to the Messiah. The "temptations," including the vision of political power entailed in the sight of "all the kingdoms of the world," may well reflect Jesus' real experience as he wrestled to discover the true nature of his calling.

Jesus' personal traits, as revealed in the Synoptic Gospels (Matthew, Mark, and Luke), show one who exercised enormous yet kindly influence on his fellows, who could penetrate rapidly to the heart of a problem, always bringing the question back to concrete and personal terms. He was forgiving yet reproving. "Sin no more" was the message to the women taken in adultery. To his contemporaries, Jesus was the prophet of Nazareth, a natural leader but one who pointed a way to salvation wholly different from that of the Messiah, the priestly or revolutionary conqueror whom they were hourly expecting. The basis of his leadership lay not in any claim as an earthly conqueror but in his claim to be the one with God.

The gospel narrative begins with Jesus accepting the baptism of John in the Jordan and at first following John with a simple message of repentance and deliverance. There follows the gradual unfolding of his own gospel (good news), the message that God's forgiveness is for all, for the Samaritans, who were the Jew's rivals and enemies, and the Romans as well as the Jews. There must be a root-and-branch reform of Judaism. The reform must be carried out in God's service, not by military means, nor by the overthrow of existing society. The message of salvation extended to all mankind. Finally, in accordance with the accepted tradition that the prophet must also suffer the martyr's death, Jesus undertook the journey to Jerusalem, there to confront the established powers of Judaism, the Pharisees and lawyers, the high priesthood, and finally, the Roman governor. For reasons that can be well understood in terms of the power politics of all ages, Jesus was sacrificed by the rulers of his own people as an embarrassment and executed on the governor's orders as a potential rebel. The Crucifixion (c. 33) gave the governor, Pontius Pilate, a chance to issue a public warning to all communities in the province. The legend on the cross "This is Jesus the King of the Jews" was written in the three current languages—Latin, Greek, and Hebrew—and spelled out the perils of rebellion.

Christ's entry into Jerusalem, from an early Christian sarcophagus. The triumphant entry into Jerusalem, only four days before Jesus' crucifixion represents the danger of popularity and acceptance—a danger often forgotten after Christianity became the religion of the Roman Empire. The sense of proportion of classical Greek and Roman art is lost when one examines the relative size of the human figures and the ass.

The Crucifixion, however, was not the end of the story. Within a very short time, Jesus' disciples had rallied. They had taken back with them to Galilee, whither they had returned, the idea that somehow Jesus was not dead. The tomb in which he had been laid had been found to be empty. This in itself had not convinced them that he had risen from the dead. The experiences they now underwent, however, of actually seeing the risen Christ, some of which are recorded in John's matter-of-fact style, persuaded them. Inspired by Peter, they decided to abandon once again the workaday lives they had resumed and to return to Jerusalem. There they would establish redeemed Israel and await the return of their Lord. The Ascension found them with their hopes restored. The experience of Pentecost convinced them finally that Jesus was indeed at God's right hand and that they had a message of redemption for all Jewry.

## THE FIRST MISSION

Jerusalem was the hub of Judaism, where Jews from all over the Greco-Roman world and from Parthia and Babylon customarily assembled at the annual celebration of the Passover. There new religious ideas could be discussed and spread, and there the disciples became an active sect among their fellow Jews. They "continued with one accord daily in the temple" and lost no opportunity of preaching Christ crucified and risen.

Soon they were attracting the attention of some of the Greek-speaking Jews who had synagogues in Jerusalem. These were by no means content with the high-priestly establishment. One of their number, Stephen, spoke his mind. From the time of Abel, the righteous had been put to death. Jesus was only the final example of the prophet done to death by his own people. This was too much; Stephen was seized and lynched. Stephen, however, was merely the tip of an iceberg. Many thinking Jews had been coming to the conclusion that, for all its virtue, the Jewish law (*Torah*) was no longer adequate as a guide. "I was alive without the law once; but when the commandment came, sin revived and I died." The law of Christ and of grace had superseded the law of Moses.

## PAUL

St Paul represents this changed view of the law. He had been a persecutor of the Christians, but was converted while traveling to Damascus. Paul's importance for the rise of Christianity is second only to that of Jesus. It seems clear from scraps of information preserved in Matthew's Gospel that the original disciples had a comparatively narrow horizon for their mission. Paul changed all this. The Jewish world in which he had grown up embraced the whole area of the Mediterranean. Since the conquests of Alexander the Great, the Jews had been taking advantage of improved communications to leave the cramped confines of Palestine to form their own communities in the major centers of the Mediterranean. There were probably 50,000 Jews in Rome, and other cities also had large numbers of the *diaspora* (dispersion). Paul's birthplace, Tarsus, "no mean city," was no exception.

The diaspora was clannish. Greek, not Aramaic, was the normal language. The outward form of life was also Greek. The Jews of the diaspora were, however, regarded with suspicion by Greeks because they retained their separate institutions. Many Greeks wondered: "Why, if the Jews claim to be citizens, do they not worship the same gods as we do?" The situation was aggravated by successful Jewish proselytization. Each synagogue had its outer circle of "god fearers," sympathizers who did not, however, accept the full law. Some of these were among the earliest adherents of Christianity.

Third-century wall painting of Jesus breaking bread, from the tomb of St Priscilla in the catacombs at Rome. Catacomb art features occasionally scenes from the New Testament life of Christ but more often scenes from the Old Testament. This shows Jewish influence on the Church in Rome, as does the burial of families together.

Yet the Jews had proved themselves loyal to Rome, and when Rome extended her influence throughout the eastern Mediterranean, they respected the Jewish religion and extended to Jews a number of privileges. One of these was that a Jew could be granted Roman citizenship without being obliged to give up his previous allegiance. The Jews were the only "dual nationals" in the Roman Empire, and Paul's parents were among the Jews who had this distinction.

Though born in the Dispersion, Paul retained Hebrew as well as Greek speech. He prided himself on his membership of the tribe of Benjamin, his links with the Pharisees, and his education at Jerusalem "at the feet of Gamaliel," a famous Pharisee.

The message that he was to take with him throughout the eastern Mediterranean after fourteen years in the wilderness on the eastern borders of Palestine was to transform the Christian faith. For him, Jesus had been the second Adam, whose return at the end of the existing age of human history had been mooted among Jewish sects. Jesus had revealed to his chosen disciples (to Paul, "the saints" or "chosen ones") "the mystery that had been hid from all generations." To the pagans, Paul represented Christ as "the unknown God" whom they worshiped in ignorance. Him Paul would now explain. They had been given a final chance of understanding the mystery of creation before the existing age would end and the day of the Lord dawn. The end would not be long delayed, hence the urgency of Paul's mission.

Between A.D. 47 and 60, the Christian message was preached in the Greek-speaking world by Paul accompanied first by Barnabas and then by various personal friends. There must have been other missionaries working independently, but of them nothing is known. The situation was not free from difficulty. In Jerusalem the leadership of the Christian community had been taken over (apparently from Peter) by Jesus' brother James. James regarded Jesus as having proclaimed a new covenant to Israel, and he clearly intended this covenant to apply first and foremost to the Jews. Yet he also valued the work that Paul had done, and under his guidance the Apostolic Council, in 49, had agreed not only that gentile converts to Christianity need not be circumcised according to the law of Moses but also that there should be two missions, one to the Jews under Peter and the other to the gentiles under Paul.

It was the latter that sparked the earliest organized persecutions of the Christians. The Jews feared that the success of Paul's mission among the Greek-speaking Jews and pagans would undermine the authority of their traditions. Paul's arrival in Jerusalem was the signal for disturbances, and the Jewish lawyer, Tertellus, who accused him before the Roman governor, explained that Paul, "ringleader of the sect of the Nazarenes," was causing "sedition among all the Jews throughout the world." Paul was arrested. As a Roman citizen, he used his right to appeal to Caesar; that is, he asked that his case might be heard in Rome. To Caesar he went, arriving in Rome in A.D. 60. There he was treated leniently. He began his mission once more and had success among the freedmen associated with some of the houses of the Roman aristocracy. His end is not recorded in the Acts of the Apostles.

### THE NERONIAN PERSECUTION

In general, Rome was tolerant of the vast numbers of foreigners who had flocked into the city in the previous two centuries. These immigrants came from all over the Mediterranean, although most came from the east, and they tended to settle in compact areas. They often brought their gods and their cults with them. So long as these were practiced discreetly and caused no scandal or disturbance, they were let be.

Sixth-century mosaic from Ravenna showing Pontius Pilate washing his hands to exculpate himself from responsibility for the death of Jesus. This action led to the use of the expression, to wash one's hands of something one dislikes. Ravenna, an important Christian center, became the capital of the Western Empire and later of the Byzantine Exarchate (province) of Italy.

On July 19, 64, much of Rome was destroyed by fire. Suspicion for the great fire fell on the Emperor Nero himself. He was believed to want to rid the city of an unsightly and crowded area in order to plan it anew on a grandiose scale. Then, to quote the historian Tacitus:

> *But all human efforts, all the lavish gifts of the emperor, and the propitiations of the gods, did not banish the sinister belief that the conflagration was the result of an order. Consequently, to get rid of the report, Nero fastened the guilt and inflicted the most exquisite tortures on a class hated for their abominations, called Christians by the populace. Christus, from whom the name had its origin, suffered the extreme penalty during the reign of Tiberius at the hands of one of our procurators, Pontius Pilatus, and a deadly superstition, thus checked for the moment, again broke out not only in Judea, the first source of the evil, but also in the City, where all things hideous and shameful from every part of the world meet and become popular. Accordingly, an arrest was first made of all who confessed; then, upon their information, an immense multitude was convicted, not so much of the crime of arson, as of hatred of the human race. Mockery of every sort was added to their deaths. Covered with the skins of beasts, they were torn by dogs and perished, or were nailed to crosses, or were doomed to the flames.*

By the end of the first century, however, the writer of the Christian work known as the *First Epistle of Clement* implies that the Jews were responsible for the persecution "through envy and jealousy." It adds that Peter and Paul were among the victims.

There is some color to this. The Jews were unpopular and were suspected of being incendiaries as a means of hastening the end of the age of idolatry. One Jewish poem of the time included the prophesy, "God shall burn the whole earth and consume the whole race of men. He shall burn everything up, and there will remain sooty dust." The Jews had friends at Nero's court, however, and these may have been able to transfer the blame to their hated rivals. The Christians were charged, be it noted, less with incendiarism than with "hatred of the human race." This was a charge often leveled by the Romans against the Jews. It was a protest against Jewish clannishness.

The Neronian persecution, however, was confined to this single catastrophe at Rome. There were no immediate repercussions in the provinces; nor, when the

Jews rose against Rome in 66 and tried to establish an independent state in Judea, were there further measures against the Christians.

## THE ORGANIZATION OF THE CHURCH

What was the organization of the early Church? Who were its officers? What authority did they have? These are questions which affect the relationships among existing churches today.

In the early Church, the fact of common baptism and commitment was primary and organization was secondary. Moreover, any form of organization could be expected to find its parallel in Judaism. Naturally, the Church in Jerusalem bore some relation to the existing high priesthood. We find early a Christian Sanhedrin, or council, presided over by James, who was assisted by the twelve disciples, representing the twelve tribes of Israel, with probably an inner council of the three "pillars" (James, Peter, and John, the son of Zebedee) and deacons as assistants. From this organization springs the idea of a monarchical episcopate handing down a visible tradition to an organized hierarchy based on episcopal succession going back to the apostles.

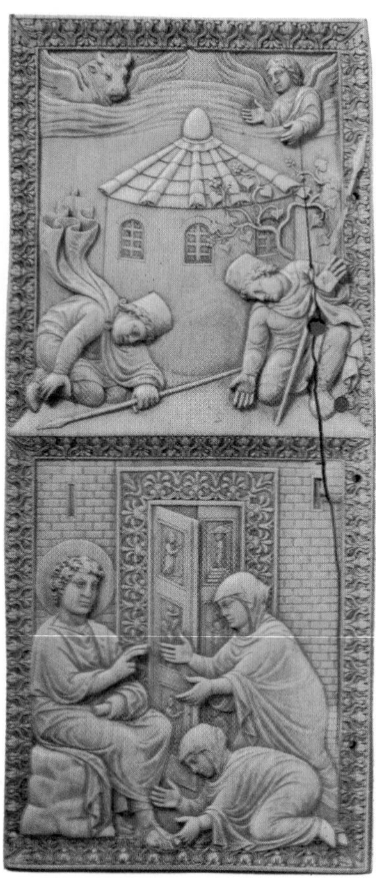

A diptych showing Roman soldiers by the empty tomb of Jesus, and the resurrected Jesus. The early Church saw the miraculous nature of the Resurrection as an argument for the truth of Christianity.

Administration by a board of presbyter-bishops was probably the earliest normal form of Church government in the missionary churches, including Rome. Paul and his immediate followers in some way or other could claim to be witnesses to Christ's resurrection. They supervised churches over great areas. When they had passed from the scene, authority automatically fell to the leaders of the resident communities they had founded. These became the Church's permanent leaders, whose position could be paralleled by the ruler of a Jewish synagogue. By the turn of the second century, the orders of bishop, presbyter, and deacon had become the established offices in the Church, with authority over each Christian community.

With the fall of Jerusalem in 70, the Church lost its natural center. Gradually, in the next thirty years, its influence in Jesus' homeland lessened. The Christians had not taken up arms against Rome, and the loyalty of the Jewish people was given to those who had, notably to the new generation of Pharisees. In the areas covered by Paul's mission, however, the Church flourished. By the end of the first century, there were Christian communities in Asia Minor far beyond where Paul had preached. This meant that from now on the Christian message would be directed westward to the Greco-Roman world. It would be preached in the Greek language, the language of Paul. It would have to make its way among the synagogues of the diaspora, and above all it would have to come to terms with the Roman state.

## CHRISTIANITY AND THE STATE

By the first half of the second century the initial impetus of the Pauline mission had flagged. Thanks, however, to the widespread character of the Jewish diaspora, the Christians had been able to establish themselves in many of the larger centers of the eastern Mediterranean and, in particular, in the Roman province of Asia (western Asia Minor). But the members of these churches displayed little interest in going out to preach among the gentiles. The "New Testament" was not yet formed into a set canon and seems to have had little effect as a means of propagating the word. Only the Christians' stubborn belief in Christ as Lord and Savior, a belief which compelled them even to welcome death, moved ordinary provincials to note their existence.

It was not until A.D. 112 that we have evidence for Christians attracting the notice of the Roman provincial authorities. In that year the Emperor Trajan (98–117) sent Pliny, an experienced lawyer, as his representative to the province of Bithynia Pontus, where there was great discontent.

Pliny's lengthy correspondence with the emperor throws light on the major day-to-day problems of Roman provincial administration. Two letters concern the Christians. Pliny had been told that the temples were in a bad way and that the blame lay with the people called Christians. He tried some of them, asking them in the customary way three times whether they accepted the accusation. Because they refused to deny it, he ordered them to be executed—for, "whatever they were guilty of, their very obstinacy deserved to be punished." A list of alleged Christians was produced. Some of them now denied that they were, and others said they had been so once but had ceased to be as much as twenty years previously. For these, Pliny applied the test of whether they would sacrifice to the Roman gods, including the genius of the emperor, and "curse Christ," that is, abjure the name and black magic attached to a demonic power. Pliny eventually reached the conclusion that he was dealing with an extravagant but basically not very harmful superstition.

Trajan's reply laid down what was to be the official line of action toward the Christians for the next century and a half. Trajan wrote:

> *You have adopted the proper course, my dear Secundus, in your examination of the cases of those who were accused to you as Christians, for indeed nothing can be laid down as a general ruling involving something like a set form of procedure. They are not to be sought out; but if they are accused and convicted, they must be punished—yet on this condition, that whoso denies himself to be a Christian, and makes the fact plain by his action, that is, by worshiping our gods, shall obtain pardon on his repentance, however suspicious his past conduct may be. Papers, however, which are presented unsigned ought not to be admitted in any charge, for they are a very bad example and unworthy of our time.*

The final sentence demonstrates the basically liberal and optimistic outlook of the age. The Jews remained a formidable internal problem. The Christians were insignificant. One could afford to be merciful.

Why had Christianity suddenly become illegal? There had been no formal law proscribing it, for had there been one, Pliny would have known of it. The situation seems to have arisen largely because for the first time it was officially recognized that the Christians were refusing to honor the emperor's genius or the gods of the communities in which they lived. They were thus putting themselves outside the close nexus of tribal, provincial, and city relationships that governed the lives of the ordinary provincials in the Roman Empire. Only Jews had a right to refuse this worship. In addition, their own closely knit organizations observed nocturnal ceremonies. It was suspected that these ceremonies were connected with black magic and therefore dangerous to the community as a whole. The Christians were anti-social. Finally, the Christians repudiated the Roman concept of the sanctity of tradition (*the mos maiorum*). This and their obstinacy deserved punishment.

Under Hadrian (117–138), another step was taken toward defining the position of the Christians. In parts of the province of Asia, they had been subjected to mob attacks. The proconsul had written to the emperor for advice. Hadrian ordered that Christians must be charged with specific crimes under due processes of law before punishment. If the charges failed, then they themselves might cross-charge their accusers under the defamation procedure. Christians were not to be treated as outlaws, but their religion was not legalized.

Moreover, when the test came, Christians proved themselves loyal to the Empire. They did not participate in the great Jewish revolt of 115–117. The Christians in the first half of the second century seemed destined to a minor role among the aberrant sects of the Roman Empire.

## The Spread of Christianity

995–1030
1155
563–597
North Sea
829–1000
440–443
Kildare
Baltic Sea
Fully Christianized by the end of the 11th Century
1100–1300
Rhine R
600–800
800–1100
Seine R
Atlantic Ocean
Alps
Rhone R
Pyrenees
Marseilles
Isle of Lerin
Danube R
Black Sea
Corsica
Rome
Thessalonica
Phillipi
Constantinople
Benevento
Balearics
Sardinia
Pergamum
Smyrna
Ephesus
Miletus
Sicily
Corinth
Syracuse
Tarsus
Carthage
Antioch
Athens
Crete
Atlas Mts
Mediterranean Sea
Cyprus
Damascus
Sidon
Caesarea
Joppa
Jerusalem
Alexandria
Sinai
Red Sea
Christians 50% of population in AD 325
Christians 5–50% of population in AD 325
Areas with few or no Christians in AD 325
Early Episcopal centers
Centers of early monastic life
Journeys of St Paul
Borders of the Roman Empire about AD300
Miles 0 500

## THE GROWTH OF POPULAR OPPOSITION

The danger to Christians in the second century came less from the authorities than from the provincials. When the political threat from Judaism ended with the collapse of Bar-Kochba's rebellion in 135, the Christians found themselves heirs to most of the popular hatred and contempt previously reserved for the Jews. In Rome, a lewd cartoon scratched on the wall of the Palatine depicts a creature with an ass's head stretched out on a cross. Underneath, a text reads "Anasseagoras worships this." The Jews were supposed to worship (and sleep with) an ass. Now the Christians were being ridiculed in the same way. Worse than this, sometime around 150 the provincials in the large centers of population in the eastern Mediterranean seem to have made up their minds that the Christians, by refusing to worship the Greek gods, were responsible for all manner of misfortunes, such as famines, floods, plagues, and earthquakes. They were atheists, and they had angered the gods further by practicing secret rites involving incest, cannibalism, and black magic (the Eucharist could be interpreted as "eating their God"). Thirty years later, Tertullian, writing in Carthage, summed up popular fears:

> *If the Tiber reaches the walls, if the Nile does not rise to the fields, if the sky does not move or the earth does, if there is famine, if there is plague, the cry is at once, "Christians to the lion." What, all of them to one lion!*

Eusebius of Caesarea (c. 260–339), the first Christian historian, records two terrible instances of popular violence directed against the Christians in the second half of the second century. In about 165 the populace of Smyrna turned on the Christians. Polycarp, their bishop, was seized and brought before the proconsul, who was presiding over ceremonial games in the city. The following scene, recorded by an eyewitness, took place:

Sarcophagus known as "The Sarcophagus of the Shepherds," another early Christian work.

> *So he was brought before the Proconsul, who asked him if he were Polycarp? He said "Yes," and the Proconsul tried to persuade him to deny his faith, urging, "Have respect to your old age," and the rest of it, according to the customary form. "Swear by the genius of Caesar; change your mind; say, 'Away with the Atheists!'" Then Polycarp looked with a stern countenance on the multitude of lawless heathens gathered in the stadium, and waved his hands at them, and looked up to heaven with a groan, and said, "Away with the Atheists." The Proconsul continued insisting and saying, "Swear, and I release you; curse Christ." And Polycarp said, "Eighty-six years have I served Him, and He has done me no wrong: how then can I blaspheme my King who saved me?"*

Detail showing three of the miracles of Jesus.

Polycarp was burned. The incident shows how little room there was for compromise between the Christians and their fellow provincials. Polycarp was a well-known and respected citizen of Smyrna. He had been bishop for nearly sixty years. Yet all this did not save him.

The second incident took place at Lyons in Gaul in 177. Eusebius cites a contemporary document (a letter sent by survivors to their parent churches in Asia Minor), which highlights not only the brutality of the mob but the weakness of the Roman authorities on the spot. Many Christians were killed, after being falsely accused of holding orgies. Their bodies were burned and the ashes thrown into the Rhone for fear that in some way or other they might be resurrected. The blood of the martyrs was the seed through which Christianity was ultimately to triumph.

## A PAGAN'S VIEW OF CHRISTIANITY: CELSUS

The gradual increase in the Church's influence in the last quarter of the second century is shown by another factor. By 178 educated pagans were beginning to take Christianity seriously as a menace to contemporary values and civilization. In that year Celsus, a Greek-speaking provincial probably living in Syria and a Platonist in outlook, wrote a full-scale attack on Christianity with the aim of awakening his fellow provincials to the danger it represented. He had taken the trouble to read Jewish and Christian works, including the Synoptic Gospels, and his *True Word* is the most important single witness of the life and attitudes of Christians during this period. Celsus made explicit what was only inferred in Pliny's letter to Trajan. His main charge was that the Christians lacked civic sense: they put their religion before their duty to the state.

In one passage, Celsus portrays vividly Christian propaganda among the less privileged sections of Greco-Roman society, the women, the slaves, and the freedmen:

> *In private houses also we see wool workers, cobblers, laundry workers, and the most illiterate and bucolic yokels, who would not dare to say anything at all in front of their elders and more intelligent masters. But whenever they get hold of children in private and some stupid women with them, they let out some astounding statements as, for example, that they must not pay any attention to their father and schoolteachers, but must obey them; they say that these talk nonsense and have no understanding, and that in reality they neither know nor are able to do anything good, but are taken up with mere empty chatter. But they alone, they say, know the right way to live, and if the children would believe them, they would become happy and make their home happy as well.*

The whole structure of customary relationships in the ancient world was endangered.

## GNOSTICISM AND THE DEVELOPMENT OF CHRISTIAN DOCTRINE

Most pagans in the first and second centuries believed in seven heavens, which were believed to form concentric circles above the earth. The most important supernatural beings were the lords of the sun, moon, and five known planets, who controlled time and after whom the days of the week were named. They and the goddess of chance were believed to rule each individual from the time of birth until his death. Christianity promised salvation from the thralldom of these elements, as Paul calls them. Should not knowledge of their true nature supplement baptism?

Out of this problem arose a number of radically heretical sects—gnostics, as they are collectively called today—centering around the belief that salvation could be achieved only through knowledge. The movement gained strength in the second century, dominating much of Christian intellectual life in the period A.D. 130–180. Because of the gnostic controversy, the Christians were forced at this time to define their essential beliefs and develop an orthodox doctrine.

The basic tenet of the gnostics was that God is not the creator of the world. This is the work of an inferior agent usually equated with the God of the Old Testament. The latter is lord of the various hostile principalities and powers that afflicted mankind. Jesus, however, was sent by God to rescue and illumine mankind and deliver men from slavery to Jehovah and his agents. In the Syrian form of gnosticism, God is associated with a female principal, the Thought (or Reflection) of God, perhaps derived from the Jewish Sophia (Wisdom) in the Wisdom literature and akin to those basic Mediterranean religious concepts that always associate a female seed or reflection of God with God himself. We see the gnostics speaking in terms like those of existentialism, probing the psychology of dreams, and we are able to separate the Jewish and non-Jewish strands in their thought.

That they stood nearer to contemporary mystery religions than to orthodox Christianity seems clear. They denied the potential goodness and reality of the material world. God was completely unknown except to themselves. Humanity was predestined to live in watertight compartments. Man could not contribute to his own salvation. It was a religion of pessimism. In addition, except by the means of subtle exegesis, Christ bore no relation to the Jesus of the New Testament, and the Old Testament had no claim to be the word of God. Jesus' ministry was not a real ministry, nor were his passion, death, and resurrection real. There was no purpose in martyrdom. The body was either to be abused or mortified. Nirvana replaced Heaven and Hell.

The most important refutation of gnosticism came from the pen of Irenaeus (c. 100–197), one of the survivors of the persecution at Lyons. The five books which he wrote *Against the Heresies* subject the gnostics to devastating criticism. Irenaeus provided an outline of doctrine, a statement of belief, and a canon of scripture that Christianity could call her own, independent of gnosticism and Judaism. By the end of the second century, the Church could begin to see its task in terms of universal mission.

One deviation escaped the lash of Irenaeus' criticism. Martyrdom and the spirit of prophecy were closely associated in his mind. In 172 a prophetic movement broke out in Phrygia (Asia Minor) inspired by Montanus, perhaps a converted Phrygian priest. He claimed direct inspiration from the Holy Spirit, which worked through Christians regardless of whether they were laymen or clergy. He also proclaimed the approaching end of the world. No one wanted to be known as a "slayer of the prophets," and Montanus' message was not unwelcome to many Christians. But his ideas conflicted with those of the leaders of the now-established Christian communities. For the first time on record, the bishops held councils and acted in common against teaching they rejected.

Gnostic gems. The term gnostic is used to explain a tendency of thought that threatened the Christian Church in the second century. Gnosticism contained many elements, religious and philosophical, taken from Platonism, Judaism, Mithraism and Zoroastrianism. Its greatest impact came from the development of Manicheism. This had extensive influence both in the western and oriental world, which characterized all physical things as being evil: only the spirit was good.

Chapter 13

# THE CRISIS OF THE THIRD CENTURY

## COMMODUS

The historian Cassius Dio says that in turning to the history of the third century he is descending from the story of a kingdom of gold to one of iron and rust. The peaceful security of an Empire bound in by a tightly contained series of peaceful provinces had passed. Barbarian invasions occurred with alarmingly increased frequency on several frontiers simultaneously, demanding the constant presence of large imperial forces. So far the forces could still repulse the invasions, but as soon as the armies withdrew, the barbarians would return. The treasuries were empty because the barbarians often had to be bought off with bribes—usually of large amounts of gold.

The story of the third-century insecurity and decline is thus set against a gloomy background of inevitability. It is questionable whether any amount of good government could have altered the prospects. But Romans blamed the government in the person of the emperor nonetheless—and, unfortunately, Commodus (emperor 180–192), the son of Marcus Aurelius, was a man who indeed deserved their criticism. Vainglorious, cruel, and stupid, he bought off barbarian tribes instead of fighting them, although a decisive military victory would have been possible. Most of his rule was taken up with the political murder of all those whom he felt were plotting against him (there were more plots against him than against almost any other emperor) but his wholesale executions, understandably, only worsened the situation. His chief enjoyments lay in perfecting his skills as a gladiator—a profession confined normally to slaves and freedmen. This earned him the disgust of the people and the senate. Eventually he was murdered. The bad rule of Commodus was more than an interlude in Roman government—it meant the end of more than half a century of peaceful succession from father to son. But now, as under the early Empire, the question rose again: should the succession fall to the man best suited to the task or to the son of the ruling emperor? It was a problem that plagued all the emperors of the third century.

After the death of Commodus there followed a period of reshuffling. Two emperors, Pertinax and Julianus, ruled briefly. Both were assassinated. It is indicative of the times that the first and most important body of people to satisfy on being elected emperor was the Praetorian Guard—the only military power within the walls of Rome.

| 200 AD | 225 | 250 | 300 | 350 |
|---|---|---|---|---|
| Severus (192–211)<br>Caracalla (211–17) | Alexander (222–44) | Philip (244–53)<br>Aurelian (270–75) | Constantine (305–37) | |
| Albinus' rising in Britain | Military emperors: economic crisis | Valerian and Gallienus (253–68) | Diocletian (284–305)<br>Christianity tolerated (313) | |
| | Goth and Persian invasions; Danube rebellion | Persecution of Christians (250) | Administrative and military reform<br>Territorial consolidation | |

The interior of the Pantheon, Rome. This is the only ancient building in Rome whose walls have been completely preserved, and is one of the greatest architectural works of antiquity. The present building was erected by the emperor Hadrian on the site of an earlier Pantheon of the first century B.C. The original purpose of the temple is unknown, but its boldness and splendor show that it was an important building. It is lit by a single large hole in the roof. In 608 the Pantheon was converted into a Christian church dedicated to S. Maria ad Martyres, and was the tomb of the kings of Italy.

## THE SEVERI

Three major rebellions had broken out during the last year of Commodus' reign. Rome could not be held, either against the Praetorian Guard or against the initiative of the talented generals employed elsewhere. Septimius Severus, who led the rising in Pannonia, struck first, realizing that there was bound to be battle between the three contenders once their common cause, the deposition of Commodus, had been achieved. He therefore made overtures to Albinus, who led the rising in Britain, promising him that he could be Caesar when he, Severus, was Augustus. Albinus agreed to this proposal. The senate, seeing the inevitability of Severus' victory, agreed to Julianus' execution, and to bestow divine honors on the dead Pertinax. Thus, when Severus entered Rome as emperor, it was as the restorer of good government, and he took care to link himself to the image of Pertinax, a sensible, senatorial ruler, under whom, had he been strong enough, the army would have been shown its proper place and limits. One of his first acts was to dismiss the Praetorian Guard. The Guard had been drawn in the past from Italians. Now they were replaced by people from his own area, who were likely to be loyal to him personally and to identify their interests with his own, rather than forming an influential opposition. Severus decided to crush his rivals. The rebel governor of Syria, Niger, was beaten. Severus attempted to wipe out all possible opposition. Antioch was razed to the ground and Byzantium's walls were demolished—two of the East's proudest cities were humbled. While in the East, Severus attacked the Persian Empire. He made inroads into Parthia, Persia's western province, in order to secure the eastern frontier.

A battle between Romans and barbarians, from the tomb of a Roman general. Although the Roman Empire in the West was eventually destroyed by barbarian invasions, for generations the barbarians had been held back or conquered by Roman armies. In general the Romans were better equipped than barbarians, and were also better disciplined. The Romans are depicted wearing helmets.

Severus decided that the only way of securing the succession was to found a dynasty. He married the famous Syrian, Julia Domna, by whom he had a son, later known as Caracalla. Severus also took the extraordinary step of apotheosizing Commodus, whose name had been condemned by the very emperor (Pertinax) whose spiritual successor Severus had originally claimed to be. Commodus had been the last member of a dynasty. The idea that heredity was the justification for succession was formally expressed later in the century as deriving from God, and then being handed down from generation to generation.

There remained Albinus against whom Severus appears to have moved without any provocation. A decisive battle was fought at Lugdunum (Lyons) in Gaul, after which Severus found that the Parthian threat once again demanded his attention. After two summers of activity he had annexed Mesopotamia as a Roman province, contravening the earlier Roman principle of not extending the boundaries of the Empire. On his return to Rome he settled down to the celebration of magnificent games and erected one of the most impressive of the arches standing today on the Roman forum, as a memorial to his Persian conquests.

Severus died in Britain, fighting a guerrilla war against the Caledonians in Scotland. He had been forced to give up the northern-most fortifications, the Antonine Wall, and retreat to Hadrian's wall. Security had lain for him in two things: the establishment of his own dynasty in order to ensure an easy succession of emperors, and the conquest of the Empire. Under his successor it was to become obvious how precarious both these principles were—both depended on good fortune, a trustworthy and competent heir to the throne, and a manageable number of barbarian attacks.

In the name of his predecessors, Severus had attempted to strengthen the defenses of the Empire, against both its external and its internal foes. His reform of government was designed in part to enable less wealthy men of talent to fill important posts and give their much needed services to the state, but in effect it tended to exclude the influential and the dangerous from positions of power. This angered many senators. Caracalla went further, throwing even superficial concern for political etiquette to the winds, defying the senate, and glorifying himself. Dio says sarcastically of Caracalla, "the fickleness, cowardice, and recklessness of the Gauls were his, the harshness and cruelty of Africa, and the craftiness of Syria." He murdered his brother, Geta, whom his father had made Caesar. On Severus' part, handing over the Empire to the care of both sons may have been due to a lack of insight into their characters; politically, however, it was a step towards admitting that the Empire was too large for one man to rule.

Caracalla, however, had his own ideas. He set about corrupting the soldiers with enormous bribes for their affections. This policy was to have far-reaching consequences for the third century, because the army grew accustomed to being able to demand money from the emperors in exchange for allegiance. Caracalla could not trust himself to enter the senate, which he had purged, without an armed bodyguard. Luckily for him, troubles in the northern frontiers of the Empire broke out, and Caracalla had to hasten there. His military talents were considerable, and, through his efforts, peace in Germany could be reestablished. Subsequently, he went eastward, securing the Danube frontier as he went, and finally making war on the king of Parthia, who refused to allow his daughter to marry Caracalla. This was indeed a cause for war to Caracalla—he had long dreamed that he would create one unified state of Rome and Parthia, or better still, all Persia. But in the course of this campaign, he was murdered by his praetorian prefect, Macrinus, who was then acclaimed emperor (217).

The "tetrarchs" from St Mark's Cathedral, Venice. The emperor Diocletian is on the right with the other Augustus, Maximian. On the left are the two Caesars, Galerius and Constantius. Diocletian's complicated division of the Empire became a model for the later division between East and West, but its complexity led to many difficulties after the abdication of Diocletian in 305.

The reign of Caracalla provides a strong link in the chain of circumstances leading to the military anarchy which was soon to follow. Autocratic rule, hatred of the senate, open arrogance to those around him, and military talent were the marks of more than one of the emperors who succeeded him. Macrinus provides the next link. A common soldier, he was the first emperor who did not come from the senatorial ranks. He was elevated entirely through his troops' assent. However, even he saw the need to base his rule on continuity of tradition, and linked himself with his predecessors by adopting Severus as his father and, strangely for one in his position, having Caracalla declared a god. He lacked, unfortunately, the military flair which Caracalla had possessed. The king of Parthia invaded Mesopotamia and Macrinus bought him off with a large bribe. The loss of currency, which Rome could ill afford, was becoming an ordinary occurrence. Macrinus was put to death through the initiative of Julia Maesa—one of the ladies of Severus' imperial family. Elagabalus, Julia Maesa's grandson and future emperor, was named after the sun god whom he worshiped. After being proclaimed emperor, this boy indulged still further the fanatical religious fantasies to which he was prone. His religion was all he cared about; the affairs of state were allowed to lapse. Elagabalus' grandmother foresaw a catastrophe, and in her ambition to maintain her position of power induced Elagabalus to proclaim his cousin (her other grandson), who called himself Alexander, Caesar. Her idea was a good one; Elagabalus hoped to be able to divide up the functions of state so that he would be able to devote himself full-time to the performance of his ritual duties. Alexander was only thirteen years old, but his friendliness earned him the affections of the Praetorian Guard. Finally, again at the instigation of Julia Maesa, Elagabalus and his mother were both murdered, and Alexander was left as sole emperor.

### Alexander

With great sincerity and tact, this boy tried to improve the atmosphere of random emotional response to political affairs which his cousin had created. For nine years there was comparative peace in the Empire. Alexander grew up—and ruled on his own. The financial situation improved with the lack of wars, and taxes could be lightened, for the first and last time in the third century. At the Senate's request he carried out reforms which had the unexpected effect of widening the membership of the senate. His great failure, however, lay in his poor generalship.

In the East, war broke out after an attempt to create a "Zoroastrian Empire." Hardly was this danger contained, than war broke out again with the Germans, who had crossed the frontier along the Rhine and Danube, presumably because the Roman defense system there had weakened during these years. This was the beginning of a recurrent pattern. Whenever the Romans were unable to maintain their frontiers, they would invade the Empire. Alexander incurred the distrust of his troops, who were mainly Illyrians, by trying to negotiate with the Germans. The Illyrians had been given parcels of land in frontier territory as part of their settlement and now, understandably, felt insecure. Because of his unwillingness to undertake an effective campaign Alexander was murdered in 235, and the Illyrian soldiers put forward an emperor from their own ranks, feeling that only such a man could represent their own interests.

## WAR AND CIVIL WAR

Maximinus, the new emperor, had never held a civilian post. He had risen through the ranks by sheer physical strength—tradition has it that he was an enormous man. He was the man, indeed, to carry out the campaign in question, but his attitude to civilian government was formed quickly as a result of a series of mutinies, instigated by men of senatorial rank. All those of senatorial rank were dismissed from office in his army.

This introduced a period of disturbance in the affairs of the Roman Empire which was to last for some time. Emperor and counter-emperor claimed the throne.

A third-century mosaic showing circus scenes. Circuses were the main organized amusement in Roman times—the equivalent of baseball, football and pop concerts. Gladiators, who were chiefly slaves, fought; chariot races were run; animals were set to fight each other or armed men. A policy of *panem et circenses* (bread and circuses) was followed by Roman emperors to keep the population of the capital content. Even in the Byzantine Empire circuses remained important: factions following the colors of the main chariot-racing groups came to dominate political life.

The senate intervened as it had rarely done and attempted to impose its own solution. The Praetorian Guard objected to this unwanted resurgence of senatorial interest and backed Gordian III whose family possessed phenomenal wealth. Eventually he emerged as sole emperor from the struggle.

However, his youth prevented him from being personally effective and he relied on his praetorian prefect. This was a critical juncture in external affairs too, because the Empire was faced with invasions from both the Persians and the Goths. Gordian met the inevitable fate of assassination and was replaced by his prefect, Philip.

Philip managed to secure peace with Persia, defeat the Goths, and mollify the senate. However, renewed trouble on the Danube produced a fresh spate of claimants for the purple. Philip outlasted his rivals, but when Decius, the general on the Danube, won success and was hailed emperor by his troops, apparently against his will, Philip refused to abandon his suspicions of disloyalty, met him in battle, and was defeated.

Decius in turn was supplanted by his lieutenant, Gallus, and emperor followed emperor in rapid succession while affairs in the Empire went from bad to worse. Plague swept through all the provinces. The Persians attacked Mesopotamia, and the Goths could not be kept out of Moesia. There was a brief respite while Valerian and his son, Gallienus, were recognized as Augustus and Caesar, but soon things grew worse. In the West Gallienus abandoned Gaul to its fate but defeated the Alemanni at Milan; in the East his father, after winning a victory over the Goths, was captured by the Persians. Gallienus, left to rule alone, made such arrangements as he could to regain control of the eastern provinces with Odenathus, prince of Palmyra. Three years later, after initial successes, Odenathus was murdered while Gallienus was fighting the Goths in Greece. Eventually Gallienus too was murdered by rebellious generals and the position of the Empire was at its very worst.

The repeated invasions had not only completely emptied the treasury, but had caused unprecedented inflation—money was minted with barely 2 percent silver content. Prices for basic commodities rose astronomically, and everywhere trade dwindled, due partly to the danger of travel during the invasions. Rome was reverting to the very basic economic system that it had left behind centuries ago.

As far as the provinces went, in the East, Zenobia, the wife of Odenathus, obstructed all attempts to regain control; in the West the enterprising Postumus had set up an independent empire in Gaul, Britain, and Spain after freeing them from the barbarians. At the time of Gallienus' death, one of his rivals was actually at Milan. Although Gallienus has been readily selected as a scapegoat it would be unfair to apportion all the blame to him. He had, however, pursued one policy which was anathema to the concept of the Empire: protecting those parts of the Empire overrun by barbarians, he left the East and the extreme West to be ruled by others without his sanction until such time that he could afford to turn to them.

## RECONSTRUCTION

The remainder of the story of the third century is the story of piecing back together the unity of the Empire, and reestablishing centralized control, which eventually became stronger than ever before.

Claudius, one of the generals who had conspired against Gallienus, was made emperor. He continued Gallienus' policy by finishing the wars against the Alemanni, and stayed on the Danube to end the Gothic threat completely. The problem of the East was left to his successors when he died of plague.

After a short interval, Aurelian, Claudius' general, took over as sole emperor. From the outset, Aurelian continued the policy of settling the barbarian threat

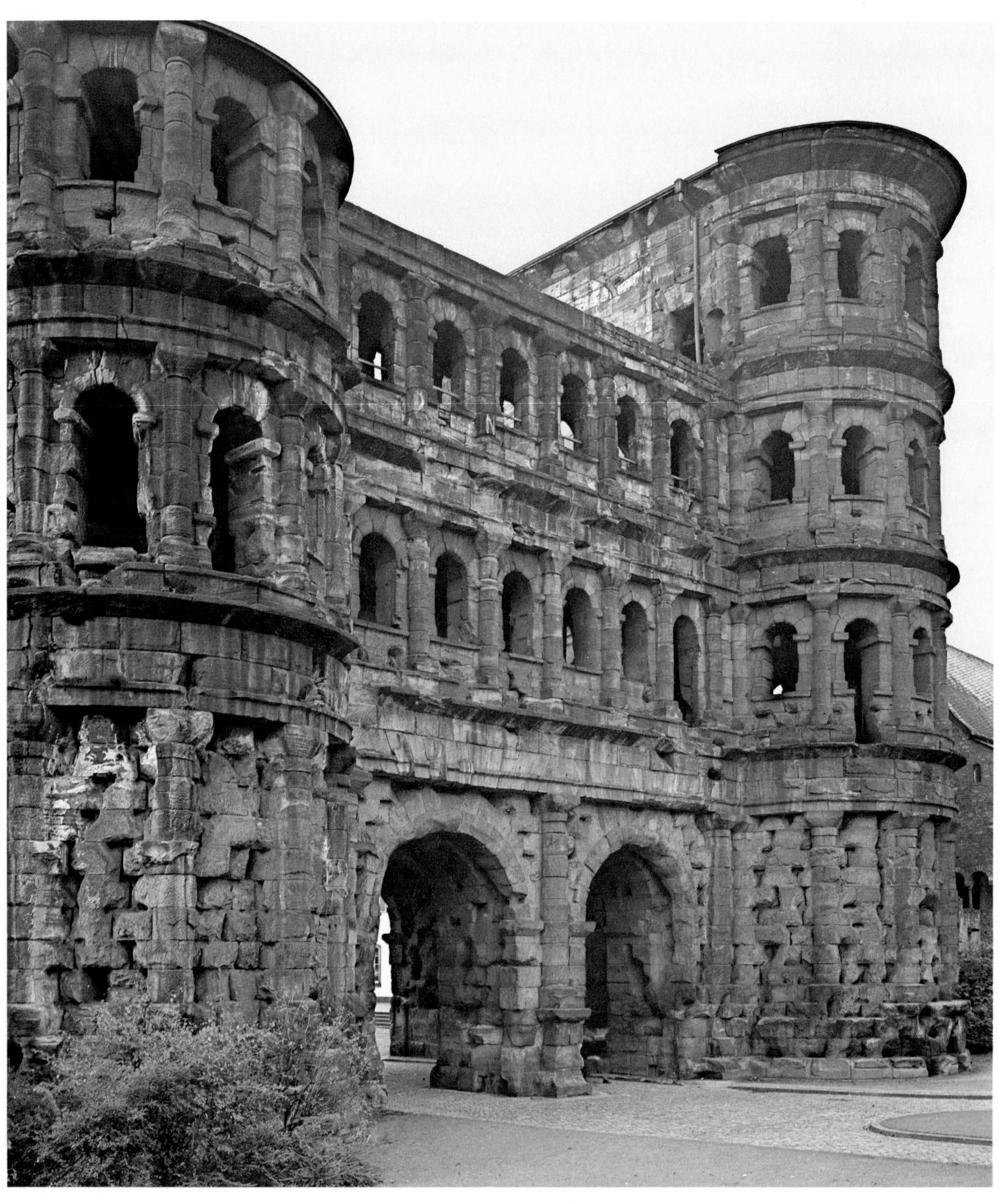

thoroughly. He moved against the tribes. In order to secure peace in the East while doing this, he recognized Zenobia's son, conferring on him all the titles which his father had had. The barbarians, instead of combining their forces, split into small bands and set out on raiding parties in Italy. Eventually, Aurelian was able to deal with them and send them back over the Alps. He rightly saw, though, that the danger lay as much within the Empire as outside it, and these last invasions resulted in a series of purges in the senate of those men who, he felt, had used the difficult situation to turn popular opinion against him, and had encouraged revolt. As a token of his desire to secure Rome itself against possible invasion, he had the city enclosed with the large walls that surround it today.

At last Aurelian could turn to the problem of Palmyra and the son of Zenobia. The question of allegiance became one of national interests. The province of Syria had, by inclination, more sympathy with the Palmyrene rulers. Asia Minor was predominantly Greek in its interests. Zenobia realized this, and acquainted herself with Greek ways, by inviting a leading philosopher of his day, Longinus, to her court. In Egypt, on the other hand, there had always been a very strong Roman element, and this was soon revived by Probus, a general of Aurelian's, later to become emperor. In two campaigns involving heavy fighting and large losses, Aurelian finally succeeded in regaining the East, and honors were showered upon him. Finally, Zenobia was captured, put on trial, and ended her days in bourgeois peace as the wife of a senator in Italy.

Aurelian was one of the first emperors with the leisure, after these campaigns, to organize a few reforms. He took further steps to reestablish a currency in which people would show some faith. He bettered living conditions at Rome. He established a new frontier in Dacia on the right bank of the Danube, leaving the devastated land on the other side to its fate. Yet even this creator of comparative peace fell victim to a plot. After two brief reigns in less than six months, the Eastern army proclaimed the ruler of Egypt, Probus, emperor. This soldier-emperor pursued the policies of his predecessor with vigor, and turned on the barbarians and on the groups of bandits who threatened both Asia Minor and Egypt. In the course of reestablishing firm rule in Mesopotamia, Probus was murdered by his troops, probably because of the firm discipline he imposed on them. His two sons were also assassinated. The soldiers nominated another emperor from among themselves, and their choice was the man under whom chaos was at last resolved, and a new system of government was devised. This was Diocletian.

*Above:* The Persian king Shapur I staghunting. Shapur, who ruled 241–272 was a highly successful general. He fought three victorious wars against the Romans. During the fighting the Roman emperor Gordian III was killed, Philip the Arab had to pay tribute, and Valerian was captured. Only after Shapur's death did Rome manage to some extent to restore its position in the Middle East.

*Left:* The Porta Nigra at Trier, a Roman gate fortress of the third century. Trier, a Roman colony from the time of the emperor Claudius, was the main trading and administrative center of north-east Gaul. From the fourth century it was at times the residence of the Western emperors.

## Diocletian

After the decisive victories of Aurelian and Claudius, the collapse of resistance in Gaul and the removal of the kingdom of Palmyra, Diocletian's legacy was not an unhopeful one. Nevertheless, it was the personality of Diocletian which lent most to the solidarity of the Empire at this time, as is evident from the way in which this coherence disintegrated after his retirement.

Diocletian soon became ruler of the whole Empire. Various attempts had been made in the course of the third century to divide the government of the Empire, the clearest example of this having been the reign of Valerian and Gallienus.

Diocletian saw the advantage of having two men working together in separate halves of the empire and soon appointed a fellow-officer, Maximian, a second Augustus. Divine authority was invoked by Diocletian's assumption of the title Jupiter, king of the gods, and Maximian's of that of Hercules, henchman of the gods. This emphasized that the second Augustus was in some ways subject to Diocletian. To divide up the task of government further and to ease the problem of succession each Augustus was granted a Caesar. When an Augustus died his Caesar replaced him, not necessarily on the principle of heredity, but of administrative experience. This was perhaps designed to exclude the inexperienced from the purple. It is uncertain whether this was the clear intention of Diocletian from the first, but it soon became clear that this was the effect that it would be likely to have.

Another great innovation of Diocletian's, of great significance to the Christian Church, was the division of the empire in to twelve *dioiceseis*, dioceses, each governed by a *vicarius* of equestrian rank. He also divided the military and civil responsibilities, assigning the former to *duces*, generals, assisted by *comites*, and the latter to *praesides*, governors. Not only church titles, but also those of European aristocracies derived from these arrangements, duke from dux, count from comes.

The divisions of rank helped the imperial status and this was further increased by the adoption of oriental ceremonial at court and the use of theistic titles. In order of precedence one descended from Augustus to Caesar to Prefect to Vicarius to Duces and Praesides. From almost all these ranks save the highest, senators were excluded. This excluded them from routine affairs of government. The system was also designed to lead to a more efficient collection of taxes and to facilitate payment of the armed forces, now all-important. An official who failed to produce enough tax was punished by confiscation of his own money.

The restored Empire was thus avowedly military in character in that all four rulers were generals. It was also bureaucratic in that all civilian forces were brought into the service of the state. The system, however, was short lived. When Diocletian and Maximian abdicated in 305, it was not clear who the new Caesars were to be, and whether or not the dynastic principle was involved. On the basis of heredity both Maximian's son and Constantine, the future emperor, forced themselves into office, the former as an Augustus, the latter as a Caesar. Nevertheless war was inevitably waged for the supreme prize, culminating in Constantine's victory. What Diocletian had demonstrated was a model for the full division of powers between East and West, even if he had not provided a blueprint for the peaceful transfer of power.

Throughout the third century, the emperors had tried to found their right to rule not only on dynastic success and military powers, but on a religious basis, by linking themselves with a god. It was now believed that there was really one supreme God, and the tendency grew in the third century to believe that this was the Sun. Aurelian made the cult of the Sun an official state religion, in the hope of its appealing, through its generality, to large numbers of provincials from different ends of the Empire. Diocletian, on becoming emperor, prayed to the sun to be witness that he had nothing to do with the murder of his predecessor. And Constantine himself linked his own worship in the early days of his rule to that of the Sun (as is described in chapter 15). Monotheism, in its many and varied forms, had become the religion of the third century. The cults still flourished and had a temporary revival as late as the reign of the mid-fourth-century emperor Julian. But even they in their third-century forms were organized around one highest principle.

Platonism flourished in the philosophical schools, some of which, by their insistence on the importance of intellectual contemplation to experience unity with an abstract principle of oneness, formed the beginnings of what is known as the Neoplatonic school of thought. Their most important exponent and founder was Plotinus (c. 205–270). It was at this period in the middle of the century, when the plight of the Empire was at its very worst, that a revival of pagan education and interests occurred together with a sense of the old values, but even these emerged under the new guise of the all-uniting godhead. The growing importance was dealt with in Chapter 11.

The sarcophagus of the philosopher Plotinus, who lived c.205–270. After his death his collected works—fifty-five in all—were published in six *Enneads* (groups of nine). The philosophical school that Plotinus founded was known as neoplatonism. Many of its ideas were taken from the works of the classical philosopher, Plato, but it was more systematic and more heavily influenced by religious aims. Although he was not a Christian, Plotinus exercised a powerful influence on medieval thought, particularly through the works of St Augustine of Hippo and a late-fifth-century writer known as Dionysius the Pseudo-Areopagite.

Chapter 14

# PERSECUTION

## THE CHURCH AND THE PAGAN WORLD

The Christians were more easily accepted in the third century than in the second, although occasional persecution took place. Christianity's chief rival was the cult of Mithras, particularly popular among soldiers. This religion had been spreading from Persia along the highways and seaways of the Roman Empire throughout the second century. At Ostia, the port of Rome, no less than seventeen sites of the cult have been discovered. Mithras was a god of light who overcame the powers of evil and darkness.

In the kaleidoscope of Roman religious life, the imperial cult played a major role as is described in the previous chapter. Even so, Christians were coming to enjoy close relations with the court. Julia Mammaea, the mother of Alexander Severus, summoned the Christian teacher Origen to Antioch in 232 to discuss religion. There were Christian freedmen in the emperor's immediate circle.

Christianity was at last also making an impression on provincial society. In the first half of the third century there were serious attempts by Christians to make their religion the religion of mankind. One such mission was that of Gregory the "wonder-worker," from Cappadocia in Asia Minor. In 236 he had thrown over a career as a lawyer to become a pupil of Origen, and then in 243 he returned to his own country where he carried out a highly successful mission for the next thirty years. In some towns, office in the Church was becoming a mark of social success. "So great," says the historian Eusebius, was the harvest of souls, "that the clergy were too few to deal with them." One great success in this period was the conversion of the royal house of the client kingdom of Osrhoene (east Syria) to Christianity. By 216 Abgar IX had become the first Christian monarch.

## THE DECIAN AND VALERIAN PERSECUTIONS

Decius, who became emperor in 249, was a man who believed that the restoration of the fortunes of the Empire depended on a return to traditional Roman virtues and a massive demonstration of the solidarity of the people with the gods. The Christians must be brought to recognize the power and benevolence of the Roman gods. In June and July 250, a general sacrifice by all households in the Empire was organized. All who participated were given a certificate, many of which survive, to attest they had done so. Many were punished because they could not produce certificates.

Christianity was still an urban religion. The great majority of its adherents had no serious desire to break with their surroundings. They sacrificed in droves or—at least—accepted certificates to say that they had done so.

After the death of Decius the Church soon regained most of the ground it had lost. Apart from the loss of life, the main problem was how to treat those who had lapsed. In 257 Valerian, who had been Decius' censor and was now emperor,

The catacombs at Rome. There are many catacomb sites in the Mediterranean world, but the largest and most extensive are those at Rome. By tunneling into soft rock along passages and galleries, tombs were excavated capable of holding as many as seven bodies arranged in tiers. The huge size testifies to the size of the Christian population in Rome. After Christianity became the official religion of the Empire they began to pass out of use as tombs and became places of pilgrimage instead.

renewed the challenge, this time directed mainly at the Church's leaders and its property. The next two years were even more destructive to the Christian leadership than the Great Persecution forty years later. In Carthage, Bishop Cyprian was brought before the proconsul on September 14, 258. He was told that "for a long time he had lived an irreligious life, drawn together a number of men bound by an unlawful association, and professed himself an open enemy to the gods and the religion of Rome." He was beheaded.

Again military events came to the Christians' rescue. The capture of Valerian by the Persians proved to be a blessing. Gallienus, who succeeded him as emperor (260–268), sent rescripts (instructions) to the bishops of Rome and Alexandria ordering the return of Church property to them and authorizing them to resume their duties. A graffito scratched on the walls of the catacomb of St Sebastian in Rome gives the date as August 9, 260. The Church was not formally legalized, but its existence was acknowledged. Its property was protected. It could develop as it chose. It had become one of the recognized facts in the life of the Roman Empire.

## CHURCHES IN CONFLICT: ROME, ALEXANDRIA, AND CARTHAGE

Public opinion was not the only factor changing to the advantage of the Church in the last decade of the second century. Suddenly, within a very short period around A.D. 190, we see the emergence of well-organized Christian communities, led by men of considerable stature, in the major cities of the Empire. Even more important was the spread of Christianity into the Latin-speaking North African provinces and the beginning of a Latin-speaking church in Rome. Formidable problems of translation arose. In addition, separate theological outlooks developed in each of the three major centers of Christianity—Rome, Alexandria, and Carthage.

### Rome

Rome was an influential and wealthy but comparatively obscure church. It was a meeting place for representatives of every type of opinion and tradition within the Church. Unlike Alexandria, and later Antioch, it never produced a theological school of its own. It had remained a Judaistic church, with Old Testament scenes and Judaistic names well represented in the catacombs. These were burial places, originating in restricted plots of land given by their aristocratic owners to their freedmen for their use for burials. The catacombs were dug into the soft volcanic rock, the lowest and often the most elaborate being the latest in date.

Rome was the center of doctrinal controversies in the third century. The churches of Christendom were prepared to accept Rome as the symbol of the episcopate, but they refused it jurisdictional rights.

### Alexandria: Origen

While Rome wrestled with problems of Church doctrine and discipline, Alexandria had established itself as the intellectual powerhouse of Christianity. The foremost among the circle of learned Christians at Alexandria was unquestionably Origen (c. 185–253), the greatest of all the minds in the Church in the first three centuries.

Origen was an infant prodigy with a great command of secular and scriptural learning, so that when he was only eighteen, Bishop Demetrius entrusted him with the headship of the Christian school. Origen's theology was based on the Greek idea of culture (*paideia*) as well as on the Bible. He believed, in contrast to the gnostics, that the whole Bible was God's word. It required deep training in philosophy to discover the spiritual meaning from the text. Probably thanks more to him than to any other influence, Christianity became aware of its universal mission and was accepted as a major religious force in the Empire.

His influence on Greek theology was profound. He was influenced by platonic and neoplatonic ideas. God's love is manifested through the "Word" (*logos*) or only-begotten Son, who is with God and in God from eternity to eternity. He was "the exact image of the Father, appearing to man in the Incarnation as Jesus, to be guide and example." Through Christ's example man had acquired the means of moving toward perfection.

### Carthage: Tertullian

The church in North Africa represents an entirely different Christian tradition from that of Alexandria. Its language was Latin. Martyrdom was a way to a material paradise. Pagan philosophical ideas were the main enemy.

Whereas the Alexandrians stressed the role of Christ as the divine Word, who reconciles all aspects of the universe with Himself, Tertullian (c. 160–240) took the opposite view. The heart of his religion lay in his emphasis on the work of the Holy Spirit, inspiring the Church. For him, there could be no reconciliation between Christianity and pagan society. "What," he asked, "has Athens to do with Jerusalem? What has the Academy to do with the Church? What have heretics to do with Christians? . . . Away with all attempts to produce a Stoic, or Platonic, or dialectic Christianity." Tertullian's theology was that of a lawyer. He was not politically disloyal to the Empire, but he had no use for the institutions of the state. "Nothing is more foreign to us than the state," he asserted.

## THE CHURCH AT THE END OF THE THIRD CENTURY

### Monasticism

Jesus' recorded advice to the rich young men to "go sell all that thou hast and follow me" reinforced the natural bias toward asceticism found in most religious

A picture from the catacomb of St Priscilla. It shows two of the Meshach triad in the fiery furnace, a theme chosen because of its allusion to martyrdom. This particular catacomb developed out of the burial area of a famous, old Roman family, the Acilii Glabrones. The catacomb became a Christian burial ground.

movements in the ancient Near East. The father of monasticism, Antony (251–356), was Egyptian. He gave away his inheritance of 300 acres, and obeying literally Jesus' injunction he migrated to the eastern bank of the Nile. There he lived for twenty years in a deserted fortress—a frugal and prayer-directed existence combatting demons. The followers who attached themselves to him were to be among the pioneers of Egyptian monasticism. A rule was developed by one of them, Pachonius. This was the basis of the rule of St Basil, which is still used in Eastern orthodox monasteries.

### Organization

In the later part of the third century, important structural changes took place in the Church. The bishops of Rome, Alexandria, and Antioch developed a status above that of other bishops. At Carthage, martyrs were not to be regarded as such until they had been "recognized by the Church." The supreme instance of Church government had become the council of bishops, organized on a provincial basis. Councils decided matters of doctrine and discipline. In addition, there was continuous if obscure debate over doctrinal matters. These debates led only to acrimony.

## THE GREAT PERSECUTION

The great test took place in 303. Diocletian had been ruling for nearly twenty years. His ideal was political and religious uniformity. The Christians, by refusing honor to the universal gods of Rome, remained outside this framework. The object of Diocletian's persecution was to bring them in with as little force as possible.

During 303 pressure was confined to the clergy and more influential Christians. Copies of the Scripture were to be handed over to the authorities for burning and churches were to be destroyed. Christians were denied civil rights. Clergy were forced to sacrifice to the gods on pain of imprisonment, but there was no death penalty. In general, the edicts were obeyed with much the same acquiescence as in the Decian persecution.

Then, at the beginning of 304, Diocletian fell ill. Power passed to Galerius, a far more convinced pagan than Diocletian. In the spring of 304, Galerius ordered a general sacrifice to be made on pain of death. The whole Christian body was now involved. In North Africa, in particular, many were martyred. The "day of incense burning" was remembered with "the day of the handing over of Scriptures" as a day of shame. In Rome, even the bishop, Marcellinus, sacrificed to the gods. This ordeal did not last long in the West. Persecution was already flagging when, on May 1, 305, Diocletian and Maximian abdicated.

*Top:* A wall painting from the same catacomb. It shows the Virgin with child. *Above:* A lady at prayer, from the cubicle of Valatia in the catacomb of St Priscilla. The practice of standing for prayer was usual in the early Church. *Right:* A bronze statuette of Jupiter. He is holding a sceptre and thunderbolt. This is a Roman work dating between the second and fourth centuries A.D. and is said to have been found in Hungary. The later the date perhaps the more unusual the work, as the Olympian gods were giving ground before the great mystery religions.

# Part III
# Roman Heritage

Chapter 15

# CONSTANTINE

## THE TRIUMPH OF CONSTANTINE

Constantine was hailed Augustus by the troops at York in 306. The next six years saw a confused struggle between Galerius and his colleagues, who wished to maintain Diocletian's system of government, and Constantine, who within a year or two veered decisively in favor of the hereditary system. Subsidiary to this was the attitude of each side toward the Christians. In the East, the persecution was continued by Galerius, but gradually popular opposition mounted. The historian Eusebius was an eye-witness and describes the situation in Upper Egypt:

> *And we ourselves also beheld, when we were at these places many killed, all at once in a single day, some of whom suffered decapitation, others the punishment of fire; so that the murderous axe was dulled and, worn out, was broken in pieces, while the executioners themselves grew utterly weary and took it in turns to succeed one another.*

Galerius realized that the situation was hopeless. In the spring of 311 he was taken ill. Deciding that his sufferings were due to the Christian God, he published an edict declaring that "the Christians may exist again." It was better that they should worship their own God than no god at all. The hoped-for relief from illness, however, did not come: On May 5, Galerius was dead.

In the West the persecution had not been renewed. There were few Christians outside Rome and North Africa and southern Spain. On his march to power Constantine had been sustained by the sun god, identified with Apollo. "To the Sun my companion," the inscription on his coinage reads. In 311 he had a vision in a temple of Apollo in which a reign of thirty years appeared to be promised to him. But he was beginning to look for favors from the Christian God. When, early in 312, he crossed the Alps in a bid to capture Rome from Maxentius, who had established himself since 306 as ruler of Italy and North Africa, he was accompanied by Hosius, bishop of Cordoba in southern Spain. On October 26, his army was five miles north of Rome. That night, according to the contemporary Christian writer Lactantius, a dream inspired Constantine to order his soldiers to place the Christian monogram, representing the name of Christ, on their shields in preparation for battle. Two days later Constantine won a decisive victory at the Milvian Bridge. Maxentius was drowned in the Tiber, and Rome opened its gates to the new ruler of the West. With Constantine, Christianity triumphed also.

*Above:* Coin of Constantius Chlorus. It shows Constantius, Constantine's father, entering London. He was appointed Caesar (junior emperor) of the Western Augustus, Maximian, in 293. He recovered Britain for the Empire in 296. His death in 306 created the problem of the imperial succession.
*Left:* Head of the emperor Constantine. He was the son of Constantius Chlorus, a Caesar of Diocletian. He made himself master of the reunited Roman Empire by his defeat and execution of Licinius in 324. He is most famous to Christians, however, as the man who legitimized the Church in the Roman Empire and for convening the conference of Nicaea which was intended to deal with the Arian heresy. He also built a new capital on the Bosphorus, and named it Constantinople.

### Constantine and the Church

The victory over Maxentius had been so unexpected by contemporaries that they readily attributed it to divine intervention. "By Divine instinct" was how they expressed it on the arch set up in honor of Constantine, though the divinity may have been that of Constantine himself. When Constantine met Licinius, who had succeeded Galerius as emperor of the East, at Milan in February 313, he felt himself under a debt of obligation to the Christian God. At Milan the two emperors set out in a joint edict the right of "all men to follow whatever they desired, so that whatsoever Divinity dwells in Heaven may be benevolent and propitious toward us and to all who are placed under our authority."

For the next decade Constantine was pro-Christian—without, however, abandoning his faith in the sun god. His coinage retained the inscription *SOLI INVICTO COMITI* ("To the Unconquered Sun my Companion"), with the figure of the sun god or the sun's orb resting on a pagan altar. The "Day of the Sun" (not the Christian "Day of the Lord") became an official rest day. Yet Constantine was lavish in his gifts to churches everywhere. He was most lavish to the Church of Rome, famous for her martyrs and first in rank through St Peter. The emperor bestowed vast domains in Rome, Italy, and elsewhere in the West, together with gifts of treasure. A pagan senator remarked to a later pope: "Make me bishop of Rome, and I will become a Christian tomorrow!"

Christian clergy were freed from the obligation to pay municipal taxes or undertake burdensome municipal offices. In 321 the Church was granted unlimited right of receiving bequests and the judicial decisions of bishops were to be accepted as binding if they had been asked to arbitrate. Most important of all, Constantine placed his son under the tutorship of a Christian writer, Lactantius.

It is important to appreciate what Constantine understood by Christianity. Constantine owed his conversion to what he considered divine intervention on the battlefield of the Milvian Bridge. Thereafter, there is always a military flavor to official Christianity; it is the worship of the god of the big battalions, more easily envisaged as a generalissimo than as a crucified man. It means victory over one's enemies. But this by itself is an oversimplification, for Constantine fell under the in-

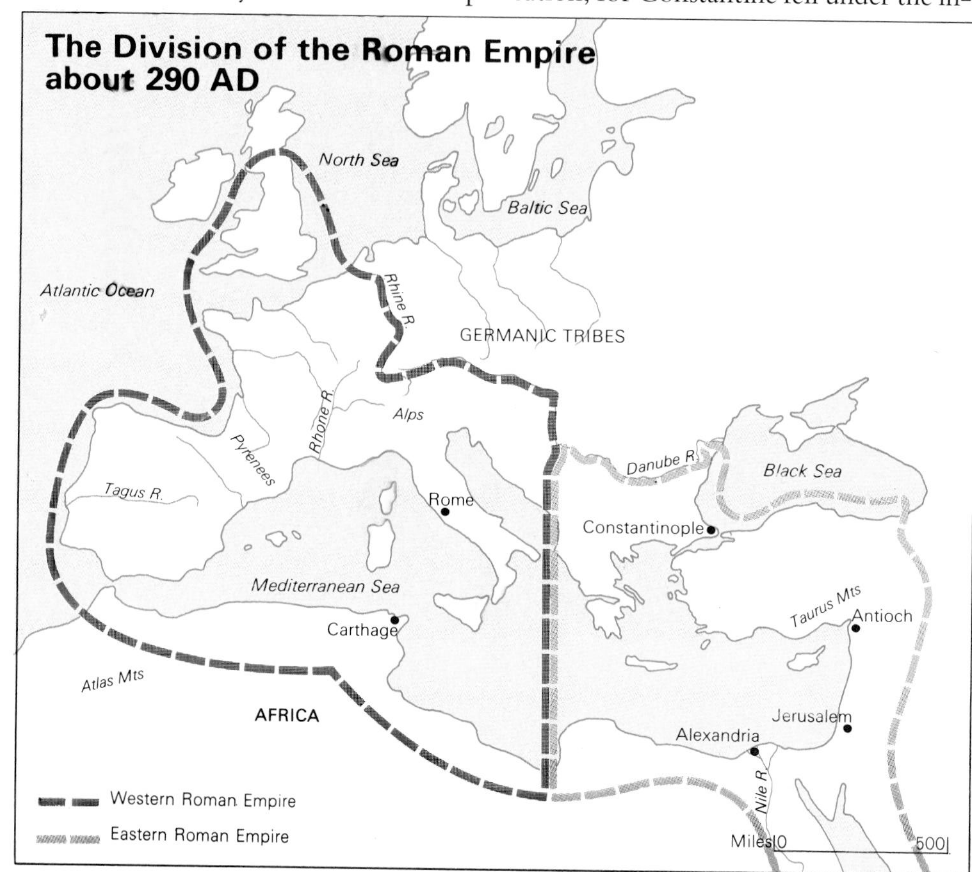

fluence of highly intelligent Eastern bishops—notably, Eusebius of Caesarea. Constantine was taught to see himself as standing in a special relationship to God, to whom he was responsible for the peace of the Church. His coins confirm Eusebius' picture of what Christianity meant to the emperor. This view was very different from that of Tertullian, who saw Christianity as a minority religion, always in danger of persecution. Endowment, not persecution, was now the threat.

A major dispute among the Christians in Africa was forcing Constantine to play an active part in Church affairs. Many of the bishops there had surrendered their Scriptures during the Great Persecution, a deed regarded by the majority as a gross act of apostasy. The surrenderers (*traditores*) had forfeited the power of grace and were unworthy of priestly office.

The crisis came in 311 when a new bishop of Carthage, Caecilian, was consecrated. Schism broke out almost at once, the opposition being led by a young Numidian bishop named Donatus, who was to be a thorn in Constantine's side for the rest of his reign. One of the bishops who had consecrated Caecilian was accused of being a *traditor*, and therefore unable to consecrate validly. Constantine ordered the bishops of Spain, Gaul, the Rhineland provinces, and Britain to decide the question. Thirty-three bishops met at Arles in France (314) and accepted Caecilian as bishop. The Donatists, supported by African public opinion, rejected the decision: the Church could not accept *traditores* as ministers. Constantine threatened to come to Africa to demonstrate how God should be worshiped. This Constantine maintained, "belongs to the very office of a prince, to expel error and destroy rash opinions, to cause all men to agree together to follow true religion and simplicity of life." Already the emperor's claims to govern the church were being stated.

Constantine never set foot in Africa. In November 316 he confirmed Caecilian in his position as bishop of Carthage, but no amount of pressure availed to oust

A relief showing the emperor Constantine and his family. He married Fausta, the daughter of Maximian, but executed her and his eldest son Crispus in 326. His three other sons embarked on typical inter-family and internecine warfare after his death.

Donatus. In the end Constantine was forced to give up, the only time in his reign he admitted defeat. The puritanical tradition of Christianity in Africa had won the day and continued to dominate until the time of Augustine, seventy years later.

Meanwhile, relations between Constantine and Licinius, the emperor in the West, had deteriorated. War broke out between them. After his victory over Licinius at the battle of Chrysopolis (324) Constantine declared himself unequivocally a Christian. His success, he stated, "starting from the sea that laps distant Britain," had been due to the aid of the supreme God.

### The Council of Nicaea

Within a few months Constantine presided over the Church's first ecumenical (universal) council at Nicaea in Asia Minor. The issue was the doctrine of Arius. This crisis, too, had developed because of the Great Persecution. Arius, a young and learned priest of Alexandria, had at first supported the party who demanded stronger measures against those who had lapsed, but later changed sides. He also concluded from Origen's theology that "if the Father begat the Son, the Son had a beginning" and therefore that "there was a time when He was not." Arius' suggestion that the Son was so separate from the Father as to belong only to the created order was condemned by an Egyptian council in 318. To deal with the new dispute Constantine summoned the Council of Nicaea. Uniformity was as important to Constantine as it had been to Diocletian.

Some 270 bishops assembled on June 19, 325. Constantine presided over the sessions. Except for Hosius of Cordoba, Caecilian of Carthage, and two priests from Rome, the Council was composed entirely of Greek-speaking bishops. The great majority were Origenists. Arius had gone too far, but their theology of Christ as the Word implied inferiority to the Father. Constantine was not happy and, perhaps advised by Hosius, proposed at a crucial moment the definition that Christ as Son of God was "of the same substance as the Father" (the term *homoousios*). This cut out Arianism but did not please the bishops. It was not a word found in Scripture. They also thought that it was dangerously close to Jewish monotheism. But the emperor had spoken; the bishops accepted the Creed of Nicaea which became and has remained the creed of Christendom.

The Council attempted to settle outstanding problems that had accumulated over the previous century. The date of Easter must be calculated independently from the Jewish calculation of 14 Nisan. The major bishoprics of Rome, Alexandria, and Antioch were granted special rights. An attempt was made finally to settle old schisms within the Church, but without lasting success. Behind this lay the emperor's resolve that the Church must be united. As "friend of God," he was called upon to rule over a united Empire aided by a united Church.

## CONSTANTINOPLE

The concept of the Christian Empire is well illustrated by the differences between Rome and Constantinople. In 330 the emperor chose as his new capital the ancient city of Byzantium, on the Bosphorus. The rebuilt city was renamed after the emperor. Although it was in many respects a second Rome, modeled on the first, there was a great difference. It was, from the first, a Christian city, unsullied by pagan cultus.

The Basilica Ostiensis at Rome. This was built by Constantine to replace a memorial chapel of St Paul. It was enlarged by Valentinian II and Theodosius the Great, and completed under Honorius.

Chapter 16

# THE DISINTEGRATION OF THE WESTERN EMPIRE

## THE BARBARIAN INCURSIONS

Although actual power in the Western Empire gradually transferred to barbarians, imperial succession continued in the West until 476. While the Eastern Empire developed a Hellenized Christian culture, the West continued in the Latin mold, less innovative and more vulnerable. After a brief pagan reaction, Julian's successor, Jovian, restored Christianity to its former position but died after only eight months. In 364 he was succeeded by a dynasty that was to rule for over ninety years. Its founders, Valentinian I and his brother Valens, began a pattern of separate Eastern and Western rule which continued virtually until the overthrow of the last Western emperor. (Even after the end of Roman rule in the West, however, the Eastern Empire claimed nominal dominion there.)

While the East preserved Diocletian's principle of a monolithic, state-serving bureaucracy, the West fell back into its customary pattern of divisive conflict. The primary political aim of the Western imperial office was defense against the barbarian, but at the same time, because of the depopulated Empire's dependence on mercenaries, barbarians were being continually invited in. In 403, for example, the Vandal general Stilicho, in the name of the Empire, defeated Alaric the Visigoth, who had himself once been a captain of the imperial mercenaries. Seven years later (410), Alaric sacked Rome, dealing a terrible blow to imperial self-esteem. For the first time in 800 years the center of the Empire was taken captive by a barbarian army. Thereafter, the Western Empire descended into political oblivion.

Meanwhile, the Empire rapidly lost ground in the crucial grain-growing provinces of Africa as a result of the machinations of a renegade Roman general in collusion with the king of the Vandals. In 455, the Vandals attacked Rome and loaded several ships with plundered works of art. Western power was assumed by Ricimer, a half-Suevian, half-Goth general who ruled through a series of puppets.

The last of the puppet emperors was Romulus Augustulus, set on the throne by his father. He lasted only a few months; Odoacer, king of an obscure German tribe, deposed him. Here Roman succession ceased in the West.

## THE VISIGOTHS

The Germanic peoples who broke into western Europe during the fourth and fifth centuries fall into two main groups. One was of West Germans, whose principal

| 325 AD | 350 | 375 | 400 | 425 | 450 | 475 |
|---|---|---|---|---|---|---|
| Constantinople E. capital (330); Constantine dies (337) | Julian the Apostate (357–63) | Theodosius I (379–95); Huns invade Europe (375); Visigoth victory at Adrianople (378) | Vandal Stilicho ruler in West; Visigoths colonize Gaul and Spain; Empire divided (395) | Visigoths sack Rome (410); W. capital at Ravenna | | Vandals sack Rome (455); Romulus Augustulus deposed: end of empire in West (476) |

Head of Attila the Hun, "the scourge of God." Attila was co-king of the Huns from 434 with his brother Bleda, whom he murdered in 445. His major campaigns were against the Eastern Empire rather than the West, but he invaded Italy and was only persuaded not to stay by the intercession of the pope Leo I. He also attacked France, but was defeated by an army consisting of Romans and Visigoths. Attila's success was largely due to the speed at which his cavalry army moved, and to the terror he inspired.

Germanic Invasion Routes in the Fourth & Fifth Centuries
North Sea
Baltic Sea
SAXONS
FRANKS
BURGUNDIANS
Rhine R.
Seine R.
Soissons
Paris
LOMBARDS
VANDALS
420
Tours
Orleans
Atlantic Ocean
443
OSTROGOTHS
Rhone R.
Toulouse
412
Narbonne
VISIGOTHS
Ravenna
397
Black Sea
410
493
Barcelona
Toledo
Rome
378
411
Constantinople
455
429
Carthage
439
Mediterranean Sea
Miles 0 500

members were Franks, Alamans, Saxons, Frisians, and Thuringians; the other was of East Germans (Goths, Vandals, Burgundians, Gepids, and Lombards). Though related, they were distinct in speech and in customs. The Goths subdivide into Ostrogoths and Visigoths.

Pastoral peoples, but cultivators in a pinch, the Goths inhabited from the third century the general area between the Danube and the Dniester. The Ostrogothic kingdom was destroyed by the Asiatic Huns, while the Visigoths were forced to cross the Danube into the Empire. In a great battle near Adrianople in 378 the Emperor Valens was himself killed. With imperial permission the Goths settled just south of the Danube.

Some of the Goths were already Christians, having been converted by a Gothic missionary named Ulfila between 341 and 348. The Christianity he learned and taught was Arianism, a distinction that was to matter when the Goths came to live among the Catholic Christians in the West.

Whatever their beliefs, the Empire was unable to hold them to their Danubian settlement area. The Visigoths pushed west, disturbing other Germanic peoples in their path and entering Rome in 410. They devastated the Italian peninsula before moving north again under Alaric's successor, and entering Gaul. Meanwhile, the withdrawal of garrisons from the Rhine to counter the threat to Italy had opened all Gaul to the Vandals and Alamans, who hastened to Spain, plundering as they went.

Mosaic from Carthage c.500, showing a mounted Vandal leaving his home. The Vandals were a German tribe who eventually made their way through Gaul and Spain to settle in Africa. Their most famous achievement was the capture of Rome in 455 under Geiseric, king from 428 to 477. He seems to have been an extremely able monarch and soldier. He made Carthage his capital and built a large fleet.

### The Visigoths Enter Gaul

In 418 the Visigoths were granted permission to settle in Aquitaine, with Toulouse as their capital, and an agreed amount of private land was surrendered to them. Some Goths certainly lived on their estates. Others lived on a permanent military footing within and around the cities they held. Only in Septimania, the corner between the Rhone and the Pyrenees, did they leave any permanent mark. This was because they were able to hold the region until the eighth century.

Society was little altered by the Gothic invasion, which meant in practice that the Gothic chieftains became as Romanized as was compatible with independent existence, while the rank and file remained the barbarians they had always been. There was a cleavage between leaders and led. Athaulf clinched the matter by marrying an imperial lady, Galla Placidia.

### Visigoths and Huns

Barbarian peoples customarily hated one another in a way that none of them hated the Romans. In particular, the Goths were hereditary enemies of the Huns, who had dispersed their eastern settlements. Under Attila, the Huns succeeded in establishing an empire in central Europe from which, for a few years, they harried the frontiers of the eastern or western parts of the Empire at will. Bought off with subsidies at one time and resisted at another, they remained a significant threat in the mid-fifth century. We have descriptions of them from the historian Ammianus Marcellinus (very hostile) and from the Greek Priscos, who visited the Hunnic headquarters on an imperial embassy and left an unforgettable description of Attila and his court.

Even a nomadic people such as the Huns could gain much in material terms from steady contact with a more advanced civilization. For example, they could obtain grain and arms.

Concentrating on the West, Attila laid claims to the hand of an imperial princess, perhaps relying on the collusion of Aëtius, Roman commander in the West and once a friend of the Huns. He determined to start by destroying the Gothic settlement in Gaul and accordingly crossed the Rhine with his main army. At the Catalaunian Field (now Moirey, near Troyes), he met in 451 an army of Goths and the imperial mercenary forces under Aëtius and was defeated. This saved Gaul. It was only the death of Attila in 453 that saw the end of this empire.

Aëtius' army had included large contingents of Franks and Goths, the latter under the command of their king. The Goths now knew that they were potential masters of all southern and central Gaul.

The Goths, of whom there must have been around 100,000, were certainly unwelcome to the Roman landlords in Gaul, even though the Gothic warriors had served them well against Attila and had a stabilizing social influence (more than once the Goths had put down risings of peasants). The Goths were even more unwelcome to the Church, since they were Arians.

An ebony diptych portraying Stilicho. The second half of the diptych portrays Serena, Stilicho's wife, and his son, Eucharius. He was supreme commander of the Roman armies in the West, and ruler in all but name from 395 to 408. He defeated Alaric and the Visigoths in 402 and 403, and in 405 defeated a horde of Ostrogoths near Florence. Despite his ability, Honorius ordered his execution in 408. Stilicho's death was one of the causes of the collapse of imperial power in the West.

For the first time, the Goths saw at close quarters that a constituent element of *Romanitas* was Catholicism, and this they would not accept. There is some evidence of what might be called persecution, but what the Church chiefly suffered from was neglect. Vacant sees were not filled, churches fell into ruin, and the Catholic hierarchy lived under suspicion. However, the Gallic Church was too deeply rooted to be seriously disturbed, and its prestige had been enhanced by the resistance of certain bishops to the early barbarian attacks on their cities. The Church was, in fact, the part of the Roman establishment that came best out of the dangerous era of disruption and swiftly weakened imperial control over the West as a whole. There were still secular officials of the Empire in Gaul, some of them little better than robber barons intent on feathering their own nests, but effectively the bishops in their cities were all that the Gallo-Romans could look to for leadership.

Sidonius Apollinaris, the bishop of Clermont, is an arresting figure. He organized local resistance in the Auvergne to the northward thrust of the Goths under their powerful king, Euric. In his surviving correspondence he vividly describes the Romanized life of the Gothic court, where much use was made of Roman expertise in the art of government and notably in law. The Gothic court was not uncivilized, but the humbler Goths of the countryside remained barbarians. Sidonius' correspondence with his friends shows how the life of a great landed aristocrat could still be led in tranquillity in the later fifth century. The aristocracy could still write to each other in excellent Latin, and the preservation of this art was one aspect of *Romanitas* they believed could be salvaged. The greater aristocracy, at least, had survived barbarian incursion and settlement to a remarkable degree. But it is likely enough that the smaller man, particularly the peasant cultivator, whether free or unfree, found life difficult.

An older contemporary of Sidonius was Salvian, who wrote a pamphlet castigating the cruelty of the landowners, the crushing pressure of taxation, and the weight of corruption and speculation that oppressed the small man. There is no need to reject this assessment but he may have heightened the colors to drive home his lesson. Salvian and Sidonius could both live quite comfortably in the large province.

## The Visigoths in Spain

From the start, the Empire had meant the Visigoths to use southern Gaul as a base from which to restore imperial order in Spain by destroying the Germanic peoples already there. This they succeeded in doing, at least to the extent that the Vandals took ship for Roman Africa, where their kingdom lasted for a century until Justinian defeated them. The Suevi, on the other hand, whose kingdom in the remote northwest of Spain was the earliest Germanic kingdom in western Europe, survived to be a thorn in the side of the new conquerors. So also did the much older settlement of the Gascons, south and west of the Pyrenees. Expelled from Aquitaine by the Franks in 507 (see chapter 18), the Visigoths treated old Castile as their main settlement area, with their capital first at Barcelona and then further south, at Toledo.

Spain was not like Gaul. It had remained Celtiberian (a mixture of Celtic and Spanish) in the countryside, with Hispano-Roman enclaves in the great villas and prosperous cities and many Jews and Easterners in the seaports of the Mediterranean coast. It was strong in its organized Catholicism.

There is plentiful evidence of the settlement of the Visigoths in the *meseta* of old Castile. Village settlements have been excavated, notably at Castiltierra near Segovia, which have yielded archaeological evidence of some 8,000 burials, covering a period of something over a century. The grave goods of the peasants are characteristic—for example, buckles with rectangular plaques. There may have been upwards of 70,000 Visigoths in old Castile. They left little trace of their occupation.

Discredited by defeat at Frankish hands, the Visigothic kingship was hard put to it to survive. Factions were bound to arise and to seek help from one or another of the many potential enemies: Franks, Gascons, Suevi, and Lusitanians (in modern Portugal), and the Empire itself. One faction successfully appealed to the Empire. Justinian sent a military expedition. Imperial forces occupied southeastern Spain from 552 to 629, when they were expelled by the Goths. The imperial forces were not welcomed as liberators by the Hispano-Romans, but they caused the Visigoth kings to move their headquarters to Toledo, whence an eye could be kept both on the troublesome north and on Byzantine Cartagena.

It was Liuvigild, greatest of the Arian Visigoths, who contained the Byzantine threat while at the same time dealing with the restless Suevi. These had already been converted to Catholicism by a great missionary, Martin of Braga. There is no evidence that Liuvigild persecuted them or any other Catholics. There was a revolt against his son, Hermenigild. From the neighboring Byzantines the rebellion secured no more than encouragement and some cash. This exhibition of local disruption made the victorious Liuvigild sterner toward Catholics in his later years, though not to Hispano-Romans as such. Indeed, the increasing Romanization of the Visigoth court was a constant irritant to the Visigoth chieftains.

Arianism lost ground. Liuvigild's son and successor, Reccared, tried to build a united kingdom upon Catholicism, thus harnessing the great provincial authority of the bishops. He saw himself as their master, a kind of Christian-Roman emperor. At a Church council in 589 at Toledo, he showed how he meant to rule Spain through its Catholic hierarchy. The Church provided the organization, the king approved or even prepared the agenda, and the nobles by their presence confirmed their adherence. No other barbarian state evolved such an instrument of royal power. The reigns of Liuvigild and Reccared mark the surrender of Visigothic kingship to the superiority of the culture that alone could give coherence to Spain. For a brief time in the seventh century that surrender was to bear remarkable fruit.

## OSTROGOTHIC ITALY

After the deposition of Romulus Augustulus in 476, to the Romans of Italy, their Emperor henceforth resided in Constantinople. An imperial structure of administration still survived in part, and still more the tradition of Roman culture. As in Gaul, the Church spoke most authoritatively for the past. But power was in the hands of barbarian chieftains with their following, anxious for land and food.

The first of these was Odoacer, whose following was a mixture of Germans, Huns, and others. Many barbarians of different tongues and backgrounds flocked to the standard of this potentially victorious warlord. For twelve years Odoacer ruled Italy, with most of his following settled in the Po Valley. He may not have ruled badly, though only a few Roman families of consideration openly supported him. His supplanter and successor was much more formidable. Theodoric, king of the Ostrogoths, entered Italy with imperial sanction and thus, though an Arian, was

*Top:* A Byzantine coin
*Above:* Detail from a frieze showing the emperor Justinian on horseback. Justinian became emperor in 527 and is perhaps most famous for his codification of Roman law.
*Right:* Tomb of Theodoric, king of the Ostrogoths, at Ravenna. Theodoric ruled over the Gothic kingdom in Italy from 493 to 526.

quickly accepted by the Roman senate and people, who saw some chance of stability under his protection.

As acknowledged ruler of the home of *Romanitas*, Theodoric meant from the start to use whatever remained of imperial provincial government. He set up his headquarters in Ravenna, the last imperial capital in Italy. There one can still see astonishing buildings of the fifth and sixth centuries, ranging from the beautiful little mausoleum of Galla Placidia to the churches of the Byzantine reconquest, rich in mosaics. Theodoric's Arian baptistry remains, and his own strange mausoleum. To the Romans he meant to be Roman. He was surrounded by Roman administrators.

One of these was Cassiodorus, who wrote Theodoric's official Latin letters. Their phraseology is that of the later Empire and their contents reveal the king's determination to rule his Roman subjects as the representative of the emperor. Cassiodorus became disillusioned as his countrymen drew away from the barbarians.

But Theodoric also ruled Goths and saw himself as a father figure among Germans everywhere in the West. He neither wished nor attempted to fuse his people with those they settled among. They were still a fighting elite, holding themselves aloof. They had their own officials, their own Arian churches and clergy, and a vernacular liturgy. There survive from this time several considerable fragments of Ulfila's Gothic translation of the Bible, and these betray the existence of a well-developed literary language. The Goths were no longer to be barbarians; neither were they to be Romans. We have no written code of Ostrogothic law, as we have codes for other Germanic peoples, but one may well have existed. Above all, Theodoric meant to appear to his own people as a sacral king, the embodiment of their past and their guarantor for the future.

It was never easy, however, for Theodoric to satisfy the Goths that he was not becoming too Romanized. He was suspicious of Roman loyalties. He came to believe that certain senators were acting as a fifth column. He took decisive action. Boethius, the embodiment of the Roman desire to be at once Christian and the preserver of antique philosophy, was disgraced and executed (525). So, too, was his father-in-law, Symmachus, the representative of a distinguished senatorial family.

Theodoric did not long survive the crisis; he died in 526. In the following year Justinian became Emperor. His desire to rule over the whole of Rome's former Empire could not be satisfied while Italy itself was in barbarian hands. In 537 the reconquest of Italy began.

But it took Justinian twenty years of hard campaigning under his best generals, Belisarius and Narses, to destroy Ostrogothic power. In part at least, this slowness was due to Justinian's commitments elsewhere (he had just reconquered Africa from the Vandals) and to his unwillingness to place enough soldiers—and soldiers well enough paid—in Italy. But in part it was also due to the spirit of the Ostrogoths, who exhibited a sense of unity as a fighting people once they recognized the Empire as their enemy. On their side, the Romans were uncertain about how to proceed. The imperial commanders wished to concentrate on the defense of the north, while the popes were anxious about the defense of Rome. All this prolonged a series of campaigns that did, indeed, destroy the Goths; but they also destroyed Italy. The imperial mercenaries did more than the Goths to shatter the prosperity of the peninsula.

In the brief time that elapsed between the defeat of the Goths and the appearance of the Lombards as the new (and uninvited) masters of Italy, imperial administration was to some extent restored, though taxation bore heavily on people already ruined by war. The Italo-Romans may not have loved the Goths, but neither did they love the representative of a distant Byzantine court that they were already coming to look upon as Greek. They were left with the papacy for their mouthpiece and the doubtful privilege of providing a battlefield for Byzantines, Lombards, and Franks.

Chapter 17

# THE CHURCH AFTER CONSTANTINE

## JULIAN THE APOSTATE

After the death of Constantine in 337 his sons ruled the Empire. The last of these, Constantine II, died in 361. There was then a pagan reaction. Constantine had been converted from paganism to Christianity. His nephew Julian, who then became emperor, was converted from Christianity to paganism.

It is easy to see, after the event, that official paganism was dead. But this was not how contemporaries saw the matter. Julian, a highly educated man with books to his credit, believed that a new paganism, ready to profit from the lessons of a successfully organized Christianity, could save the Roman idea of empire. The same view was held in the fourth century by the Roman senator Symmachus, at the time of a famous dispute with St Ambrose (340–397), bishop of Milan, over the pagan Altar of Victory in the Roman senate house. Symmachus appealed for the restoration of the Altar; it was right to maintain the religious customs of one's ancestors. He ended with his historic plea for religious toleration:

> *We plead, then, for a respite for the gods of our fathers, the gods of our native land. It is right to believe that that which all men worship is One. We look on the same stars: the same heavens are above us all: the same universe surrounds us. What matters it by what method each of us reaches the truth? We cannot by a single road arrive at so great a mystery.*

We must, therefore, take Julian's paganism seriously, as he took it. For him, successful paganism rested on two things. The first of these was a properly organized cultus, common to the whole Empire, centered upon the ritual of sacrifice. The ceaseless repetition of ritual observance struck all thinking men as the bedrock of *Romanitas*, whether one's sacrifices were beasts or the Eucharist. Zosimus, no very committed pagan, was to attribute the collapse of the classical Empire to the disappearance of ritual. Julian took sacrifice so seriously that he sometimes burned his own hands while officiating. Secondly, he believed that a mixture of philosophical neoplatonism (influential, too, with Christians) and magic would combine with the traditional literary pursuits to give men a proper sense of their place in the historical development of Rome. The guardian cults of Rome had protected her throughout her history. The well-being and unity of the state mattered more than that of the individual. But no individual, he held, should really be taken in by Christianity: it was the religion of atheists who worshiped a man—and an executed man at that. Pure in his own life, indeed an ascetic as much as a man of action, Julian knew that Christianity was too deeply rooted to be exterminated by violent means. Instead, he moved slowly, removing Christian and restoring pagan privileges by stages.

He died in battle on the Persian frontier in 363, at the age of thirty-one. He had reigned for only eighteen months. His death saw the immediate collapse of the

The anointing of David. This is the decorative motif of a silver dish found in Cyprus, dated 610 to 629.

pagan church he had so carefully nurtured. The world was safe for Constantinian Christianity. It was also the end of an energetic attempt to expand the Empire.

## POPULAR RELIGION

The progress of Christianity among the intelligentsia and townsmen was rapid, if spasmodic. Its progress in the countryside was slow. What was in question was the conversion of peasant populations of predominantly Celtic strain, whose Celtic deities had been reinforced by those of pagan Rome. This conversion had not progressed very far when a fresh pagan stimulus was added: that of the Germanic settlers, who were either pagan or only nominally Christian. Assisted by entirely inadequate staffs of clergy, bishops were faced with the task of making Christianity attractive to an illiterate population already quite clear about the functions of religion. These functions had little or nothing to do with morality. Much more, they involved the propitiation of the unseen world, periodical efforts to win the support of this or that god in the daily affairs of family life and to avoid the wrath of the spirits of evil. The Christianity that eventually triumphed took all these factors into account, and it did so by substituting Christian demigods for pagan ones.

The most celebrated of all Gallic cults in the West was that of St Martin, a soldier from Pannonia who came to Gaul in the fourth century to be a monk, but became bishop of Tours and a missionary to the Gallic countryside. Centered in Tours, his cult spread all over Gaul and further afield, gathering fresh accretions of legend as it went. What St Martin, who was indeed a great man, shared with hundreds of holy men of infinitely less importance was the capacity to work miracles. This was the proof of sanctity. Hence we read of immense crowds coming to shrines of saints to beg for miraculous help in their troubles.

Archaeology reinforces the picture. Right through the early Middle Ages, men

The Crossing of the Red Sea, from a catacomb on the Via Latina, Rome. It dates to the mid fourth century. It is another allegory against persecution, like those from the catacomb of St Priscilla which is on the Via Salaria.

and women equipped themselves with talismans and charms to ward off evil. Brooches, buckles, and rings inscribed with such charms exist in great quantity to betray one aspect of paganism that died a very slow death. Pictures on gravestones equally show how very like the pagan deities their Christian counterparts were. This adaptation of Christianity to paganism went so far that even today, in remote parts of Europe, the feasts of local saints bear a strong resemblance to those of their predecessors. In the fourth and fifth centuries the Church took a momentous step: it began the slow process of substituting not one theology for another in the peasant mind, but one kind of folk magic for another.

## THE ROLE OF THE CHURCH IN STATE AFFAIRS

The idea, fundamental among the Christians of the eastern Roman provinces, that Empire and Christendom were one, ruled by the sovereign emperor as the visible reflection of the Divine Word, was treated with reserve in the West. Although the question, "What has the emperor to do with the Church?" was asked by a Donatist, most Western Church leaders could equally well have asked it.

The great conflict between empire and papacy that dominates much of the European medieval period has a long history. Its origins can be traced to attitudes that took shape during the fourth century, in part as the result of an historic struggle between St Ambrose and the Emperor Theodosius I (379–395).

By the 370s, Rome had been replaced as the capital of the Western Empire by other cities such as Trier (Treves), Milan, or Ravenna. Theodosius, whose capital was at Milan, was a strong Nicene Christian, a good general, and a firm ruler, but he was cursed with an ungovernable temper. In 391 a riot had broken out in Thessalonica (Salonika). One of Theodosius' generals had been killed. In black rage, the emperor ordered a massacre in which 7,000 of the citizens were slaughtered.

Another early Christian frieze with biblical scenes. Probably fourth century.

Ambrose wrote to the emperor refusing him the Eucharist. His letter marked a turning point in the relationship between Church and State. Above the capricious will of the emperor, above all demands of policy, there was a higher duty and a higher code. No arbitrary destruction of life could pass unchallenged. The Church had the right to speak. Although Ambrose in general accepted imperial interference in Church matters—because it favored his cause—it is possible to see many of the seeds of medieval sacerdotal theory in his writings.

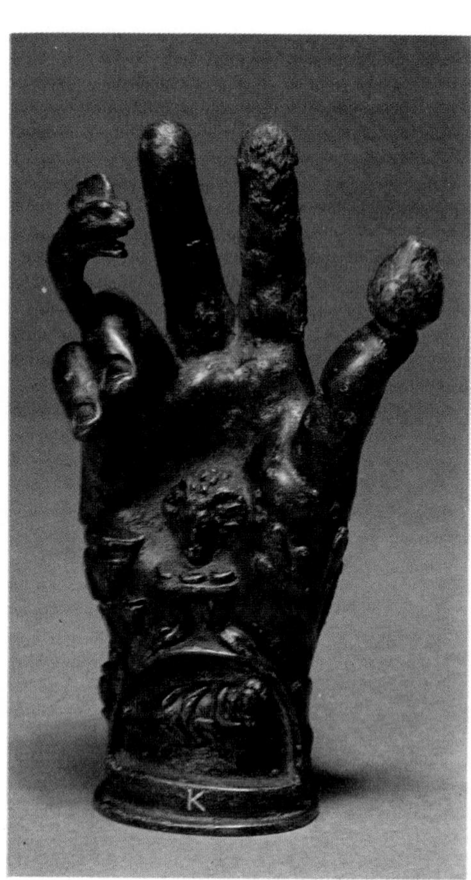

A bronze hand raised in benediction, late Roman. The additional charms on the fingers and in the palm are intended to boost the power of the talisman.

## THE SUPPRESSION OF HERESY

The Donatist heresy remained a major problem. To Donatists the Church was the body of the elect. There could be no salvation outside it, and no minister who was in a state of deadly sin could retain his place in it. The sacraments of such a minister would not only be invalid but would also be damaging to those who partook of them. It was the duty of a congregation to separate from a minister who was a sinner. In addition, it was the duty of the Christian to avoid pagan literature and pagan society. Christianity was a "law." Separation from the state was a necessity, and persecution must be accepted as part of the Christian life.

These ideals, traditional in North African Christianity, had made Donatism strong. Social and economic factors aided it also. People saw the Devil at work in the extortions of landowners and tax assessors. Protest took on a religious form. Bands of Donatist extremists roamed the countryside, burning, pillaging, and stealing. Primarily, however, they were religious fanatics. They were known as *circumcelliones* (around the shrines) as they lived near the tombs of martyrs. They offered themselves for martyrdom whenever opportunity occurred.

The Circumcelliones were the forerunners of many similar agragian movements that sprang up in medieval Europe. The members of such movements interpreted Christianity as ushering in the millennium. With this outlook the Church had no sympathy. It might be that a sacrament dispensed to someone outside the communion of the Catholic Church did not benefit the recipient, but it was a valid sacrament nonetheless.

For a time, the Donatists were regarded by Church authorities as "schismatics," and they suffered few, if any, legal disabilities. In 405, however, St Augustine (354–430) persuaded the imperial government to ban the Donatists and, by the use of existing legislation, to suppress them by force. From now on, the text in Luke relating to the Great Feast, "Compel them to come in," was to be invoked by Catholics to justify the persecution of those who disagreed with them. Another grim precedent in the religious life of Western Europe had been established.

## THE THEOLOGY OF GRACE

St Augustine was concerned with many fundamental theological problems besides that of heresy. He pondered long over the relationship between free will and grace and came to the conclusion that all virtue in man was due to grace. "Without grace it is not possible to resist concupiscence." Man was part of a "mass of sin," and only a very few were predestined to salvation. In saying this, Augustine, like the Donatists, was following the North African theological tradition of Tertullian.

Augustine's views were developed in response to the challenge of Pelagianism. Pelagius (c. 360–420) was probably the son of a Roman official in Britain and had been settled in Rome for a long time. Later tradition made him an Irish monk, but he rejected monasticism as a calling, preferring the simple title of "Christian." He believed that man, through the free will that God implanted in him, was capable of following God's commandments found in the Bible and was able therefore to live a virtuous life. "Be ye perfect, as your Father in Heaven is perfect" was to him a literal command. Pelagius did not accept either original sin or an original fall. Adam had sinned through his own fault, and his sin affected no one but himself. He would have died in any event, but his example had been a bad one for humanity. Pelagius rejected entirely the phrase that he had heard attributed to Augustine (from Book X of Augustine's *Confessions*), "Give what thou commandest and command what Thou wilt," as so much fatalism. His idea of grace was not that it is an inherent quality present with a predestined few but that it is an aid to all virtuous men to live even more in accordance with God's will.

Pelagius' ideas accorded well with what most Christians in Rome and Italy believed. Christianity there had been grafted onto a basis of Stoic values, of which the goal of a virtuous life formed an essential part. Their faith was capable of developing a social as well as a theological perspective, but it lacked the deep psychological insights of Augustine's position. The ensuing conflict between Pelagianism and Augustinianism was essentially a conflict between the North African and Italian theological traditions. In this case, thanks to Augustine and the superior organization of the North African Church, Augustinianism triumphed, with immense effects on the history of Western Europe. The Augustinian theology of grace was developed only gradually, between 413 and 426. Augustine was now elderly and, as the dispute dragged on, his worst qualities—his love of controversy and his unwillingness to concede a point to an opponent—came to the surface. By his persistent mistranslation of Romans V 12 ("*in whom* all sinned" instead of "*on account of whom* all sinned"), he exaggerated both Adam's fault and its results for humanity out of all recognition. Ten years of Manichaeanism and perhaps his frustrated desire for normal family life forced "concupiscence" (interpreted by him, as by the Manichaeans, as sexual desire) into obsessive proportions in his theology. That Western man has tended to equate sex with sin is in part due to this unhappy period of controversy in Augustine's old age. As in his Manichaean youth, he eventually affirmed that the great mass of humanity was fit only for eternal damnation.

Silver dish commemorating the Decennalia (tenth anniversary) in 388. The three emperors represented are Theodosius I, Valentinian II and Arcadius, son of Theodosius, proclaimed Augustus in 383. Theodosius was principally responsible for giving the Empire what unity it possessed at this time, though his narrow adherence to the Nicene Creed in matters religious provoked much trouble and controversy.

Before his death, however, Augustine had laid the foundations of the West's medieval political and religious thought. Predestination and free will were topics that continued to be debated by clerics and laymen in Chaucer's time as in Augustine's. The main lines of the medieval view of history and its interpretation of scripture are derived directly from Augustine and his immediate disciples. He had also tried in *The City of God* to explain the meaning of the fall of Rome in 410.

Empire and papacy, Church and world were the frames within which medieval men lived. The respective roles assigned to emperor and pope by writers in the Middle Ages had already been worked out before the curtain was rung down on the *pax romana* in the great surge of barbarian invasions during the first two decades of the fifth century. It was to take six centuries for these ideas to be fully worked out.

## THE PAPACY

The bishopric of Rome enjoyed great advantages. First, it was the see of St Peter, who had been not only Bishop of Rome but also the founder of the Church, nominated by Christ himself. St Peter's bones lay in Rome. The guardianship of those bones lay behind every papal attempt to implement Rome's claims to primacy. Every pope saw himself as the immediate apostolic successor of St Peter. Secondly, Rome was uniquely rich in martyrs, and martyrdom was the prime witness to the success of Christianity. Thus her position as the chief place of pilgrimage, rivaling even Jerusalem and the holy places of Palestine, was ensured. Thirdly, Rome was for centuries the imperial capital and retained many of the attributes of a capital long after the emperors had moved elsewhere. This meant not only that her bishops enjoyed the advantage of ready access to the senate, and on occasion to the emperor, but also that they could use the techniques of imperial administration to their great benefit. No writing office, apart from that of the emperors, was more efficient than that of the Roman bishops; no other see had records to rival Rome's. Historically orientated, it became from the beginning a see that could turn at will to written precedent and, even without any other advantage, this would have given it immense prestige and utility in the eyes of Christendom. Lastly, it enjoyed territorial wealth.

A good deal is known about the way in which the papacy ran its scattered blocks of estates in Italy, Sicily, southern Gaul, and elsewhere. As a business, the papacy was notably efficient. The popes spent their time defining doctrine and answering liturgical and administrative questions put by bishops throughout the West; taking a leading part in councils of the Church; behaving usually as loyal subjects of the Christian emperors, for whom, in effect, they ran a very important department of government. More than anyone else, they initiated the creation of the great body of written law of the Church, known as canon law.

Certain popes stand out. The see of Rome could attract the best talent. Innocent I (401–417) made abidingly clear, in a series of decretal letters to Italian, Spanish, Gallic, and African bishops, that Rome stood for the rule and interpretation of law as the emanation of divinity. In their juristic refinement, these decretals are worthy to stand beside the imperial rescripts on which they are modeled. The assumption is that no bishop can set aside a papal instruction. The pope speaks as St Peter. Innocent's contemporaries accepted that he had the right and duty to speak for the Church. His word was, quite literally, law.

Leo I (440–461) speaks with the same authority. His every pronouncement shows his familiarity with the business of civil and canon law. He stands in a great tradition, and by his firm insistence on it he does something to reveal, but not create, the gulf that was opening between Rome and Constantinople. More than this, Leo

*Above:* A mosaic design of the baptism of Christ from the dome of the orthodox baptistry at Ravenna. The baptistry was built during the pre-Gothic period of the fifth century, and was imitated by the Arian Goths after their invasion.
*Right:* Marble sarcophagus of two brothers from Rome, mid fourth century. It is decorated with scenes from both the Old and New Testaments.

was a member of the Roman embassy that met Attila the Hun near Mantua in 452 and dissuaded him from advancing on Rome. He also interceded, less successfully, with the Vandal Geiseric to spare Rome. He could speak for Italy. Indeed, he believed that he could speak for the Church. At the Council of Chalcedon (451) his *Tome* condemning monophysitism was accepted as the measure of orthodoxy. Leo regarded this as an acceptance of his juridical superiority. It is doubtful whether any Eastern bishop would have agreed.

Thirdly, there was Gelasius I (492–496), to whom it fell to define in practical terms how papal authority stood in relation to imperial power. He does not challenge the emperor's power, which, like all rule, he saw as a divine trust. But he does distinguish the division of labor. The divine majesty of the emperor remains, in theory, unimpaired.

Lastly, there comes probably the greatest of all the popes: Gregory I (590–604). He was a Roman aristocrat, trained in the business of secular administration and familiar with the ways of Constantinople. He watched over the smallest detail of the administration of the vast papal possessions. We have his correspondence to prove it. His loyalty to the emperors was never in question. Indeed, he could joyfully hail the accession of the villainous Phocas as the chosen of the Lord. But in one vital respect he was unlike his predecessors: he was a monk, and from this stemmed all that was original in his work.

A sick man, Gregory longed obsessively for the peace of the cloister he had been forced to abandon; a powerful man, he nonetheless interpreted his papal function in a monastic sense. This implied the application of his authority to a pastoral and moral end. In particular, he watched over all bishops, rebuking shortcomings and encouraging personal saintliness. He wrote a special manual on *Pastoral Care* to indicate to the clergy what spiritual rule entailed.

*Above:* Mosaic showing Christ giving the keys of Heaven to St Peter. Peter, according to Roman Catholic belief, was the first bishop of Rome, and was also the gatekeeper of Heaven. The keys form part of the badge of the papal insignia. *Left:* Ivory book cover from North Italy, sixth century. Most prominent among the Biblical scenes illustrated is the figure of a lamb, which has become a traditional symbol both of Jesus and of the Church. In Greece the lamb had been associated with Hermes. There are several statues of Hermes as *kriophoros,* carrying a lamb—literally a ram. The title and idea of "shepherd of the people" also dated back to Mycenaean times. The adoption of the lamb—like the timely canonization of local cult deities—may have been a deliberate ploy by the Church to christianize pagan beliefs and symbols.

Moreover, he faced the now Germanic West as a challenge to the missionary enterprise proper to the papacy alone. Indeed, he was as much concerned with Germanic kings as with emperors. Somewhat hesitantly, he organized the first mission to the pagan Anglo-Saxons in Kent, judging that the Celtic church had failed to proselytize among them. But he was equally concerned about the moral state of society in Merovingian Gaul, and he expressed delight at the conversion of the Visigoths of Spain from Arianism to Catholicism. In a word, he accepted the fact of Germanic Europe and spoke to the Germans as their spiritual lord.

His interventions were often, as he would have put it, *ratione peccati*—made with the object of rebuking sin. This overriding concern with the sin of society emerges in his other writings. As a commentator on the Book of Job, he demonstrates his power to penetrate to great psychological depths. He understood, as few men have, the nature of sin as it affects ordinary men and women. The end of the world, he thought, was not far distant. To save souls now was his aim. It is the moral quality of the great monk that set a new standard for his office.

Ivory diptych panel of second quarter of the fifth century. It belonged to a Roman consul, Felix, whose name may be seen in the Latin genitive case, Felicis, at top left of the figure. The two halves portrayed a deacon (illustrated) and an anti-pope.

Over two centuries the popes had learned what to say and how to say it in a world now formally Christian. What matters most is their sense of continuity of rule and of cumulative experience. Each pope, successor to St Peter, spoke against the background of recorded tradition. It never occurred to any one of them that he was founding a new papal empire to replace the Empire of Rome, for his empire was not secular but sacred. Each attempted to define his duties in terms of what he held to be old. The Church needed defending against great perils, not expansion into a monarchy. The last and greatest of the series, Gregory I, had no doubt that he was trying to salvage a rotten ship, not launch an armada.

## MONASTICISM

The West first learned what monasticism was through Eastern monastic rules. Eastern rules were for ascetics, and that they were of great strictness we know from the teachings of the early monastic centers at Lerins and Marseilles in southern Gaul. As they were applied in the West, however, by early fifth-century teachers such as John Cassian and St Augustine, they were more moderate.

It is remarkable that the Western recruits of the fourth and fifth centuries tended to be drawn from aristocratic families. A sense of disgust impelled them to leave society and the public duties that would naturally fall to them. It was not so much that they feared the collapse of society as that they felt revulsion at its self-seeking, its greed, and its corruption. The more self-indulgent a society becomes, the more asceticism will appeal to its better sons. This certainly cost society the services of some remarkable men, and it was a point that did not escape the notice of responsible pagans who still held that an educated man's duty is the service of the state. Perhaps worse, monasticism equally attracted well-born women who, by entering nunneries, forwent their natural function of bearing good sons for the state. This was a real loss. There was a loss in another way: an established monastery was a territorial loss. Lands given as endowment could never be recovered by founders' kin; indeed, they were constantly added to.

The aim of a monastery was the uninterrupted service of God in prayer and worship. To this end, it was necessary to control the daily life and even thought of every monk. This was the purpose of the rule that every monastery observed. The monastery was a community of worship through which the monk might learn to come to grips with sin and attain systematic knowledge of God. Not surprisingly, the early monasteries attracted many whose intention was merely to escape the pressures of society—to escape, for instance, from the consequence of disinheritance or difficulty in finding employment.

To some extent, bishops could control the monasteries within their own dioceses, and they were the more likely to do so if they had themselves been monks. An impressive number of the best bishops of the fifth century had started as monks. But apart from the quality of the monks themselves, they were constantly threatened by the kindred of their well-meaning founders, who rather naturally continued to regard monasteries on family land as family possessions. How could a monastery still dependent on patronage, tell the local landowner that he had no right to place his family in the cloister, let alone impose an abbot on it? How, above all, could this be explained to a pious king?

Monasteries were by their nature immunities, cut off from society; and immunities were to be a dominant feature of early medieval life.

## St Benedict

Some of the greatest men of the fourth and fifth centuries were monks or had legislated for monks. There was St Augustine of Hippo; there was Caesarius bishop of Arles, in whose surviving sermons we can catch a missionary spirit like that of Pope Gregory; and there was Cassiodorus, who in his old age founded a monastery on his estate in southern Italy, drawing up for its guidance a reading manual, secular and sacred, that was to have a lasting effect on the intellectual side of monasticism. Here for the first time was clearly set out the instruction proper for monks, based on a thorough knowledge of the Bible. It is the Bible that now moves to the forefront as the book of the Middle Ages, the one indispensable source of history, poetry, and inspiration, the book of the chosen people.

Another ivory diptych showing a poet and his muse, c.500. The muse was a pagan theme dating back to classical Greek and Roman times. The Christian poet would surely have sought his inspiration from God. However, the idea of inspiration by the muses has lingered on and they have been invoked throughout the ages, from Homer in the first line of the *Iliad* to the seventeenth-century poet, John Milton, and even to later writers. The Church adopted the idea of muses in its angelogy.

More influential even than Cassiodorus on the course of Western monasticism was St Benedict. Curiously little is known of this remote Italian. Pope Gregory, who devoted a whole book of his work on the miracles of the Italian saints to Benedict, treats him simply as a holy man, the popular image of the orthodox miracle worker, stemming directly from the New Testament. He does not even mention what he almost certainly knew, that Benedict was the author of a monastic rule. Its earliest form is unknown, but in the slightly later recension in which we have it, we can see at once that the compiler was a legislator of genius. Taking other rules, particularly the anonymous *Rule of the Master*, and using them as he thought best, Benedict put together, in seventy-three short chapters, a way of life for his own monks. It omits nothing essential and contains nothing that is irrelevant or of purely incidental application. By the side of the great ascetic rules of the past, it may look deceptively moderate. But, in fact, it looks what it is—livable—though it demands everything. Rooted in stability and obedience, the monk will learn to seek God through a carefully ordered life of worship, prayer, meditation, and manual labor. His thoughts will be anchored in the Bible, as he hears it read every day of his life, and most notably in the Psalms. His obedience to the rule requires the total surrender of his will. The will of the community is that of its father, the abbot.

What is new about the rule is Benedict's sense of community. The community is itself a worshiping unit; it has a purpose of its own. We are a long way from the kind of monastery that is no more than a collection of monks, each bent on his own salvation. Benedict said that his rule was for beginners. He meant that those who proved able could eventually turn to the sterner rules that demanded the solitary life of the hermit.

Although nearly lost during the first century of its existence, when Italy was a prey to ravaging barbarians, Benedict's rule was to survive and ultimately become simply through its merits, the great monastic rule of the whole Western world. Monte Cassino, Benedict's monastery on a hill above the road from Rome to Naples (where it can still be seen), was to remain its heart.

Chapter 18

# THE FRANKS

The Franks were not a people at all but a collection of West Germanic tribesmen living, by the first century, in the general area of the lower Rhine and its tributaries. As imperial auxiliaries and federates, they had penetrated into modern Belgium by the fourth century and settled on deserted Roman lands. Some Roman towns they also took over—as, for example, Tournai. Some of them undoubtedly penetrated yet further south to settle in northern Gaul by the mid-fifth century.

Their graves can sometimes be distinguished from those of other barbarians. Wrapped in his cloak (the metal buckle of which survives), the Frank was laid facing east, uncoffined, with his pots and weapons around him. He was buried with a short sword (the *scramasax*) and a throwing hatchet (the *fransisca*) or, if a man of rank, a long sword. The workmanship of these weapons is of high quality.

Already, it is clear, their society was hierarchized. There is no question of any free and equal Germanic community. These men and women had ranks, ranging from what they called kings down to slaves. To what extent rank was hereditary or was founded on service or landed possessions is a debated question. Their graves contain evidence of ceremonial decapitation and ritual fires.

The chieftains of Tournai managed to establish a dynasty. An early member was Merovech, whose name later became associated in legend with the magical origins of his house. At all events, his descendants were known as Merovingians. His son, Childeric, was more troublesome to the Gallo-Romans. There survive the much-pilfered remains of his burial at Tournai. His ornaments, weapons, and coins, to say nothing of strange cult objects that defy interpretation, suggest a rich man with wide contacts in the Roman world. In brief, he was a king, if only of the Franks of Tournai. He, in turn, left a son to succeed him: Clovis (more correctly, Chlodovech), a leader of heroic stature.

## Clovis

As always with barbarian heroes, legend soon enveloped Clovis. Nonetheless, in the great Frankish history written a century later by Gregory of Tours, certain parts of the historical figure can be unraveled. He emerges, through a series of clearly differentiated victories, as a warrior, who knew in what order to take his enemies. The earliest to fall to him seems to have been the last Roman ruler of northern Gaul, whom he defeated near Soissons. This opened to him the whole of the province of Belgica Secunda and made penetration to the Seine and further west a relatively easy matter. Though chronology is uncertain, he seems to have devoted himself to subduing the rival chieftains of Frankish settlements as far away as the Rhine. This he did by a mixture of guile, bribery, and assassination. Securing his rear in this way was of vital importance for his further campaign against the Burgundians, settled in eastern Gaul (effectively, the Rhone valley), and the

Frankish tombstone of a dead warrior, seventh century. The Franks carved out a huge kingdom in France, Belgium and Germany under Clovis (king, 481–511). The Franks owed their military success more to energy than to anything else. Clovis' descendants quarreled among themselves. Although it was not seriously threatened by external enemies the Frankish realm nearly dissolved several times in civil war. This was encouraged by Frankish inheritance law: a father's possessions were equally divided among his sons. Frankish customs encouraged war: every spring a meeting known as the *Campus Martius* (Field of Mars) was held, and this was normally a prelude to war.

Alamans, a much more formidable Germanic people across the middle Rhine, whom he defeated at Tolbiac.

Clovis now turned his attention to the Visigoths, who held most of France south of the Loire. With this was associated the conversion of Clovis to Catholicism, rather than to the Arianism of the barbarian peoples. The story of the conversion as it comes down to us is suspiciously reminiscent of that of Constantine (see chapter 15). It was a battlefield conversion, when defeat was turned into victory through the intervention of the Christian God. But it is made likelier by the long time of doubt, particularly about the reaction of his warriors, that passed before Clovis was prepared to be baptized. His conversion was a victory for his Catholic queen and for Remigius of Reims, the most influential bishop within his territory. It was also a risk, but like all those that Clovis took it was a calculated risk. His principal warriors accepted his decision, and he won at a stroke the wholehearted cooperation of the Gallic episcopate, without which Gaul was difficult to govern.

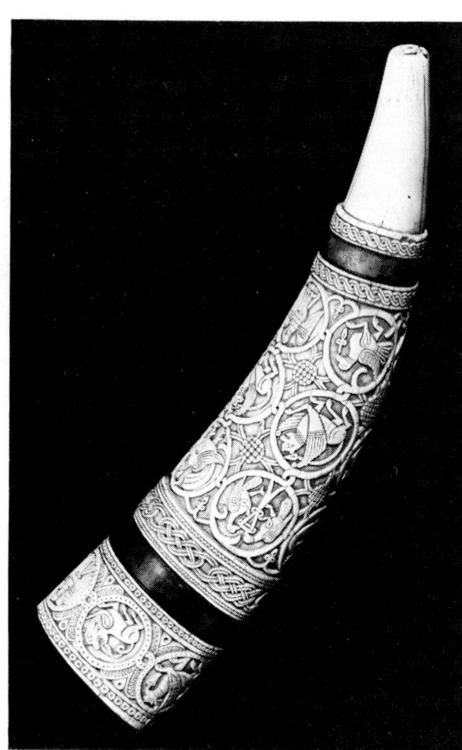

An ivory horn. The hunting horn was a symbol of nobility. In 778 after an unsuccessful attack on Muslim Spain, a group of Charlemagne's nobles were ambushed at Roncevalles in the Pyrenees. This incident was the basis for the *Song of Roland*, in which Charlemagne's general, Roland, is attacked but refuses to blow his hunting horn to summon Charlemagne to his aid. Only after his enemy has been annihilated does he sound the horn with his dying breath, and is rewarded by hearing Charlemagne's battle-cry, *Montjoie*, as the king attacks the Muslims.

But the Franks as a whole were not converted overnight. Written sources and archaeology agree that they remained pagan for a long time, some for centuries. They were countrymen, not townsmen, and so beyond the reach of a primitive parochial organization. Moreover, they had settled among Celtic rustics (the vast majority of the inhabitants of Gaul), to whom Christianity may not have penetrated to any great extent under Roman rule. Together, these two pagan elements may have given rise to something approaching a pagan renaissance.

Missionaries struggled with this intractable problem throughout the Frankish period, and we can see from inscriptions and carvings on gravestones, as well as from the contents of the graves themselves, that there was a long period of intermediate belief, part Christian and part pagan. Experience taught the Church in Frankish Gaul and elsewhere that the best approach was to win over the peasant by adapting Christianity to a pagan background, insisting only on the essentials of the new faith and especially on a cessation of blood sacrifice.

The cult of local saints throughout Gaul reveals an additional approach. The shrine of the holy man was often a local center of worship, where the saint's protection could be invoked and his miraculous healing powers won by offerings, much like those that pagan deities had expected. In brief, Christianity to the peasant seemed more a matter of propitiating a local demigod than of worshiping an abstract God who was infinitely remote. But it would be a mistake to suppose that this approach was confined to the countryside. Christianity was equally a religion of miracle and emotion, not of dogmatic persuasion, to men of substance and intelligence. In no other way can we explain the proliferation of monasteries and churches endowed by private benefactors and the enormous number of saints' *Lives* that characterize Frankish religious literature.

Clovis himself was as credulous as his warriors and peasants. A baptized Catholic, it was under the aegis of St Martin and St Hilary that he undertook his final campaign against the Visigoths. Foreseeing trouble, the Gothic king, Alaric II, had promulgated a code of law (known as the *Breviary*) to placate his Roman subjects, and this was to be the basis of all subsequent achievements—and they were splendid—in Visigothic law. He had also appealed for help to Theodoric in Italy. And certainly not all Gallo-Romans were ready to support the Catholic champion. This did not, however, save Alaric from defeat at Vouilé, near Poitiers. Aquitaine was at the mercy of the Franks, and Clovis sent a force to take over Toulouse and seize the Gothic treasure there. The Goths were now confined to Septimania and Spain. Clovis himself returned to Tours to give thanks to St Martin, and there he was invested with the insignia of a Roman official and hailed as Augustus. Whatever the technical meaning of this, the Empire had recognized him as an ally. He proceeded to summon a Church council at Orleans (511) to deal with problems in the south, an act that demonstrated who was to be master of the Church in Gaul.

To the end of Clovis' reign belongs the composition of the *Lex Salica,* a collection of Frankish customary law put together by Roman lawyers for the king. They are the customs of a peasant society and reveal little about those of the higher ranks. What they do reveal is the prominence, right through the social structure, of the feud or vendetta, a feature common to all Germanic society. The feud emerges in *Lex Salica* not as a bloody free-for-all but as an orderly way of settling local disputes between kindreds. Bloodshed was the ultimate sanction against which a system of acceptable tariffs for compensation could operate. Self-interest would have dictated that a family might rather find the means to pay off an offended neighbor than risk a running fight in which men connected by blood with both parties would be faced with a difficult choice of loyalties. Compensation, if accepted, would also save the ravaging of hard-won land. The king defines this process of compensation but does not invent it. There is new and old material in his law. Most of all, it demonstrates that he is the source and guarantor of written law. A Frank is a man who accepts the law. Clovis collects together some of his followers' customary practices, puts them in writing, and calls them his own. It is a piece of propaganda for a dynasty that is feeling its way from war leadership to the harder task of rule in settled conditions.

When he died, Clovis was buried in his own church in Paris, not in a barbarian grave like his father's. His kingdom was divided between his sons on the traditional Germanic principle that a man's conquests should be disposed of among his heirs as he thought best. Each was to have his own share, and no share was precisely delimited as a nucleated territory. We can see the seeds of future trouble here, and probably Clovis did, too. It was a barbarian way.

*Above:* Dagobert I, king of the Franks. Dagobert became king of Austrasia in 626, and by 630 had established control over Neustria and Burgundy, the other two regions of Francia. He recovered land lost to the Church and to great nobles, invaded Spain, and attacked the Slavs. He began the tradition of patronage of the arts that came to flower under the Carolingians. After Dagobert's death in 639, his possessions were divided. He was the last effective Merovingian king.
*Left:* Ivory carving. Monasteries in the Carolingian era became centers of ivory carving, and work of very high quality was produced, usually under Byzantine influence. But ivory carving of a cruder kind had existed under the Merovingians.

Clovis, king of the Franks. Clovis was the first king to rule all the various groups that made up the Frankish federation. In 486 he beat Syagrius, the last Roman general in Francia. He went on to conquer all France north of the Loire, and Belgium. In 496, Clovis became a Catholic and was the only Christian monarch in the West who was not an Arian. When he attacked the Visigothic kingdom in Aquitaine his religion brought him the support of the Catholic clergy, which eased his conquest of southern France in 506. Clovis died in 511.

The political development of Francia in the sixth century was little more than the working-out of the consequences of Clovis' partition. There was one *Regnum Francorum*, but generally more than one king reigned at a time. Each found himself drawn to local interests and problems. Thus the ruler of Austrasian, or eastern, Francia was particularly concerned with the problems of the Rhineland and the Germanic peoples east of the Rhine: Thuringians, Alamans, Bavarians, Saxons, and to the north, Frisians. It is a tale of campaigns, subsidies, and colonization. Moreover, prolonged interest in such a region inevitably meant contact with, and at times an implied challenge to, the Empire. Frankish extension of interest into west-central Europe was primarily an Austrasian affair. Similarly, the Frankish rulers of Burgundy were sensitive to the affairs of southern Germania, Provence, and ultimately Spain. Those who ruled Neustria, the northern and western areas of Francia, were most alive to happenings in the former Frankish homeland around the Rhine estuary and further north. All three participated in the control of Aquitaine and were invariably sensitive about the regions where their domains met and their capitals lay—namely, the area bounded by Soissons, Reims, and Orleans (Paris was treated as a special case). Their quarrels were the outcome partly of disputed inheritance, partly also of particular family disagreements, and partly of different views on what we should call foreign policy. One king might wish to lead an expedition into Italy, another into Saxony, and a third into Spain. But each to some extent was under pressure from local interests that were not operative elsewhere.

The interest of the period really lies in social development, in the emergence of a class of Frankish warrior-landowners and colonists. The growing power of this class is apparent in law, in the founding of churches and monasteries, and in intermarriage with the Gallo-Romans. The French language begins to emerge as a latin vernacular impregnated with Frankish loan-words. At the same time, it must be remembered that the regions of Gaul retained much of their former identity, and the degree of Frankish settlement varied from place to place. Most intense in the north, it had very little effect on Aquitaine and Provence and none on Gothic Septimania. Over all broods the Church as the one Gallo-Roman institution that the new society could build upon. Without it, the continuing life of the city would have been unthinkable, and equally without it, Merovingian kingship would have remained mere war leadership.

### Two Observers

Sixth-century Francia is illuminated for us, as is no other Germanic society, by the writings of two remarkable men, contemporaries and bishops. One was an Italian refugee named Venantius Fortunatus. For two years he was, in effect, court poet to the Austrasian Franks, producing panegyrics and short pieces in prose and verse that argue an extraordinary appetite for polite literature among the Austrasian nobility. Beyond the flattery lay the recipients' desire to be seen as heirs to the Roman tradition.

Moving on to Poitiers, where he became first a lay agent to the great abbess Radegundis and finally bishop, Venantius showed how literature could be turned to the service of religion, and in particular of religious women. He was inspired by Radegundis to write poetry that heralds the birth of medieval mystical writing in one of its most popular forms. Visions of heaven, the fruits of virginity, the ecstasy of renunciation, and the cooperation of nature in God's purposes are all themes of his compositions. To this must be added his contribution to what was then the most vital of the forms of religious literature—the saint's *Life*, designed to be read at the annual feast to the crowds gathered together to acclaim his patronage. Venantius' most important *Life* was his version of an older *Life* of St Martin of Tours, patron of Gaul and then of Francia. Factually it adds nothing, but in spirit it shows us how the sixth-century Frank liked to conceive of his greatest miracle worker. Venantius' numerous and varied compositions tell us much about him and much about the society that sheltered him.

A greater man was Venantius' contemporary, Gregory of Tours. A Gallo-Roman of senatorial rank, Gregory looks at first glance like a typical collaborating bishop, somewhat contemptuous of the barbarians he must live among and obey and constantly aware of what separates his class from that of the Frankish chieftain. His huge saints' *Lives* demonstrates the riches of the Gallo-Roman past, but it is designed for the service of the Gallo-Frankish present. As bishop of Tours, he was the guardian of the national shrine of St Martin, before which even the wildest Franks quailed. It was due to him more than to anyone that St Martin was accepted as the patron of the Merovingians. But the work for which he is justly most famous is what is now known as his *History of the Franks*.

Gregory's history belongs to a class of historical writing that stems from the Christian tradition of Eusebius, not from the classical tradition of Thucydides. It is salvation history, written to show how God's purpose emerges from the history of a people. Bede was to do the same for the Anglo-Saxons, Isidore for the Visigoths, Jordanes for the Ostrogoths, and Paul the Deacon for the Lombards. But Gregory's history is certainly the vividest of the collection. His Latin, direct and even rustic, does for history what Gregory the Great's Latin did for pastoral theology. It makes its points through a series of brilliantly imagined stories. One sees the thing as it happens. His history has a hero, Clovis, who is shown as God's heroic instrument for the conversion of the Franks. And there is a moral: warriors who serve the Catholic God will have their reward on earth as well as in heaven. The Catholic king is victorious over his enemies, as Constantine was. Thereafter, Gregory plunges into what looks like the political chaos of the reigns of the sons and grandsons of Clovis. He highlights tales of violence, not to distinguish Franks from Gallo-Romans but to prove that hostility to the Church brings ruin and support of it brings prosperity. We are reminded that the Church was a great proprietor.

Woodcut of the victory of Clovis over the Alemanni at the battle of Tolbiac, 495, and his baptism at Reims, sixteenth century. During the battle of Tolbiac Clovis is thought to have seen a vision. After his victory he decided to become a Christian. He was baptised in Reims cathedral by the archbishop, St Remigius, on Christmas day, 496, with 3,000 of his followers. It is not impossible that Clovis saw the political advantage that he would get from being a Catholic rather than an Arian.

Gregory is not much concerned with doctrine, though he still fears Arianism. His real concern is the direction of public authority. It must be exercised in the interests of the Church, and the bishops must be listened to. He has his villains and his heroes. But all whom he describes are real men and women and not personifications of virtue or vice. We see them in their daily lives, sometimes earning good marks and sometimes bad. The whole is a magnificent essay in social morality as seen by an intelligent observer who fears the worst. Gregory felt that Francia was doomed for the sins of her rulers, whereas in fact she was at the beginning of a long era of prosperity. Isidore of Seville was to occupy the opposite position in relation to the Visigoths: he believed they had a splendid future, whereas the Arabs who were to destroy them were already in motion.

## RETROSPECT

How did western Europe of the age of Gregory the Great differ from western Europe as Constantine left it, three centuries earlier?

Politically, imperial control had disintegrated, yielding to barbarian pressures it lacked the means to resist. But it had not disappeared. Nobody believed that the emperor in Constantinople did not, in theory, enjoy authority over the West. It would be wrong to underestimate the nature of Justinian's reconquests. His successors held much of Italy against the new Lombard invaders, secure in their southern bases and in Ravenna. South-eastern Spain was still theirs, and so also North Africa. Imperial fleets could still dominate the western Mediterranean from their many island bases. Even in Gaul, the authority of the emperors was felt to be a reality. None of this seemed impermanent, as it does to us.

Culturally, too, the Roman heritage still counted for much. Apart from a brief renaissance in southern Italy, the study of Greek was dead; but Latin literature continued to be taught in its traditional forms among the aristocracy. Boethius witnesses to the deep desire of the West to salvage what was best of the Greco-Roman tradition of letters. Nor was this confined to those of Roman stock.

Socially, the influx of Germanic settlers made only local differences. They were in a tiny minority. Leaders of successful war bands, who settled widely on abandoned Roman estates, no doubt adapted themselves to the forms of traditional economy dictated by the land itself. There was no technological revolution. We should rather envisage the replacement—though not everywhere—of Roman landlords by barbarians and the downgrading of independent workers of the soil to servile status. Towns, too, continued an existence of sorts behind their walls. They neither flourished nor disappeared.

In religion there were marked changes. Germanic Arianism and paganism yielded slowly to Catholic missionaries, and both had some effect on the nature of western Catholicism. The Church, believing in the approach of Armageddon, turned to the task of conversion and instruction, and first it turned to barbarian kings. Christianity, to be attractive to warriors became a religion of war and victory and miracle. And it is the miraculous that predominated in its teaching. One cause of the dissolution of classical culture was certainly the attitude of the Church. Culture and education were in its hands to an increasing extent. They were the weapons of religion, designed to fit a man to fight the Devil, not to write polite verse. In all this, the remnants of classical culture could play only a restricted role.

We must conclude that the Germanic West wished to be Roman and largely believed that it could be. But *Romanitas* reached it through a Church that was Roman in a new way.

Frankish casket of whalebone, eighth century. The detail shows the adoration of the Magi. Other scenes from classical and German mythology, rather than Christian tradition, are portrayed in the casket.

# Medieval Christendom

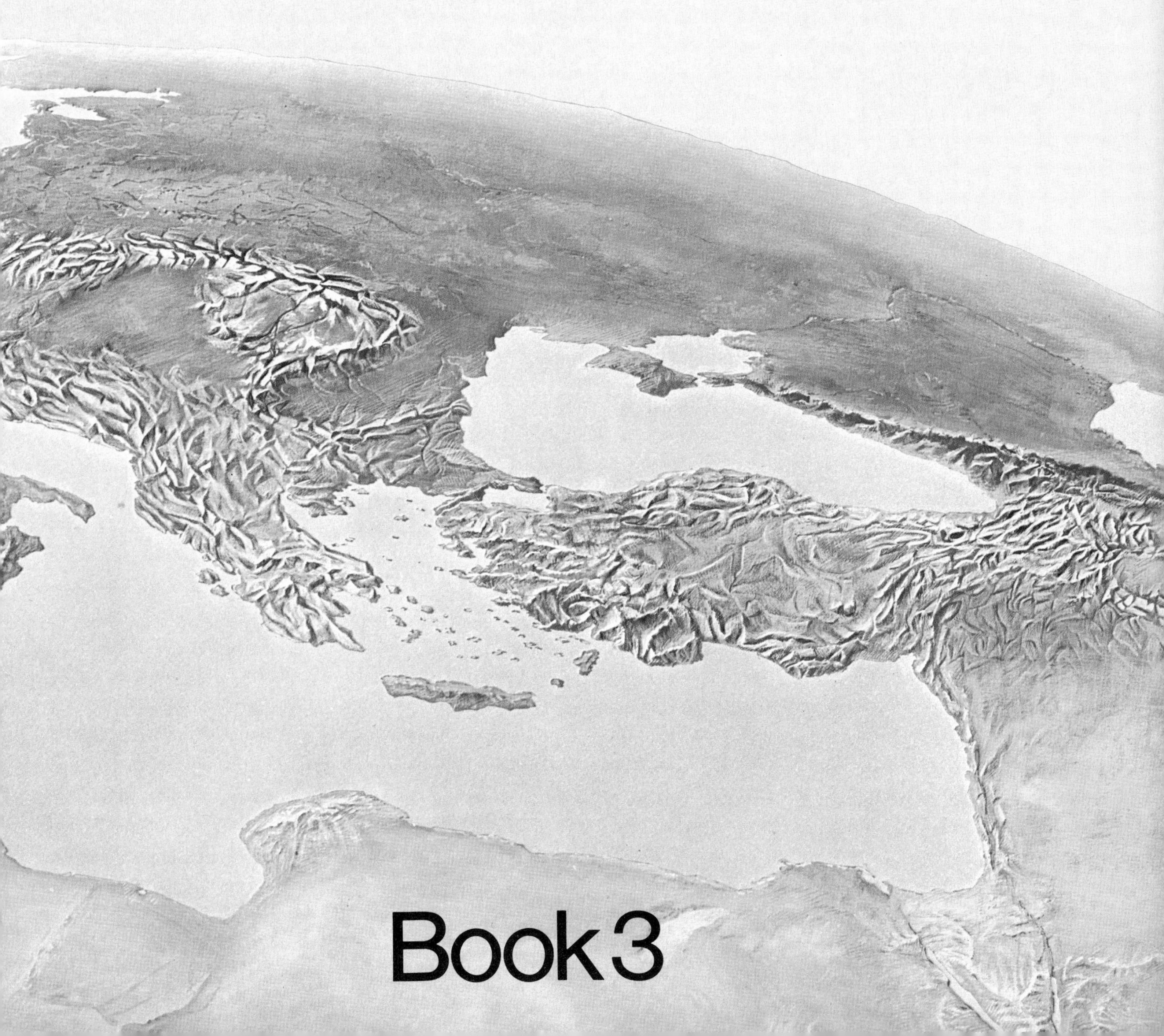

# Book 3

# Introduction

Nothing discussed in this book begins less than five centuries ago. The beginning of the story told in it goes back another thousand years or so. Yet, far off though it is, the subject is the making of Europe in a shape that is still basically the one with which we are familiar. What is called the Middle Ages in European history—and the term could not make sense in the chronology of any other continent—is because of this a recognizable chapter in world history.

This is so because European civilization is both the source and the pattern for a way of life which is more and more the general pattern in every corner of the world. Of course, much that makes up that way of life is very modern even in Europe itself. The wearing of much the same sort of clothes in New York, Bangkok and Johannesburg, or the presence of big factories in Nagasaki, Dortmund and Patna are the products of an industrialization and a technology that had only been in being for a couple of centuries. Nonetheless, it appeared first in Europe and, because Europe was already different from the rest of the world, it took forms there which were later to determine world history.

One of the ways in which Europe was already Europe was that her intellectual and social elites, sharply distinct as they are to our eyes, nevertheless shared a common way of thinking about and assessing much of their experience. This rested fundamentally on a common faith. The idea of Europe grew out of the idea of Christendom. Whatever their precise beliefs, the first Europeans thought of themselves as different from other men because they were Christians. Their faith gave their civilization great dynamism and thrust. It also gave it a profound moral and institutional imprint. The Church made Christians of barbarians; in so doing, it began to make them Europeans and consolidated its position as the central structure of civilized life for a millennium. The long rearguard action of the Church since the Reformation is a testimony to its dominant position in the centuries discussed in this book.

The Church always had rivals, of course. There is nothing monolithic about the unity of the Middle Ages. Another of the great themes that identifies this period as the origin of modern Europe is that it was then that there emerged the first modern European nations. Spain, France, England (and in a slightly different sense Germany) were made in the Middle Ages. They are with us still, the first three with not-very-different geographical definition and one of them with a continuity of organization that has sometimes been the pride and sometimes the despair of its citizens; the descent of the English crown and the continuity of parliament give Great Britain a political history whose continuity is outdistanced only by the papacy. On such foundations was to be built the nationalism of a later era; paradoxically it was to shatter the medieval synthesis that formed it. But that is another and later story.

By the material standards of our own day, medieval men lived poor lives. In part this was because they chose to invest their economic surplus in great buildings for worship; the option of going to the moon was not available to them. But more fundamentally it is because the surplus in an agricultural economy at that time was small. In this the life of medieval Europe resembled the life of most cultures we have so far considered. Abundance is a modern idea. This meant that catastrophe was often near at hand to medieval man. When it came—as it often did, in the shape of war, pestilence or famine—the repercussions were enormous. Recovery was often slow. This is one illustration of the slowness of change in medieval times; over a millennium the lot of many ranks of society can have changed hardly at all. The technology of daily life must have been much the same to the peasant in 800 as one in 1500 in many parts of Europe. Yet tiny though the increment of civilization was, it was all the time building up like a coral reef. On it was to rest the spectacular acceleration of history that is its characteristic from the sixteenth century onwards.

EXODVS

AECSUNT Cap
NOMINA
FILIORU
ISRAHEL
QUIINGRES
SISUNTIN
AEGYPTU
CUMIACOB
SINGULI
CUMDOMI
BUS SUIS
INTROIE

# Part I
# After Rome

## Chapter 1

# THE EASTERN ROMAN EMPIRE

"When Rome, the head of the world, shall have fallen," wrote Lactantius in the third century, "who can doubt that the end is come of human things, aye, of the earth itself?" By the fifth century, the Empire had come to be regarded as an institution ordained by God Himself—an earthly reflection of the divine principle of unity. To its Christian inhabitants, the fifth-century Empire, West and East together, was sacred, eternal, and indivisible. It should not be surprising, therefore, that the deposition of the boy-emperor Romulus Augustulus in 476 did not spell, for the people who lived at the time, the end of anything. Imperial authority in the West passed to the emperor Zeno in Constantinople, but since he was already the supreme ruler of the Empire, the event was not one of great significance. The fact that Romulus' deposer, the German chieftain Odoacer, felt the need to have Zeno recognize him as *patricius* of Rome is an indication of just where people believed the real power still resided.

Both as a concept and in fact, the Roman Empire continued for many centuries after its "fall." In the West, the imperial tradition was kept alive by the Church; in theory, until the time of Charlemagne, the emperors in Constantinople were acknowledged as having secular authority over all mankind. In the East, the imperial tradition was kept alive by the emperors themselves; the eastern sector of the Empire was to survive for another thousand years, its continuity unbroken until the capture of Constantinople by the Turks in 1453. Throughout this long period, the Roman origins were deliberately preserved: the emperors called themselves *Augustus*, and the subjects of the Empire were *Romaioi*. In fact, however, the culture of the Eastern Empire was essentially Greek, and its people were an admixture of races, languages, and national sympathies. Greeks, Egyptians, Syrians, Armenians, Slavs, and Bulgars all contributed to the varied and distinguished civilization that came to be known as Byzantine.

The Eastern Roman Empire after the sixth century is usually called the Byzantine Empire, or Byzantium, a name derived from the Greek town that Constantine had selected as the site of his new capital. (The town of Byzantium had been founded in the seventh century B.C. by Greeks supposedly under the leadership of a man named Byzas.) The capital of Byzantium, however, continued to be called Constantinople (the City of Constantine) until the Turks renamed it Istanbul in the fifteenth century.

Until its decline in the eleventh century, the Byzantine Empire was the foremost military and naval power in the Mediterranean. It formed a bulwark against the East, protecting the medieval West from some of the force of external attacks—from Huns and Persians, from Arabs in the early Middle Ages, from the Mongols later, and finally, from the Turks, by whom it was eventually destroyed.

In addition to its role as protector of Christianity, the Byzantine Empire served

A relief showing the emperor Theodosius the Great attending the games at the hippodrome at Constantinople with his sons Arcadius and Honorius. Theodosius was one of the most effective of the later Roman emperors, ruling the Eastern Empire 379–395. Theodosius' belief that he should control the Christian Church foreshadowed later Byzantine attitudes. The games in the hippodrome were one of the major occasions in the life of Constantinople.

also as the guardian and preserver of the classical world. Through all the long centuries of the Empire's existence, Byzantines in schools and libraries copied and recopied the scientific, philosophic, and literary masterpieces of the classical Greek and Hellenistic periods. Classical Greek was the language of scholarship, and educated Byzantines read the works of Homer and Euripides, Plato and Aristotle in the original. Without Byzantium, many of these works would have been entirely lost or would exist for us only in stray quotations in anthologies. It is difficult to imagine what our civilization would be like today without this inheritance from the classical world.

*Above:* The emperor Constantine II and his wife.
*Right:* A view of Constantinople, showing its strategic position on the Bosphorus. The city dominates the sea route between the Mediterranean and Black Seas, and stands at the junction between Europe and Asia. Its short land face was heavily protected by huge walls, while the Golden Horn, the inlet above the center of the picture, provided a natural harbor. The conquest of Constantinople by the Turks in 1453 changed the city's face: minarets were added to the huge church of Hagia Sophia when it became a mosque, and the Blue Mosque (foreground) was built.

## JUSTINIAN'S VISION

The reign of Justinian the Great (527–565) was a landmark in the fortunes of the Roman Empire and a high point in the early history of Byzantium. It was part of Justinian's conception of his responsibilities as emperor and sole ruler of the world *(Autocrator)* that he should reunite all of Rome's Mediterranean lands, re-creating the territorial unity of the *pax Romana* (a unity that was by now, in fact, unmanageable). He reorganized the military districts of the Empire, repaired and extended the border forts, and embarked on a series of lengthy and costly campaigns. His armies reconquered North Africa from the Vandals, Italy from the Ostrogoths, and southern Spain from the Visigoths. On the Eastern front, he kept at bay the Persian enemy and established the Roman right to control the eastern shores of the Black Sea. He did not, however, manage to prevent the Slavs from trickling across the Danube to devastate the Roman provinces in the Balkans.

Justinian's vision of a restored Roman Empire did not succeed: in the century following his death, most of the areas he had reconquered were again lost. A far more lasting achievement was the code of law that bears his name. The Justinian

Code, which condensed 3 million lines of imperial Roman law into a compact 150,000-line compendium, was in time to become the single most influential body of law in the West. All that was still relevant in the unwieldy mass of Roman law that had accumulated during a thousand years was embodied in the code—rearranged, codified, brought up to date. It was an impressive accomplishment. When the study of law was revived by the teachers of Bologna in the twelfth century, they took Justinian as their basis, and to this day, Roman law means primarily the contents of his code.

Justinian is also remembered as the emperor of the "First Golden Age" of Byzantine art. Many of the superb mosaics at Ravenna date from his reign and include portraits of Justinian himself and of his empress, Theodora. The cathedral of Hagia Sophia ("Holy Wisdom") in Constantinople—the "noblest church in Christendom"—was built under Justinian's patronage and enriched by him with the spoils of many conquests.

The events of Justinian's reign and of the century following his death determined both the character and the extent of the medieval Empire. Although Justinian's conquests were largely lost, some areas, such as the southern part of Italy, remained under Byzantine control. In the Balkan peninsula, tribes from north of the Danube—Slavs and Bulgars—invaded the frontier and harried the imperial provinces, reaching at one time even as far as the Peloponnese in southern Greece. These invaders were eventually converted and brought within the imperial and Christian orbit, but their permanent settlement in much of the Balkans introduced significant racial changes in that part of the Empire.

One of the greatest dangers to Byzantium during this early period of its history came from the Arabs. In an incredibly short period of time, Muslim forces had not only defeated Byzantium's archenemy, the great and powerful Persian empire, but

*Above:* Theodora, wife of the emperor Justinian, from a mosaic in San Vitale, Ravenna. After changing the laws forbidding patricians to marry actresses, Justinian married Theodora, an actress and harlot. The empress, beautiful, imperious and ruthless, provided a fitting wife for her husband, whose ambition it was to conquer all the land that had formerly belonged to the Roman Empire. *Left:* A procession at Justinian's court, from a mosaic in San Vitale, Ravenna. The emperor is about to present a gold plate to the archbishop of Ravenna, on his right.

had deprived Byzantium of its provinces in Syria, Palestine, Egypt, North Africa, and Spain. The rise of the Islamic empire in the seventh and eighth centuries was to have enduring effects on the Christian world, both West and East.

The altar and apse of the church of San Vitale. San Vitale was seen by Justinian as being a chapel of the imperial court. His vision of a restored Empire made it necessary to have a capital in the west. Ravenna, with its greater wealth and security, its communications with Constantinople, and its imperial tradition, made a more natural capital than Rome. It became the capital of the Byzantine exarchate (province) of the west, and was not lost to the Empire until the eighth century.

### Islam

Islamic civilization and its expansion will be examined in Book IV, but it is useful to know at this point what kind of a foe Christianity was facing. Islam was founded by the Prophet Mohammed, who was born in Mecca, on the Arabian peninsula, about 570. Mohammed devoted most of his life to the conversion of the unruly and largely nomadic Arab tribes to a new faith that had been revealed to him through the Word of God. By the time of his death in 632, he had succeeded in bringing most of the peninsula under one rule and one religion, the religion of Islam. Mohammed's successors almost immediately embarked on a holy war (*jihad*), obeying Mohammed's injunction that Muslims should seek the conversion of the infidel—and also, apparently, responding to the pressures of an expanding population. Within the brief span of ten years, all of Palestine and Syria and most of the Persian Empire had been conquered. The rich province of Egypt fell between 640 and 646, and the Arabs began to push across North Africa. Constantinople was besieged in 674–78. By 720, all of the Middle East (except Asia Minor), all of North Africa, and most of Spain were under Islamic domination.

In 717, the Arabs again laid siege to Constantinople. The Byzantine emperor Leo III, with the aid of a new secret weapon, Greek fire (an incendiary mixture of unknown composition), turned them back. It was a significant victory. In checking the Arabs, Byzantium managed to save not only itself but probably Europe also from falling before the Muslim expansion. Asia Minor, Greece, and most of the Aegean islands remained within the Empire. The political continuity of the Roman Empire in its medieval form was maintained. The basic core of the Greco-Roman world was preserved.

During the centuries that elapsed between the founding of the "new Rome" by Constantine and the final collapse of the Empire in the fifteenth century, the fortunes of Byzantium alternated between disaster and triumph, victory and defeat. There were always enemies pressing in from East and West. There was the ever-present danger of internal disintegration; the varied peoples that made up the Byzantine world were from the beginning in constant conflict, even within the capital itself. Separatist movements, both political and religious, threatened Church and emperor. Feudal chieftains rebelled, were suppressed, rebelled again. Yet the Empire survived, retaining its integrity in the Balkan peninsula and Asia Minor until the eleventh century, when it entered upon a long and final decline.

No attempt will be made to trace these oscillations; the political history of Byzantium is too complex to be unraveled in a brief survey such as this. Instead, this chapter will concentrate on the civilization itself, on its administrative and social structures and its culture. It was an important civilization, not only because it wielded enormous influence among the peoples of Eastern Europe but also because it left a lasting impression on the West. Its effects can still be seen today.

## HOW THE EMPIRE WAS ADMINISTERED

The long life of the Empire would have been impossible without both tenacity and flexibility; the view that it was a rigid, fossilized, late-Roman structure is mistaken. It is true that certain fundamental principles continued to the end. It remained a Christian monarchy ruled by an emperor who was the representative of God. The ruler of this earthly state was absolute; he took complete responsibility for all aspects of government, directing policy and providing the final court of appeal.

(He was not, however, necessarily an irresponsible despot. From a purely practical point of view, efficient government was essential, because the Byzantine Empire was perpetually threatened by external enemies on almost every side.) Although theoretically the emperor was elected by senate, army, and people, this was usually little more than a formality.

In the Byzantine conception of the imperial office, the ruler was closely associated with the Church. He was crowned by the head of the Greek Orthodox Church, the patriarch of Constantinople. He both supported the Church and was supported by it. Indeed, the whole routine of the imperial household was closely linked with Christian liturgical life. Every detail was provided for in the careful and detailed instructions laid down in a *Book of Ceremonies* which has survived from the tenth century, and life in the court was conducted according to strict protocol.

An absolute ruler both in theory and practice, the Byzantine emperor was nevertheless bound by more than the high traditions of his office. Citizens of the Empire were governed in everyday life by a long-standing code of justice as determined by Roman legal principles, and in addition, there were many local and private compilations, or collections relative to particular needs. One of these is the Rhodian maritime law, which provides an amusing picture of hazards at sea, ranging from pirate attacks to the danger of fire from travelers cooking on deck. Legal proceedings then, as now, were expensive and often long and drawn out. The final appeal lay in the imperial court, though a man would have to be extremely persistent, and probably wealthy, to get as far as this.

Throughout the history of the Byzantine Empire, there was a sophisticated administrative system. The routine of government continued, whatever the external pressures. Civil servants, though not excessive in number by modern standards, covered all the varied needs of state, from the imperial secretariat to the billeting of troops or collection of taxes and the execution of justice. At the top of the scale, ministers of state controlled the important departments of government and the commanders-in-chief and admirals were responsible for army and navy. These great figures had their specific titles (though these changed from time to time) and their own special place in court protocol, which often gave a clue to the needs of imperial politics—for instance, the military commander of the East took precedence over the commander of the Western troops.

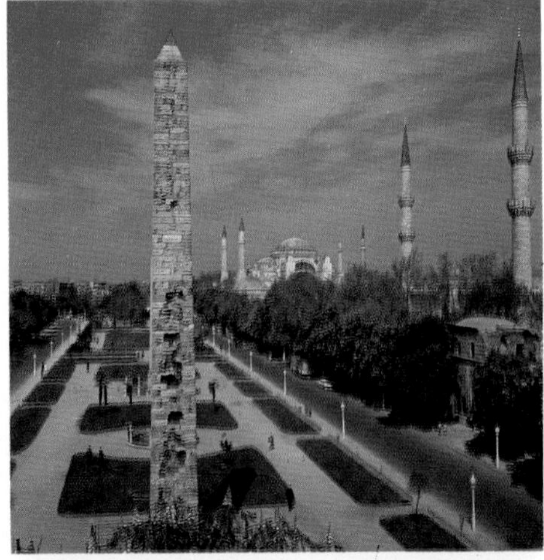

*Top:* The hippodrome gardens at Constantinople with Hagia Sophia in the background.
*Above:* Interior of Hagia Sophia, the cathedral of Holy Wisdom at Constantinople. The greatest achievement of Byzantine architecture, Hagia Sophia was rebuilt by the emperor Justinian after an earlier, smaller church had been damaged during rioting in 532. The dome of the new building, designed by the architects Anthemios of Tralles and Isidorus of Miletes, collapsed in 558. Despite reinforcements and buttresses the dome collapsed again in 989. Nevertheless, this huge dome, 144 feet in diameter, is one of the marvels of ancient architecture.

### Byzantine Diplomacy

Since Byzantium was always subjected to external pressures, defense was of prime concern. Diplomacy, however, was always considered preferable to warfare, and diplomacy was a highly developed art in Byzantium. The principles of the Byzantine foreign office in the tenth century are clearly set out in a manual entitled *On Imperial Administration*, which lists the enemies that are to be especially feared and placated and makes suggestions for playing off one foreign power against another or for weakening potentially dangerous neighbors by fomenting civil strife. In its foreign policy, Byzantium also drew on all the resources of its magnificent civilization: impressive receptions of foreign embassies, splendid presents sent by ambassadors—illuminated manuscripts, fine brocades, carved ivories, and enamel work —and, probably more effective still, lavish subsidies paid in gold. In addition, there was a far-flung and efficient secret service; all, from missionaries to merchants, were pressed into gathering information about enemy plans and resources. By means such as these, battles and loss of life were avoided where possible. The Byzantines had no use for the reckless headlong attacks sometimes favored by Western feudal knights. They preferred more sophisticated methods.

## THE BYZANTINE CHURCH

When the Arabs conquered Syria, Palestine, and Egypt in the seventh century, the patriarchates of Rome and Constantinople were alone left uncaptured. The pope in Rome and the patriarch of Constantinople all too often found themselves in disagreement. This conflict arose partly because of differences of doctrinal interpretation but still more by reason of political problems and rival interests. In the ninth century, for example, the Greek and Latin Churches competed in the Slav mission field. The revived papacy of the eleventh century clashed with the patriarch of Constantinople in the dramatic episode of 1054, when an arrogant Roman cardinal threw down in Hagia Sophia in Constantinople a bull of anathema against an equally arrogant patriarch. The cleavage was accentuated by the crusading movement, with its ravaging of the Byzantine Empire that culminated in the capture of Constantinople in 1204. The rift was never healed.

Normally the emperor and the patriarch of Constantinople worked closely together. The patriarch was virtually appointed by the emperor, and the emperor, in turn, gained enormously from patriarchal support. It was the patriarch who gave formal blessing to the imperial accession at the coronation service.

As the representative of Christ in an Empire that was regarded as a copy of the heavenly kingdom, the Byzantine emperor naturally had a unique and powerful position. But some functions he could not perform; these were reserved to the clergy, particularly the bishops, with their apostolic mandate. The Byzantine Church and Empire were each an indispensable part of a single whole.

The internal organization of the Byzantine Church was similar to that of the other leading Christian churches. At its head was the patriarch of Constantinople. Under him were the metropolitans, who were in charge of the provinces, and under them were the bishops, each responsible for a diocese or region. In the small

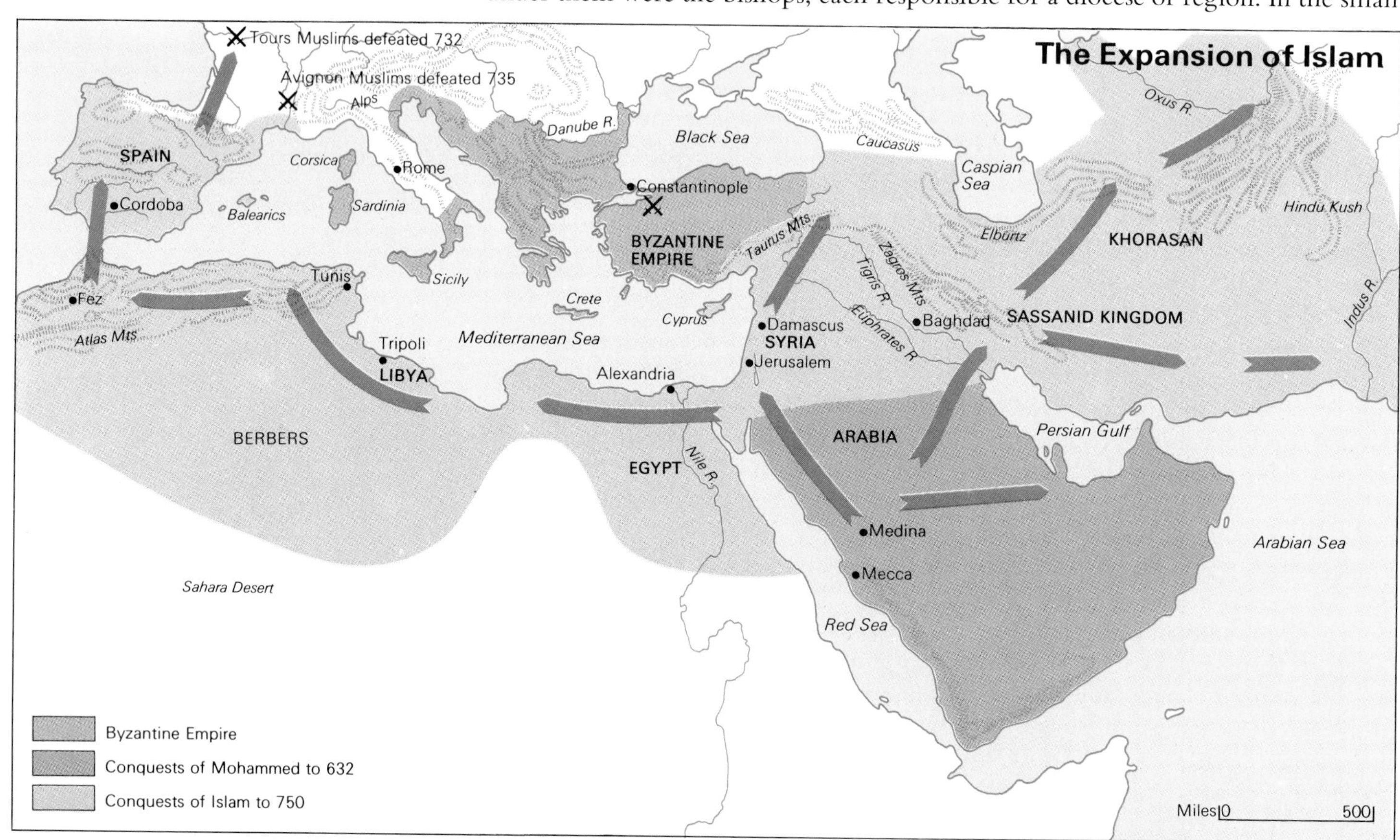

towns and villages, the priest (called the *pappas*) was a married man. Not all villages had a parish church; villagers often had to use the church of a neighboring monastery. The rich might have their own chapels on their estates or might have a special interest in the churches of some monastic foundation they had endowed, where they and their families would be remembered in the prayers of the monks. Some cathedrals had rich endowments—perhaps, like Hagia Sophia, by reason of imperial patronage or perhaps because of an association with some particularly venerated saint.

### Missions in the Balkans and Russia

Among the great achievements of the Byzantine Church were its civilizing missions. It was the Byzantine missionaries, bishops and priests, who brought Christianity to the Turkic peoples moving from central Asia into the southern steppes of Russia and, in the case of the Magyars, thence to the circle of the Carpathian Mountains and the plains of present-day Hungary. More important still was the conversion of the migrating Slav peoples. From the ninth century onward, the Byzantines worked continuously among the Slavs newly settled in the Balkans. Scholar-missionaries, such as at Cyril and Ametudius, helped them to find an alphabet so that they could translate the Greek church services into their own tongue and have a vehicle for their own literature. The successes of the Byzantine Church also included the conversion of the rulers of the Kievan state and with them their subjects, partly Slav and partly of Scandinavian stock (the Rûs).

Originally Scandinavian invaders from Sweden, the Rûs conquered the Slavonic population around Novgorod at the end of the eighth century. By the 860s they had penetrated to the Black Sea; they appeared at Constantinople first as pirates and then as traders. The Norse rulers of Novgorod and Kiev began to send

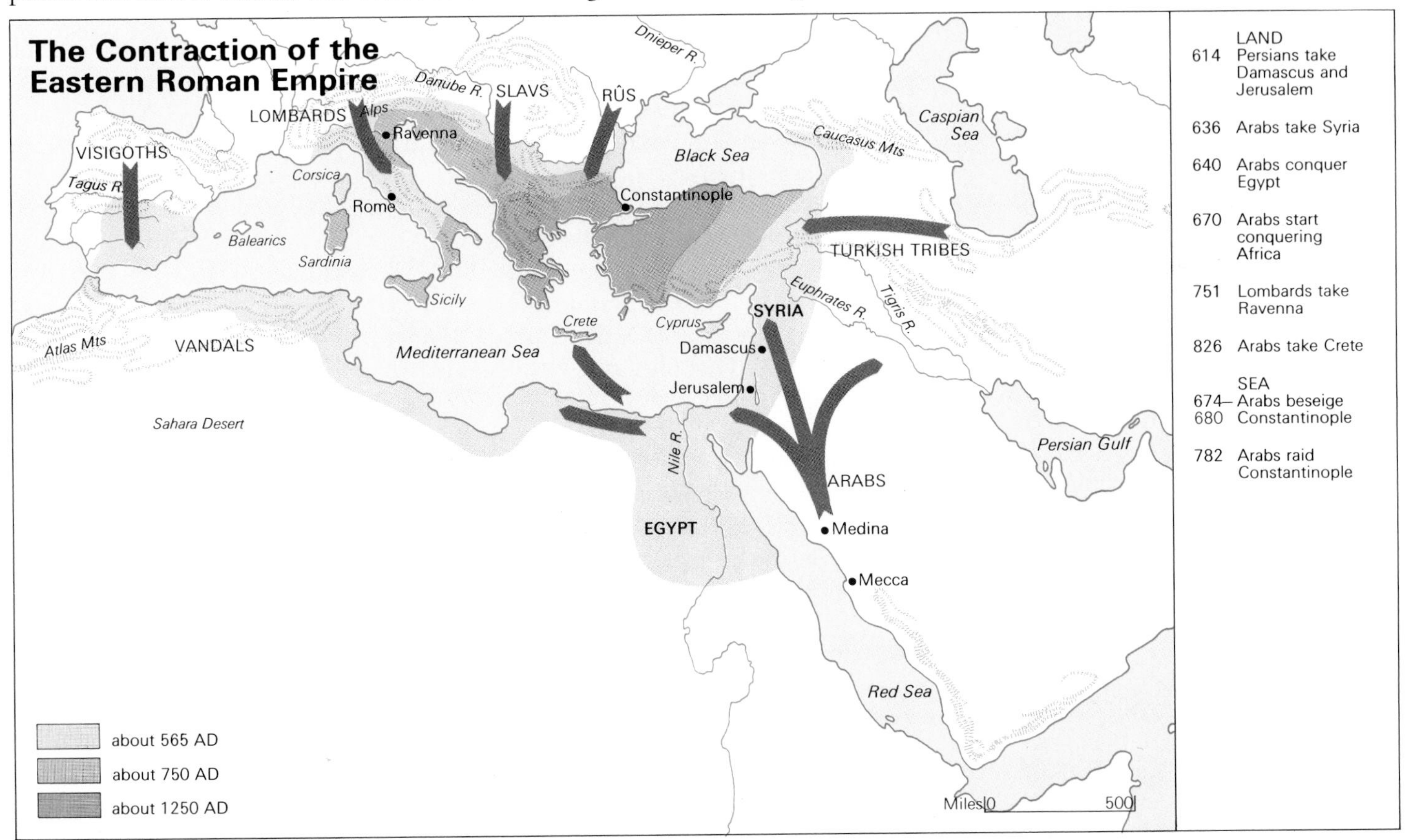

trading fleets to the capital regularly, and in the late-tenth century the Russian ruler Vladimir the Great accepted Greek Christianity for himself and his people. (He also married the sister of the Byzantine emperor.)

Adherence to the Greek faith brought the Rûs under the spiritual headship of the Byzantine patriarch. The Cyrillic liturgy and alphabet, too, were introduced into Russia as a result of Vladimir's conversion. Russian rulers later began to call themselves *czar*, in imitation of the Roman title *Caesar* used at the Byzantine court, and they revered Constantinople as *Czargrad*, capital city of the Caesars. In this formative period, Russian culture was shaped to a considerable extent by Byzantium. Even the subsequent subjection of Russia by the Mongols could not eradicate the strong Christian orientation acquired in her earliest history.

Admission of the Balkan Slavs and the Russians into the Christian circles of the Byzantine world had far-reaching significance by no means confined to its religious implications, important as these were. Byzantine law, administration, education and learning, art and architecture, all influenced these young developing countries. The debt of what has been called the "Byzantine Commonwealth" goes very deep. These countries owe to the Byzantines their introduction to a Christian polity, monarchical in character, based on a highly developed administration and with roots deeply embedded in the Greco-Roman and east Mediterranean worlds.

*Top:* The east Roman emperor Romanus II and his wife Eudocia crowned by Christ, mid tenth-century ivory relief. *Above:* Roger II of Sicily crowned by Christ, mosaic from the church of the martyrs in Palermo, Sicily. Byzantine architecture, mosaic, and sculpture formed the model for Western artists, even after the West had all been lost to the Empire. Sicily and eastern Italy were more strongly influenced than other parts of the West, as can be seen from this late twelfth-century mosaic. The idea that the ruler is crowned by Christ is of Byzantine origin.

## BYZANTINE SOCIETY

The Byzantine Empire was essentially multiracial. It was bound together by its Christian faith, its imperial tradition, and its cultural roots in Greek antiquity. Though it kept its Hellenic character to the end, it was open to many outside influences. Arab influence ranged from imperial palaces in the style of the Caliphs to stray fragments of Kufic lettering on plaques let into the walls of small Greek country monasteries, as at Holy Luke. Slaves from the inhabitants of cities captured by the Arabs might include highly skilled specialists, such as those who taught the Byzantines the art of making decorative wall plaques in faïence. Similarly, Byzantine architectural features adapted to local conditions are found in Armenia and Georgia, as well as in the Balkans. Border districts, with their frequently changing frontiers, seem to share a common idiom, as is obvious to anyone passing from present-day northern Greece into the southern Macedonian regions of Yugoslavia. Byzantine neighbors on all sides both gave of their own native traditions and also took much from the continuity and tradition of Byzantium.

There was no racial discrimination in the path to promotion, though a knowledge of Greek was an essential requisite. Emperors might come from the Balkans or from north Syria; the astute Armenians constantly rose to top positions in the army and in politics.

### City and Countryside

The capital city, Constantinople, was the envy of both the civilized and the barbarian worlds. It was admirably sited for international trade, commanding the Aegean and Black Seas and providing an excellent harbor in the inlet called the Golden Horn. Built in imitation of the elder Rome, it had its imperial palaces, senate, and hippodrome and its splendid churches crowded with relics. Within the vast complex of the great palace, visitors were received in accordance with an impressive protocol. Indeed, complicated ceremonial accompanied all aspects of court life and provided for every season in the Christian year. But there was also a polo ground in the palace precincts; emperors had their favorite boats near at hand and often enjoyed hunting in the countryside beyond the great fortified walls on the western, landward side of the city.

For those with ambition the capital was their goal, for it was here that positions and promotion, as well as education, could usually be best obtained. The well-to-do also owned property in the countryside. For the majority, land and agriculture were vital elements in their budget. The government took its land taxes and the country magnate drew much of his wealth from his estates. The poor, with their subsistence farming, depended entirely on a good harvest; floods, droughts, or wolves could reduce them to penury, so that they either became tenants of some wealthy landowner or fled to the nearest city to swell the throngs of homeless beggars lurking in every alleyway.

Some glimpses of Byzantine country life are provided by rural laws, which were extremely strict. In the seventh and eighth centuries, the "Farmer's Law" punished a slave thief who drove a sheep from its flock at night by decreeing that he be hanged as a murderer. Robbing or uprooting another man's vines resulted in the amputation of the thief's hand. But a clear distinction was made between poor beggars and thieves: "Where people enter another man's vineyard or figyard, if they come to eat, let them go unpunished; if they are there to steal, let them be beaten and stripped of their shirts."

The countryside was also much less stable than the capital. To be sure, danger lurked just beyond the walls of Constantinople at all times: Huns and Bulgars were constant threats, as were the Saracens and the Russians. (In the eighth century, every citizen was required to store a three-year supply of food, so greatly was disaster feared.) But while the residents of Constantinople were worrying about invaders, rural dwellers actually confronted them. Slavs, Bulgars, and Saracens continually ravaged the countryside around Constantinople destroying villages and monasteries. Saracen pirates were endemic along the coastline; ninth-century saints' lives are full of accounts of refugees fleeing from their raids.

*Above:* Cyrillic inscription on a tombstone in Macedonia, Yugoslavia. The Orthodox Church sent missionaries to many parts of eastern Europe. The apostles to the Slavs were St Cyril and St Methodius. Cyril translated the Bible into Slavonic; the writing he used is known as Cyrillic, and is the basis of modern Slavonic writing.
*Left:* The Fourth Ecumenical Council, sixteenth-century mural from the church of St Sozomen, Galata, Cyprus. Church and state were closely linked in the Byzantine Empire, and the emperor tried to control ecclesiastical affairs.

## Trade

Medieval Byzantium appears to have had a flourishing economic life in a number of cities apart from the capital. Thebes and Corinth were well-known centers of the silk industry. Cherson, to the north of the Black Sea, provided a link with the traders of Russia, who had a special trade treaty and found a market for their furs, wax, honey, and slaves. The specialties of Byzantine industry were luxury goods of high quality: superb brocaded materials much coveted in the West, portable objects in gold, silver, and ivory, such as book covers, small religious statues, and church ornaments and plate. Something of ordinary everyday selling and buying within Constantinople is known from the tenth-century book of the city prefect, which regulated such activities as bread making (where fire was always a real hazard), the fish market, and the various stages of silk manufacture. Customs dues were carefully organized by officials posted at various points along the borders.

*Above:* Joseph filling his brothers' sacks with corn, a sixth-century relief from Ravenna. Corn was of great importance to the economy of the Byzantine Empire. Until the loss of Egypt to the Arabs, most of the corn was imported from there. Bread was distributed free in the hippodrome at Constantinople during May, to mark the anniversary of the foundation of the city.
*Right:* A twelfth-century portrayal of an evangelist. Byzantine art, particularly its religious art, became highly stylized, but despite this it never lost its vigor.

## Scholarship and Art

The keynote of Byzantine civilization, as in Byzantine politics and administration, is continuity characterized by constant change. Even in the most difficult days of external attack, there was always an educated minority, normally the wealthy, but by no means excluding those from the middle and lower classes. Education was not obtained exclusively through the Church; there were also secular schools and private tutors. In Constantinople, in addition to the usual primary and secondary schools, it was possible to find tutors for more advanced study or to become attached to some wealthy patron. There was also a state-subsidized university, which had faculties for philosophy and law and for training civil servants.

Books were in constant demand, and this meant copying from manuscripts. Our present knowledge of classical and late-Greek authors is derived from these medieval copies. Byzantines also made their own literary contribution, particularly in the field of history. Byzantine histories were usually contemporary accounts based on first-hand knowledge. Two of the best known (which can be read in English translation) are the brilliant pen-portraits of the court circle by the eleventh-century scholar and politician Michael Psellus and the history by Anna Comnena. This learned princess gives a striking picture of Byzantine reaction to the crude but courageous Frankish feudal lords of the First Crusade.

Byzantine writings on the Christian spiritual life are outstanding in their insight, directness, and power of expression and many of these are still read in Christian circles. Their liturgical works, particularly hymns to be included in the church services, are also still in use. Music was closely linked to these hymns. A considerable body of this music survives, and its notation has now been deciphered.

The art of Byzantium, like its literature, was both secular and religious. Very little domestic architecture has survived—a few fragments of imperial buildings, such as the Great Palace and the "palace" of Constantine VII, great underground water cisterns in Constantinople, and the ruins of the palaces on Mistra, the late-Byzantine city on the slopes of the Taygetus Mountains above Sparta. There are a number of surviving churches, and many are still in use. Some of the finest surviving examples of Byzantine art and architecture—apart from Hagia Sophia in Constantinople—are in isolated monastic churches, such as Holy Luke in the hills of Phocis in central Greece and the New Monastery in the central uplands of the island of Chios. It is remarkable that in the disastrous days of the late Middle Ages, when the Empire was splintered and reduced in size, Byzantine cultural activities were in no way diminished. Amid Latin occupation and civil wars, the Byzantine could still produce the superb mosaics and frescoes which decorate the fourteenth-century church and mortuary chapel of the monastery of Chora in Constantinople.

COGITQ: FATERI
CONFERRI DONA SUPERNA
LAM CUM PROLE DOCET QUIBUS IN
DIFFUSUM FIDEI DONUM DUPLICAVIT

Chapter 2

# BARBARIAN STATES

## Francia

The change from old times to new is nowhere more apparent than in seventh-century Francia. Gregory of Tours, who died in 594, gave expression in his life and writings to the existence of two peoples and two cultures, Gallo-Roman and Frankish. A generation later the fusion was to all intents and purposes complete, except in outlying regions such as Aquitaine, which remained predominantly "Roman," the land of the *Langue d'Oc*, and the north, which was predominantly "Germanic," the land of the *Langue d'Oil* (*hoc* and *oil* being their respective words for yes), though its linguistic frontiers reached as far south as the Loire. Regionalism was to remain a vital factor in French history. The unification of Francia was neither a fact nor an objective, even when rule was in the hands of one king.

*Above:* St Guthlac on his journey to Crowland abbey, from the Guthlac Roll, twelfth century. The Middle Ages delighted in writing at great length, and with many flourishes, the lives of the obscure saints.

*Left:* Episodes from the life of St Jerome in the Bible of Charles the Bald. This Bible was produced in 845 for the king at the abbey of St Martin of Tours, one of the main centers of manuscript illumination at the time. The top picture shows Jerome, the translator of the Bible into Latin, leaving Rome's port of Ostia to travel to Bethlehem in 385.

## The Last Great Merovingians

For a brief time in the early-seventh century, Francia was ruled by one king—first by Chlotar II, a Neustrian, who was prepared to acknowledge the independent spirit of the Austrasian magnates by giving them his son Dagobert I as subking, and then in due course by Dagobert. Both kings, though still warriors of the older tradition, had no doubt that the prosperity of their house depended on their unwavering support of the Church, in the higher offices of which we now find men of Frankish and of mixed Gallo-Frankish blood. Both kings spent much time campaigning or in progress from one royal estate to another, but they were also quite often in Paris, though one cannot yet speak of Paris as the capital of Francia.

In and around Paris were many royal properties, including churches and monasteries. Of particular importance was the abbey of St Denis, from now on to be closely associated with the fortunes of the Frankish kings. Chlotar and Dagobert were generous to the Church and could afford to be so. The old imperial fiscal estates, to which much more had been added by confiscation and conquest, were in their hands, and they could replenish their treasure by foreign expeditions and by taxation. (The remnant of the Roman system of provincial taxation was still in working order, though often evaded.)

Merovingian gold coinage at the time of Chlotar and Dagobert was fairly plentiful. Soon, however, it was to be supplemented by a silver coinage, more suitable for the middle-distance trades now developing. Dagobert showed that he

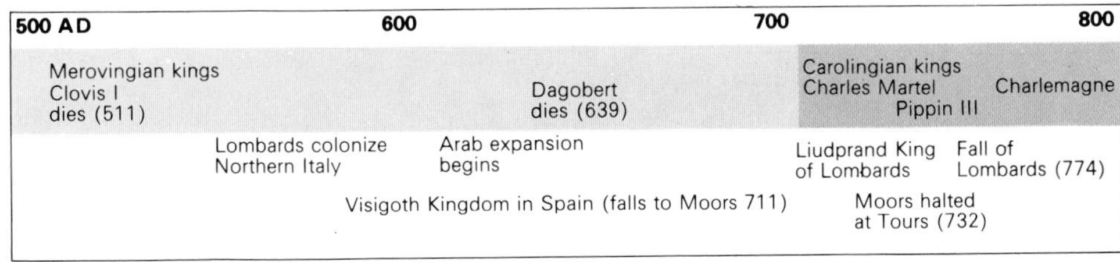

understood the shift in trade by his encouragement of an annual fair at St Denis, where goods from the north were marketed; by siting a trading post with a mint at Duurstede, near the mouth of the Rhine; and by establishing beyond the Rhine at Utrecht a strongpoint and a church.

Merovingian eyes were now firmly fixed on the pagan Frisians and on the Scandinavian and Saxon peoples living beyond them. The Rhine becomes a trade artery rather than a barrier, the route to Frankish colonies in western and central Germany, a rich belt of new family properties and churches very sensitive to periodical sorties by Saxons and others from the forests. A Frankish merchant named Samo carved out a kingdom for himself at about this time among the Slav population of Moravia and defied Dagobert, his nominal overlord, to do his worst. One way or another, Frankish power was reaching deep into Germany.

Hand in hand with this militant colonialism went the endowment of churches and monasteries. The calm of the Frankish Church had been shattered by the unfamiliar ascetic customs introduced by Irish missionaries—chief among them St Columbanus, whose austerities attracted large endowments, royal and aristocratic. The abbey of Luxeuil and her daughter houses became centers of fresh missionary and intellectual efforts. At court, too, churchmen of a new stamp gained influence. One group of promising young men who were trained there later became bishops of important missionary sees, especially in the north.

The church of the abbey of Corvey and the river Weser in northern Germany. The ante-chapel, begun in 873, took twelve years to complete. Although the Church is now heavily decorated with seventeenth and eighteenth century art, it remains one of the finest examples of Carolingian architecture. During the Carolingian era there were about 300 monks at this abbey, which was a center of culture.

### The Carolingian Mayors

Dagobert died in 639. He was the last great Merovingian. After him came the long series of rulers, Neustrian and Austrasians, known to history as the *rois fainéants*, the "do-nothing kings." Several died very young, some were assassinated, and physical degeneracy may be suspected. But this did not deter the Franks from clinging tenaciously to their royal dynasty, in which they recognized the perpetuation of some magic essential to national good fortune. Moreover, these kings were not entirely idle, as extant charters show. What they increasingly lacked were the means to buy and retain loyal service. Booty from distant expeditions was harder to get, and royal estates were constantly alienated as outright gifts, without being made good. Poverty of this kind was bound to prove fatal to any dynasty in the long run.

On the other hand, some of their subjects and many of their churches grew richer as the kings grew poorer. Two Austrasian families in particular rose to power and wealth in their own localities: the Arnulfings, centered on Metz, and the Pippinids of the Ardennes. The alliance in marriage of the two produced a dynasty of more than local significance: the family to be known as the Carolingians.

The rise of the Carolingians was not thought to be inimical to the Merovingians. On the contrary, they were welcomed as the natural protectors of a vital area of the Rhineland. The time came when, having won their way to ascendancy in Austrasia over competing families, they could bring their military power to bear on the politically unstable regions under immediate Merovingian control. The dynastic feuds that lay behind this rise to power are difficult to unravel because future historiographers, writing in the Carolingian interest, made it appear that they were divinely chosen to achieve what they did achieve.

As mayors of the palace, Pippin II and his son Charles Martel (Charles "the Hammer") effectively controlled the crown while not taking it themselves. Had they done so, they would have stirred up sharp resentment among many Neustrian and Burgundian magnates. They would also have antagonized the Church of which they were generous benefactors.

These Carolingian mayors were warriors. They could defend Francia from external attack. They could hold the pagan Frisians in the area north of the Rhine estuary and support there the missionary work of a formidable Anglo-Saxon, St Willibrörd. Colonization and frontier control, although of a necessarily haphazard kind were carried on. Punitive raids deep into Germany were made. The peoples of the central region were subdued and an overlordship was imposed upon the powerful Bavarian dukes.

The subjugation of Germany—the Saxons alone retaining their independence—meant collaboration with churches old and new, and also with the papacy. It was as a papal emissary that the greatest of the Anglo-Saxon missionaries, St Boniface, undertook the task of reforming the churches of the Rhineland (often the preserves of the local aristocracy), reorganizing the Bavarian Church, and finally reforming the Frankish Church itself. None of this would have been possible without the support of the Carolingians. In his extensive correspondence, we can catch the spirit in which St Boniface faced his work. An exile and a pilgrim, he fought a lone battle against hereditary bishops, lapsed Christians, and general neglect. But the making of the German Church was his, and without this it is hard to see how Germany as we know it could ever have assumed the shape that embraces Saxony in the north and Bavaria in the south. Worn out, he made a last and deep penetration into the extreme north of Frisia with a handful of friends and was killed by pirates near Dokkum. It seemed like a martyrdom. Mainz, his see, and Fulda, his monastery, quarreled over his remains. Fulda won, and there, in the abbey, is preserved the mutilated book with which he had tried to ward off the attack.

Lombard brooch of silver, seventh century. Lombard art was highly derivative, but it had a refreshing vigor.

Charles Martel supported Boniface more consistently than did his son, Pippin III. But however pious, Charles saw the Church also as a vast nucleus of immune territories. On some of these he laid hands to reward his faithful followers in areas where he most needed support. He earned a bad name by doing so, although many of these churches had been overendowed. On the other hand, he saved Francia, and so the Church, from the most northerly of the Arab raids from Spain. In the Battle of Tours (732), near Poitiers, he won a victory that seemed God-given. He had decisively checked the Muslim advance to the northwest, though the Rhone valley remained theirs.

When Charles Martel died in 741, the lands he ruled were divided between his sons, Carloman and Pippin III, as if he had been a king. But he was not. The Merovingians still had their supporters.

### Pippin III

The Carolingian family had more than Merovingian loyalists to contend with. There were also dissident Carolingians who had failed to get a share of the spoils. The abdication of Carloman in favor of his brother led to deep discontent. It was the Church, and above all the papacy, that saw Pippin through from a kind of glorified marcher-lordship to the Frankish crown. This he obtained in 751 after consultation with the pope. To mark the occasion—which necessitated nothing less than the forcible removal of the last Merovingian to a monastery—a new ceremony of kingmaking was employed to supplement more traditional ways. Pippin was anointed king in an analogy to the Old Testament kings. He had no magic in his veins, like the Merovingians, but he and his family could be sanctified in this new way. In effect, he was to be a priest-king. The cost was that he was liable to be told by his anointers what it was proper for him to do. But for this, the Church might never have sanctioned a coup d'état that had no other theoretical justification. More immediately burdensome must have seemed the moral obligation he was under to protect the papacy from Lombard and other attacks on its possessions.

Pippin remained a warlord, but a warlord with a difference. He could pose as the Anointed of the Lord, king of a new Chosen People, commander of the armies

TERRA

of a New Israel. The parallel was much in men's minds. The enemies of the Carolingians were henceforth the enemies of Christ. Wherever Pippin's armies went—into Italy to protect the papacy or into Aquitaine to face the Arabs—they were the host of the new David.

It was under Pippin that Septimania at last fell to the Franks, though at the cost of stirring up a spirit of Aquitanian independence that took Pippin seven years to control (it was never extinguished). An experimental king, he made Carolingian power felt throughout the old territory of Gaul. He was even strong enough to hand on that power to his sons, Carloman and Charles (better known as Charlemagne). His objectives had been entirely traditional, and his power lay in the loyal service of his armed followers. But the justification for that power was new.

## SPAIN: THE VISIGOTH KINGS

The efforts of the Visigoth kings of Spain, as of the Ostrogoth kings of Italy, to build a viable community upon the dichotomy of barbarian and Roman, Arian and Catholic, had been a costly failure. For Spain, the experiment was abandoned at the conversion of Reccared to Catholicism in 589. This, too, was to be a failure. Gothic chieftains might accept Catholicism, but they could not become Hispano-Romans or accept the implications of Catholic kingship.

Yet to Roman churchmen it seemed that a new age had dawned, and indeed for a short time they had reason to believe so. Pope Gregory the Great wrote a belated letter to Reccared to express his delight. Isidore, bishop of Seville, summarizing the exploits of recent Visigothic kings in his *History of the Kings of the Goths, Vandals, and Suevi*, thought that Spain was poised for a splendid future. He apostrophizes here in extravagant language. All the warfaring of the Arian Visigoths had led up to this happy state of affairs; Spain was united under a Catholic king—a warrior, moreover, replete with the right virtues, "so that he seems not so much to have waged wars as to have trained his people." Equally prosperous were the succeeding kings: the learned Sisebut, Isidore's own patron, and Swinthila, "who is worthy to be called not only the ruler of peoples but the father of the poor." They were God's ministers, faithful servants of the Church who had added a new dimension to kingship.

We must pause to look at Isidore, for he was the author of one of the most influential books of the Middle Ages. A busy bishop and much at court in Toledo, he yet found time to write what he considered a basic intellectual guide for the new Spain he saw emerging. He called his book *Etymologiae* (Origins). It is an awe-inspiring compilation, for long dismissed as a ragbag of nonsensical learning but nowadays seen in its true light as a great creative work. It is a systematic attempt to break down knowledge into the words of which it is composed, and to reveal the meanings of the words. Isidore's approach to words was very unlike that of the traditional grammarian. Indeed, it is emotional and even mystical—an approach to language as revelation for a people's guidance. He arranges his words in classes: the seven liberal arts, the Bible, God and the bonds that hold Him to man, man and his earthly organizations, human anatomy, the animal world, inanimate nature, and finally odds and ends such as metals, weights and measures, agriculture, war, games, ships, buildings, food, furniture, and instruments. In brief, there is a plan.

The *Etymologiae* was quickly and widely disseminated over Europe. But it is very Spanish. Like contemporary Visigothic churches—as, for example, the startling little church of S. Juan de Baños—it is an artifact constructed of old materials that say something new. The book is sharply transitional, poised between antiquity and the Middle Ages, but to Isidore's contemporaries it was original and useful. Isidore builds everything into his structure, whatever its provenance, just

*Above:* The dedication page of a seventh-century manuscript of Isidore of Seville's *Of the Catholic Faith, against the Jews.* Isidore was one of the most popular authors of the Middle Ages, and preserved much classical learning. *Left:* The cover of the Echternach Evangeliary. The covers of Bibles and liturgical books were often highly decorated in gold and jewels or ivory, and portrayed religious scenes. The Echternach Evangeliary was produced in about 990, and is unusual in portraying Christ as bearded. Monasteries were centers of all the arts that could be used to glorify God, and monks produced most of the fine examples that have survived.

as architects were using late-Roman capitals and shafts to build their churches. And so Isidore produces a compendium of knowledge for the new Spain—not a mere mosaic of what he can find in his library but an adaptation for a particular purpose and an exposition of a point of view. He has defended and reinforced the Latin language, the crucial tool of any culture he could imagine.

Seventh-century Spain produced a succession of notable ecclesiastical writers after Isidore. Their tone, somehow, is "Spanish," as if they thought in a national vacuum not easily permeated by outside ideas. Their most obvious external debt was perhaps to the scholars who fled from Africa in Vandal times. But the rapid flowering of Visigothic culture can also be seen in art. The treasure of Guarrazar, near Toledo, comprises several gold crowns, two of them bearing the names of kings. They are breathtaking pieces, blazing with sapphires, pearls, agates, and rock crystals. As we have them, they are adapted for hanging by chains, perhaps as votive offerings. Conceivably they were buried for safety at the time of the Arab invasion. At the least they bear witness to the symbolic splendor of the seventh-century kings. The nobles, too, leave evidence of their taste in finely wrought buckles and brooches. Only one illuminated Visigothic manuscript survives, but that—the Ashburnham Pentateuch—is in the highest class of book illumination. It is a wonderful book, not surpassed by the equally famous manuscripts of the so-called Mozarabic period of the ninth to the eleventh centuries, when Spanish Christians were still able to produce magnificent books under tolerant Arab rule.

A ninth-century nobleman. In order to strengthen his position Charlemagne increased the power of the nobility as well as that of the Church.

This culture affected only a comparatively small element of the population of Spain. The Gothic aristocracy remained isolated in their highland fastnesses, emerging only to intervene in the choice of new kings. Aristocracy and Church agreed at least in wanting strong kings, irrespective of their blood. They rarely succeeded. The situation was markedly unlike that in Francia, where heredity mattered most. The Church did what it could by inaugurating the anointing of kings as a safeguard against violent dispossession, but this did not prevent the spasmodic formation of cliques of magnates who hoped to secure the crown for one of themselves.

It was this clannish approach to the crown that caused the political downfall of the Visigothic kingdom. One clique invited the intervention of an Arab force from Africa to overthrow Roderick, the Visigothic king. In a single battle (711) in southern Spain, Roderick's army was routed. Spain lay open to Arabic penetration. Strictly, the defeat of the Visigoths was military, but it was political, too. Those who welcomed the Arabs did not fare too badly from the conquest; the conquerors did not overlook the reason for their sortie into Spain. But the kingdom of Toledo was not restored. The Goths, apart from such as were prepared to follow a small party of royalists into the mountains of the extreme northwest, had no center to turn to. They had remained true to themselves and had in the end rejected the political solution to chronic unrest proposed by the Church.

## ITALY: THE LOMBARDS

The Lombards (*Langobardi*) had migrated from northern Germany to the area of modern Czechoslovakia in the early fifth century. For a time they were subject to the Huns, but they regained their independence and moved to the north bank of the Danube, where some of their graves may still be seen. The contents of these graves suggest that there is already an inclination to adopt the skills of other peoples. Refusing to come to the help of the hard-pressed Ostrogoths, they preferred to bide their time and reorganize themselves into warrior bands (*farae*) under dukes. Like the Ostrogoths at a similar stage of development, they were nominally Arian in belief with a solid substratum of paganism.

They may have planned to pounce on Italy once the Ostrogoths were defeated, but their move south in 568 under their leader Alboin could equally well have been caused by the pressure of the Turco-Mongol Avars, with their subordinate Slavs immediately to the north. At all events, they moved easily into the Po Valley—Ravenna alone remaining in imperial hands—and then sent two expeditions south to Spoleto and Benevento. These established large duchies that were to remain virtually independent of royal Lombard control.

The early Lombard settlements in fortified places (*castella*) near cities do not suggest much readiness to have dealings with the local populations or to trust them. They had brought their families with them and intended to remain on a war footing. The Lombard kings set up their headquarters in Pavia, a walled Roman city that commanded the central plain. There they learned some of the ways of Roman administration, though at the beginning it was as much as they could do to resist the attacks of imperial armies backed by Frankish mercenaries.

Inevitably, the Lombards made contact with Rome. Gregory the Great was in close communication with them. As on other occasions, Gregory made his most useful contact through a woman. Theudelinda, the Lombard queen, was a Bavarian princess and a Catholic. She was prepared to listen to Gregory and use her influence at court on his behalf. At Monza is preserved one of the gifts that the pope sent to Theudelinda: a model in silver gilt of a hen and seven chicks. If it has symbolic meaning, it is lost to us. Also preserved is the diadem of the queen's crown. More directly associated with Theudelinda was the Irish missionary St Columbanus, who came to the Lombards as a refugee from Francia. There in Italy, in 614, he founded his monastery of Bobbio, which was to have a lasting cultural significance for the western world; and there he died in the following year.

The conversion of the Lombards was complicated, however, by a doctrinal dispute among Catholics, which alienated many north-Italian clergy from Rome. The schism cannot have impressed the Arians. Perhaps for this reason the Lombards remained officially Arian till the latter part of the seventh century. They retained their barbarian characteristics, at least until then. We have their grave goods to prove it.

Roman influence on the Lombards is most apparent in their written laws, starting with the *Edict* of King Rothari. Like other Germanic law codes, it is a Roman creation out of barbarian material and encapsulates the king's claim to rule his people. Indeed, it starts with a list of Lombard kings. Its 388 chapters enable us to see Lombardic society, with its ranks and privileges, at close quarters. As elsewhere, detailed tariffs for the settlement of blood feuds occupy much space. Rothari also deals with offenses against the peace, with the law of inheritance, with the position of women, and with the manumission of slaves. In a word, his approach is fairly sophisticated, though many of his regulations betray a persistent barbaric conservatism. In due course, Rothari's *Edict* was supplemented by further royal legislation, notably that of King Liudprand.

The *Edict* shows, on the whole, a yielding to the pressures of Catholicism and Western civilization. It shows, too, that the Lombards loved gold and knew the use of gold coins, which they minted. The following values, computed in gold *solidi*, are revealing: for causing the miscarriage of a mare, a fine of 1 *solidus*; the price of half a house, 9 *solidi*; the price of an olive orchard, 8 *solidi*; for a horse with trappings, 100 *solidi*; the fine for breaking open a burial vault, 900 *solidi*; and the fine for killing one's wife, 1,200 *solidi*. Basically, one suspects that the Lombards, like other Germans, lived by barter. Their economic life was centered on mills, pastures, flocks, horses, orchards, and slaves. Such, at least, is the impression left by the laws.

Part of a diptych showing pope Gregory the Great. During his pontificate at the end of the sixth century, Gregory had compiled a *Sacramentary* (a book containing parts of the liturgy), which with modifications became the service book of the Church in Rome. In 785, when Charlemagne wanted to standardize liturgical practice in the churches of his kingdom, pope Hadrian I sent him a copy of the *Gregorian Sacramentary*. Hadrian, the head of the palace school at Aachen, made some modifications to it, and its use was made obligatory by decree in 785.

The Lombards in Pavia were able to use the Roman scribes, or *notarii*, whom they had inherited from the Ostrogoths and the overrun imperial administration. In addition to writing down the laws, the scribes could prepare the excellent series of charters that equally well demonstrate the growing authority of the kings, most notably of the great Liudprand (712–744).

Liudprand did more than any other Lombard to push back the imperial frontiers in Italy; eventually, the exarch (the civil and military representative of the emperor) was effectively confined to Ravenna. In the south, however, Naples was tenaciously held by the Empire against the menace of the neighboring Lombard duchy of Benevento. The culture of southern Italy remained largely Greek. It seems unlikely that Liudprand had a clear objective of conquering all Italy. He knew what enormous resources the Empire could command so long as it controlled the sea routes. The last emperor to visit the West was Constans II, who entered Rome at the head of an army in 663, only to retire to Sicily, where he was assassinated. But who was to say that he would be the last?

*Above:* St Idelfonso arguing with a Jew. The Jews were usually an unpopular minority in western Europe during the Middle Ages. Often they were legislated against, and banned from all work other than lending money.
*Right:* Early medieval helmet.

The papacy, for its part, was in an awkward position. Spasmodically threatened by Lombards and frequently losing territory to them, it had small hope of active assistance from Constantinople. It was not "anti-Greek." Indeed, there was something of a Hellenistic revival in Rome between 600 and 750. Several popes were Greek-speakers. But culture is one thing and military support another. The day was clearly coming when Rome would have to appeal for military support to a power nearer to hand. That power could only be the Frankish armies of the Carolingians.

More than the Franks or even the Goths, the Lombards remained themselves. Whatever of *Romanitas* they absorbed—and evidence of this can be seen in their artifacts and churches as well as in their writings—they were always aware of the danger that surrounded them. This sense of separateness is clearly brought out by their great historian, Paul the Deacon. A native of northeast Italy and probably educated at Benevento, Paul moved to Francia after Charlemagne's victory over the Lombards and was much esteemed by the Frankish court for his learning. He finally retired to Monte Cassino and there composed a history of his people from their remote origins (for which he had some written evidence) to the death of Liudprand. He either did not care or did not dare to go further. He expresses no shame at the eclipse of the native Lombard dynasty and appears ready to accept another German, Charlemagne, as *rex Langobardorum*. The fact was that the Lombard people remained in Italy, though watched over by Frankish officials. It was better than being ruled by Greeks.

It has been said that the memory of the Lombards can still be recaptured in the beautiful little eighth-century church of S.Maria-in-Valle, at Cividale in Friuli. This is true, and the Byzantine influence so apparent in its sculptures does not make it less so. But the essence of this people is better expressed in a surviving relief in gilded copper from a helmet. It shows the bearded King Agilulf in his court. Armed warriors stand about his throned figure, and winged victories introduce barbarians bearing tribute in the shape of crownlike helmets. He may be firmly established in a Roman province—indeed, the most Roman of all—but he remains a Germanic warlord conscious of mastery. The mastery faded, but not the spirit behind it.

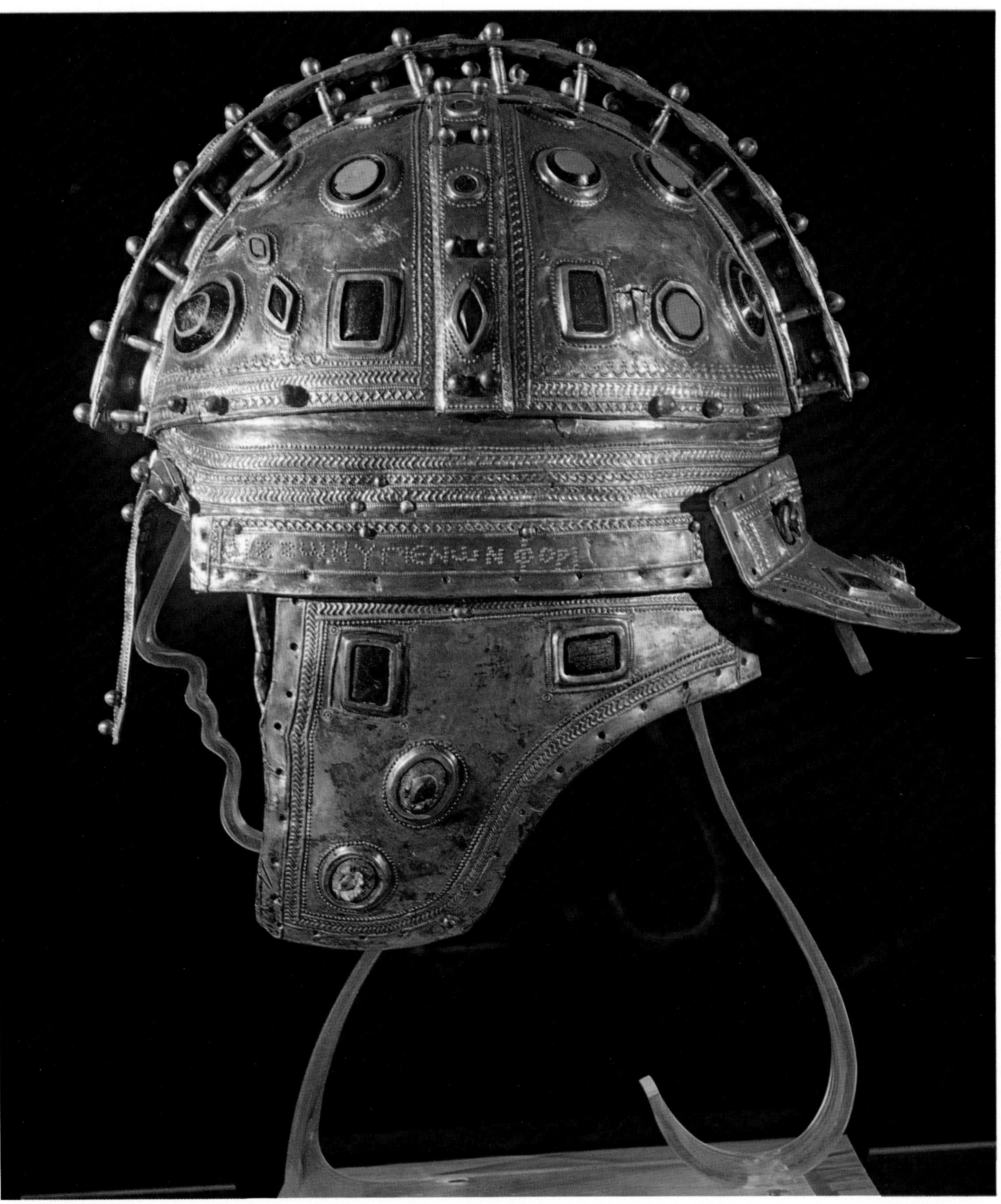

The Carolingian Empire
SCANDINAVIA
SCOTLAND
IRELAND
North Sea
KINGDOM OF DENMARK
Baltic Sea
ANGLO-SAXON KINGDOMS
WALES
CORNWALL
Dokkum
FRIESIANS
Elbe R.
SAXONS
Utrecht
AUSTRASIA
Paderborn
Saucourt
Aachen
Fulda
Corbie
Echternach
Mainz
BRITTANY
St. Denis
Rheims
Wurzburg
Paris
Lorsch
NEUSTRIA
Seine R.
Metz
Fleury
Rhine R.
Regensburg
Tours
Loire R.
MORAVIA
Poitiers
Reichenau
BAVARIA
SLAVS
Santiago de Compostella
PANNONIAN MARCH
AQUITAINE
BURGUNDY
LOMBARDY
Cividale
Oviedo
Monza
KINGDOM OF ASTURIAS
Rhone R.
Pavia
AVARS
NAVARRE
Roncesvalles
Bobbio
SPANISH MARCH
Ravenna
Saragossa
Danube R.
Ebro R.
CATALONIA
BULGARS
Lisbon
CASTILE
Toledo
PAPAL STATES
DUCHY OF SPOLETO
BULGARIA
ARAGON
Barcelona
CORSICA
OMMIAD EMIRATE OF CORDOBA
Merida
Rome
Monte Cassino
Constantinople
Naples
DUCHY OF BENEVENTO
Cordoba
SARDINIA
Seville
MURCIA
Mediterranean Sea
SICILY
Kingdom of Charlemagne, 768
Acquired by Charlemagne to 814
Areas tributary to Charlemagne's Empire
Byzantine Empire
Monasteries
Miles 0 500

Chapter 3

# CHARLEMAGNE AND THE FRANKISH EMPIRE

## CHARLEMAGNE

At the death of Pippin III (768), the Frankish Kingdom passed to his two sons, Carloman and Charles, later known as Charles the Great (Charlemagne). Carloman was dead within three years, once again leaving behind a group of Carolingian dissidents of whom the official records say as little as possible. Charlemagne was to rule alone for many years. He, too, was an anointed king who took the theoretical basis of his power very seriously. It enabled him to mount a long series of campaigns as the defender of western Christendom—in Frisia, Saxony, Bavaria, Italy, and Spain. Apart from his major decision to subdue the entire Saxon people and make their land a permanent defensive march, there was nothing in this that could not be called the traditional war business of the Franks.

Whatever threat Charlemagne saw, he met. In Italy he was successful to the point of annexing the Lombard crown; in Spain he stretched his resources too far and extricated himself only at the cost of a rearguard defeat in the Pyrenean valley of Roncevalles at the hands of the Gascon mountaineers. Yet there was unrest at home and even revolt. The parvenu dynasty still excited suspicion. His real trouble, however, was the task of controlling so extensive a group of territories with inadequate resources. His machinery of government was comparatively primitive, and he depended in the last resort on the loyalty of his Austrasian friends and the men they could bring into the field. Constantly on the move, he could be sure of commanding obedience only where he was present. For the rest, he had to chance his luck.

Charlemagne's paternalistic outlook on rule, implicit in the teaching of the churchmen he listened to, found expression in a series of remarkable administrative edicts, known as *capitularies*, promulgated at the meetings of his general councils. The gist of these capitularies was that his officers everywhere were to see that justice was done to all, that armed bands were not to be formed, that the decrees of the Church were to be rigorously observed, and so on. Their mere repetition shows how difficult it was to enforce them.

Frankish advances deep into neighboring lands naturally stirred up the peoples living beyond them. Charlemagne's methods could be draconian, as in Saxony. For him, subjugation entailed the acceptance of Christianity, and this was passionately resisted. Central Germany became a zone of missionary churches and monasteries, centers of exploitation liable to fierce counterattack whenever Charlemagne's attention was engaged elsewhere. In the course of several expeditions into Saxon territory, the Saxons were decimated and forcibly converted. Their leaders turned to their northern neighbors, the Danes, who now entered increasingly into Frankish political calculations. Germanic paganism was to prove very resilient, and it was an inevitable rallying cry against the Franks.

Paderborn was the king's advance headquarters for campaigning against the Saxons. Another, for the central area, was Mainz. At the abbey of Lorsch, Charlemagne's council chamber survives more or less intact in the guise of a gatehouse—a unique secular building. Regensburg was the imperial headquarters in southeast Germany for expeditions against the Slav-Avar peoples of the middle Danube, and another route led up from Italy. One Frankish expedition captured a great Avar treasure hoard in Hungary and brought it back to Francia in triumph.

More significant was the fact of confrontation between the West and the Slav masses who had moved into central Europe in the seventh century. Indeed, that movement is as significant for the separation of East from West as is the disruption of the Mediterranean by the Arabs, for it placed a permanent Slav belt across central Europe from the Baltic to the Balkans.

## THE CAROLINGIAN RENAISSANCE

In 789, Charlemagne issued a major statement of Church policy, called the *Admonitio Generalis*. It summarizes the needs of his Church and ranges over many topics. But what it envisages is more significant: the integration of the Roman and Frankish churches and the victory of the rule of St Benedict as a unifying monastic principle. Frankish society is Christian society and should be at peace within itself. This unity did not come about, but it was seriously intended as a practical program. However, one facet of the program did have lasting effects—the implementation of what is called, not entirely inaccurately, the Carolingian renaissance.

Charlemagne, from a coin issued in the first part of his reign. Charlemagne became joint king of the Franks in 758, and after the death of his brother sole king in 781. His conquests in Germany, Italy, France and Spain gave him a unique position in western Europe—a position recognized by the papacy when he was crowned emperor by pope Leo III on Christmas day, 800. Coins issued after 800 usually show Charlemagne crowned with a laurel wreath and with the legend "Carolus Imp Aug" (Charles Emperor Augustus).

Of what was there a renaissance? Certainly there was a turning back to the literature of classical antiquity; not a few of the classical texts that we have go back to copies of the early-ninth century. But Charlemagne's principal educational object was the provision of a trained clergy, capable of conversion work along the pagan frontiers and of teaching standardized religion to men nearer home. Texts were urgently needed of the basic books of this religion: the Bible, commentaries, liturgies and so forth, written in a clearly understandable script that could be accurately copied. Hence the reform of handwriting and the making of books were fundamental to the renaissance of learning and education.

Also fundamental was the employment of the best scholars in Europe. Charlemagne's court at Aachen attracted a group of men who made his palace school a wonderful center of learning and book production. A surprising number of these palace texts survive, though now widely scattered. The greatest contribution was made by the Irish and the Anglo-Saxons, most notable among them Alcuin, trained in the school of York.

The major Frankish monasteries, many under the direct patronage of Charlemagne, now began to build up libraries. We may mention Tours (Alcuin's own monastery), St Denis, Corbie, Fleury, Reims, and further afield, Echternach, Lorsch, Würzburg, Reichenau, and Fulda. None was as immediately productive as the palace school, but the movement of the renaissance was clearly out toward the periphery. Its effects lasted for at least a century if we place its beginnings in the early years of Charlemagne's reign and its end at the close of the reign of his grandson, Charles the Bald. At the heart of this huge and very practical endeavor was the Bible, the book that lay behind the Carolingian claim to rule. Revised texts were prepared by Alcuin and also by a Visigothic scholar, Theodulf of Oréans.

## THE IMPERIAL TITLE

Alcuin's Bible reached Charlemagne in Rome at Christmas, 800, when he was on the point of becoming an emperor. Emperor of what? Intensely practical as always, he saw himself for what he was: a high king ruling many peoples, many of whom were not Franks. In fact, his rule was roughly coterminous with what had once been the Western Empire. The title of Emperor best expressed this reality, even if the Eastern emperors looked at it askance. Inevitably it had Roman undertones, and Charlemagne was aware of the example of the Christian-Roman emperors from Constantine onward. The pope played a leading part in the ceremony. But in practical terms, Charlemagne was emperor of Western Christendom, ruling a Christian empire from Aachen with the support of the pope in Rome.

Charlemagne's imperial title certainly helped him in Rome and perhaps in Italy, but north of the Alps it counted for little. To his followers at home he remained the great Germanic warlord, ruler of the Germanic world. Such is the burden of a famous poem called the *Paderborn Epic*. At Aachen, attractive to him for its hot springs and excellent hunting facilities, he built what amounted to a capital. Indeed, he moved materials from imperial Ravenna for the purpose. The buildings of the palace itself have disappeared, but the palace chapel remains intact—a splendid octagonal building where, from his throne in the gallery, he could watch the high altar during divine service.

Seal of Elisabeth, queen of France, ninth century.

Here in the north, during the remaining fourteen years of his life, he faced increasing unrest. Exacting oaths of fidelity in various forms from his subjects was an admission that fidelity was hard to win and harder to keep. It did not always prevent local revolts or ensure that the imperial agents could enforce "justice." Not even the regular visitation of regions by special inspectors called *missi dominici* could do this. In the last resort, Charlemagne could count on only a limited circle of men bound closely to his service by a solemn oath that made them his "vassals." They, in return, had the opportunity to found great landed dynasties.

The administration of such extensive estates, whether secular or ecclesiastical, demanded estate management of some sophistication. In a famous capitulary, *De Villis*, we can see Charlemagne himself or his son Louis making such provision for a group of imperial estates. Comparable documents survive for monasteries. The Carolingians could deal with what was their own with notable efficiency, but they had no enduring machinery of government for doing more.

Charlemagne's will could be enforced only by the terror his name inspired, and as he grew older and less mobile, it inspired correspondingly less. For a while he planned to leave his lands divided among his three legitimate sons in the traditional way, saying nothing of the imperial title, which he obviously considered personal to himself. There might have been no second emperor if two of the three sons had not predeceased him. The remaining son, Louis of Aquitaine, in the end got everything including the imperial title, which, however, was bestowed on him by his father and not by the pope.

## CHARLEMAGNE'S ACHIEVEMENT

The records of Charlemagne's reign are numerous and good, but the most precious of them is a biography of him from the pen of Einhard, a member of the court circle who knew him well. The *Vita Karoli Magni* was written some years after Charlemagne's death, in disturbed times, to show the emperor's descendants what a real ruler was like. It is the first secular biography of the Middle Ages. Modeled on Suetonius' *Lives of the Twelve Caesars* and drawing factually upon contemporary annals, it is an original and vivid composition. Because the prevailing picture of ideal kingship was of a virtually sacerdotal office, Einhard's book must have seemed secular indeed. For his intention is to show that a great ruler, however pious, proves God's favor by his success in battle and his paternal care for his people. Einhard's Charlemagne has all the traditional virtues—liberality, moderation, constancy, and so on—but what really made him a great king was *potentia* on the battlefield and *magnani-mitas* in his dealings with men. These were what proved God's approbation, as they had for Charlemagne's forebears. Victory was what mattered. It was the doctrine on which a whole school of historical writers justified Carolingian rule. Thus Einhard portrays a great warrior.

The other side of the picture is Charlemagne as father of his people and director of Christian life and morals. We can watch the old man in the daily round of his life —judging, hunting, praying, feasting, even trying to learn to write, though not very successfully—and always secure in his family circle. He stands before us as a real and very formidable person. Something of this is recaptured in the little statue of him on horseback, known as the Carnavalet Statuette, though there is the possibility that it was meant for his grandson, also Charles. At all events, it is a Carolingian king dressed in traditional Frankish costume and prepared to rule the world. Let it pass for Charlemagne.

If we ask, in the end, what was new about Charlemagne's achievement, the answer must be that he had extended Frankish power almost to the breaking point and kept it intact over a long reign. A Clovis or a Dagobert might have attempted the same, given the same loyal service. But Charlemagne had a different objective, which was to make an empire of which Christianity was the cement. God had shown that Europe was to be united under the Carolingians; Charlemagne would bend all the resources at his command—military, legal, and educational—to make this unity a reality. It was the emperor, not the pope, who was head of Western Christendom. He got away with it, though only just. The fissiparous elements of his empire were almost more than he could deal with. Unfortunately his successors could not deal with them at all.

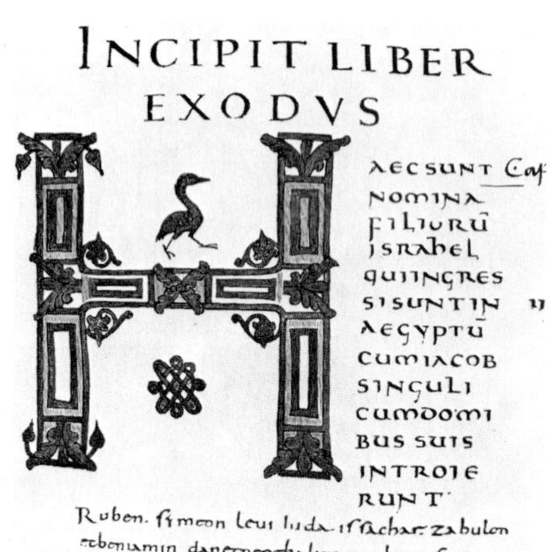


The beginning of the book of Exodus, from Alcuin's Bible. Alcuin (c.735–804) was the key figure in the Carolingian Renaissance. Born and educated at York in England, he became abbot of Tours in 796, and was Charlemagne's adviser on religious and educational matters. The Carolingian Renaissance led to a revival of interest in classical learning and to the foundation of many schools. Although Carolingian scholars were rarely original thinkers, they attempted to codify what they knew. Alcuin regarded the calculation of Church festivals as the chief use of mathematics.

## IMPERIUM CHRISTIANUM

Louis the Pious, Charlemagne's successor, certainly brought to his task a more developed view of the Christian content of imperial rule than Charlemagne ever professed. He was much under the influence of reforming monks such as Benedict of Aniane from his former kingdom of Aquitaine. But the contrast can be overstressed. Charlemagne had a stronger religious bent than he is sometimes credited with, whereas Louis was in some ways the more effective administrator, to judge at least from his capitularies. Louis was physically powerful and a good hunter. The only contemporary portrait we have of him shows him dressed as a Roman emperor equipped for war. His measures to defend the ports and coastal approaches of the West against marauders were at least as effective as his father's. In brief, he saw the day-to-day tasks of his office much as any other Frankish ruler had seen them. But his means were very limited. He had small reserves in treasure and men, unreliable servants, restless subjects distressed by plague and famine, and increasing external pressures on his defenses. He lacked his father's personal glamor, his touch was uncertain, and his temperament was unbalanced. The political and economic scene was darkening all the time.

Louis surrounded himself at Aachen with friends who were not his father's. Fierce religious reformers, they taught him that the substance of power lay not in a glorified high kingship but in a Christian *universitas* of which he was protector, not master. He ruled Christians, not Franks or Romans. He calls himself *piissimus* in his documents, where Charlemagne had preferred *gloriosissimus*. The distinction in outlook was radical.

But behind his friends with their high ideals were the lay magnates of the Empire, disaffected and disillusioned at the change in direction. Inevitably these feelings coalesced at the regional level around Louis' sons: Lothar, who became co-emperor and successor-designate; Pippin, who succeeded his father in Aquitaine; and Louis "the German." An additional complication was Bernard, the Emperor's nephew, who ruled Italy.

A plan of division issued in 817 envisaged a unitary Christian Empire of the future, with one emperor and a group of independent kings bound to him in brotherly affection. They were to act as one in any matter that affected them all. Bernard revolted and was harshly dealt with, Lothar taking Italy. Worse still, the Emperor took a second wife—a Bavarian named Judith—by whom he had a son called Charles, after his grandfather. All attempts to find Charles, the future Charles the Bald, a fitting inheritance were bound to impinge on his brothers' agreed shares. It was the last straw. The ideal of Empire and most of its reality dissolved in an entirely traditional civil war. Louis' prestige suffered irreparable damage. The prestige and the strength of local dynasties of magnates, on the other hand, was enhanced as Louis' declined.

Though self-help was the order of the day, we should not attribute to Louis' sons and their supporters any motives less worthy than those of the Frankish warlords of an earlier generation. They wanted security—the security that came of consistent and reliable kingship. Louis could find no way out of his difficulties. His only means of buying loyalty was by wholesale alienation of royal lands, which could not be replaced. Ecclesiastical lands he refused to touch. He and his successors became progressively poorer, just as the Merovingians had done.

Louis was for a while deprived of rule (in effect, self-deposed). Under pressure, he acknowledged his shortcomings, which had led to civil war. He was confined to a monastery to do penance. But his sons' treatment of their father was more than those who remembered Charlemagne could stomach. Louis was restored to power. His reign certainly created new problems. Above all, and more significantly, it revealed the personal and therefore evanescent nature of what Charlemagne had created. A stronger man than Louis might have done better for a while, but not for very long.

*Above:* The cathedral of Aachen (Aix-la-Chapelle). This building was originally the chapel of Charlemagne's palace, and is the only part of the palace to survive. The chapel, designed by Odo of Metz, was begun in 792 and consecrated by the pope, Leo III, in 795. Its inspiration was partly the Byzantine buildings of Ravenna and partly Roman buildings. Possibly Charlemagne's intention in building his palace and chapel was to construct a new Rome that would rival the old one.

*Left:* Moses giving the ten commandments to the Israelites, from Alcuin's Bible. This highly idealized picture transforms the desert surroundings of Mount Sinai in the Egyptian desert into a Carolingian palace. It is not unlikely that Charlemagne was seen as a new Moses, a civil and religious leader who legislated for the vast empire he had created in western Europe.

## THE CHURCH AND THE EMPEROR

### The Sons of Louis the Pious

The treaty of Verdun in 843 (three years after Louis' death) was a carefully prepared solution to the problem of partition, but it came to grief, like every other solution. Its essence was the creation of a middle kingdom centered on the Rhine, which Lothar was to rule. It had no historical or ethnographical justification. Both East and West Francia were bound to covet the lands of the new kingdom, especially since they contained the Frankish capital, Aachen. France and Germany, already drifting apart linguistically, were born as political rivals from the creation of this bone of contention.

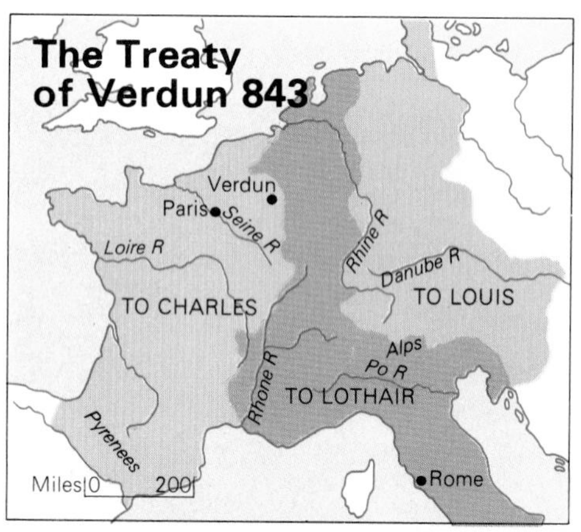


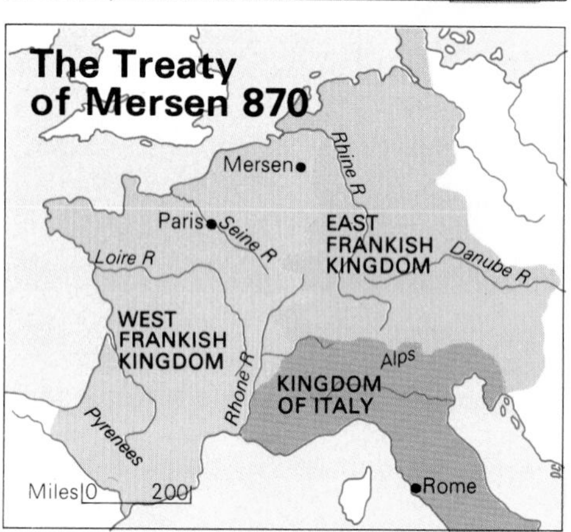


The political situation of the middle years of the ninth century was that Lothar ruled the middle kingdom, and after him his son, the Emperor Louis II, whose time was spent mostly in defending Italy from Arab attacks; Louis the German ruled Germany and Charles the Bald ruled western Francia and Aquitaine. The complex series of campaigns and arrangements to which this led need not detain us. Loyalties constantly changed, undermining the fragile structure of personal trust erected by Charlemagne. But the situation pleased nobody. Some measure of what men really respected is provided by the development of the cult of Charlemagne. Almost as powerful in legend as in life, the old Emperor was looked back to as the ideal Christian ruler. His true achievement, so admirably delineated by Einhard, was soon lost in a mass of local accretions. He was well on the way to becoming the father figure of the *Song of Roland* (see Part II, Chapter 5). He was what men wanted but could not find in the circumstances of endemic civil war.

### Charles the Bald

The most interesting of Louis' successors was Charles the Bald. A warrior and legislator with a keen sense of the past, he had to listen attentively to what the Church told him. Partly this was because his bishops could dispose of so many loyal men and so much land, but also it was because the Church was now feeling a new power and responsibility. It had, in a short time, replaced the Merovingians by the Carolingians, made an emperor, and launched a cultural revolution. It had had to think about the obligations and limitations of the kind of rule it had inaugurated and sustained. So it spoke with a new tone of authority. We can catch that tone in the utterances of the most remarkable of Charles' supporters, Archbishop Hincmar of Rheims.

Ecclesiastically considered, Rheims was a barrier principality stretching across western Francia to the Channel. It came to Hincmar as a reward for services rendered as a monk at St Denis, where he had done much to tighten the links between crown and abbey. He was a scholar of wide attainments, especially in canon law, and a man of strong personality. At Rheims he was prepared to use his authority to the full.

One of Hincmar's objectives was to involve the Carolingians in the defense of his exposed province against Viking attacks. Another was to enhance the prestige of his master, Charles the Bald, by binding him closer to the Church. On more than one occasion, Hincmar composed a special coronation service for Charles' use. These *ordines* are extremely revealing. They show how a complex ritual of king-making was evolved during the ninth century. One result, if it was not an object, was to place the interpretation of the royal office in the hands of the clergy. It was the natural outcome of a faraway event—the unction of Pippin III in 751. It seems doubtful whether Charles saw this as circumscribing his power; he may have welcomed it, since it bound his anointers to him as firmly as it bound him to them.

Hincmar was strong enough to keep the West Frankish clergy loyal to Charles when the kingdom was threatened by Louis the German. Louis was told not to interfere. So, too, was the great Pope Nicholas I, who thought he had business with

Hincmar's suffragans. In brief, Hincmar was a new type of archbishop: master of his own province and suffragans, no longer a kind of respected chairman. It was the Anglo-Saxons who had introduced this concept to the continent. It was a short step from Boniface to Hincmar.

What Rheims did for the West Franks, Fulda did for the East. The annalistic records kept by the two monasteries, each from its own point of view, are proof of the importance contemporaries were attaching to the keeping of official historical records. Fulda also kept alive, as did no other house, the learned tradition of Bede and the school of York as transmitted through Alcuin. The last phase of the Carolingian renaissance was particularly the concern of German monasteries.

We have two contemporary pictures of Charles the Bald, one of which is a striking representation of him on the occasion of his second marriage. He much needed a healthy male heir and was hoping that the Church could work a kind of magic to ensure this—which it proved unable to do. The picture suggests a rather Byzantine ruler, which indeed sorts well with other evidence that his court was subject to Byzantinizing influences. A *Christus Domini* could hardly be expected to look like a simple warrior, even though King David, the favorite biblical examplar of king, had been both.

Toward the end of his reign, Charles journeyed to Rome and was made Emperor by the pope. Rome was not again going to allow emperor-making to slip from its hands. The Frankish magnates did not welcome this, feeling that their own problems required the constant presence of their king. But he did not long survive his imperial coronation.

Silk shroud for the tomb of Charlemagne, showing elephants in medallions.

## THE DECLINE OF THE CAROLINGIANS

Charles the Bald was the last considerable Carolingian. The dynasty was to linger on, on both sides of the Rhine, for some time yet, but Carolingian power, like the sources that fed it, was spent. Other families were rising to prominence, ducal and comital dynasties identified with the successful defense of marcher regions against external attack. The Capetians in France and the Saxons in Germany were to achieve kingship for precisely the reason that had once favored the Carolingians: they had the power and the resources to attract loyalty and put down trouble. But just as the Merovingian name had not ceased to stir emotions after 751, so the Carolingians were long remembered. Loyalties of this kind have their own political momentum. At the Battle of Hastings in 1066 the song that was on the lips of the Normans was about Charlemagne—not the historical Charlemagne but a white-haired, mysterious warlord, almost a second Woden and the idealized figure of a heroic past.

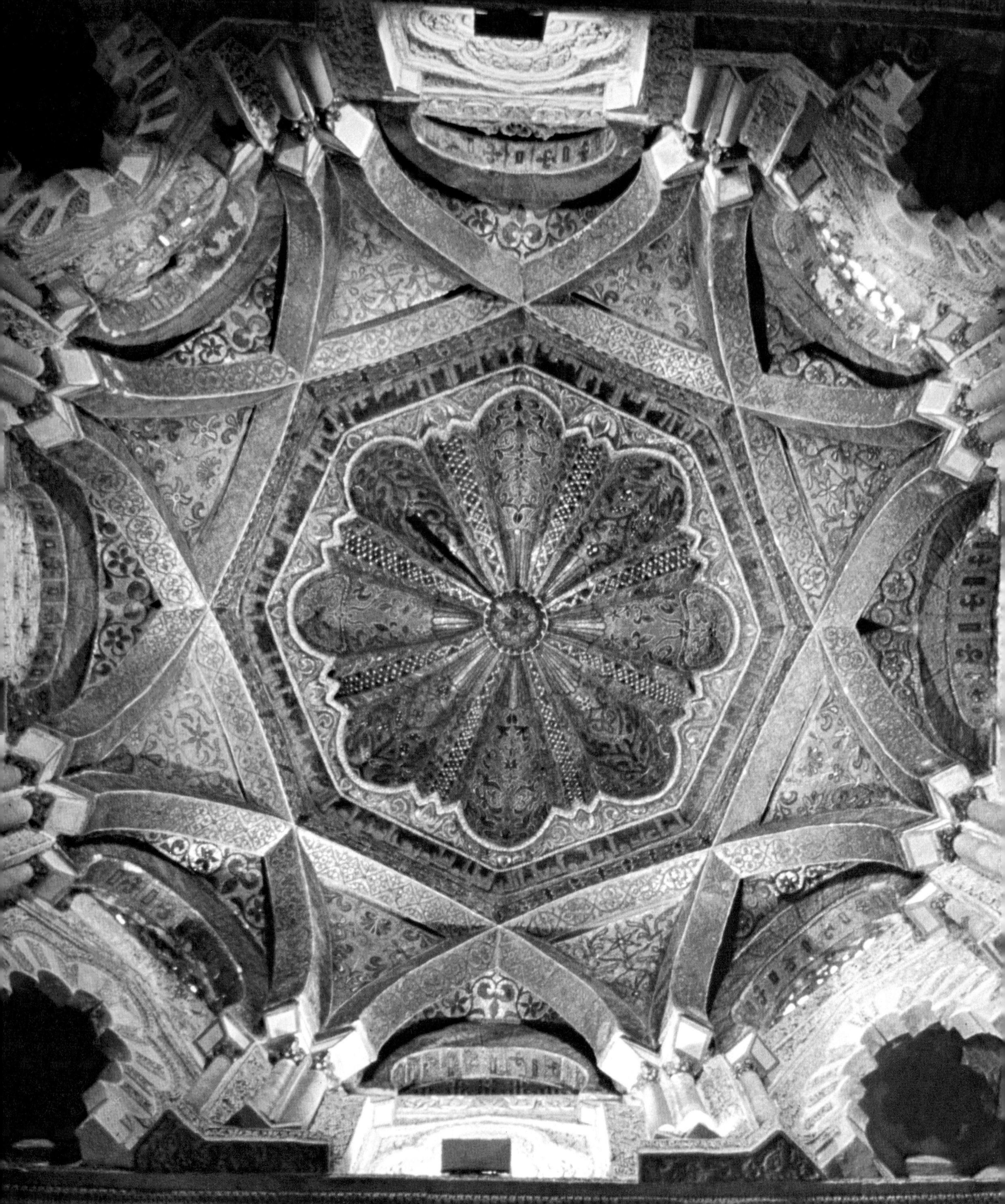

Chapter 4

# NINTH-CENTURY EUROPE

## THE WESTERN ARABS

The Arab expedition under Tarik to Spain in 711 was a small matter. It had not been planned and was not sanctioned by Musa, the Arab commander in North Africa. But it was successful. The Arab forces could advance as they wished, taking towns as they could and improvising terms when they did. Under the Arabs was a large body of mercenary Berbers. These, always troublesome, were eventually settled on lands unattractive to the Arabs in Old Castile.

Some towns, probably including Toledo, gave up without a fight. Others put up a stout resistance. The treaty made between the Arabs and Theudemir, overlord of Murcia, survives. Its terms are generous. The Christians of Córdoba, the Arab capital, seem to have enjoyed privileges originating in a treaty.

There was no persecution of Christians till 850, and even then they may be said to have brought it on themselves. Neither were the Jews persecuted—understandably, since they probably reacted against Visigoth persecution by giving active help to the Arabs. On the other hand, the fiscal advantages of conversion to Islam were considerable. Many Christians of the Arab south—Al Andalus—turned to Islam within a generation or two. Others, especially in Toledo, remained firm in their faith, which they continued to practice. But they were cut off from Christendom. Their faith accordingly developed in isolation. Heresy was to be the characteristic of Mozarab (Christian Arab) belief, at least according to Carolingian theologians.

Beyond the south and east of Spain, the Arabs either could not or would not settle in large numbers. Life in the south was more like what they were used to—hot and refined. The north remained as unsubdued as it had been before.

Islamic Spain was always aware of intellectual developments in the East. Before the end of the eighth century, Arab pilgrims were bringing back to Spain accounts of the new Islamic sciences. From such beginnings grew the reputation of Spain as an intellectual clearing house between East and West. Spain's role was to be of vital importance for medieval Europe. But it was immediately of importance for Spain herself. The court of Córdoba became in the ninth and tenth centuries a great center of Islamic theology and jurisprudence, controlled by an intellectual aristocracy.

The Arabs were not only in Spain. From Africa it was an easy matter, as the Vandals had found, to raid profitably along the coasts of Provence and Italy. The coastline was too long for effective defense against attacks in the emirate of Tunisia, which could strike anywhere. Byzantine Sicily fell in 902 after a long and bitter struggle. The Italian mainland, however, found a champion in the Emperor Louis II, who managed, over several years, to confine the Arabs to the south. But for him, Italy would have suffered the fate of Spain and the Alpine passes would have been open to the Arabs. Naples, Gaeta, and Amalfi organized a successful common defense. Other cities, including Rome, suffered more severely. In Provence the Arabs made a stronghold of St Tropez, from which, for many years, they raided far afield

The "La Kebla" cupola of the great mosque at Córdoba. This makes an interesting contrast with the dome of Aachen cathedral. Tenth-century Còrdoba was the scene of an intellectual flowering even more remarkable than the Carolingian Renaissance. This Muslim city was described by a contemporary as "the center of learning, and the beacon of religion." Under the caliphs Abd-al-Rahman III (912–961) and Al-Hakam II (961–975) a huge library of 400,000 volumes was assembled, and the visual arts flourished as beautiful mosques were built and decorated. It was in great part from Córdoba that knowledge of classical writers began to emerge in western Christendom.

for plunder and captives to ransom. Trading went hand in hand with piracy. But the Arabs could pay in gold for what they chose to buy, and thus the balance was not entirely unfavorable to the West. Nor were the Arabs always unattractive as masters. But the general picture is clear: Europe felt itself to be threatened by a pagan world and, in meeting the threat, learned to identify its own values.

## THE VIKINGS

We do not know why the Scandinavian peoples erupted in the later eighth century. Land hunger, population explosion, discontent with autocratic kings, even the movement of herring shoals have been advanced as reasons. But there is little evidence for any of them. All that we know for certain is that groups of young warriors, well equipped with weapons and boats, set out in search of adventure, plunder, and land. They may have been following routes already taken by predecessors who had combined trading with piracy in a familiar medieval mixture. Moreover, the same reasons may not explain the eruption of all those we classify as Vikings. The Swedes sailed northeast along the Baltic, penetrating German and Russian rivers as they went, until they finally set up a trading post at Kiev. Their future as a Russian kingdom was to be tied to Byzantium's, and so they cease to be our present concern. The Norwegians, probably even better equipped, with boats of real sophistication, sailed in a great arc around Scotland to Ireland, the Faroes, Iceland, Greenland, and Newfoundland. To the Icelandic settlement in particular we are indebted for an incomparable epic record of the heroic Scandinavian past. The Danes moved toward Anglo-Saxon England, Frisia, Spain, and the western Mediterranean. It is not unlikely that Carolingian penetration into Frisia and northern Saxony may have alerted them to opportunities as well as dangers, though it would be another matter to argue that the Franks caused the Danish irruption. Certainly the Carolingians lost no opportunity to fish in troubled Danish waters.

The Medina Az Zahara, the remains of tenth-century Córdoba. Córdoba was a cosmopolitan town with a population of perhaps 250,000. The population was made up of Christians and Jews as well as Muslims from Spain, Arabia and Africa. Visitors were amazed by the number of public baths (around 400 in all) and the richness of the mosques. After the death of the emir Al-Hakam in 975, a reaction set in. His successor, al-Mansur, destroyed his library, and much of the vigor departed from the city's cultural and intellectual life.

Charlemagne faced the early stages of the Danish penetration of his northern territories, but it was Louis the Pious and Charles the Bald who bore the brunt of serious attacks down the length of the Frankish coastline. Hit-and-run raiding based on island retreats gave place to the landing and establishment of armies capable of raiding far up the river courses. Naturally, churches and monasteries fell an easy prey to them. It followed that the churchmen whose records tell us of these raids made them sound terrible, and no doubt they had an inflated idea of the numbers involved. Nevertheless, monasteries were sacked, men were killed, lands were ravaged. It was perhaps less the actual destruction than the threat of it that caused social instability. No one knew upon whom they would next fall. But it would be absurd to suppose that the churchmen got it all wrong and that the Vikings were in reality peaceful explorers anxious to buy land.

There is also a religious side to it. The victims saw the Vikings as pagans first and foremost. As Scandinavian religion comes to be better understood, we can see why. The warbands were the servants of Woden, who demanded bloody sacrifice. The blood eagle was a gruesome ceremony. Woden's service was no mere lip service but something requiring sustained ecstasy, even intoxication. The pagan Danes, said Archbishop Wulfstan somewhat later, are more careful about their sacrifices than Christians are about theirs. And this was very much how Hincmar saw the Vikings as they ravaged his province of Reims. The section he wrote of the so-called *Annals of St Bertin* is full of alarm. Charles the Bald personally led the defense of his own monastery of St Denis against their assault. They were not invincible. Whenever a proper army could be put into the field against them at the right time and place, they could be held, as at the Battle of Saucourt. Maine and Britanny, where they tried to settle, were denied them, though Normandy was not.

On the other hand, the Vikings could settle down quite quickly when allowed to do so. Recollections of their past soon faded in Normandy, where for all their practical independence, they blended into the local population and learned to speak its language. Settlement brought with it fairly rapid conversion to Christianity and adaptation to local ways. They could be intelligent businessmen and good farmers.

Not every threatened landlord put national or royal interests before his own when he was offered a fair deal. It might be possible to offer successful resistance to a raid if you had the money or the men, but it might not come off, as those of the Seine-Loire region found in 859 when they banded together in self-defense and got massacred. Resistance or capitulation really rested with the men on the spot.

The Carolingians could do little more than defend their own. In practice, this meant putting up stout resistance in the Paris region and a few other districts. Indeed, they had no higher view than this of their royal duty. The surprising thing is that the Frankish world resisted as well as it did for a century. Much was lost. Displacement of population from threatened areas certainly took place; weaknesses were revealed in the political structure. Perhaps the Frankish Empire would have come even better out of the ordeal if it had not at the same time faced comparable dangers from the Arabs in the south and the Slavs, and later the Magyars, in the east. The total effect, though politically disruptive, was to give the western world a feeling of being beleagured, of being unlike what lay outside. The medieval outlook was born.

## THE PAPACY

It is ironical that Gregory the Great, least politically intentioned of popes, should have launched his successors on a course that looks singularly political. Their chief preoccupation throughout the seventh and eighth centuries appears to be endless negotiation for the defense of Rome and her patrimony of estates against the Lom-

A typical Viking figurine, perhaps of Thor, one of the ancient Norse gods. From the eighth century Viking attacks disturbed the calm of Europe. Not until after the Norman conquest of Sicily in the eleventh century could Europe hope that no further attacks would come from the wild invaders of Scandinavia. Originally pagans, the Norsemen had worshiped a pantheon of gods, including Woden, Thor and Fria (after whom Wednesday, Thursday, and Friday are named), until their conversion to Christianity, which helped to civilize them.

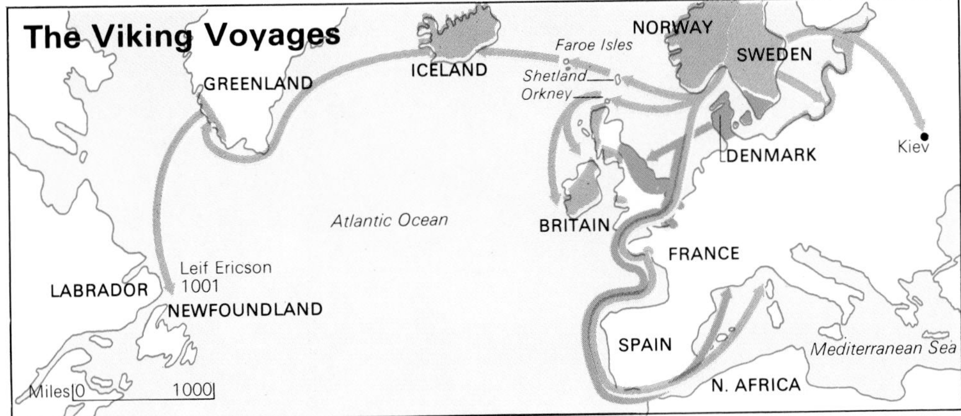


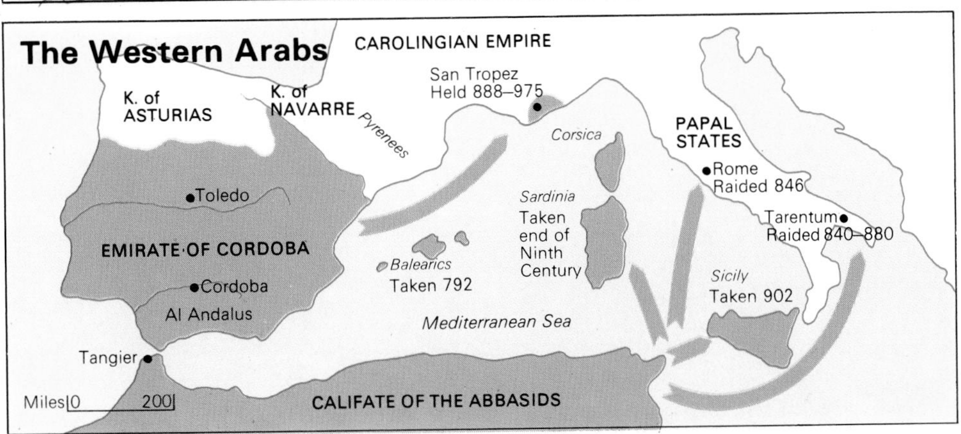

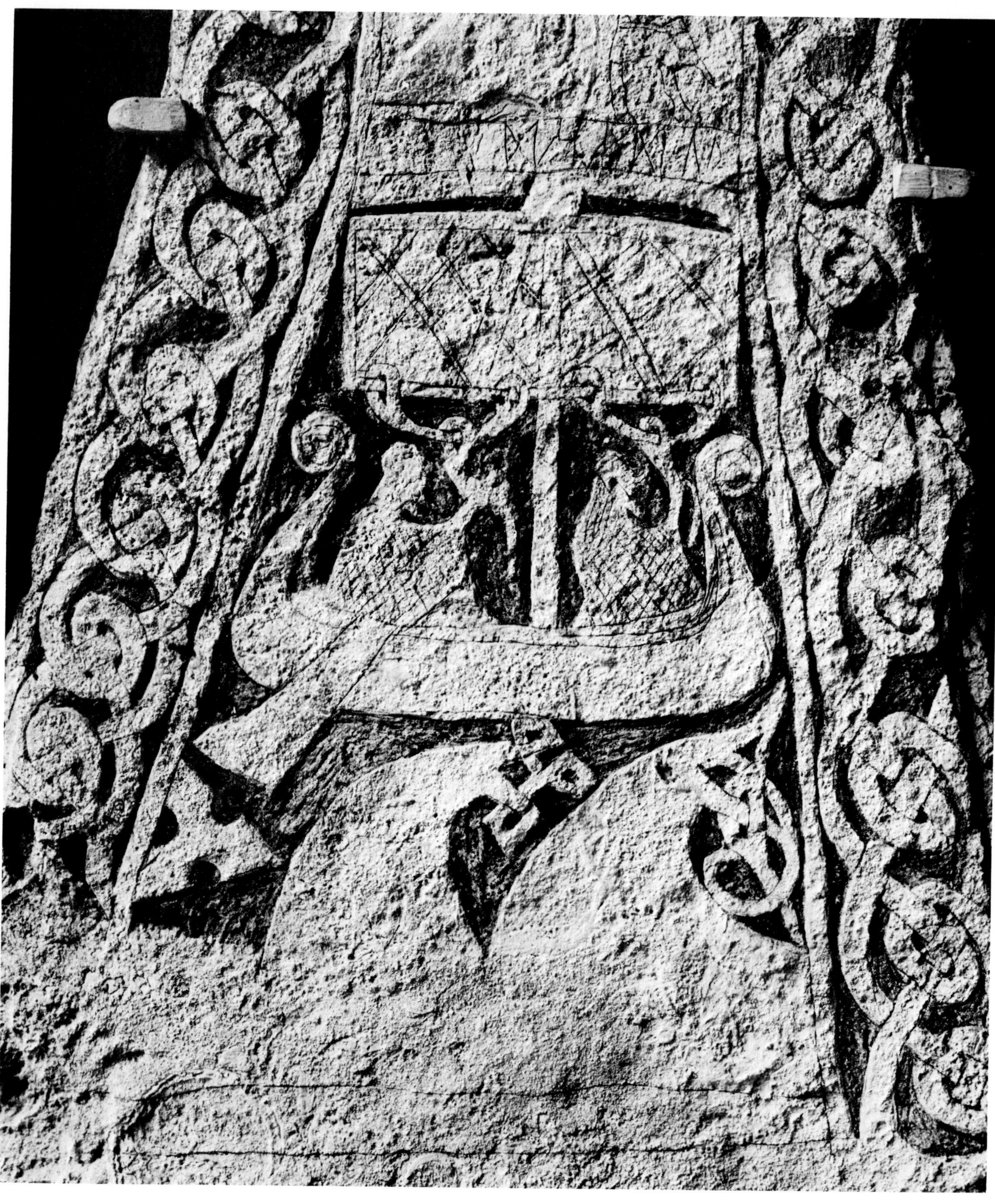

bards; in the ninth, it is against Arabs and local magnates. To exchange Byzantine protection for Frankish did not solve many problems and created some new ones. But this is only part of the truth. Gregory was also the great exemplar of a missionary pope. Thus, eighth-century Germany owed as much to the popes as to St Boniface, who considered himself their servant, and quite apart from their supervision of his labors in central Germany and the Rhineland, the popes had their own links with the Bavarian Church. From this center it was natural to extend their influence further east along the Danube, among the Slavs of the Balkans. The Balkans were disputed territory between East and West, and the papacy was not prepared to forego intervention in an area where Byzantium was pushing her claims.

Each pope could look back to the record of the struggles and achievements of his predecessors in the *Liber Pontificalis*, the series of papal biographies kept up in the papal palace of the Lateran. He could frame his policy with an eye to the past. Conservation is, not surprisingly, the keynote of papal policy. It matters more than the slow and uncertain formulation of a view on the relations of Church and state brought about largely by Rome's compact with the Carolingians. Two great popes of the ninth century were Nicholas I and John VIII.

*Above:* A Viking tombstone found in London, England.
*Left:* View of a Viking boat. In their longboats the Norsemen sailed and rowed enormous distances. They explored the coast of the Baltic Sea, traveled round the Northern coast of Scandinavia into the ice-bound Barents Sea, raided and eventually conquered England and Ireland, crossed the Atlantic Ocean to Iceland and Greenland, and even discovered North America, which they knew as Vinland. Boats provided a livelihood for the Vikings, but they were thought to help the dead also. On many gravestones, such as this, boats were shown carrying the dead to the other world.

The biography of Nicholas (pope, 858–67) is a major piece of writing. It is the work of Anastasius, the papal librarian. Like Gregory, Nicholas was "one of us," a Roman brought up to be an administrator and well in with the emperor. Also like Gregory, he was a natural ruler whose initiatives were generally responses to the actions of others. He could deal with an appeal from the clergy and people of Emilia against an extortionate archbishop; he could adjudicate at the Byzantine emperor's request in the matter of the deposition of one patriarch of Constantinople and the appointment of another; he could intervene over the projected divorce and remarriage of the Western Emperor, Lothar. The law of the Church is in the pope's hands, and it must not be misinterpreted by distant kings and bishops. He hears an appeal in Rome by the bishop of Soissons against his archbishop, Hincmar of Rheims. In reply to an appeal from the Bulgarians, he writes them a long and famous letter on the subject of conversion—a papal, not Byzantine, specialty, he is at pains to make clear. In brief, Rome was to be arbiter in all matters affecting the Church. Anastasius describes these great issues graphically and places them firmly against a local background of Roman intrigue, papal supervision of *domuscualte* (farms), and day-to-day administration of the see. Nicholas is a legislating pope, deeply versed in canon law and ready to adjudicate, arbitrate, teach, convert, and rebuke sin. In his energy he looks new, yet he was a living demonstration of orthodoxy and continuity.

Nicholas was a good model for the future, and almost at once for John VIII (pope, 872–82). Equally determined to be master in his own house, John had vision and statesmanship. He saw to it that a careful register was kept of his large correspondence. Records were vital. Though much involved in local disputes, he kept a keen eye on European events and made himself felt when a vacancy occurred in the Western Empire. Charles the Bald was his personal choice as emperor against fierce local opposition. In 875 Charles had to make an unpopular journey to Rome to be crowned by John in St Peter's. But none of this solved the problem of endemic rivalry, exacerbated by the nearby Arabs, among the Italian nobility for the control of Rome. The rivalry was the key to so much. However actively John negotiated for the survival of the Western Empire, he was increasingly in the hands of powerful factions at home. A long history of papal independence ended with his death in 882. The papacy had become politically too important to Italy not to attract the ambitions of cupidinous families.

Behind this growing political turmoil lay a deeper reality. The popes were the guardians of the bones of St Peter and of the martyrs of Rome. They presided over the most sought-after goal for pilgrims in the whole Western world. Their consistent implementation of the claims implicit in this guardianship was their first duty. And it was a duty that won affection and respect. Different as they were, the early medieval popes all stood or fell on this. Politics and legislation were secondary. Things were to be very different in the Middle Ages proper.

## WESTERN ECONOMY

It is no difficult matter to find out what kinds of economic exchange prevailed in the early Middle Ages, but it is impossible to say how much of a particular kind there was at any one time. The reason for this is scarcity of evidence. No statistical conclusions such as modern economic historians reach are possible.

At least we can be certain that there was no sharp break at the point where antiquity becomes the Middle Ages, wherever we may place it. An economy based on the land was as characteristic of the one period as of the other. Nor could it be otherwise without a technological revolution, which did not take place. It can be shown that over the centuries towns declined, money became scarcer, population decreased, and long-distance trade became more difficult, but these processes start far back in antiquity. The land remained the same. On it all livelihoods ultimately depended, and its possession was the best of all investments.

The Germanic invasions certainly affected the landholding shape of the West. The additional population could comfortably be absorbed, if at the cost of some expropriation. The *villa*, as the common unit of agricultural exploitation, was not abandoned, although it sometimes changed its shape. Germanic owners replaced Roman. Place-names reveal how frequently the one took over from the other. Still the land was cultivated by servile or semiservile labor. The Germans were perhaps keener than the Romans on hunting and horse raising, and hence we occasionally find them in upland country, as in Spain or Aquitaine, where a Germanic chieftain would settle on land a Roman landlord had neglected. We also find colonization on forestland in the form of *vici*, or village settlements—as, for example, around Paris in the seventh century. There was nothing planned about any of this. No one, not even a victorious king, could long hold what he had won or inherited without giving away substantial parts to loyal servants or to the Church. Immunities arose everywhere, lands from which the public service ceases to benefit in one way or another. Moreover, lands held as payment for service, such as a count might hold, tended to be treated as private and to be disposed of as hereditary possessions. To replace a royal official by one not of the same family often required armed force. All offices, even ecclesiastical ones, tended to be looked on as hereditary. But the exploitation of the land goes on much as before. Some marginal land goes out of cultivation, but new land comes into cultivation as a result of colonization. This was notably true of the Merovingian and Carolingian drive eastward over the Rhine, with the Church participating actively at all stages.

St Dunstan of Canterbury kneeling in prayer at the feet of Christ. Dunstan, a monk of Glastonbury abbey, was archbishop of Canterbury from 959 to 988. After a visit to the abbey of Cluny during a period in exile, he helped restore the monastic life to an important place in the English Church, and established monasteries at Peterborough and Ely. He also persuaded the Anglo-Saxon king Edgar to carry out political reforms, but after Edgar's death Dunstan's influence declined. During the last years of Dunstan's life the Danish invasions further reduced his influence.

The Roman West, or at least its monied elements, depended on a steady Mediterranean trade with Africa and the East. This was the route for olive oil, grain, and luxury goods such as spices and silk. The Church did not lose its taste for such things, and the barbarian warlords quickly acquired it. But the Vandal occupation of Roman Africa made a difference, and so later did that of the Arabs. Neither Vandals nor Arabs deliberately disrupted trade, but the seizing of cargoes and the threat to ports presumably caused merchants to think carefully about alternative markets. Once the Eastern Empire had developed Asia Minor, thus making good the loss of Egypt and Syria, such a market was available. Eastern goods were still reaching the West in the seventh and eighth centuries, but spasmodically. The Byzantine fleets that blockaded vital areas of the Mediterranean may themselves have added to the difficulties. On the other hand, the Arabs were quite prepared to do business, especially in the purchase of slaves, and thus some Arab gold certainly entered Europe to replace its failing supplies. But gold is hard to interpret. To the early medieval mind it appeared primarily as treasure—a precious commodity to be hoarded away. It could be converted to any use the occasion required, decorative or commercial. It could often change its shape and purpose. It cannot, then, whether as money or otherwise be a very safe guide as evidence of trade. A coin hoard may indeed signify a commercial transaction, but it may equally well be part of a subsidy or a gift. What we unearth may represent no more than a man's *wergeld*, or personal price at law. It was no accident that the contemporary mind liked to see dragons as guardians of treasure.

Trade with the Mediterranean, then, became more spasmodic as time went on. Simultaneously, though not necessarily as a consequence, northern trade showed signs of flourishing. It was financed by silver rather than gold. New ports supplying the Rhineland developed fast, and increasing business was done in towns and fairs, as at St Denis. Again, the Church played a big part. Charlemagne reformed his coinage as a consequence of this trade. We know that he negotiated with the Anglo-Saxon King Offa to ensure a regular supply of cloth of the right kind and length for his kingdom, and the wide diffusion of Offa's silver pennies over southern England argues a connection with the same business. To a large extent this trade, and other trades such as fish, fur, and amber, were in the hands of Frisian merchants. They were the great movers of northern wares until the Viking attacks of the ninth century disrupted their ports. But the Vikings were themselves traders. They knew, for example, how to foster the northern wine trade to their own advantage, and their ports were considerable places. To all this must be added regional trades, such as the armaments business along the eastern marches, the salt trade along the Danube (until interrupted by the Slavs), and the metal, textile, and glass trades of the Rhine. Above all, there was the slave trade. Large consignments of captives were moved south in convoys from the Rhine or the Danube to the Mediterranean ports for shipment to Arab markets. The rise of Venice, the first center of mercantile capitalism, was in part connected with this.

St Matthew from the gospel book of Mac Durman, ninth-century Irish. Ireland and Scotland helped keep Christian and classical culture alive when they were threatened with extinction on the continent. Irish missions founded monasteries in Europe. Irish illuminated manuscripts were one of the influences on the Carolingian schools.

But in the end we are left with an agricultural scene, with king, churchmen, and lay magnates learning to manage estates in an efficient way—that is, in a bookkeeping way. There is enough documentation to prove that they did it. Land had suffered greatly from invasion and the threat of it. The future lay less with the Church as landlord than with the many rising families of *seigneur* who had carved out for themselves estates that could support dynasties. But this, the emergence of feudal society, has to do with more than economic considerations.

## PROTOFEUDAL SOCIETY

"Feudalism" is a modern word that would have meant nothing to the early medieval mind. "Feudal society," on the other hand, has some meaning, provided we never regard it as static or as identical in any two areas at any one time. It is the name we give to a society predominantly organized around the fact of the *feudum*, or fief—that is, a society in which one man holds a commodity such as land from another man in return for specified services and with the hope that the arrangement will hold good for the heirs of both. The holder is the *homo* ("man"), the person of whom he holds is the *dominus* ("lord"), and their contract will be entered upon with much solemnity. It rests in the last resort on the good faith of both parties.

Such an arrangement had ancient roots, both Roman and Germanic. In the later Empire it was common practice for free men to seek the patronage of greater men who could protect them. To use the technical term, they "commended" themselves to their patrons. The bond between them was felt to be moral. This could also mean that the lesser man surrendered his property to the greater, receiving it back as a *precarium*, sometimes called a *beneficium*, a free gift, though this was a legal wangle. But it was not a contract. It could easily be revoked. The practice of Roman patronage took many forms, of which surrender of land was only one.

The Germans entered quite naturally into these social arrangements. One soon finds Germanic words used as equivalents of the old Latin ones: for example, *patrocinium* becomes *mundiburdis, fidelitas* becomes *trustis*, and so on. Indeed, the process appears to gather momentum. More and more free men felt the need to commend themselves for the sake of protection.

There survives at least one early formula for the ceremony of entry into patronage. Clergy as well as laymen recognized its benefits. The patrons most often sought were kings. The general responsibility of Germanic kings to protect all their subjects, especially the weak and oppressed, was not enough. It was safer, if you could, to place yourself more directly under royal protection—in brief, to commend yourself. This was done by placing your hands between the king's hands and swearing a solemn oath. He thus became not only your king but your *senior*, your patron.

Precarial grants, too, were becoming even commoner and perhaps more difficult to annul without a struggle. But still the parties to such grants were not bound by any oath. Each agreement was particular to the occasion. Quite often, it would envisage a concession lasting three generations. So advantageous was this thought to be that magnates as well as small men would seek them, especially with churches.

The services a commended man could render his lord varied enormously, but the most obviously valuable one in an age dominated by warfare was military service. Germanic kings had always surrounded themselves with warriors, who were the spearhead of their fighting forces as well as their natural companions. One cannot envisage a Germanic king in any other context. The Merovingian king had his *trustis* of attendant warriors, each of whom entered upon the relationship by a hand-oath of fidelity. It could be the making of an ambitious young man. Magnates, too, had the same need for groups of armed companions to protect and avenge them.

One way of rewarding the service of an armed retainer was by a grant of land, whether outright or as a *beneficium*. The change from the Merovingian to the Carolingian age is chiefly one of terminology. A new word, *vassus*, comes into use. Originally Celtic, it meant no more than servant and was perhaps first used by royal commended men to mark their sense of deference. But the Carolingian vassal entered upon his career with a new ceremony, called *hommage*. Stripped of his arms, he knelt before his lord to place his hands between his lord's hands and, possibly, to kiss his feet. He went on to take his oath of fidelity upon the Gospels or relics. It was a contract meant to last for life, in token of which the lord made a symbolic gift. The Carolingians were greatly attracted by the possibilities of vassalage. They liked to have large followings of vassals and used them freely on royal business. The vassals' reward was to be *casati*—enfeoffed with royal or ecclesiastical lands. Moreover, these lands were immunities outside the control of local officials. When vassals fought, they did so directly under royal command and not as part of any local contingent. It was a wonderful safeguard, at least in theory, to have such men in areas where the loyalty of officials could not be depended on. It also seemed helpful to kings to have their great men surrounded by their own vassals. It was a reinforcement of royal power, not an infringement upon it, for a local lord was responsible to the king for the loyalty of his vassals, who were thus bound more closely to the king than before. We can see the danger implicit: that a lord's vassal would in the end place his immediate loyalty to his lord before his loyalty to a distant and powerless king. But the Carolingian could not see it.

Local magnates, though royal vassals, naturally thought in local terms, especially in distant marcher zones, where their followings were constantly in arms. The magnate might hold his office and lands from the crown, but he would nonetheless expect his son to succeed him in both. By the mid-ninth century it was becoming extremely difficult for any king to deny this. But it would be wrong to attribute the breakup of the Carolingian world into a ring of marcher lordships solely to the growth of vassalage. Vassalage did in the end strengthen the moral links of man to lord at the expense of the crown, but it did not create the political conditions in which this took place. Although relationships were increasingly expressed in terms of the lord-man relationship, it must not be overlooked that many free men continued to hold their land of no lord; they were owners of personal property, *alods*, and these came in all sizes.

The immediately significant aspect of this protofeudal society was not tenure or service but social relationships. Men and women of all ranks except the lowest were now thinking in terms of the lord-man bond and its reciprocal loyalties. It was not merely prudent to serve one's immediate lord with heart and soul; it was right to do so. The feeling begins to affect family relationships and to be reflected in literature. What could be worse than disloyalty? A lady named Dhuoda, wife of the Marquis of Septimania, wrote to her son in 843 to urge on him the significance of fidelity: "... maintain toward the king and his service in all things a devoted and certain fealty both of body and soul ... May the madness of infidelity be ever far from you. ... Read the lives and words of the holy men of former times, and you will find there how to serve your lord and be faithful to him in all things." Easier said than done. Loyalties could not quickly be determined or maintained in the ninth century. But the moral bite of what we call the feudal relationship is there already. It was something to hold onto in a dissolving world—and it was not itself

An Anglo-Saxon king and his court. Increasingly during the troubled times of the tenth century kings tried to give their nobles a say in governing their country in an attempt to ensure loyalty. The duty and privilege of the nobility to advise their king became more important. Also, in order to secure an untroubled succession, the oldest son of the king was often associated with the king during his lifetime—even if, as in the picture, he was only a child.

OTTO·PRIM
RATOR·ROMANO

the solvent, as is sometimes claimed. The powerful links of the kindred, supported by blood feud, had nearly disappeared; the loyalty to kings preached by the Carolingian Church had not withstood political strain. Society was left with lord and man, bound to each other in solemn moral contract and armed to face the Middle Ages as best they could.

## An illiterate age

"Eternal Trinity, deliver thy Christian people from the oppresion of the pagans." This was the prayer of western Europe after the collapse of the Carolingian Empire. During the century after 850, the West was ravaged by what has been described as the "second wave" of barbarian invasions. The Franks, Germans, and English, who had centuries before settled within the old Roman lands, were now themselves subjected to devastating raids by Northmen, Magyars, and Saracens. The damage and demoralization were great, especially as the raids were accompanied by a collapse of the peace and order which had been precariously maintained by the Carolingians.

The answer to the prayer came in the form of the Saxon, or Ottonian, ruler of Germany. Henry I (919–936) united under his control the eastern provinces of the former empire. In modern geographical terms, although these would not have been used at the time, he established a kingdom of Germany. His son and successor, Otto I (936–973), extended the influence of his family throughout much of Europe. Italy was united to the German monarchy, and the Holy Roman Empire was revived. Otto was crowned Emperor at Rome in 962. The West Frankish kingdom ("France" in our terms) was made subordinate, extensive lands were conquered from the Slavs on the eastern border, and the Magyar menace was finally crushed at the Battle of the Lech in 955. Ambassadors traveled to Spain and Byzantium, and missionaries journeyed into Russia and the Slavonic lands of the East. The story of the successors of Otto I is not one of uniform success, for their projects were ambitious and their power overextended, but their claims are vividly expressed in the portrayal of Otto III (983–1002) receiving the homage of the various regions of Europe. Without doubt, there was considerable reality in these pretensions.

The brilliant monarchy of the Ottos was essentially a successor state of the Carolingian Empire, but it had distinctive features of its own. It is obvious that the center of political control and activity had shifted markedly toward the east. Another tendency was an increased stress upon the "sacred" or "divine" character of the monarchy, an emphasis already clear in the empire of Charlemagne. It is significant that Byzantine influences were very strong at the Ottonian court. Otto III, who by birth was half-Greek, adopted Byzantine ceremonial and titles and exaggerated the idea of divine kingship to a point which would have created uneasiness even at Constantinople. Otto III was portrayed in manuscripts and imagery more appropriate to Christ, and Conrad II was addressed as "the vicar of Christ." The emperors saw themselves as divinely appointed rulers of the Church.

The existence of this monarchy, drawing its culture consciously from German, Frankish, classical, and Byzantine sources, must not, however, be allowed to conceal from us the character of the society over which it ruled. This was an illiterate age. It was illiterate not merely in the sense that relatively few people could read and write—although this was certainly true—but in the more profound sense that it used ritual, symbol, and gesture where we would expect to use words. Writing was unusual in many of the transactions for which we would think it indispensable. Judgments in legal cases were not committed to writing; the government did not maintain systematic records or issue written instructions to its agents; land transactions were often unrecorded. The use of language in literature—and, for that

The emperor Otto I, from the shrine of Charlemagne at Aachen cathedral. Otto was proclaimed emperor after his victory at the Lechfeld against the Magyars in 955. His coronation seven years later in Rome was the beginning of the Holy Roman Empire as an institution that was to continue until 1806. The Ottonian emperors rebuilt a Germany that had been shattered by civil wars and barbarian invasions. Like Charlemagne's vision of empire Otto's was selfconsciously nationalistic; just as Aachen had been intended to be a Frankish Rome, so Otto tried to make the cathedral city of Magdebourg into a Germanic Rome.

matter, in prayer—remained lapidary, statuesque, and without fluency. The dramatic gesture replaced verbal communication. The authority of the king was expressed by sitting in majesty, wearing his robes of office. Appointments in the church were made by "investiture"—the gift of a ring and staff, the exact significance of which was undefined. Land was granted in a series of striking ceremonies which said little about the precise powers which were being transferred. In matters of religion, great importance was attached to the solemn enactment of rituals, and kings thought their patronage well bestowed when it provided for the liturgy on their behalf. Their government has been called, with some justice, "the liturgical state." So dominant was this ritual character of the age that, by a paradox, words themselves became endowed with a formal, ceremonial significance rather than a practical, explanatory one. The manuscripts written in German monasteries for successive emperors were not designed to convey information but were, in the fullest sense of the term, "holy books," treated as precious objects, almost as relics.

The age was not only illiterate. It was also in many ways very local in its attitudes. The symbols of Empire might speak mutely of a universal dominion, but the communities over which the Ottonian house ruled lacked an international outlook. The Church, which so often in the Middle Ages provided the expression for a general Western culture, did not do so in this period. The Church of each region was governed primarily by the archbishop or metropolitan. Supervision by the pope was almost nonexistent, and the canon law (the general law of the Western Church) was, in the tenth century, ill defined and little studied. The most important form of monasticism, the Benedictine, was also very local in character. Although it had a common rule, this provided no central organization but anticipated that each abbey would be separately administered. The rank and file of the clergy, married, subject to no very distinct body of law, and with little by way of distinctive education, were closely integrated into the society of their region.

Lay control within the Church was extensive. Most churches were private churches, *ecclesiae propriae*. A private church had an owner, originally the lord who had built it, although it could also be sold or given away. The rights of the bishop were slight compared with those of the local landowner, who could use his churches to advance his family or as an inducement for favors. To make matters worse, the lord who had provided the church naturally expected a cut from the profits, rather as he would from the mill or the oven. Almost everything in the church was for sale—baptism and communion, appointments, consecrated oil—and the lord took a share of the proceeds. In practice, therefore, lay control of the Church inevitably involved simony, or the sale of spiritual benefits.

The emperors saw themselves as God's representatives on earth, and they also owned many "imperial" or "royal" churches in the manner of the private-church system. It is not surprising, therefore, that their way of dealing with the Church was a masterful one. From 962, when Otto I was crowned emperor, to the death of Henry III in 1056, the emperors were frequently involved in the appointment of popes. Many popes, indeed, were simply imperial nominees. On the whole, the appointments were good ones and a few were distinguished. The influence of the emperor, however, was very strong, and it reached its most dramatic expression under Henry III, at the Synod of Sutri in December 1046. At this time, there were no less than three claimants to the papal title. Henry removed them all and appointed his own nominee, a German who had already been prominent in his service, as Clement II. On the face of it, 1046 would appear to be the extreme instance of the bankruptcy of the papal office and the need of imperial authority to regulate the affairs of the Church. But appearances were deceptive. Already, the climate had begun to change.

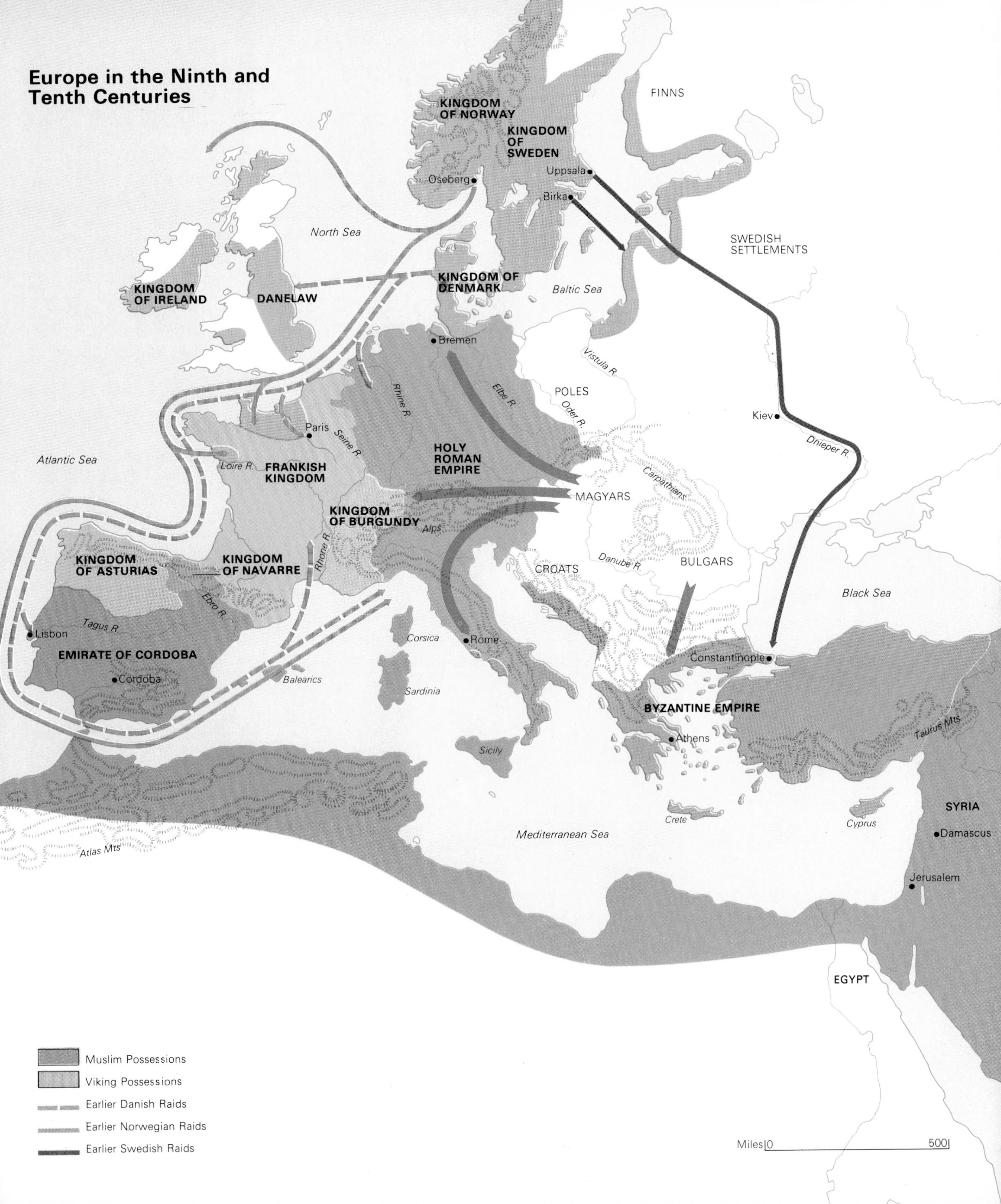

Europe in the Ninth and Tenth Centuries
KINGDOM OF NORWAY
KINGDOM OF SWEDEN
FINNS
Uppsala
Oseberg
Birka
North Sea
SWEDISH SETTLEMENTS
KINGDOM OF IRELAND
DANELAW
KINGDOM OF DENMARK
Baltic Sea
Bremen
Vistula R.
Elbe R.
Rhine R.
POLES
Oder R.
Kiev
Paris
Seine R.
Dnieper R.
Atlantic Sea
Loire R.
FRANKISH KINGDOM
HOLY ROMAN EMPIRE
Carpathians
MAGYARS
KINGDOM OF BURGUNDY
Alps
KINGDOM OF ASTURIAS
KINGDOM OF NAVARRE
Rhone R.
CROATS
Danube R.
BULGARS
Black Sea
Ebro R.
Tagus R.
Lisbon
Corsica
Rome
Constantinople
EMIRATE OF CORDOBA
Cordoba
Balearics
Sardinia
BYZANTINE EMPIRE
Athens
Taurus Mts
Sicily
SYRIA
Crete
Cyprus
Damascus
Mediterranean Sea
Atlas Mts
Jerusalem
EGYPT
Muslim Possessions
Viking Possessions
Earlier Danish Raids
Earlier Norwegian Raids
Earlier Swedish Raids
Miles 0 500

DOMINVS ECCLESIAE
CONSER PVDENTI
VATOR ANAE
L

# Part II
# Growth and Change in the Middle Ages

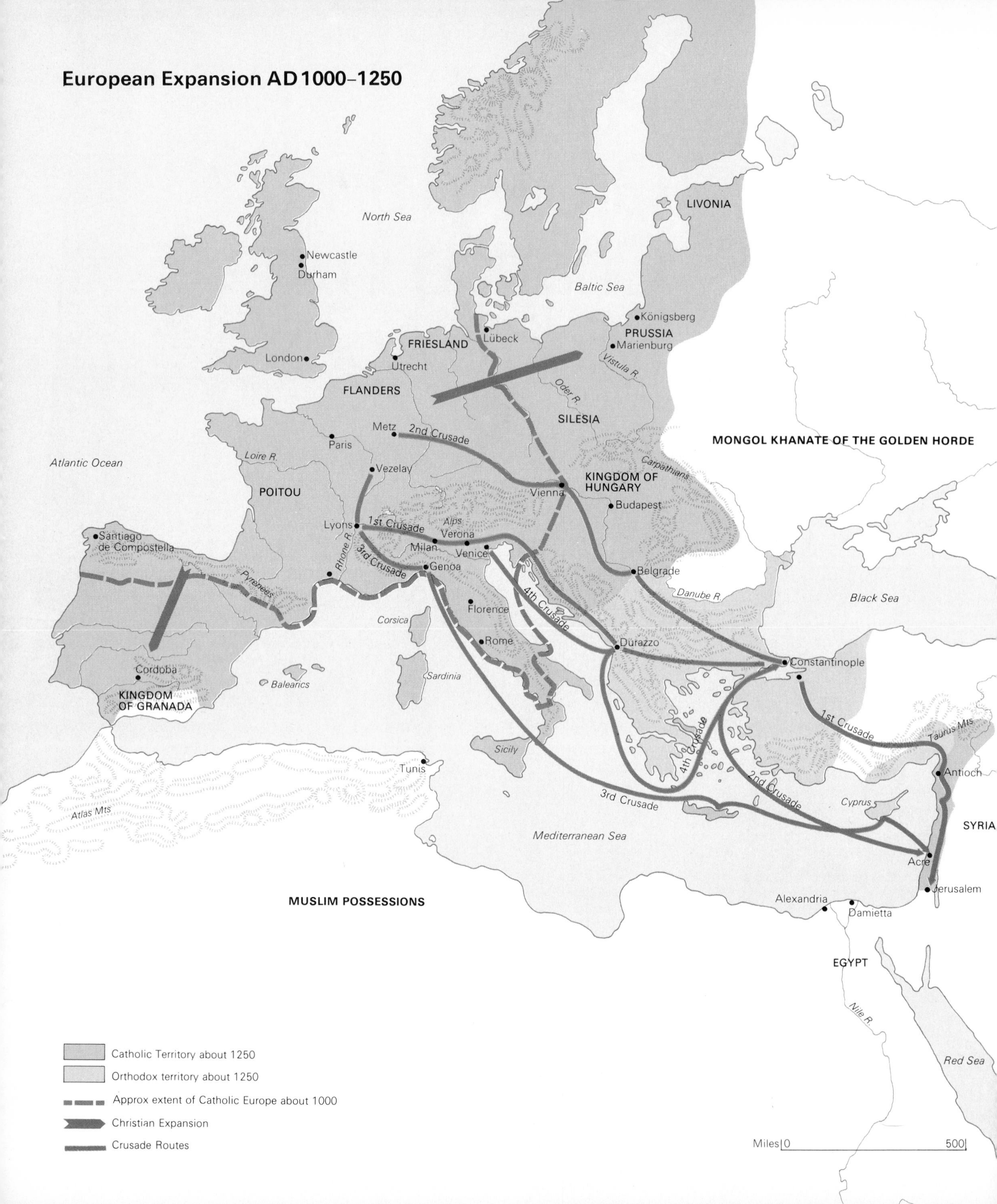

European Expansion AD 1000–1250
North Sea
Newcastle
Durham
London
Baltic Sea
LIVONIA
Königsberg
PRUSSIA
Marienburg
Vistula R.
FRIESLAND
Lübeck
Utrecht
FLANDERS
Oder R.
SILESIA
Metz
2nd Crusade
Paris
MONGOL KHANATE OF THE GOLDEN HORDE
Atlantic Ocean
Loire R.
Vezelay
Carpathians
KINGDOM OF HUNGARY
Vienna
POITOU
Budapest
Lyons
1st Crusade
Alps
Verona
Santiago de Compostella
Milan
Venice
Rhone R.
3rd Crusade
Genoa
Belgrade
Pyrenees
Danube R.
Black Sea
Florence
4th Crusade
Corsica
Rome
Durazzo
Constantinople
Cordoba
Sardinia
Balearics
KINGDOM OF GRANADA
1st Crusade
Taurus Mts
4th Crusade
Sicily
Tunis
Antioch
2nd Crusade
3rd Crusade
Cyprus
Atlas Mts
SYRIA
Mediterranean Sea
Acre
Jerusalem
MUSLIM POSSESSIONS
Alexandria
Damietta
EGYPT
Nile R.
Red Sea
Catholic Territory about 1250
Orthodox territory about 1250
Approx extent of Catholic Europe about 1000
Christian Expansion
Crusade Routes
Miles 0 500

Chapter 5

# THE YEARS OF GROWTH 1000-1250

## THE YEAR 1000

There was little cause for optimism in Western Europe in the tenth century. The continent was still in the throes of a series of external assaults which had shattered its defenses and undermined its social and political organization over the last two centuries. The very future of Western Christendom was still in doubt: at best, it might survive as a landlocked, underdeveloped, besieged continent; at worst, it might be overrun by its enemies and its tenuous links with its Roman and Christian traditions be finally broken.

The enemy was closing in on all sides. In the south, the Mediterranean—which the Romans had so proudly called "our sea"—was firmly under the control of the Arabs, and its trade was thereby stifled. Sicily had been conquered by the Saracens, and so had almost the whole of Spain. Marauding bands of Saracens were plundering the cities of mainland Italy and waylaying pilgrims and merchants in the Alpine passes. In the east, the Magyars presented an equally forbidding threat. Their skill as horsemen was unparalleled, and their lust for plunder insatiable. The sphere of their raids encompassed the whole of Western and Central Europe, from the gates of Kiev to those of Nimes in southern France and from the rich abbeys of Lorraine to the richer valleys of northern Italy. The Vikings were the terror of the northern seas. Indeed, the Vikings were the most persistent and successful of all the raiders on Europe's frontiers, for they came not only as plunderers in search of wealth but also as settlers in search of land. They set up a duchy for themselves in Normandy in France and a kingdom in Dublin; they conquered the islands and highlands of western Scotland and colonized extensively in eastern England. In 1016 the greatest prize of all came their way when King Canute added the crown of England itself to the long list of Viking conquests.

The prospects for Europe at the outset of the eleventh century were very gloomy politically and militarily; they were equally gloomy culturally and psychologically. Western Europe's culture was little more than the tattered and half-understood remains of the classical and Christian heritage of the past; its monasteries, which had been its outstanding cultural outposts, were now the obvious targets of marauding raiders and greedy princes; its kings were regarded as barbarian upstarts in the cultured courts of Christian Byzantium and Moslem Spain; its cities were mere villages when compared with the splendors of Con-

| 950 AD | 1050 | 1150 | 1250 |
|---|---|---|---|
| Otto I crushes Magyar threat (955); Canute King of England (1016–35) | Normans conquer England (1066) | | |
| E. Europe converted to Christianity | Gradual Christian reconquest of Northern Spain | | |
| German wars against Slavs and Poles | Growth of trading cities in Italy | | |
| | Western colonization of Eastern Europe (to 1350) | | |
| | 1st Crusade (1096) | 2nd Crusade (1147); 3rd Crusade (1189) | 4th Crusade (1202) |

# The Normans

William the Conqueror and Henry I, from a fourteenth-century manuscript. The Norman kings of England provided a century of firm government and outward-looking policy.

At the end of the eighth century, the Vikings began their dramatic outburst from Scandinavia and quickly became the terror of Europe. Places as far apart as Constantinople and Dublin, Pisa and Cadiz, knew the horror of their swift raids. Their fierce-prowed ships reached Iceland and even Vinland (as the Vikings called America). The plea "From the fury of the Northmen, Good Lord deliver us," was offered up in the Litany. While the people prayed for deliverance, their rulers did their best to protect their lands. Sometimes they fought the Vikings, at other times they tried to bribe them. In France one of the last of the Carolingian rulers, Charles the Simple, a weak and ineffectual king, made a treaty with the Vikings in 911 at Clair-sur-Epte. This treaty made a virtue of necessity by granting the Vikings the area around the Lower Seine, in which they had already settled. Thus the Duchy of Normandy, which became the home of the Vikings, was born.

With these origins it is hardly surprising that the Normans were a vigorous, adventure-loving people, but they had in addition a tremendous ability to adapt themselves to the life of the countries that they conquered, and to develop the countries' institutions to their own ends. This ability eventually led to the loss of their separate identity. Once established in Normandy, the Northmen changed from a group of pirate bands into a feudal society. Although they were still turbulent, they were soon stronger than any other group in France. They were a prolific race, and because their adopted system of inheritance left the younger children in a family without any land, they were also land hungry. This problem could only be solved by new conquests, and so there occurred their spectacular conquests of England and Sicily.

Tancred de Hauteville was a Norman knight with a modest estate and many sons. What distinguished his family from many similar ones was that it carved out and created the Norman principality in southern Italy and Sicily. Tancred's grandson, Roger II of Sicily, ruled the most mature and absolute state in western Europe. Nothing shows more clearly the vigorous skill and initiative of the Normans. Southern Italy was ruled by the Byzantine Empire and Sicily by the Moslem Arabs, when a handful of Normans first arrived to fight as mercenaries. Rapidly, in a series of bandit-like adventures they gained control of their former masters and drove them from their lands. Robert Guiscard was the greatest of Tancred's sons. As a brigand leader he was not above staging a mock funeral in order to get his followers inside the walls of a town that he wanted to attack. By such cunning he became the ruler of all southern Italy before his death in 1085, and even had his position recognized by the papacy. So the Normans established their principality. They also proved that they could govern it. They were excellent administrators and statesmen. They exploited to the full the rich, varied culture that they found and were successful in welding the heterogeneous population of Greeks, Arabs and native Sicilians into an efficient state. The kingdom was taxed and administered by a centralized network of officials, and all the different races were eligible without prejudice. The Normans mixed and intermarried with their subjects. Hence they benefitted to the full from the heritage of their land. Under this influence the king lived in eastern luxury and splendor at his court in Palermo. Frederick II even surrounded himself with a harem and eunuchs.

In England the Norman achievement was less spectacular, but it was more lasting. The conquest of 1066 was a more organized affair than the rather haphazard conquest of Sicily. Far more men were involved, and the expedition was led by the Norman duke, William. He had been lucky to survive at all, for when his father had died he had been only seven years old, and he was also illegitimate. Despite the unruliness of his barons, he had succeeded in pacifying his own lands. He began to plan the invasion of England, which was ruled by his kinsman, Edward the Confessor, who had no direct heirs. After Edward's death he landed and beat his rival for the throne, Harold, at the battle of Hastings. He preserved many features of Anglo-Saxon government which helped to create one of the strongest kingdoms in Europe. The Norman achievement merely underlines the chameleon-like qualities of adaptability that the Normans possessed.

stantinople or Córdoba; and its social and political organizations manifested the breakdown of public authority. Whatever its own pretensions may have been, Europe in 1000 was a barbarian continent in the eyes of civilized observers. Furthermore, it was a continent which lived with a deep conviction of the impending end of the world: "We who have been placed at the end of time," as one bishop put it. Once the Roman Empire finally ended, so contemporaries believed, the reign of Antichrist would begin; and the accumulated fears associated with the year 1000 and the news of the destruction of the Holy Sepulchre in 1009 seemed to indicate that the last days were indeed at hand. The real fears of heathen invasions from without were matched by an equally real inward conviction that the end of the world was nigh.

## NEW FRONTIERS

Already by 1000 the battle for the survival of Europe had, in fact, been won, even if the victory remained to be secured. In the east, the Magyars suffered a crushing defeat at the hands of Otto I at the battle of the Lech in 955, and henceforth they ceased to be a serious threat to Europe. Instead, they settled down to a more sedentary, agricultural life and to the establishment of a kingdom of their own in Hungary. In the south, the Arab control of the Mediterranean was increasingly and successfully challenged by the naval power of the Italian cities, and the supply lines of the Arab kingdoms in Spain were broken. In the north, the great waves of Scandinavian invasions had temporarily stopped, and when they were resumed at the end of the tenth century, the Vikings were much more prepared to be assimilated into the cultural and religious life of Christian Europe.

Not only had Europe survived; it was increasingly switching to the offensive in its relations with the outside world. In that offensive the skill of the warrior was forged with the zeal of the Christian, and wars were thereby converted into holy campaigns for the propagation of the faith. Europe had entered the age of the crusade, the age of the Church militant.

### The Reconquest of Spain

The offensive began in Spain. For three centuries almost the whole of Spain had been ruled by the Moslem caliphs from their capital of Córdoba, whose beautiful mosque—now the cathedral—remains as a standing tribute to the splendor of their civilization. Their rule had on the whole been highly tolerant and enlightened, but in the mid-eleventh century the kings of the small Christian states of northern Spain took the initiative in a crusade of reconquest against the Moslems. It was a long-drawn-out crusade, lasting for over four centuries. Christian warriors came from across the Pyrenees to seek adventure and eternal salvation in the holy war against the infidels. Spain became a land fit for heroes and a worthy setting for heroic literature.

The *Song of Roland*, one of the greatest and most popular of medieval epics, took the struggle between Saracen and Christian on the borders of Spain as its theme, and one of the heroes of the reconquest, the great Castilian warrior El Cid (c. 1040–1099), became the central figure in a great poem of the twelfth century. The *Song of Roland* and the *Poem of the Cid* are the literary products of an aggressive Europe confident of its faith and of its military prowess. And in this story of aggression the aid of the saints was summoned to strengthen the hands of the heroes: one of the tympana of the great pilgrim church of Santiago (St James) at Compostella displays the saint himself busily slaughtering the Moslems, and the legends of St George likewise attributed to him and his white horse a central role in the defeat of the infidel in Spain.

The occupations of the months, from an eleventh-century calendar. Agriculture was the way of life of most of the population of Europe during the Middle Ages. In most places the economy was a subsistence one, providing little more than the bare necessities of life for the farmers. This was due partly to technological backwardness—heavy plows were only introduced late in the Middle Ages—and partly to inefficient techniques. The disruption caused to the agricultural economy by war and invasion was enormous: men who were needed on the land had to go and fight and crops were damaged or stolen.

By 1250 the reconquest of Spain was virtually complete, and only the emirate of Granada remained under Moslem control. Spain was once more firmly part of Christian Europe; indeed, it was to become more intolerantly Christian than any other country in Europe.

### Conquest and Colonization in Germany

Spain was one of the borderlands of Christendom; the eastern frontier of Germany was another. And here also the men of Europe—princes, soldiers, monks, and settlers—were displaying their new-found confidence. By 1350 the map of medieval Germany was dramatically extended by the conquest and colonization of an area equivalent to two-thirds of the Germany of 1100. This German movement eastward was quite as dramatic and as far-reaching in its effects as the opening up of the American West in the nineteenth century, and like that movement, it often rode roughshod over the rights—and lives—of the native population. It took the borders of Germany from the River Elbe to the River Oder and beyond. It was the establishment of new towns, such as Lübeck (1143) and Königsberg (1255); villages and hamlets sprouted by the thousands—over 1,200 were founded in Silesia alone in a mere 150 years. Settlers flocked from the overcrowded towns of Flanders and Germany to colonize the virgin lands of the east, attracted by the low rents and liberal terms offered by the landlords.

Much of the colonization was peaceful, but occasionally the native population proved recalcitrant and had to be bludgeoned into submission both to their new landlords and to their new religion. Nowhere was this more obviously so than in Prussia and Livonia, where the Teutonic Order, a body of knights bound by monastic vows, asserted their authority and their religion in a series of brutal crusades. The Order's massive castle at Marienburg on the River Vistula demon-

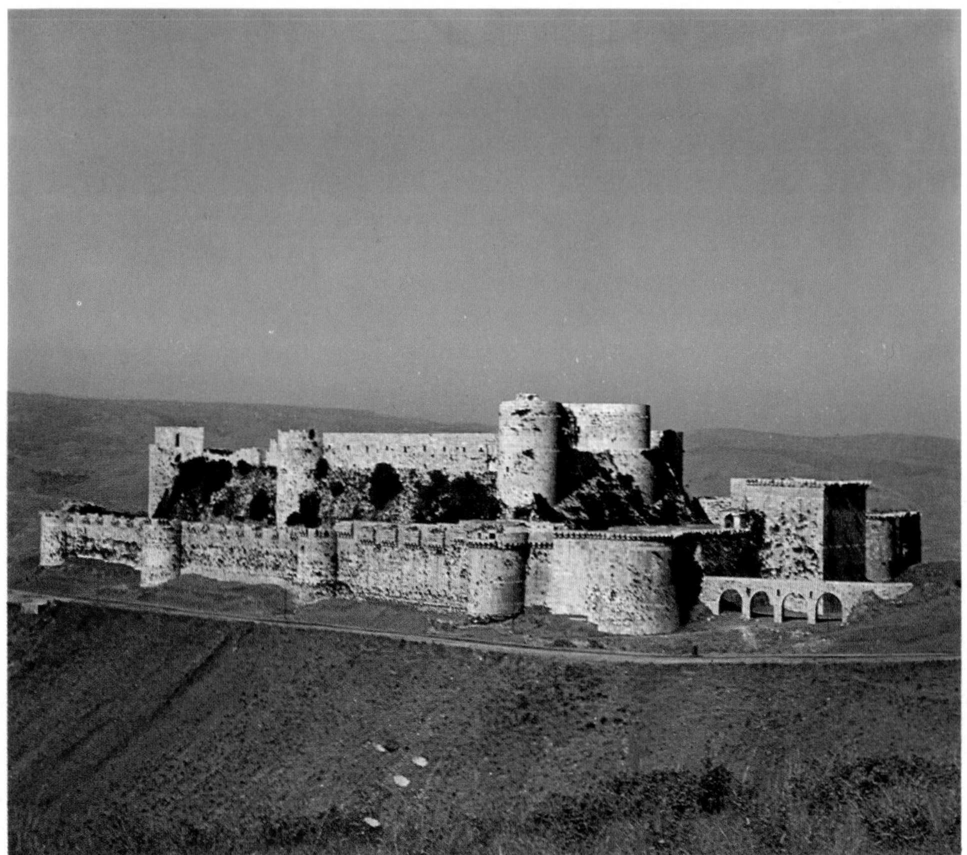

Krak des Chevaliers from the southwest. The crusading movement restored Palestine to Christendom but this created enormous problems of defense. From across the Syrian desert, from the depths of Arabia, and from Egypt the Christian kingdoms and counties were vulnerable. Lack of manpower led to the formation of semi-monastic orders of knights who dedicated their life to the protection of the Holy Land and of pilgrims. They built dozens of castles, of which Crak is the largest and most impressive, in a vain effort to hold back the Muslim counter-attack on Jerusalem, a city as holy to Islam as it was to Christianity.

strated quite clearly to the natives that this race of Christian warriors ruled firmly and ruled by the sword.

### Crusades Overseas: The Holy Land

Just as Europe was rapidly pushing back its frontiers in Spain and eastern Germany, so was it also asserting its mastery of the Mediterranean. In the eleventh century the Italian cities wrested the control of the sea from the Arab fleets and the Normans brought Sicily once more within the fold of Christian Europe.

Now that the control of the Mediterranean was assured, the warriors of Europe lifted their sights even higher. What nobler vision could there be for the knights of Christ than to take up the Cross and win back the Holy places of their Lord? The frontiers of Europe were now to be extended to the Holy Land itself; Europe indeed was looking outward. On July 15, 1099, the crusaders marched into Jerusalem, their mission achieved. A series of crusader kingdoms were established in the Holy Land, and the institutions of Western Europe were transplanted for the first time onto alien soil. Even today, the mood of militant confidence that inspired the knights of Europe to such feats can be recaptured in the ruins of the great crusader castle of Krak des Chevaliers (Castle of the Knights). Europe was asserting itself overseas.

The attempt was premature, for within less than two centuries the crusader kingdoms had collapsed. Jerusalem had been lost within a hundred years. But this did not deter the Europeans from establishing another new frontier overseas; they took Constantinople in 1204. The Byzantines were not heretics, but they were schismatics and the Westerners therefore regarded them as a fair target for their crusading zeal and territorial ambitions. The capture of Constantinople was the seal on Europe's expansionist drive; the great capital of the Eastern Empire and the

A scribe at work. Until the beginnings of printing in the fifteenth century the only way in which books would reach a wide audience was by making copies by hand. The cost of this laborious process ensured that books were a rare and expensive commodity, and that literacy was the preserve of a tiny minority. The Church was the home of the educated, and it was in monastic houses that most books were copied. Medieval scribes and illuminators showed an amazing attention to detail and pictures in their manuscripts are often a valuable historical source, showing how people lived.

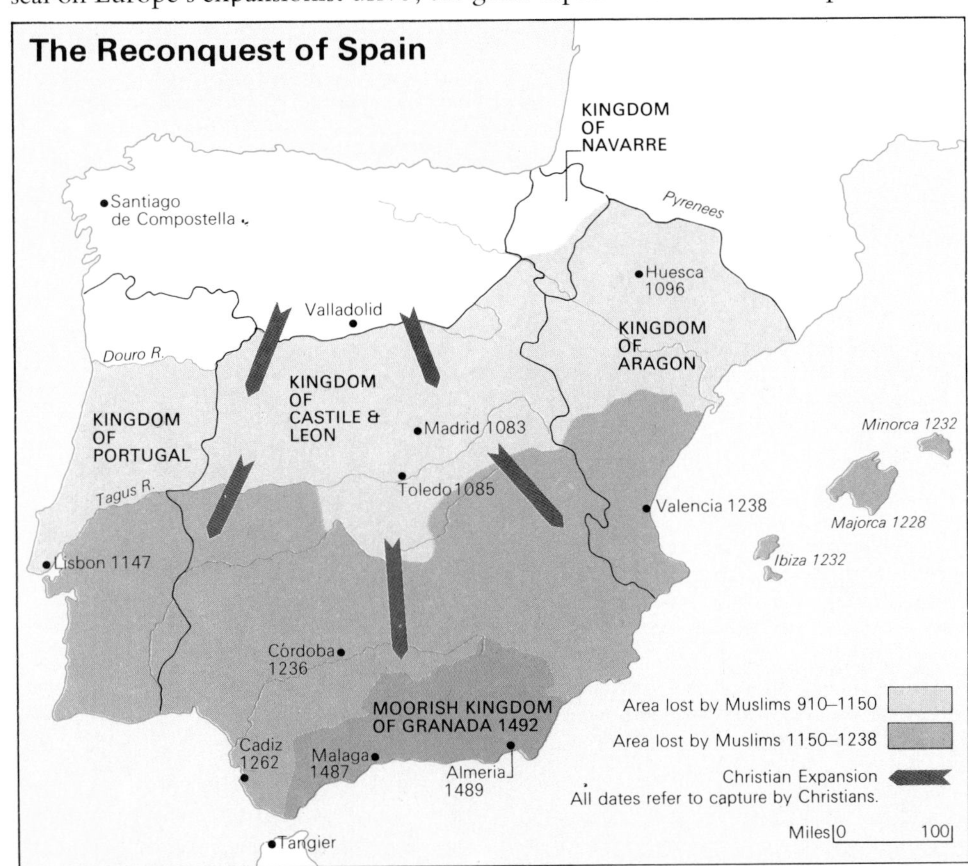

# Recapture of Jerusalem

Crusading warfare in the Middle Ages. The expansion of Christendom eastward into the Holy Land, and Byzantine Empire and the Baltic countries, and southward into Spain, put great pressure onto Europe's economy. Fighting methods had to develop: for example the longbow *(above)* provided a more efficient weapon than the crossbow: naval attacks became more efficient *(right above)*; armor, and in particular helmets, developed and was strengthened—sometimes at the cost of mobility (far right above); siege weapons, largely ignored since Roman times, once again became important (far right below). But, despite all developments, men died: the funeral of France's St Louis IX in 1270 *(below right)*.

The crusading movement was at its peak in the twelfth century. The reasons for its popularity are not hard to find. By going on crusade a man could satisfy his religious fervor as well as his desire to fight. Thus the laity, and especially the military aristocracy, was given an ideal opportunity to serve the Church. Men could attack the heathen, enjoy the excitement of battle, perhaps win some land, and at the same time assure their spiritual future. The East was famed for its riches, and many an uneducated knight must have dreamed of the streets of Jerusalem being paved with gold and probably flowing with milk and honey as well.

In November 1095 Pope Urban II launched the first crusade. He appealed to Christians to take up arms to recapture Jerusalem from the Moslems. He had been prompted by an appeal for help from Alexius Comnenus, the Byzantine emperor, who was troubled by Turkish attacks. The relief of Constantinople was, however, a secondary issue to the crusaders. Jerusalem, where Jesus was crucified, was their main objective. Why this sudden enthusiasm to recapture a town that had not been in Christian hands for over four centuries? Alexius' appeal was the result of the invasions of the Turks, who disrupted the stability of the Middle East. He wanted mercenaries to help him retake Asia Minor. In the event he got more than he asked for. He was like a man who prays for rain only to find himself swept away in a flood.

Urban himself was unprepared for and suprised by the results of his appeal. From all over Europe men set out in groups, usually led by local lords such as Count Raymond of Toulouse and Bohemund, the son of Robert Guiscard of Sicily. They made their way separately to Constantinople. First to arrive in 1096 was a rabble of ill-armed peasants, including many women and children, who had been roused by Peter the Hermit, a fanatical preacher. Alexius watched their riotous behavior with fascinated horror. As soon as he could, he shipped them out to Asia Minor, where they quickly met a sorry end, butchered by the Turks in their first battle. The main body of crusaders was slightly more orderly, but from the beginning there was no love lost between them and the Greeks. They envied the Greeks, and were regarded by them as uncouth barbarians. Alexius quickly moved the crusaders on. Undaunted by hardship, they made the long journey through Asia Minor, and captured Antioch in Syria without a fight. But once in the city they fell victim to plague and were attacked by a Turkish army. Their spirits were restored by the miraculous discovery of the holy lance that had pierced Jesus' side on the cross. With this carried before them they drove off the Turks. On June 28, 1098, they entered Jerusalem after a fierce battle. Their goal was achieved. In a fever of joy they massacred the Jewish and Muslim inhabitants of the city.

Land won had also to be governed. By 1100 four feudal states had been set up, at Antioch, Edessa, Tripoli and Jerusalem. Many of the crusaders had returned home, and defense became a problem. The long desert frontier was difficult to protect, even after the construction of a chain of huge castles. The military orders of the Hospitallers and Templars were too undermanned to hold the frontier. In 1144 Edessa fell. A second crusade was sent out, but proved to be disastrous. The disunity that had characterized the Moslems at the time of the first crusade had vanished. The Turkish leader Saladin united the Muslim world in 1174. In 1187 he captured the city of Jerusalem. The third crusade, under leaders such as Richard Coeur de Lion (the Lionheart), proved unable to recover the city.

The hostility in religious matters that existed between Rome and Constantinople made further efforts at crusading into little more than pirate raids. The fourth crusade in 1204 concentrated on the capture of Constantinople instead of Jerusalem. The weakness of the Byzantine Empire in the later Middle Ages was largely a result of this. Jerusalem remained in Muslim hands until the twentieth century.

BELLVM·INTER·

gateway to the Black Sea and thereby to the trade of central Asia was now in Western hands. And so it remained, along with much of Greece, for the next fifty years. The borders of Western Christendom had reached the Bosporus. In whatever direction we look, the map of Europe had been transformed between 1000 and 1250. The frontiers had been pushed outward. Furthermore, those countries on Europe's periphery which in earlier centuries had presented such a threat to its safety—Scandinavia, Poland, Bohemia, and Hungary—were now firmly integrated within the structure of Western Christendom. By 1250 this great movement of European expansion, comparable in so many ways to European expansion overseas from the sixteenth century onward, was drawing to its close. By then it was clear that the Europeans had overreached themselves in their attempt to open a new frontier in the eastern Mediterranean, while in eastern and central Europe the remarkable growth of Mongol power had closed the frontier to further expansion in that area. Nevertheless, almost all the territorial gains which had been made in the last two centuries were retained, and in the process the map of Europe had assumed the shape that it was to keep for many centuries ahead.

The sanctuary knocker at Durham Cathedral, England. In the Middle Ages a criminal had a right to protection for a limited time (usually forty days) if he took refuge in a church. Since the criminal had to take an oath of abjuration and to leave the country within forty days, this right was only used for serious crimes. Normally it was sufficient for a criminal to take refuge in a church, but in some churches it was necessary to touch the altar, a sanctuary-stool, or some other object. At Durham the criminal had to touch the knocker on the north door.

## INTELLECTUAL EXPANSION

The saga of European expansion from 1000 to 1250 was more than a matter of geography. It brought Western Christendom face to face with the challenge of other cultures and other religions, and it thereby profoundly affected Europe's intellectual development. The response to the challenge varied. For the most part, it was a response of complete incomprehension and intolerance. The incomprehension sprang in good measure from the inferiority that Westerners must have felt when confronted with the far superior civilizations of Muslim Spain and Orthodox Byzantium. The intolerance was much more dangerous; it sprang from the Westerners' conviction that whatever they lacked by way of polish in their culture was more than made up by the orthodoxy and zeal of their faith. It was a zeal which justified and even encouraged massacres and brutality on a massive scale, whether by the Teutonic Knights against the pagan Prussians or by the crusading armies against the Muslims of Spain and the Holy Land.

Yet there was more to the relations between Western Europe and the outside world than an aggressive religious intolerance. There was even an attempt on the part of a few scholars to base their knowledge of Muslim religion on a surer basis than that of prejudice. It was in this spirit that the abbot of Cluny commissioned a translation of the Koran from the Englishman, Robert of Kertan. The great scholar Roger Bacon went so far as to suggest that the gap between Muslim and Christian should be and could be bridged by teaching and preaching. Such enlightened tolerance was very much the exception, not the rule; but there was bound to be at least a good measure of mutual influence, especially in those areas where Christian and Muslim communities coexisted, as they did in Spain and the Holy Land. It has been suggested, for example, that the etiquette of Western chivalry was deeply influenced by knowledge of the customs of Muslim noblemen. Even more significantly, the pointed arch, which is such a central feature of the Gothic style of Western Europe, is seen by some art historians as a direct borrowing from Muslim architecture by way of the crusading armies.

But it was, above all, in the field of scholarship that Islam had a great deal to teach the Western world, and in spite of their religious scruples, the Westerners learned avidly. Not only did the Arab world produce great thinkers of its own, such as Avicenna (980–1037) and Averroes (1126–98), whose works were studied by Western scholars, but it was also via the Arabs that medieval Europe once more recovered the scientific and philosophical writings of ancient Greece, especially those of Aristotle, Euclid, Galen, and Hippocrates. The scholars of Europe traveled to Sicily and Spain, the two most important meeting points of Christian and Moslem culture, in order to translate the Greek classics into Latin from Arab manuscripts. In Sicily in particular, they could find scribes who knew Greek, Arabic, and Latin, as contemporary manuscript illustrations show. In the early years of the twelfth century, for example, an English scholar, Adelard of Bath, traveled in Sicily, Spain, and even the Near East in search of manuscripts, and among his many enterprises he discovered and translated an Arabic version of Euclid's *Elements*.

This process of translation from Arabic and Greek sources was of momentous importance for Europe's intellectual development, for the corpus of Greek, and in particular of Aristotelian, learning became the basis of university syllabuses in Europe for the next five centuries. The works so translated were, of course, non-Christian in character, and it was to be one of the great intellectual achievements of thirteenth-century Europe that its leading scholars, such as Albert the Great or Thomas Aquinas, were able to integrate the newly acquired learning of ancient Greece with orthodox Christian theology. Looked at from this angle, the European expansion of the twelfth and thirteenth centuries was much more than a matter of crusades and new frontiers; it was equally a process of intellectual expansion and particularly of the reconquest of Greek thought. And in that process the Arab and Jewish philosophers had played the vital role of intermediaries.

Eleventh-century masons at work. During the Middle Ages, as architectural styles grew increasingly complex, and as the size of churches grew too, stone-masons tended to form associations. Conditions of work were uncomfortable and dangerous, and the associations sought to alleviate these problems. The secret masonic lodges of our own day are the descendants of those early trade unions.

No single incident sums up more vividly these twin processes of geographical and intellectual expansion than a meeting which took place in 1254 at the court of the Khan, the king of the Mongols, in central Asia. There William of Moerbeke, a Flemish philosopher, debated with a Muslim, a Buddhist, and a Nestorian Christian about the validity of their respective faiths—and he floored all three of them by his use of Aristotelian logic. The location of the meeting and the result of the debate epitomize both the adventurousness and the intellectual confidence of Western Europeans during their first age of expansion.

## THE GROWTH OF MONARCHICAL POWER

Europe's external expansion in the period 1000 to 1250 was matched by profound changes in its social and political structure. In 1000 its political organization was of the loosest kind; it was an unhappy amalgam of Roman traditions on the one hand and barbarian institutions on the other. The gap between theoretical claims and practical power was immense, and nowhere more so than in the central institution of kingship. The pretensions of kings were very great indeed: Otto III (983–1002) even called himself "august emperor of the world" and engraved the words "Renewal of the Roman Empire" on his seal. These fine words were not borne out by political reality. Kingdoms were breaking up, and new ones were proliferating. New royal houses were usurping the place of old ones, as happened in France in 987 and in England in 1016. Monarchical power was proving increasingly ineffective in its twin duties of dispensing justice and providing defense, and more and more of the reality of power was passing into the hands of local nobles and ecclesiastics. Contemporaries were well aware that Otto III's words were, indeed, vain boasts. "Today," remarked one of them, "instead of kings we have kinglets; instead of kingdoms, mere fragments. . . . The state is on the verge of collapse."

And yet it did not collapse. On the contrary, there was in many respects a remarkable resurgence in royal authority between 1000 and 1250. The state, through its king, came to occupy an increasingly important role in the life of Europe. How did this come about? In the first place, monarchs, however weak they might be, never allowed their subjects to overlook the fact that their power was

# Universities

*Above:* A musician and a dancer. *Right:* St Thomas Aquinas, the *Doctor Angelicus* (angelic doctor) of the medieval Church, by Francesco Traini. Aquinas, a Dominican friar, was the most important of all medieval theologians. He managed to incorporate much of the teaching of the classical philosopher Aristotle into the Church's teaching without being condemned for heresy. His *Summa Theologica,* perhaps the most significant work of systematic theology ever written, shows a masterly grasp and great intellectual flexibility. Although the *Summa* was left unfinished at the time of Aquinas' death in 1274, it was accepted as the official teaching of the Roman Catholic Church in 1879.

Modern students might well be surprised if they were spirited back in time to the thirteenth century to glimpse the young universities of Paris or Oxford. In some ways students life has changed little: then as now, some students were poverty-stricken, others frittered away time on sensual rather than intellectual pleasures. Yet to modern eyes it would appear strange that there were no imposing buildings, libraries or lecture halls. Instead rooms were hired for lectures, and the university was not restricted to any one place. This made a mass migration to a different city easy to accomplish, if any difficulty arose, for the university consisted only of the community of masters and students. Moreover since Latin was the lingua franca throughout Europe, medieval students of all ages, could wander between universities as they pleased.

The twelfth century was a time of cultural and intellectual renaissance. In France most cathedrals had schools; some schools, such as Orleans, Chartres and Paris, rose to prominence because of the fame of their teachers. It was the teacher who made the school, and on his death, students would often move to another, somewhere else. Paris, however, gained permanent popularity through a series of famous masters, who drew flocks of students to the city. Of these Peter Abelard (1079–1142) was the greatest. As a student he drew attention to the flaws in the reasoning of his master, William of Champeaux. This endeared him to his fellows, but hardly to his master!

In the late twelfth century, the masters of the school at Paris' Cathedral of Notre Dame formed themselves into a private corporation, like a town guild, to regulate teaching and to prevent charlatans from practicing; thus the university was born. From the first it was under the authority of the chancellor of the cathedral who although not a member of the corporation, granted the teaching licenses. Gradually, inception into the masters' association, when a new master was officially recognized by his fellow, became as necessary for teachers as the chancellor's license.

Most universities benefitted from the protection and patronage of a monarch or the papacy, and Paris gained formal privileges from both. The Capetian kings and the popes aided the young university in its struggles to free itself from the chancellor, and from the provost of Paris. Its first charter of privilege was gained in Philip II's reign as a result of the first of many "town and gown" disturbances. A brawl in a tavern, during which students beat up the proprietor, was followed by an armed attack on a student hostel by the provost and other citizens. Several students were killed. Appeals to the King brought Philip firmly down on the side of the university, and the Parisians had henceforth to respect its privileges. A similar tavern brawl in 1229 resulted in the dispersion of the whole university from Paris. It reassembled in a few years with increased privileges but in the meantime, many students had crossed to England, swelling the younger foundations of Oxford and Cambridge. Both these universities developed in a fashion similar to Paris, yet with characteristic academic patriotism and in total disregard of the facts some historians of Oxford have attributed its foundation to King Alfred, and Cambridge, not to be outdone, has been known to claim the legendary King Arthur as a benefactor.

Paris was the great center of theological teaching, but the two other earliest universities were Salerno and Bologna, specializing respectively in medicine and legal studies. Bologna differed from northern European foundations in that it had a corporation of students rather than masters, with the result that the latter fell into a state of such subservience that they were fined by the students if they began lectures late. They could not even marry without student consent, although as most were clerics this was not often a problem.

The subject choice at a medieval university was narrow, but the course was broad. A student began in the faculty of arts, where the principal subject of study was logic or dialectic, a legacy from the ancient world. It took about seven years to become a master of arts, and a scholar might then progress to one of the three superior faculties: medicine, law or theology. To complete one's studies at this level could take as long as fifteen years. Of all the pagan classical writers studied it was Aristotle, known simply as "the Philosopher," who had the greatest influence. The reintroduction of the main corpus of his work into western Europe, during the thirteenth century, had the most profound effect on intellectual development, and also caused much controversy. The majority of Aristotle's writing had been lost to the West until it was rediscovered, via Arabic philosophers, mainly through increased contact with the Arab world in Spain. Toledo became a great center of translation and the "new" Aristotle burst upon Europe, opening whole new realms of knowledge. Yet because it came via the Arab philosophers, Averroës and Avicenna, and intermingled with their writings, some of the most anti-Christian elements of Aristotle were emphasized, such as the denial of individual immortality. As a result Aristotelianism was banned by the Church as heretical, and at Paris its teaching was forbidden. That this state of affairs did not endure was principally the result of the work of St Thomas Aquinas (c. 1225–1274). He more than anyone made Aristotle acceptable, and pressed his work into the service of the Church, so that it became an authoritative confirmation of the Catholic faith.

In some respects, as has been noted, student life through the ages has not varied greatly. Yet the medieval scholar did face additional hardships: his examinations were conducted orally in Latin and were sometimes so difficult that there were penalties for students who knifed the examiner. Teaching was by lecture and disputation, beginning very early in the day, and whilst the master commented laboriously on the prescribed texts, the students scribbled notes on scraps of parchment. Yet if they became bored they could move on. To travel from Oxford to Paris to hear a particular master was probably cheaper than buying one of his books. Books were extremely expensive because in the days before printing they had to be copied by hand. There are contemporary complaints of students gambling, drinking, love-making and rioting, but many successfully pursued their studies and the institutions of which they formed a part have survived as the greatest contribution of the middle ages to our educational heritage.

divinely ordained. Dukes, counts, and nobles owed their position, at least theoretically, to the king; the king owed his only to "the grace of God." At his coronation the king was anointed with holy oil as an expression of the sanctity of his power, and from this ceremony of anointing, the kings of France and England came to claim that they had the power to cure certain illnesses by the royal touch.

By such methods, the uniqueness of kingship was actively fostered. "Anointed kings," as one contemporary put it, "are not in the same position as mere lay people; they are above it." That in itself was a promising start, but a more substantial basis was needed for a real advance in royal power. In a landed society the only secure basis of power is land, and it was by consolidating their estates that kings normally enhanced their position. In France, for example, the kings increased the size of their estates fourfold between 1100 and 1300, and their authority grew commensurately. Gradually, in terms of his resources as well as in terms of his sanctity, the king was setting himself apart from the rest of his subjects. Nor did the growth of monarchical power end there, for the king's authority began to intrude increasingly into his subjects' lives and into their income. His judges took his justice to all corners of the land, and his court was the final court of appeal. His coins with his image on them circulated throughout the country, sometimes exclusively so. His armies were recruited on the basis of a claim that he could demand military service from all his able-bodied subjects. And increasingly he came to claim that he could also ask for a share of his subjects' wealth by way of taxation.

This growth of monarchical power was slow and fitful, and its pace was very uneven from one part of Europe to another. Yet the growth itself cannot be doubted. Nothing, perhaps, conveys it more vividly than the writs which the kings of England were dispatching by the thousands annually by 1250. The writ was a royal letter conveying a command from the king, often a command which expected a reply. The very numbers of these writs remind us that England was already a much-governed country. They remind us also that government depended increasingly not so much on the king's personal presence but on the delegation of his work to his servants, both professional and amateur. Finally, the fact that the writ was a written command reminds us that government had passed from the stage of oral command to that of written orders. In the process, the political community was gradually welded together more tightly into something that increasingly resembled a modern nation. "The king of France," said an observer at the end of the thirteenth century, "is both pope and emperor in his kingdom." That was a medieval man's way of saying that the king was truly sovereign in his realm. It was a far cry from the dishevelled state of affairs in 1000.

## THE DEVELOPMENT OF AN ARISTOCRACY

The centuries between 1000 and 1250 saw the establishment of monarchical power in a fashion that was to last in Europe until the end of the French Revolution; this period also saw the formation of a nobility and an aristocratic culture that was to be equally long-lived and influential. Europe in 1000 had no true nobility of blood. In most parts of the continent, life was too insecure and short for the effective establishment of noble families, and very few of the nobility had genealogies which extended beyond two or three generations. Military skill rather than gentility of blood was the hallmark of nobility. And it is not surprising that this should be so, for in an age of invasion and chronic insecurity, it was natural that pride of place should be given to those who were skillful in the arts of war. The nobles had no monopoly on the right to fight, but they were immediately and clearly distinguished from the common soldier by the fact that they alone fought

The crown of the Holy Roman Empire.

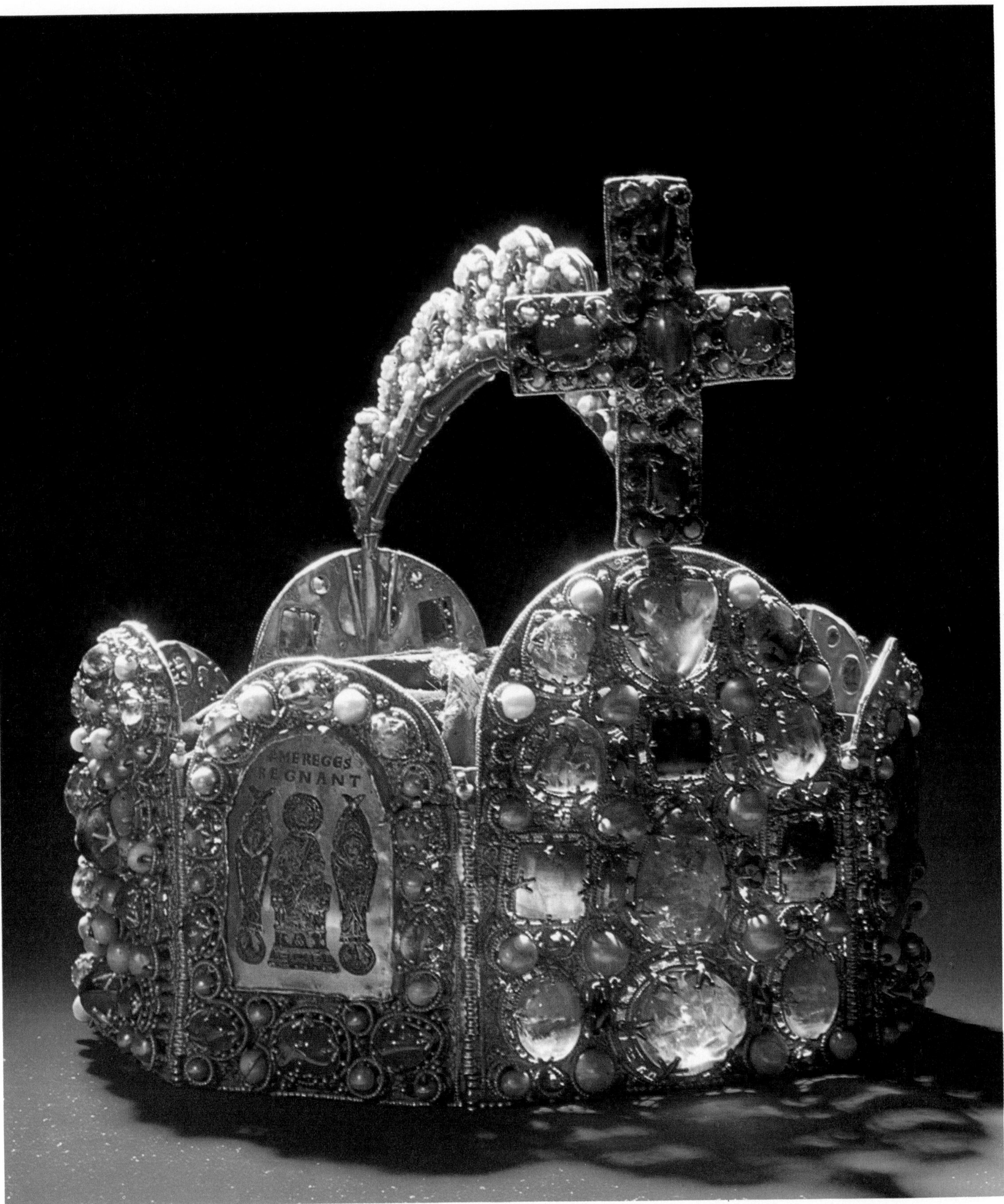
MEREGES
EGNANT

# Medieval Science and Technology

*Above:* Laborers building a wattled enclosure. This was probably for use as a sheep pen. Wattle was used for building houses as well as fences: it was covered with dried mud or clay, and could then withstand fairly severe weather. Few houses in the Middle Ages were built of brick or stone; wood or wattle and daub were far more common, because they were both cheaper and easier to use. Transporting goods by water *(right above)* and cart *(below right)*. Due to the high costs of transport, few goods traveled far from their point of manufacture. Long-distance transport was a rarity until the rise of Venice and the Hanseatic League to a dominant position in international trade. Most people's knowledge of the world extended no more than a few miles, and all that they bought was locally manufactured from locally produced materials. However, some trade existed: the east of England grew rich from wool exports and France exported large quantities of wine. For long distances, sea transport was cheaper than land transport and was also quicker.

It is not easy to put the contribution of medieval European civilization to science into perspective. Even the most enthusiastic medievalist would hardly claim that the years A.D. 300–1500 were a heroic age of scientific achievement. By contrast with the golden era of Greek science, the "Dark Ages" do indeed seem rather dark. However it is possible so to exaggerate the Glory that was Greece, and so to minimize medieval science, that both the decline of classical civilization, and the scientific Renaissance of the sixteenth and succeeding centuries, become inexplicable historical phenomena. In fact, they can both be seen as natural consequences of the evolution in social organization that occurred during the medieval period.

The primary contribution of medieval European civilization to science was that it progressively removed the social, economic and ideological barriers to scientific progress that classical civilization had erected. As it did so, it admittedly erected some barriers of its own. However, throughout the later medieval period (say from A.D. 1200) one can detect a "background noise of low technology," which gradually swelled up to a crescendo in the sixteenth century. The conceptual advances that mark the "scientific Renaissance" were built on this material basis.

The decline of Greek science had largely been due to internal inadequacies. Rome's contribution to science had been mainly technological. Bridges and aqueducts were built, but little scientific study had taken place. The establishment of Christianity and the disruption caused by barbarian and Islamic invasions virtually destroyed classical scientific knowledge. The early Church, emphasizing the importance of revealed truth and the imminence of the world's end, had little time for scientific interest. The distrust of "pagan" knowledge could lead to the destruction of libraries and of academies, such as that of Athens which was suppressed in 529. The warfare and social disruptions that took place in the fifth to tenth centuries destroyed so much that the destruction of books was unnoticed.

During this period of decline and fall, only a handful of classical texts were preserved in the West, and these were Latin compilations of the learning of the Greeks—notably Pliny's *Natural History*. These survivals were due to the Church, whose attitude to learning was ambiguous rather than wholly negative. Christian writers, such as Cassiodorus (died 526), Boethius (c. 475–525), and Isidore of Seville (c. 570–636), incorporated much from Aristotle, Euclid and Ptolemy in their own works. Irish monasteries and Benedictine abbeys built up libraries and became centers of learning, even during the darkest ages. Constantinople was a treasurehouse of manuscripts, many of which were brought to the west after the seizure of the city by the crusaders in 1204. More useful still was Arab science. In Moslem lands classical learning had survived, and from the eleventh century this began to reach the West, mainly through Muslim Spain. At first this new knowledge was received with suspicion. It was soon recognized, however, that there was no incompatibility between the classical scientific and biblical accounts of natural phenomena, and the search for scientific facts and explanations then became respectable. It did not at once become popular, a fact lamented by Roger Bacon (c. 1214–1294) who accused his academic contemporaries of "undue regard to authority, habit, prejudice and false conceit of knowledge."

The foundation of universities in the west and the revival of Aristotelianism provided a suitable background for a resurgence of scientific thought. The dialectical methods of Peter Abelard (1079–1142) were useful. In the early twelfth century Adelard of Bath held that to search for natural meaning did not detract from God. "Everything that exists does so because of him. But nature is not confused and without system, and so far as human knowledge has progressed it should be given a hearing. There should be recourse to God only when that fails." In the thirteenth century there was a great flowering of science. Roger Bacon emphasized the importance of experimentation. The court of the Emperor Frederick II was a center of interest in biology, of which Frederick's *Art of Falconry* with its detailed zoological introduction is an example.

Chemistry and astronomy tended to be dominated by alchemy and astrology, but nevertheless real advances were made. Techniques of distillation were improved, and alcoholic spirits made. Nitric and sulphuric acids were also discovered. The earth was regarded as the center of the universe, but Western astronomers realized that the earth was revolving. The main purpose of astronomical observation was for the construction of calendars, but other developments were made. For example in 1092 an Englishman, Walcher of Malvern, calculated the difference in longitude between England and Italy from the time of an eclipse. Trigonometry was developed in Oxford in the thirteenth century.

Other advances were made, particularly in the late Middle Ages. Science was again, as it had been in ancient Greece, of interest to scholars. Philosophical developments played a great part in making possible critical analysis of the newly available scientific works. "Occam's razor," the principle that "entities should not be multiplied unnecessarily," was introduced by the philosopher William of Occam (died c. 1350).

It would be wrong to overemphasize the advances made. Scientific attitudes took time to develop, and advances were not always accepted at once. On the methodological side, the answer seems to be that medieval scientists had not yet learned the technique described by Descartes as "dividing the question." They expected every new fact to fall into place in one vast conceptual scheme, modeled on their theology, and they were unreasonably impatient of small-scale partial theories which did not attempt to explain everything. On the social and economic side, medieval society was not yet sufficiently prosperous to afford scientific research. There was no large body of middle-class tradesmen. Kings did not bestow substantial patronage. On the intellectual side, it has to be recognized that to reconcile Greek and Christian theology at all was a heroic undertaking; in the process, Greek science was incorporated rather uncritically. It took a long time to identify and eliminate the nonsense.

on horseback. They were the knights, the cavalry elite of the armies of the day. Their leadership in war was their claim to nobility, and from leadership in war they passed easily and naturally to leadership in peace, to the control of land and the exercise of power. The European nobility of the eleventh century was most certainly a warrior aristocracy. We can see this clearly in the epic poetry of the time, which proudly recalls the nobility's feats in war. We can see it even more vividly in the Bayeux Tapestry, which provides a contemporary impression of the prowess of the Norman knights at the Battle of Hastings (1066).

The nobility of Europe in 1250 still retained this military aspect; the profession of arms was still the only vocation that a noble would deign to undertake. Indeed, he was expected to undertake it. Furthermore, his home was military in character, for the European nobility lived in castles, whether in the tower of the Italian towns or in the castles of the countryside of north Europe. Castle building began in Europe at the end of the tenth century, and by 1250 the continent was covered with castles. They evolved from the simple motte-and-bailey fort, which could be erected in a few days, such as may be seen at Berkhamsted, to the grand concentric castles, such as the one that the Earl of Gloucester built at Caerphilly in Wales. Their primary purpose of defense gradually gave place to an increasing emphasis on domestic comfort and architectural elaboration, but their presence in the countryside was still a reminder that prowess in war and defense was of the very essence of nobility. This military aspect is further revealed in the fact that it was as warriors that the nobility cared to be remembered in the seals on their letters and in the effigies on their tombs. Even in peacetime, their military tastes were catered to in the tournaments and jousts that became such a prominent feature of aristocratic society in the twelfth and thirteenth centuries.

### Courtly Love

The nobility of Europe still remained military warriors to some degree in 1250, but they were now more than that. They were a hereditary class whose claim to title was based on blood descent and whose pride in that descent was amply demonstrated in their coats of arms. They were united by a code of conduct that increasingly set them apart from the rest of society in peace as well as in war. Nowhere was this code stricter and more influential than in the rules it laid down for the noble's conduct toward women, and nowhere does the contrast between the nobility of the tenth and thirteenth centuries appear more clearly. There was little room for the woman in the desperately heroic world of the tenth and eleventh centuries; in the epic literature of the period, the place of women was at best inferior and peripheral. By 1250 this situation had been totally transformed, and in the noble circles of the time the woman was placed on a pedestal. It was in her honor that tournaments were fought, and the quest for the love of a noble lady became the consuming passion of knightly society.

It is little wonder that in literature, the epic, which had sung the praises of heroic warriors, was replaced by the romance, which treated of the virtues of noble ladies and which laid down an intricate code of courtly love for the instruction of the knight. Noble society was now distinctive not only in the way it fought but also in the way it lived and loved. Noble etiquette had been born, and this gentility of manners was to remain one of the most distinctive features of aristocratic society until the First World War. Furthermore, now that Europe was in every way more thoroughly integrated, this aristocratic code of conduct was truly international in character. Courtly love was as much the vogue in England as it was in southern France or Italy, and so was courtly literature. Nothing exemplifies this more clearly than the amazing way in which stories of King Arthur became the theme of a vast literature in every country in Medieval Europe. King Arthur was the idealization of heroic bravery and courtly chivalry; he epitomized the virtues of the European nobility of 1250.

## POPULATION GROWTH

Europe in 1250 was ruled by kings and nobles, but the roots of its wealth and the whole basis of its expansion lay in the lower orders of society. Its geographical expansion was made possible only by an even more remarkable economic expansion in agriculture and trade. The most fundamental manifestation of this economic expansion was a marked growth in population throughout Europe between 1000 and 1250. In England, for example, it has been calculated that the country's population as a whole increased fourfold and even possibly fivefold during this period, and in the case of the Flemish city of Ghent, the city boundaries had to be extended five times to cater for the growth of the population between 1163 and 1299. The story was the same in almost every part of Europe, even if the pace and chronology of the movement varied. As a result, Europe in 1250 was, in terms of an underdeveloped, preindustrial economy, a thickly populated continent: parts of the Lincolnshire fenlands, for example, had a population level in 1250 which was not regained until the nineteenth century; some Italian towns, such as Siena and San Gimignano, have in fact never recovered their peak medieval population levels.

### Colonization and Migration

In order to absorb this growth in population, more and more land had to be colonized for the first time in Europe's history. Old villages grew until they almost burst at the seams. Marshland was drained and forest cleared to provide new homes and new farming land. In the overpopulated districts of Europe, families were driven to migrate in search of cultivable land. In the fenlands of England, for example, about 100 square miles of land was inhabited for the first time between 1086 and 1350. In the lowlands of Poitou and in the Po Valley in Italy, marshy river valleys were put to the plow for the first time in history, while in Holland in the twelfth and thirteenth centuries, land hunger drove peasants to cultivate the salt marshes and to build dikes against the ravages of the sea. Massive as was this movement of internal colonization, it was not enough to cope with the increase in population, and so it was that the search for new land took the peoples of Europe beyond the old frontiers of the continent. It led to the colonization of eastern Germany beyond the Elbe and to the opening up of the interior of Spain. Prospectors in virgin land enticed settlers to come to live on the margins of Europe; Count Adolf of Holstein, so a contemporary account tells us, "sent messengers to every country, to Flanders and Holland, Utrecht, Westphalia, Friesland to invite anyone who was suffering from land hunger to come to receive ample and good land, fertile, well stocked with fish and flesh and good pasture for cattle." Such a prospectus was guaranteed to appeal to an overpopulated continent; it was the propaganda of an expanding Europe.

### Improvements in Agriculture

Europe was able to cater for the sudden increase in population in good part by internal colonization and external migration, but it did so also to some extent by improving its agricultural productivity. Land was more intensively and rationally cultivated by the adoption of a regular system of cropping and fallow. Soil exhaustion was thereby limited, and crop yields more than doubled between the ninth and thirteenth centuries. Air photography has recently revealed to us with a new vividness the way in which the medieval peasant exploited his arable land to the

# Feudalism

*Above:* King giving justice at a gate, eleventh century. All justice was supposed to flow from the king, which often created difficulties if the crown was a party in the law suit. In practice decision in legal cases was left to judges appointed by the crown. Here a judge assists the king in reaching a decision. Because justice was supposed to be open to all, trials were often held at the gate of a palace. *Right:* Coronation and investiture of a king, c.1250. The divine character of kingship was emphasized by the ceremonies of coronation. It also gave the Church a measure of control over kings.

From the chaos and disorder of Europe's dark ages there emerged a form of society that was to form the basis of modern parliamentary government. Although the term "feudalism" has been greatly overworked by historians, it was not a word in medieval usage at all. It was first employed by a seventeenth-century French historian who derived it from the Latin *feudum* (fief). There is no comprehensive definition of feudalism with which every historian would agree. No feudal system existed: only a group of relationships.

Feudalism involved a chain of relationships linking each level of society together with bonds of mutual obligation. The vassal knelt before his lord and swore "never to do ought by word or deed that should grieve him." He promised "aid and counsel" to his lord. The former was usually military service, at the vassal's expense, for forty days each year. Sometimes military service was commuted into a money payment or scutage. It became customary for a vassal to assist his lord financially on certain occasions, such as the knighting of the lord's eldest son, by paying an "aid." Attempts by King John of England to raise frequent aids were one of the baronial grievances that led to Magna Carta. A lord also demanded a payment of "relief" when a new vassal took possession of an estate through inheritance, and also, if the vassal was a child, exercised the profitable control of wardship. A vassal gave counsel to his lord by helping to settle disputes: with his peers he gave judgment in his lord's presence. At a national level, this gave the major nobles the duty and the right to meet in council to advise the King. In his turn the lord promised to protect and defend his vassal, and to see that justice was done to him; then he invested him with a symbol of his estates.

If either party broke the contract, then the other was no longer bound by his promises. For example, in 1202, King Philip Augustus of France declared King John of England deprived of the right to his French lands.

The tenant's place in the social scale depended upon the kind of service he performed. At the lowest level, the villein held strips of land on condition that he worked on his lord's estate; higher up, the knight held a manorial estate on condition that he did military service for his lord; whilst the magnate held a collection of estates on condition that he supplied a fixed quota of knights to fight, at the King's command. Yet this is a simplified view of the feudal pyramid. In the twelfth century, loyalties had become very complicated and many men held estates from several lords of varying rank. A man might hold one estate from the king and thus be a tenant-in-chief, and another from a tenant, as a sub-tenant. In some cases a tenant was far stronger than his lord. The Norman kings of England were vassals of the king of France, in respect of the duchy of Normandy. Yet the kings of England were often far more powerful even in France than their nominal overlords.

The roots of feudalism were deeply embedded in Roman and Germanic custom and can be traced in the late Roman Empire and in Merovingian France. It developed gradually and haphazardly. The main development occurred in the ninth century when the central authority of the Carolingians collapsed in the face of Viking, Saracen and Magyar attacks. Personal freedom ceased to be a privilege and power fell to those who could offer protection from the invaders, when emperors and kings proved incapable of doing so. Under these circumstances men surrendered their lands and became vassals in return for a guarantee of protection. During the dark ages mounted knights had become the main fighting force and since they were more expensive to arm and maintain than infantry, fiefs were granted to knights so that they could equip themselves.

This process developed most rapidly in France. The kings granted away powers that they could not exercise, by creating "immunities." A magnate (or, more often, a church) was given complete authority, military, judicial and fiscal in his estates. Fiefs tended to become hereditary. By the tenth century, the French monarchy had almost disappeared amidst independent feudal states. Yet the king still had a place at the apex of the feudal pyramid. In theory he remained the universal overlord, the owner of all the land. The idea of monarchy was kept alive.

In England the situation was made very different by the Norman Conquest. Although certain characteristics of feudalism had existed in Anglo-Saxon England, feudalism was imposed from above by William the Conqueror, who claimed all land and granted estates to his followers in return for knight service. Subinfeudation occurred when the great magnates granted parts of their estates away to vassals, to ensure that they would be able to provide their quota of knights. The English king—unlike the French—maintained control over subtenants as well as over his tenants-in-chief.

Feudalism is sometimes regarded as an anarchic system, with no ordered government, and private feuding rife throughout society. This is not a true picture, for although a feudal society was geared to war, this was because it had developed to meet the needs of a particular situation, when central government was weak. The great fiefs provided a framework of government until national monarchies were strong enough to assume control. But a strong monarchy could use feudal institutions, as can be seen in the crusading states in Palestine and Syria.

In fifteenth-century England, during a period when the monarchy was weakened by dynastic feuding, a form of "bastard" feudalism arose. This was not based on land tenure and hereditary ties but on self-interest. Nobles bound bands of soldiers to them by written indentures and a retaining fee. It became necessary to have a patron in order to gain any protection in the general lawlessness that resulted from the lack of strong royal authority during the Wars of the Roses. This development, which has often cast a slur on feudalism as a whole, was only curbed after the accession of Henry VII.

Although feudal institutions survived into the modern period in some places in Europe—in France until the French Revolution—as a force feudalism declined in the fourteenth century when the mounted knight lost his dominant role in warfare. Yet the effects of feudalism reached far beyond this. From the obligation of a vassal to give counsel to his lord, arose tribunals such as the Parlement of Paris, the French Estates, and Parliament in England. Moreover the feudal idea of a contract between lord and vassal foreshadowed the modern theory of a limited monarchy.

full by laying it out in long strips for maximum efficiency in plowing, and his efforts have thereby left a permanent imprint on much of the countryside of England in the form of a corrugated pattern of ridge and furrow.

New technical skills were also employed in an effort to boost agricultural production. The most significant of these was a much greater use of iron instead of wood, especially in the making of agricultural implements. Europe was entering its second iron age. Nowhere was this more important than with regard to the plow. The early medieval European swing plow, still in use in parts of southern Italy, was a most primitive implement. Its major virtue was that it was cheap and easy to make; its major defect was that it was uncontrollable and barely did more than scratch the surface of the soil. Gradually, from the eleventh century onward, it was replaced in northern Europe by a much heavier plow, made of iron and in every way more complex. This new kind of plow made far greater demands on peasant resources since it needed a team of six or eight oxen to draw it, but the returns were well worthwhile. The heavy plow cut deep, and for the first time in history it was possible to exploit the dense but fertile clay soils of the river valleys.

The introduction of the heavy plow and of the water mill—which also became popular in Europe at this time—makes this period one of the most vital in the development of agricultural technology before the eighteenth century. These improvements helped medieval Europe to tackle its first major experience with the population problem.

*Above:* St Martin giving half of his cloak to a beggar. The fourth-century saint, noted for his generosity to the poor, was a popular figure in medieval hagiography. *Left:* The choir of Amiens cathedral, one of the finest gothic churches in France. In twelfth-century France a great era of cathedral-building began. Most of the cathedrals—Chartres, Paris, Laon, and Amiens for example, were dedicated to Notre-Dame, and these palaces of the heavenly queen were far more magnificent than those of any earthly queen. The cathedrals, financed largely by wealthy citizens are examples of civic pride, and dwarf the buildings around them.

### New Building

Europe in 1250 was an intimate continent compared with the Europe of 1000. It was a much more densely populated continent, and thanks to the improvement in its communications, its peoples knew one another better. New towns bristled in its landscapes, and their names are still with us—*New*port, *New*castle, *New*land, *Franche*ville, and so forth. We can date the birth of some of them with precision, as in the case of Villafranca near Verona, which was established in 1185 when a village of 180 households was set up to colonize 800 acres of virgin land. In other cases, as in that of Ludlow in Herefordshire, the growth of the new town was relatively stunted, and we can still trace clearly the neat, geometrical street plans of the original town planners. This was indeed an age of new towns; some 100 were founded in England alone.

To the modern observer, however, this age will always remain preeminently the age of new cathedrals. And it is right that this should be so, for in no other buildings did Europe wear more clearly and confidently the aspect of its prosperity and expansion than in its splendid cathedrals. The names of Durham and Amiens and any other church or abbey of this period are not only great building and mechanical feats, representing a remarkable investment in eternity, but are also, in their grandeur, a reflection of Europe's expansive spirit. Contemporaries were well aware of what was happening. "One would have thought," said one of them, "that the world was shaking itself to cast off its old age and was clothing itself everywhere in a white robe of churches. Then nearly all the churches . . . were reconstructed more beautifully than before." There could be no more apt comment on the rebirth of Europe.

## THE EXPANSION OF TRADE

The expansion which characterized population, agriculture, town life, and building was equally evident in trade. European trade in 1000 was a paltry affair. The continent was largely landlocked since the seas were controlled by its enemies, and international trade was restricted to a few luxury goods, such as spices, which the largely self-sufficient manors could not produce. Europe's retreat from trade had been accompanied by and was manifested in its abandonment of gold, the currency of international trade. Such merchants as existed were mere peddlers or members of communities who lived on the fringe of European society—Jews, Syrians, Frisians, and Vikings. It is little wonder, therefore, that in contemporary analyses of society there was no role for the merchant alongside the priest, the peasant, and the warrior.

From this commercial stagnation Europe, and especially southern Europe, recovered with remarkable speed, particularly in the geography of trade. In the first place, northern and southern Europe were gradually bound together by a system of roads—and it was in 1225 that the St Gotthard Pass through the Swiss Alps was opened—which made long-distance commerce feasible and safe. Fairs could now be organized for more than local retail trade, and none was more vital in the commercial integration of Europe than the great fairs of Champagne in eastern France, for it was in these fairs that the merchants of Italy made their first appearance in the commercial life of northern Europe.

Roads were one of the arteries of trade, but the sea was an even more important one, for it provided a cheaper and quicker route for the transport of bulk commodities. That is why 1277 is such a key year in the annals of medieval European trade, for it was the first occasion that an Italian galley made the round trip from the Mediterranean through the Strait of Gibraltar and thence to the ports of northern Europe. The sea link between northern and southern Europe had been renewed, and Bruges in Flanders became the terminus for this great seaborne trade. Bruges was also the terminus for another vital commercial sea route, namely, that which bound the Baltic to the North Sea. It was the German cities of the Hanseatic League—Lübeck, Hamburg, and so forth—that opened up this trade route and ensured

Weighing coins in the royal treasury, mid-twelfth century. Control over the coinage was one of the main ways in which kings were able to expand their power.

that Scandinavia, the Baltic, and even parts of Russia came within the orbit of Europe commercially.

What is immediately apparent from a commercial map of Europe in the thirteenth century is that Europe, once a continent of isolated communities, is now enmeshed in a web of trade routes and that its commercial frontiers had expanded in step with its political boundaries. Indeed, in the Mediterranean the frontiers had expanded much farther, for by 1250 the Italian merchants had penetrated into the Black Sea, Persia, and central Asia in search of goods. Nothing can perhaps convey more vividly the commercial expansion of Europe than to note that Chinese silk was on sale in Genoa in 1257 and that an Italian trade manual of the period regarded the journey from the Crimea to Peking, taking 284 days, as a safe and desirable one for European merchants.

As the trade routes of Europe proliferated, so did the quantity of trade grow to cater to the needs of an expanding population. Furthermore, trade was increasingly in bulk commodities and raw materials rather than in a few luxury items. Most of the trade of the Mediterranean world, for example, was concerned not with high-priced oriental spices but rather with the transport of large quantities of cereals and wine to meet the needs of populous cities such as Venice, Florence, Constantinople, and Alexandria. Even more significant for the commercial development of Europe was the growth of areas of specialized production that catered to a national and international market rather than a local one. It was, for example, during this period that the major wine-producing areas of Europe became defined for the first time, especially those which are still the best known today—Bordeaux, Burgundy, the Moselle, and the Rhineland—and their wine now found an international market. By 1300, to give one example, more than 18 million gallons of wine were exported through the port of Bordeaux (as much or more than is exported today), and the wine of the Bordelais accounted for over 30 percent of England's imports. Wine was a vital commodity in European trade, but cloth was even more important, for cloth was the key commodity that restored the balance of trade both between northern and southern Europe and between western and eastern Europe. It was in search of Flemish and English cloth that Italian merchants came to the fairs of Champagne or sent their galleys to Bruges and London; this cloth, in its turn, found its way into the bazaars of the Levant and Asia in exchange for spices, perfumes, and dyestuffs. Cloth, wine, and some other commodities such as salt and cereals were accelerating the commercial integration of Europe. They were also affording it its first experiences as an industrialized society, for production for an international market was matched by the growth of an industrial proletariat in the cities of Flanders and Italy.

### Merchant Organizations

This rapid growth of trade also inevitably involved the growth of a merchant class, vigorous in the pursuit of its privileges and governed by its own law. In the new world of international trade and finance, merchants began to cooperate and to form associations to further their interests both at home and abroad. At home, the government of most of Europe's leading cities and towns passed into the hands of a merchant oligarchy; abroad, merchants united in groups to secure trading privileges and monopolies. Some of these associations were national or international in character—such as the Hanseatic League, to which many of the towns of the Baltic and of Germany belonged and which had major trading stations and privileges in London, Bruges, Bergen, and Novgorod. In southern Europe, many of these mercantile associations took the form of tightly knit family companies—such as the Bardi company of Florence—with trading and financial enterprises and

Medieval commerce
To Iceland
Bergen
NORWAY
SCOTLAND
Stockholm
SWEDEN
Riga
North Sea
IRELAND
COAL
Dublin
York
DENMARK
Baltic Sea
CORN
TIMBER
ENGLAND
Lübeck
Danzig
Königsberg
FISHERIES
Hamburg
LEATHER
FURS
HONEY
Atlantic Ocean
Oxford
Cambridge
Amsterdam
Bremen
Stettin
London
COAL
Brunswick
Magdeburg
Vistula R
Bruges
TEXTILES
Dortmund
SALT
Leipzig
Frankfurt am Oder
Warsaw
WOOL
Cologne
GERMANY
POLAND
Paris
Breslau
Seine R
Frankfurt
Oder R
Rheims
Elbe R
Chartres
Provin
WINE
Nuremberg
Cracow
Angers
Orleans
Troyes
PAPER
Rhine R
Lagny
Loire R.
Augsburg
Vienna
PRECIOUS METALS
AGRICULTURE
Basle
SALT
Pest
WINE
TEXTILES
FRANCE
WINE
Buda
Milan
Vicenza
Santiago
Lyons
Piacenza
Modena
HUNGARY
Bordeaux
WINE
SILK
Leon
Vercelli
Venice
Garonne R
Rhone R
SILK
Toulouse
Montpellier
SILK
Genoa
SILK
METALS
Palencia
Pamplona
Bologna
Danube
Reggio
Narbonne
Ebro R
Marseilles
Ragusa
Salamanca
WOOL
WINE
MERCURY
SUGAR
Lerida
Corsica
Lisbon
Barcelona
Rome
PAPER
SPAIN
Valencia
Balearics
Naples
Seville
Cordoba
Salerno
Sardinia
Tarentum
Cartagena
Granada
Malaga
Almeria
Tangier
Athens
Reggio
Sicily
GOLD
IVORY
SLAVES
from
Africa
Tunis
NORTH AFRICA
Mediterranean Sea
Sahara Desert
Tripoli
Trans Sahara Routes to Black Africa
Towns Trading through the Hanseatic League
Hanseatic League sea trade routes
Venetian sea routes
Other trade routes
Universities founded before 1300
Fairs in the Champagne region
Areas of relatively dense population
Areas of moderately dense population
Areas of comparatively sparse population

The late tenth century geographer Muqaddasi lists the goods imported through the Volga as:
SABLE
GREY SQUIRREL
ERMINE
MINK
FOX
BEAVER SKINS
SPOTTED HARE
GOAT SKINS
WAX
FALCONS
SWORDS
SHEEP
ARROWS
BIRCH BARK
FUR CAPS
FISH GLUE
FISH TEETH
AMBER
HONEY
HAZEL NUTS
ARMOR
SLAVONIC SLAVES
FURS
Novgorod
Moscow
RUSSIA
Kiev
Volga R
Don R
Astrakhan
SILK from China
Rostov
CORN
SALT
Dnieper R
Kaffa
Sudak
Caspian Sea
Derbent
Black Sea
Poli
ARMENIA
Trebizond
Sinope
Astrabad
L Van
L Urmia
Tubriz
ASIA MINOR
MESOPOTAMIA
Imports by Muslim Merchants from China included:
AROMATICS
SILK GOODS
CROCKERY
PAPER
INK
PEACOCKS
HORSES
SADDLES
FELT
CINNAMON
Antioch
Aleppo
Euphrates R
Tigris R
Cyprus
PAPER
Baghdad
COPPER
Tripoli
PAPER
SYRIA
SUGAR
Beirut
Damascus
Jerusalem
SPICE ROUTE
Alexandria
EGYPT
Cairo
Arabian Desert
GOLD
IVORY
SLAVES
from Central Africa
Nile R
SPICE ROUTE to Zanzibar
ARABIA
To Mecca
Persian Gulf
To India and the Far East
Miles 0 500

agents in every part of Europe and beyond. Whatever the form of the commercial organization, the merchants of Europe were no longer a peripheral group of peddlers; they were now central to Europe's economic life. The confidence of that economic life in 1250 is reflected in the new gold coins. Gold was the currency of international trade, and it is indicative of Europe's commercial reawakening that in 1248 Venice struck its first gold ducat and that Genoa and Florence followed suit four years later with their gold florins.

### Venice: An Empire Built on Trade

It is singularly appropriate that Venice should be the first city to return to gold, for it was also the earliest and greatest of Europe's commercial cities. Its history epitomizes Europe's medieval commercial revolution. Venice was a city built on trade in an age in which most wealth was based on land. Its greatest asset in its early history was its geographical position. In wartime, its islands and lagoons were a safe haven against the raids of barbarian armies; in peacetime they formed an admirable springboard for commercial expansion. Detached from the struggles of mainland Italy, Venice looked to the sea for its prosperity. She first claimed the Adriatic and then turned her attention to the Mediterranean, firmly asserting her naval supremacy by completely annihilating the Egyptian war fleet in 1123. For a city whose wealth depended so exclusively on commerce, control of the sea was a prime condition of survival, and from an early date the Venetians recognized this fact symbolically in their magnificent ceremony of "the wedding of the sea," celebrated annually on Ascension Day. They also recognized it by forbidding Venetian citizens to acquire estates on the mainland of Italy; theirs was to be an empire of the sea.

It was also an empire built on commerce. Other towns owed their wealth to the fact that they were episcopal or royal headquarters or university centers; Venice owed its prosperity exclusively to trade. Its distinction was that it was the first city of Western Europe to establish strong trading contacts with the eastern Mediterranean and thereby with Asia and the Orient. Already in the tenth century it enjoyed a favored trading relationship with the Byzantine Empire, and by 1150 some 10,000 Venetians were already living in Constantinople and exploiting their trading privileges to the full. This monopoly of eastern Mediterranean trade was vastly extended from 1204 with the fall of Constantinople into European hands. The merchants of Venice now had direct access to the Black Sea and to the Persian and Asian trade routes that lay beyond. In the carving up of the Byzantine Empire, Venice secured great possessions in the eastern Mediterranean, including Rhodes, Crete, Corfu, and Chios. It was highly appropriate that Venice's first empire was built overseas in the very area in which it had made its commercial fortune.

Just as the merchants of Venice built a commercial empire abroad, so likewise they dominated the internal politics of their native city. Venice was governed by a commercial oligarchy, which ensured that the city's policies were directed to the furtherance of trade. The city government was headed by a *doge* (duke), but his powers were limited and there was no danger of his being allowed to become an autocratic and hereditary monarch. The great merchants retained effective control and finally in 1297 entrenched their power in law. Never before in European history was the whole life of a great city so exclusively geared to the maintenance and expansion of commerce as was that of medieval Venice. "You Venetians," said the doge on one occasion, "are the only people to whom land and sea are alike open. You are the canal of all riches, your provision the whole earth; all the universe is interested in your prosperity; all the gold of the world comes to Venice." It was justified pride, and it admirably sums up the achievement of Venice, the capital of Europe's commercial rebirth.

The center of Venice. One of the largest and wealthiest cities in medieval times, Venice built itself into a great trading empire. In addition to control over much of northern Italy and Yugoslavia, Venice held possessions in Asia Minor. The fourth crusade (1204) was diverted from its purpose of attacking Muslims in the Holy Land, into an attack on Constantinople, as a result of Venetian greed. Venice was one of the few Italian republics not taken over by princes in the late Middle Ages: it retained its oligarchic control by the doge (duke) and senate until the nineteenth century.

Chapter 6

# THE CHURCH VICTORIOUS

The traditional picture of the medieval Church is of a static hierarchy striving to maintain a fixed and unchanging order. There were, indeed, real elements of caution and conservatism evident, but on the whole the hierarchy was among the forces which welcomed, and strove for, change. What we can see in the century from 1050 is a papal "revolution," which created medieval Catholicism in its familar form, and this revolution was probably of more profound importance in the history of the Church than was the Reformation.

It is not often appreciated how many of the elements of later Catholicism were established in the course of the eleventh and twelfth centuries. Individual confession to a priest, for example, was, before 1050, an unusual practice characteristic of some forms of monastic piety. In 1215, it became an annual requirement for every member of the Church. The term transubstantiation, as an account of what happens at the consecration of bread and wine at mass, was wholly unknown in 1050. By 1150 the application to the mass of the distinction between "substance" and "accident" was established, and by 1215 transubstantiation had become the official doctrine of the Church. Even more striking was the emergence of a new way of thinking about Christ on the Cross. For the first time in the long history of Christianity, he was shown in the crucifix, not alive and triumphant, but as a dying man, and stress on *compassion* for the dying Lord (an idea which the early Church would have found shocking) now became commonplace. It is vividly expressed in a hymn by Peter Abelard, written about 1135:

*For they are ours, O Lord, our deeds, our deeds.*
*Why must thou suffer torture for our sin?*
*Let our hearts suffer for thy passion, Lord,*
*That sheer compassion may thy mercy win.*

## THE PAPAL REVOLUTION: 1050–1150

The foundations of the papal revolution were laid during the years after 1046. The popes appointed during the reign of Henry III of Germany (1039–1056) were all in a real sense imperial nominees, but a very conscious and active program of reform was launched by Pope Leo IX. Leo created the nucleus of the papal reform group by assembling around himself a remarkably talented and effective body of advisers. They include the northerner Humbert of Moyenmoutier, whom Leo, a man of Lorraine himself, must have known previously, and the talented Hildebrand. The reforming party was thus well entrenched in the central government of the church; its program may be described as clerical, international, and papal.

Firstly, the program of reform was *clerical*. Its aim was the liberation of the church from lay control and the establishment of the clergy as a distinct group, set

The cathedral of Notre Dame at Chartres. Widely regarded as the greatest masterpiece of gothic architecture, Chartres cathedral expresses the spirit of the Middle Ages in all its fervor. After the previous, romanesque cathedral had been destroyed by fire in 1194, the present church with its cluster of columns, simplicity of line and feeling of height and air was built. The stained-glass windows, which bathe the cathedral in infinitely rich colored light, were designed to express the Christian message for those who could not read the Bible.

apart from the rest of society. The first target was simony, the sale of ecclesiastical appointments, which was forbidden repeatedly from its condemnation by Leo IX in 1049 onward. Together with the attack on simony there developed a similar offensive against clerical marriage. This institution was so firmly established that it took a long time to eliminate, but by 1200 clerical marriage had become not only illegal but also unusual in Western Europe. The third element in this clericalization of the Church was the prohibition of lay investiture. The title *investiture contest* has been given to the whole conflict between Empire and papacy in this period. It is something of a misnomer, because a determined attempt to eliminate lay investiture did not really begin until the 1090s. By 1122, a series of compromises had ended the practice in the greater part of Europe. Laymen no longer bestowed ecclesiastical offices in such a simple and direct way.

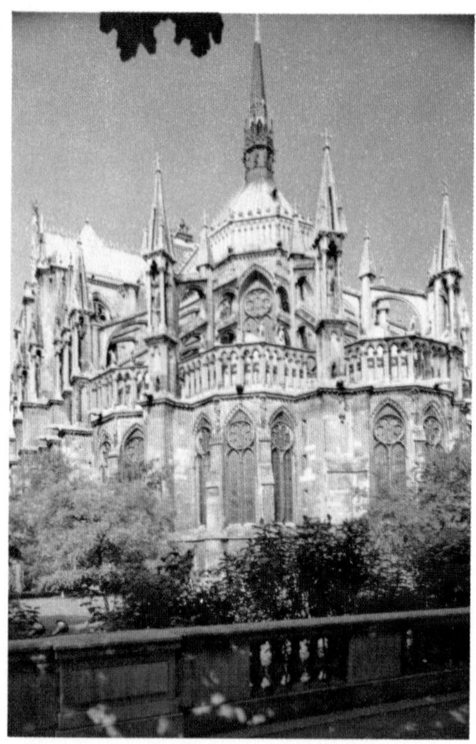

The east end of Reims cathedral. Reims, heavily influenced by the architecture of Chartres, was begun in 1212. Reims was the ancient ecclesiastical capital of France, and the French kings were crowned there. Beyond the high altar, in the round east end are small chapels for the celebration of private masses—a characteristic of medieval worship. Reims was the first major cathedral to use external flying buttresses. The cathedrals of Amiens and Reims are more developed than Chartres. They show a change of emphasis and express the utopian ideas of scholasticism, instead of man's sense of awe and mystery in the face of the infinite.

The reform movement was also *international*. It brought into being a whole range of international institutions that helped to standardize the culture and civilization of Western Europe. New monastic orders came into existence which (unlike the older Benedictine order or even the Cluniac houses) were centrally administered, with uniform usages in many lands. Perhaps the first new-type order was that of the Hospitallers, which existed to care for the needs of pilgrims to Jerusalem. Its first rule was approved in 1113. A still more influential example was the Cistercian order. Its first abbey, Citeaux, was founded in 1098. By 1115, its four senior daughter houses had been established, and by 1153 it had 350 houses, stretching from Norway to Spain. Its phenomenal expansion was partly a tribute to the outstanding personal influence of St Bernard, abbot of Clairvaux, who had become a Cistercian in 1112, and was partly due to its success in expressing the aspirations of the age. Its worship and architecture were remarkably standardized throughout the entire order.

Another international institution was the crusading movement. The First Crusade was proclaimed by Pope Urban II at Clermont in 1095, and his call to the Cross was answered from many countries. A chronicler listed a vast number of participating peoples:

> *Whoever heard of such a mixture of languages in one army? There were present Franks, Flemings, Frisians, Gauls, Allobroges, Lotharingians, Suabians, Bavarians, Normans, English, Scots, Aquitanians, Italians, Dacians, Apulians, Iberians, Bretons, Greeks, and Armenians.*

The First Crusade culminated in the capture of Jerusalem in 1099, and by 1110 most of the Syrian coastline was in Christian hands. The frontiers of Christendom had, as a result of cooperation among the various nations and classes of the West, been extended to include the Holy Places where the Lord lived and died.

The reform movement took place within the context of the universities, another major international development. There was a community of scholarship in Western Europe that today we would find hard to imagine. The great schools of Paris and Bologna received students from every part of Europe. Through the teaching of these schools, international legal codes were developed, which were regarded as having very wide application. At Bologna, the study of Roman law was revived, and the law was analyzed and codified under Irnerius and his successors. Even more important was the growth of the scientific study of canon law (the law of the church). The great textbook on this subject, the *Decretum* of Gratian, was completed before 1150, and upon it was based the whole subsequent development of an integrated law for the Western Church.

The most remarkable of the new international institutions, however, was the *papacy* itself. In spite of the vast power claimed by the Roman Church, it would be a great mistake to think of the papacy as an Italian institution, governing from Rome. The popes themselves were of many nationalities—German, French, Italian, and even an Englishman, Hadrian IV (1154–1159). They were rarely in occupation of their own supposed see of Rome and, in fact, provided for the church a traveling government. Their claims to authority were enormous. Gregory VII referred to "blessed Peter the apostle, whom the Lord Jesus Christ has made prince over the kingdoms of the world." This was not intended to be a mere titular headship. Papal legates, traveling as official representatives of the pope, began to make decisions about a wide range of issues within the local churches, while bishops were cajoled, persuaded, or commanded into making regular visits to the papal court. By 1135, for example, almost every English bishop had been there at least once, some of them several times.

The emergence of these new ideals, and this new power, did not go without a challenge. The parties most directly affected were the powerful local clergy, who expressed vigorously their resentment at papal innovations. Archbishop Liemar of Bremen complained about Gregory VII:

> *This dangerous man takes it on himself to give orders to bishops as if they were his stewards. If they do not do everything he wants, they either have to go to Rome or they are suspended without trial.*

The clergy of Liege complained in 1103:

> *The pope, who ought to be praying for the king, even if he is a sinner, so that we can lead a peaceful and quiet life, makes war on him instead*

Such complaints remind us that it is wrong to see these quarrels as "Church against State." The clergy were by no means all in sympathy with the reformers who were directing papal policy. It was a "revolution from the top," which provoked deep resentment in the local churches, whose clergy feared for their independent authority, for the benefices they had purchased, or for their family lives in the face of this campaign against clerical marriage and simony. Nevertheless, it was the local monarchies who had the effective power to resist the papal demands, and there were clashes with most of the royal houses: with France in the late eleventh century and with England in the early twelfth, when Henry I and Archbishop Anselm were at issue over the question of royal investiture.

The longest and most critical conflict, however, was that with the German emperors. Both sides put forward theoretical claims which they could not easily renounce. Both had interests, and allies, in Italy, which they could not abandon. In 1076, the Emperor Henry IV finally broke with the papacy. At the Council of Worms, he proclaimed the deposition of Pope Gregory VII—who, in turn, excommunicated Henry. The events of 1076 opened a period of almost half a century of hostility between pope and emperor. Attempts at reconciliation proved ineffective. In January 1077, Henry and Gregory met in person at Canossa. Although Henry did penance and received absolution, there was no settlement of the issues of policy which divided the two men. By 1080, the chasm had opened between the two sides. Pope and antiking (Rudolf of Suabia) confronted king and antipope (Clement III).

The papacy depended for its political effectiveness on its allies among the German princes and the Italian powers, and at first things did not go well. Henry IV was able to secure his coronation at Rome as emperor, and Gregory VII died in exile at Salerno. Henry's government in Germany and in parts of Italy remained in general effective, but successive popes held resolutely to the validity of his deposition. The controversy continued until the Concordat of Worms in 1122, a com-

The rose window at the west end of Reims cathedral. The rose window, a romanesque invention, was taken over with enthusiasm by gothic builders. This was because of its symbolism—the rose was the emblem of the Virgin Mary. Its circular shape raised enormous problems when associated with the use of the painted arch, which is the chief characteristic of gothic architecture. At Reims the buildings simply incorporated the window into the arch. There were more usual solutions to the difficulty: at Chartres and Amiens the window was simply set into the wall; at Paris and Laon the window was put into a rounded arch.

promise in which Henry's son and successor, Henry V, gave up the main bone of contention, investiture by the lay power, while obtaining reassurances about continued royal influence in the German Church.

## THE TRIUMPH OF THE CHURCH: 1150–1250

It would be simple-minded to say that the popes "won" any of the direct clashes with the royal courts during the years from 1076 to 1122. When they gained their point, they usually did so as a result of considerable compromise in detail. There can, however, be no doubt of the transformation of the position of the papacy in European society. The church had perhaps reached its greatest period of influence about the middle of the twelfth century. At least, this was the period at which its authority was most widely respected. Papal policy was influenced, and at times even controlled, by scholars and monastic reformers. The secular powers were well disposed toward the reforming papacy. In France, at least after 1144, Louis VII was a consistent friend of the church. In Germany, Lothar III and Conrad III were both friends of reform and allies of papal policy. The leading churchmen received immense respect from public opinion. The papacy could be found at the heart of many of the major enterprises of the age; it encouraged monastic reform, legislated for the Church as a whole, and proclaimed the First and Second Crusades. The authority ascribed to the popes, as successors of St Peter, knew almost no limits.

The Church continued to enjoy, during the century after 1150, both theoretical importance and practical influence. A modern man, if he were translated to that century, would be astonished by the predominance given to this one institution. Its power can be seen not only in the extent of its possessions and the influence of its teaching but in directly visible symbols. A favorite theme of sculpture was the "majesty." Here, Christ in glory, or Christ on his mother's knee, is seen ruling in splendor over the whole creation. The actual buildings often express this authority. A huge church would stand, majestically constructed in stone, towering over an impoverished community, which huddled at its feet. It was an age that believed in hierarch, and the evidence suggests that many people did not resent, but rather welcomed, the application of the surplus of a primitive economy to the provision of buildings, which had no practical use but expressed the majesty of divine order and the power of the Church, through which God was made known to man. The years from 1150 to 1250 might well be described as "the triumph of the Church."

*Above:* The figure of the Greek philosopher and mathematician Pythagoras, from Chartres. In the Middle Ages it was believed that the Virgin Mary must have studied the seven liberal arts (grammar, rhetoric, dialectic, music, arithmetic, geometry, and astronomy). At Chartres, dedicated to the Virgin, a representative of each of the arts is included: Pythagoras represents geometry.
*Left:* The abbey of Mont-Saint-Michel, on its peninsula off the coast of France. Parts of the abbey, built out from a natural mound, collapsed in 1776.

On closer inspection, however, the triumph appears a hollow one. As we examine it, we must notice two weaknesses in the position of the Church, even at its time of greatest success. The first of these was the existence of large groups within society which, in one way or another, did not recognize its authority. There were the heretics, who formally repudiated it; the poor and ignorant, who did not understand it; the secular monarchies, which declined to give its teaching political application. The second weakness was the presence of an inner self-contradiction in the life of the Church itself. On the one hand, the Church was a rich propertied corporation with vast political influence. On the other, it was a body called to preach the Christian Gospel and to advocate a renunciation of riches and splendor. This awkward dilemma was never resolved. It was analyzed by Bernard of Clairvaux in his book *On Consideration*, which he wrote about 1150 at the request of Eugenius III. In Bernard's view, the power of the pope was of a very peculiar kind:

> *The world is your inheritance. But . . . I do not think you have inherited the world absolutely, but with certain limitations.*
> *Your power does not lie in possessions, but in the hearts of men.*

*On Consideration* was a favorite book with successive popes. We shall now observe with what success they applied its searching paradoxes in the age of the triumph of the church.

### The Friars

The hierarchy was well aware of the limitations of its power, and it devoted a great deal of attention to what might well be described as a "church extension program." Preaching and the confessional were important means of reaching ordinary people and of guiding them to an understanding of the Catholic faith. At the beginning of the thirteenth century, the church developed almost the ideal instrument for the application of these methods: the friars. Of these, the most original and radical were the Franciscans, who received verbal recognition as an order from Innocent III about 1210 and formal confirmation in 1223. Their founder, St Francis, saw them as vowed to complete poverty and called to preach and serve the poor. He ascribed to them a very high place in God's plan for the church:

> *The fellowship and life of the Little Brothers* (Friars Minor) *is a feeble flock which the son of God in these last days has requested of his heavenly Father, saying: "Father, I wish that you would create and give to me in these last days a new and humble people, differing in humility and in poverty from all those who have gone before, and content to have me alone.". . . For this reason the Lord wished that they be called Little Brothers, because they are the company of people whom the Son of God asked of His Father.*

Christ on his heavenly throne, from the church of San Pudenziana, Rome. Throughout the Middle Ages pilgrims flocked to Rome to visit the tombs of St Peter and St Paul, supposedly buried there. Like a modern tourist center, the city became rich. With the wealth that the pilgrims brought, new churches were built and decorated magnificently. Four of Rome's churches are as old as San Pudenziana, which dates back to the second century. The mosaics were made in the fourth century, when the church was rebuilt. St Peter is believed to have celebrated the eucharist on a table in the church.

By the time of St Francis' death in 1226, his friars had already appeared in most countries of Western Europe and even beyond it. Their impact upon the age was dramatic. They were comparable in the reactions they provoked with the revolutionary groups of our own era. It is not unfair to see Francis in this light, with the very important qualification that he wholly rejected the use of violence and aimed at personal conversion as the means by which society was to be transformed. That the papacy should have authorized, and actively supported, such a movement provides clear evidence that the popes were by no means reactionary autocrats.

The other great order of friars, the Dominicans, was no less important in the life of the medieval church. It was directed to a more clearly defined end than that of the Franciscans: the preaching of the Gospel and the study of the faith. The Order of Preachers, as it came to be called, had reached its distinctive form by about 1229, and its members rapidly established themselves in Western society and especially in the growing universities. Preaching, the confessional, the friars—all had an important role in bringing to the people the Church's ideals (see inset page 362).

### The Cathedrals

A different aspect of the extension of the church is to be seen in the great building program. "Building big" was a relatively new idea; very large churches were rare before 1050. Moreover, until about 1150, most major architecture was monastic. The picture that we think of as typically medieval, of a city with its great cathedral towering above it, is in most cases the creation of the years after the middle of the twelfth century.

A series of new cathedrals was built in the towns of northern France, culminating in Chartres, Reims, and Bourges. The emergence of these buildings undoubtedly reflects the growth of the cities themselves and the availability of the huge sums of money required for conspicuous expenditure on this scale. It also expresses a genuine concern for the popularization of Christian worship. There is ample evidence that lay people, as well as clergy, were devoted to the ideal of "building big." At Chartres, windows were presented by many of the local trade guilds, and at Paris, the guild of prostitutes offered to donate a window, suitably devoted to Mary Magdalen—an offer which the bishop indignantly rejected. Sometimes, the building went on amid scenes of religious revival, with noble and peasant alike helping to haul the carts with their burden of stone. If this extreme participation was unusual, it is nevertheless true that these great building schemes often evoked wide popular support. The design of the cathedrals was, moreover, intended to appeal to the public. Their vast naves provided covered processional spaces in which the people could have easy access to the relics when they were carried on festival days. The large numbers of pilgrims who came to major centers to adore the relics gave rise to a new design for the east end of the cathedral: the inclusion of an ambulatory, which made it possible for visitors to circulate in an orderly way.

The cathedrals also served as a means of formal teaching. They were, as has so often been said, "the Bibles of the poor." The level of literacy was low, and men thought more readily in terms of images than of arguments. Churches were filled with sculpture and glass recording the events of the Old and New Testaments, illustrating their symbolism, or narrating the miracles of the local saint.

Boniface VIII, pope 1294–1303. Boniface was an upholder of the most extreme claims of papal power. He quarreled with the king of France, Philip the Fair. In a series of "bulls" (officially sealed letters), Boniface condemned Philip. The final bull *Unam Sanctum* (1302) claimed papal jurisdiction over all creatures, and asserted that both the spiritual and temporal "swords" (power) had been given to the popes by Christ. Philip responded by capturing Boniface who was at his birthplace, Anagni. Although he was quickly released, Boniface died a month later. Anagni showed that the growing power of national states could not be ignored by the papacy.

### Heretics

The extension of the Church naturally brought it into collision with those who consciously rejected its teaching: the heretics. Medieval Europe was full of heresy. The most successful of all the heretical groups were the Cathars (also known as the Albigensians and the Bougres). The various sects among them held somewhat differing views, but fundamentally they were dualists. In place of the Christian concept of one God, they believed in two opposite principles of good and evil. The material world had been created by the evil principle and was therefore in itself evil. As a consequence, the Cathars rejected the sacraments, including marriage, as being concessions to the evil flesh.

In the second half of the twelfth century, Catharism spread rapidly in southern France and northern Italy. By 1200, Cathar bishops had almost replaced Catholic ones in parts of Languedoc, and large sections of the population of the Italian cities had fallen into the Waldensian heresy. The local Church had proved itself incapable of dealing with the problem. The machinery of coercion, at the local level, was not designed to overcome opposition on this scale. Preaching campaigns by visiting Catholics proved much less effective than the preaching of their opponents, and the heretics were now obtaining important support from lay powers. Under Innocent III, the development of the friars provided the church with a better means of witness and propaganda than before, but Innocent was also driven to the conclusion that persuasion was not enough. It had to be supported by force. It is fair to say that he came reluctantly to suggest the use of violence and that its adoption was partly the result of violence by heretical sympathizers themselves, as shown in the murder of the papal legate Peter of Castelnau in 1208.

When the Pope did turn to force, it was terrible and effective. In 1209, the Albigensian Crusade was proclaimed. The lords of the north of France invaded the south, slaughtered the populace of Béziers in a terrible massacre, and began to seize the lands of the southerners, irrespective of their religious convictions. The struggle in the south was to continue for a long time, but a fatal blow had been struck against the political security of the Albigensian heretics.

The Albigensian Crusade was followed by the creation of the most famous of all the institutions of religious persecution: the Inquisition. The essence of this was the removal of heresy trials from the local church courts and their transfer to specialist groups of traveling investigators—a step which was taken in the 1230s.

# St Francis

St Francis of Assisi, founder of the Franciscan friars.

St Francis was born Giovanni di Bernardone in 1182, in Assisi, Central Italy. During his youth, his position as eldest son of a prosperous merchant of the town enabled him to live a riotous life. But as the result of a serious illness, he decided to take up a life of religion in 1206, and in this he was warmly supported by the bishop of Assisi, Guy.

Despite the scorn which he incurred for repudiating a wealth that was envied by many, Francis pursued the life of a hermit with single-minded devotion, traveling around Assisi. After having a dream in which he was told that he should rebuild the Church, he started rebuilding two local churches, San Damiano and Portiuncula, which were in a state of disrepair. Soon he met men who were inspired to follow his example and join him, and gradually the small community began to preach, and go on missionary journeys. He saw that his mission, to rebuild the Church, should be understood to apply to the whole Church, not merely to bricks and mortar.

The aim of Francis' religious life was to recapture the spirit of the gospels; and there are countless parallels in his life with that of Christ. Francis wished to pursue a life of poverty, depending for his living on alms as evidence of God's charity, and "taking no thought for the morrow." This ideal of apostolic poverty represented a turning away from the increasingly legalistic and political preoccupations of the contemporary Church; and there is a joyfulness too about the Franciscan concept of religion which had largely been missing before their time. This is particularly evident in the saint's poetry, the *Cantico delle creature* (Canticle of all Created Things).

By 1210 there were twelve men altogether, and Francis felt it was necessary to lay down a set of rules for their life together. He therefore tried to compile a list of the ideals for which they were striving, and the twelve men traveled to Rome, to ask the pope, Innocent III, to ratify the order, and give the brothers the tonsure (the status of ecclesiastics) and permission to preach.

This permission was not given lightly, particularly since the stress that Francis laid on absolute poverty could easily be mistaken for heresy. The Albigensian heretics were notorious for their belief that God had created only the spirit, and that everything material was the work of the devil. However, it was soon apparent to Innocent that Francis wanted to return to the gospels and was not denying the Incarnation or the sacraments. Innocent had a dream in which he saw Rome's cathedral, St John Lateran, in danger of falling until it was saved by the small figure of Francis himself: this decided him to ratify the order.

After the visit to Rome, the order continued to grow, and missionary activity increased. In 1212, Francis encouraged Clare Scifi, a girl who wished to take up a similar religious life. A new order of nuns was set up. St Clare and her sisters established themselves at San Damiano, and the spiritual relationship between the two orders remained close. While both the orders remained based at Assisi, the Franciscans went abroad to spread their missionary efforts further afield. Some friars were martyred in Morocco, and unsuccessful journeys were made to France, Germany and Hungary. However, Francis did reach the Holy Land, and preached among the crusaders in Egypt, and even before the Sultan. The nuns, who came to be known as "Poor Clares," however, were encouraged to stay in their nunneries. However, disagreements arose over the rule and Francis composed a new one.

A measure of the increasing divisions within the order can be realized through the fact that there were disputes about the final form of this new rule from the time that it was finished in May 1221 until November 1223. Francis and the other early Franciscans were aware of the growing tendency of their junior colleagues to prefer study to physical work. This tendency was not shared by all the brothers; a sharp division was growing between the Conventuals, who wished to study, and the "Spiritual" Franciscans, who carried the ideal of poverty to the borders of heresy.

After the death of Francis and the original brothers, it became necessary to record the stories concerning their careers. Then there grew up the corpus of stories known as the *Fioretti* (Little Flowers), of which some dealt with Francis and his contemporaries, and some, added later, continued the tradition in telling of later Franciscans' lives.

The death of Francis himself saw the end of the original impulse of the order; the leaders after that time abandoned the early ideal of evangelical poverty. The Church of San Francesco at Assisi is the living record of the change in the Order after the death of its founder.

The Dominicans provided many of the inquisitors, although some of the most brutal (including Conrad of Marburg in Germany and Robert le Bougre, himself a converted heretic, in France) were not, in fact, friars. The proceedings of the inquisition were not as ruthless as its reputation suggests, and the supreme penalty of burning was used very infrequently considering the large numbers of heretics. Yet there is no denying the use of torture, and above all there is no denying the fact that this machinery was designed to repress not actual opposition but simple dissent and divergence of opinion. It enjoyed considerable, but not complete, success. Heresy was never eliminated, but the danger that parts of Europe might lapse altogether from the Church receded for several centuries.

### The Secularization of Church Policy

During the period from 1150 to 1250, the resources of the papacy were increasingly channeled into the achievement of political purposes, and the result was that the papacy began to be viewed as a secularly minded institution—the very thing that it wished to avoid. It is a paradox that during this hundred years, when the government of the Church reached an elaboration previously undreamed of and when papal control of this government was unusually secure, the papacy was threatened by the growing power of the monarchs. The national kings were able to benefit, in exactly the same way as did the papacy, from the improvement in governmental skills. The elaboration of canon law was balanced by the codification of the Roman civil law and of the codes of the various countries of Europe. The universities, which provided popes and bishops with skilled administrators, provided them also to the royal courts.

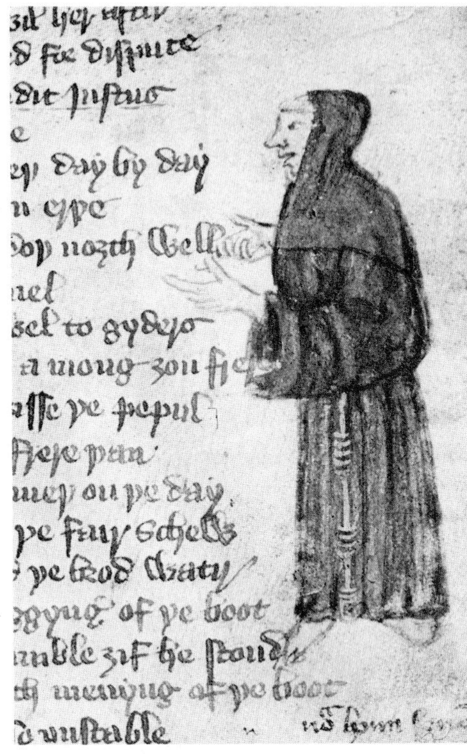

A Franciscan friar, from a manuscript of William Langland's *Piers Plowman*. Langland was a cleric born c.1332, and was the most important English poet in the generation before Geoffrey Chaucer. *Piers Plowman* is a poetic enquiry into the nature of salvation. In his search for the Christian life, the poet meets two friars, who tell him to compromise his ideals. The book is among other things an attack on the corruption of the religious orders.

Some of the most famous and effective secular rulers of the Middle Ages belong to this period. Henry II of England (1154–1189) was lord not only of this powerful kingdom but also of large territories in western France. Germany was governed by three great Hohenstaufen emperors: Frederick I Barbarossa (1152–1190), Henry VI (1190–1197), and Frederick II (1212–1250). All these kings were personally orthodox Catholics, with the possible exception of Frederick II, but they were devoted to a policy of limiting the privileges and power of the clergy in general and the papacy in particular. The French royal house was notably different. Throughout the greater part of the twelfth and thirteenth centuries, this family, the Capetians, founded its policy on active cooperation with the papacy.

The most dramatic confrontation between clergy and king took place in England and turned primarily on the issue of clerical privilege. Henry II had shown increasing concern about the growing extent of the jurisdiction of the Church: the widening competence of the Church courts, the abuses which accompanied their enquiries into lay morality, the growing volume of appeals to the papacy, and the exemption of the clergy, even when they committed serious crimes, from the normal penalties to which laymen were subject. Henry probably hoped for a favorable settlement of these issues from Thomas Becket, who had been royal chancellor and the personal friend of the king and who became archbishop of Canterbury in 1162. In practice, Thomas proved to be a vigorous defender of the rights of the church of Canterbury and of the English clergy, and within two years he had quarreled openly with Henry. From 1164, he was in exile, under the protection of the French king. He returned to Canterbury after six years but without any settlement of the issues at stake. In 1170 he was murdered in his own cathedral by four knights who were acting on some ambiguous instructions from the king. The settlement that followed this sacrilegious act was a compromise, but the details are less important than the symbolic standing of the martyred archbishop. He became a representative of the Church's resistance to royal tyranny. Canonized in 1173, he was venerated throughout Europe, and his life was written by many contemporaries. Innumerable pilgrims thronged to his shrine in Canterbury cathedral.

It seems reasonable to conclude that the Church emerged victorious from almost all its clashes with royal power during the century between 1150 and 1250. True, the papacy was only rarely in a position to dictate terms. But it was able to defend against royal attack most of the things it regarded as essential. The freedom of papal elections was maintained against imperial attempts to overrule it. The legal privileges of the clergy were (by and large) preserved intact, and indeed were extended. The attempts of successive emperors to establish effective control in Italy, and thereby to threaten the independence of the papacy, were frustrated. Moreover, the power of the French kings, the traditional allies of the papacy, had increased greatly. After the death of the Emperor Frederick II, St Louis of France (1226–1270) was unquestionably the most powerful layman in Western Europe.

These triumphs of the papacy were in part real, but they were also in part illusory. This was true even in a political sense. The years after 1250 were to show that the popes, in their struggle to avoid being dependent on the emperors, had become dependent instead on France. Within a fairly short time, dependence would turn into subordination. At a more fundamental level, too, the victory of the Church was more apparent than real. The growth of papal government and of episcopal government locally had greatly improved the efficiency of administration, but efficiency is not the same thing as spirituality. Increasingly, influential positions fell into the hands not of the theologians or humanists but of canon lawyers. The papal court, the bishops, the archdeacons, and all their subordinate officers were increasingly concerned with the administration of law. Already in 1150, St Bernard had complained that in the papal court one heard more of the laws of Justinian than of the law of Christ, and by 1250 the process had gone much further. The reform movement had abolished the cruder expressions of lay control and of simony, but the reality was still there: careerism, the search for promotion in the administration of Church and state, the accumulation of benefices by the nobly born or the highly talented. Preachers and satirists lamented that pastors had been replaced by lawyers:

*Now the shepherd's seat is turned*
*Into a tribunal.*

In the opinion of contemporaries, moreover, the upper orders of the Church had not merely been legalized, they had also been secularized. Excommunication, crusading vows, the offerings of the faithful, propaganda, and preaching—all were pressed into service to achieve an objective that was essentially secular. This had always been part of papal policy, but it was on the way to becoming the major part. The pope had forgotten that his power was not in possessions but in the hearts of men.

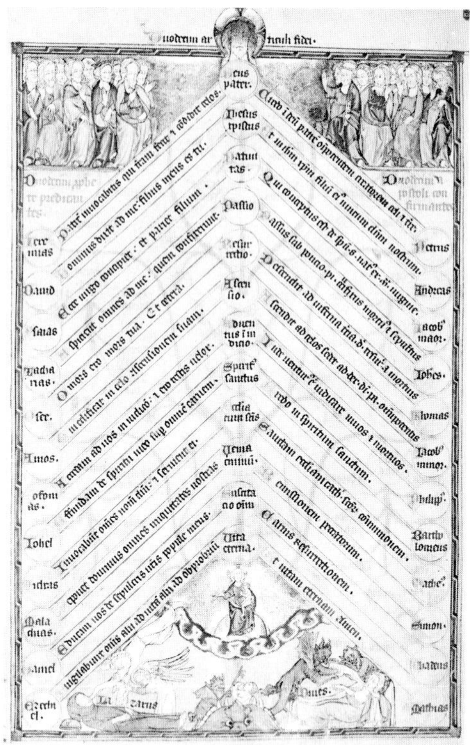

*Above:* A diagrammatic representation of the Church. In the left-hand column are twelve "Preachers," Old Testament figures who foretold Christ's coming; in the center column, twelve articles of faith, taken from the creed, running from belief in God the Father to the eternal life; in the right-hand column, the twelve apostles. The picture at the top shows angels taking souls from the righteous dead, while below devils take the souls of those condemned to hell.
*Right:* The entombment of Thomas Becket, archbishop of Canterbury. The murder of Becket in his cathedral on December 29, 1170, by four nobles of King Henry II, shocked Europe.

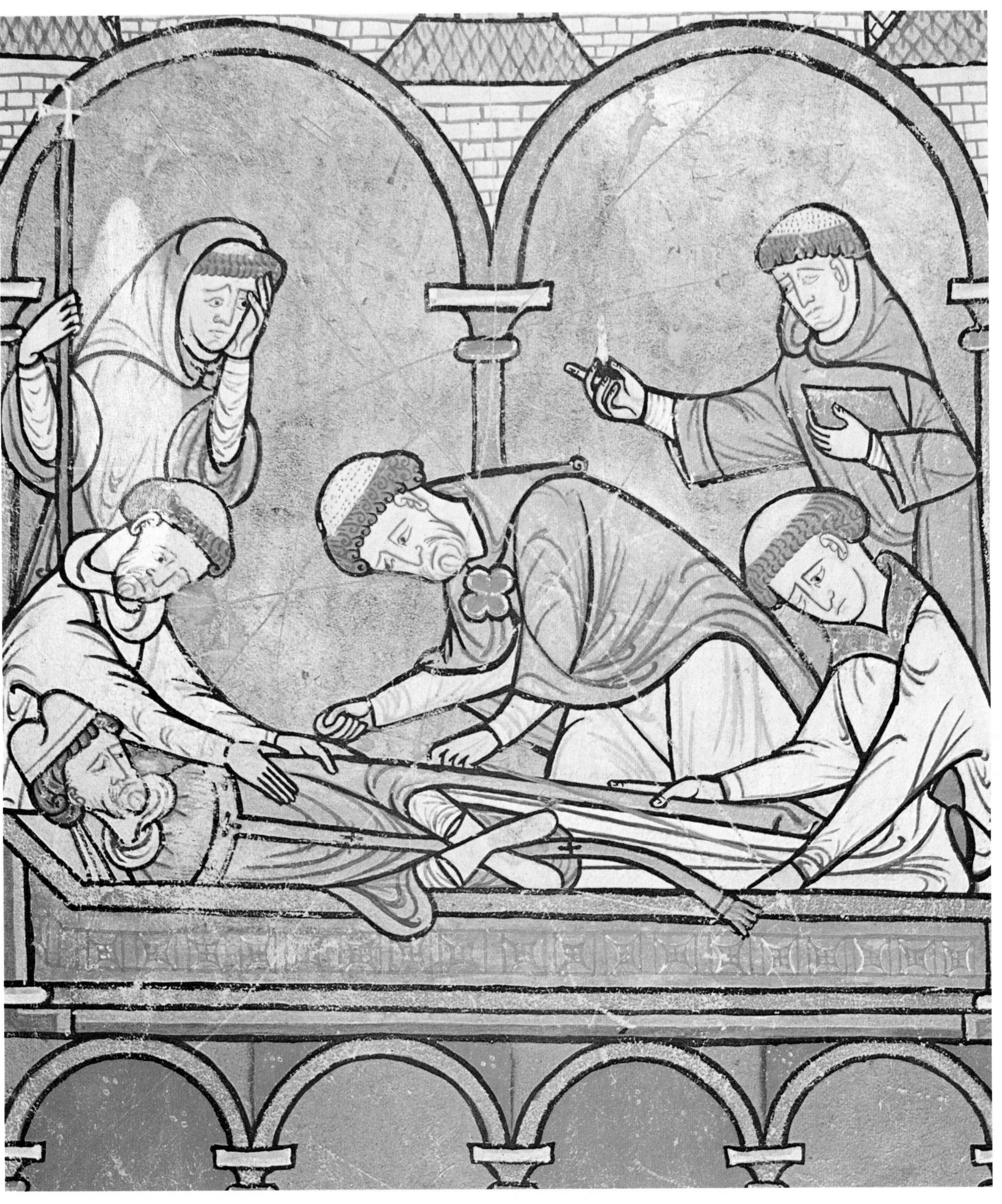

Chapter 7

# A PERIOD OF CRISIS AND CHANGE: THE FOURTEENTH AND FIFTEENTH CENTURIES

The epidemic of bubonic plague (the Black Death) that ravaged Europe in the years 1348 to 1350 was the greatest natural disaster that has ever been recorded in European history. Even the wars of the twentieth century killed a smaller proportion of the population. Historians now accept that in the terrible years of the mid-fourteenth century, in much of Europe between one-third and one-half of the population died. This epidemic did not occur in isolation: quite apart from local famines and epidemics, there were at least three general recurrences of the plague in the period between 1350 and 1400, and there had been earlier episodes of high mortality, notably in the famine years of 1315 to 1317.

Some historians have drawn a gloomy picture of European society in the fourteenth and fifteenth centuries. Undoubtedly our sources contain descriptions of physical decay—of unoccupied land, deserted villages, and shrinking towns. The psychological effect of the high death rate has been linked with the religious crises of the late Middle Ages, particularly the spread of heresies. Political and social conflicts became more bitter, resulting in the devastation by war of large areas of Europe, especially in France and Bohemia.

However, this picture of decay and destruction can be exaggerated, and some areas of expansion can be identified. While old centers of prosperity, such as Florence and Paris, declined, new ones, such as Antwerp, Nuremberg, and Seville, developed and expanded. New industries arose, especially rural cloth manufacture, and some sectors of agriculture continued to develop, as in the wine-growing areas of Spain.

Those historians who stress the elements of decline and those who allow for some expansion agree, however, in this respect: the fourteenth and fifteenth centuries saw profound changes both in the geographical distribution of wealth and in its distribution among different classes of society. These changes have been attributed to changes in the environment—a long-term deterioration in the climate and the spread of the plague bacillus—that lay beyond human control. An underdeveloped, peasant economy of the type that prevailed in medieval Europe was vulnerable to such environmental changes, since subsistence agriculture and unhealthy living conditions made bad weather and epidemics major killers. However, the failure of European society to recover rapidly from the setbacks of the fourteenth century suggests that fundamental social problems lay at the root of the problem, rather than accidents of nature.

Burying the dead at Tournai, Belgium, during the Black Death, 1349. In many parts of Europe, because of the huge number of deaths bodies were thrown into mass graves without even being placed in coffins. In some areas as many as 30 percent of the population are thought to have died.

## FAMINE

In the period around 1300 in many parts of Europe, the end of a long period of expansion had been reached. The numbers of people, the amount of cultivated land, and the size and number of villages and towns had all been rising steadily for at least three centuries. To take a single example, the village of Kempsey in Worcestershire, England, had tripled its population, from about 200 to about 600, in the two centuries between 1100 and 1300. Woodlands had been cleared and heaths plowed up to provide arable land to support the increased numbers of people. New hamlets had grown up within a mile or two of the parent village. But in spite of the development of new areas of cultivation and settlement, the share of land available to each peasant household had dwindled, and most of the peasant families worked only between three and fifteen acres of plowed land.

Already by the late thirteenth century the social crisis developing from this shortage of land began to have its effect. After a long period of expansion, the population of parts of Italy and southern France showed signs of beginning to decline. In southern England at the same time, each moderately poor harvest was accompanied by an increased number of deaths from starvation or the diseases associated with malnutrition.

In the summer of 1315 heavy rains ruined the harvest all over Europe, and thousands of people died. For peasant families living from year to year, with no surplus of food that could be stored, the loss of a single year's crop meant ruin. Even more desperate situations arose in the towns, where people relied on the food that peasants brought in for sale. There was another poor harvest in 1316. In six months in 1316, 10 percent of the population of the Flemish town of Ypres died.

Between 1315 and 1317, famine had spread over the whole continent, from Italy to the Baltic. The effect of only two bad harvests was devastating. Something, apparently, was seriously wrong with the social order in the early fourteenth century; the people of Europe seemed to be balanced on a knife edge between life and death.

The dance of death from the Marienkirche at Lübeck. Reactions to the Black Death were varied. Many people saw the bubonic plague as God's punishment on an evil generation and sought refuge in prayer and fasting. Others adopted "sympathetic magic," such as songs like "Ring around the rosy," and dances, imitating the convulsions of the dying. A few sought escape in flagellation. The wealthy tried to escape by leaving the crowded towns and living in the country. The theme that death chooses his victims without regard for rank was a common one in the art of the time.

## THE PLAGUE

Although the great famine of 1315–1317 stands out as a particularly dramatic episode, famine and disease continued to take their toll of the European population in the years after 1318, and the crisis reached its culmination in the late 1340s. In that decade a series of local famines are recorded, and then came the plague itself, entering Europe from the Mediterranean coast in the last weeks of 1347, and spreading north to Scandinavia and Scotland by the winter of 1349–1350. In each district the disease lasted for some months, and the scattered records that have survived from individual towns and villages show a death rate that often exceeded a third of the population.

The spread of the plague and the resulting mortality rates reflect the living conditions of the victims. People were packed together; in many areas in north Italy and in parts of France and England, censuses and tax records show that in the preplague period the density of people was comparable to or even greater than that of the supposedly overpopulated twentieth century. Peasants and townsmen lived in houses that often provided only a single room as sleeping accommodation for whole families. Houses lacked adequate floors and had thatched roofs without ceilings. Both roofs and walls were of wattle and daub (interwoven twigs smeared with mud) and thus harbored the rats from whose fleas humans contracted the plague. (Bubonic plague is a disease of rats that spreads to humans when the rats die and the fleas transfer themselves to human hosts.) Once the epidemic developed, a rarer variation of the disease, pneumonic plague, was spread by direct contact with other infected humans. Other diseases, such as dysentery, may have accompanied these two forms of plague and contributed to the high death rate.

The death of so many people in such a short time caused an immediate disruption of normal life. Some fled, particularly from infected towns, and the survivors who remained were faced with major problems of burying corpses, arranging for

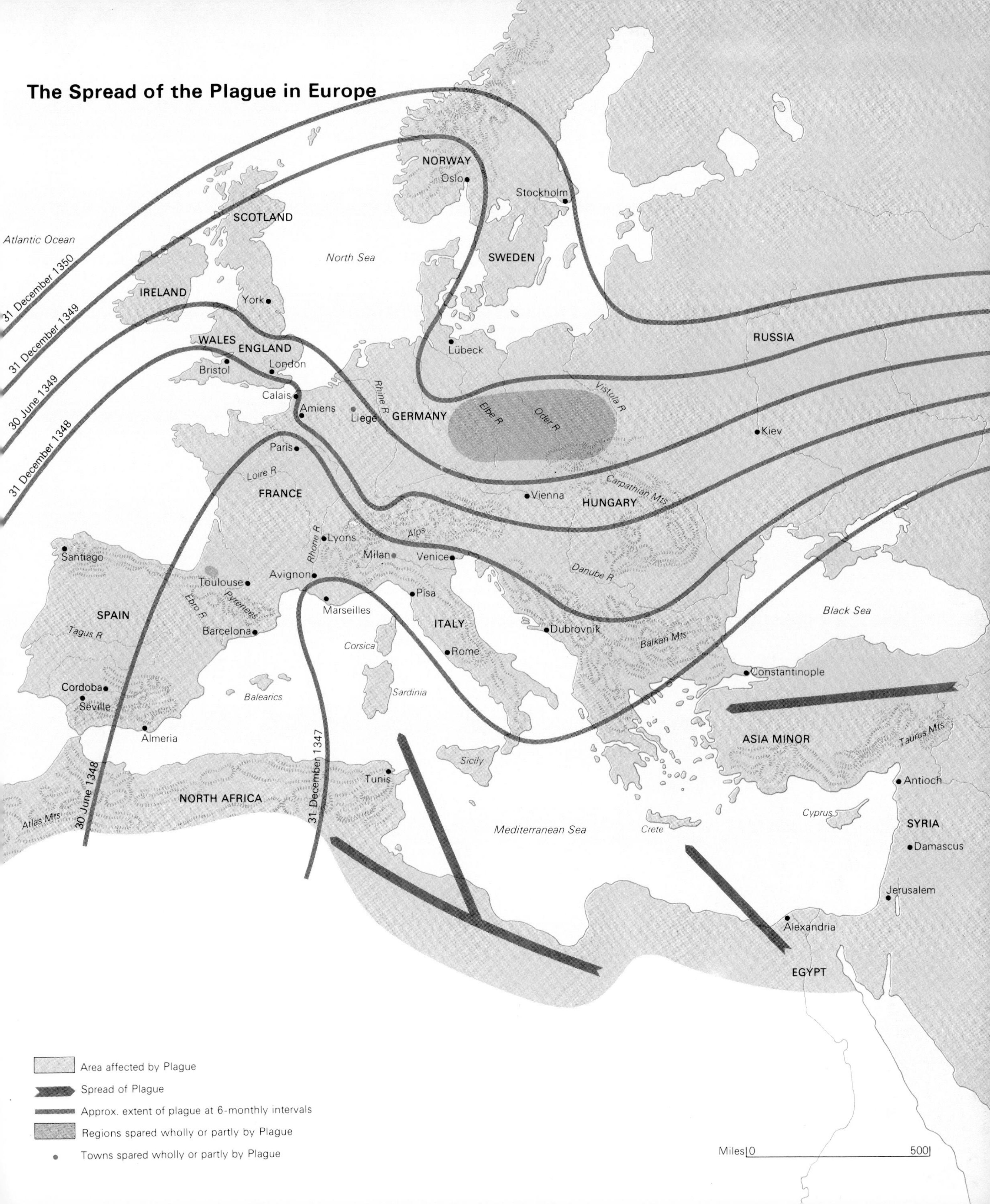
The Spread of the Plague in Europe
31 December 1350
31 December 1349
30 June 1349
31 December 1348
30 June 1348
31 December 1347
Atlantic Ocean
North Sea
NORWAY
Oslo
Stockholm
SWEDEN
SCOTLAND
IRELAND
York
WALES
ENGLAND
London
Bristol
Calais
Amiens
Liege
Rhine R
GERMANY
Lübeck
Elbe R
Oder R
Vistula R
RUSSIA
Kiev
Paris
Loire R
FRANCE
Vienna
HUNGARY
Carpathian Mts
Alps
Lyons
Rhone R
Milan
Venice
Danube R
Santiago
Toulouse
Avignon
Ebro R
Pyrenees
Marseilles
Pisa
SPAIN
Tagus R
Barcelona
ITALY
Dubrovnik
Balkan Mts
Black Sea
Corsica
Rome
Constantinople
Cordoba
Seville
Balearics
Sardinia
Almeria
ASIA MINOR
Taurus Mts
Sicily
Tunis
Antioch
NORTH AFRICA
Atlas Mts
Cyprus
SYRIA
Mediterranean Sea
Crete
Damascus
Jerusalem
Alexandria
EGYPT
Area affected by Plague
Spread of Plague
Approx. extent of plague at 6-monthly intervals
Regions spared wholly or partly by Plague
Towns spared wholly or partly by Plague
Miles 0 500

# Manorial Life: A Comparison 1300 and 1400

*Above:* Pallas and Arachne weaving, from Ovid's *Metamorphoses*, fifteenth-century Flemish. *(Right above)* A packhorse and a driver approach an inn, from Marco Polo's *Les Livres du Graunt Caam*, c.1400. Wool was one of the four commodities for which a wide market existed throughout Europe, and as a result it was exported widely from sheepgrowing areas. *(Right below)* A woman uses a distaff and spindle, while her husband sits and watches, from the *Roman de la Rose*, fifteenth-century French. On the table next to the husband is a wooden winding machine.

One of the rather better-off tenant farmers in midland England in the early fourteenth century was Walter Rusmere, who had a holding of fifteen acres. From this, he had to maintain his family, consisting of a wife and two or three children, and also apparently his widowed mother, Matilda Rusmere. Their lands formed part of the common arable of the village, with many strips scattered over larger fields. This land had to be cultivated according to traditional communal arrangements, so that only half of it was sown with crops each year, the other half being left fallow in order to recover its fertility. Even the seven or eight acres that were cultivated each year were not very productive. Rusmere probably had few animals—much of the village pastureland had been plowed over during the period of expansion of the twelfth and thirteenth centuries. There was, therefore, a shortage of manure, and the crop that Rusmere harvested each year from unfertilized land was a meager one. His family rarely ate meat; their staple foods of bread and pottage came from the grain harvested from their eight acres of arable land.

Thus a shortage of land and poor methods of agriculture kept Rusmere and his family at subsistence level. Life could then be very dangerous if the vagaries of the weather reduced the crop yields below even their normally low level.

Rusmere, and people like him, faced other problems as well. A substantial part of the crop had to be paid in feudal dues, tithes, rents, and taxes to his social superiors. After the harvest, before the grain was collected into Rusmere's barn, the rector of the parish church or his employees would travel around the fields collecting tithes (one-tenth of the crop). Of the remaining sheaves, some went immediately to the landlord as rent and a considerable part had to be sold so that Rusmere could pay two shillings as a fixed cash rent. He was also required to work for two days of each week, and for even more days in the harvest season, on the lord's own demesne land. By this time, lords were often demanding that peasant tenants pay money instead of performing labor services, and Rusmere may thus have incurred even greater cash payments—perhaps as much as another ten shillings.

All these regular annual payments of money and grain meant that Rusmere lost as much as half of the produce of his land before he could feed his family. The situation was made even more difficult by a series of extraordinary payments that he had to make—taxes to the king and various "fines" and taxes demanded by the lord, such as when Rusmere sold ale to his neighbors, when he took over his holding of land from his parents, or when his daughter married. The tenant also had to have his lord's permission for his daughter to marry. Peasants were often burdened with debt as a result of such demands made on their resources. Since they could afford only a restricted amount of food for themselves and their families, they can be assumed to have felt some resentment against the landlords and rulers whose exactions made a difficult situation almost intolerable.

A century later the situation was very different. Thomas Rusmere, perhaps the great grandson of Walter Rusmere, shows how far the position of the tenant farmer had improved as a result of the Black Death and the other troubles of the fourteenth century. The population of his village fell from about 600 in 1300 to between 350 and 400 in the early fifteenth century. Because of the frequent vacancies arising in the village, Thomas was able to take two holdings totaling thirty-three acres. The village pastures were capable of providing Thomas with food for many more animals than had been owned by his predecessor. In addition to his purely agricultural activities, Thomas rented a grain mill and kept an inn. He sold bread and ale to those of his neighbors who did not produce their own food and drink—presumably the wage laborers of the village, whose spending power had increased since 1350.

Like his great-grandfather, Thomas Rusmere had to hand over some of the produce of his land to his superiors. His obligation to tithes and taxes remained, but the burden of rent imposed by the landlord was gradually reduced and the urgent need for land in the village relaxed. In particular, many of the extraordinary and arbitrary exactions that had made life so difficult for Walter Rusmere were reduced or even abolished. For example, the heavy fine that had previously been paid by each new tenant on taking up a holding had become a nominal sum of a few shillings and was sometimes waived altogether.

The farming itself followed much the same pattern as it had done a century earlier. Grain-farming still formed the main part both of labor and produce. Farming was adapting increasingly to the use of a three-field—instead of a two-field—system. One strip would be used for autumn planting and another for spring planting, while a third lay fallow. Most manors were self-sufficient for the basic needs of life. Markets and fairs supplied needs that could not be satisfied within the locality, and also provided an outlet for any surplus that might arise.

Not only were Thomas Rusmere's holdings larger than Walter Rusmere's had been; because of improved agricultural methods, his yield per acre was significantly higher. His family therefore ate better than Walter's had and were even able to store some surplus for emergencies. Also, Thomas had more cash. Most important, he was allowed to keep a larger proportion of what he made. On the whole, life was much easier for Thomas than it had been for Walter.

the disposal of the property of the dead, looking after the many orphans and widows, and at the same time attempting to continue with the everyday tasks of agriculture and economic activity. The speed with which some communities returned to normal life after this first epidemic of the plague is recorded in the administrative documents of such bodies as the councils of Italian towns.

Had the plague occurred as an isolated disaster, therefore, recovery from its effects might have been rapid. The survivors were provided with opportunities in the form of untenanted land and high wages that would have allowed early marriage and a consequent rise in the birthrate. However, the epidemic of 1347–1350 marked only the beginning of a series of outbreaks. These often affected parts of Europe rather than the whole, and they were less virulent than the first attack, but most areas of Europe experienced at least three epidemics in the latter half of the fourteenth century. The population reached a low point by the early fifteenth century, and it remained at this point until about 1500. The Black Death of the mid-fourteenth century can thus be seen as an important contributor to a long-term decline in population that began in some areas as early as 1300 and continued for two centuries.

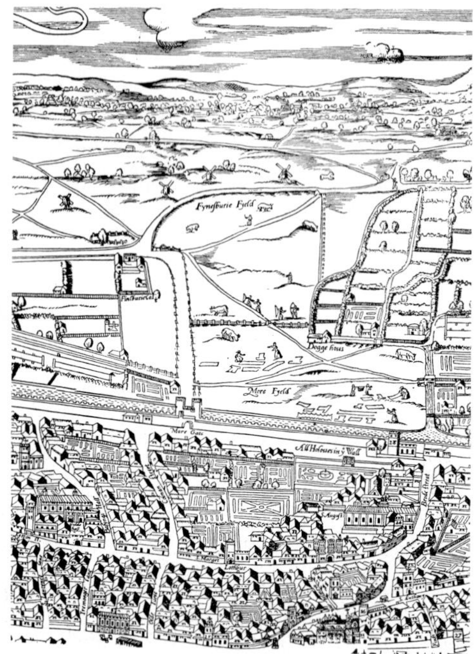

Detail from a map of medieval London. The area shown is the northeastern part of the city and the fields beyond. Medieval London was already a major trading center. The city of London itself was still a walled town. Despite the great fire of London in 1666, heavy bombing during the two world wars, and massive redevelopment since 1945, the city has retained something of its medieval character. The street plan and street names are largely the same as those shown on the map. The administration of the city, largely in the hands of livery-companies, based on medieval guilds, has also changed little.

## CHANGES IN THE COUNTRYSIDE

The effects of the decline in population can be seen in all sections of society in the period after 1350. Before the population decline a huge area of land, some of it quite unsuitable for cultivation, had produced grain crops that provided the basic food supply of the peasants and town dwellers. Much of this land was abandoned as the population shrank, and by a process of natural selection, thousands of villages were deserted in favor of more attractive dwelling places in either country or town.

A more dramatic and immediate result was a shortage of labor. This caused a rise in wages, which in many cases became a long-lasting trend. Governments attempted to resist the increases, but their efforts rarely succeeded in preventing a major improvement in the incomes and living standards of these many urban workers and the small holders or landless laborers in the countryside who relied on employment for money wages.

For peasant cultivators, the death or migration of their neighbors increased the amount of land available for cultivation by the survivors. With more land to go around, the number of small holders declined and a minority of peasants were even able to amass holdings large enough for commercial farming. As the need to produce food grains for the inflated preplague population disappeared, peasants had opportunities to improve their agricultural methods and, in particular, to keep more animals. And as the demand for land fell, landlords could no longer enforce payment of the high rents that had prevailed earlier. In Western Europe, therefore, the restrictions of servile status were gradually relaxed.

For the landlords, the situation after the plague required considerable readjustment. Up to 1300 the lay and Church nobility had enjoyed steadily rising revenues. With peasants desperate to obtain land, rents everywhere rose. A nearly continuous shortage of foodstuffs ensured that high prices could be obtained from the sale of produce, and domestic and agricultural labor was plentiful and cheap. The growing revenues of the upper classes were used to maintain a life style appropriate to their social station. Social pressures often drove aristocratic families into debt and even ruin as they indulged in conspicuous consumption of exotic foodstuffs (particularly spices), high-quality cloth, buildings, and entertainment.

The decline in population reduced many of the sources of revenue of the aristocracy. Their main income came from rents, and these fell as tenants died or migrated and the remaining tenants demanded reductions. Many of the goods produced by aristocratic lands, notably grain, declined in price, while the goods they consumed, such as cloth, spices, and wine, and the labor they employed became more expensive.

Although the nobility still maintained themselves as the wealthiest and politically most powerful section of society, they did experience financial problems. Also they lost some of their direct control over their social inferiors. Serfdom, the legal condition that institutionalized the subjection of many peasants to their lords, had begun to decline in much of Europe before 1300, but by 1500 its disappearance was almost total. The great exception lay in the lands to the east of the River Elbe, where an aristocracy independent of control by royal authority reacted to the labor shortage by imposing servile dues and subjecting a peasantry that had hitherto enjoyed considerable freedom to close personal control.

Tomb of a knight in armor.

### Peasant Uprisings

Some of the most important changes that followed the reduction in population during the fourteenth and fifteenth centuries involved the social relationships between lords and peasants. Because landlords enjoyed a monopoly of political and military power, rents and wages were not changed by a process of free bargaining of the modern type. The peasants, and particularly the serfs, had few rights and powers, though they had advantages in number and in a long tradition of communal solidarity based on their experience of life in village communities. Just as the lords maintained their position by the ultimate threat of force, so peasants had to have recourse to violence in order to press their demands.

Rebellions of peasants, often on a small scale, are recorded from the whole medieval period, but they did not break out as large and effective risings until the 1320s. Practically every European country experienced a major peasant uprising in the succeeding two centuries—Flanders in 1323 to 1328, France in 1358, England in 1381, Bohemia and the Scandinavian countries in the early fifteenth century, Italy in 1420 and 1460, Spain in 1462 to 1486, and Germany at the beginning of the sixteenth century. These were not all blind insurrections by desperately impoverished men, although the French Jacquerie has been so characterized. Elsewhere, the rebels often had defined aims, ranging from idealistic proposals for the removal of the whole ruling class of aristocrats and churchmen to much more practical and down-to-earth demands for the removal of unpopular taxes, rents, and servile status. The uprisings often involved all sections of rural society, including the more prosperous peasants. Their organization, although less effective than that of their opponents, was sometimes successful, as when the peasants of maritime Flanders virtually ran the administration of the district for five years.

The military defeat of many of the peasant risings has led historians to conclude that they were ineffective. In fact, some risings achieved their defined aims. The Spanish rebellion of the late fifteenth century ended in 1486 when the Sentence of Guadalupe removed the hated *remanca* (serfdom) and gave about 50,000 peasants their freedom. After the English revolt of 1381, the poll tax that had sparked the rising was never levied again. The shock of the risings, even after they had been savagely repressed, as after the Jacquerie of 1358, influenced the way in which lords responded to peasant demands and made them more willing to make concessions.

The rebellions took place during the period when the fall in population had improved the bargaining position of the peasantry. They were necessary because landlords and governments, refusing to recognize the new realities, attempted to use their power to maintain the old conditions. What the uprisings accomplished was to force the ruling class to remove some exactions that hindered the peasantry from taking advantage of new opportunities.

## CHANGES IN THE TOWNS

Although the towns of medieval Europe proclaimed their separateness by means of the physical barrier of their stone walls and the legal and political barriers created by centuries of privileged self-government, they depended closely on the countryside for their existence. They needed food, raw materials, and immigrant labor from the country, and they supplied the nobility of both country and town with traded luxuries and the products of urban industry. So that, although different social forms were established in the towns and cities, they were still not independent of the influences that operated on agrarian society.

However, the changes of the medieval period appear in their most extreme form in the towns. Towns grew even more rapidly than the villages of the countryside in the period before 1300. Large centers such as Paris, with its population of about 200,000 in 1300, were created, and at the same time perhaps a dozen other cities arose with populations exceeding 40,000. In the Low Countries and Italy, the process of urbanization had been particularly intense, and great cities and smaller towns clustered together; in some regions as much as a third of the population lived in an urban environment.

Recreational activities in the fifteenth century: *(top)* a game of chess, and playing ball, *(above)* music making. The increasing emphasis on luxury in the late Middle Ages led to the development of recreational activities at the courts of kings and lords. Music, in particular, advanced enormously. The court of the dukes of Burgundy was the center of fifteenth-century developments in popular music. The work of composers such as Josquin des Pres has recently been seen to be of great originality and importance. During the Middle Ages chess was imported from the east and became a popular game among the nobility.

By the early fourteenth century most towns had reached the limits of their physical expansion, and just as their growth had been more rapid than that of the countryside, so their decline was more catastrophic. Plagues and diseases such as influenza hit the towns, with their overcrowding and poor sanitation, hardest. The result was a constant high rate of mortality in the towns and a long-term decline of population. For example, the Catalan city of Barcelona fell in population size from 50,000 in 1340 to about 40,000 in 1359 and then down to as little as 20,000 in the late fifteenth century. As the population declined, the physical area occupied by the town dwindled. Some towns were virtually abandoned, but this was rare. More commonly, as houses fell into decay, the area occupied by gardens and other open spaces increased.

The economies of some towns also went through profound changes, particularly those large cities whose wealth was based on supplying the needs of aristocratic consumers. The great ports of Italy—Venice and Genoa—relied on the importation and distribution over the whole of Europe of luxuries obtained from the East, such as spices and silks. This trade was substantial in bulk (at its height, Venice was handling 50,000 tons of goods from the East every year), and the high value of the goods and the very high profit margins meant that whole communities of merchants waxed fat on it.

Every town had an industrial element in its population, and some, such as Ghent and Ypres in Flanders and Florence and Siena in Italy, specialized in the production of high-quality woolen cloth, which was traded over a large area. Many of the smaller-scale industries, such as leatherworking (a common product being saddles and other goods for equipping horses) and the metal industries, specializing in weapons and jewellery, were also aimed at providing for the needs of upper-class consumers.

Both the international trade in luxuries and the industrial manufacture of high-quality goods fell into decline in the fourteenth and fifteenth centuries. At Florence and Ypres, cloth production had by the 1370s fallen to a third of what its peak had been in 1300. The volume of goods passing through ports such as Genoa and Marseilles underwent a series of fluctuations that were influenced by local factors, but all ports apparently reached their lowest point in the middle years of the fifteenth century.

This depression cannot be blamed exclusively on the reduced population. The numbers of upper-class consumers may not have fallen very drastically; rather, it must be assumed that the nobility were no longer able to afford to drink so much wine or to line their clothes with so many squirrel furs and that they bought less fine

Ypres cloth and seasoned their food with smaller quantities of pepper. This reduced consumption of luxuries undoubtedly reflects the reduced revenue obtained by landlords from their estates. The fortunes of the established cities were linked closely with the spending power of the upper classes.

Not all of the economic changes that affected towns can be linked with plagues and famines. Some changes arose directly from the political conflicts of the period. Trade was peculiarly vulnerable to war and political troubles; wandering armies and the piratical activities of naval forces could rapidly break lines of communication. The Mediterranean, always a dangerous sea, became with the advance of the Ottoman Turks increasingly hostile to Italian shipping, and trading fleets had to travel in convoys to ward off attacks. The Flemish towns suffered badly from the political conflicts between England and France in the fourteenth century. In the late fifteenth century, the policies of the Dukes of Burgundy helped to eclipse the importance of Bruges as a center of finance and international trade and provided for the rise of Antwerp to replace it. In the twelfth and thirteenth centuries, the great fairs of Champagne had provided the hub of long-distance trade; here Italian merchants had brought their goods for sale to their northern counterparts for distribution into France, Germany, and England. With the political changes in the area, the Italians began to pass by this market, developing new and more direct routes, notably through the straits of Gibraltar.

In the towns themselves, the fourteenth century saw a succession of violent social conflicts, which were sharpest and most frequent in the most highly developed industrial centers such as Flanders and northern Italy. These towns, notably Bruges, Ghent, Ypres, Florence, and Siena, had achieved self-government under the leadership of oligarchies whose wealth and power had been based on the control of international trade and the ownership of landed property, both within and outside the

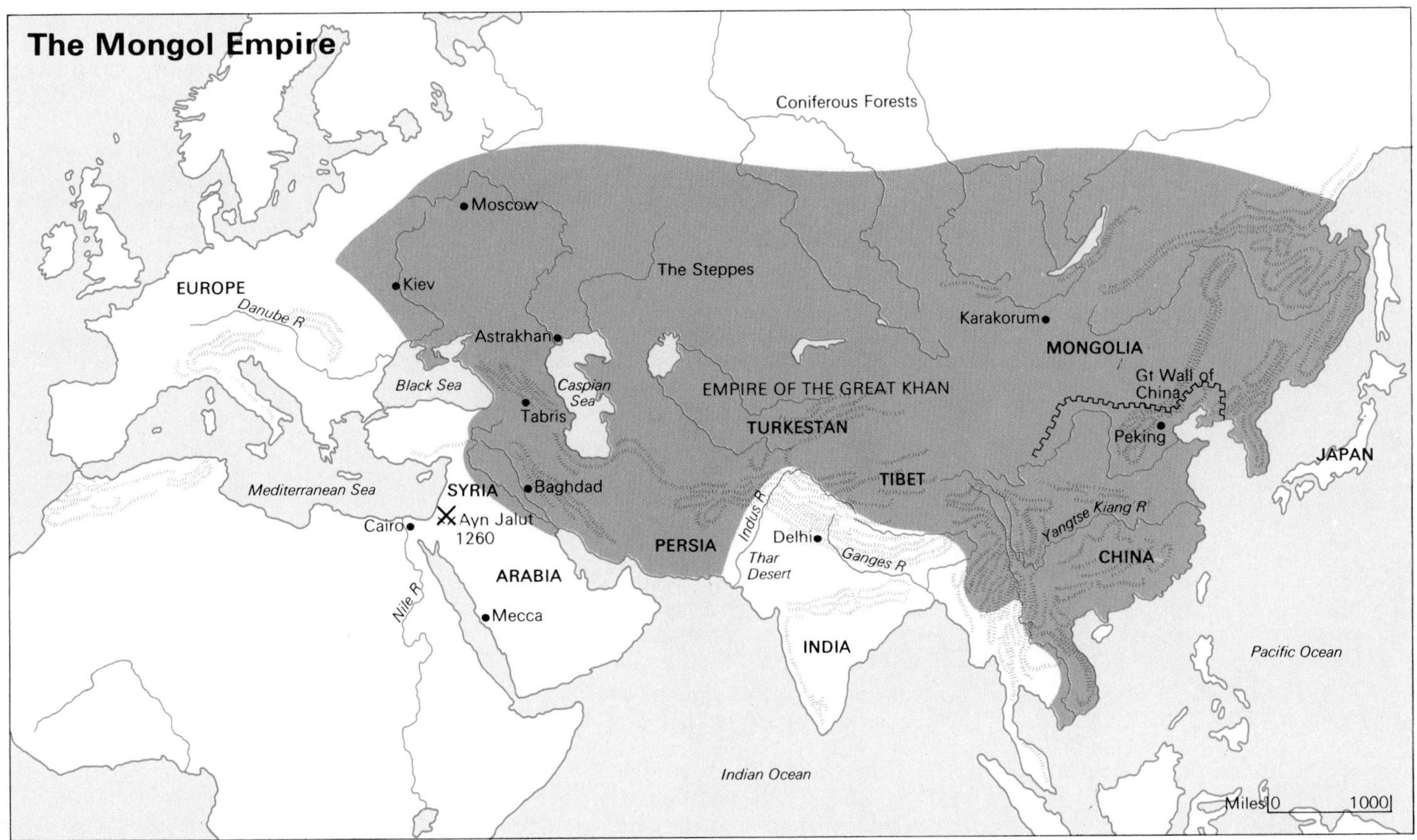

# The Mongols

*Above:* The Mongol leader, Chingiz Khan. The Mongol Empire, created by the energy of Chingiz Khan, threatened to engulf Europe. He saw the value of discipline and technology, and also the use that could be made of fear.
*Right:* Ogodei, Chingiz's successor.

At the end of the thirteenth century the Mongol empire stretched from the Pacific almost to the Mediterranean and from the Baltic to the China Sea. Only the British Empire ever reached a comparable size. But whereas Britain built on sea-links, the Mongol empire was entirely land-based.

In the late twelfth century Inner Asia was inhabited by scattered nomadic peoples. They spoke different languages, but in other respects they lived similar lives. Most were pagans although some were touched by Islam, Buddhism or Christianity. They kept herds of horses, sheep and goats, lived in tents and roamed the steppes in small family clan groups. Occasionally, for war or the great annual hunts, they would combine in larger tribal groups. But for the most part they remained politically disunited and, encouraged by the Chinese, fought amongst themselves.

The Mongols, whose pastures were on the headwaters of the Onon and Kerulen rivers, were only one small tribe among many. But, at the end of the twelfth century, they produced a leader of genius—Temujin, better known to history as Chingiz Khan. Having built up a following as an able war leader he defeated his rivals and united not only the Mongol tribe but all the other tribes of Mongolia, who thereupon took the name Mongol. Immediately thereafter he attacked the two most northerly Chinese states and in 1215 took Peking. He then turned westwards and in 1219–23 smashed the political organization of Turkestan, swept through eastern Iran and sent a detachment as far as Kiev. At his death in 1227 there was still no Mongol empire but he had forged and tested the military force with which his successors could build it.

The expansion of Mongol power under his successors was rapid. The major effort was always against China and it was only after long years of campaigning that his grandson, Khublai, in 1279 finally extinguished the last resistance of the Sung dynasty, ruled all China and extended his power into southeast Asia. By then the Mongol conquests in the west were already completed. In 1236–42 another grandson, Batu, led a great campaign that drove through southern Russia and well into eastern Europe before Batu set up, on the lower Volga, the capital of the Golden Horde, which, from its base in the southern steppes, controlled the Slav states of the northern forests of Russia. A second major campaign in 1255–58 was led by Khublai's brother, Hulegu, who conquered Iran and Iraq and overthrew the Abbasid Caliphate.

In the meantime, at Karakorum in Mongolia, the Mongols built a great new capital, furnished it with booty from their conquests, and populated it with captured artisans. To Karakorum came a stream of subject kings and princes together with ambassadors from as far as western Europe.

Contemporary victims attributed the success of the Mongols to the punishment of God for their own sins, or to the number and ferocity of the Mongols. Later historians wrote of mass migrations of hungry nomads fleeing from climatic change and over-population on the steppes. But the truth is simpler. There was no climatic change or mass migration. The great majority of Mongols returned to Mongolia after the campaigns. The armies of Batu and Hulegu had a substantial Turkish element from the beginning and, as the Mongols withdrew, their places were filled by Turkish nomads gathered up as the campaigns proceeded. Nor were the numbers so great. In no campaign were there much above 100,000 Mongols. The explanation lies in the basic superiority of light cavalry in open country in the conditions of medieval warfare. And, as light cavalry, the Mongols were unsurpassable. Their skill with bow, sword and spear came from continual practice. All they needed was unity. Once Chingiz had enforced that, his army was ready made. The clan system, with its strong patriarchal family organization, could easily be converted into a semi-feudal system in which clan leaders performed military service under the leadership of specified members of the Chingizide family. Thereafter no force could defeat the Mongols in the field. Sieges of towns were a different matter. Before they learned the techniques from captives they were obliged to blockade towns for years. Their reputation for ferocity partly derived from their weakness in this respect, because they slaughtered resisting garrisons to deter others from doing likewise.

The Mongol conquests are therefore relatively easy to explain. The empire was held together by various factors. The Mongols were nomads and therefore thought in terms of authority over men rather than territory. Accordingly a Mongol prince might receive allegiance and tribute from clans living in the territory of another prince. A common authority made this possible. Secondly, all the early campaigns were joint enterprises. Each Mongol prince contributed men from his own clan and received appropriate shares of the loot. A third factor was the communications system. To rule so large an area, speedy information was essential. To provide this, the Mongol rulers established an elaborate and extensive system of post stations and Mongol messengers achieved extraordinary speed on their journeys. Fourth, and perhaps most important, was the prestige of Chingiz's family—the Golden Family.

But although the Mongol empire held together as a reality for sixty years and nominally for much longer, it eventually collapsed. One cause was the Mongol law of inheritance, which divided a man's possessions at his death. Although one son, Ogodei (1229–41), was recognized as Great Khan after Chingiz's death, some great vassals soon became more powerful than the Great Khan himself. In 1250 the descendants of two of the four sons of Chingiz allied to defeat the others. In 1258–60 a second civil war took place. By the last quarter of the fourteenth century the empire was rent by disputes. The two great western states fought each other for possession of Transcaucasia, while Khublai was locked in a long struggle with Kaidu (d. 1301), the ruler of Central Asia and western Mongolia.

The inheritance system and personal quarrels weakened the empire. But behind its decline lay two other factors. First was the fatal attraction of the great settled civilizations with which the Mongols came into contact. Although Mongol soldiers in China lived apart from the Chinese people, the princes rapidly adopted Chinese ways. The Khans of the Golden Horde and the Il-Khans adopted Islam, and their capitals—Saray and Tabriz—became notable towns. The old Mongol religion, and, what was more significant, the legal system—the Yasak of Chingiz—was progressively discarded in favor of the more sophisticated systems of settled law. The Mongol princes were being absorbed by the cultures in which they had settled. The size of the empire was more important as a cause of decline. Like the dinosaur, the Mongol empire had grown too big to survive.

The fourteenth century saw the gradual collapse of the Mongol states. In 1368 the native Ming dynasty replaced the Mongols in China. The Il-Khans of Syria collapsed after 1340. The Golden Horde lasted longer, perhaps because it was located in a primarily nomadic area. But, in the course of the fifteenth century, it broke up into smaller units which were gradually absorbed by Russia, although the last of these, the Khanate of the Crimea was not annexed until 1783. Outside Mongolia the most enduring states were in Turkestan. There, the Turko-Mongol clans, constantly reinforced by new immigrants from the steppes, dominated the political scene until the nineteenth century. Even Timur (1336–1405) the most brilliant ruler of his time, never dared to rule in his own name, but always maintained puppet rulers of the family of Chingiz. Finally should be mentioned the Moguls of India, whose rule lasted nominally from 1526 until 1857. They were, however, Mongols only in name.

The Mongol legacy was a considerable one. In Russia they changed the course of history entirely. Their economic impact was also significant. They destroyed agriculture and industry and reversed the tide of settlement which had been encroaching on the steppes for centuries. By establishing a single political unit they fostered the growth of trade. Italian merchants like Marco Polo (c. 1254–1324) penetrated to China in search of silks and spices. Their cultural significance lies in the provision of a channel along which ideas could flow from east to west. They formed a nomadic world-bridge to breach the isolation that geography imposed upon medieval man.

towns. By the thirteenth century, industrial development had created new social groups—manufacturers, craftsmen, and laborers—who organized themselves in guilds for the regulation and protection of their interests. They were excluded from the governing bodies of the towns, which made the decisions on such vital matters as taxation without consulting the industrial element. The crafts pressed for representation in the town government but were themselves divided between employers and employees. Thus the struggles within the towns could be very complex, with all those involved in craft activities attacking the ruling oligarchy and with the wage workers, in turn, demanding better conditions from their employers. In Florence in the thirteenth century, the craft guilds gained control of the city government, but as industry declined in the fourteenth century, they, in turn, faced rebellion, culminating in the temporary seizure of control by the unprivileged cloth workers in 1378.

In Flanders the conflicts resulted in a broadening of the basis of the ruling oligarchies in the towns, but in Italy the struggle between social classes and political factions so weakened the self-governing city republics that despots were able to seize power.

A fight with pickaxes and shields.

## THE NEW ECONOMY

In spite of the decline in population and the political and economic troubles of the period, the towns emerged at the end of the fifteenth century still as a major social force. One of the most important results of the changes of the later Middle Ages was a shift in the geography of trade and industry. New industries and commercial enterprises arose as the older ones failed. Many of the old, established organizations reacted to the erosion of their position by becoming more narrow and restrictive. Thus the merchants of the Hanseatic League, the federation of German towns that held a monopoly over the trade of the Baltic, fought fiercely to keep competitors out of their sphere of influence, but the ultimate result was to strangle the enterprise of the commerce of the northern cities and to allow the initiative to be taken by their Dutch and English rivals. The most successful German towns of the fifteenth century, Augsburg and Nuremberg, and the new center of the Low Countries, Antwerp, were characterized by their comparative lack of restrictions—monopolies were not rigorously enforced, and newcomers to these towns could set up businesses without encountering serious obstacles and opposition.

Similarly, the decline of the old clothmaking centers was hastened by their restrictive regulations, as in the industrial centers of Florence and Ghent. In the country and smaller towns of England, the Low Countries, Germany, and Spain, a new cloth industry, comparatively free from close control, flourished under the management of a new type of entrepreneur.

A notable feature of many of the industries of the later Middle Ages was that they aimed at producing goods that were in general use among a wider section of society. Cloth production became much more dispersed in the countryside. Often the textiles made outside the careful regulation of the towns were inferior in quality, but they were also cheaper and could be purchased by more people. There seems also to have been an increased demand for iron and for foodstuffs, such as herrings and butter, that had previously been available only to a minority.

Also developing out of the difficulties of the fourteenth and fifteenth centuries were improvements in both industrial techniques and trading methods. In order to maintain profits in the context of the higher wage costs and reduced volume of trade, economies had to be found in the operation of commerce. In industry, where the essential need was for a reduction of wage costs, water power was introduced into the production of iron. Two developments in industries employing small numbers of men had vast repercussions: paper manufacture spread over Europe from Italy to replace parchment as the main writing material, and in the late fifteenth century, printing was invented in Germany.

Italy remained the land of the businessman *par excellence*. Here new techniques of organizing commerce arose in response to the needs for greater efficiency. Manuals were written for the instruction of traders, the flow of money was improved with the increasing use of bills of exchange (the nearest equivalent to paper money), and individual merchants and firms were able to exercise greater control over profitability through the use of double-entry accounting.

By the early fourteenth century, banking had developed as a specialized activity of certain companies, the most important being the Florentine firms of the Bardi and Peruzzi, who had branches all over Europe. They had developed their business by providing financial services for trade, but they became increasingly involved in lending to governments—a very hazardous operation, as they found in the 1340s when Edward III of England was unable either to repay the loans that had been made or to pay interest. But the subsequent collapse of these Florentine banks did not prevent the continuation of a close relationship between rulers and financiers. A new class had come into being. Merchants such as the Medici in Italy, Jacques Coeur in France, and the de la Poles in England were making their fortunes in the new markets and industries of the fifteenth century. These men were capitalists, and they were a new phenomenon.

Did the changes of the fourteenth and fifteenth centuries create a new form of society? Although the balance of social forces shifted, Europe remained an agrarian peasant society, dominated by kings, churchmen, and aristocrats as before. However, some developments, often on a small scale, prepared the ground for future transformations. Some countries emerged in the fifteenth century as more active in commerce and industry, among them England and Holland. Technical innovations, notably in shipbuilding and navigation, made preliminary voyages to the non-European world possible at the end of the fifteenth century. In Italy, advanced business methods, such as insurance, bills of exchange, and accounting techniques, aided the growth of early capitalist enterprise. The confusion and disturbances of the period also had their effect on ideas, and the philosophical and theological systems of the "age of faith" were eroded by the critical humanism of Italy and the heresies of northern Europe, which are dealt with in book 5.

Chapter 8

# POPULAR PIETY AND THE DECLINE OF PAPAL AUTHORITY

In the twelfth and thirteenth centuries, the Western Church under the leadership of the popes seemed to go from height to height, becoming with each generation better organized, better educated, more effective in its guidance of lay attitudes, more widespread in its missionary activity, and more influential in the lands of the infidel. The papacy, triumphant over the emperors, was everywhere recognized as the central institution of Christendom. Such thirteenth-century popes as Innocent III (pope 1198–1216) and Gregory IX (pope 1227–41) directed a vast international corporation that was active in every corner of Europe—organizing local churches, supervising the international orders of friars, judging cases, and directing missions. The papacy could harness to its services not only the greatest minds of the time—St Thomas Aquinas is a notable example—but also the spiritual genius of such men as St Dominic and St Francis of Assisi.

In the early fourteenth century, the papacy moved from Italy to Avignon, a more convenient location from which to exercise a centralized authority. At first, the popes seem, if anything, to have increased their power. They now had a systematic body of law, and their decrees were accepted and acted upon throughout western Europe. Their control of appointments increased steadily. Their financial resources grew larger and larger as payments from clergy in the first year of their appointments were added to the ordinary taxations of the Church. The popes, of course, had their setbacks, but such incidents did not disturb the smooth working of papal government. Theologians in general continued to attribute to the papacy temporal as well as spiritual dominion over the world.

Underlying the papal government of the fourteenth century was a new development that had great significance for the future: the emergence of a university-trained clergy. Opportunities for education had greatly increased. In 1300 only a few universities existed, and these trained a narrow elite; by 1400 there were fifty-five universities, and many more were founded in the fifteenth century. The new universities turned out a large number of solidly educated, competent, professional people, capable of administration, diplomacy, and business as well as the cure of souls. The higher clergy, many of them closely connected with lay governments, were nearly all graduates; already by 1350 at least half of the English bishops were graduates, and by 1500 not a single bishop lacked a degree.

One effect of this education was a more efficient control of parishes and lay religion. At the same time, it brought the clergy more closely together than before. The churches and monasteries of the twelfth century had lived under the shadow of patrons, often local families who filled their benefices, or "jobs," with relations and dependents. The supply of graduates made more feasible by the fourteenth century what popes had long dreamed of: an educated clergy whose loyalties were to the Church alone.

Pope Boniface VIII with the college of cardinals. The cardinals in the Middle Ages were mainly bishops of dioceses around Rome. They had substantial power, ranking as Roman princes, junior only to the pope; governing the church during papal vacancies; and electing one of their own number as successor on the death of a pope. The right of papal election by cardinals existed from 1179, but only after 1271 were the cardinals locked up during the election. Difficulties still arose occasionally, however, and the Great Schism was caused by disagreement among different groups of cardinals.

Yet it was during this period, when the papacy was apparently at the height of its power, that both pope and Church became the targets of increasingly serious attack from an ever-growing circle of critics. Indeed, one of the most striking characteristics of the age is this mounting criticism of established institutions and their personnel—monks and monasteries, friars and friaries, bishops and their officials, universities, clerical morals, and of course, popes and the papacy itself.

The religious ideas of many people, especially educated people were changing. In the twelfth and thirteenth centuries even its severest critics had conceived of the Church as the City of God, an association of Christians fighting together against the infidel or the inroads of the secular world or the ignorance and heathenism of the people. Some critics of the fourteenth century saw things differently. They, too, were awaiting the reign of Antichrist predicted in the *Apocalypse*, but they identified Antichrist with the very center of the Church—with the papacy, especially. The tide of criticism began to flow with Marsilius of Padua's *Defensor Pacis* (1324) which denied the right of the clergy to meddle in secular affairs. It came to full flood in the years between 1370 and 1440 in what was, very nearly, a first Reformation.

Monks in a herb garden, c.1400. In pagan times many herbs had been used for magical purposes, but in the Middle Ages herbs were cultivated chiefly for their medicinal effect.

Why did this happen? Apparently, the centralization of papal government, although it had the immediate result of increasing the authority of the pope, in the long run made it impossible for the vast machinery of the Church to be adequately controlled. Corruption was inevitable. More important, the centralized government was remote from the people, and the Church began to lose its spiritual authority. This was a time of great religious energy, but the springs of inspiration were to be found among the laity and lower clergy and not within the organization of the Church itself.

Thus the latter half of the fourteenth century saw the triumphant progress of the papacy falter and then fail. Papal leadership and prestige began to dissolve. The process was accelerated first by the scandal of the Great Schism (1378–1415) and then by the worldliness that characterized Church affairs in the fifteenth century. It was during this period that the foundations for the Reformation were laid.

## CLERICAL CORRUPTION

Pope Clement VI (1342–1352) was a consummate diplomat: articulate, urbane, civilized. All parties at Avignon had combined to raise him to the papal dignity in 1342. As a pope, Clement was magnificent. A great patron, clergy came flooding for promotion to his court. His new Palace of the Popes at Avignon was a center for men of letters, among whom was the poet Petrarch. Educated, charitable, easygoing, he showed how successfully, in the right hands, the late medieval Church could be governed. Yet his reign became a byword of papal corruption.

The fourteenth-century popes perfected, at Avignon, an elaborate machine of government. They exercised for the first time the right to override patrons and appoint whom they chose to every benefice in Europe. This system of *papal provisions* profoundly changed the pope's relations with secular governments, and it vastly expanded the business of the papal court. For instance in a few weeks in 1342, the Curia disposed of no less than 100,000 benefices! No single man could control this vast apparatus of patronage. In effect, though papal provisions certainly reduced the number of disreputable appointments, the popes, who were businesslike men on the whole, preferred to compromise with secular powers. Oxford University sent up "rolls of graces" at intervals, with the names of graduates who needed promotion. At the beginning of the fifteenth century, an agent like William Swan, living in Rome, could often, at a price, procure for his clients the promotion they wanted. In its heyday, the system of papal provisions was no more than a means of organizing the ordered promotion of graduates.

The critics of the Church felt strongly that the clergy was corrupt, and by corruption they meant the evils of simony (buying benefices), pluralism (holding several), and papal provisions—criticisms similar to those made in the tenth century. All these practices were elements of the centralized system that had grown up around the Avignon papacy. The bitterness of some critics can be seen in the words of Nicholas de Clamanges:

> *Avarice and blind ambition have invaded the souls of ecclesiastics; they have become the slaves of three masters who must be satisfied: luxury, pride, and cupidity.*

## POPULAR RELIGION

In the later fourteenth century a large part of the religious life of the layman lay outside the Church. Ordinary people often sought the help not of the clergy but of the supernatural.

Europe at that time was a society of villages loosely grouped around small towns; only a handful of towns had a population of more than 30,000. The inhabitants were therefore vulnerable to local conditions. The scale of some disasters in fourteenth-century Europe—the famine of 1315–1317 and the Black Death of 1340–1349—should not blind us to the yearly threat of the failure of crops or to the individual's closeness to sudden death or sickness. It was natural that men should turn to the supernatural—to magic or to the help of the saints—for security. Charms and amulets abounded, and though condemned by preachers, superstitious practices were universal. The saints, too, provided help. St Barbara protected from lightning; St Fiacre cured piles; San Rocco, patron of the poor, was powerful against plague. Everywhere devotion to the saints was the salient feature of popular religion.

A knight and a forest hermit. In the late Middle Ages many chose to reject the world, and became hermits. This was part of a movement toward personal piety. To some extent this personal piety, which took a number of forms, was a rejection of the Church's institutionalism. The Church tried to control the hermits by absorbing them into semi-hermitic religious orders. The most important of these were the Carthusians, in which each monk lived in a small cottage built off a cloister, and the Camaldolesians, in which communal ties hardly existed. Hermits only became uncommon, however in the sixteenth century.

When ordinary people needed guidance, they frequently turned to the hermits and holy men who led solitary lives near most communities throughout Europe. Richard Rolle, a contemplative in the north of England (c.1300–1349), was sometimes called in to expel devils. Such hermits were influential even with the higher clergy. The "friend of God of the Oberland," who lived in the Alps behind Berne leading a life of austerity for the sins of the world, once visited Pope Gregory XI at Avignon and severely adjured him to undertake the reform of the Church.

In the religion of the laity can be found the origin of many of the abuses condemned by reformers. For instance, the papal practice for granting indulgences, or remission of the penalty for certain sins for a specified number of years, grew up only because of the great demand for them from laymen. Also, excesses of image worship were a manifestation of popular religion. Sometimes, especially after such catastrophes as the Black Death, religious feeling was expressed in wild and hysterical exhibitions. One of the strangest of these excesses was the flagellant movement. The flagellants were bands of men who went from town to town, especially in Italy and Germany, scourging themselves with sharp spikes. In such times of crisis as 1349–1350, they had a terrifying impact on the population, and processions of many thousands roved from place to place.

It was from concern with the state of popular religion that ecclesiastical authorities encouraged the production of simple guides to religion in the vernacular. In 1362, for instance, Archbishop Thoresby of York produced his *Lay Folks' Catechism*, which had the Lord's Prayer and the Ten Commandments in English with simple explanations. Probably more influential on popular religion were the preachers. The fourteenth and fifteenth centuries were an age of mass preaching. The two huge churches of S. Maria Mormosa and the Frari in Venice were built for this purpose. St Vincent Ferrer, a Dominican friar, made extensive preaching tours in

France and Spain, attempting to draw the attention of the laity away from the cult of saints and relics and to concentrate it on Christ. The career of Savonarola, the Dominican friar who dominated Florence in the 1490s, shows how important these preachers could be.

## "MY INNER LIFE IS MY OWN"

The fourteenth century was an age of mystical literature. In Germany, a powerful school of mystics grew up in the wake of Meister Eckhart. In England, there were Walter Hilton, Juliana of Norwich, and the author of the *Cloud of Unknowing*; in the Netherlands, there was Gerard Groot. Late-medieval mystics wrote largely in vernacular languages for a wide audience, often laymen. For them, religious life was a matter for the individual. Walter Hilton, at the height of his meditation, affirmed the private nature of his experience in the words of Isaiah: *secretum meum mihi*, "my inner life is my own."

The reformer John Huss being led to the stake. Huss was born in 1369, and became a master of Prague university in 1396, and rector of the university in 1409. From 1400 he had preached sermons influenced by the ideas of the English reformer John Wyclif (c.1329–84): he attacked clerical morals, and supported the idea that damnation and salvation were predestined. He also attacked the hierarchical structure of society and the right to private property. Huss was excommunicated in 1411 by Pope John XXIII. He appealed against this in 1414 to the council of Constance, and was given a safe-conduct to the council by the emperor, Sigismund.

In this spirit, many people felt strongly that it was better to worship God individually than in a religious order. In 1401, the reformer Jean Gerson advised his six sisters, who wished to devote their lives to religion, not to enter any order but to practice a devout life around the family hearth. Here we have advice that clearly foreshadows Protestant piety.

The most influential religious group of this period was a voluntary community of laymen in the Low Countries called the Brethren of the Common Life. Their single ideal was religious liberty—the freedom to pursue an inner devotion. One of the brothers was Thomas à Kempis, who wrote, about 1427, the *Imitation of Christ*. This was a "guide to paradise" for people leading active lives in the world. It instructed its readers in the various stages of contemplation. It was, and is, enormously popular.

This belief in religious life rather than the life of the Church led to heresy in the fifteenth century. The two principal heresiarchs of the period, John Wyclif and John Huss, were both, essentially, reformers. Huss was a successful academic and preacher, close to the royal family of Bohemia. He followed a long line of Czech reformers; like them, he was anxious to free religious feeling from the shackles of popular superstition. He was a sharp critic of papal centralization and, like St Vincent Ferrer, a compelling preacher. His influence in Prague in the 1400s was immense. Accused of heresy, he attempted to clear himself at the Council of Constance (a body with which he was basically in accord), but he was condemned and burned in 1415. His martyrdom made him a national figure in Bohemia; following his death, the country became engulfed in a civil war between the Catholics and two factions of Hussites. For twenty years the Hussites successfully held out against the universal Church. Thus, for the first time, an independent national Church had rejected the Roman obedience.

## THE GREAT SCHISM AND THE CONCILIAR MOVEMENT

The real crisis of the Church, which no educated churchman in Europe could ignore, came at the center, in the papacy itself. This crisis was the Great Schism of the West, which began in 1378 and was finally resolved by a council independent of the pope. For thirty years there were two popes in Christendom, and for another eight years there were three popes. The Schism arose from a papal effort at reform.

In 1337 Pope Gregory XI returned to Rome from Avignon after a papal exile of more than sixty years. He did so, although the government of the Church was much more convenient at Avignon, in response to critics who attributed the corruption of the papacy to its residence at Avignon. Pope Gregory died in Rome on March 27, 1378. On April 7, the cardinals, perhaps under pressure from the Roman mob, elected as his successor Bartolommeo Prignano, Urban VI. It was the first election of an Italian since 1303. The cardinals were themselves a closely knit group, largely of French origin, and their loyalty to the new Pope was stretched to the breaking point when they discovered his violent temperament and his determination to reform their morals. Within a few months, the cardinals met again and elected Robert of Geneva as Clement VII. There were now two popes; Clement VII, the "antipope," established himself at Avignon, and Urban VI remained at Rome.

What perpetuated the Schism was the attitude of the European sovereigns, who took opposing sides—France, Aragon, and Milan for the Avignon pope; England, Germany, and Naples for the Roman. Each secular government decided which pope to support, and the Church's international authority, which had for long labored to reconcile the opposing parties in the Hundred Years' War of England and France, gave way, even urging the champions of the two popes to further hostilities.

At this point some cardinals of both camps took the lead, proposing that a new council of the Church be convened to settle the problem. That they turned to the idea of a council was a fact of immense importance for the future. General councils had met before, the most recent at Vienne in 1312, but they had never had a standing independent of the pope. Now a council, with delegates from every diocese, every religious order, and every secular ruler, was to meet and determine the affairs of the Church without having been summoned by a pope. Though the papacy, once united, inevitably regained the initiative, councils were never again an instrument of the popes except in cases of dire necessity (for example, the Council of Trent after the Reformation), and right up to the time of Vatican II they were to present a standing threat to papal authority.

In an atmosphere of high hopes and in the absence of either pope, the General Council met at Pisa on March 21, 1409. Temporarily, the Council only made things

The martyrdom of John Huss. When the Czech reformer Huss arrived at Constance he was arrested despite the emperor's safe-conduct. He was found guilty of heresy for his views on predestination and property. After his condemnation by the council, he was burned on July 6, 1415. His death made him a national hero in Bohemia, and he was regarded as a martyr by the university of Prague. At the time of the Reformation he was regarded as a forerunner of the protestants.

# Monasticism

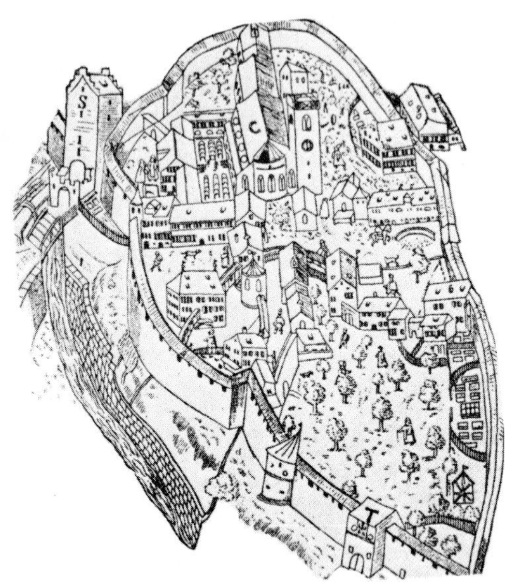

*Above:* Plan of the abbey of St Gall, one of the most important monasteries in late-Carolingian times.
*Right above:* St Simeon Stylites, from a tenth-century manuscript. The fifth-century hermit, Simeon, was the earliest of the stylites (pillar-saints). The way of life he founded continued in the east until the fourteenth century, but never became popular in the West. Sleep was only possible by leaning against the parapet, and food had to be passed up in a basket.
*Right below:* Monks in the Egyptian Thebaid. Western views of eastern monasticism bore little relation to reality. The Egyptian desert could not be cultivated like a vegetable garden.

The rule of St Benedict orders that "when any newcomer applies for conversion, an easy entrance shall not be granted him." Yet "conversion"—the rejection of the values of the world and entry into a monastery—was not made too difficult in medieval Europe. There were hundreds of thousands of monks and nuns in the monasteries that were scattered across the continent.

The aspiring monk had a choice of two ways of life, both of which involved "dropping-out" of society. The first was that of the hermit. This existence involved renunciation of the things of this world, and an active concern for the reform of society. Solitary monks criticized the revenues and lands that maintained established monasteries. Many Celtic monks abandoned their monasteries to become wanderers, "exiles for Christ." In tenth-century Italy, St Romauld of Ravenna became a hermit after his father, a landlord had killed a neighbor in a quarrel. If owning property could lead to murderous quarrels, St Romauld reasoned, he was not prepared to do so. A twelfth-century Dutch saint, Norbert, wrote, "I will not dwell in cities, but rather in deserts and uninhabited places."

The second face of monasticism was that of withdrawal into a stable community, living a cooperative life of prayer, work and study. The monks, who had mostly been recruited in childhood, benefitted the community by their labor, charitable work and prayers.

The two attitudes did not necessarily lead to the foundation of separate institutions. Most monks in the Middle Ages lived under the Rule of St Benedict, but at meal times *The Collations* of John Cassian, a collection of lives and sayings of Greek hermits, was read to them. The life of the hermit was often regarded as a higher vocation than that of a monk, but it was a vocation for a few only.

The Benedictine rule did not overcome older forms of monasticism rapidly. In the sixth century strange forms of monasticism flourished in northern England, Scotland, and Ireland. Monasteries followed rules based on the asceticism of the earliest monks of the Egyptian desert. Instead of diocesan organization under bishops, great monasteries, such as Iona in the Hebrides and Lindisfarne in northern England, provided the sole basis for Church order. Indeed the early Church in northern Britain is regarded by some historians as a monastic Church. Something of the extravagant character of this Celtic monasticism can be seen from the superb manuscripts that survive, such as the Book of Kells and the Lindisfarne Gospels.

Gradually the more moderate life ordered by the Benedictine Rule came to be regarded as the norm: indeed Benedict's Rule came to be regarded as "the Rule." The history of medieval monasticism is largely the story of a conflict between corruption and reform, and this conflict centered upon the Rule. The monastic ideals of poverty, chastity and obedience and the additional vow of stability (to continue in the one particular monastery until death) were always in danger of being ignored. Each abbey was an independent organization and in many the Rule was very liberally interpreted. Many abbeys managed to become independent of the authority of the local bishop, and outside control was impossible. Attempts at reform, such as that of St Benedict of Aniane (c.817), were frustrated by the independence of the abbeys.

Monastic life was built around frequent appearances in church. Every few hours during the day, and sometimes in the middle of the night as well, the monks met for short services, seven in all. In addition they had to attend mass. Services were often sung, usually to plainsong, a form of chant developed originally by Gregory the Great (pope 590–604).

A more significant reform movement was begun by the abbey of Cluny in Burgundy. Cluny's power grew rapidly from its foundation in 910. Instead of allowing daughter houses to become independent abbeys, the abbot of Cluny retained central control. For the first time it was possible to speak of a monastic order, instead of a group of monasteries. However, although the monasticism of Cluny was reformed and well ordered, it was also a privileged way of life. Its emphasis on the solemn performance of the mass and the liturgical hours endangered other essential aspects of monastic life. The monks of Cluny spent most of the day in their huge church—which was perhaps the largest church ever built—while other aspects of the Rule, such as manual work, were ignored. Work was left to lay brothers, whose life was divided almost completely from that of the "choir monks," a characteristic of medieval monasticism.

Further reforms followed. Many of the values of established monasticism were questioned, and new orders were created to express new ideals. There had already been a revival of the hermit's life in Italy under the influence of men such as Romauld. In the twelfth century orders of semi-hermits were set up, with the brethren living in separate cells from which they emerged only occasionally. The largest and most successful of these was the Carthusian order.

Other orders had more practical purposes. The Premonstratensians were a sort of "Cistercian canons." In the Holy Land the Hospitallers took care of pilgrims, and the Templars were military monks, devoted to protecting the Holy places from the assaults of Islam. All of these orders had rules based heavily on that of Benedict.

The most successful of the new orders was created by a thorough reform of the Benedictine Rule. The abbey of Citeaux was founded in 1098. Within fifty years there were almost 350 Cistercian abbeys spread across the whole of Catholic Europe. The Cistercian success was largely due to St Bernard (1090–1153), abbot of Clairvaux, a brilliant publicist and writer as well as an outstanding religious leader, who insisted on the Benedict's Rule, and strongly objected to grandiose or ornate monastic architecture.

In the later Middle Ages monastic wealth became a source of envy to both the secular clergy and the laity, while monkish morals became a source of scandal, as can be seen from many of the stories in Giovanni Boccaccio's *Decameron*. The life of medieval monks seems hard, with regular hours, rising in the middle of the night to go to church, and frequent fasting. But it seemed less hard to most people in the Middle Ages. Many monks—particularly if they came from a poor family—lived an easier and more comfortable life than they could have done otherwise. Education, medical attention and regular meals were not available to all in the Middle Ages. The luxury of monastic life was condemned by many critics.

The reforming initiative that had characterized the monastic movement up to about 1200 gradually died out. Or perhaps it would be truer to say that it was differently directed. Two new institutions, the universities and the orders of friars, had begun to take hold in medieval Europe: both sprang from monastic origins.

worse. While both popes retained their shrunken obediences, the Council, after deposing them, elected a third—Alexander V. On his death in 1410, a disreputable soldier, Baldassare Cossa, was elected as Pope John XXIII. He commanded little respect and obedience, and for the next four years the various national Churches continued, in effect, to go their own ways. Finally, a new council was summoned to Constance in 1415. Its program was to depose all three popes, to make a stand against the Hussites, and to reform the government of the Church. It was a vast assembly, representative of the whole mass of educated churchmen: academics, bishops, and representatives of secular princes.

The first two tasks were achieved with varying success. While the Hussites waxed stronger than ever, the Council deposed the three popes and elected Oddo Colonna as Martin V. The third task was fraught with difficulty. Everyone recognized that reform of the Church "in head and in members" was desirable. Yet everyone depended upon the system; Pierre d'Ailly, for example, the most eminent of the reformers, owed his advancement to successive popes. And since nobody could devise an alternative to papal government that preserved the international character of the fourteenth-century Church, the only reform achieved was the decree *Frequens*, which ordered the holding of a Council every five years—and even this proved impossible to enforce. When the Council was dissolved in 1418, the idea of reform had been indefinitely postponed.

At first sight, conciliarism was a failure and the papacy was restored. The age of the Renaissance was glorious for the popes. Nicholas V (1447–1455), a great patron of learning, planned the rebuilding of Rome and founded the Vatican Library. Pius II (1458–1464) was the first genuine humanist to become pope. Sixtus IV (1471–1484) began the Sistine Chapel, and the infamous Borgia pope, Alexander VI (1492–1503), restored order to the papal states. The popes commanded more wealth than ever before and spent it, in the new St Peter's, on as magnificent an expression of the Christian religion as the world had yet seen. Yet, in many respects, the crisis of the Great Schism affected the Church almost as much as the Reformation was to in the sixteenth century. After the Schism, Frenchmen felt themselves part of a "Gallican" (French) Church, and a similar feeling of nationality was developing in England and elsewhere. Already at the Council of Constance, the delegates had not voted individually. So much were they under the influence of secular rulers that they naturally formed into "nations," national blocs which voted as single units—French, Italian, English, German, Spanish. The popes soon recognized this political reality. At the end of the Council of Constance, Martin V made a series of agreements with secular rulers about their national Churches that gave them, in effect, control over appointments. Though these were modified from time to time, the real power remained with the lay authority in all the European states. The conciliar movement effectively destroyed the papal leadership of Christendom.

For this reason, the reform movements of the fifteenth century, and there were many, developed independent of papal authority. To achieve their aims, the reformers looked to the cooperation of lay powers. Thus Cardinal Ximenes, in his great reformation of the Spanish Church at the end of the century, sought the support of his sovereigns Ferdinand and Isabella. Such local congregations as that of Windesheim in Germany (a group of reformed abbeys for Augustinian canons) developed without more than formal reference to the pope. The sense of unease and impending doom felt so strongly at the end of the fourteenth century had given way, by the end of the fifteenth, to a confident independence among religious reformers in every part of Europe. The age of Luther and Calvin was beginning.

A page from John Wyclif's translation of the Bible. Wyclif, born c.1320, influenced the protestant Reformation more than any other medieval heretic. His attacks on religious forms, and sacraments made him unpopular, while his sophisticated attacks on "dominion" (private property) were widely misinterpreted. Perhaps his greatest achievement was to inspire the first full translation of the Bible into English. The translation, from the Latin Vulgate version, was literal, but aroused a storm of hostility. The Church was very suspicious of vernacular translations because it became possible for ordinary people to read the Bible without understanding the critical views of scholars.

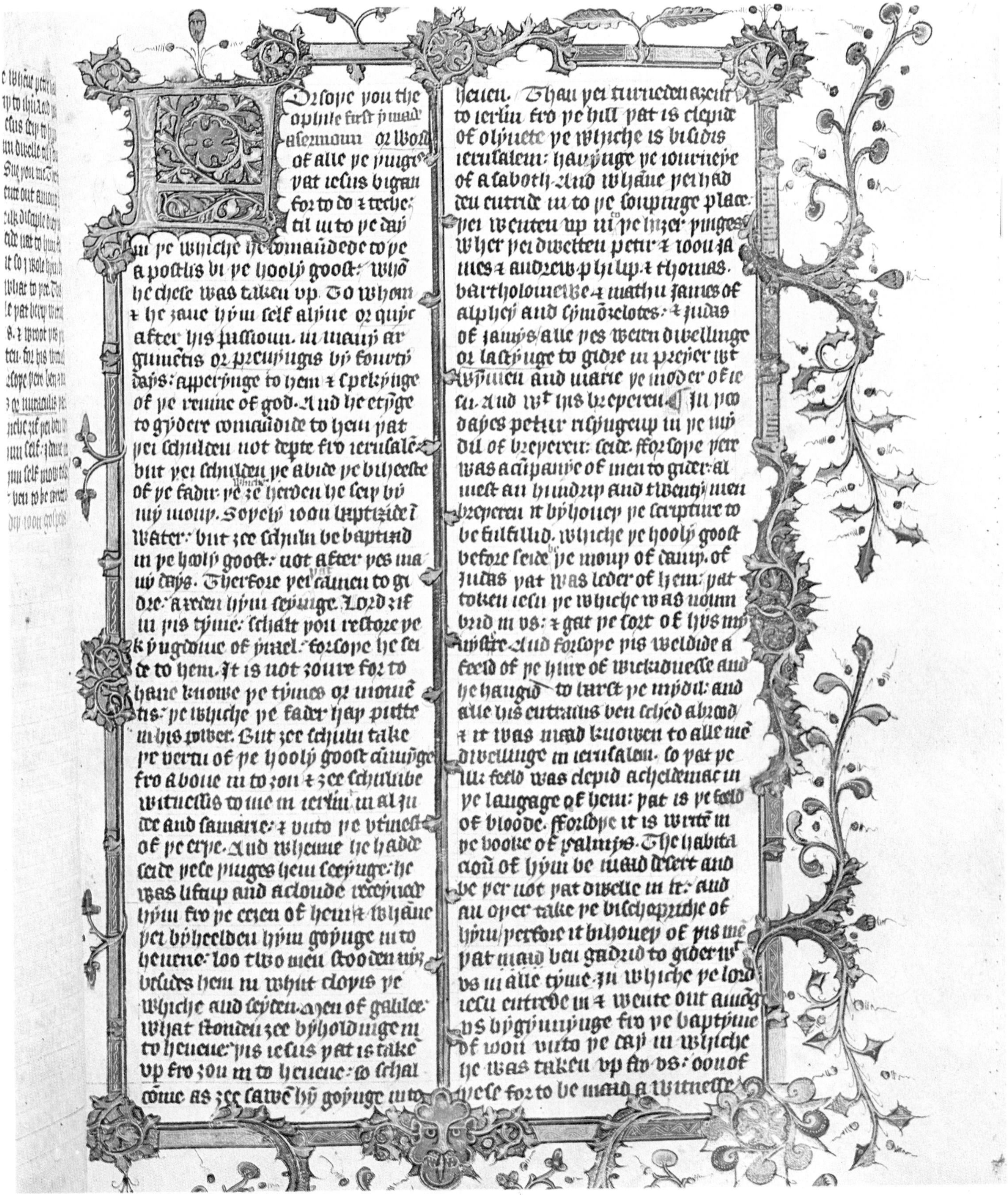

Forsoþe þou the ofilie first I made a sermoun or word of alle þe þinges þat iesus bigan for to do & teche: til in to þe day in þe which he comaundede to þe apostlis bi þe hooly goost: whom he chese was taken vp. To whom & he 3aue hym self alyue or quyk after his passioun in many argumentis or preuyngis by fourti dayes: apperynge to hem & spekynge of þe rewme of god. And he etynge to gidere comaundide to hem þat þei schulden not depte fro ierusalem but þei schulden abide þe biheeste of þe fadir: þe which 3e herden he seiþ bi my mouþ. for ioon baptizide in water: but 3ee schuln be baptisid in þe hooly goost: not after þes many dayes. Therfore þei þat camen to gidre: axiden hym seyinge. Lord 3if in þis tyme: schalt þou restore þe kyngdome of israel. forsoþe he seide to hem. It is not 3oure for to haue knowe þe tymes or moumentis: þe whiche þe fader haþ putte in his power. But 3ee schuln take þe vertu of þe hooly goost cumynge fro aboue in to 3ou & 3ee schulen be witnessis to me in ierusalem in al iudee and samarie: & vnto þe vtmest of þe erþe. And whanne he hadde seide þese þinges hem seeynge: he was lift up and a cloude resceyuede hym fro þe eyen of hem. & whanne þei biheelden hym goynge in to heuene. loo two men stooden wiþ bisides hem in whit cloþis þe whiche and seyden. men of galilee: what stonden 3ee byholdynge in to heuene: þis iesus þat is take vp fro 3ou in to heuene: so schal come as 3ee sawe hym goynge in to heuen. Than þei turneden a3en to ierusalem fro þe hill þat is clepid of olyuete þe whiche is bisidis ierusalem: hauynge þe iourneye of a saboth. And whanne þei hadden entride in to þe soupynge place: þei wenten vp in þe hi3er þinges wher þei dwelten petir & ioon james & andrew philip & thomas. bartholomewe & mathu james of alphey and symound zelotes: & iudas of james. alle þes weren dwellinge or lastynge to gidre in preier wiþ wymmen and marie þe moder of iesu. and wiþ his breþeren. In þo dayes petir risyngeup in þe myddil of breþeren: seide. fforsoþe þer was a cumpanye of men to gidere: almest an hundreþ and twenty men breþeren it bihoueþ þe scripture to be fulfilled. which þe hooly goost before seide bi þe mouþ of dauiþ. of iudas þat was leder of hem: þat token iesu þe whiche was noumbrid in vs: & gat þe sort of þis mynistrie. And forsoþe þis weldide a feeld of þe hire of wickidnesse and he hangid to brest þe myddil: and alle his entrails ben sched abrood & it was mad knowen to alle men dwellinge in ierusalem. so þat þe ilk feeld was clepid acheldemac in þe language of hem: þat is þe feeld of bloode. fforsoþe it is writen in þe booke of salmys. The habitacioun of hym be maad desert and be þer not þat dwelle in it: and an oþer take þe bischopriche of hym. þerfore it bihoueþ of þis men þat maad ben gadrid to gidre wiþ vs in alle tyme. in which þe lord iesu entrede in & wente out among vs bigynnynge fro þe baptyme of ioon vnto þe day in which he was taken vp fro vs: oon of þese for to be maad a witnesse

Chapter 9

# THE TURKS AND THE FALL OF CONSTANTINOPLE

The power of the Byzantine Empire never recovered after its sack in 1204 by the greedy pirates who made up the fourth crusade. By 1450 the once-great Empire had been reduced to a small area around the capital and to parts of Asia Minor. But even these possessions were coveted by the Turks. In 1451 an energetic new sultan succeeded to the Ottoman sultanate. Mehmed II, although only twenty-one, had shown signs both of ability and of ambition. His over-riding ambition was to conquer Constantinople.

Although he promised the Byzantine emperor, Constantine XI, that he would not attack Constantinople, he broke his word almost at once. He built a large fortress, Rumeli Hisar, ten miles north of the city. This threatened communications between the capital and the Greek possessions on the southern coast of the Black Sea. It became obvious that Mehmed's messages of peace were false, when he had the Byzantine ambassador executed.

Early in 1453 a Turkish army of about 100,000 marched from Adrianople (Edirne) to the Turkish capital. It reached Constantinople on Easter Monday, 1453. The city was guarded by 7,000 men, many of them westerners. The city was easy to defend, being surrounded by water on two of three sides—to the south and east the Bosphorus, to the north the Golden Horn, a huge natural harbor—and with mighty walls on its third side. The Golden Horn was protected by a boom and by the suburb of Galata to the north, which was Genoese and therefore neutral. But its walls covered over fourteen miles, and Constantine's garrison was as ill-equipped and disciplined as it was small.

After two months of siege, Mehmed, whose army was running short of food, pulled off a master stroke. He transported seventy ships into the Golden Horn by having them dragged across land behind Galata—a two-mile journey. This allowed easy communication with the troops on the northern side of the Golden Horn, effectively held down the Byzantine fleet, and also increased the length of wall that had to be guarded.

During the siege, the walls of the city had been pounded by heavy artillery, including a cannon capable of firing cannonballs of over half-a-ton. The gates had been attacked. The garrison had lost many men. The population was starving. Desperate appeals had been sent to the western states, and to the papacy and Venice in particular: it now became clear that no help could be expected. At last on May 29, 1453, Mehmed ordered a general assault. While the main attacks were repelled by the demoralized garrison, the city fell by misfortune. A small postern gate was left unguarded and the Turks managed to get in and attacked the defenders from behind. For two days the city was sacked. Mehmed then rode to the great Church of Hagia Sophia, which had been rededicated to Islam, to pray. The Byzantine Empire, heir to that of Rome, had fallen. Its Greek and Christian tradition gave place to a new

*Above:* The siege of Belgrade (1523). The Turkish advance into Europe, held up for centuries by the Byzantine Empire, was able to continue unchecked after the fall of Constantinople in 1453. As late as 1683 the city of Vienna was besieged by the Turks, and the whole of the Balkans formed part of the Ottoman Empire. It was only in the nineteenth-century, that the Balkan world began to achieve its freedom.

*Left:* Map of Constantinople, early sixteenth century. The building of minarets and mosques after 1453 changed the city's appearance.

empire, centered also on Constantinople. The tradition of the Ottoman Empire was Islamic and Turkish.

## OTTOMAN CIVILIZATION

Ottoman civilization proved remarkably long enduring. Until the relief of Vienna in 1683 all Western Europe lay open to the threat of conquest by the Turks. It was only after World War I that the Ottoman Empire was destroyed.

In the eighth century the Turkish-speaking peoples of Inner Asia, who were, at that time, beginning a long drift westwards in search of new and better pasture lands, had encountered Islam. The Turkomans, as they were known later, were pagans, and led a nomadic life, dependent upon their animal herds.

Mehmet II in the hippodrome at Constantinople. The hippodrome had ceased to be used for chariot racing after the crusaders' conquest of the city in 1204. The crusaders had damaged it, but it was privately restored in the fifteenth century, and used for horse racing. Shortly after the conquest, the Turks destroyed the hippodrome, and it is now a public square and garden.

Large numbers of the Turkish herdsmen settled in the broad steppe lands of southern Russia and the Ukraine. Others crossed the Muslim frontiers or entered the service of Muslim rulers as slave soldiers or mercenaries. Many of these accepted Islam and its civilization and, often with tribal assistance, set up new dynasties. One of the most notable of these was the Great Seljuk Sultanate, established in Baghdad in the eleventh century.

In the northwest of their dominions, on the eastern borders of Asia Minor the Seljuks came into conflict with the Byzantine Empire. In 1071, at the battle of Manzikert, the Byzantines were heavily defeated by the Seljuk Sultan, Alp Arslan and the way was open for Turkish penetration of eastern and central Asia Minor.

The Turkish tribesmen and frontier warriors formed small independent states, but rulers from the Seljuk family eventually succeeded in establishing a loosely organized state with its capital at Konya. This state, known as that of the Seljuks of Rum (Rome) endured, with fluctuating fortunes, for about 200 years from the late eleventh century until the end of the thirteenth century, outliving its parent, the Great Seljuk Sultanate. The Seljuks of Rum played an important role in preparing the way for the much greater state of the Ottoman Turks. They succeeded in imposing their rule over a large area, and provided settled conditions in which agriculture could flourish. They inflicted on the Byzantines a decisive defeat at Myriokephalon (1176), which ended Byzantine hopes of recovering Asia Minor.

The golden age of the Seljuks of Rum is usually considered to have been the reign of Ala al-Din Kay-Qubad I, who ruled from 1220 to 1237. After that time the state declined rapidly. The Seljuk state was swept away by new invaders. Many small independent states were formed. The states in western Anatolia are usually called *Ghazi* states. A Ghazi is a hero in the religious war, the *jihad.* To the Ghazi rulers Islam was a way of life, enshrined in various institutions—political, economic and social. Inevitably, since the circumstances of various peoples were quite different, there came to be, in effect, several different Islamic civilizations, coexisting under the same label. There was the classical system, expounded by learned men of Islam, the *ulema.* There was also a popular Islam, best expressed by the itinerant preachers, the Sufis. Sufism was strong among the Turkish warriors of the Ghazi states. Personal inclination, economic necessity and religious injunction all combined to suggest to these men that their main objective should be to prosecute the holy war against infidels. By this means they could win renown, booty and lands in this world and the prospect of an exalted position in the next. Comfortable Seljuk rulers in Konya might and did hope for a stable peace with Byzantium but the Ghazis maintained their continual border raids. Tension existed, as it always had, between the frontiersmen and the men of the settled heartlands of Islam.

With the breakdown of Seljuk authority these states were free to pursue their aims. The largest, Karaman, in the south, tried to replace the Seljuks in Konya. In the west, the warriors of the states of Menteshe and Aydin took to the sea to war against the ships and islands of the Christians. But eventually they were checked by the combined efforts of the Knights of St John on Rhodes, of Venice and Cyprus. The Ghazi state that came to be most successful was the small community of warriors ruled by the family of Osman (hence Ottoman). This state lay in the extreme northwest of Asia Minor, right up against the Byzantine frontier.

The date usually accepted for the foundation of the Ottoman state is 1300. Its first major acquisition was Bursa (1326), which became the new capital. Nicaea (Iznik) and Izmid followed in 1331 and 1377. But the possibilities of jihad in Asia Minor was now limited by the small size of remaining Byzantine territory and the future really lay in Europe. The acquisition of Gallipoli (1354) opened the way and the second half of the fourteenth century was one of rapid expansion into the Balkans. The Ottomans drove northwards to Sofia (1385) and westwards into Macedonia and Serbia.

Sultan Mehmet II. In 1453 Mehmet led the successful attack on Constantinople that finally destroyed the Byzantine Empire. Although principally a warrior, Mehmet was a generous patron of learning and the arts, and spoke six languages. He issued a law code, which was the basis of many later Ottoman law books. Because of his military successes in Constantinople, Serbia, Bosnia, Greece, the Black Sea region, and Dalmatia, Mehmet was known as *Fatih* (the Conqueror). His main purpose, largely achieved by his death in 1481, was the consolidation of the Ottoman Empire.

The Ottoman successes in the Balkans were made easy by the dissensions among the Balkan princes and by the general unpopularity of Byzantine rule. Byzantium had three problems to which no satisfactory answers could be found. These were the shortage of manpower which forced her to rely more and more upon imported soldiers; the tensions between the great landowners and the central government, which contributed to the increasing discontent among peasantry and landowners, and religious dissension between Orthodox, Latins and heretics. Accordingly, just as the Turks were often welcomed in Asia Minor, so the Ottomans found their path to power in the Balkans smoothed by local populations and rulers.

The Mongol invasion under Timur in 1402 was a temporary setback to the Ottoman Empire. By the reign of Murad II, who ruled from 1421 to 1451, the tide of Ottoman progress flowed again. Power was recovered in western Asia Minor and the campaigns in Europe were resumed. The way was open for his successor, Mehmed II, to take the last step necessary to complete the edifice of the new empire—the conquest of Constantinople.

Three centuries of settlement had made Asia Minor largely Turkish and the tide of migration had now flowed into the Balkans. The new state was more than just a new Turco-Islamic dynastic structure. A very large part of its subjects were Christians, and Constantinople was the center of Orthodox Christianity. The new empire was multi-national and multi-religious and seemed to have established, in what was once the capital of the Roman Empire, a new formula for world empire.

## Chapter 10

# THE RISE OF NATION STATES

During the later Middle Ages there emerged all over Western Christendom new political structures, states characterized by princely power, by a centralized bureaucracy, and by territories situated within defined frontiers. Inside these boundaries the prince exercised his sovereignty in political, politico-religious, judicial, financial, and military matters. These states were not, however, "absolute" monarchies, for the prince's actions were limited or controlled by the different estates of society represented in assemblies and by the very nature of the administrative organs that served him. Nor were they all "nation" states, since they were not all based on or supported by national sentiments. Some historians have seen in them an intermediate stage between the medieval and the modern state and have christened them "Renaissance" states.

From the tenth to the mid-thirteenth centuries, the political life of Western Europe had been dominated by feudalism and feudal monarchy. Feudal relations, based on the fief and the personal bond of vassalage, played the essential role in political affairs. The power of the prince was based on personal ties, privileges, and duties rather than on territory, and it was limited by the claims of both pope and emperor. By 1300 the political importance of feudalism and papal and imperial claims to authority throughout Western Christendom were in decline, and while fiefs and vassals, the Western Church, and the Empire continued to exist, the states of Western Christendom in the fourteenth and fifteenth centuries were certainly not feudal and the power of the princes who controlled them was subject to increasingly little outside interference. How did this come about?

Those who think of the later Middle Ages as a period of decay are inevitably impressed by the decline of imperial and papal authority. After the death of the Emperor Frederick II in 1250, and in particular during the period from 1250 to 1273, when there were two rival kings claiming the imperial throne, imperial power sadly declined; all over Europe princes assumed sovereignty in their lands. While it would certainly be wrong to conclude that the universal claims of the Empire ceased to count for anything after 1300, for they remained very much alive in men's minds well into the fifteenth century, nevertheless there can be little doubt that from the beginning of the fourteenth century, they no longer had any basis in reality.

| 1200 AD | 1250 | 1300 | 1350 | 1400 | 1450 |
|---|---|---|---|---|---|
| Sicily under Frederick II (1212–50): model of secular state | | Popes at Avignon (1309–77): Papacy loses power to secular rulers | | | France and England nation states |
| 4th, 5th, 6th, 7th Crusades (1221–48) | | Growth of cities and urban economy | | | Gutenberg printing (1453) |
| | | | Hundred Years' War (1339–1453) | | |
| | | | Black Death (1347) | | |
| | | | Peasant risings in Western Europe | | |

*Above:* Bishops and nobles at the election of the emperor, and *(below)* the imperial coronation by three archbishops. The Holy Roman Empire was a great secular power, but it was also to some extent an ecclesiastical state. The emperor was elected by seven "electors," great princes, of whom three were archbishops. By the fifteenth-century the election had become a formality and the emperors were always Hapsburgs.
*Left:* The battle of Agincourt, 1415, where England's Henry V beat a large French army. This apparently decisive victory did not bring the English ultimate triumph in the Hundred Years War, and by 1453 the French kings had at last won control of their country.

The papal threat to the development of princely sovereignty arose from the pope's claim to universal rule as vicar of Christ which had been proclaimed by both Innocent IV (1243–1254) and Boniface VIII (1294–1303). Certainly, neither of these two popes contested the autonomy of temporal powers, but they asserted their right to intervene in temporal affairs by reason of their *plenitudo potestatis*, that is, their total and unlimited sovereignty. During the course of the fourteenth century these claims became patently meaningless. The Great Schism (1378–1417) finally made nonsense of them. Thus in the fourteenth and fifteenth centuries, outside the limits of the Holy Roman Empire kings all over Europe assumed full sovereignty within their territories, and the same process was at work within the three kingdoms of Germany, Italy, and Burgundy which made up the Empire.

## IMPERIAL AUTHORITY IN GERMANY AND ITALY

Dante and his guide Virgil, from a thirteenth-century manuscript of the *Divine Comedy*. The city-states of northern Italy encouraged patriotic and nationalistic feelings long before other regions. Dante Alighieri (1265–1321) was a leading citizen of Florence: he took part in embassies, became a magistrate, and was banished for his political activities. He was also the leading writer of his time, and the *Divine Comedy* is perhaps the greatest work of Italian literature. It describes the journey of his soul through hell and purgatory to heaven: it also passes judgment on Dante's enemies and criticizes many political institutions of his time.

To investigate the emergent state in late medieval Germany, we must look to the towns and territorial principalities, for it was increasingly there that the real power rested. The elective nature of the monarchy, the smallness of the royal domain, and inadequate financial resources made it impossible for the Emperor to support a royal administration or an army; nor had he any obvious capital in which to build up central institutions and a bureaucracy. Of necessity, he had to renounce power in towns. Strasbourg and Nuremberg both proclaimed their sovereignty and had it recognized. Leagues of towns were formed throughout Germany. The most important of these, the Hanseatic League, had at its height more than 70 full and 100 associate members, of which the chief city was Lübeck.

However, the future ultimately lay with the territorial princes. Bohemia had become a kingdom as early as 1198, and the hereditary principle was recognized there in 1216. Although such concessions were exceptional, the first of a large number of privileges were granted to the ecclesiastical and lay princes very shortly afterward—in 1220 and 1231, respectively. But without doubt the most important step in the devolution of political authority in Germany was the Golden Bull of 1356, which transferred almost all the Emperor's regalian rights to the seven electoral princes and ratified their position as virtually independent rulers. Offenses against them were to rank as treason, appeals could not be made from their courts to that of the Emperor, and they were to have complete control over currency in their own lands.

It would be wrong, however, to conclude that after 1356 imperial power was at a discount and the territorial princes had established themselves, for this was far from being the case. It took time for the princes to consolidate their principalities and even for many of them to see that as their goal. The interests of towns and nobles, often represented in estates, were too firmly entrenched to allow of immediate change, and the German princes had a hard fight before they emerged as masters of their territories in the later fifteenth and early sixteenth centuries. The notion of Empire and attachment to it persisted into the late fifteenth century almost everywhere within the imperial territories except in the Low Countries and Bohemia. But the Empire was becoming, to all intents and purposes, a German empire. Reduced to Germany, it was nevertheless not a state, as France and England were states, for a sense of nationhood and the state did not coincide. Formed within the Empire were a number of different and lesser states: the kingdom of Bohemia, the Swiss Confederation, the territorial principalities, and the leagues of towns.

In Italy at the beginning of the fourteenth century, the question of the Emperor's role continued to divide the inhabitants into rival factions of Guelph and Ghibelline, even though imperial power there was rapidly dwindling. For although imperial authority remained manifest in the use and teaching of Roman law, the absence of any royal domain, royal administration, and royal capital in Italy made the occasional presence of such emperors as traveled there little more than an anachronism. The one area in which the continuity of imperial authority was evident was in the granting of vicariates (delegations of imperial authority), such as those granted to Florence in 1355 and Venice in 1437, and titles, of which the first was granted to Giangaleazzo Visconti, who was made Duke of Milan in 1395. The emperor was thus becoming to Italians little more than a machine to legitimize and reinforce, for a payment, the *de facto* political entities. He did so for political reasons, and against a background of growing national sentiment. This new nationalism is evident, for instance, in the poetry and prose of Dante Alighieri (1265–1321), Francesco Petrarca (1304–1374), and Giovanni Boccaccio (1313–1375), which made Tuscan the main language in a country which had no written tradition or uniformity in the vernacular. But, as in Germany, the emergent political framework was fragmented. Power passed to city-states—Venice, Genoa, Lucca, Siena, and Florence are examples—and to principalities such as Savoy, Mantua, and Milan.

Frederick II's octagonal hunting lodge, Castel del Monte. The emperor Frederick II (1194–1250) was the son of Henry VI and the Queen of Sicily. Frederick's court at Palermo drew together strains of Jewish, Byzantine and Islamic culture as well as that of Western Christendom. He supported the medical school at Salerno and the university of Naples. He spoke six languages and was widely known for his scientific interests. He also codified Sicily's laws. As a soldier he was less successful: the papacy felt threatened by his huge German and Italian possessions.

## PRINCES AND THEIR SUBJECTS

The relationship between the princes and those over whom they exercised their authority was at first limited to the feudal relationship, to the suzerainty which a prince eventually came to exercise over all sections of the feudal hierarchy. But from around the 1260s, as a result of the influence of Roman lawyers, the kings of France and England began to transform this suzerainty into sovereignty, which made the king supreme in his realm over all others. The attributes of royal sovereignty were many, although they were not all immediately obvious. Royal sovereignty had the character of supreme power, not restricted to the world of vassals but extending to all the inhabitants of the kingdom. Thus a clearer definition became necessary of the territories and persons over which this sovereignty was exercised. The exterior limits of the feudal state had been indeterminate and had had only jurisdictional significance, with hardly more importance than internal feudal boundaries. Once the prince extended his judicial, fiscal, and legislative powers outside the feudal framework, the need for the development of frontiers between states became obvious.

The growth of princely sovereignty and a more precise definition of frontiers had two other important consequences: they necessitated a nonfeudal definition of the inhabitants of the lands over whom the prince exercised his authority, and they made the distinction between "native" and "foreigner" more evident. The concept of "subject" appeared together with that of "vassal" quite early in France and England, although its use in Germany has not been recorded before the later fourteenth century. Nevertheless, the transformation from vassal to subject did not occur overnight; for a long time, the two concepts coexisted. Thus, whereas Charles VII of France (1422–1461) expected to be "obeyed by his vassals and subjects," his successor, Louis XI (1461–1483), neglected the feudal argument altogether and demanded from even his great lords the obedience only of a subject.

## THE CONCEPT OF NATION

An early sign of nationality occurred when people found a name in common for the country they inhabited. The word *Francia* appeared very early, though we must be careful to distinguish what contemporaries understood by it. *Polonia* had appeared by about the year 1000, and *Teutonia* or *Alemania* in the middle of the twelfth century. Certainly, by the end of the thirteenth century, many states in Europe expressed an elementary collective conscience in a name. These states were no longer artificial constructions based on marriages, conquests, and successions.

Once it became conscious of itself, a nation sought to justify its present from the past, and during the course of the twelfth century the first national histories appeared in the West. In 1135 Geoffrey of Monmouth wrote his great *Historia regum Britanniae*. In the second half of the twelfth century, Saxo Gramaticus produced the first national history of Denmark, and between 1185 and 1204 the monks of St Denis in France compiled a *Historia regum Francorum*. All these works, in one way or another, evoked a sense of national pride by tracing the invariably fictitious origins of each people, finding glorious ancestors in antiquity or in more recent personages, such as Charlemagne and King Arthur.

"National" saints were also being adopted, and governments were soon able to persuade their subjects that to fight for their country was to defend God. In Bohemia, the cult of King Wenceslas, who was assassinated by his brother on September 28, 929, had already begun in the tenth century; in the eleventh century September 28 became a national feast day, and it was particularly cultivated by Charles IV (1346–1378) and John Huss (1369–1415). In France, St Denis was adopted as special protector of the monarchy in 1120 by Louis VI, who placed the banner, or *oriflamme*, of the abbey of St Denis at the head of his armies; the cult of the saint was well established by the thirteenth century. In England, the council of Oxford, of 1222 ordered the feast of St George to be celebrated as a national feast, and in the reign of Edward III (1327–1377), St George was adopted as the official protector of the realm. By the later Middle Ages, most European states had been placed under the protection of such a "national" saint.

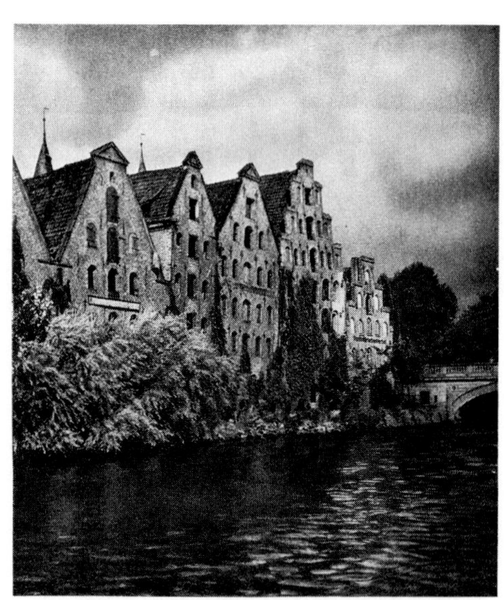

Salt warehouses in Lübeck. Founded in 1143, Lübeck quickly became the chief city of the Hanseatic League. Salt and herrings were its main exports. The *Deutsche Hanse* (German League) was a federation founded to protect the export trade of North German cities. Baltic trade was a Hanseatic monopoly, from the mid thirteenth-century. Ships from the Hanseatic towns traded all over northern Europe. As a result the towns developed strong civic ideas and became very wealthy. The League only declined in importance in the sixteenth century.

Toward the end of the thirteenth century, princes all over Western Christendom began to regard their subjects as forming a nation, and some princes attempted to secure linguistic uniformity within their states. But the concept of nation was still sufficiently indistinct so that the chronicler Jean Froissart (c. 1337–c. 1404) could write of the nation of London and an anonymous citizen of fifteenth-century Paris, writing in his journal, could refer to his city as a nation. George Chastellain (d. 1475), who was appointed the official historiographer of the house of Burgundy, spoke of "the nations of the kingdom" under Charles VII.

Most people in the Middle Ages regarded their country, or *patria*, as primarily the region, town, or village in which they were born. Only slowly did they come to regard the state in which they lived as their *patria*, the center of their loyalties and affections, and it should be noted that the word *patriotism* did not come into use before the eighteenth century.

## THE DEVELOPMENT OF THE NATION STATE IN FRANCE

On the surface, it seems remarkable that a country like France should emerge as one of the nation states of Europe at the end of the fifteenth century. For much of the later Middle Ages the great fiefs and appanages (estates), many of which coincided with the historic provinces—Brittany, Flanders, Burgundy, Guyenne—remained the effective political units of the day and were the centers of loyalty and patronage. In many ways their autonomy and independence were enhanced by the events of the fourteenth and fifteenth centuries; Burgundy, much greater in sheer size than any German principality, could vie with France herself. However, in France, unlike Germany, the monarchy had become hereditary. Moreover, for more than three centuries, from 987 to 1328, the crown had passed in unbroken succession from father to son, and the kings of France had thus enjoyed the singular advantage of being able to increase the royal domain and establish an administration. They were based in their capital in the rich wheat-growing region of the Ile-de-France.

That France, together with England, was to emerge as one of the nation states of later Medieval Europe may have been evident in 1500, but it was by no means sure in 1300. Certainly, by the beginning of the fourteenth century some Frenchmen thought of themselves as belonging to a French nation, which corresponded more or less to the boundaries of the state, but these convictions were not at all widespread; they were limited to a small intellectual elite in the king's government and entourage, and they were not shared by the majority of Frenchmen. The events of the fourteenth and fifteenth centuries in France could have fostered the growth of independent principalities there just as much, if not more, than they did in Germany. It remains to be seen why this did not happen.

### The Hundred Years' War

The factor that most influenced the development of national sentiment and the nation state in France, and to a lesser extent in England, was without doubt the Hundred Years' War (1337–1453). In the feudal structures of the eleventh to the

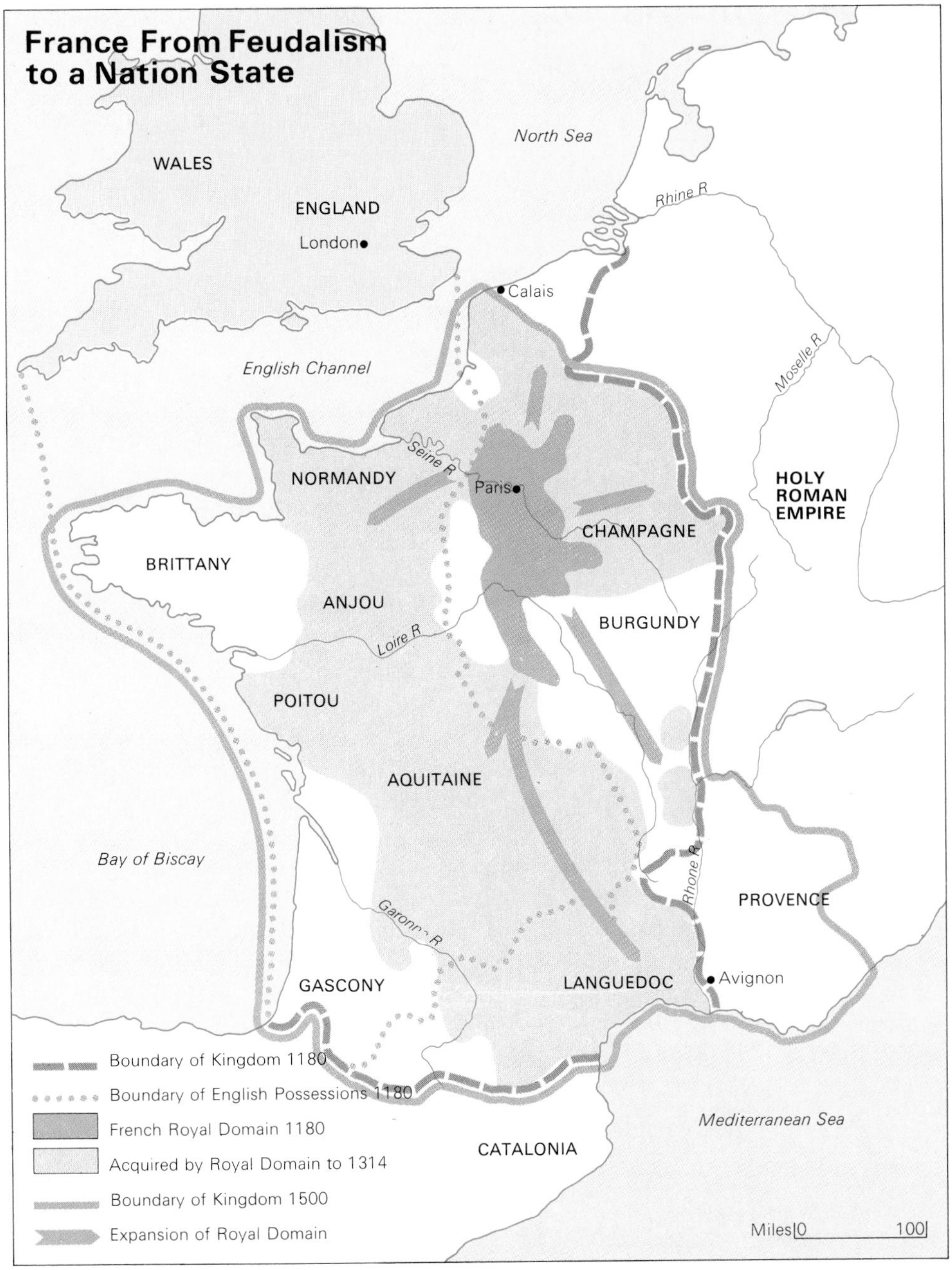

Roofscape of Siena. From 1125 Siena tried to preserve its independence as a city-state, before its eventual capture by Florence in 1555. Military insecurity did not prevent Siena from being one of the great centers of Renaissance art. Duccio de Buoninsegna (c.1260–1318), and Simone Martini (1283–1344), and Ambrogio Lorenzetti (c.1300–50) are the most important artists of the large Sienese school. Pope Pius II (c.1405–64), a native of Siena, was one of the leading art patrons of the fifteenth century; he and his nephew, Pius III, both left memorials.

thirteenth centuries, the king of England was the vassal of a French suzerain for the territories which he held in France. This relationship became increasingly outmoded and inadequate in the second half of the thirteenth century, when both kings were in the process of centralizing their political authority and extending their competence in judicial, financial, and legislative matters beyond the feudal framework. The Hundred Years' War was essentially a conflict between the kings of these two countries for ultimate sovereignty over the territories which the king of England held in France. To this conflict there was ultimately no political solution, since the French refused to renounce sovereignty over any part of their kingdom and the English refused to accept a settlement based on anything less than the cession of territories in full sovereignty. In the years between 1337 and 1492, England and France were in a continuous state of war or truce. The impact of long-drawn-out war on the economy, society, and political structures of the two countries irrevocably confirmed—though it did not create—the tendency toward centralized nation states.

The coronation of Edward the Confessor, king of England. The last English king before the Norman conquest was widely regarded as a saint in medieval England. The crowning of English kings in Westminster abbey developed from his patronage of that church. In the late Middle Ages the palace of Westminster became the seat of parliament, and has remained so to the present.

In dealing with the economic and social repercussions of the war in France, the first thing to note is that it was destructive of both lives and property and that it encouraged, and in some cases set in motion, migrations of the population from the open countryside to the relative security of walled towns and from the frontier and devastated regions of the kingdom to more secure provinces. This had the effect of breaking down provincial prejudices and loyalties. At the same time, the hardships and suffering which the war brought about united in a bond of common misfortune the regions that had been trampled by men-at-arms and encouraged a hatred of the soldiery. Government pamphleteers and propagandists were, in the fifteenth century, able to turn this hatred into national feeling against the foreigner.

Before the last two decades of the fourteenth century, concern for the sufferings of the people had not been linked to hatred of the English, but in the poems of Eustache Deschamps (c. 1346–c. 1406), which were mostly written after 1380, the two were clearly brought together. In the fifteenth century the point was given added potency in the writings of refugees from English-occupied Normandy, who sought to bring Frenchmen closer together, to settle their differences, and to put the national interest first. One of these writers, Jean Chartier, reflects, in his *Quadrilogue Invectif* (1422): "What has become of the constancy and loyalty of the French people, who for so long have been renowned for their firm and entire loyalty toward their natural lord?" The moral was clear.

In England, threats of invasion from France in the 1330s, 1370s, and 1380s, raids on the south coast and over the Scottish border, interference with English merchant shipping in the Channel, and suspected collusion between the Avignon popes and the French monarchy all had the effect of producing a bellicose national consciousness and a hatred of all foreigners—in particular, the French and the Flemings. These feelings are seen, for instance, in the songs of Lawrence Minot, which were composed between 1333 and 1352. They are also found in the *Libel of English Polycie*, written in 1437, at a time when the Duke of Burgundy was enforcing an economic blockade of English merchandise bound for the Low Countries and was attempting to invest Calais. The author stresses the necessity of English control of the Channel:

*Keep then the sea about in special*
*Which of England is the round wall*
*As though England were likened to a city*
*And the wall environ were the sea.*
*Keep then the sea, that is the wall of England.*

In the political sphere, the war provoked the state to intervene in many areas which had hitherto been outside its purview. In particular, from the time of Charles V (1364–1380), the French government sought to control more municipal affairs, to dismantle or take over seignorial castles, and to have the suburbs of many towns destroyed which might give cover to the enemy. It appointed captains, castellans, and regional governors in places and provinces where it had before had no authority. In attempting to control prices, it placed prohibitions on the export of food from one region to another. It circularized all parts of the realm to encourage the people against a common threat. Above all, it dramatically extended its competence in the field of extraordinary taxation. The years between 1356 and 1369 were crucial for the development of direct taxes (the *taille*) and indirect taxes (*aides*, *gabelles*, customs), and they saw the first steps toward the recruitment of a standing field army, made permanent in Charles VII's great military *ordonnance* of 1444.

In England, too, the war had profound political consequences. The growing powers of Parliament, and particularly of the Commons, were intimately linked with the demands for war finance and the debates over war policy that those demands entailed. Already in the fourteenth century, English national consciousness was represented by a wide cross section of the community in a national assembly.

When the war was over, a massive program of reconstruction took place in France: land was recovered from forest and waste, churches and houses were rebuilt, deserted areas were repopulated, men were restored in their property. It was a national program.

## THE EMERGENCE OF THE STATES OF EUROPE

In the later Middle Ages, new centralized states were emerging all over Western Christendom from a feudal past. Not all of them were nation states like France and England; in Germany and Italy, for example, the boundaries of the new states did not coincide with those of the nation, and city-states were almost the norm. Nor were their origins the same. In France, the growth of the state preceded that of the nation, which was largely brought into being by the action of the state itself; in Germany and Italy, the nation preceded the state, which did not appear before the nineteenth century. Elsewhere in Europe—in Sweden, Spain, and Portugal—new national monarchies were emerging. But whereas in France the definition of the nation was political, religious, and historic, in Germany it was linguistic, in Italy historic, and elsewhere primarily economic. In France the principal role was played by the monarchy and the servants of the state; elsewhere, it was the merchants, nobles, and peasantry who brought the nation into being. By the end of the Middle Ages, all these nations except Germany and Italy coincided with the state.

*Top:* Charles VII, king of France. During the early part of Charles' reign, his cause seemed hopeless, and the English and Burgundians were only beaten after Joan of Arc encouraged him to fight. Charles' eventual coronation in Reims cathedral in 1429 marked a start of the revival of the French crown's fortunes.
*Above:* The coronation of Charles VIII at Reims in 1483. The ceremony of coronation at Reims was of great importance for the French kings, as it marked them as the rightful lords of France. Charles VIII's reign marked the eventual victory of the French crown over the nobles.

Chapter 11

# THE GROWTH OF REPRESENTATIVE ASSEMBLIES

In the eighteenth century Montesquieu observed that the origins of representative institutions in Europe "must be sought in the remoteness of the German forests." His comments were just, in the sense that medieval monarchy was never absolute. From the earliest times kings had recognized the need to seek counsel from their leading men, and this was implicit in the political habits and customs of the Germanic peoples and subsequently in the conventions and rules of feudal society. The duty of a vassal to give his suzerain counsel and aid was added to the right of consent implicit in the Germanic monarchies, and this was done in assemblies which were variously called curiae, concilia, colloquia, conventus, placita, tractatus (council), whose composition and functions for long remained imprecise.

## PARLIAMENTARY ORIGINS

Gradually, these assemblies also came to be known as parlamentum or parliamentum. To begin with, the word was used only in the general sense of conversation, conference or assembly, and it appears more frequently in chronicles than in official records. Already in the eleventh century it was used in a technical sense by the papacy, and to describe the general assemblies of citizens which were held in the north Italian communes; but it was not until the thirteenth century that it became common in official records. It was first used in England and France in the 1230s, in England to denote an enlarged session of the king's court or curia, and in France to describe a judicial session of the same body; but it was not used exclusively to designate these gatherings, nor was it the only word used for them before the fourteenth century, by which time it was current in the more restricted sense elsewhere in Europe.

The functions of these early assemblies were various. They provided a forum for witnessing royal acts: they acted as a supreme judicial court (restricting themselves in France and Castile to judicial business); they assented to royal legislation; they were consulted over political affairs; they assented to taxation.

It was this latter function which, in particular, led to the adding of representatives of the towns, and, in England, the shires. In most countries the prelates, nobles and burgesses came to meet and deliberate in separate "estates," and were most usually referred to as the "Three Estates." In France, during the first half of the fourteenth century, when the parlement of Paris was definitively organized as a sovereign judicial court, the words were used of a variety of representative assemblies called by the king, of which the largest have been referred to somewhat misleadingly by historians as the "Estates-General."

The need for representation of corporate bodies had first been felt in the Church where, with the revival of interest in Roman Law in the twelfth century, canon lawyers fell upon a phrase in a sixth-century law code of Justinian dealing with

A fifteenth-century view of the parliament of Edward I. Most of the features of the modern House of Lords in England are already present in this picture. Representative assemblies developed at much the same time throughout Europe. The Church was the main influence on medieval parliaments. Bishops and abbots often formed a majority in Parliament.

private law, and isolated it from its context: *quod omnes tangit ab omnibus approbetur* (what touches all shall be approved by all). During the thirteenth century it was used in the Church to prove that the clergy could not be taxed without their consent. This was implicit in a canon of the third Lateran Council of 1179, and was specifically referred to in a canon of the fourth Lateran Council of 1215. In its councils and synods the Church also pioneered the techniques of representation by procuration, in which the proctors (representatives of the lower clergy) secured *plena potestas* (full powers), to bind their constituents to the decisions of these assemblies. This was an important development, since as long as the elected representatives only had power to "hear and report" upon the proceedings of the gatherings they attended, the assemblies could have little power.

Louis XI of France presiding over his parliament. Even despotic rulers such as Louis XI were forced to take the advice of their subjects.

The Church thus offered a working example of representation, and illustrates the main motive why, in the second half of the thirteenth century, representatives equipped with full powers were increasingly summoned to secular assemblies. All over Europe princes were faced with an increasing number of problems—administrative, political, military, and above all financial. They could not hope to solve these without enlarging their traditional assemblies and, for their part, their subjects wished to be brought together to defend their interests. Town representatives first appeared at royal assemblies in the Mediterranean countries, especially in Italy. This was primarily because of their precocious commercial and mercantile development, but also because the nobility were town-dwelling, many towns were under seignorial control and could thus be represented as fiefs, or else they had become immunities possessing public authority. Representatives of the Italian communes were summoned to imperial diets as early as 1154 and 1158. In Aragon the towns were represented in royal assemblies by 1164, in Leon in 1188, in the Papal States in 1200, in Languedoc in 1212, in Sicily in 1232, Germany in 1255, northern France in 1263, and England in 1265. A further development, peculiar to England, was the election of representatives of the shires. Whereas on the Continent the counties had been absorbed by the great fiefs and private jurisdictions, and the idea persisted that the feudatories represented their vassals, in England the shire had survived as a community, and in each shire the freemen came to be represented by two knights. Knights of the shires had been summoned to royal assemblies on administrative business as early as 1226 and 1227, and they were subsequently summoned to parliament for political purposes in 1261, 1283, 1295 and 1307, as well as to Simon de Montfort's parliaments of 1264 and 1265.

Thus by around 1300 representative assemblies had emerged in most European states, and for much of the fourteenth and fifteenth centuries a dialogue existed between the prince and his people, in which the people came to play an important role in political, judicial, financial and legislative affairs.

### Judicial, financial and political functions

Many historians have insisted upon the primarily judicial functions of parliaments in the thirteenth century; but it would be wrong to dismiss the political propagandist element in the early representative assemblies, or to neglect the financial aspect that is the essential key to the expansion of their competence in the fourteenth and fifteenth centuries. The propagandist purpose is evident in the timing of the assemblies—at the beginning of a new reign, to announce the king's intentions and to associate opinion with him, or to promulgate new laws. Thus in 1295 and 1307 representative parliaments were assembled in England to enlist support against Philip the Fair of France and the pope, and in 1302 and 1308 Philip called together the French Estates to secure backing in his quarrel with the pope, Boniface VIII, and for his suppression of the Order of the Temple. However, the role of representative assemblies in the political affairs of the later Middle Ages was primarily connected with war and war finance, for by the middle of the fourteenth century most princes had recognized that they could not levy direct taxes without the consent of their subjects. In England, the same was true of indirect taxes, mainly on wool and cloth; after 1362 they too had to be approved by parliament and thereafter all extraordinary taxation required parliamentary assent.

This control of taxation gave the assemblies their bargaining and legislative powers. In England, the knights and burgesses assembled together in the Commons sought to appropriate the taxes they had voted, to secure an audit of accounts, and to appoint special treasurers to handle the moneys raised. After 1327 they presented collective or "common" petitions before approving taxes, and these invariably led to the making of new law by parliamentary statute. In the kingdom of Aragon financial bargaining power gave the representative assemblies, the Cortes, a voice in drafting and elaborating provincial privileges and liberties. Although nothing quite like this occurred in France where, as we have seen, the Estates largely lost control of taxation after the crisis of 1356–58, royal demands for subsidies frequently led to the presentation of grievances, of *doléances*, at meetings of both the provincial and more general Estates. These grievances often resulted in the promulgation of royal *ordonnances*, or reforms, by the king's lieutenants. Moreover, the burden of war finance and the necessity of defense positively fostered the development of provincial Estates in France, either by leading to the creation of new assemblies, such as those of Poitou in 1372 and Vivarais in 1381, or by enhancing the powers and prestige of older ones, such as those of Normandy in the fifteenth century.

Parliament of Richard II. Medieval parliaments tended to be informal.

However, the effectiveness of representative assemblies depended upon their duration and frequency, and there were wide variations from one country or province to another. Some assemblies were brief and irregular, like the larger French Estates, and most Continental gatherings only lasted for a few days. Elsewhere they were more frequent and regular, as in England, where parliaments were held annually for much of the fourteenth and early fifteenth centuries, and lasted for about three weeks.

Yet, in the second half of the fifteenth century, the assemblies lost their powers in most parts of Europe; in some places they had already disappeared before then, and everywhere the position of the prince was growing stronger. In France, the Estates of 1439 was the last large assembly to have any say in taxation; thereafter Charles VII (1422–61) and Louis XI (1461–83) raised direct taxes without consent and reinforced their position with a standing field army. In Germany, the Landtage became an instrument in the hands of the princes, and even in England the king regained the initiative in parliament, which was summoned less frequently by Edward IV (1461–83) and Henry VII (1485–1509), and the powers of the Commons had atrophied from an even earlier date. There were several reasons why the prince regained the initiative. In France, a lack of social and geographic unity had long made the king's subjects indifferent or even hostile to the more general assemblies; they preferred to negotiate with the king's representatives direct, either in provincial assemblies or at the more local level of the *balliage* or the town. Moreover, both there and in Spain, the exemption of the nobility and clergy from the more onerous taxes (the *taille* in France and the *alcabala*—a general sales tax—in Castile) made them largely disinterested in the fate of the assemblies. But the most important single factor was the improved financial position of the monarchy. This was caused by the general economic recovery of Europe after more than a century of troubles and difficulties in the later decades of the fifteenth century, and by an improved exploitation of the ordinary resources of the crown, better financial administration and, particularly in England and France, the conclusion of the Hundred Years' War.

Chapter 12

# CITY LIFE IN THE RENAISSANCE

Behind the cultural achievements of Renaissance Europe lies the medieval town, for the urban milieu was conducive to artistic production, literary activity, technological improvement, and scientific advance. In order to understand the role played by the towns, it is necessary to understand the rich quality of urban life. And in order to understand the overwhelming contribution of Italy to these developments, it is essential to grasp the unique position of the Italian city-states.

Towns were the product of trade, the centers of industry, and the headquarters of commerce. The commercial revival of the eleventh and twelfth centuries had produced a rash of towns all over western Europe. During the later Middle Ages, some of these towns had outstripped others in size, prosperity and influence. By 1500 the areas of outstanding urban development were in the Low Countries, Germany, and north and central Italy. These areas were marked off from the rest of Europe by the number and size of their towns.

*Above:* An illustration to Psalm 127: "Except the Lord build the house, they labor in vain that build it." In the earlier Middle Ages the chief benefit of city life was defense in time of war, but from the thirteenth century onward economic advantages became more important.
*Left:* The harbor at Naples by Pieter Breughel (1525–69). North Italy was the most densely populated region in Europe, but Naples in the south was the largest city in the whole of Europe.

## GREAT CITIES

Toward the end of the Middle Ages, about 10 to 15 percent of the population of western Europe was concentrated into towns. In the heavily urbanized regions, particularly in Holland and Brabant, the percentage was very much higher. Even so, very few towns were big. Of the 3,000 towns in Germany, well over three-quarters had populations of under 1,000. The largest town in Germany was Cologne, with about 30,000 inhabitants. In the Low Countries only Ghent, Bruges, Brussels and possibly Antwerp could match it for size. By these standards some Italian towns were giants: Genoa, Bologna, Rome, and Palermo all had populations of about 50,000. But even these were dwarfed by Venice, Milan, Florence, and Naples, all of which had populations approaching 100,000.

The biggest towns were in Italy. And so was the biggest business. The populations of these Italian towns were sustained by immense industrial, trading, and commercial enterprises. Rome was the center of Christendom, whose chief source of income was the papal curia. Bologna was a university town of international repute, whose law school attracted students and money from all over Europe. Venice was the hub of a huge commercial empire. Its income was based on importing and exporting, and it had a near monopoly of trade with the East. Its Arsenal was the most extensive industrial plant in Europe. Florence was a great industrial town, whose textile works were probably Europe's biggest employers. In the 1330s when the population of Florence was about 100,000, probably 30,000 were engaged in the manufacture of woolen cloth. Like Genoa, Florence was a leading money market, a center for international credit and exchange. Its chief bank, the Medici Bank, was the largest in Europe. The firm had branches in London, Bruges, Avignon, Lyon, Geneva, Basel, Milan, Venice, Rome and Naples, and agencies throughout the

Continent. Its biggest customer was the Church, its outstanding account that of the pope. Big business yielded big profits. Between 1435 and 1450 the Bank earned over 290,000 florins. Earlier Florentine banks, such as the Bardi and Peruzzi, had financed kings. The house of Medici provided two popes, and married into other royal lines, as well as supplying a line of grand dukes.

The business interests of these towns were on a truly international scale. Italian merchants dealt in expensive commodities, and operated long-distance trade. Italian bankers had cornered European high finance. Compared with the scale of the Italian towns, urbanized areas outside Italy had only small-scale economic enterprise. Most German towns were concerned mainly in local trade, short-distance traffic and regional markets. Even the industrial centers of the Low Countries, and the Hanseatic ports around the Baltic were unable to compete with the scope and extent of the Italian concerns. And their magnates and merchants were unable to make comparable profits. For size, wealth and influence the monster towns of northern and central Italy were unrivaled.

## INDEPENDENCE AND CANNIBALIZATION

Unlike towns elsewhere in western Europe, those in Italy were barely inhibited by monarchical control. They had developed institutions of self-government, and had become established communes. During the later Middle Ages, each of the major towns had subjugated its surrounding territory and formed a *contado*—a valuable source of grain, troops and cash. Eventually the towns with the biggest appetites looked greedily at their neighbors. Enmity between towns was nourished by commercial rivalry. In this jungle situation the weaker fell victim to the stronger. Only the fittest survived to become city-states. By the late Middle Ages, much of northern and central Italy was controlled by the monster towns of Venice, Florence and Milan.

*Above:* The Palazzo Vecchio in Florence. Florence was one of the most important and successful of the north Italian city-states.
*Right:* Statues in the Piazza Signoria, Florence, with the dome of the cathedral below. Civic pride led to patronage of the arts. Cathedrals were built in a spirit of rivalry in fifteenth century Italy: each town tried to build a more magnificent cathedral than its rivals. Among the statues visible is Michelangelo's David (second from right).

These towns had survived and grown fat by cannibalism. Florence had gobbled up Fiesole, Volterra, Arezzo, Pistoia, and Pisa. By the end of the fourteenth century, Milan had digested most of the towns of Lombardy. And in the fifteenth century, Venice devoured Treviso, Bassano, Vicenza, Verona, and Padua. The victims suffered: Pisa, which had once had a population of 30,000 had wasted away to a sickly backwater of under 10,000 by 1500.

By the late Middle Ages, the monsters were fat and attractive. They preyed on each other. At the end of the fourteenth century, Milan was planning to gobble up Florence, a big mouthful. When Milan collapsed shortly afterward, Venice fed off the remains. And, early in the sixteenth century, Florence and Milan combined in an attempt to dismember Venice. By then the Italian city-states were themselves the prey of even greater predators, the king of France and the Holy Roman Emperor.

During the later Middle Ages most of the Italian communes—formerly republics—had succumbed to the rule of a *signore*, or lord. Dynastic lordships became common: Padua succumbed to the Carrara, Verona to the Scaligeri, Bologna to the Bentivoglio, Ferrar and Modena to the Este, Mantua to the Gonzaga, Modena to the Montefeltri, and most notably, Milan to the Visconti and later to the Sforza. Very few communes survived the trend. The most conspicuous of these that did were Venice and Florence. When Milan grappled with Florence, the struggle assumed the added dimension of tyranny versus republican liberty.

The friction between the city-states generated immense civic patriotism. City chronicles and panegyrics became an established literary form. Writers extolled the city's size and situation, delighted in the number and variety of its products, the precocity of its inhabitants, the beauty of its buildings, and the quality of its amenities. In the fifteenth century a citizen of Florence thanked God that he had been born in such a great city.

Such civic pride was often appropriate, for the rich quality of urban life was a civic achievement. Town councils, in Italy and elsewhere, aimed to regulate essential services: steady supply of unpolluted water; hygenic conditions; ample grain at a reasonable price; cleaners to sweep the streets; and police to scour them. Moreover, the city fathers tried to regulate the minutiae of civic life: to curb reckless gambling, restrict lavish dress and extravagant make-up, control the size of dowries, prohibit sodomy, and control funerals. Painstaking paternalism of this strict sort was not confined to Italian towns. At Nuremburg, municipal workers were allowed an hour off each week so that they could attend the municipal baths.

Civic patriotism was probably most developed and articulate in cities that retained republican institutions, and where political power was relatively widely distributed. Participation in government encouraged citizens to identify with their town. The fortunes of the individual and the city were then closely identified. The public career of Jacopo di Piero Guicciardini, a Florentine citizen, shows the continued involvement of a citizen with his city. Between 1452 and 1490, Guicciardini was a captain of Arezzo and of Pisa, and held other administrative posts in the Florentine *contado*. In addition he served as ambassador to Naples, Venice, Milan, and the papacy. He sat on several civic committees concerned with coinage, public safety, justice, the contract of mercenaries, and the conduct of warfare. Exposure to such varied diplomatic and political experience was an education in government. Such an education produced the doctrinaire political thinker, Niccolo Macchiavelli, and the more practical historian, Francesco Guicciardini.

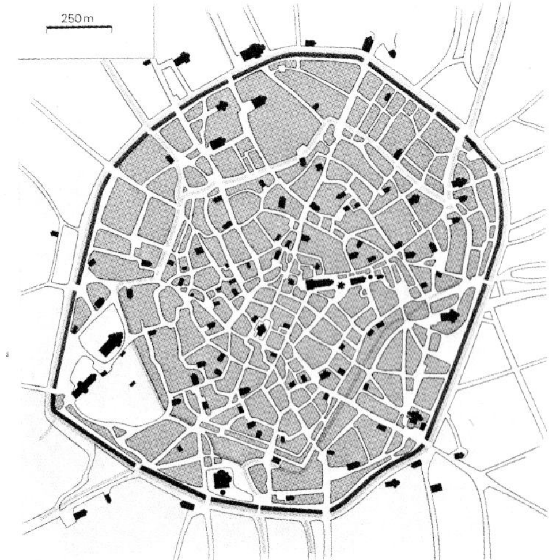

*Top:* A plan of Milan in the Middle Ages. Most medieval towns had many churches. Not all were parish churches: there were chapels and monasteries also. Organized religion played an important part in the city life.
*Above:* Building a palace. In the later Middle Ages there was a great upsurge of buildings, particularly in Italy. It was in the large cities of northern Italy that the Renaissance began.

## PATRIOTISM AND DISUNITY

Although civic power was widely distributed in the city republics, eligibility for civic office was still restricted to a patrician minority. In a monster city like Florence, only about 3,000 citizens were qualified for civic office. The mob was entirely excluded.

Civic patriotism did not exclude civic disunity. It may even have encouraged it. Political instability was an ingrained feature of city life. The return of the Medici to Florence in 1434, after a term of exile, and the subsequent banishment of their rivals, the Albizzi, is a celebrated but typical example of the frenzied politics of an Italian city-state. Cities were prone to internal faction. They were also susceptible to outbreaks of violence. The mob, undernourished and underpaid, rioted frequently. Often these riots were antisemitic, because Jewish pawnbrokers were an easily identified target for dislike. Not surprisingly, civic discord and social unrest nourished doctrines of civic unity.

Municipal concern, public amenities, and civic pride were features common to all European cities. But in Italy the quality of urban life was noticeably enriched by the tremendous rivalry that persisted between the city-states. Cannibalism promoted culture. This is most marked in the case of architecture. Inter-city rivalry bred municipal sensitivity about the visual impact of cities, and encouraged investment in building. Town councils became patrons and planners. They cleared streets, ordered demolitions, and encouraged the construction of town houses. They sponsored civic architecture—town halls, public squares, monuments, and churches. These projects were usually conceived and organized by civic committees, and were financed from public funds by means of special taxation. The great cathedral-building projects vividly illustrate the municipal mentality and the keen competitive spirit. The Florentines planned their duomo in the last decade of the thirteenth century; it was to be "the most beautiful and honorable church in Tuscany." In the next century, the Sienese, close neighbors and rivals, answered the challenge with an even more ambitious cathedral project. It was designed to eclipse that of Florence.

The Marriage Feast at Cana by Paolo Veronese. During the Renaissance period crowded buildings and narrow streets jammed into a walled enclosure for protection gave way to wider perspectives and broader vistas.

Toward the end of the fourteenth century, Gian Galeazzo Visconti, Lord of Milan, planned a new cathedral for his city. It was to be the largest in Europe. Such huge projects enhanced prestige, stiffened diplomacy, and boosted morale.

Cannibalism added other colorful ingredients to city life in Italy. Each year on Holy Thursday the Venetians celebrated their victory over the patriarchate of Aquileia during the Dark Ages. Other Italian towns had similar festivals, most of which represented the submission of the contado towns to the city. At Florence, on the feast of St John the Baptist, the city's patron saint, the feudatories of the contado carried heavy wax candles in procession through the city. The cannibalization of neighboring towns also provided occasions for festivals and pageantry.

### Religious initiative

Civic interest in cathedrals, and civic promotion of festivals illustrate another basic facet of urban life: municipal direction of the Church and initiative in religion. In many cities the building of a new cathedral was closely associated with the expulsion of the bishop by the civic authorities. During the later Middle Ages the bishop's authority was gradually supplanted by that of the city council, which assumed local control of the Church. This development was common to cities in Italy, Germany, and the Low Countries. The local clergy were deprived of the immunities from taxation and justice, and town councils made appointments to benefices, as well as supervising rectors and administering Church property. Moreover, the civic authorities claimed—and exercised—responsibility for many spiritual functions. They organized processions and sermons, and provided fish for Lent. They managed charities and hospitals, homes for the destitute, the old, and orphans.

View of a city by Ambrogio Lorenzetti.

### Country Life

The distinctive qualities of urban life can only be appreciated against its rural background. In the countryside, the tempo of life was slower than in the towns, and the range of activities more limited. The predominantly industrial occupations of urban communities contrast sharply with the mainly agrarian concerns of the country. And the facilities for urban religion were in marked contrast to the spiritual starvation of the countryside. Moreover, the degree of literacy in the towns was substantially higher, and this contributed another dimension to the urban experience. Townsmen relished jokes at the expense of country bumpkins. Boccaccio's *Decameron* is full of such jokes, and assumes a wide reading public among the urban laity.

But it would be misleading to insist on too sharp a distinction between town and countryside. The city walls often enclosed sizeable areas of undeveloped, agricultural land, and many townsmen commuted daily to work in the countryside. Moreover, it was usual for wealthy citizens to retire to a country villa for the summer months. And profits made in commerce and industry were invested in land. The returns were lower, but the investment was safer. The real-estate holdings of Neri di Gino Capponi, a Florentine citizen of the mid-fifteenth century show a typical division of interest between city and countryside. In his tax return of 1451, he listed a city residence, two other town houses, together with a country villa, twelve farms, three cottages, and an isolated parcel of land.

The medieval town was behind the cultural accomplishments and religious innovations of early Modern Europe, for the political situation and economic circumstances of the towns supplied the incentive and opportunities for artistic and literary activity. And the complexion of urban religion, together with the practice of municipal salvation, were very receptive to the diffusion of Protestant doctrines. Without the medieval town, there would have been no Renaissance and little Reformation.

MARGARIT' RITIO ME FECIT

Chapter 13

# THE DIFFUSION OF EARLY RENAISSANCE ART

Between the end of the thirteenth and the middle of the fifteenth century the arts underwent an astonishing transformation. What changed was not subject matter; this remained overwhelmingly religious. The change was one of style. Painters and sculptors moved from commemorating an idea to re-creating an incident in believable human terms, from a symbolic to a more realistic way of reminding men of the place of religion in their lives. But it is best to move at once from definitions to the objects themselves: four treatments of the same theme, the Madonna and Child, will show the change that occurred.

The painting by Margaritone, done around 1270, is a fair example of the style that was to be supplanted. It is signed at the bottom; the painter was firmly aware of his own identity and the value of his work. But he was not concerned to give individual identities to the figures he painted. The virgin's face is not based on the observation of a real woman's face but on an assembly of features—eyes, nose, chin—derived from Byzantine tradition; together they spelled "face" rather than "so-and-so's face." The body is little more than a pair of hands thrust through a robe; there is no sense of its weight; rather than sitting on a throne it appears to be propped against a fence. The child, one hand raised in the gesture of a teacher, is less a child than a very small man. The figures pointing out the significance of Mary, the mother of a God transformed into a man to teach "real" men the way to save their souls, hover beside her like little cut-out dolls. We are not being invited to look out of a window, but are being reminded of a lesson of crucial importance.

The purpose of this description is not to disparage the painting as a work of art but to prepare the way for charting the changes that are to occur in the way in which this scene is to be depicted by artists of the early Renaissance. The changes were to be so great that later Renaissance artists looked on works like Margaritone's with scorn and revulsion. And *their* approach to the treatment of the human body, the relationships between the various figures in a composition and the space in which they dwell, has been so influential that it is only during the last two or three generations that men have stopped echoing that scorn. Thanks to the fact that we inherit not only a realistic but an abstract and decorative approach to painting, we can find Margaritone's work both impressive and beautiful.

His work shows the medieval tradition closing in somewhat crude strength. Cimabue's, painted about 1280, shows it ending in a more refined and poetic way, a way which already reflected the increasing naturalism, or truth to life, that was to take its place.

The Virgin's face is still composed from the Byzantine vocabulary of separate features, but they have been smoothed out. The child still teaches but he is more believably of an age to be held on his mother's knee. The note of tenderness in their relationship was not lacking in Margaritone, but it is stronger here. The throne is

*Above:* Madonna and Child by Cimabue.
*Left:* Madonna and Child by Margaritone.

reasonably three-dimensional, but the Virgin's body is still hung against, rather than sitting on it. The size of the Old Testament prophets is still dictated by their being of less importance than the Virgin they foretold, but they are not just marginal notes. However, if the picture were brought suddenly to life they would drop away, the Virgin slide down the front of the throne, the throne through the supporting angels' hands. We would be left with angels on an empty sheet of gold.

Twenty years later the revolution had already begun. Giotto's figures not only have weight but are securely anchored within the picture frame. The Virgin's clothes drape a real body; she sits firmly on her throne. The "witnesses" are still on a smaller scale than she is, but they neither hover in the air nor are glued on at the bottom. We are at the beginning of an art that was less interested in making symbols—"mother of God," "God made flesh," "prophecy"—roughly resemble real people, than in giving real people an added symbolical significance.

Madonna and Child by Masaccio.

In another hundred years the revolution had reached a stage that still permits endless experiment—but on its own terms. Whatever follows will take humanity as its starting point. Painters will distort the human figure. They will deny it gravity. They will deliberately frustrate our inclination to read a painting as though it were a scene from real life. But they will not again think of symbols first and human beings afterwards as did Margaritone and Duccio and the artists of their time.

Masaccio's Madonna was painted in 1426. She sits with an ease that is new, but, as with Giotto, it is on a throne whose architecture makes us think of whole buildings (the many churches dedicated to her) rather than a chair. The child is at last a real child. But the grapes he clasps are there to remind the onlooker of the wine, symbol of the mature Christ's blood, that the priest drinks at the altar. The symbolic element is there, but it is now an adjunct, a clue, not the formal subject of the painting. Margaritone's Christ is both child and man and therefore like nothing in nature. Masaccio's is a real child reminding us through a real thing (the grapes) of what is to happen when he is a man. The Christian message is identical. The way in which it is conveyed has been transformed.

One more comparison between works by the two men whom posterity has come to accept as the giants of the revolution of the early Renaissance—Giotto (c. 1290–1340) and Masaccio (1401–c. 1428)—will show how both men dealt with narrative and the outdoors.

Giotto's Nativity combines two episodes. On the right, the shepherds listen to angels telling them of the event which is happening in the middle and left of the painting, where Mary receives the baby Jesus from the midwife while Joseph sleeps —for he is only the foster father of a godchild sired by the Holy Ghost. The shepherd's backs are a manifesto of the revolution. The idea of catching anyone *unawares*—as if with a camera—is quite new; they are no longer part of a message, they are part of a story. Giotto is not indifferent to the message, but he is interested in how the news first came and how it was received. There is a historical sense that is new and a new willingness to seize the moment—even at the cost of informality. And if we forget the artificial coexistence of two episodes, we can read the painting as a satisfactory whole: people in a landscape which, by making a minimum of imaginative readjustment, we can see as real in intention, if not in appearance.

Masaccio's Tribute Money is also a fresco (a wall painting). It contains not two episodes, but three. Christ and the apostles have arrived at Capernaum. It is a Roman city and they are asked to pay an entrance toll or tribute. As Jews, in their own homeland, they argue—in the central episode—about the rights and wrongs of this imperialist imposition. Again we have a character, the gatekeeper, with his back to us to help transport us to the time when the argument took place. The apostles, with Peter foremost amongst them, protest. But Christ, intent on his mission, cuts the argument short. He tells Peter to cast a line in the lake of Galilee—as he does in episode two on the left—"and when thou hast opened his mouth, thou shalt find a piece of money: that take, and give unto them for me and thee" (Matthew XVII 27). In the third episode, Peter hands over the money to the gatekeeper on the right.

As with Giotto's Nativity, we read the scene as a whole, though we are aware that there are two gatekeepers and three Peters. But now the landscape which bridges the gap between unity of setting and multiplicity of event, no longer just reminds us, but shows us what is real. And whereas the architectural element in Giotto (the stable) was sketched in almost apologetically, Masaccio brings us confidently to the fringe of a real town. And Masaccio goes further yet. To his grasp of physical reality he adds a sense of political reality to the Bible story. While he was planning this fresco Florence was under the threat of military defeat by Milan. Taxes to raise defensive armies were essential. Not only Christ's but every Florentine's opportunity to "do his own thing" depended on freedom from outside dictation—on paying cash to authority to preserve the individual spirit's freedom of action. The scene as a whole sends the observer back to the Bible. The episode on the right must give pause to every would-be revolutionary. With this flexibility of reference, rooted in observed reality, painting came of age in a new phase of artistic mastery.

This drive to woo the viewer's imagination away from real life to its significance, rather than from a symbol to its meaning, was also reflected in sculpture. And sooner—because the classical art of ancient Rome, which stressed the actual appearance of things, continued to exist in the form of carvings, while its paintings had perished or, as in the cases of Pompei and Herculaneum, been buried.

Madonna and Child by Giotto.

It was under the influence of an ancient sarcophagus that Nicola Pisano created his montage of the birth of Christ in 1260. Each character is better portrayed as an individual than in any contemporary painting. That is the classical influence. But the influence of medieval painting has led to four episodes being so jammed together that the scene as a whole is quite unrealistic. At the top left is the Annunciation—against a Roman temple facade. At the top right angels announce the birth of Christ to (now headless) shepherds. Bottom left, the midwives bathe the newborn Jesus, while Joseph sleeps. On the middle right Mary watches beside her baby, now placed in his cradle.

If we move from this sculptor, who was a contemporary of Margaritone, to the work of Donatello (1386–1455), who was a contemporary of Masaccio, we can see the effect of the change in artists' approach to their subject even more dramatically than we could in painting. In this bronze relief of c.1425 we have, again, more than one episode shown simultaneously. In the Bible story (Matthew XIV 6–11) Salome's dancing so pleased Herod that he said that he would give her anything she asked for. Prompted by Herodias, her mother, she asked for the head of John the Baptist. Here she is still dancing on the right, while the head is shown to an appalled Herod on the left. The costumes show that again, like Andrea Pisano, Donatello has looked at ancient sculpture, and his debt to ancient art is intensified by the careful study of Roman architecture reflected in the arches and columns of Herod's palace.

The difference between the works emerges most strikingly in two respects: expressiveness and viewpoint. The drama is not only reflected in the faces of individuals and the attitudes of their bodies, it drives the observer to follow it from the calm groups on the right to the reactions of the terrified children on the left, past Herod to Herodias's grim triumph to the sickened guest on her left. And this circle of emotions is made all the more impressive by its contrast to the normal life of servants and musicians glimpsed in the main body of the palace. The expression of emotion was not in itself new. Such a degree of credibility and such a linking of individual feelings in a coherent narrative of emotion was, however, without precedent.

Also new was the rigorously logical way in which Donatello used a perspective based on the recession of lines and planes (floor, table-legs, walls) to a single vanishing point imagined in the distance beyond the sculpture. The use of perspective to organize the component parts of a work of art and encourage the spectator to feel that he is viewing "real" space was perhaps the most important technical innovation of the Renaissance revolution.

A single building by Filippo Brunelleschi (1377–1446), a third member of that astonishing generation of early-fifteenth-century innovators, will show how far architecture, too, had grown away from the gothic and Italian romanesque formulas of the fourteenth century. Donatello had illustrated an imaginery Roman palace in his Salome relief, and his square, fluted columns and round arches recur in this real chapel begun by Brunelleschi early in the 1440s. The sense of airy clarity—for the white walls were designed to be kept clear of frescoes, contrasting only with grey stone and coloured terracotta plaques; the symmetry and harmony of the building as a whole; the lucid, mathematically calculated relationship between each of the architectural elements: all these features were to become characteristic of the new architecture. And, like Donatello, Brunelleschi borrowed motifs from ancient Rome without producing anything the ancients themselves would have recognized as akin to their own spirit.

This account of early-Renaissance development in the arts has concentrated on the most striking innovations. Work of comparable beauty and, indeed, of superior delicacy or decorative effect was produced by many other Italians. Fra Angelico's gentle Annunciation was painted three years after Masaccio's Tribute

*Above:* The birth of the Savior, detail from the pulpit of the Baptistery, Pisa, by Nicola Pisano.
*Right:* The central portion of The Payment of Tribute by Masaccio.

Money. Ghiberti's Jacob and Esau was cast a decade after Donatello's Salome. Outside Italy, Jan van Eyck's Giovanni Arnolfini and his Wife, loving, poetic, yet drastically faithful to the physical appearance of things, was painted in 1434. But if we think of artists who led the visual imagination forward and whose influence was to be greatest in the later stages of the Renaissance throughout Europe as a whole, we must stress the contribution of Italy. And not simply "Italy." Every Italian name mentioned here is that of a Tuscan. Why Tuscany? The sixteenth-century art historian Vasari said—well, it was a miracle. Social historians are still trying to prove him wrong.

The appetites both to record the world directly, as the eye sees it, and to use art to reveal more about men's feelings, their emotions, were both revealed in vernacular (that is, non-Latin) literature and, again, most successfully and most directly in Italy.

For literature, this Italian leadership was new. Before 1300, literary forms and literary subject matter had overwhelmingly reflected French taste. French chivalrous romances, in prose or verse, in the original or in translation, were the most popular reading matter throughout western Europe. The earliest stories, based on the Emperor Charlemagne or on the crusades, were tales of war, loyalty and treachery, hewn from the black-and-white values of the feudal nobility. In the thirteenth century the Arthurian stories added the strangulated sexuality of the chivalrous code of love.

It was the extraordinary achievement of the Florentine Dante (1265-1321) to produce in the *Divine Comedy* a work that combined an enticing "quest" or grail-like narrative with the intellectual and argumentative grittyness associated with the scholarly Latin treatise and with a series of settings and characters more graphically realistic than any landscape or individual in the romances. This double

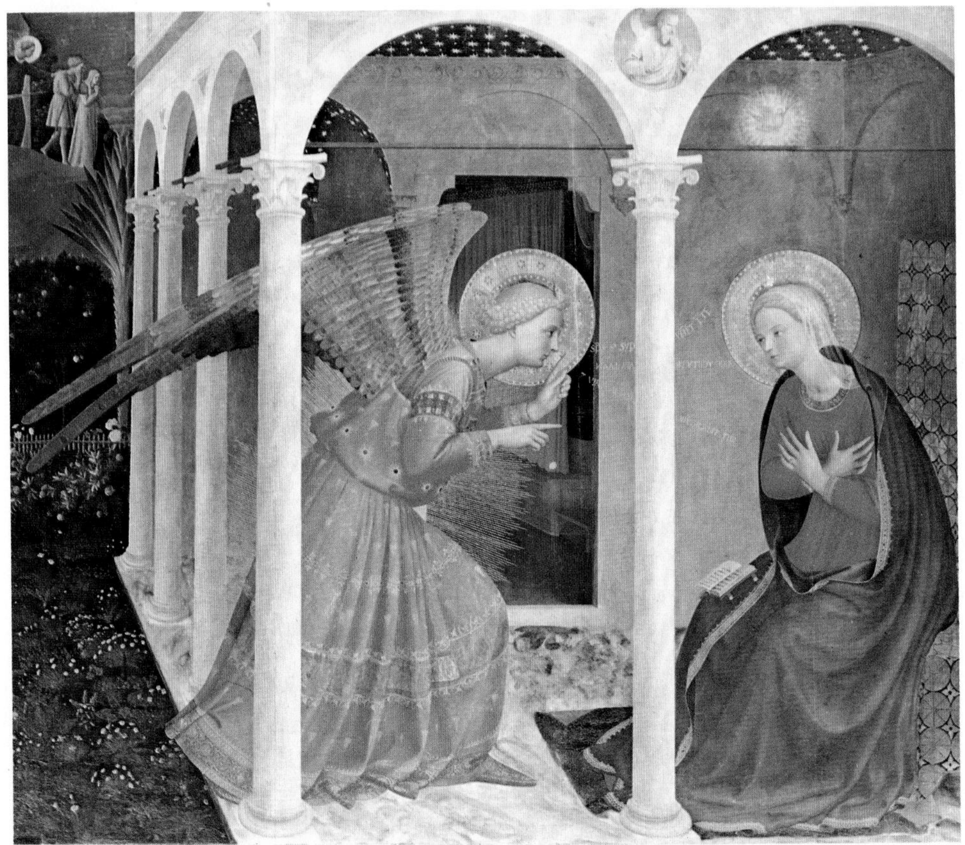

*Top:* Roof of the Pazzi chapel at San Croce, Florence by Brunelleschi.
*Above:* Herod's Feast by Donatello.
*Left:* The Annunciation by Fra Angelico.

appeal to the mind and to the mind's eye, enforced by a poetic style clamped close to the sense, opened a new era of expressiveness.

No one can feel at ease praying in Esperanto. What a man is able to say is determined by language. The more flexible that language is, and the more natural it seems to him, the more fully he can express his feelings. The most significant writers are those who both express "new" feelings—feelings that have hitherto lacked a vocabulary for their nuanced expression—and at the same time offer a model which others can use.

Dante was such a writer. Another was Petrarch (1304–1374), whose sonnets helped his readers define their own conflicting sensations about love, loss, self-confidence and nature. And for better or for worse, his sonnets had such gracefulness and shapeliness that generations, indeed, centuries of poets all over Europe were to rephrase his feelings. And if Dante helped express one instinct, to relate self to the cosmos, to "the scheme of things," and Petrarch to express the sensation of a particular moment, Giovanni Boccaccio (1313–1375) helped to develop a similarly basic need: to enjoy the flavor of anecdote. How basic that need is was demonstrated by the variety of his sources: Asiatic, classical and medieval. But his collection of stories, the *Decameron*, added a psychological and social verisimilitude that was new, instantly advancing the timeless anecdote to the status of the realistic short story and in some cases preparing the way for the novel.

*Above:* Jacob and Esau by Ghiberti.
*Right:* Giovanni Arnolfini and his wife by Jan Van Eyck.

Apart from this Italian triumvirate, only one writer of comparable creative power worked within this period: the English poet Geoffrey Chaucer (c.1340–1400). He knew much of their work (but not the *Decameron*) and there is no doubt that the examples they offered of what to say and how to say it helped his own genius and knowledge of life to produce the *Canterbury Tales* and *Troilus and Cressida*, and thus to ensure that his version of the English dialects spoken in his day would come to underlie the language of Shakespeare and the King James Bible.

In the realm of music, Italy remained a borrower throughout this period as far as actual innovation is concerned. For most of the fourteenth century the leadership was, again, French, its nature summed up in the earliest of musical manifestoes, the *Ars Nova* (c.1320) of Philippe de Vitry, and its leading exponent Guillaume de Machaut. Early in the fifteenth century the innovating energy began to flow from the Netherlands, especially from the widely influential works of Guillaume Dufay (c.1400–1474) and Gilles Binchois (c.1400–1460), who transformed the nature of French music while absorbing the influence of the first thoroughly creative school of English composers headed by John Dunstable (c.1390–1453). Thanks to the fact, however, that composers, singers and instrumentalists traveled widely to work at courts and cathedral music schools, the actual music performed throughout western Europe was more uniform in style than was the case with art or literature.

The chief drift in music was in the direction these other forms of creative communication were taking: towards increasing the expressive potential of the medium. The single line of the early medieval Gregorian chant had already had other lines—choral, orchestral or both—added to it. An emphasis on rhythm, an interest in adding variety by letting the voice parts now "run over" one another, now sound clearly in unison: these and other devices densened and complicated musical texture. Indeed, in its more extreme forms, the music of the "Ars Nova" became a sort of sonorous puzzle in which the sense of the words became trapped. And it was the glory of the Netherlands school that while not renouncing this opulence of sound they once more lay bare the text beneath it, thus not only throwing the listener a thread to guide him through the labyrinth of polyphony but imposing a challenging discipline on the organization of the music itself.

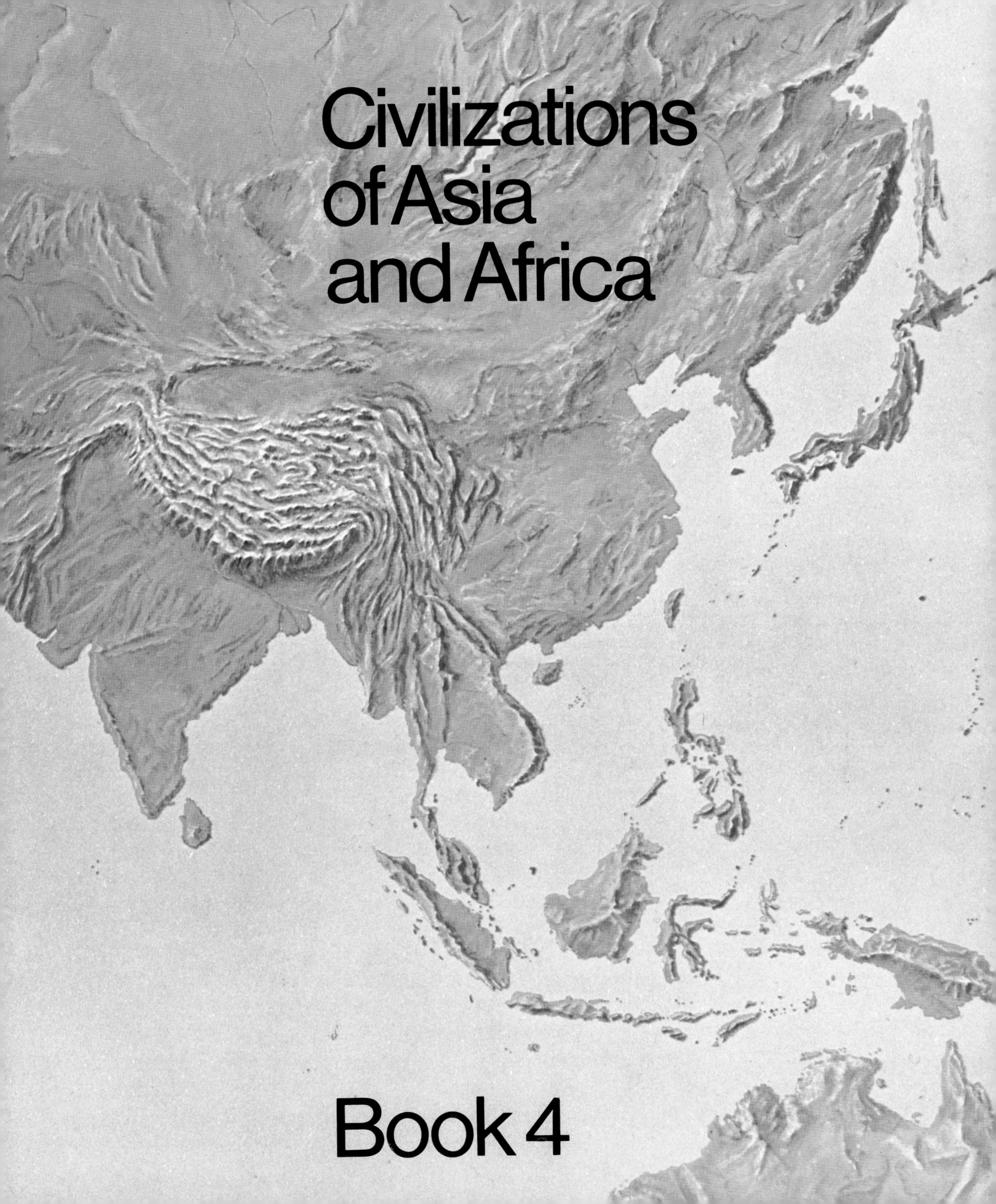
Civilizations
of Asia
and Africa
Book 4

# Introduction

This Book goes back toward the beginning of our story. During the 1,500 years that elapsed while the classical world turned itself into medieval Christendom, the great civilizations of India and China were evolving steadily to rhythms quite independent of that development. The African continent was never again to produce anything so impressive as ancient Egypt, but continued living its own history at its own pace. By about A.D. 1500, the great sub-Saharan spaces were still almost completely isolated from Europe. There was very little reciprocal effect; if these great tracts of the earth's surface were untroubled and unaffected by what was going on in the emerging nations of Europe, so were those nations virtually untroubled by what went on in other continents. The occasional traveler penetrated them; and their products, in small quantities, titillated the appetite of wealthy European consumers in commercial centers such as Venice and London, but that was all.

Or nearly all. There was one colossal exception. Attention has already been drawn to the way that it affected Europe in Book 3. But it affected Asia and Africa as well. This exception was the coming of Islam, the first great world religion to appear since Christianity. Its historic heartland has remained the semitic Near East, the land junction between the three continents. But Islam spread outwards from its source into all three continents. In north Africa it swept around the Mediterranean shores. It has retained its hold in north Africa, and in west Equatorial Africa is still an advancing religion. In Asia conquest and conversion established a great empire in India, and large Moslem populations in China and Indonesia. Islam is one of the great ideological success-stories. But it does not much alter the pattern of a world isolated from Europe before 1500, because although the relationship between Islam and Europe was close and continuing, it was also basically antagonistic.

This is another reason why it is sensible to bring together here the stories of the civilizations which follow their own scenarios during the period of Europe's crucial evolution, and not to try to fit them to that plot as it unrolls. Their chronological patterns are totally different. They make nonsense of such conventional and useful building-blocks as Greece, Rome and the Dark Ages. Sometimes these civilizations move at a faster pace than Europe, sometimes at a slower. Often they were capable of achievements far beyond those of their European contemporaries (no European feat of engineering described in this volume can surpass the Great Wall of China), and this, like their art and wealth, sometimes bemused the few Europeans who came to find out about them.

Meanwhile, still other parts of the world were moving on even more independent historical courses. This book does not discuss all of them. Some of them—the peoples of Oceania, for instance—have left so little evidence that it would be difficult to know what to say. In the case of others, their absence is explained by the fact that they were even less integrated with an evolving pattern than those that are described in this Book. The obvious example is the Americas. The origin of civilization there was explained in Book 1. Thereafter their history is best explained at the point at which they come into the mainstream of world history. This unhappily was also the point at which they disappeared from it as independent cultures, at the time of the European conquest of the sixteenth century. That was the beginning of an age that would crumble in some measure the integrity and uniqueness of all the traditions described in this volume. It would be an age when Europe would export its own preoccupations and quarrels world wide. Willy-nilly, other peoples would have to put up with it even when it meant, as an English historian once put it, that red men would scalp one another beside the shores of Lake Erie and brown men would kill one another because a European king wanted to rob his neighbor. But that is another story, and it forms the subject of much of Volume II.

را بنوازشهای بی اندازه مخصوص ساختند

# Part I India

Chapter 1

# INDIA'S EARLY HISTORY

## THE ARYAN INVASION

From about 2000 B.C. onward, the ancient world was thrown into turmoil by the invasion of warrior hordes from the steppes of southern Russia and central Asia. Destroying or radically altering the ancient cultures of the lands upon which they fell, these peoples spread out over Europe, the Middle East, and India. In India, the newcomers called themselves Aryans.

The arrival of the Aryans in India during the second millennium B.C. is described in book I, part II, chapter 6. Overrunning the declining Harappan civilization, the Aryans spread from the northwest to the Punjab and Gujarat. The fusion of Harappa culture with that of the Aryans to become part of the classical Hindu pattern was a gradual process.

The main center of Aryan culture was the Punjab plain, especially its eastern part. With their horses, chariots, and well-designed bronze weapons (the theory that the Aryans arrived somewhat later than is generally believed and brought the first iron to India is not yet accepted) they subdued the Punjab. They were primarily interested in rearing cattle and horses, although they lived in permanent or semi-permanent villages and practiced some agriculture. Cattle rustling was an accepted activity in Aryan life, and when not fighting the original inhabitants of the Punjab, they often fought among themselves.

*Above:* Soapstone figure of a *yakshi* (tree-nymph), second century B.C. In contrast to the asceticism of Buddhist doctrine, the sculptured figures of *yakshis* express a forthright sensuality. The *yakshi* was originally a fertility spirit worshiped by barren women.
*Left:* A huge statue of the Buddha in a cave-temple at Sokuram. The impact of the Buddha's ethical teachings on the India of the sixth and fifth centuries B.C. may be likened in some respects to that of Christianity on the decadent Roman Empire, the earlier simplicity of the Vedic religion having become increasingly complex, and ritualized.

## THE RIG-VEDA

Because the early Aryans lived in small settlements and did not build in stone or brick, they have left few archaeological remains. Their most important monument is a collection of more than 1000 hymns to their gods. These hymns, intoned at the sacrifices which formed the most important element of Aryan religious life, were composed by *rishis* (seers) and were passed on by word of mouth.

Perhaps around 900 B.C., 1,028 of the hymns were collected in the Rig-Veda, the oldest and most sacred text of Hinduism. It was still not written down, but because it was thought dangerously sacrilegious to tamper with the text, special mnemonic techniques were devised to keep it pure. It is almost the only text of ancient India that has not undergone accretion and alteration.

The text of the Rig-Veda contains no clear reference to the earlier home of the Aryans beyond the mountains of the north-west, or to the Harappan civilization.

| 1000 BC | 900 | 800 | 700 | 600 | 500 | 400 |
|---|---|---|---|---|---|---|
| Aryan invaders of Punjab expand east and south to Ganges Valley, Bengal and North Deccan | | | | | | Persia invades Indus Valley |
| Agricultural progress. Intermingling with native races. Important cities | | | | Buddha (567–487) | | Jainism Mysticism Yoga |
| | Rig-Veda hymns | | | | | |
| | | Use of iron | | | | |

Thus it seems that even the earliest hymns were composed well after the Aryans arrived in India. Because they were a warlike people, the emphasis of the Vedic hymns is on the man's part in life and on the male virtues of courage, loyalty, truthfulness, and generosity. The hymns were sung in honor of many gods, the most important being Varuna, Indra, Agni, Surya, and Soma.

Varuna, the god of the heavens, controlled the order of nature (*rita*). The Aryans regarded him with awe, for his spies watched all men's actions and those who broke his laws suffered dire punishment. But he was also just and true to his word, and rewarded the righteous.

Indra increased in importance as Varuna declined. The personification of the tough Aryan warrior, he slew a mighty dragon named Vritra at the beginning of time, thus releasing the heavenly waters and creating the cosmos. Most strongly stressed was the production of water as a result of his victory. The defeat of Vritra was repeated every year, with the coming of the monsoon. As well as being a rain-maker, Indra was a war-god, the leader of the hosts of heaven against the demons, and the Aryans prayed to him for victory in battle.

Agni was the god of fire. (The word *agni* in Sanskrit simply means "fire," and is related to the Latin *ignis*.) He was important as the intermediary between gods and men, for the sacrificial fire carried offerings to heaven. The sacred hearthfire was kept constantly burning in each home, for through it Agni protected the family. He dwelt in the heavens also, as lightning, and in the fire-sticks which produced him when rubbed together.

Surya was the most important of several sun-gods. Every morning he was awakened by the beautiful dawn-goddess Ushas, harnessed his steeds to his chariot, and drove across the sky. At the end of his journey he gave the world into the care of the night-goddess Ratri. Ushas and Ratri are among the few goddesses referred to in the Rig-Veda and they were not taken very seriously. The moon, Chandra, played little part in the earlier religious life of the Aryans.

Soma was the god of the *soma*, a plant with a narcotic sap from which a hallucinogenic sacred drink was prepared. Drunk only at sacrifices, it was believed to confer immortality on its drinkers and to allow worshipers to commune with the gods. The soma plant is now believed to have been a kind of mushroom, the fly agaric.

## THE EXPANSION OF ARYAN CULTURE

From the Punjab, the Aryans steadily expanded east and south. They were aided by their possession of a new metal, iron, which first appeared in India around the beginning of the first millennium B.C. The period from 1000 to 500 saw fairly rapid development, and by 500 the Aryans had become agriculturists, with a number of important cities on which their political and commercial life centered. However, modern archaeology cannot, as yet, clearly explain this process of development.

Certainly the expansion of Aryan culture was partly due to the conquest of new territories, but there is also reason to believe that much of it was brought about through the adoption of Aryan ways and Vedic religion by indigenous peoples. Moreover, although the Aryans tried to keep their race pure, there was much intermarriage between Aryans and the older inhabitants of the Ganges valley.

Religious practices became more complex. Three more *Vedas* were composed, and these were followed by lengthy prose treatises, the Brahmanas. These were still orally transmitted, but the priests had such highly developed mnemonic techniques that they were able to pass the texts on fairly accurately. This religious literature reflects a culture much preoccupied with sacrificial ritual. The belief that the world had been created by the gods through a great sacrifice at the beginning of time led to the emphasized importance of earthly sacrifices in maintaining the process of creation. Animals of many species were sacrificed, but human sacrifice was not widely approved and seems to have been almost entirely given up towards the end of the period.

### The Class System

Aryan society was divided into the four *varnas*, classes or orders, which still survive as the theoretical basis of the Hindu social system. The highest position was claimed by the brahmans (priests); followed by the *kshatriyas* (rulers and warriors); the *vaisyas* (free tribesmen); and, at the bottom of the social ladder, the *sudras* (servants and slaves). These four classes were thought to have resulted from the creative power of the primeval sacrifice and thus to be an essential part of the cosmic order.

The influence of the brahman at the head of the class system increased with the

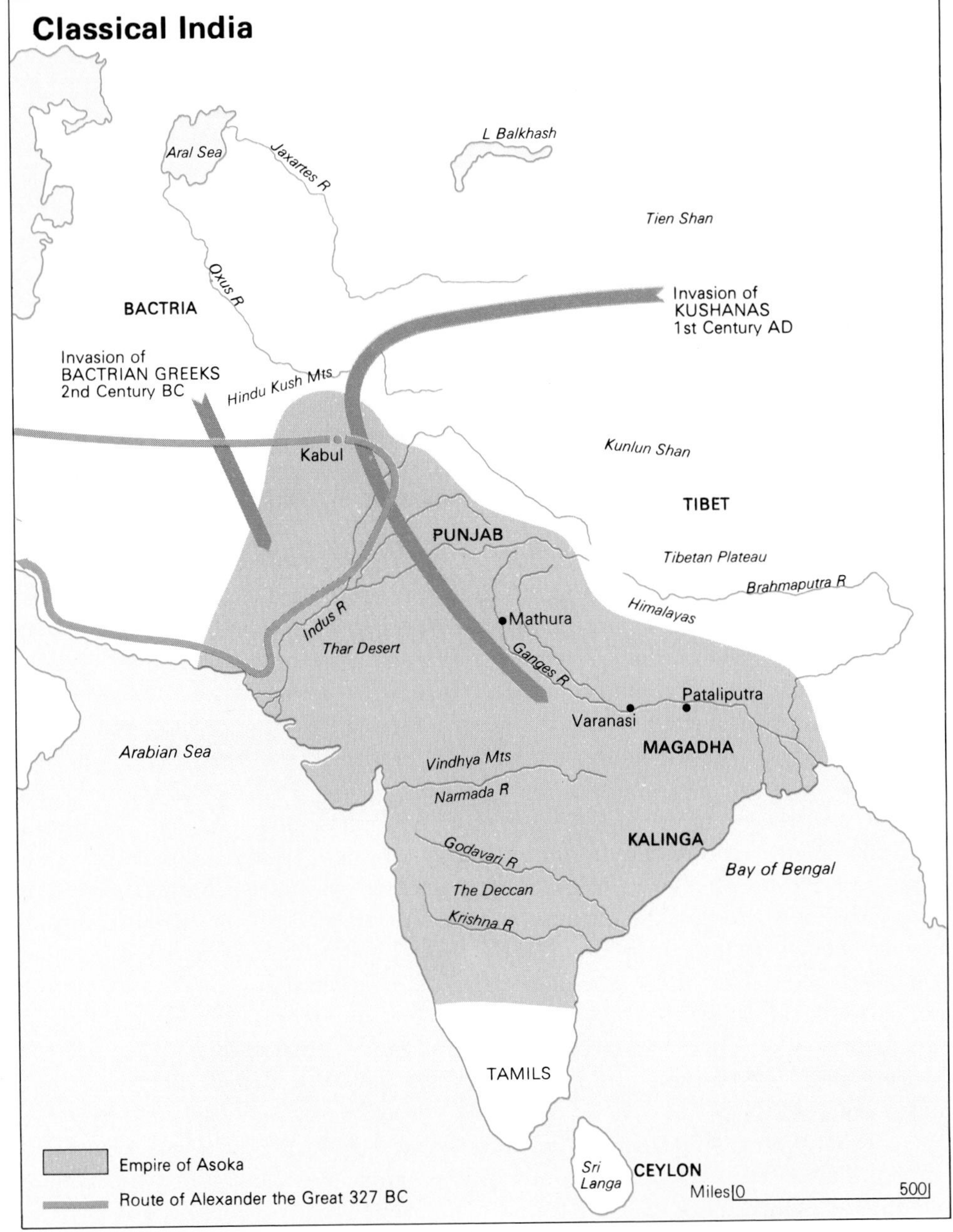

The carved figure of a *Bodhisattva*, a Buddhist saint. According to the doctrines of Mahayana Buddhism, the *Bodhisattvas* were those who had delayed their own life-cycle on the threshold of Nirvana in order to help others along the way to supreme knowledge. Although the Buddha himself was always portrayed with short hair and wearing a monk's robe, symbolizing his total renunciation of the world, the *Bodhisattvas* were shown in fine clothing, wearing scarves and jewelry, as a reminder that before renouncing the world Buddha himself had been a prince.

years. The *kshatriyas* also gained in power. As culture became more complex, the *raja* (tribal chieftain) developed into a king. Faintly reflected in the religious literature of the period, and in the legends of the great epics which were composed in their present form at a later date, is the conflict of tribes and their amalgamation into regional kingdoms. The kings were supported by the brahmans, who benefited from royal patronage, and although the brahmans claimed preeminence, they were often subservient to royal authority.

As the tempo of change and expansion quickened, the center of Aryan civilization shifted from the Punjab to the Doab, the region between the Jumna and Ganges rivers dominated by the tribe of the Kurus (Kauravas). Later it moved farther east, to the eastern parts of modern Uttar Pradesh. By the mid-sixth century B.C., Aryan culture had spread throughout the Ganges valley as far as northern Bengal and had penetrated south to the Narmada River, the northern boundary of the Deccan. By this time, systems of writing and coinage may have been in use, although there is no good archaeological evidence. The rise of the Persian empire brought India more closely into touch with western Asia. In about 515 B.C. much of the Indus valley was conquered by Darius, including the city of Taxila which, as a center of learning, had much contact with Aryan lands farther east.

## MYSTICISM AND RELIGIOUS REFORM

At a time of cultural and political expansion, religion and philosophy might be expected to reflect the same tendencies. In India, the reverse occurred. While kings expanded and consolidated their power, craftsmen introduced new techniques, and merchants developed trade and commerce, thoughtful men tended to turn away from the everyday world to search for spiritual security. Many factors influenced this attitude.

The sacrificial religion had become pessimistic. The Aryans had formerly believed that by performing sacrifices and observing traditional customs and ethics they would be assured of rebirth in heaven, where they would feast with their ancestors for ever. Now the belief developed that even in heaven there was no escape from death.

The composers of the latest hymns of the Rig-Veda expressed doubt of the traditional myths and speculated freely about the origin and nature of the cosmos. Such speculation increased in the later Vedic period, when the literature contains numerous attempts to establish a single creative entity or principle. New gods, such as Prajapati and Brahma (the two are sometimes identified), were postulated as the ultimate beings from whom the other gods and the universe emerged. Some sages maintained that the ultimate had none of the attributes of man, but was impersonal.

The speculative trend may have begun with orthodox brahmans who still upheld the Vedic sacrificial religion, but the questioners began to doubt the value of the sacrifice itself. They considered that although the world might have been created through sacrifice, the ultimate and absolute existed before the creation and the sacrifice, and that to draw closer to the primal being required mystical meditation, often accompanied by penances such as fasting. Training to produce trance states at will, called *yoga*, came to be looked on as an integral part of the religious life of those who strove to transcend the religion of the ordinary man. These features, developed in the later Vedic period, have remained characteristic of Indian religion.

Another feature appearing at this time, together with mysticism, was belief in the rebirth of the soul. The way in which the doctrine of transmigration found general acceptance is not clear. It is first plainly enunciated in the texts known as

Upanishads, prose and verse passages appended to the Brahmana literature which describe the new mystical doctrines. These texts mark the transition between the older Vedic religion and emergent Hinduism.

The doctrine of transmigration spread rapidly. By about 530 B.C., when the Buddha began to preach, it was almost universally accepted, and was taken for granted in his doctrines. Linked with the doctrine of *karma* (work), it acquired a moral quality: a man fared in his next life according to his behavior in this. If he lived an exemplary life, his soul might spend a long period in one of the heavens before rebirth on earth in more favorable conditions than before. But the soul of a wicked man would suffer long agonies in a purgatory and many rebirths as a lowly animal, until his evil deeds had been purged and he won another chance as a rational being.

A corollary of the doctrine of transmigration was that all things were interlinked. The soul inhabiting a dog was no different than that of a saint. Only the material coverings of the two were different. This led to the doctrine of *ahimsa* (non-injury), the belief that it was wrong to injure or kill any living thing. It was most strongly supported by heretical groups such as the Jains, but its increasing acceptance by the orthodox meant that in later centuries most Hindus of higher castes became vegetarians. The doctrine of transmigration also gave strong support to the growing practice of seeking enlightenment through mystical disciplines aimed at achieving a state of bliss absolutely free from change or fear of change, from the constantly repeated cycle of death and rebirth, and from the sorrows and evils of everyday life.

From the seventh century onward, an increasing number of men became ascetics, although many did not wholly reject the authority of the Vedas and the brahmans or the validity of sacrifices. The ascetics developed the mystical doctrine

*Above:* Late twelfth-century Japanese wood carving of the head of Amida Buddha, ruler of the western paradise in Mahayana Buddhist theology. Early in the Christian era, Mahayana (the Great Vehicle) Buddhism spread from northern India into China, reaching Japan around the sixth century.
*Left:* Relief carving from Gandhara, northern India, dating from A.D. 200–400, depicting the birth of the Buddha, which took place in 566 B.C. Earlier Buddhist art depicted the Buddha symbolically, and it was probably in Gandhara that he was figuratively depicted for the first time.

of the identity of the human soul and the absolute being, called Brahman. (This name must not be confused with the brahman priest, the Brahmana texts, or the god Brahma.) They held that the man who realized the absolute truth of this doctrine, by deep and long meditation, would be freed from the cycle of transmigration. Other sages taught that the absolute was a personal god, and began to practice mystical devotions which would unite them with him. These mystics did not cultivate the greater gods of the Rig-Veda, who were slowly losing prestige, but were mainly devoted to two minor gods, Vishnu and Shiva (the latter then more often called Rudra).

As well as the hermits and wandering ascetics who did not break completely with orthodoxy, there were more revolutionary thinkers who opposed the brahmans, denied the authority of the Vedas, and opposed sacrifices and other ritual practices as cruel and useless. Most of them also rejected the belief that the world was created by a supreme being, teaching instead that it came into being as a result of natural law. They believed in supernatural beings and survival after death, but held that the gods themselves were subject to the laws of the universe and were liable to decay. Considering the world an evil and unhappy place, they taught that release from it lay in disowning all possessions and worldly ties and living a life of self-denial. Some even gave up their clothes and went about naked, begging their food or relying on the support of lay followers. Many of them followed a discipline laid down by a leader, thus forming the world's first monastic orders.

## THE BUDDHA

Of the several ascetic orders of this kind, few made much impact on posterity—but one developed into a world religion. This was the order founded by Siddhartha Gautama, known to his followers as Buddha, "the Wide-awake" (sometimes

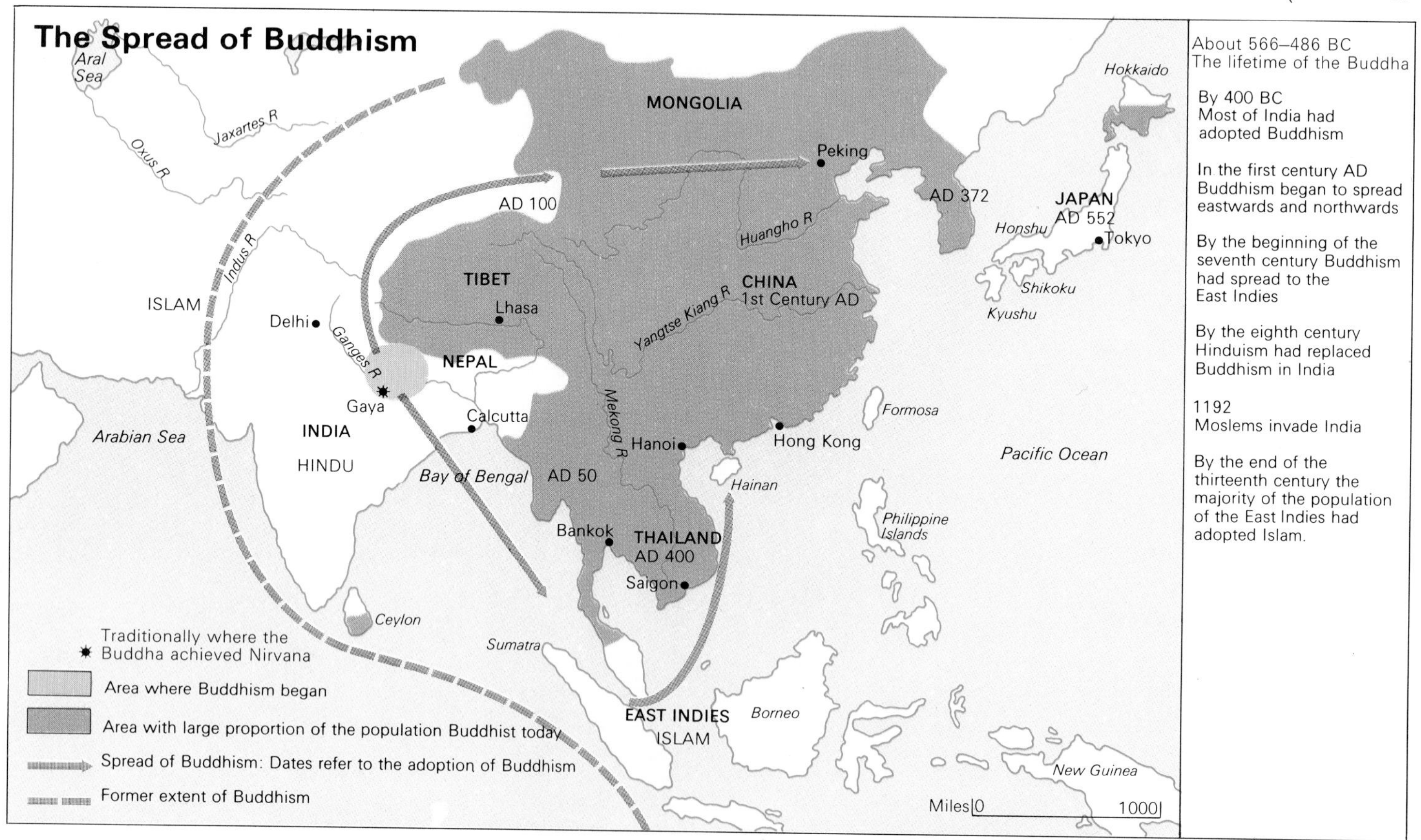

translated as "the Enlightened"). Although his followers left a great deal of literature purporting to give the texts of his sermons and to describe incidents of his life, many of these documents are unreliable. However, the broad outline of his life is fairly clear. He was the son of a chieftain of the Sakya, a republican tribe dwelling on the northern fringe of the Ganges plain, and was born at what is now Rummindei Garden, near Paderia in Nepal. Like many intelligent young men of his time, he grew disgusted with the world and left his home to become an ascetic. After years of searching for the truth, and finding it to his own satisfaction, he began to preach, gathering a band of yellow-robed disciples who came to be known as *bhikshus* (beggars). He traveled widely in the Ganges plain, preaching, disputing with opponents, and making converts. His dates, probably from 566 to 486 B.C., are the earliest in India that can confidently be given to within a few years.

The Buddha sought to understand suffering, its cause, and its cure. He came to the conclusion that sorrow stemmed from desiring what one does not have and clinging to what one already has for fear of losing it. The world, for the Buddhist, is in a state of constant flux; man tries to stop the flow of events and suffers in the process. Although man imagines that he has a permanent, unchanging soul, the core of his personality, he is really a mere chain of composite events. When he fully realizes this truth, he achieves the state known as *Nirvana*, ceases to exist as a person, and is released from rebirth. But to arrive at this state takes many lives. It can only be reached by abandoning all sense of self. Perhaps surprisingly, the austere teachings of the Buddha developed into a religion which now has hundreds of millions of followers.

The first Buddhist monks had to consider the inclinations of the laity who supported them and from whom they recruited new members, so they adapted popular religious practices to Buddhist ends. Sacred trees were common all over India while in the Ganges valley people worshiped the mounds in which the ashes of ancient heroes were buried. Similarly, the pipal tree was adopted as the sacred tree of Buddhism, for it was under such a tree at Gaya in Bihar that Buddha achieved full enlightenment; and the burial *stupa*, a large hemispherical mound, marked his final entry into *Nirvana* on his death. Pipal trees were planted and *stupas* erected in the monasteries, and the laity was encouraged to come and worship them and listen to the preaching of the monks, who told tales of the life of the Buddha or of his earlier incarnations. Simple liturgical passages were also devised, for laymen to learn and repeat.

## THE JAINS

Of the heterodox sects of the sixth century B.C., the only survivor is Jainism, now the religion of 3 or 4 million Indians. Its founder, Vardhamana Mahavira, who had the religious title of *Jina* ("Conqueror"), was a contemporary of the Buddha. He taught that all living things, including plants and apparently lifeless objects such as stones and flames, consisted of individual souls imprisoned in matter. Men should strive to set their souls free from matter, and thus avoid rebirth and dwell in bliss forever. This ultimate state was to be achieved by penance and strict non-violence, which is perhaps more strongly emphasized by Jainism than by any other sect.

One other group which deserves mention is that of the materialists, followers of Ajita Kesakambali, a contemporary of Buddha and Mahavira, who founded a philosophical school that rejected religion entirely. His followers did not believe in the gods or in the survival of the personality after death. Little is now known about them, but they were a factor in Indian life for over 1,500 years.

Chapter 2

# PRE-ISLAMIC INDIA

## THE GROWTH OF INDIAN EMPIRES

At the time of the Buddha, the kingdom of Magadha (south Bihar) was ruled by a king Bimbisara, who appears to have had very progressive political ideas. Bimbisara consolidated his small kingdom and organized an embryonic bureaucracy which was more efficient than the quasi-feudal system of government, through sub-kingdoms and local chiefs, which prevailed elsewhere. Under Bimbisara's successors, Magadha steadily expanded its frontiers, absorbing other kingdoms and tribal republics throughout the Ganges valley. When Alexander of Macedon invaded India in 327 B.C., the area from eastern Punjab to the Bay of Bengal was more or less under the control of the king of Magadha, whose power may also have extended to north Deccan. Soon after Alexander's retreat, the throne of the Magadhan empire was seized by Chandragupta Maurya, who set to work to expand the empire and improve its government. He was aided by a brilliant "prime minister," Kautiliya, whose name has been given to ancient India's most important political text, the *Kautiliya Arthasastra* (in fact, a compilation of somewhat later date).

Chandragupta gained control of the Punjab and wrested most of Afghanistan from Alexander's successor in Asia, Seleucus Nicator. Megasthenes, Seleucus' ambassador to the Mauryan capital of Pataliputra (modern Patna), has left the earliest important account of India written by a foreigner, although his text only survives in fragments. Both Seleucus and the *Kautiliya Arthasastra* provide a picture of a stern ruler of a state organized on thoroughly bureaucratic lines. A large, well-disciplined army and police force maintained the peace. The people, although taxed fairly heavily, enjoyed justice, security of life and property, and rudimentary social services. The state's part in the economic development of the country, which was very prosperous, included such works as irrigation schemes.

When he died, soon after 300 B.C., Chandragupta's empire extended over north India and what is now Pakistan (with the exception of Assam), and probably included part of the Deccan. Little is known of Bindusara, who succeeded him, but Asoka (c. 269–232), the third Mauryan emperor, is one of the best documented figures of ancient India.

All over the subcontinent, from Kandahar to Mysore, are inscriptions on rocks, pillars, and stone slabs, recording the decrees of Asoka. These are the earliest

400 BC | 300 | 200 | 100 | AD | 100 | 200 | 300 | 400 | 500 | 600

Mauryan Empire (323-185)
Greek principalities in Northwest India
Kushan Empire in Northwest India
Guptan Empire (320-590) Classical Hindu culture
Alexander invades India (327)
Development of Hindu Kingdoms in Ganges Basin
Rise of Mahayana Buddhism and Hinduism
Sanskrit grammar
Decimal system
Huns invade India
Asoka (273–232)

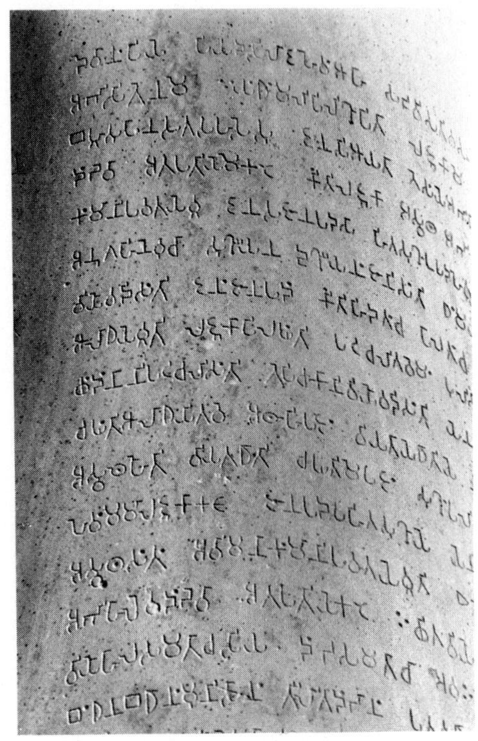

*Above:* The edicts and inscriptions of Asoka (c. 269–232 B.C.), the third Mauryan emperor, survive on carvings in northern and central India. In *Brahmi* script, they are the earliest surviving significant Indian writings. This inscription concerns religious law, medical aid and welfare.

*Left:* Eighty-five temples were built at Khajuraho, near Allahabad in northern India, around A.D. 1000. The sculptured friezes which ornament the twenty remaining temples are famous for their erotic subject matter. To the pious Hindu, sexual union symbolizes the union of the worshiper with his god.

significant and intelligible Indian writings to survive. The script of the Harappa people appears to have been forgotten, but writing was rediscovered some centuries before Asoka. The inscriptions reveal that when Asoka had been emperor for eight years he embarked on a bloody war in Kalinga (modern Orissa), but afterwards underwent a great change of heart, abandoning military ambitions and attempting to develop his empire as a kind of welfare state. He sent envoys west as far as Macedon, urging other rulers to follow his example and give up war. During his reign there was a great Buddhist council at Pataliputra, which sent out missionary monks all over the subcontinent. It was as a result of these missions that Ceylon (recently renamed Sri Lanka) became a Buddhist country.

The Mauryan empire at its greatest extent was the largest Indian empire until the days of British rule. But soon after Asoka's death—if not before—it began to break up. It lingered on for about fifty years, but its force was spent. The same pattern may be traced in the rise and fall of later Indian empires: a century or more of brilliant success, followed by a rapid decline.

A sandstone figure of a *yakshi*, dating from the second century A.D. This is work of the school of Mathura (modern Muttra) on the Jumna River. Mathura was a center of religious art from the second century B.C. onward; the red sandstone which supplied material for so many of its artists was quarried at Sikri, near modern Peshawar, Pakistan.

## THE INVADERS

Around the middle of Asoka's reign, the Greek colonists of Bactria, which lay between the upper Oxus River (the modern Amu Darya River) and the Hindu Kush, became independent of the Seleucid empire. Early in the second century B.C., they began to attack northwest India, soon establishing their rule over most of what is now Pakistan. They were followed by tribes from Central Asia, the Sakas or Scythians, semi-nomadic peoples of Iranian stock who had been set on the move by several factors, notably the consolidation of China under the Qin and Han dynasties. Parthians from the eastern part of the Arsacid kingdom also found their way into the Indus valley. They were followed, in about A.D. 30, by the Kushanas, another central Asian tribal people, who had slowly trekked westward from the borders of China to Bactria.

The Kushanas penetrated deeply into India, reaching at least as far as Varanasi (the recently revived Sanskrit name of what was formerly called Benares) on the Ganges. Their greatest ruler was Kanishka, the date of whose accession is much disputed, estimates ranging from A.D. 78 to 144. He was the overlord of an immense empire, reaching far into central Asia and prospering because of its control of the overland routes from both China and India to the West. Like Asoka, Kanishka is remembered as a great patron of Buddhism, and under the Kushanas Buddhism spread in central Asia, whence it soon found its way to China.

The age of invasions was one of fierce and bloody battles. However, in the east of the Ganges plain, Hindu kingdoms emerged from the ruins of the Mauryan empire. The invaders, even the culturally advanced Greeks, soon came under the influence of Indian culture and made no attempt to change the ways of the people. The prosperity of the times is proved by the remains of many splendid religious buildings, chiefly Buddhist, with inscriptions testifying to liberal donations towards their erection, not only by kings and chiefs, but also by merchants, craftsmen, and even peasants.

The invasions opened India to the rest of the world even more than Alexander had done. India appears in Chinese records for the first time in 129 B.C., when an envoy of the Han rulers reached Bactria. The expansion of the Roman Empire, and the demand for Asian luxuries on the part of its wealthier citizens, led to further contacts. As well as spices, jewels, and fine textiles, Indian stories, fables, and probably some religious ideas, found their way to Europe. Western influence on India, chiefly in the fields of art and astronomy, was soon assimilated into distinctively Indian systems.

## THE DECCAN AND THE TAMILS

Until Mauryan times, references to peninsular India are few and vague. The epic *Ramayana* describes it as a wild, thickly forested area, inhabited mainly by demons and monkeys. But Asoka's empire reached as far as Mysore, and by Asoka's time Aryan civilization had influenced the more populous areas of the Deccan, although it had hardly begun to affect the southern plain, the home of the Tamils.

Although indigenous dynasties took over from the Mauryas in the Deccan, their rulers supported the northern religions—Hinduism, Buddhism, and Jainism—and their official language was Prakrit, which had been used by the Mauryans for public pronouncements. No doubt the Mauryan conquest much encouraged the Aryanization of the south, but it is likely that the main agents in the process were wandering religious ascetics from the north, and merchants who risked crossing the wild Deccan plateau to obtain the jewels and spices of the south. Aryanization ultimately extended throughout the peninsula and, later, beyond India to southeast Asia.

The Tamils are the only important race of India to have a literature which predates full Aryanization. Dating back to the beginning of the Christian era, this literature reflects a people divided into small kingdoms constantly at war, worshiping nature divinities with orgiastic rituals. There was a softer side to Tamil life, however, and hints of the intense devotion of later Tamil religious poetry are to be found even in the earliest collections.

The ports of the peninsula were active from the first century A.D. Indian ships sailed west to the Red Sea and east as far as Canton, and India was visited by merchants of many nations. The large number of Roman coins found in south India and Ceylon is clear evidence of commercial contacts.

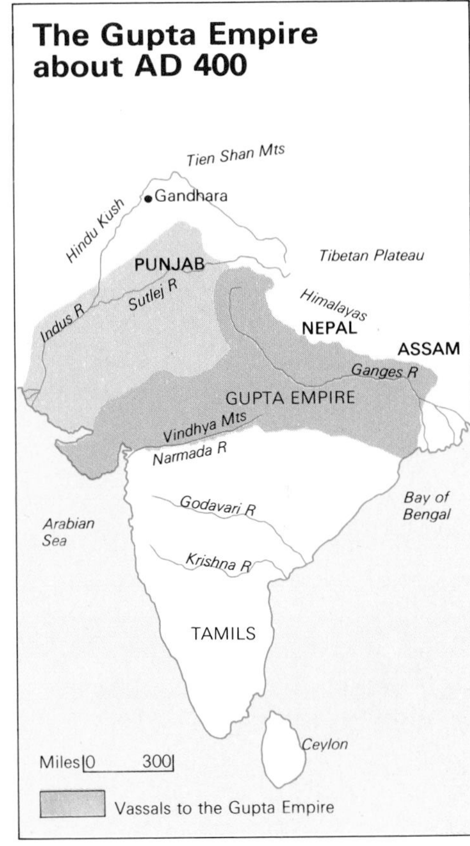


## THE GUPTA PERIOD

In A.D. 320, another Chandra Gupta came to the throne of a small kingdom in the Ganges valley and began to build another great empire. The process was continued by his two successors (Samudra Gupta, c. 335–376, and Chandra Gupta II, c. 376–415), until once again north India was governed by a single ruler whose power extended from sea to sea. Most of the Ganges plain, and some other areas, were directly controlled. Other regions were held by vassal kings. On the fringes of the empire, in places such as Assam, Nepal, and parts of the Punjab, the Gupta emperors claimed suzerainty, but probably had little real influence. Their power was occasionally felt to the south, but never extended for long beyond the Vindhya Hills.

The Guptas were in some respects more successful than the Mauryas. Their dynasty lasted longer, and more of its literature and art survives, reflecting a high level of culture and a way of life which, though it had its somber elements, achieved a degree of urbanity rare in the world's history.

The end of the Gupta empire came partly through the tendency of its local governors to change their status to that of vassal kings, thus setting up small dynasties which soon became independent. The process was much accelerated by further invaders, called *Hunas* in Indian accounts. The word is a variant of *Hunni* (Huns), the Latin name for the fierce horsemen who were devastating much of Europe at about the same time, but it is doubtful whether the two people were closely akin. About A.D. 500, Hun chieftains occupied all of what is now Pakistan and much of western India, raiding almost to the borders of Bengal. Their power in India did not last long, but its effects were considerable. Much of the northwest was laid waste and the Buddhist culture of Gandhara (in the Kabul valley) never fully recovered. In western India, many old ruling families disappeared and were replaced by the ancestors of the thirty-six clans of the Rajputs of medieval times, some of whom may have been Indianized invaders. The Gupta rulers continued to control the east Ganges plain until the middle of the sixth century, and another line with the surname Gupta, not closely related to the main one, persisted there for 200 years longer.

## The Social Order

A wooden figure representing the *avatār* (incarnation) of the god Vishnu as the boar Varaha. Vishnu, the supreme spirit in Hindu theology, has eight other *avatāras*: Matsya, the fish; Kurma, the tortoise; Narasinha, half man and half lion; Vamena, the dwarf; Parashurama, the hero with an ax; Ramachandra, hero of the epic *Ramayana*, Krishna; and Buddha. A tenth *avatār*, as Kalki, a white horse with wings, is yet to come.

It was in the Gupta period that Hindu culture entered what may justly be called its classical phase. It is necessary to interrupt the chronological sequence here to discuss some of the period's distinctive features. Many features of the Gupta social order remained in operation in India until recent times.

Any account of the Hindu social system must make a clear distinction between *varna* (class) and *jati* (caste). The two are of separate origins. The four classes of society emerged at the end of the Vedic period. Castes, whether theoretically included in one of the classes or left outside the system altogether, have come and gone, have risen or fallen in the social scale. They have tended to increase in number —in the nineteenth century there were at least 3,000 castes.

Of the four classes, the first three—brahmans, *kshatriyas,* and *vaisyas*—were "twice born," that is to say that males underwent investiture with the sacred cord, after which they could study the Vedas. The *sudras* were not allowed to learn or even hear the Vedas, but members of the higher *sudra* castes, known as "clean" *sudras*, might receive certain ministrations from the brahmans and hear and learn religious literature of lesser sanctity. Below these *sudras* were others, considered so impure that they were not allowed to enter the temples. These were untouchable in varying degrees, and included such humble yet socially important folk as leather workers, sweepers, and funeral attendants.

Caste, as distinct from the system of the four classes, was not recorded in India until the latter part of the first millennium B.C. Its origins are uncertain and are the subject of many theories. Some of the earliest known castes, like those mentioned in the *Lawbook of Manu*, compiled early in the Christian era, bore the names of ancient tribes, suggesting that the caste system was a survival of tribalism.

A caste was distinguished by three main features: it was endogamous—its members must marry within the caste; it was commensal—its members must not eat food cooked by members of a lower caste, or eat in the company of members of a lower caste; and it tended to be craft-exclusive—its members usually followed the same profession or group of professions.

Castes were organized through local committees or *panchayats*, consisting of the most respected members of the caste, usually heads of families. The caste *panchayat* could fine or ostracize members who infringed its rules, and Hindu rulers recognized its authority. Caste hierarchy was controlled by the local ruler, and there were sometimes fierce disputes between one caste and another over questions of precedence. The duty of the king as the preserver of caste and class is emphasized very strongly in Hindu ethical and legal literature; any infringement of the rules was looked on as a grave sin, likely to endanger the whole social system.

Few modern Indians have much good to say for the caste system, for it tended to perpetuate social inequality, and members of the untouchable castes suffered grave disabilities. But it must not be forgotten that it gave stability to Indian social life. The caste was a source of security, both psychological and economic, giving its members a sense of belonging to a corporate body. It assisted those who fell on hard times, and cared for widows and orphans.

Even more important than class or caste in the life of the ordinary Hindu was the family, for few people had so strong a sense of kinship. A family formed a closely knit corporation, the joint owner of ancestral property under the control of the paterfamilias. Family solidarity was strengthened by the rite of *sraddha*, periodic offerings which were believed to help the ancestors in the next world and by numerous domestic rituals, especially marriage.

In theory, women had few rights. They were subordinate to their fathers in childhood, to their husbands in marriage, and to their sons in old age. In classical Hinduism, a woman had legal ownership only of her clothes and jewelry. Divorce was not allowed, for marriage was a religio-magical rite joining husband and wife for ever—but although monogamy was morally desirable in normal circumstances, it was possible for a dissatisfied husband to marry again while his first wife was living. Indeed, if she were not capable of producing male children it was his religious duty to do so, for without a son he and his ancestors would suffer in the next life and the family line would be broken. The supernatural bond between husband and wife was not severed by the husband's death, and a widow was not permitted to remarry. She was expected to devote the rest of her life to prayer, fasting, and penance, in order that she might at last join her husband in the next world. These religious norms, laid down in the socio-religious texts known as *Dharmasastras*, were applied with increasing rigidity. The practice of *satī* or suttee (the widow burning herself to death on her husband's funeral pyre) was very rare until after the Gupta period, but its frequency increased thereafter.

However, it must not be imagined that in classical India a woman was a mere chattel. She had rights in law, and the ill-treatment of women was looked on as reprehensible. Even as woman's legal status declined, and social custom progressively restricted her freedom, within the home she was much respected, especially if she was the mother of sons. Secular literature, moreover, shows that there were many women who were not bound by the rigid ties of convention, including actresses, singers, and entertainers, who were normally prostitutes.

In the *Mahabharata*, the great Hindu epic of (around) A.D. 600, the hero, Krishna, is a central figure of the section known as the *Bhagavad-Gita*, but the Krishna-figure is of more ancient origin—possibly a fertility spirit worshiped in southern India.

## THE EVOLUTION OF HINDUISM

In the religious life of India after the Mauryan period, the old gods such as Indra and Brahma lost support, while Vishnu and Shiva gained ground. By the Gupta period, one or other of the latter pair was looked on as the creator by most Indians.

The rise of Vishnu is mirrored in the two great epics, the *Mahabharata* and the *Ramayana*, which were based on earlier poems, but only now took their present shape. The former, much edited and expanded, became the world's longest poem. Among its interpolated episodes is the Bhagavad-Gita, now the most important Hindu scripture. This beautiful poem was composed partly as a counterblast to the pacifistic and equalitarian tendencies encouraged by Buddhism and Jainism. One of its central messages is that men can most speedily achieve salvation by carrying out their traditional class duties (*dharma*) in a truly religious spirit, without thought of personal reward.

From the theological point of view, the most significant feature of the Bhagavad-Gita is its identification of a legendary hero, Krishna, as the incarnation of Vishnu, who from time to time has taken human form in order to rid the world of evil. The god Vishnu, not an impersonal absolute entity, is the ultimate source of all creation. The Bhagavad-Gita does not reject outright such traditional religious activities as sacrifice, repeating the Vedas, penance, and meditation, but it maintains that these are less effective than *bhakti*, simple devotion to a god, as a means of obtaining final bliss.

Because worshipers found Vishnu's incarnation as Krishna both attractive and intelligible, the cult of Krishna grew through the centuries. At first he was looked on as the type of the savior hero, helping his devotees in their troubles and hardships as the Krishna of the *Mahabharata* helped the five Pandava brothers. Later, other aspects of Krishna developed: Krishna as a handsome youth, playing his flute in the moonlight and dallying with the milkmaids of Vrindavana (modern Brindaban), became the symbol of god calling the souls of men to him; Krishna as a boy, the darling of his foster-mother despite his pranks, satisfied maternal instincts. Indeed, the complete Krishna legend contained something to meet every psychological need.

The doctrine of *avataras*, in which the god took living forms in order to save the world, led to the acceptance of ten heroes and minor divinities as incarnations of Vishnu. After Krishna, the most important was Rama, the hero of the epic *Ramayana*. Rama lacked Krishna's breadth of appeal, but he was worshiped as the prototype of the faithful son and husband, and the righteous and benevolent ruler.

*Bhakti*, devotion to a personal god in place of penance and meditation, and *puja*, the worship of a god by chanting hymns and offering flowers and fruit, made headway also among devotees of other gods. The later *Upanishads* show the beginnings of these tendencies, which came to the fore in the *Svetasvatara Upanishad*. This saw Shiva as the sole origin of the universe, who should be worshiped with devotion to obtain release from transmigration. Shiva, however, was a less colorful divinity than Vishnu. In none of his legends does he take on the life of a man, and he was most frequently worshiped in the image of an upright post, the *linga*, a phallic symbol.

*Top:* A yogi, follower of a mystical discipline of meditation and fasting, sitting in front of a temple at Varanasi (Benares), the greatest pilgrimage center of India.
*Above:* A Hindu wedding ceremony. Despite the lowly position of women in Hindu society, marriage is an important and complex ceremony, for the reincarnation cycle depends on begetting children.

## SCHOOLS OF PHILOSOPHY

The religious developments of the Gupta period were accompanied by the growth of philosophy in the strict sense of the term, as distinct from the mystical speculations of the *Upanishads* and the earlier Buddhist scriptures. As well as the heterodox systems, six schools of philosophy were recognized as orthodox, each claiming to put forward the simplest and most effective means of obtaining release from the transmigration cycle. The six comprised *Nyaya*, a school of logic; *Vaisheshika*, which maintained that the structure of the material world was atomic; *Sankhya*, which proclaimed a doctrine similar to Jainism, emphasizing the distinction of soul and matter; *Yoga*, a school of training in meditation and mystical disciplines; *Mimamsa*, which attempted to justify faith in the Vedas by logical means; and *Vedanta* ("the end of the Vedas"), which provided logical arguments for the typical doctrine of the early *Upanishads*, that the individual soul (atman) and the impersonal world spirit (*Brahman*) were really one and the same. Vedanta had most influence on later times, through its greatest teacher, Shankara (early ninth century), who wrote commentaries which have provided a basis for intellectual Hinduism to the present day.

With the universal acceptance of the doctrine of transmigration, new ideas about the nature of the cosmos developed. The doctrine of time cycles held that the universe went through an infinite series of cycles in which it was alternately created and reabsorbed by the supreme being. The Indian philosopher recognized that the universe was immense in extent, infinite in duration, and its decline inevitable. However, man could improve his situation by spiritual and physical efforts. In staving off the consequences of cyclical decline, much was thought to depend on the king. If the ruler observed the sacred law, his people would follow his example, and their righteousness would beneficially affect the whole order of nature. Thus, the Hindu world view was not fatalistic; religious texts exhort men to make strenuous efforts for their own and their fellow's welfare.

A red sandstone head of the *Bodhisattva* Avalokitesvara (the Lord who Looks Down), dating from around the fifth century A.D. Avalokitesvara is the most frequently portrayed of the many *Bodhisattvas* in Mahayana Buddhist art: he is always shown with a headdress which bears an image of Amida Buddha.

## MAHAYANA BUDDHISM

The early Buddhist monks had adapted their beliefs to meet the needs of the laity. This trend was furthered by new doctrines which explicitly attributed divinity to the Buddha. According to the older system, a man should strive to reach *Nirvana* by the quickest route, living many lives of selflessness and benevolence, but this aim began to seem selfish to some Buddhists. Instead, they maintained, a man should strive to reach the very threshold of *Nirvana*—and then turn back and use his great spiritual power to help others, thus bringing many to salvation instead of only himself. The adherents of the new doctrine called the old system *Hinayana* (the Lesser Vehicle), as compared with their own *Mahayana* (the Great Vehicle).

The Mahayanist strove to become a *Bodhisattva*, a term used by the Hinayanist only to denote a previous incarnation of Buddha. Mahayana taught that many Bodhisattvas already looked down from the heavens and poured their compassion and help upon all living things. One of these, particularly concerned with mankind, was the gentle Avalokitesvara (the Lord who Looks Down), who was worshiped by many simple believers as a kind of savior.

According to the older sects, Buddha was an ordinary man who achieved supreme knowledge and thus found the way to *Nirvana*. But the Mahayanists taught that the earthly Buddha had been the manifestation of a heavenly Buddha, Amitabha, one of many such Buddhas presiding over different regions of the universe. Later, the belief arose that these heavenly Buddhas were the manifestations of a single primeval Buddha, equivalent to the world-soul of Hinduism.

Mahayana beliefs apparently took final form in northwest India while the invaders were in control, and may owe something to the influence of the Iranian religion of Zoroastrianism. They quickly spread, not only within India but also to central Asia and finally to China and Japan, where in local forms they still survive. In its popular manifestations, Mahayana Buddhism is a religion of faith and devotion; one need only call on the name of Amitabha with sincerity to join him after death in his heaven, to be reborn no more.

Together with the new theology, the Mahayanists devised subtle philosophical systems. *Madhyamika*, or *Sunyavada*, the most important of these schools, was founded by the teacher Nagarjuna, who maintained that the universe as man knows and sees it was not truly real. The only absolute reality was *Nirvana*, while all material things were *sunya* (empty), void of all essential being. By subtle arguments, Nagarjuna sought to prove that there was no essential difference between *Nirvana* and the material world, that *Nirvana* was present everywhere, all the time, if only man could realize the fact.

In India, Mahayana Buddhism gradually supplanted Hinayana. All Hinayana sects have now disappeared, with the exception of *Theravada*, which was established in Ceylon in the time of Asoka and resisted the efforts of Mahayanists to undermine it. It spread in later times to many parts of Southeast Asia, replacing the Mahayana Buddhism and Hinduism which had previously prevailed there.

The great religious changes in India during the early centuries of the Christian era embraced both subtle philosophy and simple devotion to the gods. The latter aspect led to the appearance of image worship and temples. Religion as a whole became more colorful and vivid as members of the upper classes were more and more influenced by the simple faith of the lower orders and lavished their wealth on temple buildings and image making.

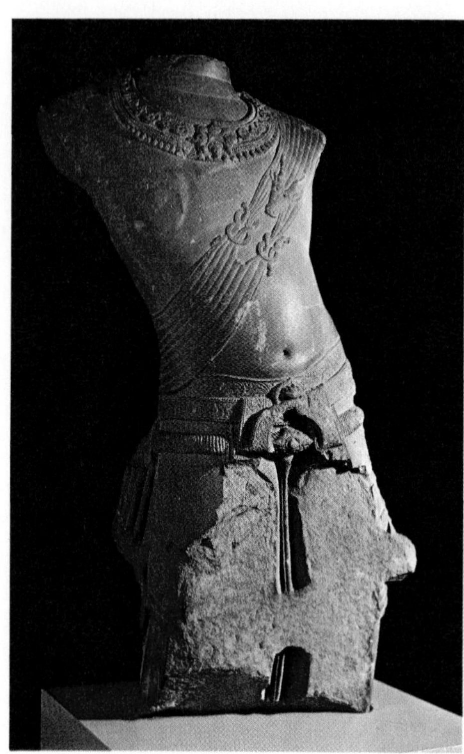

The torso of a *Bodhisattva*. This is a carving in the Gupta style of the fifth century A.D., but it comes from the great complex of Buddhist *stūpas*, burial mounds, at Sanchi, Madhya Pradesh, which dates from the second and first centuries B.C.

## CULTURAL LIFE: SCULPTURE AND ARCHITECTURE

Works of art dating from the fall of the Harappa culture to the Mauryan period are almost completely lacking. From the Mauryan period, there are a number of highly polished stone columns with finely carved capitals, several engraved with Asoka's edicts. Archaeologists have found no evidence of a developed craft of stone carving before the Mauryan period, and certain similarities, especially the high polish, suggest that the Mauryan school of sculpture arose through the influence of Iranian craftsmen, perhaps refugees deprived of their livelihood by Alexander's invasion.

The sculpture of the Mauryan period gave way to a more popular style, subservient to architecture. In the centuries before and after the birth of Christ, there were great developments in *stupa* building and the excavation of artificial caves, chiefly in the service of Buddhism. Small *stupas* of roughly hewn stone were enlarged, faced with well-cut masonry, and surrounded by stone railings with finely carved gateways at the four cardinal points of the compass. These constructions prove that building and carving in stone was a relatively new craft, for both *stupa* railings and the facades of cave temples clearly imitate wooden buildings, and the earliest stone sculpture shows the influence of small-scale carving in ivory or hardwood. The achievement, however, is impressive. The gateways of the *stupa* of Sanchi (Madhya Pradesh), carved around the time of Christ, perhaps mark the apogee of this phase of Indian art. Many of the reliefs illustrate Buddhist legend, but their relaxed vitality seems to reflect the everyday life of the times rather than the formal doctrines of Buddhism.

Meanwhile, in the northwest, influences from the Mediterranean were felt. Under the Kushanas, there arose in Gandhara a school of sculpture much influenced by the West. Most surviving products of this school are Buddhist works, and it is possible that here the Buddha was depicted for the first time. Earlier Indian sculpture never portrays the Buddha, but symbolizes him by such emblems as an empty throne or a pair of footprints. The first portrayals of the Buddha appear at about the same time in Gandhara and Mathura. The latter site has produced many fine figures made in the early Christian centuries, in a style chiefly indigenous but showing some Gandharan influence. At first the treatment of the Buddha's image showed considerable experiment, but by Gupta times it had taken the forms which survive to the present day.

From the Mathura school developed the typical sculpture of the Gupta period, which perhaps has never been excelled in India. The vitality of the older indigenous schools was harmonized with influences from Gandhara and transmuted into a style perfectly adapted to the expression of the Indian spirit. The most famous product of Gupta sculpture is the Buddha from Sarnath (near Benares), where he preached his first sermon. It is typical of the art of the period in its contrast of smooth surfaces with detailed ornamentation.

By the Gupta period, the Hindus also were producing fine sculpture. Much has now disappeared, but enough remains to show the magnitude of the achievement. The colossal relief carving of the boar incarnation of Vishnu at Udayagiri (Madhya Pradesh) is a splendid composition; the upward thrust of the boar's body contrasts with the limp female figure, symbolizing the earth, clinging to its tusk.

The god Vishnu in his *avatār* as the boar Varaha—a carving from the friezes on the temple complex of Khajuraho.

Architecture was highly developed when Megasthenes visited India in about 300 B.C., for he wrote of Chandragupta's splendid palace at Pataliputra—but mentioned that it was built entirely of wood. At that time forests of hard timber stood near every city, but in the alluvial Ganges valley plain stone was less easily obtainable, and stone buildings appeared late on the Indian scene. Free-standing stone temples, as distinct from cave temples, were not common until the Gupta period. Most of those that survive are simple structures in out-of-the-way places, but the great Buddhist temple at Buddh Gaya in central Bihar, built near the end of the period, is an exception. From the sixth century onward, free-standing stone temples were built farther south, in the Deccan and Tamil Nadu. Sculpture had already developed in the south, through the influence of Buddhism.

Literature records that painting was a popular art, but little has survived. The most outstanding exception is the series of mural paintings in the Buddhist caves of Ajanta, north Deccan. Some date from about the time of Christ, but most were painted during the Gupta period or shortly after. All depict Buddhist themes, but many incidentally illustrate the life of the times, especially court life. The style shows a realism and a sense of space and movement rare in the painting of the ancient world. Other paintings from the Gupta period survive at Bagh, near Gwalior, and at Sigiriya, in Ceylon, where the Ajanta style is reflected in the pictures of demi-goddesses on a great rock once crowned by a royal palace.

### Literature

The history of classical Sanskrit literature begins with the grammarian Panini, who analyzed and standardized the Sanskrit language, probably in the fourth century B.C. He produced a grammar of an accuracy unequaled anywhere in the world until the early nineteenth century.

In succeeding centuries the epic *Mahabharata* was compiled from earlier material. The main story is told in simple Sanskrit verse. Reflecting the martial life of earlier times, it contains many exciting passages, but its immense length and numerous didactic interpolations make it rather tedious reading. The second epic, the *Ramayana*, is shorter, and the main narrative seems the work of one man, traditionally the sage Valmiki. It is composed in a much more sophisticated style and has achieved greater popularity.

The *Ramayana* is close in style to the formal long poem, the *Kavya*, which became one of the main expressions of educated literary taste in later centuries. The courtly style, highly artificial and employing the many tricks of Indian poetry such as alliteration and punning, originated early in the Christian era and achieved its most perfect expression in the work of Kalidasa, who lived about A.D. 400, when the Gupta empire was at its height. Kalidasa's poetry, though technically sophisticated, is full of feeling. He is especially adept in his treatment of women and their ways. The scenery of India, its birds, beasts, and flowers, find an important place in his work, as does the splendid ceremonial of the Gupta court. There were great poets after Kalidasa, but their longer poems tend to become shapeless displays of ingenuity. From post-Gupta times, the most attractive poetry is chiefly in the form of four-lined stanzas.

To modern taste, the best ancient Indian writer of prose fiction was Dandin, who lived around A.D. 600. His *Dasakumaracharita* ("Tales of the Ten Princes"), a collection of short stories which vividly reflect the ordinary life of the times, has been translated into many languages.

The Lingaraja Temple of Shiva at Bhubaneswar, Orissa. Dating from around A.D. 1000, the Lingaraja celebrates Shiva (who is, with Vishnu, the leading deity of later Hinduism) as lord of the lingam (male sexual organ) which symbolizes the creative power of the god. Standing out among the hundreds of temples that make up the Bhubaneswar complex, the Lingaraja temple rises to a height of 180 feet.

### The Theater

One of ancient India's greatest literary achievements was the development of a theatrical tradition. The earliest surviving dramas are probably no earlier than A.D. 100, but there must have been a much older popular drama out of which the Sanskrit theater developed. The plays are composed according to strict conventions, in a polished style combining prose and verse. Many themes were freely adapted from religious and heroic legend, but others—tales of political intrigue or court love affairs—were invented by their authors. There were also farces and allegorical dramas. Exceptional is *Mrichchhakatika* ("The Little Clay Cart") by Sudraka, a vigorous melodrama of middle-class life in an ancient Indian city. The greatest Sanskrit dramatist was also the greatest poet, Kalidasa, who has left three plays. The best-known is *Sakuntala*, an idyllic tale of legendary times, which has been performed in translation on the American and European stage.

The dramas were normally performed by professional actors of both sexes, on a stage without scenery and with a minimum of "props." Acting technique was probably extremely formalized, using a complex language of gestures to express a wide range of ideas and to reinforce the power of the spoken word.

### Music and Dance

The history of Indian music is too complex and specialized to deal with in detail here. As in modern Indian music, all performances were improvisations based on a brief succession of notes called *raga*, the number of which has increased over the years. The names of some great musicians survive, but because they had no system of notation capable of recording their performances, their music is lost forever.

The instruments of later Indian music were not all known in the classical period. Several stringed instruments such as the *sitar*, now well-known in Europe and America, were introduced from western Asia in medieval times. The main stringed instrument in the Gupta period was a bow-harp, like that of ancient Egypt and Mesopotamia. This has now disappeared in India, but still survives in Burma.

The evidence of surviving literature, painting, and sculpture, shows that the subtle and complex dance system now generally known as *Bharata natyam* was already in existence early in the Christian era, although perhaps in a somewhat less developed form.

## OTHER ASPECTS OF CLASSICAL INDIAN LIFE

Rural life in some ways has changed very little in India until quite recently. But many of the crops now widely grown in India were unknown in classical times. The chili pepper came only at the end of the sixteenth century, along with tobacco and the potato. Other crops introduced by the Portuguese from America were maize, the papaya (paw-paw), and the pineapple. The state taxed the peasants heavily, and they were compelled to hand over an appreciable portion of their crops (theoretically one-sixth, but usually more) to the king. In return they could expect protection from criminals and help with irrigation.

In the larger towns, especially at the great pilgrimage centers such as Varanasi (Benares) and Mathura, peoples of all the races of India met each other. In Hindu life, Varanasi played almost as great a part as Mecca does in that of the Muslim. If a man died in Varanasi, it was believed that his sins would be washed away and he could be sure of a long rebirth in heaven. Aged people of both sexes came to Varanasi (as they still do) to end their days in one of the special infirmaries. The dying were brought there and immersed in the Ganges at the moment of death.

Representatives of the leading merchants sometimes formed a sort of town council which was recognized by the royal government and had considerable say in the control of the city and surrounding countryside. Merchants and craftsmen formed guilds recognized by law as corporate bodies with rights over their members. There was much trade between cities.

The technical achievement of classical India was considerable. In western Asia, Indian steel was famed for its toughness. A splendid memorial to Indian metallurgy survives in the Iron Pillar of Delhi, a column about twenty-three feet high, made of a single iron casting, which has resisted corrosion from the fifth century A.D. to the present day.

Indian textiles, particularly muslin and silk, were much in demand in the Roman Empire. The art of weaving fine cotton fabric was preserved through the ages; Indian muslin was again exported to Europe from the seventeenth century onward.

The Indians had little knowledge of experimental sciences, but through observation and speculation their achievement was considerable. In the field of

*Above:* Ram Gopal, one of India's leading dancers today. He performs in a style based on the *Bharata Nātyasāstra*, a textbook on drama, music, and dancing compiled in the first century A.D.
*Left:* The cave temples at Ajanta in the Deccan region of Hyderabad. These are the most important sites of Buddhist art in India. The wall paintings, most of which date from the sixth century A.D., combine physical beauty, spiritual insight and depth of feeling. As well as scenes from the lives of Buddha and his followers, the paintings provide information on the court life of the period.

astronomy they received many ideas from the classical West, but developed a system of their own which was more accurate than that of Ptolemy. In mathematics they outstripped other peoples of antiquity, largely through their invention of the decimal numeral system. The decimal system was taken over by the Arabs, from whom it spread to late medieval Europe.

The knowledge which ancient India had of human anatomy and the functions of the internal organs was perhaps inferior to that of classical Europe, because religious prohibition of contact with cadavers prevented dissection. But Indian surgeons excelled in superficial operations; they could extract stones from the bladder and perform the Caesarian section. They were also skilled in plastic surgery.

In the range of its drugs and therapeutic methods, the Indian medical system was unexcelled by any in antiquity. The Indian physician was receptive to new ideas, and so profited from contacts between India and the outside world. As time went on, drugs from southeast Asia, the Middle East, China, and finally Europe and America, were added to the Indian physician's pharmacopoeia.

From the above, it will be seen that ancient India was not wholly taken up with religion, but had its practical side. Deeply religious folk were numerous, but there were also anti-religious materialists in India. There were many others whose interests lay in this world rather than the next and who carried their religion lightly, among them educated and wealthy people who formed an urbane, secular intelligentsia. Their activities are reflected in many Indian texts, such as the *Kamasutra*, which as well as being a manual of erotic technique mirrors the life of the cultured elite.

The general pattern of the sexual life of ancient India cannot easily be reconstructed. In contrast with the *Kamasutra* are many passages commending celibacy and advising married men to exercise their sexual prerogatives sparingly if they wish

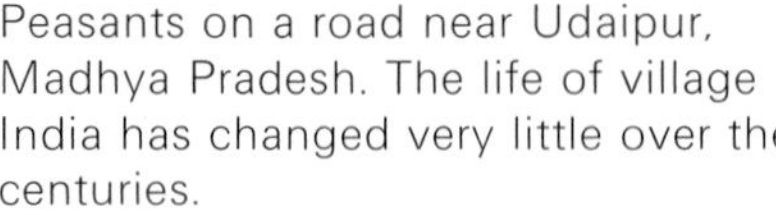
Peasants on a road near Udaipur, Madhya Pradesh. The life of village India has changed very little over the centuries.

to produce healthy, intelligent, and virtuous children. There was evidently an ambivalent attitude, with the orthodox tending to restraint and the more worldly taking open pleasure in sex. Such ambivalence may be explained by reference to the doctrine of *caturvarga purushartha* (the four aims of man), which throws light on many early Indian values.

The doctrine taught that there were four aims which a man or woman should pursue. The first, *moksha* (salvation), or release from transmigration, only indirectly affected ordinary people, but was the direct concern of those who had "given up the world." The other three aims affected all human beings. They were: *dharma* (virtue), strictly observing religious and social duties in order to achieve a happier rebirth; *artha* (material gain), gaining wealth of which part should be devoted to worthy causes and part to enjoying the good things of life; and *kama*, which implied the fulfillment of desires, sexual or otherwise.

These three aims were all valid, all worth achieving, but the moralists made it quite clear that they were in descending order of precedence. The ideal to strive for was the balanced life, giving each of the three aims its due place, in order to achieve a rebirth nearer to the final aim of salvation. The doctrine of the four aims was not puritanical. Piety, profit, and pleasure, all played a part in the ideal life, and all were thought worthy of pursuit.

## AFTER THE GUPTAS

With the end of the Gupta empire, northern India was again divided, as the south had always been. In the seventh century, Harshavardhana, king of Kannauj (Uttar Pradesh), on the upper Ganges, succeeded in gaining loose control of most of the north, except what is now Pakistan, but his empire died with him. His reign (606–647) is interesting, because in the latter part of it the country was visited by

The Ganges River at Varanasi (Benares). Varanasi, which is regarded by Hindus as Shiva's capital city on earth, stands on the most hallowed stretch of the holy Ganges. More than 1 million pilgrims come every year to purify themselves in the holy waters, and the river's banks are lined with ghats, or steps, where bodies are burned and their ashes cast into the Ganges.

the Chinese Buddhist pilgrim, Hśuan Tsang, who left a long account of India.

The complex political history of the succeeding centuries, during which numerous dynasties controlled the various regions of India, are of little interest except to the specialist. The kingdoms were almost constantly at war with one another, but the wars were rarely decisive because they were fought according to standards of chivalry which strongly condemned the "uprooting" of a conquered dynasty or the outright annexation of territory. Conquered kings were usually required only to do homage and pay tribute to their conquerors, and then were permitted to retain their kingdoms as vassals. Officials were normally rewarded by grants of territories from which they were entitled to collect taxes. In theory, such grants were usually held at the king's pleasure, but they tended to become hereditary, and the tenant achieved a status comparable to that of a vassal chief. The system encouraged the development of a society similar to that of the Western feudal system of the Middle Ages.

Details of the sculptured friezes on the temples at Khajuraho. Many of the erotic techniques pictured in these carvings reflect those described in the *Kamasutra*, the manual of the arts of love which is said to have been compiled by Vatsyayana around A.D. 100.

During the seventh century, the center of cultural activity tended to shift to the south, where the lettered classes had by now become thoroughly Aryanized and quickly adapted northern concepts to their own tastes. From 600 onward, south Indian art, architecture, religion, and philosophy developed apace, while the north tended to stagnate. However, the period was not one of complete degeneration in northern India.

Great armies were involved in expensive and bloody warfare, but the effect of war on the economic and cultural life of the country seems to have been remarkably slight, probably because victories were rarely pushed to their logical conclusion. The ethics of Hindu warfare proscribed looting, unnecessary injury to non-combatants, and impossible demands on the conquered, and although such principles were not always observed, they had considerable effect.

From the tenth century onward, larger and more complex temples were built, many of which still survive in southern India. In the north, however, such temples are rarely found near the main political centers, where the Muslims later exerted direct control. In eastern Orissa are the remains of the largest Hindu temple ever built, the great temple of Surya the sun-god at Konarak.

## RELIGIOUS DEVELOPMENTS

Certain new religious trends became noticeable towards the end of the Gupta period and grew stronger thereafter. Although mother-goddesses were ancient objects of worship in India, the upper classes had taken little interest in them. The gods had wives, but they were quite unimportant. Now temples to goddesses were built. Parvati (also called Devi, or Durga), the spouse of Shiva, was the most highly respected of these goddesses, and by 600 her cult was widespread. Its theologians explained that the goddess represented Shiva's active and immanent aspects, his *sakti* (power). Moreover, the transcendent and absolute god could not have created the world without the help of his manifest and active wife. It was an idea as old as the Vedas that the universe came into being as a result of the primeval coitus of the first being and the spouse whom he created out of himself. Such theories were now revived. The view was put forward that the first creative sexual act of Shiva and his wife was mystically repeated in the human sexual act. Groups arose among whom sex became ritualized as part of the cult. The system of these sects—generally also worshiping the mother goddess and believing in the magic of *mantras* (mystical utterances) which were thought to have immense power—is generally known as Tantrism, from Tantras, the word these worshipers preferred to use for their scriptures. Some Tantrists practiced their sexual sacraments privately with their wives, but others developed rituals in strange and, to the orthodox, obscene ways.

Tantrism affected Buddhism as well as Hinduism (indeed, the movement may have originated among Buddhists). The heavenly Buddhas and Bodhisattvas were also provided with wives, and sexual rituals developed around them. Other, more unpleasant, aspects of popular Indian religion also became prominent about this time. Animal sacrifice was to some extent revived in a non-Vedic form, especially associated with the cult of the mother-goddess. The burning of widows, child marriage, and female infanticide became more frequent, although strongly opposed by the Tantrists, who, as goddess worshipers, held women in high regard.

Another feature of religious life which developed as the golden age of Indian culture declined was *hatha yoga*, that form of yoga involving difficult acrobatic contortions. It was based on a physiological mythology concerning a mysterious "serpent power" at the base of the backbone, which was raised to the top of the skull by a long course of suppressing the breath while contorting the body. It had little in common with the yoga of the classical period, sometimes known as *raja yoga*, a system of training the mind and soul to achieve deeper meditation. The system of hatha yoga sometimes produces most striking results: its most advanced practitioners gain sufficient control of the automatic and reflex actions of the body to perform remarkable feats. These feats, which include fasting or being buried alive for long periods, have not yet been satisfactorily explained, although some of the more extravagant claims made by the devotees of hatha yoga are pure myth.

However, the most important religious development was the rise of popular devotionalism. This began in the south with the appearance, from about 600 onward, of devotees of Shiva and Vishnu who approached their chosen god in an impassioned, emotional manner, chanting hymns in their mother tongue, Tamil, rather than in formal Sanskrit. The *Nayanars* and *Alvars*, as the singers of Shiva and Vishnu respectively were called, produced some of the best poetry ever composed in India, and their popularity soon affected orthodox intellectuals. A very important text, the *Bhagavata Purana*, composed in south India in Sanskrit in or soon after 800, told the story of Krishna in verse which encouraged the attitude of deeply emotional faith. Like some Christian and Jewish mystics, the south Indian hymnodists often used erotic terminology to express the love between worshiper and deity. Like the sexual rites of Tantrism, this emotive poetry, composed in a language which all could understand, provided a safety valve in a society where social norms were becoming progressively more rigid, where children were often married to partners whom they had never seen, and where the easy relationship reflected in the *Kamasutra* corresponded hardly at all with social reality.

In spite of their use of erotic imagery, these hymnodists, whose influences spread all over India, tended to encourage a puritanical, ascetic attitude. Many proclaimed that "giving up the world" was not the only way to salvation, and that the worshiper could obtain complete union with the deity in the course of everyday life. But because the layman must devote all possible attention to his god, wealth was a dangerous distraction and the pleasures of the flesh even more so. The old commonsense doctrine of the four aims of life appeared less frequently in the literature of the medieval period.

The most famous of the theologians who interpreted the new devotionalism in philosophical terms was Ramanuja, a south Indian brahman who lived toward the end of the eleventh century. Working on the same texts as those used by Shankara, he interpreted them to mean that the absolute being from whom the universe stemmed was a personal god, Vishnu, and that devotion to Vishnu was the most effective means of salvation. Shankara had taught that the human personality was completely lost in the absolute, since it was part of the "unreal" world of the senses. Ramanuja affirmed the full reality of the world and of human personality.

*Top:* The marriage of Shiva and Parvati, a carving of the Pala period, dating from about the ninth century. Parvati represents the benevolent aspect of Shiva's spouse: she was also worshiped by Tantric sects, in sadistic and bloody orgies, as Kali or Durga, the terrible goddess of death and destruction. *Above:* An event from the life of the Jain holy man, Kalaka. Among the earliest and finest surviving examples of Indian miniature painting are illustrations from manuscripts of the Jain sect, produced in Gujarat, between the thirteenth and sixteenth centuries.

امی شاه پرسیدند و ایلچی را بنوازشهای بی اندازه مخصوص ساختند

Chapter 3

# THE SULTANS AND THE MOGUL EMPIRE

## THE IMPACT OF ISLAM

An account of the doctrines and early history of Islam is contained in part III. However, it may be stressed that if one set out to devise a religion which, while remaining theistic, should be as different as possible from Hinduism in its doctrines and practices, that religion would be something like orthodox Islam. Islam abhors many of the tenets of Hinduism. It is rigidly monotheist; it forbids the worship of images or even symbols; it has no priesthood; and it generally rejects asceticism. It is, in theory, equalitarian, giving all believers the same rights in the faith. Any distinctions of class or caste that have crept into Islamic society, in India or elsewhere, have no justification in the Koran or the early teachings of Islam.

The impact of Islam on India was complex and varied in its effects. The first encounter came early in the eighth century, when the Arabs conquered the Hindu kingdom of Sind. For some time, the Arabs attempted further conquest, but after a century or so they settled down in their own domains and no longer troubled their Hindu neighbors. It was through the Arab kingdom of Sind that much Hindu medical, astronomical, and mathematical lore was transmitted to western Asia.

A more serious threat was presented by Mahmud of Ghazni. The northwest frontiers of India, including Afghanistan, had become a melting pot of Central Asian peoples as the original Indian inhabitants were conquered in turn by Persians, Bactrian Greeks, Scythians, Parthians, Kushanas, and Hunas, all of whom left traces in the racial and cultural makeup of the area. After the Hunas, various waves of Turks found their way into the borderlands, where most became Buddhists or Hindus. Meanwhile the Muslims were pressing on Afghanistan from the west, where Islam was making headway. In the latter part of the tenth century, a Turkish Muslim chieftain, Sabuktigin, established a kingdom at Ghazni, south of Kabul. His son Mahmud (997–1030) expanded his kingdom until it was the most powerful state between Byzantium and China. Sultan Mahmud did not leave India out of his plans; from 1001 onward he made seventeen raids on the subcontinent, penetrating as far as Gujarat in the south and western Uttar Pradesh in the east, and obtaining much loot and many slaves. As a result, the area now called Pakistan became part of Mahmud's empire. Those Hindu rulers who were unaffected by Mahmud's raids took the opportunity to expand their power at the expense of those who had suffered more severely.

AD 700 800 900 1000 1100 1200 1300 1400 1500 1600 1700

Arabs conquer Sind from Hindus (711)

Other Hindu states left in peace

Turkish Muslim Kingdoms of Ghazni and Ghor

First Sultanate of Delhi

Mogul Empire

Battle of Tarain (1192): Ghor defeats Hindus

Tamerlane sacks Delhi (1398)

Akbar (1556–1605)

Shah Jahan

Chola ascendancy in South India
Flowering of Tamil culture

Breakaway Hindu states in South
Portuguese arrive

The Mogul Emperor Akbar receiving an ambassador from the Shah of Persia, around 1562.

When Mahmud died, the Ghaznevids gave no further serious trouble to the Hindu kings on their eastern frontiers, and for nearly 200 years the kings of north India continued to rule as though nothing had happened. Although his impact was greater than that of Alexander, Mahmud seems soon to have been forgotten and no lessons were learned from him. The last two centuries of Hindu India saw the increase of Tantrism and decline of Buddhism in most of India. When the land was finally conquered, Buddhism had almost vanished from most regions.

The caste system, Hindu non-violence and vegetarianism, and the division of the land into many rival kingdoms are often blamed for the victories of the Muslims in India. These factors contributed to the ease and speed with which the Muslims imposed their rule, but they won battles simply because their military methods were far more efficient than those of the Hindus. The armies of the Hindus were generally larger than those of the Muslims, but they were slow-moving and clumsy in maneuver; they relied too heavily on the easily frightened elephant; and they had nothing to match the fast, light cavalry of the Turks, whose horsemen could shoot arrows with deadly effect while in full gallop.

The twelfth century saw the rise of another Turkish kingdom in Afghanistan, based on the city of Ghor (Taiwara), to the west of Ghazni. The Ghorids captured Ghazni, wiped out the Ghaznevids, and then turned their attention to India. In 1192 at Tarain, in the watershed between the basins of the Indus and the Ganges, was fought one of the most decisive battles of Indian history. Muhammad, brother of the sultan of Ghor, soundly defeated Prithviraj Chauhan, the Hindu king who controlled most of Rajasthan and the region of Delhi.

Muhammad returned to his homeland after the battle, leaving his Indian conquests in charge of his general Qutb-ud Din Aibak, technically a slave, who made his headquarters at the small, fortified town of Delhi. Qutb-ud Din and other

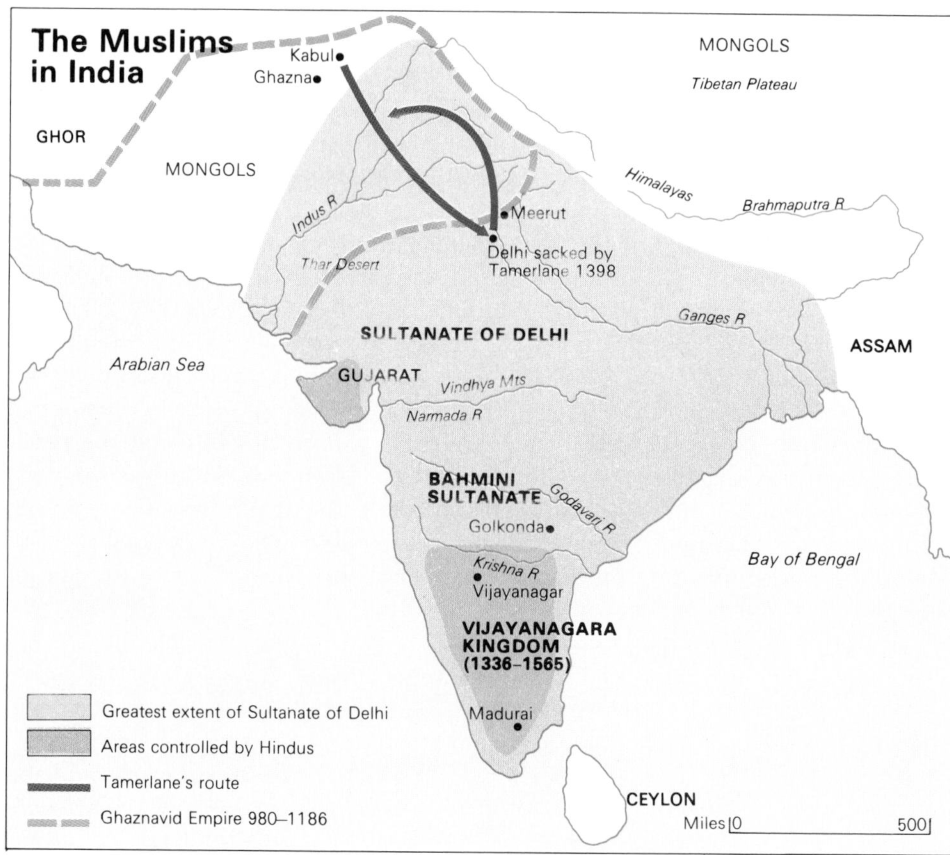

Turkish generals, over a period of about twelve years, gained control of the Ganges as far as the sea. In 1203, Muhammad became sultan of Ghor on the death of his brother, but two years later he was assassinated. In 1206, Qutb-ud Din proclaimed himself sultan of Delhi and his former masters recognized his independence.

The history of the next 300 years is again one of constant warfare—but it was mainly warfare between Muslims. The larger Hindu kingdoms of northern India were annexed by the Turks, but many smaller ones, in less accessible regions such as Rajasthan, survived, with their rulers paying tribute to Muslim overlords. The land was controlled by a form of feudalism not very different from that of the Hindus; the Turkish generals received large regions as *iqta̱* (grants) in payment for their services, and subdivided these among their underlings in the same way. But the Muslim system laid less stress on the hereditary principle than had the Hindu. It was quite common for lands to be reclaimed by the overlord on the death of his vassal, or even before.

Qutb-ud Din died in 1210, and was succeeded by his brother-in-law, Iltutmish (1211–1236), also an ex-slave, who was the real founder of Islamic power in India. He managed to reduce all the Turkish warlords to obedience, and organized a rudimentary civil service in the directly governed area around Delhi. His memorial is the splendid 234-feet-high tower at Mehrauli, outside modern New Delhi, the *Qutb Minar*, formerly the tallest building in India.

The Muslims do not seem to have been motivated by religious zeal in their campaigns. It was not for the glory of Islam that they remained as rulers of India, but for their own advantage. They were Turks, and it was a Turkish empire they tried to found, with non-Turks, whether Muslim or Hindu, excluded from all high positions. But with them came the *ulema* (doctors) of Islam, prompt with advice on how the state should be governed. The influence of these learned religious men varied from reign to reign. In general, they encouraged the sultans to take a tough line with Hindus; to forbid the performance of Hindu rituals in public; to demolish temples and replace them with mosques; and to impose the *jizya* (tax) on unbelievers.

The conquerors were also followed by *sufis*, the mystics of Islam. Some were as rigid in their orthodoxy as the *ulema*, but others were mild, gentle men, who emphasized the love of Allah for all creation, even infidels. The more tolerant *sufis* soon influenced some Hindus, and it was probably through the *sufis* that many Hindus were converted to Islam.

However, there is no clear picture of how conversion came about or of the speed at which it took place. What is now Pakistan had been under Muslim domination for two centuries or more by the time of Qutb-ud Din, when its population must already have contained a large Muslim element. Hindus with a tradition of government service would sometimes become Muslims in order to gain preferment. Forcible conversion is recorded in the chronicles, and may have accounted for numerous conversions. But probably the majority of the converts were low-caste Hindus who became Muslims because they were attracted by the faith's simple equalitarian doctrines.

The Turks could not maintain their racial dominance for long. In their wake came Muslim adventurers of many races. In the days of Iltutmish, the great conqueror Chingiz Khan established Mongol power as far as the west bank of the Indus. From that time onward, Mongols frequently raided the Punjab and moved into India. Because there were few Turkish women in India, the Turks often married non-Turkish wives, even captive and converted Hindu girls. Thus Turkish hegemony was slowly undermined. More and more non-Turks obtained high positions, until in 1451 an Afghan, Bahlol Lodi, became sultan of Delhi.

The correct treatment of their Hindu subjects was a problem which often preoccupied the rulers of Delhi. In general their tolerance and benevolence varied inversely with the influence exerted by the *ulema*. The ruthless and efficient 'Ala-ud Din Khalji (1296–1316), was a free thinker and flouted the *ulema* on several occasions. He exacted heavy taxes from the peasants, but treated Hindu and Muslim much alike. On the other hand, Firuz Tughluq (1351–1388), essentially a kindly man but extremely pious, demolished temples, forbade all public practice of Hinduism, and strictly imposed the tax on unbelievers. He was also largely responsible for breaking Turkish hegemony, for, in accordance with the principles of Islam, he treated Muslims of all races as equals, and gave preferment even to African freedmen (*Habshis*) and Hindu converts.

Oxen dragging siege guns to Akbar's attack on the fort of a rebellious Hindu prince in Rajasthan, in 1568. When Babur, the Mogul ruler of Kabul, invaded India in 1526, his soldiers won decisive victories over Indian armies ten times as large, partly because of the greater efficiency of the Mogul troops and partly because of their possession of cannon, a weapon new to India. Babur's grandson, Akbar, was also a great military leader.

Early in the fourteenth century, thanks largely to the military genius of 'Ala-ud Din's general, Malik Kafur (a converted Hindu eunuch and former slave), the power of the sultans reached into the Deccan, where Hindu kingdoms were annexed. For a few years the troops of Delhi even held Madurai, the sacred city of the far south. But the success of the Delhi sultans in the peninsula was shortlived, for their triumphant generals were so far from Delhi that only the most energetic sultans could maintain control over them. In 1347, a Turkish officer proclaimed his independence in the Deccan and founded the Bahmani dynasty, which broke up into five independent sultanates at the end of the fifteenth century. The Deccan sultanates were very prosperous and one of them, Golconda, near modern Hyderabad became famous even in Europe for the magnificence of its court, which profited from the nearby diamond mines.

At about the same time as the foundation of the Bahmani dynasty, officers of a conquered Hindu state managed to establish their independence at Vijayanagar (modern Hampi) in eastern Mysore, where they held out against all Muslim attempts to overthrow them. They gained control of what is now Tamil Nadu and Kerala, as well as the southern parts of Mysore and Andhra Pradesh. Vijayanagar was the last of the great Hindu kingdoms. Its rulers learned much from the Muslims in military organization. Vijayanagar remained a great Indian power until 1565, when it was sacked by a coalition of the five Deccan sultans. The kingdom survived in an attenuated form much longer, and the extreme south never came fully under Muslim control.

A great disaster struck the Delhi sultanate in 1398, with the invasion of Timur (or Tamerlane, from Timur-i-lang, Timur the lame) the Tartar ruler of Samarkand, whose fame as a ruthless conqueror spread to Europe, where he became known as Tamburlaine mainly through the medium of the play of that name by the Elizabethan dramatist Christopher Marlowe. Timur slaughtered noncombatants without compunction, but was careful to preserve the lives of as many skilled craftsmen as possible. These men were enslaved and sent back to Central Asia. Delhi was plundered for five days, with great destruction and bloodshed, and the inhabitants of the city of Mirath (Meerut), which Timur attacked on his return march, were all slaughtered.

Humiliated and weakened, the sultans were in no position to assert control over their generals and provincial governors, who soon claimed independence. In order to consolidate their power, the new sultans were compelled to come to terms with their Hindu subjects, and in general their policy tended to be more liberal towards the Hindus than that of Delhi.

## MUTUAL INFLUENCE OF ISLAM AND HINDUISM

For a generation or two, the conquerors of India looked on themselves as foreigners. At home they spoke a form of Turkish, using Persian for official and literary purposes. But when Chingiz Khan (1162–1227) overran their homeland, the fact that it was now under alien control attached them more closely to India. Gradually, they began to look on themselves as Indians.

The *bhakti* movement, stemming from popular devotional cults, has already been mentioned. A possible example of the mutual influence of Hindu and Muslim ideas is seen in its development at this time. One of the most interesting *bhakti* poets was Kabir, who lived in the fourteenth and fifteenth centuries. Many legends are told about him, but few can be authenticated. From his name, and from the legend that he was a brahman boy brought up by Muslims, it seems that he was of Muslim parentage. A humble weaver, Kabir sang of the love of god and the brotherhood of man. He disapproved of asceticism, image-worship, pilgrimage, priesthood, ritualism, and caste distinction. His favorite term for god was Ram (in Sanskrit, Rama), the legendary hero who, like Krishna, was accepted as an incarnation of Vishnu and an ideal type of justice and mercy. Ram's popularity grew rapidly after the arrival of the Muslims, and he was widely worshiped by simple Hindus.

Kabir is sometimes put forward as the most important example of the mutual influence of Islam and Hinduism, although probably the only aspect of his teaching for which precedents cannot be found in older Indian religion is his opposition to image-worship. He believed in the doctrine of transmigration, and most of his teaching is couched in Hindu terms. The medieval order of *yogis* known as *Nath* or *Gorakhnathis*, and the late Buddhist teachers known as *Siddhas*, whose verses became widely popular among Hindus, sometimes put forward doctrines rather similar to those of Kabir.

An Indian artist's view of the capture by Akbar of the Rajput fort at Jodhpur, Rajasthan. After Akbar had broken the independent power of the Hindu princes, he consolidated his empire—and won the goodwill of many of his Hindu subjects—by appointing the Rajput leaders to high posts in his armies, his provincial administrations, and in his own advisory council.

Muslim influence on the Hindus is to be found rather in social life than in religion. The common speech of most parts of India was enriched by many Persian words. The cookery of northern India was much affected, especially by Persian sweetmeats. Male Hindus often adopted Muslim dress, and women of higher castes, always limited in their freedom of movement, took to the Muslim *pardah*, or *purdah*, avoiding men not of their own family and never appearing in public without a veil over face and figure. For all the efforts of the *bhakti* reformers, caste restrictions and ritual observances seem to have grown stricter.

Hindu influence on Islam in India was probably greater than that of Islam on Hinduism. Although most present-day Indian Muslims must be descended from Hindu converts, they have preserved fewer ancestral traditions than have, for instance, the Muslims of Indonesia and Malaya. In earlier times, however, this was not always the case. Many medieval poems, written by men with Muslim names in Indian language and script, borrow themes from Hindu legend and tradition and refer to the Hindu gods with respect. In Bengal in the sixteenth century, an attempt was made by local Muslims to show that Krishna, whom Hindus believed to be the incarnation of god, was in fact a prophet (*nabi*) in the line of the Muslim prophets of whom Muhammad was the last and greatest. In Kashmir, there appeared a local school of *sufis* who were strict vegetarians and called themselves *rishis*, like the ancient Vedic seers.

The converted Hindu was not always satisfied with the austerity of worship in the mosque. He sometimes found a substitute for the old gods in the tomb of a local *sufi* elder of high repute. Even in their lives, some of the *pirs* (literally "old men") gained a reputation for miraculous powers, and on their deaths their tombs became objects of pilgrimage for many miles around. Whatever the *ulema* might say, the simple Muslim believed that the *pir* looked down with affection from heaven upon the scene of his earthly labors and could be a potent help to those in trouble. So the *pirs* became part of popular Indian Islam, and even found worshipers among Hindus. The cult of *pirs* may have gained converts to Islam.

## Artistic Influences

In art and architecture, mutual influence is clear. The Muslim invaders brought few craftsmen with them, and Indian influence is visible even in their earliest buildings. Orthodox Islam forbids the imitation of any human or animal form, so the Hindu sculptor was much restricted in his designs if he worked for a Muslim master. However, he made good use of the many traditional abstract or floral patterns of Hindu culture, and thus Indian Muslim architecture differs significantly from that of other Muslim countries.

The Muslims probably introduced the use of the arch and the dome to India. Distinctive regional styles of Muslim architecture arose in the provincial sultanates, showing the influence of the Hindu tradition roughly in proportion to their distance from Delhi. Because sculpture languished, even the carving done for Hindu patrons deteriorated in style and became stiff and formal. The most remarkable stone carving of the period is to be found in the delicate arabesque tracery of the stone windows of some of the mosques at Ahmedabad, built at the end of the fifteenth century.

The earliest Muslim painting in India, probably the work of foreign artists, is purely Persian in inspiration. Painting on a large scale declined, although the period saw the beginnings of the great schools of miniature painting which flourished in later centuries. The earlier phases of miniature painting in India are obscure, because the prepared palm-leaves then used for writing and painting generally disintegrate after four or five centuries in the Indian climate. The oldest surviving Indian miniatures are delicate pictures of Mahayana Buddhist divinities, illustrating palm-leaf manuscripts, painted in Bihar and Bengal from the eleventh century onward and later taken to Nepal, where the cooler climate has preserved them. The school of miniature painting in eastern India faded away with the

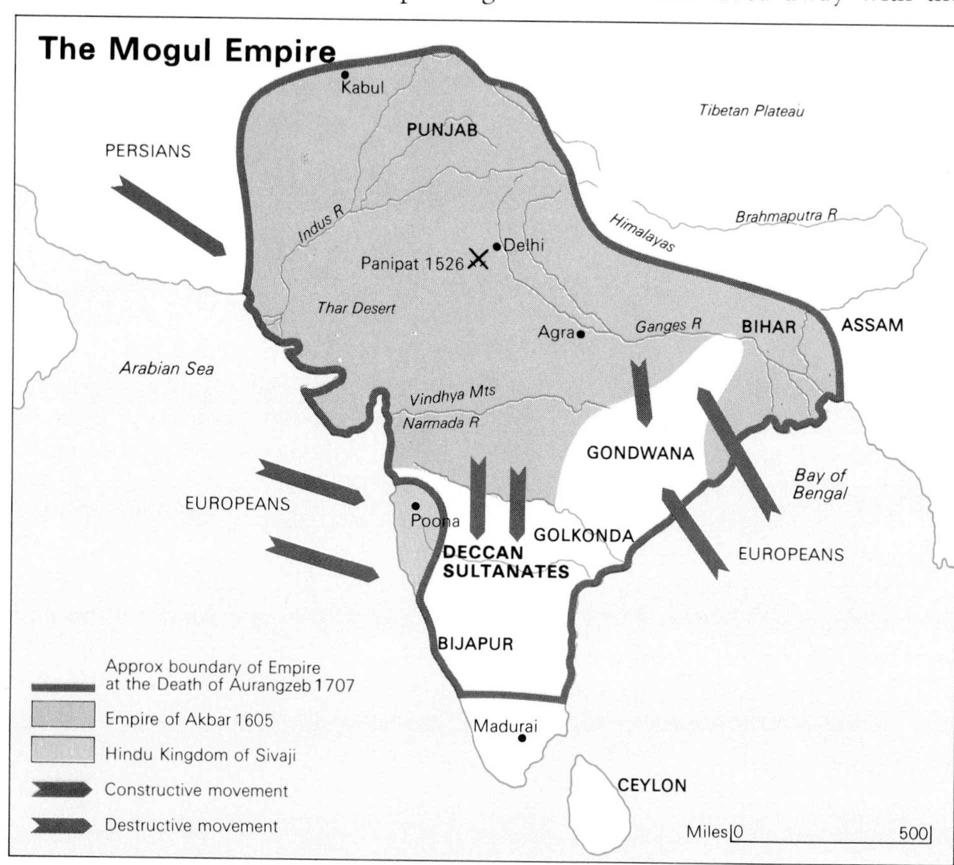

decline of Buddhism, but another school appeared in Gujarat in the fifteenth century; its products are less delicate and less realistic than those of the eastern school, as though the artists were making a fresh start from a folk tradition.

## THE MOGUL

The Turkish sultans of Delhi gave way to the Lodis, a dynasty of Afghans. The Lodis had gained power with the aid of other Afghan chiefs, but when they became arrogant and denied their racial ties, their fellow Afghans turned against them. The third Lodi sultan, Ibrahim (1517–1526), so antagonized his compatriots that they invited the ruler of Kabul, Babur, to invade India. In 1526, with Afghan support, Babur defeated and killed Ibrahim Lodi at the battle of Panipat. Ibrahim's army was defeated by an invader which it outnumbered by perhaps ten to one by virtue of the invader's great military efficiency. Babur had excellent cavalry, together with a new weapon which had hardly been heard of in northern India at the time—cannon.

Babur was a descendant of Timur and his stock was referred to as Mogul, from the Persian Mugul ("Mongol"), although the original Mongol blood had become much diluted by intermarriage. Babur had had an adventurous career before he conquered India; he had been constantly campaigning, mainly in Central Asia, with no lasting success. He was also a man of letters, who wrote poetry and found time during his short reign in India to write his autobiography, which has literary merit as well as being an important historical source.

Babur died in 1530 with his conquest only half completed. He controlled Afghanistan, the Punjab, and the Ganges plain as far as the borders of Bihar, but to the east many Afghan chiefs were unsubdued, and the Hindu Rajput princes were up in arms in Rajasthan and the hills south of the Ganges. The task of consolidating

A Mogul picture of the Emperor Shah Jahan (1627–1658) out riding. The power and magnificence of the Moguls reached their peak under Shah Jahan, although the demands of a corrupt revenue system weighed heavily upon the mass of the people, leading to widespread banditry and famine. Among the great architectural monuments of Shah Jahan's reign are the Taj Mahal, the Jama Masjid mosque, and the forts of Delhi and Agra.

the Mogul empire fell to Babur's son, Humayun, who inherited his father's attractive character and literary tastes, but not his energy and force of will. Humayun suffered also from a problem which beset several of his successors—brothers whose ambitions outweighed their family loyalty. In 1540, Sher Khan, a brilliant leader of the Afghan chiefs who still controlled Bihar and Bengal, inflicted a crushing defeat on Humayun, who was compelled to evacuate Delhi.

Sher Khan, now known as Sher Shah, reigned for only five years after his victory. Had he lived, the later history of India might have been very different, for his short reign saw a complete reorganization of the administration, making his kingdom more soundly governed than it had been for over 200 years. He is also remembered as the builder of the Grand Trunk Road, still one of the main communication routes, running from Bengal to the Indus. Sher Shah's son, Islam Shah, reigned for about eight years. His death was followed by a succession dispute, giving an opportunity to Humayun, who with Persian support had reestablished himself in Afghanistan. In July 1555, Humayun reoccupied Delhi and Agra. In January 1556, he died. His eldest son Akbar, was a boy of thirteen.

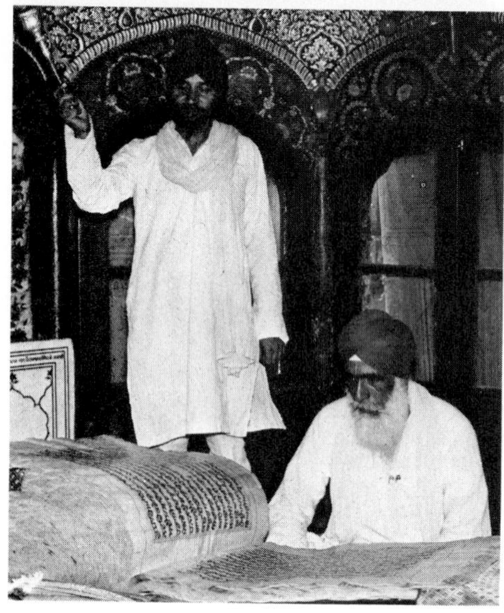

*Top:* The Golden Temple at Amritsar, west Punjab, central shrine of the Sikh religion. Its construction was completed by the guru Arjun (died 1606), and in the nineteenth century the Rajput prince Ranjit Singh brought marble panels from the sack of Jahangir's mausoleum at Shadara to add to its splendor.
*Above:* Reciting from the *Guru Granth Sahib*. In the Shish Mahal, a small chamber in the Golden Temple at Amritsar, a recitation of the *Granth*, the holy book of the Sikhs, goes on continually. The *Granth* is the focus of Sikh worship because the religion forbids the making of images.

## AKBAR

Akbar was an intelligent but lazy boy, who never learned to read properly and could barely sign his name. At the time of his father's death he was titular governor of the Punjab, and his prospects of a long and successful reign must have seemed rather dim. Yet his reign was a little longer and quite as successful as that of his approximate contemporary, Queen Elizabeth I of England.

On his accession, Akbar's main assets were his tutor, Bairam Khan, and his personality, which even in his boyhood won him the loyalty of his friends and the respect of his enemies. Bairam Khan, a Turk, had served Humayun faithfully. As Akbar's guardian, he had been *de facto* governor of the Punjab and on the boy's accession to the throne he became virtual regent. It was he who, on Akbar's behalf, organized the resistance to the Afghan chiefs, who quickly intensified their attacks on the Moguls when they heard of Humayun's death. For a while Delhi was lost once more, but Bairam soon recaptured it and steadily restored the Mogul position. In 1560, however, Akbar, then eighteen, dismissed Bairam and assumed full control. For two years Akbar did nothing, leaving the management of the kingdom to his mother's favorites. Then he awoke to his responsibilities and steadily established his personal control of affairs. From 1564, his reign really began.

Intensely ambitious and tolerating no political rivals, Akbar aimed to build up an all-India empire, and his armies were almost constantly at war on his frontiers. But, more clearly than any Muslim ruler who preceded him, he increasingly realized that if he was to build a durable empire it must ultimately depend on the consent of the governed. Such consent could only be achieved by efficient and just administration and by the abolition of all religious and racial preferences within the state.

Akbar's reorganization of the administration produced a system which lasted with little change until the end of the Mogul empire. It was a strange hybrid of bureaucracy and feudalism, but it worked well. The realm was controlled by provincial governors, holding office at the emperor's pleasure and bound to provide soldiers for the emperor's service. The same was true of the lesser *mansabdars* (state officials), who were graded according to the number of troops they were expected to provide. Land tax was reassessed on a fairer basis and the standard rate fixed at one-third of the crop, although special factors might lead to a reduction. Bribery, corruption, and extortion were put down sternly. The record books kept for each province have not survived, but they were utilized by Akbar's secretary, Abu'l Fazl, in compiling a detailed survey of the imperial system called Ain-i-Akbari ("The Akbarian Institutes"), a most important source for knowledge of Mogul administration. It was a sign of the religious toleration of the time that the minister who, under the emperor's general guidance, planned and executed these reforms, was a Hindu, Todar Mall.

Akbar was predisposed to liberal religious views. His father, Humayun, had extended tolerance to the Hindus, and Akbar found some of his strongest supporters among the feudatory Rajput princes. At the beginning of his reign he made some show of orthodoxy, but soon he realized that to create a stable empire he must conciliate all religious groups. A series of edicts put this policy into effect. In 1563, he abolished the tax on pilgrims to Hindu sacred places. The *jizya*, the tax on non-Muslims, was abolished the following year. In 1579, he set himself up as the final arbiter in all matters concerning the Muslim religion.

Akbar's faith in Islam waned. He loved listening to discussions between members of the various schools and sects of Islam, and from 1579 he took to inviting members of other faiths to expound their beliefs in his presence. Theologians of all religions—Hindus and Muslims, Jains and Parsees from Gujarat, and Jesuit fathers from the Portuguese colony of Goa—attended his court. In 1582, he instituted the *Din-i-Ilahi* (Divine Faith), an eclectic religious system combining elements of Islam, Hinduism, and Zoroastrianism. Because the emperor's new religion did not include the Muslim confession of faith ("There is no God but God and Muhammad is the Prophet of God") in its liturgy, Akbar cannot be considered a Muslim, even a heretical Muslim, from this time onward. The Divine Faith was accepted by many courtiers and its rituals were regularly performed during Akbar's lifetime, but no serious attempt was made to spread it among the masses, and on his death it soon disappeared.

Many Muslims were outraged by Akbar's religious policy and his personal rejection of Islam, but he managed to keep his enemies at bay. Several revolts took place during his reign, but his throne was never really in danger. He was a despot, but he cared for his people and listened to their complaints. He had terrible fits of anger, when he might act with extreme ruthlessness, but soon he would come to his senses and regret his actions. He was never calculatingly cruel, but was generally just and merciful according to the standards of his time.

Akbar was also a passionate lover of music, art, and architecture, and his greatest memorial is the palace complex and mosque of Fatehpur Sikri, a few miles from the city of Agra, which the Moguls made their second capital. The court soon moved back to Agra and the palace was deserted, but much of it still stands intact.

A Sikh army officer. The tightly knit discipline of the Sikhs proved invaluable when they were forced to become a semi-military community in the face of persecution from the Mogul emperor Jahangir. The military tradition has persisted among the Sikhs to the present day; they are reckoned to be among the finest soldiers in Asia.

## SUCCESSORS OF AKBAR

Jahangir (1605–1627), Akbar's son and successor, was weak rather than evil, and was addicted to alcohol and drugs. It is not surprising that the court should have become corrupt and full of intrigue in his reign, and that revolts should have broken out in the provinces. It says much for the system founded by Akbar that the machinery of government continued to function, although local officials often became more oppressive.

The next emperor, Shah Jahan (1627–1658), was a stronger man, but extremely extravagant. To supply the needs of the court the revenue system was revised at the expense of the peasantry. This led to banditry, which was rife in many provinces until it was ruthlessly suppressed by Mogul troops. There were several famines, one in Gujarat, in the early 1630s, so serious that people were driven to cannibalism. Abdul Hamid, a court chronicler, records that the emperor gave 150,000 silver rupees for relief measures and remitted one-eleventh of the annual land tax—figures that show how rapacious the Mogul system had become since the days of Akbar.

Nevertheless the Mogul empire continued to expand, chiefly at the expense of the independent sultanates of the Deccan. In 1636, the emperor appointed his third son, Aurangzeb, viceroy of the Deccan, and in the following years Aurangzeb consolidated and further expanded Mogul power in the south.

The reign of Shah Jahan also saw a revision of Akbar's religious policy. During the reigns of Akbar and Jahangir, a Muslim divine, Shaikh Ahmad Sirhindi, had preached strongly against toleration. He had little influence in his lifetime, but his views gained support after his death. There was a growing feeling among some courtiers, strongly backed by the *ulema*, that Akbar's religious policy had gone too far. In 1632, Shah Jahan ordered that no new Hindu temples were to be erected and that those under construction were to be demolished. This edict was fully in accordance with Islamic law, but it is doubtful whether it was generally put into effect. Hindus were not subjected to other disabilities, and many continued to hold responsible government positions.

Shah Jahan's reign marks the apogee of the splendor and pomp of "the Great Moguls." Its most famous memorial is the Taj Mahal of Agra, the tomb of the emperor's favorite wife, Banu Begam, known as Mumtaz Mahel (the Adornment of the Palace). When she died in 1631, Shah Jahan planned a mausoleum of unequaled beauty and splendor. The building of the Taj Mahal began in 1632 and lasted for twenty-two years.

The first half of the seventeenth century also saw the finest work of the school of miniature painting at the Mogul court in the time of Akbar. By this time European art had begun to have some influence, notably on the Indian artists' attempts at perspective effects. The work produced during Jahangir's reign is particularly attractive in its remarkable feeling for flowers, birds, and animals.

The end of Shah Jahan's reign was tragic. Among his four sons the eldest, Dara Shukoh, was his father's favorite and was expected to inherit the throne. Dara was an intellectual with a great interest in theology and religious debate and a tendency to mysticism. He studied the Hindu scriptures as well as Muslim literature and would undoubtedly have maintained Akbar's religious tolerance. But his arrogant and irascible personality made him many enemies among the courtiers. Aurangzeb, Shah Jahan's third son, was a calculating politician, inspired by an intense devotion to orthodox Islam, who could justify his most ruthless actions by reference to Islamic principles. In 1657, when it seemed that Shah Jahan was dying, Aurangzeb embarked on eighteen months of complicated plotting and succeeded in eliminating his three brothers. Shah Jahan, who had not died after all, was kept in confinement in Agra fort until his death in 1666.

## Aurangzeb

Aurangzeb was proclaimed emperor in 1658, when he was about forty. His reign lasted nearly fifty years, to 1707. He was a man seemingly motivated by two overwhelming drives: personal ambition, which he sought to satisfy with skill and cunning, and passionate attachment to orthodox Islam. He sought to carry out every minor ritual action and to follow even the most insignificant provision of his faith in an exemplary manner, and promoted its welfare by every possible means. Where there was a conflict between his two drives, the religious generally triumphed. He could justify even his revolt against his father and his fratricidal warfare by appeals to Islamic principles.

In accordance with his faith, Aurangzeb had simple tastes. One of his first measures was to reduce the luxury of the Mogul court. The excesses of tax collectors were curbed, so the impoverished peasants may have benefited from his orthodoxy. But Aurangzeb's ambition led him to attempt territorial conquests, and meanwhile revolts broke out within the empire. Some were more than mere rebellions of disgruntled provincial governors or Rajput princes; they had about them the character of popular risings, hitherto very rare in India.

In 1669, in spite of these troubles, Aurangzeb, in order to serve his faith, antagonized the majority of his subjects. Prompted by the news that certain brahmans had been preaching in public and that their sermons had been attended by Muslims, he ordered the destruction of all Hindu temples throughout his realm. How far this order was put into effect is disputed, but certainly great temples in the cities of Varanasi and Mathura, referred to in earlier sources, are no longer to be found there, and mosques from Aurangzeb's time have replaced them. The destruction of temples was followed in 1679 by the reimposition of the *jizya*, the poll tax on unbelievers. By now Hindus were virtually excluded from all the more important official positions, and the *jizya* formed an added inducement to conversion. As a devout Muslim Aurangzeb had no strong racial prejudices, and the convert was treated with honor. But this led to great resentment among both non-Muslims and Muslims, who disliked the favors shown to turncoats.

The *jizya* may not have been a very heavy burden, but the Hindus had enjoyed a century of equal treatment and were no longer ready to accept a position of inferiority. There were demonstrations and protests. Most of the Rajputs, who in the main had remained loyal to the Moguls, now turned against Aurangzeb, and gave shelter to his rebel son, Akbar. Aurangzeb's religious policy was not the sole cause of the breakup of his empire, but the divisive tendencies of the time were much strengthened by it.

The greatest threat to the Moguls came from the Deccan, where a minor but energetic chieftain, Sivaji, built up a kingdom centered on Poona. Sivaji died in 1680, and in the following year the aging Aurangzeb decided to lead the Deccan campaign in person. He succeeded in conquering the two surviving Deccan sultanates, Bijapur and Golconda, while the Mahrattas were driven into the south. But his victories were not decisive. The Mahrattas linked up with bands of Muslim freebooters, the remains of the armies of the Deccan sultanates, to harry the countryside. Aurangzeb kept up his constant campaigning until his death in 1707 at the age of eighty-nine. On his death-bed, he appears to have been oppressed by feelings of guilt, for he left letters which reflect some recognition of his shortcomings as a ruler.

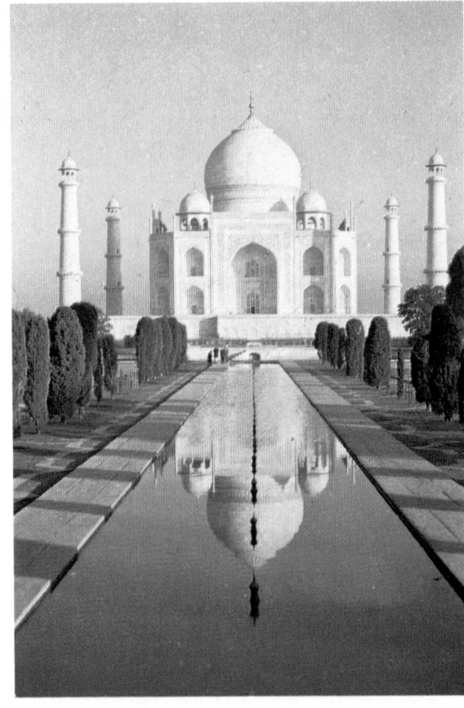

The Taj Mahal at Agra. "A thing of perfect beauty and of absolute finish in every detail," wrote the American poet Bayard Taylor in 1853—and although other critics have attacked it for "a deficiency of fancy" (Aldous Huxley) and other imagined faults, it remains perhaps the most widely admired building in the world. Built in 1632–54 at the command of Shah Jahan, as the tomb of his favorite wife, its design is sometimes credited to a Persian or Turkish architect called Ustad 'Isa. It is set among superb gardens and pools, and is best viewed by moonlight.

## THE SIKHS

A new force which appeared in India almost on the eve of European domination was the religion of Sikhism, whose adherents form a very important minority in India. Around the beginning of the sixteenth century, a Punjabi hymnodist named Nanak began to travel through India (and, according to legend, beyond it as far as Mecca), proclaiming his own brand of devotional religion in fine poetry. His message was largely that of Kabir: simple faith, devotion to god, and brotherly love towards men of every creed are the ways to salvation. He attracted a band of followers who called themselves Sikhs (disciples). Nanak became their acknowledged Guru (teacher), and before he died in 1538 he appointed one of his closest disciples, Angad, as his successor.

The Sikhs continued to grow in the Punjab as a peaceful sect, a reformed branch of Hinduism, with no caste system and worshiping without images or other sacred symbols. The fifth Guru, Arjun, who attracted the admiration and patronage of Akbar, combined the hymns of Nanak with his own and those of other Gurus and devotional poets to form the first part of the *Granth*, the Sikh sacred book. It was in Arjun's time also that the Golden Temple of Amritsar, the central shrine of Sikhism, was constructed. Arjun suffered at the hands of Jahangir, for he was accused of supporting the revolt of the emperor's recalcitrant son, Khusru, and was put to death in 1606. Although his execution seems to have had no religious motive, it tended to alienate the Sikhs from the Moguls. Moreover, they now became more inclined to take up arms in defense of their faith. The ninth Guru, Tegh Bahadur, was also accused of rebellion. Captured by Aurangzeb, he refused conversion to Islam and suffered martyrdom in 1675. His son, Gobind Singh, became the tenth Guru.

Guru Gobind completed the conversion of the Sikh community into a military brotherhood. He instituted several reforms which welded the Sikhs together as a close-knit, disciplined community, representing a third religion, neither Hinduism nor Islam. The most striking of his innovations was the five *kakaras*, items which constitute the uniform of the male Sikh: *kesh*, long hair which must never be cut; *kangha*, a comb to hold the hair; *kripan*, a short sword (generally omitted by modern Sikhs); *kachh*, short underpants replacing the Hindu *dhoti* (which might work loose in battle, with unfortunate results); and *kara*, an iron bracelet. Gobind also introduced a form of baptism and communion meal, the latter intended to break down all vestiges of caste prejudice. He encouraged his male followers to hunt and eat meat, but strictly forbade wine, tobacco, and drugs. All Sikhs were given the surname *Singh* (lion). The Sikhs gained strength rapidly under Gobind; they were transformed into disciplined fighters and were a constant thorn in the side of the later Moguls.

The Sikh religion contains elements of both Hinduism and Islam, and its baptism and communion meal may have been inspired by Christianity. It is monotheistic, but it admits some of the lesser divinities of Hinduism to the status of angels. It rejects the undue subordination of women, but permits polygamy. It shows its debt to Hinduism in its belief in rebirth and *karma*, and the influence of Islam is seen in the extreme respect paid to the *Granth*. Guru Gobind, unlike his predecessors, did not appoint another Guru to succeed him. Instead he told his followers that after his death the *Granth* would be their Guru. So the sacred book is known as *Guru Granth Sahib* ("Teacher Book, the Master") and is the focus of worship in every Sikh temple.

## THE MOGUL DECLINE

At Aurangzeb's death, the Mogul empire seemed ready to break up. It was further weakened by a twelve-month war of succession among his three sons. The eighteenth century saw the Mahrattas emerge as the kingmakers of India, with the Sikhs also a constant threat to the Moguls. Invasions of Persian and Afghan warlords resulted in the sack of Delhi on two occasions and the loss of the Mogul territory west of the Indus. The Europeans, already established in small trading posts on the coast, began to take part in the confused politics of the time. The European conquest of India is fully examined in the second volume of this series.

The conservatism of the Moguls was a potent factor in their decline. The new invaders of India triumphed with new weapons and new fighting methods which the Moguls shunned. Even in practical, everyday matters the Moguls were conservative. When Jesuit fathers at the court of Akbar showed the emperor samples of printing and offered to set up a press with movable type, Akbar refused, because the cursive *nastaliq* variety of Arabic script, in which Persian was traditionally written, could not be adapted to printing. In contrast, the Mahrattas of the Deccan learned some of the new methods. Sivaji developed a small navy and improved his army along European lines. It was their readiness to learn from their enemies that raised the Mahrattas to a dominant position in India in the eighteenth century.

However, it should not be assumed that the mismanagement and oppression of the latter part of Aurangzeb's reign brought confusion throughout India. Many areas were comparatively little affected, although experiencing more frequent warfare and rather less security of life and property than in the seventeenth century. The weakened Mogul emperors, often dependent on Mahratta and Rajput support against their own rebellious officers, soon abandoned Aurangzeb's anti-Hindu policy. New temples were built in the areas where they had been destroyed, but these new buildings were far inferior to those of earlier days. A decline in taste is evident in most aspects of creative activity. Muslim art reflects the same decline; although mosques and palaces were erected in this period, they were far inferior to the buildings of earlier days. Literature also languished. The great devotional poets found few successors in the eighteenth century, and most of the writing of the age is dull and imitative. Yet the eighteenth century was not wholly unproductive. Two unexpected bursts of creativity occurred. One followed the capture of Delhi in 1739 by the Persian, Nadir Shah. His troops looted and slaughtered mercilessly, carrying off the magnificent Peacock Throne of Shah Jahan and annexing all the territory west of the Indus. The remnants of the Mogul state were impoverished and demoralized by the terrible blow, and this may have been one of the reasons why, around this time, some writers at the Mogul court began to compose verses in their mother tongue, Urdu, rather than in Persian.

In the Deccan, Urdu verse had been written since the end of the sixteenth century, but now, first at the crumbling imperial court of Delhi and later at Lucknow, at the court of the Nawab of Avadh (Oudh) who was practically independent of the emperor, other schools of Urdu poets appeared. Their verses, although based on Persian models, were Indian in inspiration and showed great beauty and much originality. Three Urdu poets, Sauda (1713–1781), Mir (1724–1810), and Mir Hasan (1726–1786), were the greatest Indian literary figures of the century. Though their poetry was primarily written for the Mogul nobility, it was intelligible to the ordinary man, for it was composed in his own language.

The second development was in the realm of art and was even more surprising. Miniature painting at the Mogul court continued after Shah Jahan, but produced nothing equal to the works of the early seventeenth century. However, the courts of the Rajput kings and chiefs also had their painters, inspired partly by local folk art but also owing a good deal to the Mogul school. As Mogul painting declined, so that of the Rajputs advanced. The touch of the Rajput artists became progressively more delicate, their use of color more sensitive, their feeling for their subjects more sympathetic. Then they too began to decline. By the end of the eighteenth century, many of the great Rajput princes had seen something of Western art, and encouraged their painters to break away from the old traditions. The results were unhappy hybrids with little to be said for them.

In general, the social divisions of the Hindus hardened, and the more objectionable practices of Hinduism, such as *sati*, female infanticide, and child marriage, became more common. The same conservatism affected the Muslims, upon whom Aurangzeb's rigid orthodoxy, although no longer enforced by the state, had made a deep impression.

In the eighteenth century, non-Muslim forces were gaining strength. Both the Mahrattas and the Sikhs were generally tolerant of Islam, but in their territory and those of the Rajputs many Muslims found themselves ruled by unbelievers, with the titular Mogul overlord too weak to help them. Consciousness of their declining fortunes gave Muslims a deep sense of insecurity. This gave rise to a new puritanical movement, led by Shah Waliullah, a preacher active around the middle of the eighteenth century, which encouraged Muslims to keep themselves to themselves and to avoid all practices and beliefs not justified by the early traditions of the faith.

The division between Muslim and Hindu, which was later to be encouraged by certain aspects of British policy, played an important part in the establishment of European domination over India.

# Part II China and Japan

Chapter 4

# CLASSICAL CIVILIZATION IN CHINA

To consider the history of China is to consider also the lives of around one-third of all the people who ever lived before A.D. 1800. And for a proper understanding of modern China—indeed of the modern world, since Chinese culture forms a considerable proportion of the sum of human experience—it is necessary to have some knowledge of the traditional Chinese culture which flourished for more than 3,000 years.

The early development of Chinese civilization, down to the time of the Shang dynasty (c.1600–1066 B.C.), has been traced in book 1. The account here follows its course from the Zhou (Chou) period to the establishment of the Qing (Manchu, or Ch'ing) dynasty in A.D. 1644, concentrating on key periods of change rather than on the rise and fall of dynasties. Chinese society in the eighteenth century, a period which saw the highest development of the traditional system before the prolonged crises of the nineteenth century, is examined in some detail. Although the old "dynastic" approach to Chinese history has been discarded, the names of dynasties are still used by scholars, as they are here, as convenient labels. For Chinese names, the standard system of romanization promulgated in 1958 is used throughout, but the more familiar older spellings are given in parentheses where they differ from the new.

*Above:* A bowl of the neolithic Yang-shao culture, which flourished in the Honan area of west China until about 1500 B.C. The significance of the part-man, part-fish figure is not known, although fish—always an important Chinese staple food—provides a frequent theme in Chinese art. The Yang-shao culture is sometimes known as the Painted Pottery culture, to distinguish it from the Lungshan, or Black Pottery, culture which flourished in northeast China at roughly the same time.

*Left:* An ornamental brick house in the form of a gateway dating from the Han period. Although the Han period, around the beginning of the Christian era, was one of internal strife, it was also a time of great development in traditional Chinese architecture, centering on the western Han capital of Ch'ang-an (modern Sian).

## THE SHANG LEGACY

Certain important legacies of the Shang dynasty survived its fall in the eleventh century B.C. Among them were: a capital city that was essentially an extension of the ruler's palace; a written language that was primarily the preserve of officials; and a general acceptance of a Chinese society ruled by a monarchy which combined administrative and ritual functions. Among the aspects of Shang political order retained by the Zhou, the most important included the system of parceling out the kingdom to local feudal lords, whose duty it was to provide soldiers for the rulers' service in return for the right to local political control. But eventually the Zhou rulers were unable to prevent the feudal lords from winning more and more independence of central control and engaging in internecine warfare as each struggled to absorb his neighbor. From about 700 B.C., endemic war began to exert revolutionary pressure on Chinese society.

| 500 BC | 250 | AD | 250 | 500 | 750 | 1000 | 1250 | 1500 |
|---|---|---|---|---|---|---|---|---|
| Warring states period | Qin Dynasty (221–207)<br>Han Dynasty (206 BC–AD 184) | | Intermediate Period | | Sui Dynasty (581–618)<br>Tang Dynasty (618–909) | Song Dynasty (960–1279)<br>Kin Dynasty in North | Yuan (Mongol) Dynasty (1279–1368) | Ming Dynasty (1368–1644) |
| Confucius (551–479) | Bureaucratic administration instituted | | | Spread of Buddhism Hun invasions | Block printing of books. Bureaucracy formalized | | | Portuguese arrive (1514) |

## FROM ZHOU TO UNIFIED EMPIRE

The theme of the last two centuries of the Zhou dynasty was one of change induced by war. Chinese society and culture underwent a long crisis in which social and political structures, economy, thought patterns, values, technology, and environmental relationships were profoundly changed. The period was in many ways akin to the modern age: powerful and ruthless governments struggling for supremacy while traditional values and ways are discarded and the economy is changed to meet the needs of war.

The Chinese states, no longer feudal except in name, had to be ruthless to survive now that their relations were no longer governed by the king and the old morality. Those that observed the old chivalrous conventions of war, such as not attacking an unprepared enemy, were defeated and destroyed. In the struggle for survival, a ruler had to entrust his armies to the ablest commander, irrespective of whether or not he was a hereditary aristocrat; and this served to undermine the former aristocratic monopoly of high positions. War also demanded a large population to man, feed, and equip ever-larger armies. In consequence, rulers sought for the first time to exercise direct control over their subjects.

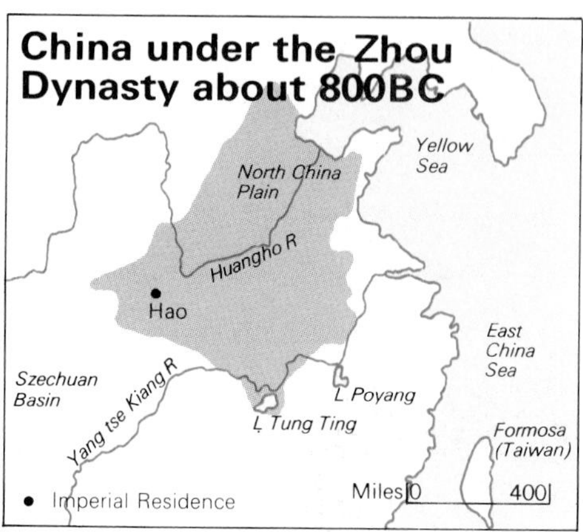


It was during this period that the Chinese discovered how to make cast iron—a technical breakthrough not achieved in the West until nearly two millennia later. The technique depended on the development of furnaces capable of reaching the temperatures of 1,400° C, needed to liquefy iron, which was then poured into molds to make cheap, strong agricultural tools and other implements. Because bronze had been too rare for use in agriculture, the peasants now made a rapid transition from implements of wood, stone, shell, and bone to iron tools, with a consequent leap forward in productivity. The rulers of the states began to mobilize their populations in public works of military value, such as canals and walls, and in the cultivation of

A bronze tiger's head inlaid with silver, Zhou dynasty.

heavier soils, made possible by the new tools. Agriculture was also boosted by the introduction of improved methods of cultivation, including the widespread planting of soya beans, which not only yielded far more protein to the acre than stock-raising, but also helped build up the soil's fertility.

## CONFUCIUS AND POLITICAL PHILOSOPHY

The troubled society of the late Zhou period and the Warring States, which drew to a close towards the end of the third century B.C., gave rise to a period of intellectual ferment the like of which was not seen again in China until the irruption of Western influences in the nineteenth century. From this period, in which so many schools of philosophy sought for a way to political and social stability that it is sometimes called the period of the "Hundred Schools," the name of Confucius (551–479 B.C.) must be singled out for special mention, for a political, administrative, and ethical code largely based on Confucius' teachings or on interpretations of those teachings dominated Chinese society for some 2,000 years.

In formulating his theories, Confucius looked back to an early, near-legendary Chinese society in which the social order was maintained by every man knowing his place and striving to make the best of his allotted task. At the head of society stood the ruler, directly responsible to heaven. The ruler's advisers, scholars, were responsible for guiding his "right conduct" and for administrating a centralized bureaucracy through a structure of graded officials. In effect, Confucius' system relied on traditional virtues—patience, reason, respect for ancestors, respect for family elders, and respect for scholarship—to reinforce an overall pattern of acceptance and preservation of the established order. By respecting and obeying his superiors—who claimed superiority through their moral worth—a man gained in virtue and, presumably, happiness. This held good for everyone from the ruler down to the most minor bureaucrat. Even the lowest peasants had a part to play—that of accepting their lot gladly, observing morality, and feeding their rulers by their toil.

The bureaucracies of the new Chinese states needed literate men who would be reasonably trustworthy, and the philosophy of Confucius and his followers was well-suited to the production of such men—men who located themselves within the long tradition of Chinese culture, who valued good behavior, and who felt an obligation to be loyal to their superiors. A quotation from the important collection of Confucius' teachings made in the fourth century B.C., the *Lun Yu* ("The Analects of Confucius"), will serve to give an idea of the way in which his ideas were expressed.

Confucius defined the attitudes and behavior of a "gentleman":

> *A gentleman does not compete.*
>
> *The gentleman loves virtue; the little man loves land.*
>
> *The Master did not use a net when he fished, nor did he shoot at a sitting bird.*
>
> *If wealth were to be had by seeking after it, I would even become a market constable. But if it is not to be sought, I shall do what I like doing!*
>
> *There can be happiness in eating coarse grain, drinking water, and sleeping with only one's arm for a pillow. Wealth and honor gained through wrongdoing would be mere drifting clouds to me.*

Confucius' teachings did, in fact, insist upon the right and duty of the individual to uphold the ideals of "right conduct," even if this might, in theory, mean challenging authority which had strayed from the path of virtue. But reforms inspired by Confucian ideals were likely to be aimed at a return to what were thought of as the traditional virtues, rather than at innovatory attempts to change society for the

*Top:* A portrait of Confucius (551–479 B.C.) taken from a marble slab found near a Confucian temple. The pragmatic traditionalism of Confucian thought conditioned Chinese social behavior and political development for some 2,000 years.
*Above:* Si-ma Guang (1019–1089), a leading Confucian statesman of the Song period, in his official hat and robes. Under the Song, whose rule ended with the Mongol invasions of the thirteenth century, the Chinese state took on the pattern it was to retain until the nineteenth century.

better. And Confucian ideals, revised to some extent by such of his followers as Mencius (c.372–c.289 B.C.), tended to become increasingly rigid in application, leading to policies of extreme conservatism.

## LAO-ZI AND DAOISM

The less worldly teachings of the semi-legendary Lao-zi (Lao-tzu), possibly a contemporary of Confucius, were also of importance. The mystical and poetically expressed doctrines of Lao-zi and his followers were collected in the sixth to fourth centuries B.C. in such books as the *Dao-de jing* (*Tao Te Ching*) and the *Zhuang-zi* (*Chuang-tzu*). They stress the subjectiveness of human values and the limitations of human perception, and prescribe retreat from a competitive and over-organized society to seek unity with *Dao* (*Tao*, "the way") through deep meditation. In various forms, Daoism (Taoism) has exerted a considerable influence on Chinese thought, although its social and political importance has been nothing like as great as that of Confucianism.

Like Confucius, the author of the *Dao-de jing* looked back to an idealized past, albeit a rather different one, in which nothing happened: the ruler would make a virtue of inactivity, and his subjects would be kept in blissful stupidity. This is well illustrated in the following quotation in which the author suggests ways in which to counteract what he saw as undesirable tendencies in late Zhou China:

> *Reduce the size and population of the state. Ensure that even though the people have the tools of war for a troop or a battalion they will not use them; and also that they will be reluctant to move to distant places because they look on death as no light matter.*
> *Even when they have ships and carts, they will have no use for them; and even when they have armor and weapons they will have no occasion to make a show of them.*

The *Zhuang-zi* reinforces the teachings of the *Dao-de jing* by means of colorful and easily-understood "parables." An example from *Zhuang-zi* must suffice to give some idea of the style and import of these moral tales.

> *Rush, the King of the Southern Ocean, and Hurry, the King of the Northern Ocean, used to meet on the territory of Unformed, King of the Center. Unformed entertained them so well that Rush and Hurry, wanting to repay Unformed, said: "Everybody except Unformed has seven holes through which to see, hear, eat, and breathe. Let's try boring him some." Each day they bored one hole; on the seventh day Unformed died.*

Later Daoism included elements of folk religion and of alchemy; adepts of this kind of Daoism tried to find an elixir of immortality and adopted arcane sexual practices which were thought to lengthen life. In general, Daoism offered a way of escape to the tired official, and indicated a sense of resignation and acceptance when things went wrong. In some ways, Daoism prepared the way for Buddhism, which, when it first appeared in China, was often regarded as a new kind of Daoism.

Other thinkers were more subversive, among them the redoubtable Mo Zi (Mo-Tzu), whose traditionalist rejection of military aggression took the extreme form of leading his followers to the active defense of states under attack. Another school, known as the Legalists, pitched their appeal to the monarch who wanted to make his power absolute at home for the sake of subduing his enemies abroad. Theirs was the calculating cynicism of men who held human nature in low esteem and were concerned not with morality but with results. They offered the subject honor and wealth only on condition that he served the state in peace as well as in war. Any failure to do so was to be mercilessly punished. Related to the Legalists were the theoreticians of the art of war, of whom the most realistic and brilliant was the author of the military manual *Sun Zi*, a work still studied by soldiers in China, Japan, and even the Pentagon. At the opposite pole to the Legalists were thinkers who advocated a return to rustic simplicity or to a mythical, ideally peaceful past.

## THE QIN AND HAN

In the last centuries of the Zhou period, aptly known as that of the Warring States, the seven major powers within China fought it out in shifting patterns of alliances. Finally the most ruthless and totalitarian, the state of Qin (Ch'in) in the west, destroyed its rivals. Within a very short time, the Qin regime unified currency, weights and measures, and script throughout the states, and imposed a centralized bureaucratic rule on the whole of China. But the speed and harshness with which these measures were carried out alienated not only the old aristocracies but also the peasants, who were dragooned into forced labor projects, and the intellectuals, whose dissenting voices were ruthlessly silenced.

Although the Qin regime lasted only until 221 B.C., collapsing within years of the death of its first emperor, the centralized empire and civil service ruling the whole of China were principles retained by all later dynasties. Subsequent regimes, however, made more concessions to local landed power and modified the Legalism of the Qin state system with Confucian conservatism.

One of the contributory causes of the Qin collapse was the series of revolts sparked off by forced labor and militia duties along the northern frontiers. These frontiers were particularly prone to attack because the pastoral peoples of the Inner Asian steppes, having coalesced to form their own state structure, could muster large bands of horsemen to invade the rich lands of north China. To guard against

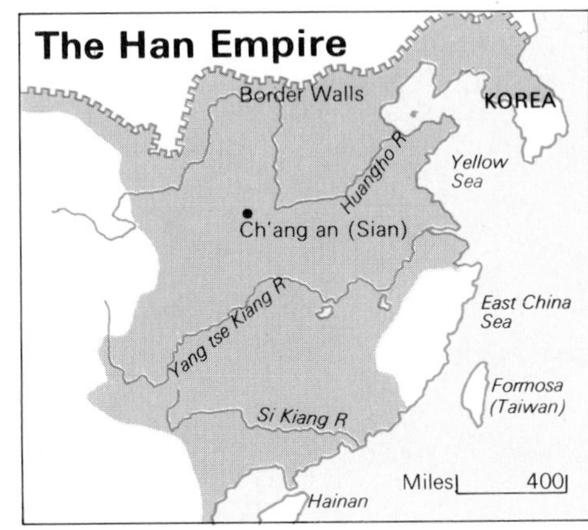


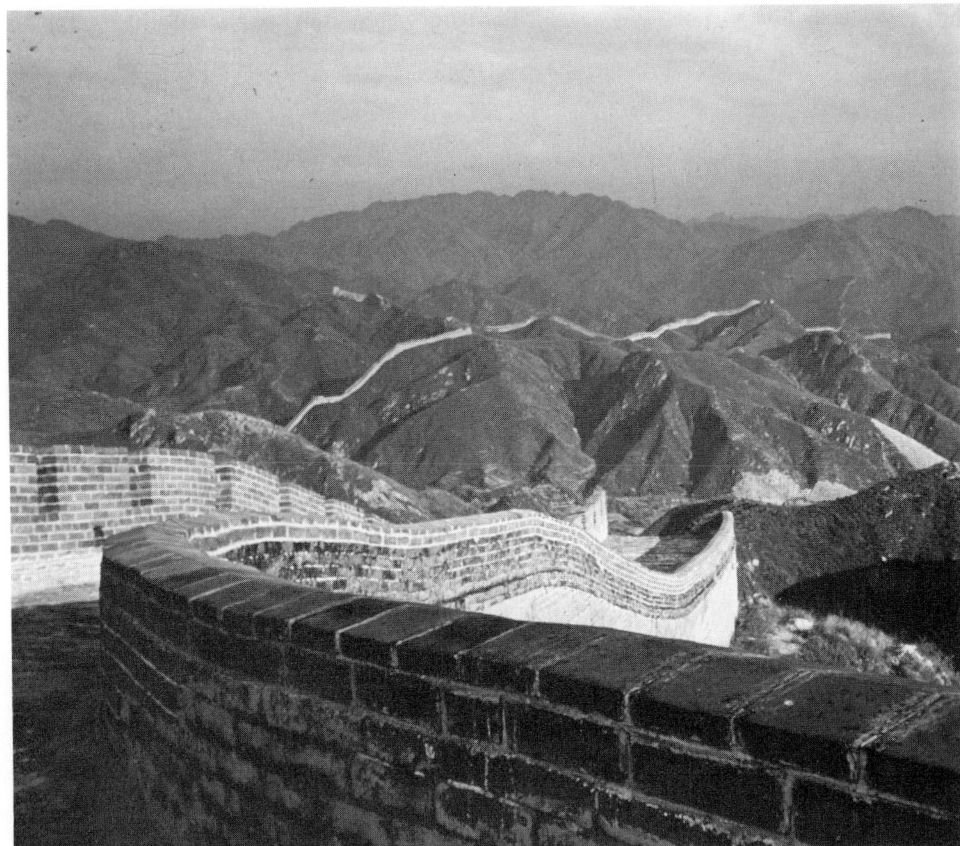

Only a state as firmly centralized as the Qin could have mustered the immense labor force needed to build the Great Wall as a defense against the northern barbarians. At the order of the Emperor Shih Hwangti (246–209 B.C.) defenses already built in the northern provinces were incorporated into a wall running 1,500 miles, from Kansu in the northwest to Shanhaikwan (modern Linyu) on the Gulf of Liaotung in the east. The Great Wall, which has been extensively rebuilt in modern times, varies in height between fifteen and thirty feet; its base is twenty feet wide, narrowing to twelve feet at the top.

these attacks millions of soldiers and peasants were mobilized to build, maintain, patrol, and supply the defense lines which were eventually joined together to form the Great Wall. (The surviving parts of the Great Wall, however, date mainly from the Ming period, A.D. 1368–1644.) Only a strong state could garner the manpower and wealth needed for this defense. The Han emperors who took the throne after the fall of the Qin were only able to meet such needs for the first of the four centuries of their rule. After that time they were unable to control the powerful families at the head of the local communities within China, who naturally resisted central control. As a result, the Han were forced to attempt to maintain national defenses by bringing into China some of the very tribal peoples whom the wall system had originally been intended to exclude. And when these peoples found themselves treated not as honored allies but as contemptible barbarians, the seeds were sown of the disastrous race wars that devastated north China in the fourth and fifth centuries A.D.

## DISUNITY AND TANG REUNIFICATION

The political history of the four centuries following the effective collapse of Han power at the end of the second century A.D. presents a complex and bewildering list of short-lived dynasties. Most of those north of the Huai (Hwai) River were non-Chinese or depended on non-Chinese military support. In the north, the disasters of war and the low level of commercial activity did not prevent further refinements of the techniques of dry-land agriculture. From the late fifth century onward, the state managed to gain some control over the allocation of land, thus safeguarding the revenues in grain and cloth it needed for the support of huge standing armies and magnificent capital cities. In the south, Chinese regimes brought increasing areas under control through piecemeal conquest and absorption. For most of this period the south was under unified regimes, and northern settlers and refugees were fused

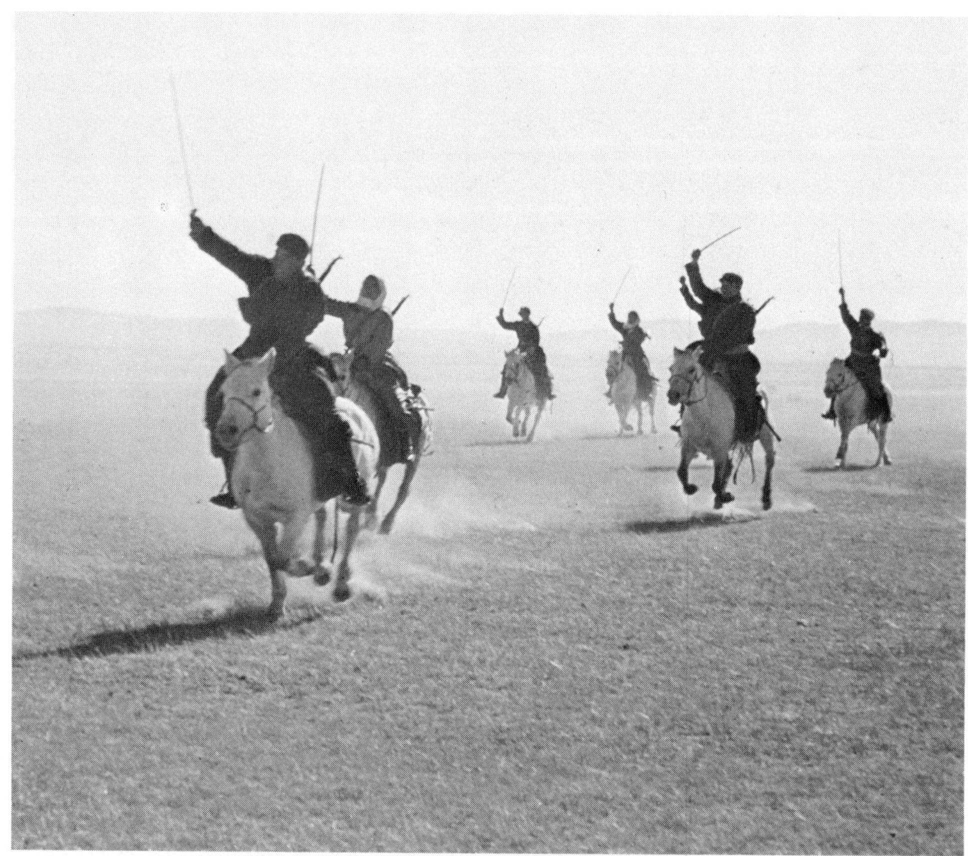

The Great Wall, built to guard China against the incursions of nomadic horsemen like these. Military defense was reinforced by financial appeasement, but in the fourth century A.D. the barbarians broke into north China and, after a period of fighting among themselves, were united under the leadership of Fu Chien. In 383, Fu Chien led his armies to the conquest of south China, but he was defeated and his followers were gradually assimilated into Chinese society.

with or absorbed the indigenous peoples of the Yangtse valley, the Szechuan (Szechwan) basin, and the Canton region. For some time, the southern state was strong enough to resist northern invasions, but it finally succumbed at the end of the sixth century, when China was once again reunited. The wealth of the south had become so great that the new dynasty of Sui found it worthwhile to mobilize the largest labor force ever recorded in Chinese history to dig the 900-mile-long Grand Canal linking the Yangtse (Yangtze) valley with the north. Every year huge quantities of grain were shipped up the canal to feed the capital and armies of the northern frontiers. The canal also served to bind north and south China together far more closely than had been the case under the Han.

During the period of disunity between the Han and the Tang up to the last years of the sixth century, the Chinese were more open to foreign influences than they were to be in the following millennium. Disunity meant that there was no overall state-supported orthodoxy, so Buddhism was able first to penetrate the Chinese and non-Chinese ruling classes and then gradually spread among ordinary people, in much the same way that Christianity spread during and after the collapse of the Roman Empire. In contrast to the West, however, religion in China never became institutionalized to the extent that it could legitimize the state, let alone challenge its power. Throughout the period of disunity both northerner and southerner alike maintained a common sense of being Chinese, and both laid claim to the legacy of Han.

Silver and gold wine flask of a horse trained to dance while holding a wine bowl in its mouth, Tang dynasty. A troop of such horses was one of the marvels of the Tang court at a time when its capital at Ch'ang-an (modern Sian) rivaled Baghdad as a center of cultural exchange. The large horses of western Asia were much admired by the Chinese and were imported at great expense, although the sturdy steppe pony remained the standard cavalry mount of the Chinese armies.

Educated opinion welcomed the restoration of unity under the Sui and the gradual strengthening of the Confucian state system under the Tang. The comparative peace of the first 150 years of Tang rule led to a period of great prosperity and the cultural interaction of northern and southern traditions flowered in literature, especially poetry, and the visual arts. Buddhist power was attacked and limited, and Buddhism itself became diffused among China's other popular religions. Among the elite, Confucianism was greatly strengthened by the introduction of the principle of selecting officials because of ability (judged by Confucian norms) through a complex examination rather than aristocratic birth.

But the fundamental problem of how to counter-balance the power of the non-Chinese soldiers needed for the defense of the northern frontiers was not solved. Within a year of the outbreak of military rebellion in 755, much of the regime's achievement collapsed. The rulers were unable to regain effective control over the frontier zones, a weakness which eventually led to their downfall.

## FROM HWANG HO TO YANGTSE VALLEY

Most historians are agreed that the changes taking place between the eighth and tenth centuries, clearly visible for the first time in the Song (Sung) period, went beyond the changes usually associated with the breakdown of one dynasty (in this case the Tang) and the establishment of its successor. To begin with, the overwhelming majority of the Chinese people now lived in south China (centered on the Yangtse valley) rather than in the older heartlands of Chinese civilization (centered on the plains of the Hwang Ho, or Yellow River). Gradual colonization of the south had been going on for centuries, occasionally dramatically accelerated by conquests of the north by the peoples of the steppes, but it was under the Song, especially after the conquest of all north China in the tenth and eleventh centuries, that the consequences of this population shift became clear.

The south is a land of much greater productivity than the north, and its plentiful water supplies provide not only convenient sources of irrigation but also cheap means of transport and communication. As Chinese farmers moved south, they brought with them the techniques of dry-land millet and wheat cultivation upon which they depended in the north. These techniques were now combined with southern techniques of rice cultivation to produce a tremendous increase in production. At the same time, dikes were constructed and new permanent fields were built, sometimes on terraces carved from the hillsides. New crop strains were introduced, and by the end of the eleventh century it had become possible to harvest rice as often as twice a year.

Increased productivity and cheaper and simpler transport led to an intensification of trade and a notable increase in city populations. Craft and merchant guilds began to appear, large quantities of money began to circulate (including early forms of paper money), and for the first time Chinese merchant and naval ships began to dominate the coasts and waters of southeast Asia. In the cities, the invention of printing gave rise to the growth of a written popular culture far removed from the classical studies of the Confucian scholar-officials.

The beginnings of an urban culture were, however, easily contained (and at times suppressed) by the newly-reformed Confucianism of the age. The great Confucian systematizers were members of the new class of wealthy landowners who replaced the old northern aristocrats of the Tang. The new gentry not only upheld and expanded the strongly anti-merchant ideology, they also supported and contributed to the increased power of the emperor, whose men, as successful civil-service candidates, they had become. With the passing of the old aristocracies, the old militia systems went too, and the power of the central government was strengthened by the creation of a centralized professional army under bureaucratic control.

Chinese state and society emerged from the chaos of the late Tang period and the wars of the tenth century in a form much like that they were to retain down to the nineteenth century. The changes which took place in China between the eighth and tenth centuries have been compared to similar changes in the West associated with the shift from the great Mediterranean empires to the new states of northern Europe. New groups came to the fore, the state system was reinvigorated and strengthened, and a new secular urban culture began to flourish. The analogy must not be pushed too far. In China, the structure of the empire emerged stronger than ever before; the new gentry took their ideology from the past and successfully contained the merchants. There was change—but it was change within the Confucian tradition.

A sixteenth-century wood-block illustration to the popular novel *Shui-hu zhuan* showing one of its bandit heroes, Li Kui (the Black Whirlwind), wielding two battleaxes as he fights his way to the rescue of his comrades from the executioner. The frustration of the peasant classes, in China as elsewhere, expressed itself in the many popular tales glorifying the exploits of outlaws of the "Jesse James" stamp.

## MONGOL INVASION AND LATE IMPERIAL RECOVERY

Chinese civilization received a serious setback in the twelfth and thirteenth centuries. In the twelfth century, just at the time when the state had greatly strengthened its central executive organs by curtailing the powers of its provincial and frontier generals, new confederations of warlike nomadic peoples broke out of the usual

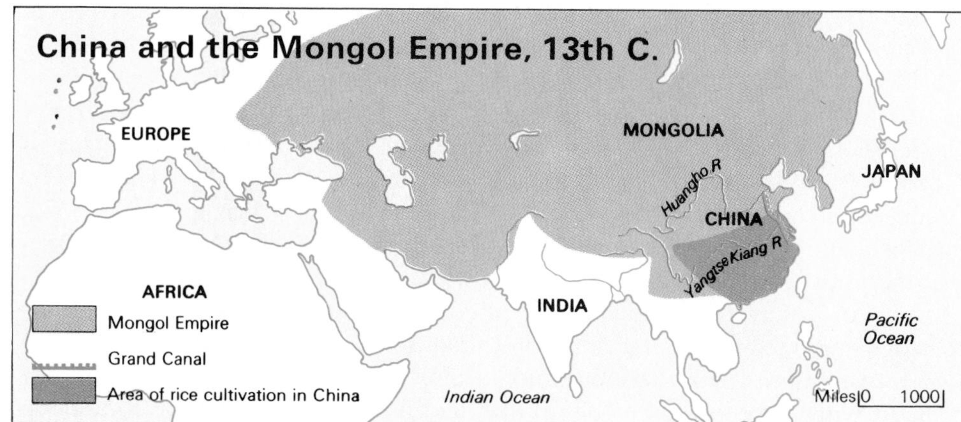

pattern of raid and trade and successfully conquered not only north China, as their predecessors had done, but south China as well. The Mongol state of Chingiz Khan and his successors was by far the largest of the nomadic empires; at its height it linked backward Europe for the first time directly with the advanced civilization of China. To a European merchant-adventurer like Marco Polo (c.1254–c.1324), the splendors of China were far superior to anything in the Europe of his day. Such early contacts helped to stimulate new advances in the West, especially in technology, but they brought few advantages to the East. Although the Mongols were eventually persuaded not to turn north China's farmlands into pasture for their horses, and although the Mongol Yüan dynasty (1279–1368) was shortlived, the Mongols left an ineradicable scar upon Chinese national consciousness. Henceforth, the Chinese were more narrowly traditionalistic, far more suspicious of foreigners, and far less open to innovation or change than at any previous period.

While reacting in these ways to the shock of the Mongol conquest, under the Ming dynasty (1368–1644) the Chinese also took practical steps to try to ensure that such a disaster would never be repeated. In effect, this called for neglect of the expanding southern sea frontier in favor of the northern border defenses. Early in the fifteenth century, when Chinese fleets had just reached the coasts of Africa, further oceanic exploration was curtailed, overseas trade was forbidden, and the capital was shifted north, from Nanking back to Peking. Chinese culture began to turn in on itself.

In time, these measures proved ineffective, for by the end of the sixteenth century the Ming dynasty had become so corrupt and short of funds that it was unable to control the classic combination of ever-larger internal popular uprisings with an external threat, this time from the Manchus, a former tribal people who had established a unified state on the Chinese model in Manchuria. The Manchu conquest of China was completed by 1644, and the new rulers quickly secured the cooperation of the Confucian gentry. They were particularly successful in maintaining a ruthlessly enforced Confucian orthodoxy. The remnants of the Ming forces were easily defeated; some fled to Taiwan, a course followed by the survivors of the fallen Chiang Kai-shek regime in the twentieth century.

In many ways, the Manchu Qing (Ch'ing) dynasty saw the authoritarian Chinese imperial system at its most efficient: it successfully crushed or contained competing elites within China, and at the same time launched a series of victorious campaigns against the steppe peoples along the northern frontiers and the Vigurs and Tibetans to the west. Indeed, the very success of the system was to make it very difficult to introduce change, let alone fundamental reforms, in the face of the new dangers presented by the arrival of Westerners and Japanese in the nineteenth and twentieth centuries.

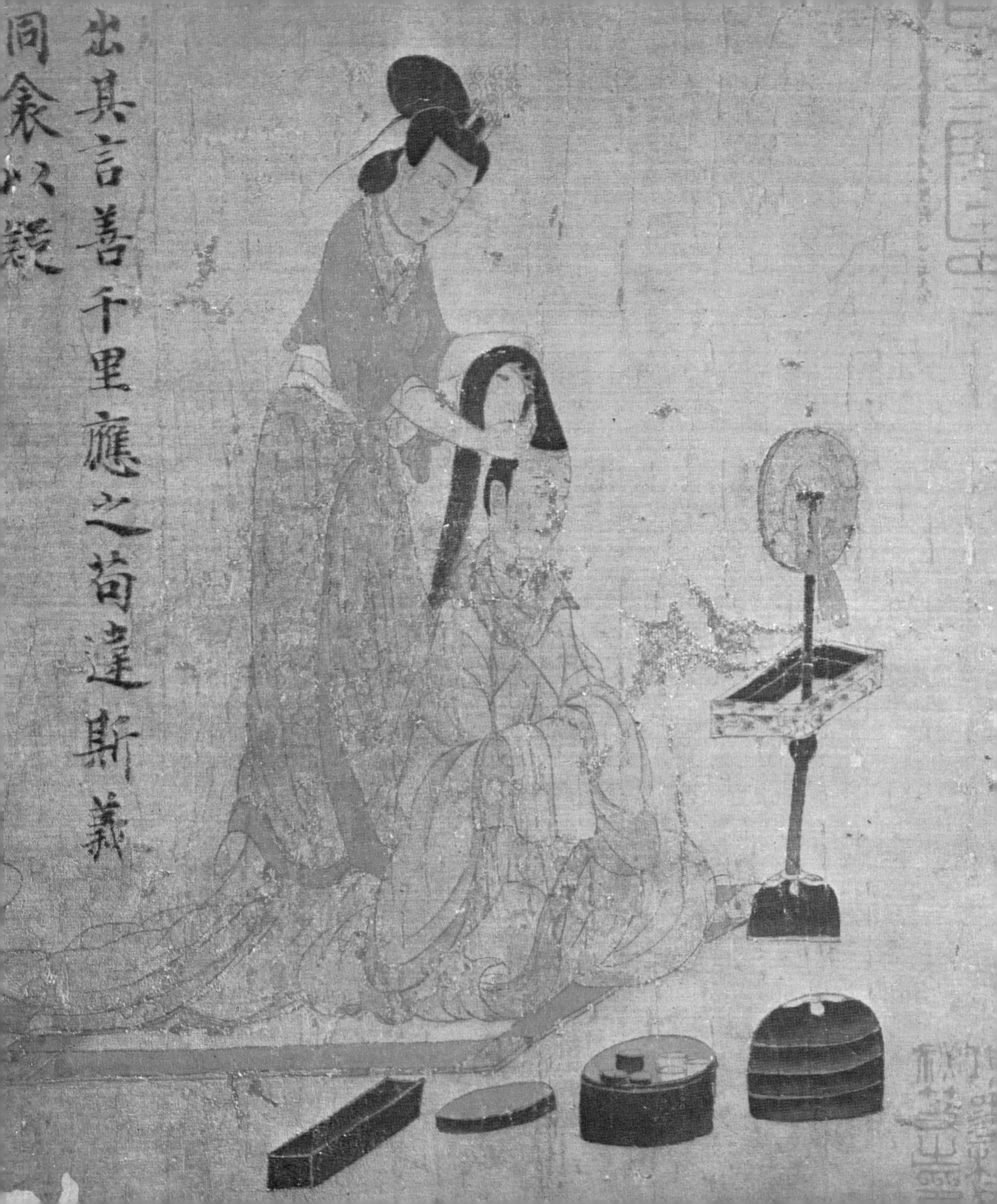

出其言善千里應之苟違斯義
同衾以疑

Chapter 5

# CHINESE SOCIETY IN THE EIGHTEENTH CENTURY

Having traced the main stages of China's development down to the nineteenth and twentieth centuries, it is now desirable to embark upon a more detailed examination of the main groups in Chinese society at a point in time. The eighteenth century is a convenient point, for it is well documented; it also marks the final stage of the traditional Chinese society which was soon to be transformed out of recognition. An appreciation of Chinese society in the eighteenth century not only helps toward an understanding of Chinese history; it also furthers an understanding of the later revolutionary transformation of that traditional society.

## THE PEASANTS

In the eighteenth century, as in all previous periods, the vast majority of the Chinese people were peasants. The basic unit of social and economic organization was the small family of father, mother, and children, which typically did not break up until the death of the parents. Family land and movable property were then equally divided among the sons, a form of inheritance which stands in marked contrast to the systems of primogeniture found in most feudal societies, including medieval Europe, Japan, and early China itself. The social ideal was to have five generations under one roof, but this was not possible for the peasantry, who were unable to afford the various forms of lineage and clan enforcement organizations used by the gentry to prevent inherited wealth leaving the family.

As in all peasant societies, age was deeply venerated, for not only was age in itself something of a rarity where the average life span was short, but also it was the elders who passed on the accumulated experience of the peasant—the routine execution of a multitude of routine tasks unquestioningly accepted—to the next generation. The ideal relationship was gerontic, patriarchal, and authoritarian, characterized by group obedience and group conformity. The status of women was extremely low; a woman was married out of her own family, to a partner chosen for her, into a strange family in which her duty was to serve her husband and mother-in-law. When it came to inheritance, women received practically nothing. In times of scarcity, girl children were the first to be sold or to be put out to die of exposure. It was only by producing male offspring that a woman acquired any standing in the family and gained the hope of exercising the powers of a mother-in-law.

*Above:* A print of a peasant plowing with a team of oxen, Han dynasty. Until the later Tang period, when irrigation methods became increasingly widespread, Chinese cultivators practiced mainly dry farming with millet (seen in the top part of this picture) and later wheat as staple crops. The cultivation of rice was first carried out on a large scale in the warm, humid Yangtse basin.
*Left:* Court lady of the Tang period, with a hairdresser in attendance.

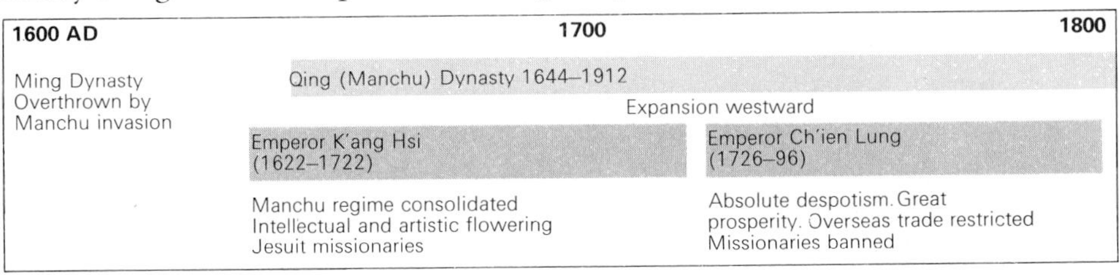

Peasants also cooperated in groups larger than the family. They came together for such activities as crop-watching, irrigation, and invocation of local deities. These activities received the sporadic patronage of the gentry and also, on occasion, of the local officials, who were anxious to control any form of organization which might be potentially seditious. In south China, where greater wealth led to the formation of lineages and clans, the peasants provided the bulk of the membership of these organizations without controlling them.

Most of a peasant's life was lived within the confines of the village or the market, serving a group of villages, to which he brought his produce. At times, endemic unrest, caused by such factors as bad harvests, high rents, or official corruption, would escalate into larger uprisings led by such fringe members of peasant society as bandits, migrants, ex-soldiers, or smugglers. If the conditions were ripe, as at a time of regional or national dislocations and disasters, the uprising might gain further momentum, attracting dissident gentry and officials, until eventually the peasants would briefly enter the national political arena as the force leading to the toppling of the old dynasty and the founding of a new one—when some might enter the new ruling elite, while the great majority returned to their old lives in the villages. Such a course of events happened several times in Chinese history, providing one of the many, and certainly the most dramatic, means whereby the Confucian state system constantly renovated itself. Although Confucian political theory regarded uprisings, like natural disasters, as calamitous, and although Confucian scholar-officials were active and ruthless in their repression, Confucian theory was that a regime which, by misgovernment, provoked rebellions it could not control, deserved to be replaced.

If an extremely hard-working and successful peasant managed to accumulate a little extra land he (or more likely his descendants) might eventually be able to hire extra labor. Then, if his wealth continued to increase, he might even become a small landlord, renting out parcels of land to tenants. A recent study of the account books of a small landlord in east China in the eighteenth and nineteenth centuries shows just how difficult and precarious such a climb from the ranks of the peasantry must have been. It took the family in question all of 200 years to build up an estate of just over thirty acres; each generation narrowly managed to accumulate enough to offset the losses which would attend the partition of the land when the next generation inherited. Luck might play a part in land accumulation; there are many popular tales of sudden windfalls, such as the discovery of buried treasure or the timely murder of a wealthy traveler, leading to a poor peasant acquiring wealth and eventually becoming a landlord. But most never made it.

There were other ways of becoming a member of the wealthy landowning class. One was through trade or money-lending—but where was a peasant to get capital for such activities? Another was to become an official (recruitment was by open examination discussed below)—but where was a peasant to find the leisure to study for the fifteen or twenty years needed to master the curriculum of the Confucian classics and the niceties of a learned language? For most peasants, the struggle to make ends meet and lay aside a small store for bad years were the primary concerns.

By the end of the eighteenth century, even these limited objectives were becoming ever harder to reach. Thousands of years of agricultural development had transformed the Chinese landscape. Where once the whole of China had consisted of scattered village economies, with a total population of hundreds of thousands only, by the eighteenth century agricultural production was at a level of intensity which astounded contemporary European observers. The population had risen to a total of some 400 million, of which about 30 to 40 million lived off the agricultural surplus of the peasants, in hundreds of towns and cities.

The level of population reached in China's greatest cities in the eighteenth century is indicated in a passage from the *Memoirs of Father Ripa during Thirteen Years' Residence at the Court of Peking in the Service of the Emperor of China.* Here Father Ripa, an Italian Catholic missionary, is addressing an English merchant:

*"Have you ever seen Canton from the top of the great tower?"*
*"Yes, I have," he answered.*
*"How large did you think it?"*
*"At least twice as large as London."*
*"Which of the two cities is the most thickly inhabited?"*
*"Canton, by far: its thoroughfares being at all times obstructed with people."*
*"Is it men or women who chiefly form the crowd?"*
*"Oh, no woman is ever seen in the streets of Canton."*
*"Then," said I, "if London contains eight hundred thousand inhabitants, as you say, surely Canton, being twice its size, and with a male population sufficient to throng the streets, must have sixteen hundred thousand; and if Canton contains sixteen hundred thousand, Peking, which is far larger, and more thickly peopled, cannot fail to have at least two millions."*

Although the peasants continued to open up new lands, plant new crops, and raise the yields on already cultivated land, the limits of expansion had just about been reached. Ever-smaller landholdings, however intensively cultivated, produced ever-diminishing margins. At last, in the nineteenth century, massive rural poverty was to be the background to the greatest peasant uprisings the world has ever seen. It is at such points that the peasants enter history—but the tensions and struggles within the various strata of the peasantry were always present, as the constant groundswell to the well-documented lives of the ruling classes.

The teeming city of Kaifeng, on the Hwang Ho (Yellow River) in Honan province, from the *Qing-Ming shanghe* scroll. Kaifeng was the Chinese capital during the eleventh century.

## THE GENTRY

The leading economic and social class in the local communities was the gentry, whose wealth was largely invested in, if not necessarily derived from, landholding. Among smaller gentry members, immediate household needs were usually met from estate produce, and the remainder of the income from land rented out. By the eighteenth century larger gentry tended often to be absentee landlords who left the management and control of their estates to stewards and rent collectors. Other economic activities usually engaged in by the gentry included money-lending and commerce, activities which had always been frowned upon in Confucian ideology as unbefitting a gentleman, but which nevertheless gave the rich the quickest return on investment among the credit-hungry peasantry. Large gentry households would often be situated in the local country town, while the biggest landlords of all would be found operating their many interests from large establishments at the provincial and national capitals. Unlike the peasantry, the gentry constituted large families, with many servants and followers, held together by special endowments to pay for the ceremonial and other supports needed to overcome tensions between family members—especially when parents died and family wealth was divided among sons. Such complex human situations with incidental indications of the economic foundations of a huge gentry household are brilliantly portrayed in one of the greatest Chinese novels, the eighteenth-century *Dream of the Red Chamber*.

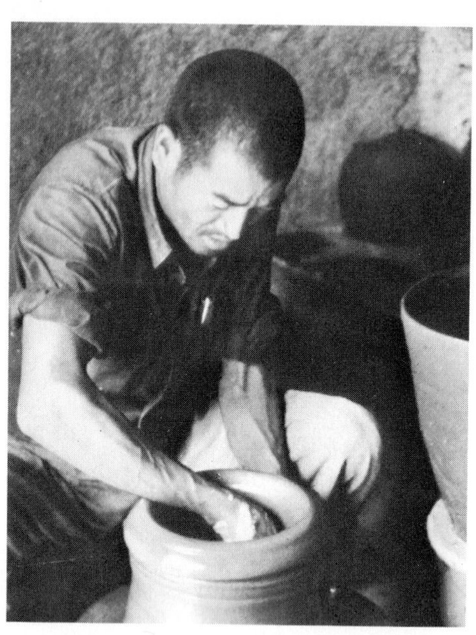

A potter at work. China has long been famous for its ceramics, and among the wares most prized by collectors are those produced in the Song period. Green-glazed pottery of the kind known in the west as "celadon" was a popular Song product: it took its western name from a green-clad shepherd called Celadon who appeared in a pastoral play in Paris in 1610. In Arab countries, it was popularly held that celadon ware would crack if a liquid containing poison was poured into it.

## LOCAL AND NATIONAL OFFICIALDOM

Wealth alone did not decide the status of a gentry family, or qualify its members for entry to the national political elite. Education was the great criterion—and by the eighteenth century education had become completely integrated with the system of civil service examinations. For this reason, a newly rich landlord would urge his sons to study; many gentry households set up special educational bursaries to finance clan schools and family tutors to coach their offspring for the state examinations. If one of its members could not master the examination system, a family might purchase one of the many available honorary degrees or titles, and thus gain some place in the ranks of officialdom. The importance of examinations is apparent even in poetry:

*What agony it was thirty years ago*
*At Peking, waiting for the lists to appear!*
*I was staying for the night at Mr Ni's house,*
*And was hurrying home, prancing along through the dark.*
*On the way I met someone who told me that I had passed;*
*I was bowled over by this thunderclap of joy and surprise . . .*
*Parents, however much they love a child,*
*Have not the power to place him among the chosen few.*
*Only the examiner can bring the young to notice,*
*And out of darkness carry them up to heaven!*

Officials of the imperial bureaucracy ("mandarins") had the unchallenged prestige derived from expressing and embodying the sovereign power of the state. They were regarded as exemplifying those key political and moral values of society whose guardianship was their jealously guarded prerogative. They also had unique opportunities for gaining and conserving wealth. They were accorded legal, fiscal, and sumptuary privileges which, together with the pomp and ceremony which invariably surrounded them, effectively marked them off from the rest of the population. Their main functions were judicial; military; administrative (running the imperial bureaucracy, collecting taxes and so on); ideological (upholding Confucian orthodoxy); and managerial (over-seeing the running of the local communities). It is one of the distinguishing characteristics of Chinese traditional society that entry into officialdom was virtually the only means of gaining high status.

The official elite was extremely small in relation to the total population. In the eighteenth century there were approximately 20,000 ranking civil officials and about 7,000 military officers. To these must be added all those qualified to hold office but awaiting appointment, as well as retired officials and holders of official titles, to arrive at an overall figure of around 80,000. Taking into account the fact that an official's privileges were extended to his immediate household, the total number of the official elite in any one generation (taking five as the average household size) was 300,000. Thus, compared with a population which had risen to a total of about 400 million by the end of the eighteenth century, the official elite appears remarkably small.

However, the tiny number of officials in relation to total population is readily understandable in terms of the functions of officials and their connections with the local elites. More than half the total number of incumbent officials were classified as "officials to oversee officials," and mainly posted in the national capital at Peking. It was only at the lowest rung of the bureaucracy that the 2,000 or so district (or county) magistrates (classified as "officials to oversee the people") actually came into contact with the "people." Even at this level, the district magistrates did not come into direct contact with the populace, but tended to rely upon the informal managerial and governmental service provided by the gentry, the leading class of the local communities. For it was from this class that the officials themselves had been drawn, and it was to this class that they would return upon retirement. Both groups shared a common ethos, and both belonged to the ruling strata in Chinese society. One eighteenth-century magistrate wrote about how useful his contacts with the gentry proved to be:

A nineteenth-century photograph of a local official presiding over a court of law. Although the legal system was well organized, China's was not a legalistic society: disputes and minor crimes were usually dealt with in the local community according to local custom.

> *When I arrived at Ning-yuan (a district in south-west Hunan where the writer was district magistrate for four years) I was like an ignoramus. So whenever guests arrived I humbly questioned each of them about local conditions and asked for the names of rowdies and ruffians. . . . Secretly I prepared a small notebook in which I carefully noted everything my guests told me as soon as they departed. Concerning pettifoggers, bullies and thieves, I put on record age, features and abode. Every time before going into the court hall I glanced through my notebook, and if I saw people bearing a resemblance to those recorded in it, I picked them out and gave my instructions. Everybody was dumbfounded. Thus the law was enforced without offense and before the end of the year I knew the essential facts about the territory under my jurisdiction. . . .*

Actual day-to-day administration was handled by an unofficial, local, sub-bureaucracy of clerks, *yamen* (official residence) runners, and the like, whose numbers may have reached more than a million by the eighteenth century. Although unpaid and accorded little or no status, this sub-bureaucracy played a vital part in handling the details of local business which the local magistrate could not hope to master, for he was usually only posted to a district for two or three years and often might be unable to speak the local dialect.

While the local gentry mediated between the officials and the general populace, the elite of national officials stood between the emperor and the gentry. Much of the political tensions and clashes of interest in Chinese history arose from the varying stresses between the emperor, the imperial bureaucracy, and the local elites, stresses which were exacerbated by the fact that officials were also members of their own local elite. For this reason, officials were forbidden to hold posts in their native provinces or to buy land where they were serving, and no two members of the same family were allowed to serve in the same province or in the same department of the central government. But despite regulations designed to combat localism and nepotism, regional cliques often formed within the bureaucracy, and many officials used their office to advance the interests of their kin.

As a group, Chinese officials (and the educated members of the gentry from whom they were drawn) were characterized by an adherence to a traditional humanistic ethic—Confucian orthodoxy—which stressed the importance of understanding, embodying, and regulating social relations (especially familial relations) according to norms laid down in the Confucian classics and their commentaries. A Ming writer summed it up: "Maintenance of moral tradition is the main task in government." A proper understanding of the "moral tradition" was considered the most important qualification for entry into officialdom, and thus formed the main subject matter of the civil service examinations. By the eighteenth century, this led to a stereotyping of traditional learning at the expense of innovation. This was wryly expressed by the author of China's finest comprehensive summary of traditional technology, when he said in the preface to his work, *Tian-gong kai-wu* (1637),

> *An ambitious scholar will undoubtedly toss this book onto his desk and give it no further thought: it is a work that is in no way concerned with the art of advancement in officialdom.*

An itinerant barber at work in a Chinese town. The queues of hair, popularly known as pigtails, worn by the men in this picture were imposed on the Chinese as a mark of servitude by the Qing conquerors from Manchuria in the seventeenth century. The pigtail was abolished when the Chinese Republic was founded in 1912.

The peasantry and the gentry (ignoring the various sub-divisions within them) were the two main classes in Chinese society in the eighteenth century. The peasantry were as old as Chinese history itself; the gentry had finally emerged as a non-aristocratic local and national elite by the time of the Song dynasty. No description of Chinese society in the eighteenth century, however, would be complete without discussing the role of the imperial elite, at the apex of society, and the various groups of outcast people at its base.

## THE IMPERIAL ELITE

By the eighteenth century, the aristocracy in China had long ceased to exist as a political force. Aristocratic power had been at its height during the latter part of the Zhou dynasty. It was to make spasmodic appearances thereafter, but it was gradually and effectively replaced by the ever-increasing power of the emperor in alliance with a non-hereditary bureaucracy recruited from the local gentry.

During the Song and later dynasties, including the Qing, the aristocracy had no independent existence apart from imperial favor: hereditary titles, privileges, and stipends were conferred upon members of the imperial clan and upon those who performed exceptional services for the emperor, but, significantly, both the imperial and non-imperial nobility were supervised by special departments of the bureaucracy. Certain ranks of nobility might place their holders at the apex of privilege in society, but the titles in themselves carried no real power. Indeed, the downward mobility of most of the imperial clansmen and hereditary imperial nobility had become so great by the late eighteenth century that special routes into the regular bureaucracy were opened for them. Hereditary privilege only carried political power in the small, closed circle of the emperor's immediate relatives and only in the arena of imperial court politics.

Although China never had a caste system, there existed in all periods small caste-like groups of hereditary slaves and menials. What distinguished these small groups from the rest of the population was their supposed inherent moral baseness, reflecting the Confucian view that society was divided into the "good," who formed the vast majority, and the "base," a small minority. By the eighteenth century, the main categories of "base" people were uprooted elements such as beggars, actors, or prostitutes, or menial workers such as barbers, household servants, or chattel slaves. Other categories included certain servants of officials and various regionally defined base people. The origins of the base people are often obscure, but they included unassimilated ethnic minorities, defeated rebel groups, families of criminals, those sold at times of famine, and the like. Base people were not allowed to marry into the families of "good" people; they were also the only members of the population prohibited from entering officialdom, either by taking examinations or by purchase. However the comparatively small number of the base people indicates the weakness of notions of hereditary privilege or closed-caste status in eighteenth-century China.

## MERCHANTS AND CRAFTSMEN

One class remains to be examined, that of the merchants and craftsmen. By the end of the eighteenth century, China's urban population numbered between 30 and 40 million. The problem of feeding and equipping this huge non-agricultural population gave rise to many pursuits associated with trade and specialized handicrafts, conducted by a large number of merchants and craftsmen.

Chinese craftsmen had extremely high standards; they were unrivaled in many fields, including bronze-casting, porcelain- and paper-making, silk weaving and jade-carving. Apart from village and cottage handicraft industries, which served local needs for pots and pans and rough, strongly woven clothing materials (of which cotton was the most important), townsfolk were catered for by small handicraft workshops, numbering a dozen or so masters and apprentices. The biggest groups of craftsmen characteristically were those working under direct bureaucratic control in the imperial kilns, craft workshops, silk and brocade factories, and other establishments, which produced magnificent and costly trappings for the emperor, his palaces, and his court.

A European artist's impression of a dinner party at the home of a mandarin, or local magnate. The scholar-gentry constituted a local elite in traditional Chinese society: their political and administrative functions, won through the examination system and sanctioned by the emperor, were reinforced by their large holdings of land and capital. The Chinese name for a local official is *kuan*; "mandarin" was the term applied to them by Portuguese traders, and is a form of the Hindi or Malay word *mantri*, a minister of state.

Although ranked below the craftsmen in official ideology, merchants played a ubiquitous and vital role in the economy at every level, from the local peddler with his entire capital on his back to the wealthy state monopolist. Like their medieval Western counterparts, Chinese merchants engaged in money-lending and usury; they also pioneered the use of paper money and developed banking institutions and monopolistic guilds. But unlike their Western counterparts, Chinese merchants never developed a sense of their own identity and worth to set against the anti-commercial values of the scholar-officials. They were never able to challenge the power of the Confucian state system which, while granting the necessity of commerce, accorded merchants comparatively low status and controlled them strictly. Chinese urban centers never became the base for a politically powerful "middle-class" situated between the aristocrats and peasants, as in Europe, but remained centers of Confucian learning and administration and of the great gentry families. No matter how wealthy a Chinese merchant became, he could only attain political power and social status by urging his sons to study and pass the state examinations, by purchasing a degree, or by patronizing the arts of the Confucian literati: calligraphy, painting, classical scholarship, book-collecting, and so on. There was no question of the merchants offering a challenge to established values—values which, for the most part, they enthusiastically endorsed.

In a consideration of the overall characteristics of Chinese state and society in the eighteenth century, it may first be noted that the existence of a single dominant

# Chinese Science

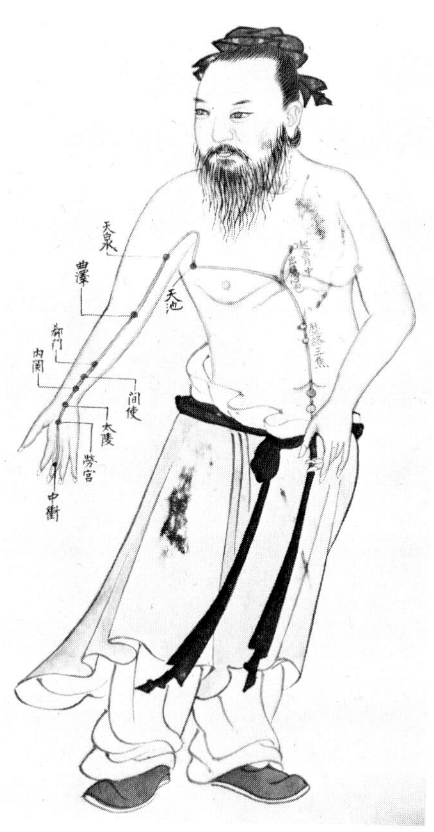


*Above:* Series of acupuncture points used in the combat of diseases of the heart and sexual organs, eighteenth-century watercolor. Acupuncture, an ancient Chinese medical practice, has not yet been fully evaluated by western scientists.

*Right above:* A traditional blowing-engine for a forge and furnace, taken from the *Thu Shu Chi Chhang* encyclopedia of c.1726. The technique of making cast iron was discovered in China as early as the beginning of the first millennium B.C.

*Right below:* Classical Chinese silk-weaving machine, from the *Tshan Sang Ho Pien* of Sha Shi-An, a technological work published in 1843. Also described in the eleventh-century *Tshan Shu* of Chhin Kuan.

It is a remarkable fact that in the history of mankind there are only two essentially independent scientific traditions. One tradition has its roots in the Middle East in the third millennium B.C., passed from there to classical Greece, thence through the Arabs to Western Christendom, and finally, with the scientific renaissance, spread out to embrace the earth. The second tradition has its roots in the plain of China's Yellow River, flourished outstandingly in the Han and Tang dynasties, and then gradually withered away, without ever acquiring the internal dynamic that ensured the survival of science in the West. Both the successes and the failures of Chinese science are significant, the more so because China provides the only available testbed for historical theories that purport to explain the evolution of science in the West.

Although Chinese science broadly parallels western science in the *order* in which subjects were opened up—arithmetic, algebra, astronomy and medicine in the early period, and optics, magnetism and chemistry rather later—the *dates* at which particular discoveries were made by no means match up, and until the scientific renaissance the Chinese were generally ahead, often by many centuries, particularly in the more "applied" aspects of the subject. Reference has already been made to the discovery of the technique of casting iron during the Zhou dynasty: the principal achievements of the Han dynasty likewise anticipated the West by several centuries. Decimal-place-value arithmetic was already established by the first century B.C.: Chinese artisans were by then checking their work with decimally calibrated calipers. Chinese observational astronomy was also several centuries ahead: they were recording sunspots in the first century B.C. and making lists of nova, meteors and comets by the seventh century A.D. at the latest. Their astronomical instruments were superior—for example they had developed a mechanical clock mechanism, and were using it to align instruments with astronomical objects by the first century B.C. They were worrying about the cause of magnetic declination (the tendency for a compass needle to point slightly *downwards*) long before the Europeans ever knew it pointed north. They constructed the first practical seismograph (c. A.D. 130).

In parallel with these strictly scientific achievements came a wealth of developments in technology—the construction of efficient horse-harnesses, the discovery of the co-fusion and direct oxidation processes for making steel, the invention of the differential gear, gunpowder, paper and movable-type printing. Unlike their scientific work, which in good approximation had no effect upon developments in the West, their technological advances did spread by diffusion, particularly during the Yuan and early Ming dynasties (thirteenth and fourteenth centuries) when China briefly passed through an outward-looking phase. However, their self-imposed isolationism in the succeeding centuries successfully protected them against infection by the Renaissance spirit, and there was never a Chinese Galileo.

The reasons for this failure of the Chinese scientific tradition, and indeed for its initial successes, can perhaps be found in their social structure. Reference has already been made to the centralized bureaucratic regime which was established in China during the Qin dynasty, a mode of government which was consistent with the Confucian social philosophy and which in fact survived only minor modifications up to the nineteenth century. It is perhaps significant that the two most successful periods of Chinese science—the Han dynasty (202 B.C.–A.D. 220) and the Sui and Tang dynasties (A.D. 581–906)—occur respectively immediately after the the establishment of this bureaucracy in the Qin dynasty, and after its reformation in the Sui dynasty so that its officials were selected on "merit" by examination. Although this more democratic mode of selection of officials—the "mandarins" as they came to be called—undoubtedly made some difference, it remained broadly true that there was a great and almost unbridgeable social gulf between this stratum of society and those whom they governed. Higher still in the pecking order were the immediate relatives of the imperial household, and these had a significant impact on the development of Chinese science.

Liu An, the Prince of Huainan (who ruled in about 130 B.C.) with his entourage of naturalists, alchemists and astronomers, is one of the most famous figures in Chinese history. Another Han prince, Liu Ch hung, who ruled in about A.D. 170 invented the grid sight for the crossbow, and the late-eighth-century

Tang prince Li Kao was interested in acoustics and physics and was responsible for the development of a paddle-wheel warship. The patronage of science by rich men of leisure such as these was certainly one of the factors that favored the development of science in China as compared with the West. However, the mandarin stratum of society was unquestionably more important in determining the overall flavor of Chinese science. Their activities were broadly comparable to those of the scientific civil service today: indeed, during the Han dynasty most of the trades that possessed the more advanced techniques were "nationalized." For example, there was a "Salt and Iron Authority," and a string of "imperial workshops" in each of the main provincial cities. In organizations such as these, teams of artisans worked under the supervision of a senior civil servant, and some of the most striking achievements of the Han dynasty resulted, including the development of the seismograph by Chang Hêng and the introduction of the water-powered metallurgical blowing-engine by Tu Shih in about 31 B.C. This pattern continued in later dynasties and, for example, Shen Kua in about 1080 in his charming scientific book *Dream Pool Essays* ascribes the invention of movable-type printing to a technician, Pi Shêng (about 1045) and says that after his death his font of type "passed into the possession of my followers, among whom it has been kept as a precious possession until now." This account illustrates both the strength and the weakness of the Chinese bureaucratic society as a milieu for scientific and technological advance. On the favorable side, Pi Shêng enjoyed the encouragement, security and state financial support which a complex task such as the development of printing requires: on the unfavorable side, he was a commoner, on the wrong side of a great social divide, and was perhaps never given adequate scope to exercise personal initiative on an intellectual plane. The men who had this scope—the officials—lacked the practical experience of the real world of the commoners that they directed (the long fingernails of the mandarins somehow symbolize their attitude to practical endeavor) and so the great fusion of abstract intellectual thought and planned experiment which brought about the scientific renaissance in the West never took place in China.

set of authoritarian values, backed by a single dominant class, made China a very different place from the pluralistic Europe of the same period. The key managerial and functional elite in China, the gentry and the officials, performed many of the roles undertaken by specialized groups in Europe. Thus, the gentry had a quasi-religious monopoly not only of political values, but also of the accepted moral values of society. There was in China no institutionalized church standing apart from the state and at times providing shelter for important dissident groups and ideas as in Europe. Buddhism was kept under strict state control. There were only the scholar-gentry and the officials. Compiling indexes of prohibited books and investigating and purging heterodox ideas were as old as the Chinese empire. But far more important than these punitive means of maintaining orthodoxy was the linkage of learning and scholarship with political power and social esteem, making these the rewards for adopting fully the values of Confucian orthodoxy. It was a rare man—almost a social deviant—who strayed from the narrow confines of accepted thought. It has been shown that aristocracies, the Buddhist religion, the army (led by the great border generals), the merchants, in short all possible countervailing elites which might have developed a competing set of values, were destroyed or absorbed, and their place taken by the scholar-gentry and officials.

Many of the institutions of the Confucian bureaucracy were later adopted in the West. The concept and practice, for example, of graded examinations as a means of testing merit for entrance into the civil service were only adopted in Europe in the nineteenth century, while the practice of institutionalized criticism from within the bureaucracy (provided in China by the censors) lies behind the twentieth-century function of the ombudsman. The development of the Confucian state was a slow one (although by no means the oldest, China's is by far the longest continuous political culture), and this may help to explain the unusual degree to which the values of the gentry permeated all classes. It should also be remembered that general suffusion of Confucian values was greatly aided by the lack of institutionalized barriers between classes.

The very success of the Chinese system, and its undisputed preeminence for so many centuries in east Asia, was to make it extremely difficult for the gentry and officials to accept that fundamental adjustments were required to meet the Western influx of the nineteenth century. Radical change was only to come with the growth of new elites capable of repudiating Confucianism and overthrowing its gentry supporters.

## ELITE AND POPULAR CULTURES

An excellent way of working towards an understanding of Chinese civilization is through an examination of its literary and artistic achievements. A wide range of art books and translations of Chinese literature is now available, and collections in American museums and galleries house some of the finest works of Chinese art (the loss of which the Chinese keenly resent), so these are aspects of China's culture that Americans are well placed to explore for themselves.

It has been estimated that before A.D. 1500 more books were published in China than in the rest of the world put together. Although much has been lost over the centuries, a huge quantity of Chinese literature still survives. The main reason for this considerable survival is that by the eleventh century the Chinese had already begun to print books on paper with movable type. Although the majority of the population remained illiterate until comparatively recently, this meant that copies of books were produced fairly cheaply and in large numbers. The consequent mass of material defies brief summary, but three of the most important aspects of Chinese literature—history, poetry, and popular fiction—are considered here.

### Historiography

No culture has been more concerned with historical record than the Chinese, whose historians—generally officials writing either in their capacity as government historians or privately—have left a great deal of organized evidence, often presented in convenient form, for the study of political history at the top level. In addition, provincial and district histories (of which about 7,000 survive) provide much information on local elites. The facts they give are extremely reliable, but the sense of history of Chinese officials usually made them particularly careful to reveal only such information as suited their purposes. Anything not falling within the purview of Confucian historiography was simply left out: thus, the fact that a certain scholar made a fortune through managing a chain of pawnshops would be passed over in silence, and the lives of those who were not scholar-officials or active in national politics were rarely mentioned. Another characteristic of Confucian historiography was its view that although details alter from time to time, essence remains the same. History was not normally regarded as a process of qualitative change, but rather as a compendium of administrative and political case studies to be used by the wise bureaucrat as a guide to future political action. The modern scholar must sift carefully through the processed materials left by the Confucian historians, asking very different questions from those posed or answered by the original compilers.

### Poetry and the Visual Arts

It was not only in historiography that past precedent was held in deep esteem; this was also true of the other arts. Freshness, abandon, or spontaneity were not usually regarded as desirable qualities by the elite. This did not mean that there was absolutely no creativity; but rather that imperial China's value system stressed order, tradition, and established morality. Individuality, freedom, and innovation were regarded as dangerous, because they were potentially disruptive. The Chinese saw no point in attempting to improve on the ancients if they had done something well. Thus, if a style of poetry had reached a height of perfection there was every reason to emulate it rather than to seek a new mode. During the Tang dynasty, a great deal of fine poetry was written in the *shi* style, a form developed under the Han and based on folk poetry. As a result, *shi* continued to be written in the Tang style for the next thousand years, despite the fact that the language had changed so much that Tang rhymes had to be reconstructed with the aid of rhyming dictionaries. Eventually the Tang *shi* became a deliberately archaic form, mastery of which was required as part of the syllabus of the civil service examinations. (The *shi* style retains its popularity in modern China: Mao Tse-tung himself writes *shi* poems.) Outside the classical forms, folksong and ballads developed along with the living language, and the elite even turned to the lyrics of popular music from western Asia for new inspiration. Even so, the poet was characteristically a scholar and an official, and the criteria for judging literary innovations included moral ones. Fortunately, the Confucians did not have it all their own way: there is far more variety and individuality to be found in Chinese poetry than the strict Confucian would approve.

The influence of Confucian moral criteria was also strongly felt in the visual arts. Even in calligraphy, the pre-eminent art of China and the most abstract of the visual arts, the many years of rigorous practice required for its mastery were held to reflect the moral caliber of the calligrapher. In painting too, the work of professionals was less highly regarded than the amateur work of the Confucian scholar-gentlemen. By Ming times the mere expert was despised; and the professional painter in China never enjoyed the prestige (and with it the greater freedom) gained by his counterparts in the West during and after the Renaissance. By Ming times, the division between gentlemen-painters, who prided themselves on being above mere technical facility, and professional artists who tended towards the decorative and intricate, was a wide one—and both sides suffered in consequence. Despite these unfavorable circumstances, much fine work was done, although the influence of accepted canons and past styles continued to be strongly felt to the end of imperial times and even beyond.

Much of the Chinese art that now attracts most admiration in the West, such as the great range of ceramics produced from Neolithic times onward, was the work of unknown craftsmen. Their works, like those of the weavers and dyers of silks and cottons, are among the productions of Chinese culture that make the most immediate appeal.

A fan painting of the Song period. The materials used by Chinese painters were the same as those used for calligraphy—the two arts are so closely akin as to almost be one in China—bamboo brushes tipped with hairs of varying thicknesses were used to apply colors and washes. Ink was produced by grinding sticks made from a mixture of pinewood charcoal and gum on a wetted stone.

The values of ruling-class culture—restraint, tradition, morality, scholarship, refinement, and so on—were shared to some extent by the mass of the population. At the same time, the common people had their own traditions, and these sometimes stood in opposition to those of the high culture, although related to them. When, for example, an official or landlord hung a scroll picture on his wall, he would probably choose an ink study of a landscape or plant, typically selected for its moral symbolism: a bamboo for its ability to adapt itself by bending without breaking: a mountain pine standing rugged against the storm; a winter blossom for its capacity to flower in adverse circumstances. But a peasant would choose something colorful to brighten his home, with a theme that would cheer him up and bring good luck, such as fat sons, or fish to symbolize abundance. He would also want pictures of fierce warriors, which were thought to keep away demons.

Popular culture had few inhibitions regarding violence. The village storytellers were more likely to glorify "have-sword-will-travel" outlaws than mild-mannered scholars. Often, the deeds of such heroes were based on the real-life exploits of those regarded as bandits or rebels by the officials; as a consequence, efforts were made to prevent such stories circulating. In the villages, peasant boys would gaze with admiration at displays of swordsmanship and acrobatics by professional teachers of the martial arts. This aspect of the popular culture found its way into print in the great cities of Song times and later, where there were readers sufficiently rich and literate to buy books but not necessarily interested in studying the classical curriculum of the civil service examinations. The most famous of the picaresque stories of adventure eventually took the form of a novel, *Shui hu zhuan* (translated as *Water Margin* or *All Men Are Brothers*), which is still immensely popular today. Not the least of the attractions of the popular novels was the fact that they were written in a style not too far removed from everyday speech. By contrast, the literature of the scholar elite was written in a style which took years of study to master.

## Popular Religion

In the field of religious beliefs, there were even stronger contrasts between elite and popular practices. Although most people were imbued with the Confucian values, the intellectual forms of Buddhism or Daoism to which the educated turned for consolation had little general appeal. The religion of the peasantry varied widely in different parts of the country, depending on different combinations of Chinese and pre-Chinese beliefs. It was essentially a series of practices designed to keep at bay the supernatural equivalents of the landlord, the bailiff, the official, the bandit, and the host of clerks and constables in the local government offices. With gods, as with men, it was a question of knowing whom to bribe, how much, and when, in order to avert disaster.

There was also a latent underground religion that surfaced at times of natural disaster, war, exceptional misgovernment, or the breakdown of order. This underground religion, which provided much of the ideology for the great popular rebellions, took many forms: Daoist, Buddhist, Nestorian, and even, in the nineteenth century, Protestant Christianity. Whatever its form, the religion of these great popular upheavals was starkly dualistic. Like the millenarian movements of medieval Europe or South America, it saw the world divided between the good people and the demons. For a new era of peace and prosperity to begin, it was necessary for the forces of good to struggle with and destroy the forces of evil. The underground religion, repeatedly suppressed for 2,000 years, especially in the aftermath of the revolts it inspired, proved to be ineradicable.

## CHINA: LIMITATIONS—AND ACHIEVEMENT

Having examined some of the contrasts between the Confucian cultural values of the elite and those of the illiterate peasantry, this account concludes with two further instances of the self-imposed restraint and deliberate intellectual narrowness of the gentry. It is perhaps not surprising that in the arts of music and dance the high culture had nothing but suspicion, if not contempt, for music that was not carefully regulated, refined, and rhythmically restrained. There were professional musicians, but they never overcame the stigma of "baseness" attached to their profession as entertainers. The lively and rhythmic music and dance of Chinese central Asia, the choral singing of some of the peoples of the south, and the haunting melodies of Chinese folksong have survived to the present despite, rather than because of, the efforts of the ruling elite. To the Confucian gentleman, the outward display of most emotions was a regrettable indulgence. Not surprisingly, the gentry expressed public abhorrence of the appeal of strong rhythms, seductive tunes, and the human body in motion; if they enjoyed such things, they preferred to do so in private.

The author of the most extensive work on technology in traditional China was quoted earlier as remarking that scholars would simply discard his book because it had nothing to do with getting on in officialdom. Most Confucian scholars tended to regard technology as something best left to the peasantry, because it had nothing to do with the moral and political questions which were the scholars' main concern. This attitude may help to explain why, although China was technically the world's most advanced civilization until at least A.D. 1400, the Chinese never developed a full scientific method: the educated elite by and large was not interested in such questions. Despite this drawback, it should not be forgotten that many Chinese scientific and technological discoveries were made far in advance of the West and played a vital part in the transformation of Europe from the late middle ages onward. In this connection may be mentioned cast iron; various types of mill and water-powered machinery; gunpowder; the mariner's compass, and many aspects of ship design that made possible the nautical expansion of Europe; paper and printing, including the use of movable type; and the technology of canals. But the list calls for constant extension, for many of China's contributions to world technology and science are only now beginning to receive due recognition, and some of them, such as the medical technique of acupuncture, have hardly begun to be evaluated in the West.

The Chinese of the twentieth century have rejected much of their old culture as feudal, or useless in the new technologically oriented society. But much still remains, either in its original form or blended with western and other styles. And many of the old values, unaltered or in a new form, still mold Chinese behavior today.

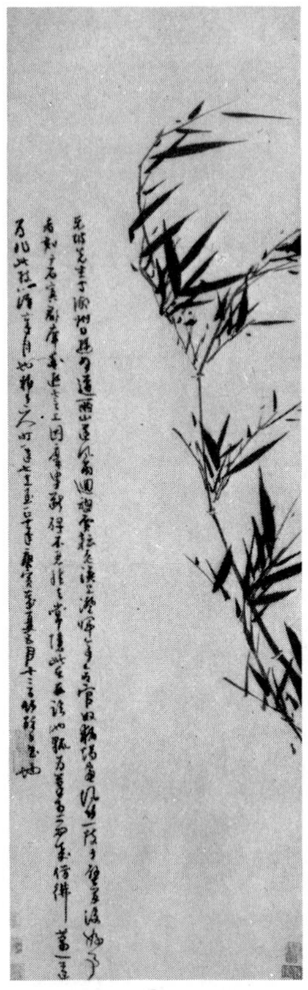

A bamboo bending in the wind, a traditional theme of Chinese art, by Wu Zhen (1280–1354), together with a specimen of classical Chinese calligraphy. Calligraphy, which has gradually evolved from pictorial signs, has been one of the main forces maintaining Chinese unity, for it is not affected by regional differences in language and dialect and its basic character has remained unchanged for some 2,000 years. Written Chinese contains around 50,000 characters, although only between 2,000 and 4,000 are in everyday use, and since 1956 large-scale calligraphic reform has been undertaken.

Chapter 6

# JAPAN IN THE EARLIEST TIMES

## JAPAN IN THE EARLIEST TIMES

A brief notice on Japan in the *Wei Chih*, the chronicles of the Chinese kingdom of Wei compiled in A.D. 297, suggests that at that time the Japanese were still little influenced by Chinese culture. Chinese visitors to Kyushu, the southernmost island of Japan, describe the Japanese as being much concerned with taboos, ritual cleanliness, and class distinction. Thus, lesser mortals encountering important men on the road were required to withdraw to the roadside. Notables often had four or five wives, who were reported to be faithful to their men. The people were fond of dancing, singing, and drinking. There was no theft.

It is interesting to notice how many of the above characteristics—some associated with the native religion now known as *Shinto*, are still to be observed in modern Japan. A further characteristic, also associated with Shinto, is the love of simplicity and of nature so often encountered in the cultural history of Japan. Traditional Japanese society consisted overwhelmingly of peasants and fishermen living close to nature in largely self-sufficient, cooperative villages. The social structure formed by this kind of life and by the beliefs which attend Shinto have created a hard core of "Japaneseness" which has never been completely eroded, despite the massive importation and adaptation of Chinese civilization which led to the high culture of classical Japan in the Nara and Heian periods (A.D. 710–1184), and despite the modern importation of many aspects of Western civilization.

The origins of the Japanese people are the subject of much conjecture and controversy, but a general outline is fairly widely accepted. Physically, the Japanese are Mongoloid people with some admixture with the Ainu, a Caucasoid people unaccountably found in central and north Japan from earliest historical times. Korean, Chinese, and southeast Asian types are still recognizable in the population. As with physical origins, cultural origins are largely north Asian, with a secondary element from southern China and southeast Asia.

The earliest extant Japanese historical chronicles were written in the early eighth century in a mixture of Chinese and Japanese-Chinese characters being used phonetically to write Japanese. Japanese was an entirely different language than Chinese but had some structural affinities to Korean and the Altaic languages of northeast Asia. Although later borrowings from Chinese greatly enriched its vocabulary, Japanese has remained essentially the same structurally.

| 600 AD | 700 | 800 | 900 | 1000 | 1100 | 1200 | 1300 | 1400 | 1500 | 1600 |
|---|---|---|---|---|---|---|---|---|---|---|
| | Nara period | Heian period | | | | Era of the Shoguns (to 1868) | | | | |
| Buddhism introduced<br>Shintoism (native)<br>Main period of Chinese influence | | | Feudalism. Warring lords<br>Power of Emperor declines | | | Kamakura Shogunate<br>Mongols fail to conquer Japan | Ashikaga Shogunate | Civil wars | Portuguese arrive | Tokugawa Shogunate<br>Japan sealed off |

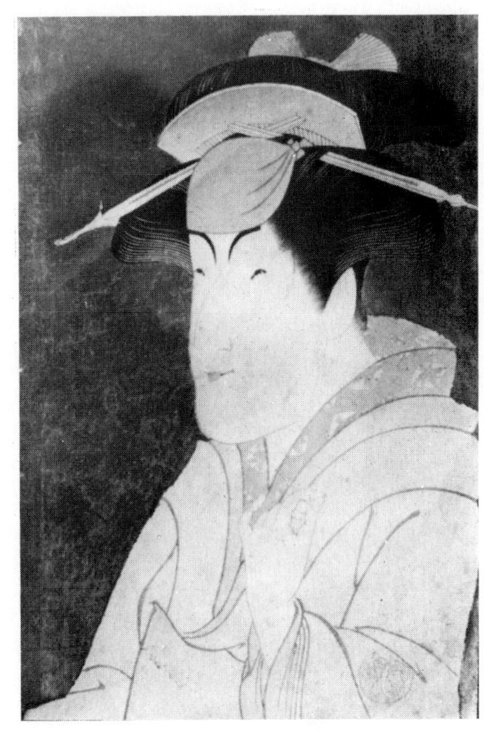

*Above:* A portrait of an actor whose elaborately pinned hairstyle suggests that he is depicted in a female role. This work is in the style of Toshusai Sharaku, whom many authorities consider to be the greatest of the Japanese print masters. Little is known of Sharaku, who was active in 1794–95: it is thought that he may himself have been an actor in the traditional *Nō* theater.

*Left:* Minamoto Yoritomo, the first of the shoguns, military governors, who gave Japan strong semi-feudal rule in the late twelfth century. This is a copy of a painting by Fujiwara Takanobu (1142–1205).

*Top:* A village street, a detail of a painting by Ichiryūsai Hiroshige (1797–1858). Hiroshige was one of the finest print masters of the early nineteenth century, and certainly one of the most prolific Japanese artists: his output has been estimated at 5,460 works. Although this detail centers on human figures, it was as a painter of panoramic landscapes that Hiroshige excelled.
*Above:* Another detail from a painting by Hiroshige. The life of Japanese boatmen provided a frequent subject for the artists of *Ukiyo-e* (the Floating World) prints, which portrayed scenes from the everyday life and surroundings of ordinary folk. One of the most attractive features of Hiroshige's works is a delicate sense of humor, apparent in this sympathetic study of boatmen's children.

## GEOGRAPHICAL INFLUENCES ON JAPANESE HISTORY

"The people of Wa (Japan) dwell in the middle of the ocean on mountainous islands," begins the notice on Japan in the *Wei Chih*. And although the geographical position of Japan, some 115 miles from the tip of Korea at its closest point, is fixed, its degree of geographical isolation is not. For sailing ships, those 115 miles were very dangerous, and the consequent isolation of Japan in early historical times contributed to the attainment of a high degree of cultural homogeneity, national consciousness, and pride in political independence. Before the improvement of communications in modern times, Japan was free to choose involvement or disengagement, piracy or war, or peaceful trade and cultural exchanges with its continental neighbors.

The area of Japan is about 143,000 square miles, a little less than that of Montana, and the country is extremely mountainous. Only about 16 percent of its surface is flat enough for agriculture. Not all of that small percentage is naturally flat: much land has been leveled by human labor, most strikingly in the terracing of slopes, often to create irrigated rice paddies. Soils are relatively infertile, requiring the use of huge quantities of fertilizers.

Japan's population problem dates back for centuries. As early as 1339, Kitabatake Chikafusa (names here are given Japanese-style, with family name first) wrote that "the dynastic warfare . . . is due to the claims of an unlimited number of persons on a limited amount of land," an underlying theme of much Japanese history. There have been many famines, the last in 1837. To counterbalance the country's disadvantages, Japanese tradition has made virtues of poverty, frugality, and hard work, and a favorable climate allied to human ingenuity has enabled the country to support an ever-increasing population. Even now, with a population exceeding 100 million, Japan is virtually self-sufficient in food, having achieved the highest crop yields in the world.

The regular monsoon in June and July, bringing warm rains from the south to most of Japan, helped set the rhythm of agricultural life and made irrigated rice cultivation possible. The necessity of sharing labor and water resources molded society in a way which still has important social and political implications.

Japan's modern industrialization was achieved despite a serious lack of basic mineral resources, such as oil and iron ore. Although coal is relatively abundant, it is of poor quality and is difficult to mine. However, these scarcities were less important in Japan's mainly agrarian society before industrialization, for there was enough copper, and sometimes gold, to export to China and Korea.

## EARLY RELATIONS WITH CHINA

Japanese history may be roughly divided into three cultural periods. First, the indigenous Japanese period, before A.D. 645 when, in the Taira period, reformers began their efforts to recreate Japan in the Chinese image. Second, a long period in which Japan was, in varying degrees, under Chinese cultural influence. Third, after a remarkable but abortive period of openness to Western influences in the sixteenth and early seventeenth centuries, a period since 1868 in which Japan has been reacting as positively to the impact of the military power, technology, and ideas of the West as it did to those of China.

In Japan's bronze-iron age (roughly from the third century B.C. to the sixth century A.D.), centuries before deliberate and large-scale borrowing from China began, there was already some significant cultural influence from the continent. New military and agricultural techniques, such as the use of metal implements and better methods of rice cultivation, were brought to Japan largely by people pushed out from the mainland as the Chinese expanded southward. The success of these migrants in Japan established a pattern of receptivity and enthusiasm for new ideas from abroad which became a recurring phenomenon.

After the official introduction of Chinese script in A.D. 405, and of Buddhism, probably around 538, radical changes in society along Chinese lines became a possibility. There was a growing realization of Japan's weakness, lack of unity, and backwardness in comparison with China and Korea. Politically, economically, and culturally, Japan was still an undeveloped country compared to China under the great Sui and Tang dynasties (589–906), which was then perhaps the best governed, most prosperous, powerful, and culturally advanced country in the world. It is not surprising that China's example was extremely attractive to Japanese leaders, especially when the feasibility of a non-Chinese culture adopting Chinese ways was being demonstrated in Korea.

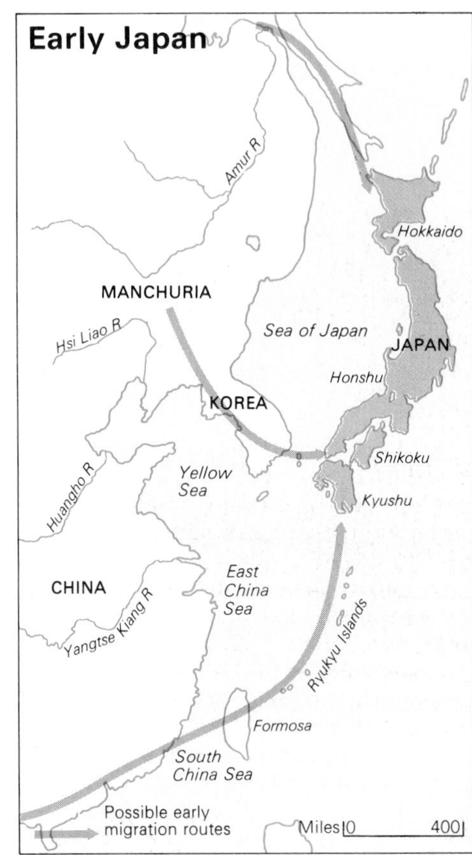


## IMPERIAL JAPAN

The Prince Regent Shōtoku Taishi (574–622) had a vision of a united and prosperous Japan under the emperor and did much to prepare for it. But the time was not ripe, for Japan was still divided into semi-autonomous clans or lineage groups (*uji*). Although these sometimes cooperated with the imperial clan, they were often involved in internecine power struggles. However, in 645, determined reformers seized control of the government in a coup d'état, and thus made possible the beginning of purposeful and effective cultural borrowing.

First, the Chinese principle of the emperor's ultimate ownership of all land was asserted, and land reform based on the government-operated "equal field" system of the Chinese kingdom of Wei began to be applied to increasing areas of rice land classified as public domain. A system of provincial government and uniform taxation was established to replace the partial and irregular methods previously operated. A centralized government structure on the Chinese model was established, in which the important clan leaders who supported the emperor were given the highest posts. Less important clan chiefs were given either lesser positions at court or posts in provincial administration.

As fields in the former clan domains were absorbed into the new system of land tenure, which distributed labor uniformly and provided regular and increasing tax revenues for the imperial government, the clan chiefs lost some of their local political autonomy. But they lost little economically, for more rational management of land and labor resulted in higher yields. They also gained in prestige as the recipients of court titles and offices dispensed by the imperial government. In all these measures, adjustments were made to suit Chinese models to Japanese conditions. But sometimes too many concessions were made to entrenched interests—and sometimes not enough changes were made to ensure the effectiveness of the new institutions.

### An Established Court

Before 710, the emperors had no real permanent residence. Death was thought to defile a house, so the imperial court was obliged to move every time an emperor died. Then, at Nara, complexes of buildings were erected to house the imperial family and high officials, so a new emperor could simply establish himself in a different building. Nara, on the fertile Yamato plain, was laid out in a rectangular grid in the manner of the Chinese capital at Sian, although most buildings were of wood rather than of the stone preferred in China. The main streets were very wide and were lined with orange trees. About 10,000 court officials resided at Nara, and judging from the poems in the *Manyōshū*, the earliest surviving anthology, they busied themselves in the creation of an ever-stronger central government, both economically and politically. A sense of pride and purpose is evident in the poems written by officials sent to govern distant provinces, to keep the Ainu at bay in the northeast, or on missions to Korea or China.

From the seventh century onward, Japanese artists quickly absorbed Chinese artistic techniques and ideas, most often those associated with Buddhist art and architecture. At Nara, and especially at Heian (modern Kyoto), artists worked towards an art less monumental, simpler, and more personal, with elements of humor—an art which can be called typically Japanese.

Buddhist establishments already in the region of Nara built fine temples, monasteries, and nunneries. The Emperor Shōmu, a devout Buddhist, built the huge Tōdaiji temple to house a fifty-three-feet-high gilded-bronze image of the Buddha, and had temples built in all the provinces as branches of this national temple. In time, the great Buddhist establishments came to wield considerable economic and political power at Nara, and it was largely to escape their influence that the capital was moved to Nagaoka in 784 by the Emperor Kammu. In 794, the capital moved to Heian, which remained the imperial seat until 1868. Heian, later called Kyoto, reached an estimated population of 100,000 in the early ninth century.

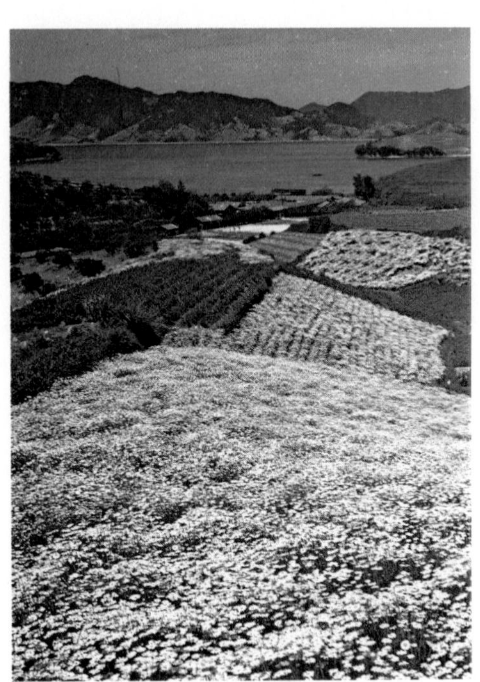

Pyrethrum blossoms under cultivation on Inno-shima Island in the central Inland Sea. The way in which the slopes of the mountainous terrain have been brought under cultivation by terracing, a widespread practice in Japan, is at once apparent. Pyrethrum are small chrysanthemums.

In the Nara and early Heian periods, relations with China continued to be close. However, after the diplomatic and trading mission sent to China in 838–839, an idea grew that China had little more to teach Japan and that, in fact, enthusiasm for everything Chinese had gone too far. Increasing departures from Chinese models began, and in 894 a proposal to send another large official mission to China was rejected on the grounds of China's increasing domestic disturbances. Although private intercourse continued for a time, with Buddhist monks, scholars, and traders coming and going, official missions were not resumed until the late twelfth century.

### Mongol Invasions

In the thirteenth century, during Japan's early feudal period, there was another era of prosperity and of active relations with China, and during this time Zen Buddhism was introduced. But the Mongols conquered Korea and China, and Kublai Khan became emperor of China. Because the Japanese refused to recognize the Mongol dynasty and send tribute, the Mongols, with the forced aid of the Chinese and Koreans, made two attemps to conquer Japan. The first Mongol expeditionary force of about 30,000 men was sent in November 1274. After one day's fighting a great typhoon struck, and the Mongol fleet was forced to return to Korea with the loss of about half its men. The next attempt was larger, with about 150,000 men, and better prepared. It was sent in July 1282 well before the typhoon season. But after seven week's fighting, in which the Japanese generally held their ground, another typhoon struck with disastrous results for the invaders. It is easy to understand why the Japanese welcomed these typhoons as *kamikaze* (divine winds) sent by the *kami* (Shinto deities). The failure of the Mongol invasions greatly increased national pride and strengthened a view of Japan as the sole country to enjoy divine protection.

Peaceful relations between Japan and the continent were not resumed until a Chinese dynasty, the Ming, replaced the Mongols in 1368. Before the Mongol invasions, Japanese traders denied the opportunity to trade in Korea had turned pirate, and the Mongol invasions gave some small justification for large-scale piracy against the Chinese coast as well. This continued sporadically until Japanese pirates were known and feared as far as the Phillipines and southeast Asia, although in the sixteenth century the Japanese were to a great extent replaced by more effective pirate-traders—the Portuguese.

For some years after 1368, shoguns belonging to the Ashikaga clan arranged peaceful trade with Ming China, but their successors found it increasingly difficult to control the piratical activities supported by the virtually independent feudal lords of southern and western Japan. However, until 1467, when the entire country was drawn into endemic wars among the feudal lords, there was renewed enthusiasm in Japan for Chinese culture. The central years of the Ashikaga period were a time of relative prosperity, economic progress, and a flowering of the arts.

The sixteenth century was marked by the arrival of the Portuguese in 1543, at a time when there was no real central government and feudal lords were competing for trade and for political control. European trade, influence, and Europeans themselves were welcomed enthusiastically and, with the help of muskets introduced by the Portuguese, the centralization of the country was achieved. But although European help was welcomed, Christianity came to be viewed as subversive of the newly-achieved order and stability. Then, at the end of the sixteenth century, ill-fated attempts to invade Korea led to a withdrawal from the continent. The beginning of the seventeenth century saw the establishment of the Tokugawa state, which was followed by intensive persecution of Christians and the sealing of the country against outside influences.

A view of the Asakusa Temple, Tokyo, by Hiroshige. Although founded in the twelfth century, when it was known as Edo or Yedo, Tokyo did not become an important city until after 1603, the year in which Tokugawa Iyeyasu, founder of a shogunate which ruled Japan until 1868, made it his headquarters. It took its present name when it became the new imperial capital in 1868.

## IMPLICATIONS OF CULTURAL BORROWINGS

Owing in part to its geographical isolation, Japan has never been successfully invaded; it had never been defeated in war until World War II. Changes in Japanese society were not imposed from outside but evolved gradually, and cultural borrowings were conscious, selective, and voluntary. Although most borrowings were of a useful kind and added greatly to the quality of Japanese economic and social life, some were hardly practical. For example, directional taboos from China were incorporated into an indigenous system of taboos and were widely practiced by the courtiers of the Heian period (794–1185), who thus believed it bad luck to travel in certain directions on certain days. A journey necessary on one of these days must either be postponed or carried out in a sufficiently roundabout manner to avoid the evil consequences of violating a taboo.

The Japanese subjected other aspects of Chinese culture, such as Buddhism and Confucianism, to a creative process, an adaptation to native cultural patterns. The result was to change both the indigenous culture and the ideas and institutions borrowed. In the Kamakura period (1185–1333), when various popular forms of Buddhism were widely adopted, Japan could conceivably have been called a Buddhist country. But it was a Buddhism so different from that of India that such a statement can only be made with strict reservations.

Conscious cultural borrowing created certain problems of national psychology. A pattern can be seen: periods of enthusiastic borrowing, followed by long periods of assimilation, and then anxiety about a possible loss of national identity with a subsequent search for "true Japanese" elements in the culture. An obvious example of what can be called a "purely Japanese" institution was the imperial house, which traced its origins back to the sun-goddess in an unbroken line, making its preservation all the more psychologically important to the Japanese. In the nineteenth century, the knowledge that much in the Japanese tradition was not of Japanese origin made it easier to jettison a great deal of it as "Chinese," and thus ineffective and undesirable, in favor of Western ways—while still preserving, of course, the imperial house.

## FROM BUREAUCRACY TO FEUDALISM

Modern Japan, like Western Europe, developed from a feudal system that had come into being to fill the political vacuum created by the decay of a centralized empire. The disappearance of the Japanese bureaucratic state was beneficial, in that feudalism did much to provide the raw materials for Japan's modernization, but unfortunate in that warfare was almost endemic during the slow evolution of feudalism, when militarism and the rule of force became established and the military hero came to be the ideal.

The Japanese failure to create a bureaucratic state along the Chinese lines, one strong enough to prevent the country slipping into feudalism, is often contrasted with Japanese success in penetrating to the essence of Chinese art and turning it to their own uses. But unlike art, ideas and methods of political and economic organization brought from a very different geographical, social, and intellectual environment were very difficult to transplant. It proved to be impossible to impose on Japan a thoroughgoing process of centralization along Chinese lines.

Most agricultural communities were located in small valleys more or less isolated by mountains. Efforts at centralization were further hampered by the strong clan tradition within these communities, the tradition of local cooperative self-sufficiency, solidarity, and self-rule. Moreover, seventh-century Japan was not culturally sophisticated enough to apply wholesale the Chinese imperial system which had taken some 800 years to develop.

Before the Taika reforms of the later seventh century, the Japanese emperor, in his two capacities as chief of the imperial clan and as the acknowledged superior of all other clans, had always to maintain alliances, often strengthened by arranged marriages, with a group of powerful clan chiefs who dominated their peers. And at times, one of these chiefs would come to the fore and gain control over the emperor. The creation of a radically reformed central bureaucracy greatly increased the power of the court; some strongminded emperors exerted real personal power. But this did not alter the basic power structure. The great clan chiefs, now better educated, more civilized, and less warlike, constituted a court nobility and enjoyed prestige and

A painted screen, dating from the first years of the Tokugawa, or Edo, period, showing European travelers landing in Japan. The Portuguese were the first Europeans to reach the country, in 1542 or 1543, when a group of merchants trading along the Chinese coast were blown off course and wrecked on the coast of Kyushu. In 1549, Saint Francis Xavier became the first Christian missionary to land in Japan.

assured incomes through largely hereditary court titles and offices. They could compete in building up the economic and political power of their own clans, chiefly by the accumulation of tax-free estates at the expense of the public domain. As the taxable public domain gradually decreased, court officials began bypassing the government and governing as clan heads rather than as officials of the central government. In this re-emergence of inter-clan rivalry, the Fujiwara clan was to become the most powerful and, in the middle and late Heian period, gained domination over the emperor.

## THE FUJIWARA AND THE MILITARY CLANS

From 645 to 858, the Fujiwara clan maintained, with varying success, close connections with the imperial clan, including intermarriage. In the latter year, a Fujiwara chief became regent for an emperor who had not come of age. In 884, the head of the Fujiwara clan assumed the title of *Kampaku*, a rank which, in effect, made him regent even for an adult emperor. Until the late Heian period, the Fujiwara leader, as grandfather or father-in-law of the emperor, was the real ruler, governing through the emperor as well as on his own behalf as head of the most powerful court clan.

Not all emperors were content with this state of affairs, and efforts were sometimes made to restore some of the imperial prerogatives. In 1086, Emperor Go Sanjo attempted to stop the growth of tax-immune estates, but was blocked by the Fujiwara chief. Subsequently, the imperial clan joined more actively in the accumulation of estates, and with these as a financial base a system was initiated whereby an emperor would retire, take Buddhist orders, and seek to control the government through the reigning emperor, his son. This undermined the position of the Fujiwara clan at court, but produced a confusion of responsibility likely to lead to power struggles in the form of succession disputes. In two such disputes, in 1156 and 1160,

A combat between two *samurai*, a colorprint by Igusa Kuniyoshi (1797–1861), who specialized in military subjects. The *samurai*, warriors whose two great ideals were loyalty to their war leaders and absolute indifference to all physical hardship, played an important role in Japanese political history from the twelfth to the nineteenth centuries.

military clans were called in by both sides. One such clan, the Taira, ended up in control of the court by defeating their rivals, the Minamoto. This marked the beginning of the political predominance of military men which was to last for more than seven centuries.

In the last years of the Nara period (710–784), it was realized that conscription of peasants had not created an effective military force to combat Ainu guerrillas, and that many abuses of the system had arisen. The system was abolished, and Japanese frontier families in the northeast were made responsible for providing permanent militia. The tough, arrogant, professional fighting men thus created became the prototypes of the later *samurai*. With the government's failure, from the middle Heian period on, to maintain the law in the provinces, a feudal society grew to fill the gap. The strongest provincial military clans were called upon by the court to suppress piracy on the Inland Sea, and rebellions in the provinces and in the capital.

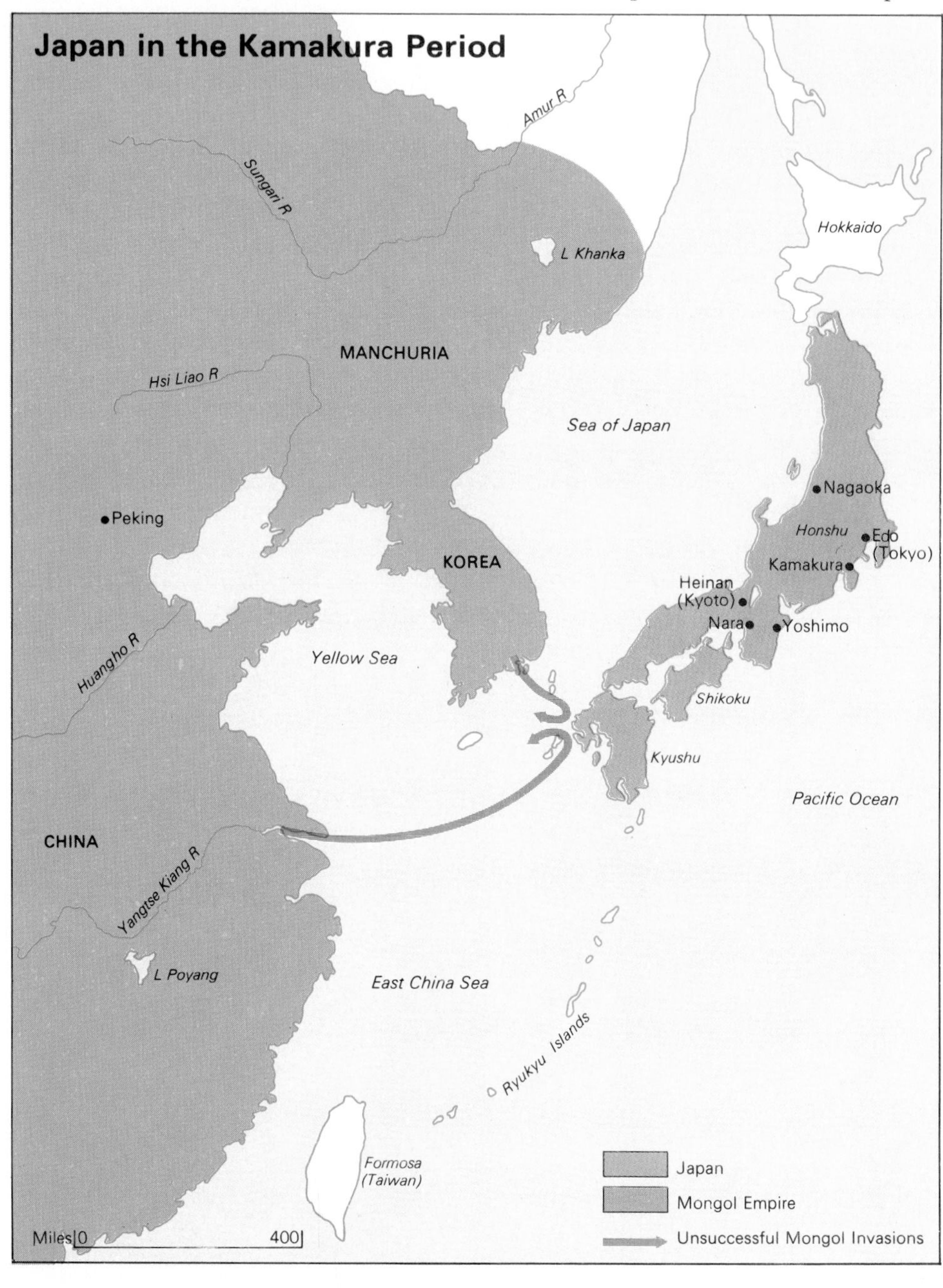

The feudal-military elements were first linked to an effective central government by Minamoto Yoritomo, a great military and political leader who succeeded in restoring the fortunes of the Minamoto clan by vanquishing the Taira in 1185, after protracted hostilities. Having consciously championed the cause of the established interests injured by the arbitrary and destructive policies of the Taira, Yoritomo carried out his promise that peace would be maintained in the provinces and that taxes and rents, often withheld from the government and proprietors, would again be delivered. After his victory, he treated the court well, obtaining the right to send his vassals to the provinces as military officials responsible only to his own clan government in Kamakura. Yoritomo was made shogun by the emperor in 1192. He saw himself as the military arm of the court, with powers delegated to him by the emperor. This dual government, in which formal prestige and economic predominance remained with the imperial court, but in which the shogun, who enjoyed the actual military power in the country, could overrule the court or dictate to it in matters which affected his interests, represented the first phase of feudalism in Japan. It lasted until 1333, when the Kamakura shogunate was overthrown in favor of an uneasy and inept imperial government under Emperor Daigo II (or Go-Daigo). For two years, Daigo II tried to rule as his forebears had once ruled, but this was impossible in a world where the real power was in the hands of military chieftains.

The Akita armor, one of the finest surviving examples of classical Japanese armor. Although the suit was not made up until 1748, when armor had become more decorative than functional, it is in a style closely modeled on ancient armor—and its helmet-crown has been identified as the work of an armorer of the late twelfth century.

In 1336, a powerful military leader, Ashikaga Takauji, broke with Daigo II, who fled south to Yoshino and set up his court there. Ashikaga established as emperor in Kyoto (the former Heian) a prince whose claim to the throne was as valid as that of Daigo II, and until 1392 warfare continued, as shifting alliances of feudal lords, grouped about the two courts, fought for supremacy. In 1392, the shogun Ashikaga Yoshimitsu arranged a negotiated settlement to his own advantage, and the southern court ceased to exist. The Ashikaga period, which lasted until 1573, was a time of widespread strife in which the feudal lords largely replaced the court, the court nobility, and the religious establishments as landowners. It was a period of more complete and more localized feudalism, in which the shogun seldom had control of very much of the country, and in which the imperial court reached a new low in political and economic power.

Anarchy and endemic warfare could not be tolerated indefinitely. After a long process of consolidation, complete ownership and control of integrated and defensible feudal fiefs finally replaced the estate system of scattered holdings and multiple ownership. It became possible for military leaders of genius to begin a process of regional and then national consolidation, resulting in the centralization of the country near the end of the sixteenth century. The unification was achieved by three remarkable leaders of relatively humble origins: Oda Nobunaga, Toyotomi Hideyoshi, and Tokugawa Iyeyasu. Iyeyasu became shogun in 1603, and the Tokugawa shogunate ruled Japan until 1868. In that year the last shogun resigned and the emperor became once more the center of an imperial bureaucracy which, in the Meiji period, set about the task of modernizing Japan.

## ECONOMIC AND SOCIAL DEVELOPMENTS

In an agrarian society, land is the key to political power. The Taika reforms begun in 645 rested on land reform, and when that broke down the whole political structure collapsed. The "equal field" system borrowed from China was a very complicated government-managed system of land tenure: rice fields were divided into units for allocation to peasant cultivators in accordance with the number of family members, their sex, and their age. Because these statistics were constantly changing, surveys and reallotments were made each six years. However, these procedures were expensive, left room for abuses, and were resisted by local families who did not wish to lose gains made in their holdings. Reallocations tended to be postponed and eventually dropped entirely, to the advantage of the well-to-do peasants. Also, ordinary peasants were offered better conditions and permanent tenure on estate lands, and as a result many abandoned their plots on public domain where the tax burden was increasing. A more workable, Japanese-originated system of land tenure eventually replaced the "equal-field" system.

In return for tax exemption, and to escape reallocation, local landholders commended their lands to powerful provincial clans, to court clans, or to religious institutions, preferring to pay rent and secure permanent tenure. Also, a magnate such as a prominent Fujiwara, with influence at court, could gain tax-exempt status for an estate and grant it as a benefice to a local family, which would pay rent to him as protector. This system proved to be a step towards feudalism, for when the need for military protection arose, the tenant was required to provide military service to his lord.

Rice field in Hokkaido. Rice has been cultivated in Japan since the Neolithic period, and it is not surprising that in a country which has almost always suffered from the pressure of an increasing population the rice plant has become a symbol of life. Hokkaido is in the north, where only one harvest a year is possible; father south, fields may be double or even treble cropped. It is estimated that some 85 percent of Japanese agricultural land is now given over to rice culture.

A money economy had been introduced in the Nara period, when the government minted copper coins, made money taxes legal, and supervised markets in the city. This continued in the Heian period. But country districts were very little affected, and in the late Heian period there was a partial return to a barter economy, which encouraged localism. However, in the Kamakura period, when Kamakura itself became an important center of population and commerce and towns throughout the country began to take on importance as military headquarters, domestic and foreign trade increased. In the Ashikaga period these trends continued, and copper coins, brought by pirates and genuine merchants alike, flooded in from China.

It may seem paradoxical that the turbulent years between the Ashikaga period, beginning in 1336, and the Tokugawa period, from 1600, saw remarkable economic growth and increasingly widespread cultural innovation and activity. But the wars of the time were mainly a matter of hand-to-hand conflict between *samurai* wielding long, slightly curved, two-handed swords with deadly efficiency. The *samurai* were later reinforced by foot soldiers recruited from the peasantry—mostly spearmen, but some armed with muskets made in Japan from Portuguese models—but even then warfare did not greatly hinder agriculture and commerce. Buildings were mostly of light construction, and could be quickly rebuilt if destroyed.

The consolidation and economic exploitation of feudal domains stimulated commerce and industry. Handicraft industries flourished and manufactured goods such as folding fans, a Japanese invention, joined Japanese swords and raw materials as exports to the continent. The large-scale military campaigns of the middle and late sixteenth century, the use of muskets and cannon, the building of large, moated castles, and the unprecedented growth of towns and cities, spurred economic expansion which continued into the eighteenth century. The total population of Japan increased from about 18 million in 1580 to around 30 million in 1750, remaining at about that level until the 1870s.

### The Clan, the Family, and Feudalism

The evidence available concerning the structure of the earliest Japanese village suggests that it was roughly the equivalent of a clan, a cooperative lineage group under a clan chief who was considered the living embodiment of the clan deity, and thus had a religious as well as a political function. There are faint traces of a matriarchy, but by historical times the clan was firmly patriarchal. The clan chief held as symbols of authority such artifacts as a Korean-style, comma-shaped bead, a straight sword, or a polished bronze mirror, of Chinese origin. Fine examples of each of these artifacts constitute the three imperial regalia, and are still the enshrined symbols of that office. The boundaries of the villages were marked by ropes, and there were often disputes over boundaries and water rights among the clans. Regular supplies of water were essential for irrigated rice culture, and the Japanese procedure was for the community to make decisions as to its use which individual families had to accept.

The prototype of government was the family—consciously so in Japan—and the clan was an extended family. The imperial clan was the most important clan of all, presiding over a national family of lesser clans (the Japanese word most often used for "nation" means, literally, "national family"). This social structure meant that, although members' wishes were consulted, once a decision was reached, individuals and individual families were expected to put aside their own interests for the greater good of the larger community. Emphasis was laid on the duties of inferiors—and ideological support for this was found in Confucianism.

A possible echo of the ancient matriarchy occurred in the Heian period among the court nobility. Important men usually had one principal wife and two or three concubines, a practice which emperors also had pursued since earliest times and which helped to assure the continuation of the dynasty. Each consort had her own residence, belonging either to her father or to herself. The husband visited his wife or concubines as he wished, returning always to his own residence. Children were raised in the mother's residence, supervised closely by the mother's parents. Thus the Heian emperors were generally brought up in the Fujiwara residence, giving that clan a unique opportunity to establish control over them and, through them, over the imperial government.

Just as political organization was based on the idea of the family, so the feudal system was fitted into this concept—in a particularly extreme form. It was essential in a feudal-military society for vassals to put their loyalty to their lords above all

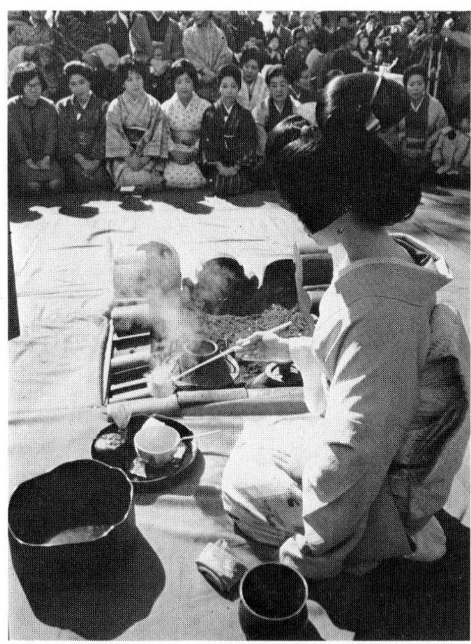

*Above:* A geisha girl performs the traditional tea ceremony outside a temple in Kyoto, where there exists a school, the *Urasenke*, that teaches this ancient art. The ceremony probably originated around the fourteenth century and it is said to have reached its peak as an art form—the ceremonial preparation and drinking of tea, a dramatic ritual lasting about two hours—under the shogun Yoshimasa (1435–90).
*Left:* A typical Japanese village. Japanese society traditionally centers on the self-contained, largely self-sufficient village society.

else, so even the loyalty of son to father, insisted upon in Confucianism as the most basic loyalty, had to be put aside in favor of loyalty to the feudal lord. The vassal was expected to sacrifice his own life for his lord in battle—and the lives of his family as well. In modern Japan before 1945, this line of thought was used to direct the subject's absolute loyalty to the emperor, as the father-figure of the state.

## Art and Literature

The greatest works of sculpture and painting of the Nara and Heian periods are Buddhist, and examples of the temple architecture of these periods still remain in and near Nara and Kyoto. All are strongly influenced by Chinese Buddhist art, but tend towards greater simplicity and elegance. Shinto architecture from even earlier times exists in the periodically rebuilt ancient shrines.

In literature, the series of anthologies of Japanese poetry beginning with the *Manyōshū* provides much information on Japanese society and culture. The poems show an interest in human relationships and a highly developed appreciation of the beauties of nature, made more poignant by the realization (a Buddhist idea) of the brevity of human life. Romantic tales of court life appeared in the Heian period, mostly written by women; men more often wrote in Chinese, which carried greater prestige. The greatest of these tales is *The Tale of Genji*, dating from around 1001–1020 and written by the court lady known as Murasaki Shikibu, a very long, complex novel. It is, perhaps, the first novel of world literature to be a highly controlled, psychological study of the development of personality. It is also a poetic evocation of the unique, hermetically sealed Japanese court society, concerned with highly refined canons of artistic taste; calligraphy and the writing of poetry (both often associated with love affairs); and almost completely oblivious of life outside the court, both that of foreign countries and that of common people in Japan.

There were two quite separate cultures in 1185, at the beginning of the feudal period. They were the classical court culture, originating in Heian, and the rough, practical, frugal, and simple culture of the warriors who, although they despised the courtiers' ineffective behavior and effeminacy, admired their education and manners. The cultural history of the feudal period is one of the fusion of these two cultures. The provincial lords began to take pride in protecting and encouraging the arts, and high culture ceased to be a monopoly of the imperial city.

In the feudal period, classic art and literature were permeated by a new vigor and realism, seen in tales of war and in the depiction of battles and the lives of warriors in the remarkable scroll paintings of the time. Zen Buddhism, which was transmitted in a very personal way from master to disciple, turned attention to the forceful personalities of Zen teachers; extremely realistic portrait paintings and sculptures made their appearance, along with increasingly powerful and realistic Buddhist sculptures of a more traditional kind.

In the Ashikaga period, Zen and Chinese influence was apparent in the development of an art of sudden, fleeting inspiration, alongside great, sustained, landscape paintings typified by those of Sesshu (1420–1506). Landscape gardening, the tea ceremony, flower arrangement, pottery making, and the classical *Nō* drama all either originated in the Ashikaga period, encouraged and patronized by the shoguns, or developed at that time to new heights of sophistication.

The huge castles built in the sixteenth century were splendidly decorated in a colorful, even flamboyant, style which was a departure from the subdued sophistication of Ashikaga art. This new style of wood carving and screen and wall painting continued in the Tokugawa period. A new indigenous art, that of polychrome wood-block prints, began to appear at the end of the seventeenth century. Wood-block printing, of which the earliest extant Japanese examples go back to eighth-

*Top:* Scene from a *Nō* play, a popular entertainment which evolved from a fourteenth-century court entertainment. Masked actors perform on an eighteen-foot-square stage, to a musical accompaniment.
*Above:* Statues of the Buddha on the island of Shikoku. Buddhism reached Japan from Korea around A.D. 538.
*Left:* A forthright sense of humor seems to have inspired the maker of this *tsuba*, or swordguard. Three great eastern religious philosophers—Lao-zi, the Buddha, and Confucius—are shown as a jolly trio around a jar of *sake*.

century Nara, experienced a very rapid development in Tokugawa times, when education spread rapidly among the lower classes. The polychrome prints were a development of illustrated, wood-block printed books, and were sold in large numbers to a growing, artistically-discriminating urban population. They depicted actors, courtesans, and other aspects of everyday life, the "floating world" of the vigorous and active townspeople. Another facet of the new urban culture was the appearance of two forms of popular theater, *bunraku* (puppets) and *kabuki* (live actors) which flourished in Tokugawa times, from the seventeenth century onward.

### Religion

The indigenous religion of Japan came to be known as Shinto ("the way of the gods") only in the sixth century, to distinguish it from Buddhism. It consisted of a great variety of cults based, to a large extent, on feelings of awe and reverence directed towards unusual, impressive, and largely inexplicable manifestations of nature. As well as aspects of nature, great men were thought to possess some divine attribute which classified them as *kami* (usually translated as "god" or "deity"). Every Japanese community had its simple shrine where the *kami* might be invoked, reported to, and asked for favors, and where pollution might be ritually cleansed. The shrine festivals, sometimes connected with fertility and gratitude for the harvest, often consisted of giving a deity a ride in a palanquin borne on men's shoulders about the village or town, attended by much conviviality. The deities required no personal commitment to belief in them, and offered no particular code of morality. They apparently wished only to be remembered at the proper times, and such commemoration was largely a community affair rather than an individual or family matter. Attendance at a festival might simply be an acknowledgment of the continuity and solidarity of the village or neighborhood. Participation in national

*Above:* A Zen Buddhist ceremony. Zen Buddhism was introduced into Japan in the twelfth century and, perhaps because of its simplicity and its emphasis on self-help, appealed particularly to warriors. Broadly speaking, the Zen Buddhist discards all formal observances and systems, all philosophical and religious writings and ideas, and concentrates on reliving the mystical experiences of the Buddha himself—thus finding enlightenment through total self-knowledge.
*Right:* A Zen garden at Kyoto. The essential simplicity of Zen Buddhism is reflected in this abstract composition of blossom and rock.

festivals connected with the cult of the emperor, which had its clan shrine to the sun-goddess at Ise, was, at least until 1946, expected in much the same way. At the least, it was a simple recognition in public that the participant was a member of the Japanese nation-family.

Buddhism was an addition to the religious life of the Japanese rather than a competitor with Shinto, and to a considerable extent Buddhism was changed to suit older assumptions. As interpreted in Japan, Buddhism is associated with funerals, prayers for ancestors, divine protection, and divine intervention in worldly affairs and troubles. For some, Buddhism offers personal salvation and hopes of heaven, which appeal especially in time of war and insecurity. The Buddhist deities, embodied in impressive statues, made a tremendous impression on the Japanese, whose divinities had never been given any visual embodiment. Although many emperors became fervent Buddhists, the Shinto rites of the imperial clan and the myth of the divine descent of the emperors from the sun-goddess were always maintained. The emperors were what most Japanese have been since—both Buddhists and Shintoists; and Confucianists as well, in matters of social and political ethics and morality.

Part of the sculptured decoration of the Kamakura hall at Heian (modern Kyoto), the imperial capital from 794 to 1868. The hall (which is popularly called the Sanjūsangendō, from the Japanese words that indicate that it is constructed with thirty-three bays) was designed to house 1,000 lifesize images of the *Bodhisattva* Kwannon (the Lord of Compassion).

The ruling classes readily accepted Buddhism, at first largely as a means to mundane ends, an emphasis which ultimately resulted in its virtual secularization. Otherworldly concerns were never strong in Shinto, and Japanese religious ideas, despite the Buddhist rejection of the world, remained firmly fixed on the here and now. During the Nara and Heian periods, the aesthetic and magical aspects of Buddhism were perhaps predominant. As a religion, it permeated gradually downward through society. In the Kamakura period, greatly simplified forms like popular Amidism and Nichiren Buddhism spread among the common people, while Zen Buddhism was embraced largely by the warriors.

During the centuries of feudalism, Buddhist institutions survived, although battered, protecting lands and economic interests with private armies, increasing revenues by protecting merchants and artisans, lending money, and participating in foreign trade. In the process, Buddhism adapted itself to conform to the hierarchical pattern of the society of the time. Among the ruling classes, Buddhism was largely replaced by the ideology of *bushidō* ("the way of the warrior"), which emphasized the selflessness of the vassal in his loyalty to his lord, and, in the Tokugawa period, by Neo-Confucianism, which imposed more of an intellectual than a religious commitment.

### Historical Development

With a tinge of self-pity, Japanese Confucianists of late Tokugawa times called Japan the "orphan of Asia," a complaint frequently heard since. They referred less to geographical than to intellectual isolation, an isolation largely self-imposed by piracy, the invasions of Korea, and the closed-country policy of the sixteenth and seventeenth centuries. When Japan was opened to outside contact in the nineteenth century, emotional commitment to Asian, mainly Chinese, culture, was, however, insufficient to prevent the Japanese from abandoning and replacing "Chinese" elements in Japanese culture by Western elements—once they became convinced that national survival depended on it. Although Japan is an Asian country with a unique culture its historical development has been perhaps closer to that of Europe than that of Asia. The logic of this development helps to explain Japan's positive response to the threat, and challenge, presented by Western intrusion in the nineteenth century.

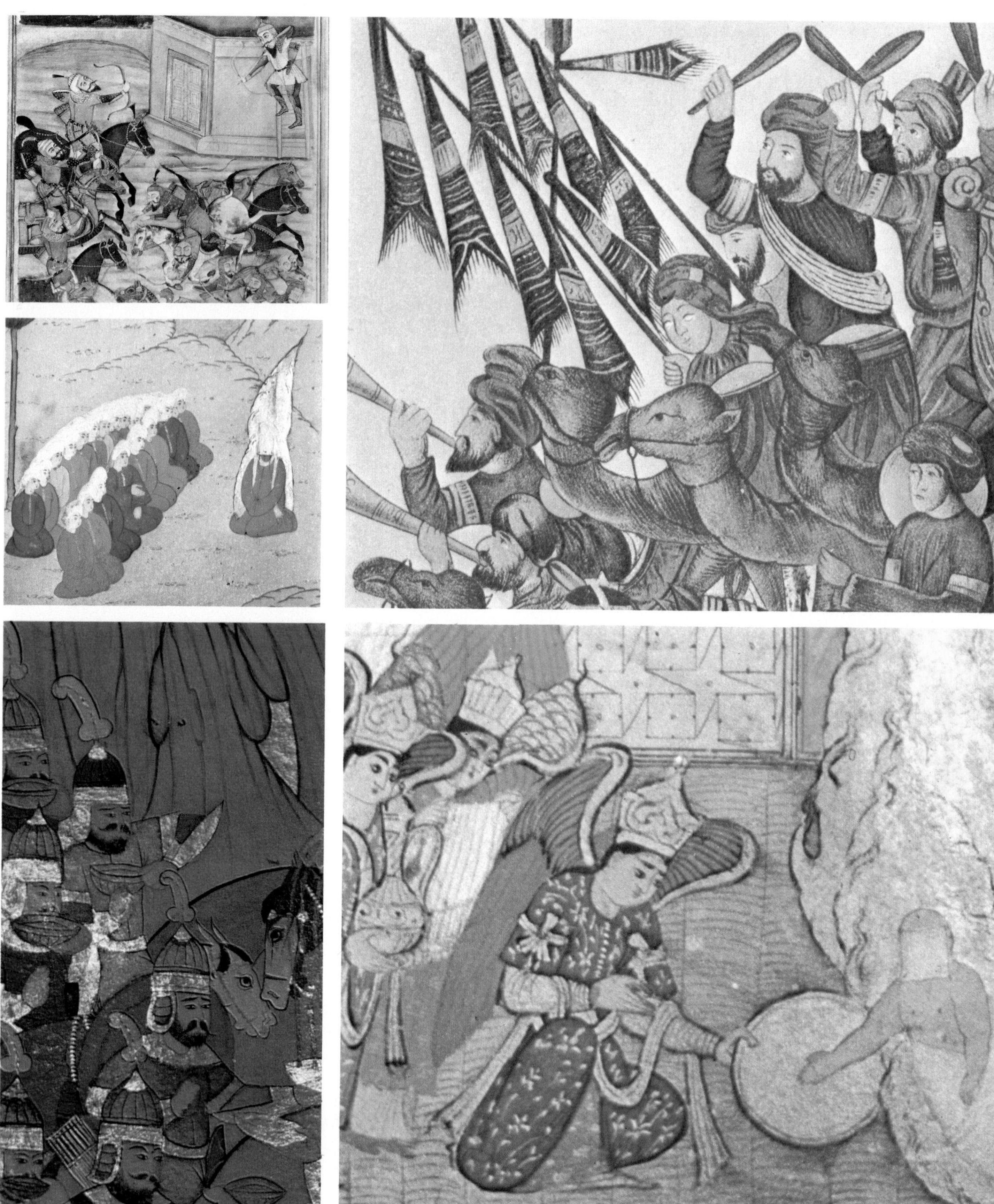

# Part III Islam

Chapter 7

# THE GROWTH OF ISLAM

## The Middle East Before Islam

At the beginning of the seventh century, Arabia was in turmoil; in most places the nomadic bedouins had prevailed over the discipline formerly imposed by sedentary kingdoms. Warfare and famine were widespread.

Arabia was a backward area. Its economy was pastoral rather than agricultural; cities were few and underdeveloped; its people were tribesmen and mostly pagans. The great Byzantine and Sassanian Empires reached only to the fringe of the Arabian peninsula.

Before the advent of Islam and the subsequent period of Arab expansion and conquest, the extraordinarily diverse region in which Islamic civilization was to develop—with its heartlands between the Nile River and the Jaxartes River (the modern Syr Darya River) in central Asia—was divided between two empires. The Byzantine, or Late Roman Empire held the west: Anatolia, Syria, Egypt, north Africa, and part of Mesopotamia. The Sassanian empire held what is now Iraq, and Iran as far as the Oxus River (the modern Amu Darya River). The Byzantine Empire was Christian. Most subjects of the Sassanians were Zoroastrians, but there were large Christian, Jewish, and pagan minorities.

These Middle Eastern empires were decentralized; it is desirable to consider each of them as a loose collection of peoples owing homage and support to one ruler. But whatever the limits on their political power, the empires served to integrate, to some extent, the many different interests and peoples under their sway. The imperial governments decided the allocation of resources and power between the central government and the provinces, between provinces, and between ethnic and religious communities. They fostered common languages and laws, encouraged social and geographical mobility, and gave their peoples a sense of common loyalties and common identity.

On this diverse region, divided into two great spheres of religion, culture, and empire, and into innumerable small and more or less self-contained communities, Islam was to impose a new unity. And this major development in the history of civilization depended on events in Arabia, a region peripheral to the main areas of civilization but one which would change the history of the world.

*Above:* A Turk reading the Koran in the Selimiye Mosque, Nicosia, Cyprus. Cyprus fell to the Arabs in 649, but was retaken by the Crusaders in 1191. In 1424 an army from Egypt recaptured the island for Islam.

*Left:* A Persian miniature painting depicting the birth of Muhammad, which took place at Mecca around A.D. 570. According to Muslim tradition, Muhammad was the son of Abdullah of the tribe of the Koreish, who died at about the same time as the prophet's birth, and of Amina, of the same tribe, who died when Muhammad was about six years old.

## Muhammad and the Rise of Islam

In Arabia, the main oases, such as Mecca and Medina, were experiencing grave social pressures. Mecca, the home of the Qurasysh tribes, was the site of the Kaaba, a holy shrine, repository of the tribal gods, and the object of an annual pilgrimage and fair. The pilgrimage made Mecca the commercial center of Arabia and the focus of an international caravan traffic in spices, aromatics, drugs, and other goods. These products originated in east Africa and the Far East and were transported from Yemen to Syria, where they were exchanged for money, weapons, cereals, and wine. As a result of this trade, Mecca was one of the few places in Arabia to have both a permanent population of clans and tribes and a floating population of individual exiles, refugees, outlaws, foreign merchants, and settlers. Meccan society had grown beyond the limitations of the clan and thus afforded more political and economic possibilities than did clan relationships.

This social heterogeneity expressed itself in a diversity of religious and social values. In Mecca, pagan animism, the polytheistic cults of the Kaaba, and the higher religions were all represented; merchants and travelers and Jewish and Christian settlements had diffused Judeo-Christian concepts throughout the peninsula. The pagan view of a fragmented universe, society, and human soul coexisted with the single god of the monotheistic religions, who had created material and spiritual order in the cosmos and had made men brothers, as well as moral and purposive creatures whose ultimate purpose was salvation. In Mecca, such competing values meant openness and freedom on the one hand, and moral confusion and social conflict on the other.

In this disturbed world, about the year 610, Muhammad received his first revelations. They concerned a great single God, Allah, a just God, who had created the world, and who required that men worship him, perform good works, and live piously. On the day of judgment Allah would review each man's life, and consign him to eternal bliss or damnation.

For three years Muhammad preached his vision privately to his family and friends. Then, in 613, he made his revelations public, engaging his religious visions with contemporary political and social realities. To Muhammad's surprise and chagrin, his preaching aroused opposition. The people of Mecca resented his assault on their traditional beliefs. He, in turn, felt compelled to clarify his purposes, and came to see himself as a prophet in the succession of Old and New Testament

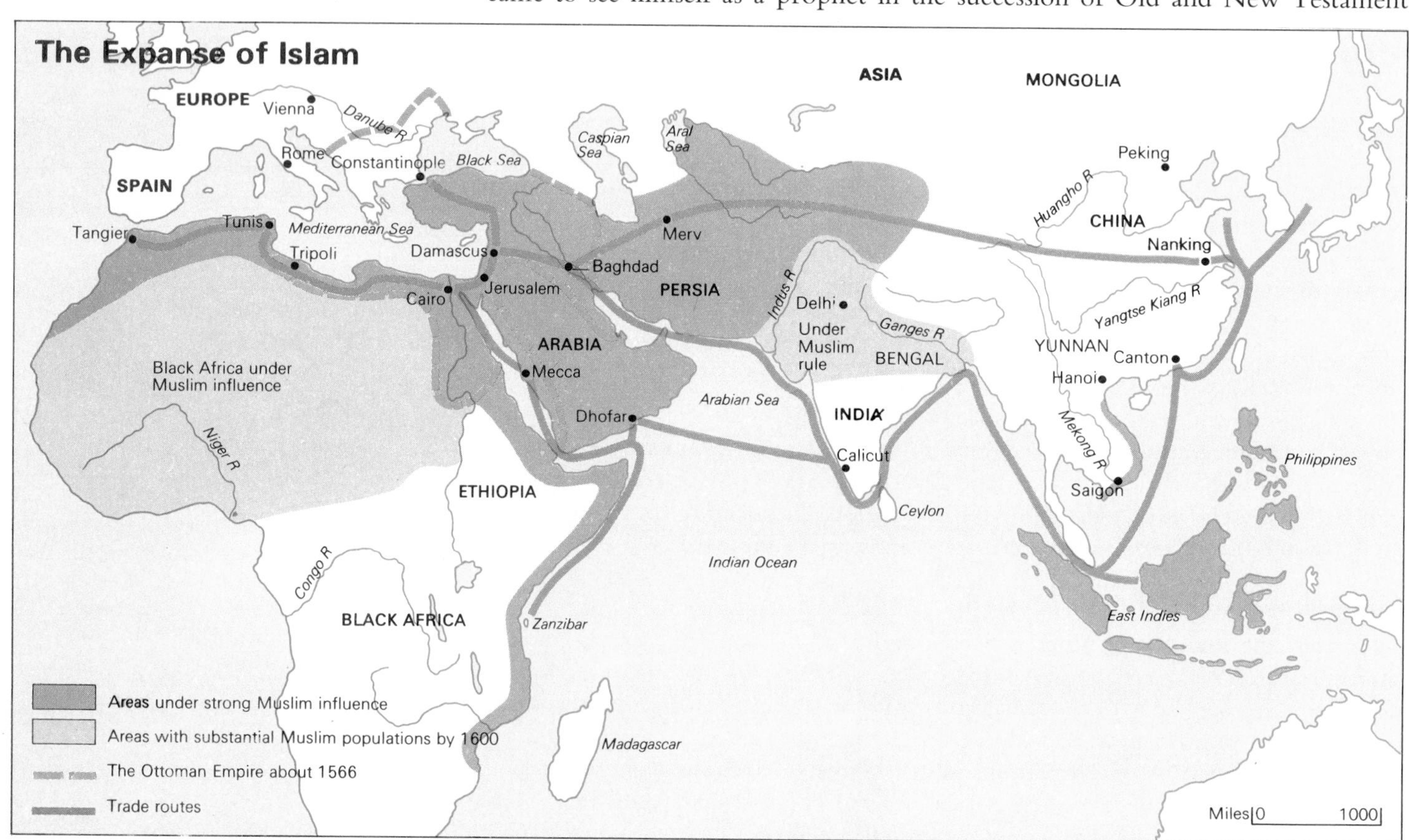

prophets—a man sent by God to reveal the divine will to the Arabs in Arabic speech. At this time, Muhammad addressed his message not only to pagans but also to Christians and Jews.

The opposition of the Meccans showed Muhammad that religious beliefs could not be separated from the life of a community. Because Muhammad believed that his mission was not only to reveal God's laws but also to guide the people in observing them, he realized that the new religion could flourish only in a new society, where God's will could be carried out in the everyday lives of men.

### The Hegira

Muhammad found himself oppressed by his opponents, dishonored in his own house, and obliged to look beyond Mecca for a foundation for a new community. At this juncture he was invited to arbitrate the bitter tribal feuds in Medina, an agricultural oasis inhabited by various clans. Like Mecca, Medina was undergoing social changes which undermined the bedouin kinship society. Medina also contained a large Jewish population, which encouraged the movement toward monotheism. In 622, Muhammad and his followers left Mecca for Medina, making the migration called the hegira which marks the beginning of the Muslim calendar era and the transition from kinship community to a society based on common belief.

A mosque in Baghdad, the capital of Iraq. Iraq, then a part of the Sassanian empire, fell to the Arabs in 637, and in 756 the Abbasid Caliph Mansur founded Baghdad as his capital. It rapidly grew to become a populous and cosmopolitan city, one of the major centers of Islam.

The Medinians saw Muhammad's leadership as a source of order and security, but Muhammad regarded the hegira as part of his missionary work, which was not to be limited to Medina alone. He strove to consolidate his authority over the Medinian clans. He first included the Jews in his nascent community, but when the Jewish clans refused to accept him as a prophet he began to stress the essentially Arabian quality of his new religion. The Jewish clans were destroyed or expelled from Medina. Islamic theory now excluded Jews and Christians; Islam became a distinct religion, separate from Judaism and Christianity. Thus by winning over the Medinian pagans and by destroying the Jewish clans, Muhammad gradually made Medina a Muslim community under his rule.

Using Medina as a base, Muhammad attempted to bring Mecca and the surrounding Arabian tribes under his authority. After a series of battles, the most important at Badr and Uhud, Mecca capitulated to Muhammad in 630 and accepted Islam. The remaining independent tribes in western Arabia followed suit. Muhammad and his followers had created a new supra-tribal political confederation, built upon loyalty to Muhammad and the authority of Islam.

The establishment of a community based on religious belief necessitated the promulgation of rules for social life, personal behavior, and religious observance. Such a framework of rules was provided by the *Koran*, the sacred book of Islam, which is said by Muslims to have been dictated to Muhammad by an angel. The Koran laid down the ritual obligations of all Muslims in "the five pillars of Islam": *salat* (ritual prayer); *zakat* (alms-giving); *hajj* (pilgrimage); the obligation to keep the fast of Ramadam; and the obligation to bear witness to the existence of the one god and to the true prophethood of Muhammad. The Koran also laid down rules for the proper conduct of business transactions and of warfare, and contained prohibitions of gambling and intoxicating liquor.

The most important Koranic social rules were those that regulated family life. In Muhammad's time, Arabian family practices were diverse; the patriarchal clan dominated in the peninsula, but polygamy, polyandry, and temporary marriage were also practiced. This diversity and instability caused confusion over the status of women and the guardianship of children. Muhammad aimed to reconstitute the family as a locus of moral living, and as an educative force for his broader religious message. Koranic law strengthened the patriarchal agnatic clan—the family of several generations under the authority of its chief—with its collective property rights, duties based on blood ties, and control of marriages. Muhammad also introduced a new freedom and dignity for individual members of the family. He tried to elevate the status of women and children from that of chattels or potential warriors to a position more in keeping with their individual rights and needs. But although he discouraged such abuses as hasty and unjustified divorce, he did not give women equal rights with men, and recommended that they be obedient and subordinate within the family. Nevertheless, his reforms encouraged some growth of mutual respect between husbands and wives, and enhanced a sense of the religious worth and ethical autonomy of individuals.

Nomadic bedouin tribesmen with their camels at Tafilelt, southern Morocco, the largest oasis of the Sahara. Before Islam arose in the seventh century to impose unity upon the Arab peoples, warlike tribesmen like these kept large areas in a state of anarchy. Even when the Abbasid administration was at the height of its power in the eighth century, the bedouin continued to fight against centralized control.

In the supra-tribal political confederation Muhammad was building, the Koran supplied ideological support: an internal reality of common worship, common social laws, common family norms, and encouragement for morally autonomous individuals who would become responsible members of the *umma* (brotherhood) of Islam. At once, Muhammad created a doctrine, a morality, and a society.

Muhammad himself was a man of profound religious vision which he put into action in a life of preaching and community-building. Although his religious doctrines stemmed partly from Judeo-Christian tradition, they stressed the utter transcendence, majesty, and omnipotence of god, and focused on the individual's total submission to god's will. Moreover, although many Islamic conceptions were derived from Judaism and Christianity, Islam was a completely different religion because it involved more than religious doctrine—it was a way of life in which religious conviction transformed traditional social practices.

Through Islam, Muhammad brought a new order to fragmented Arabia. The *umma* was a community which integrated individuals, clans, and cities. It reinterpreted traditional Arabian concepts of clan, marriage, and authority; it gave religious loyalties priority over other obligations; and it provided a new common law and political authority. The *umma* regulated the affairs of the populace in the interest of a peaceful, moral society, and for the sake of the salvation of individual souls.

### The Islamic Conquests and Empire to 750

After Muhammad's death in 632, the Arab conquest of the Middle East and the establishment of Islamic rule proceeded apace. The conquest movement itself began in the internal disruption of the Muslim community at Muhammad's death. Muhammad appointed no successor, and it was only after his death that his followers agreed to the need for a succession. They selected Abu Bakr, the prophet's father-in-law, as the first caliph (from Khalifa, "Successor"), whose duties were to maintain Muhammad's teachings, lead the *umma*, arbitrate disputes, and otherwise preserve the community as Muhammad had left it.

However, although Medina and Mecca accepted Abu Bakr as Muhammad's successor, many bedouin tribes seceded from the confederation. Opposing secession, the Muslims waged war on the tribes and the fighting soon spilled out of Arabia into Syria and Iraq. Muhammad himself had prepared for the expansion of Islam, whether consciously or not, by seeking alliances with the Arab border tribes of Iraq and by encouraging raiding and reconnaissance parties to penetrate toward Syria. As the tribes on the Arabian border were subdued, it became necessary to raid farther afield if strife within the Muslim brotherhood was to be avoided, and the subsequent expansion process was furthered when the subdued tribes sought to make up for their losses in Arabia by attacking settlements under Byzantine and Sassanian rule. The raids led to pitched battles, then to systematic conquest, and finally to a mass movement of Arabians into the fertile areas outside Arabia. Though the Muslim armies were inspired by zeal for Islam and by the prospect of rich plunder, the conquest, especially at first, was generated by the upheavals in Arabia.

On the Byzantine front, the Arabs took Syria in 633–636 and Egypt in 641, and in 643 began their century-long drive to conquer north Africa and Spain. The Arab advance into western Europe was only stopped at Poitiers, in west-central France, in 732. However, the Byzantine empire retained its heartlands in Anatolia and the Balkans and kept alive for centuries the threat of recapturing its lost provinces. In contrast, the Arabs completely destroyed the Sassanian empire. They conquered Iraq in 637, established new bases at Basra and Kufa, and methodically subdued the rest of the Sassanian provinces. They captured Mesopotamia by 641, western Iran by 644, Fars by 649, and Khurasan by 654.

The two empires were both militarily and politically too weak to resist. In the former Byzantine regions, local populations generally collaborated with the victors, but in the Iranian hill country many places had to be subdued again and again before they accepted Arab rule. The Arab victories established the first unified Middle Eastern empire since Alexander the Great.

The tomb in Cyprus of Hala Sultan, wife of the Omayyad caliph Mu'awiya, who accompanied her husband's invasion of the island in 649. Mu'awiya was the leader of the *sunni*, Muslims who held to the *sunna*, divine law, and the traditional teachings of Muhammad, as opposed to the *shii*, who upheld rather the teachings of the prophet's son-in-law Ali.

From the seventh to the fifteenth centuries, Egypt to central Asia represented the heartland of Islamic civilization. But Islam reached beyond this heartland. In the west, north Africa and Spain were governed by Islamic dynasties. From north Africa, Islam crossed the Sahara to the Sudan and the Niger region as early as the eleventh century. From Egypt, Islam crossed into Nubia, Abyssinia, and central Africa in the twelfth to the sixteenth centuries. Merchants, missionaries, migrant tribes, and conquerors carried Islam throughout Africa. In Europe, the Ottoman empire established Muslim peoples and converts in Serbia, Bosnia, and Albania; but although Turkish armies reached as far as Vienna, Muslim populations are now to be found in only a few places in the Balkans.

In the east, with the conversion of Turkish peoples, Islam reached beyond Iran into central Asia in the tenth century. Mongols in Iran and north of the Caucasus were converted at the end of the thirteenth century, and the Mongols brought Islam to China, where, from the end of the thirteenth century, a Muslim population was settled in Yünnan. Muslim influence penetrated India in the eighth and eleventh centuries, and substantial conversions to Islam began in the thirteenth century, especially in Bengal, as the combined result of conquest and *sufi* missionary activities. From Persia and India, Muslim traders and missionaries brought Islam to Malaya and Indonesia in the fifteenth and sixteenth centuries, and reached out as far as Vietnam and the Philippines. Today, Islam is the religion of hundreds of millions of people from the Atlantic to the Far East.

After their relatively swift victories, the Arabs had to organize a regular government in their new domains. In exploiting their victories, they also had to reconcile their own interests with the needs of an expanding society and had to harmonize the interests of bedouin and sedentary peoples, Muslims and non-Muslims.

The early form of Arab rule was established in the reign of Caliph Umar (634–644). Umar saw the Arabs as a governing class in an otherwise undisturbed society. Accordingly, the Arabs themselves constituted an exclusive military caste isolated from their subjects in special garrison cities, some newly founded for the purpose. No Arab could own land or engage in a non-military occupation. Instead, the soldiers received a regular stipend from taxes. The established method of administration and the distribution of power and property were left untouched, but all subjects were required to pay taxes or tribute to the ruling caste. Above all, Islam was the religion, the identifying faith, and the unifying force of the ruling caste—although subjects were not required to undergo conversion and were permitted to practice their own religions.

Thus the victors took the spoils and privileges of victory without destroying the stability of the conquered societies. With the caliph as chief of the ruling caste and emperor of the conquered peoples, the Arabs had created a new empire and a new elite. Yet their simple, conservative arrangements were fraught with deep potential for revolutionary change.

The first century of Arab rule, the period of the "rightly guided" caliphs (632–660) and the Omayyad dynasty (661–750), witnessed the progressive subversion of the conquest arrangements and the gradual transformation of Middle Eastern government, society, and religion. Arab rule did not remain stable, but was upset by internal conflicts: the members of Arab elites struggled among themselves for control of the caliphate; the caliphate contended with its own followers over the limits of caliphal authority and the distribution of taxes and booty; and other Arab factions fought among themselves. These conflicts stemmed from the effort of the caliphate to centralize its powers against the wishes of the Arab masses. The caliphs believed that effective government and imperial expansion required a centralized government with the loyal support of all Arabs. To these ends, the caliphate, which had begun as the simple religious succession to Muhammad, claimed imperial authority on the model of the Byzantine and Sassanian Empires. It built up a central army to dominate Arabs as well as conquered peoples, and streamlined fiscal administration to maximize revenues.

### Opposition to the Caliphate

As the caliphate widened its claims, its tribal followers renounced their initial support. The Arabs continued to view themselves as equal to the caliphate in the administration of the new empire and refused to recognize any authority beyond what they would freely concede. To many pious Arab Muslims, the caliph's actions

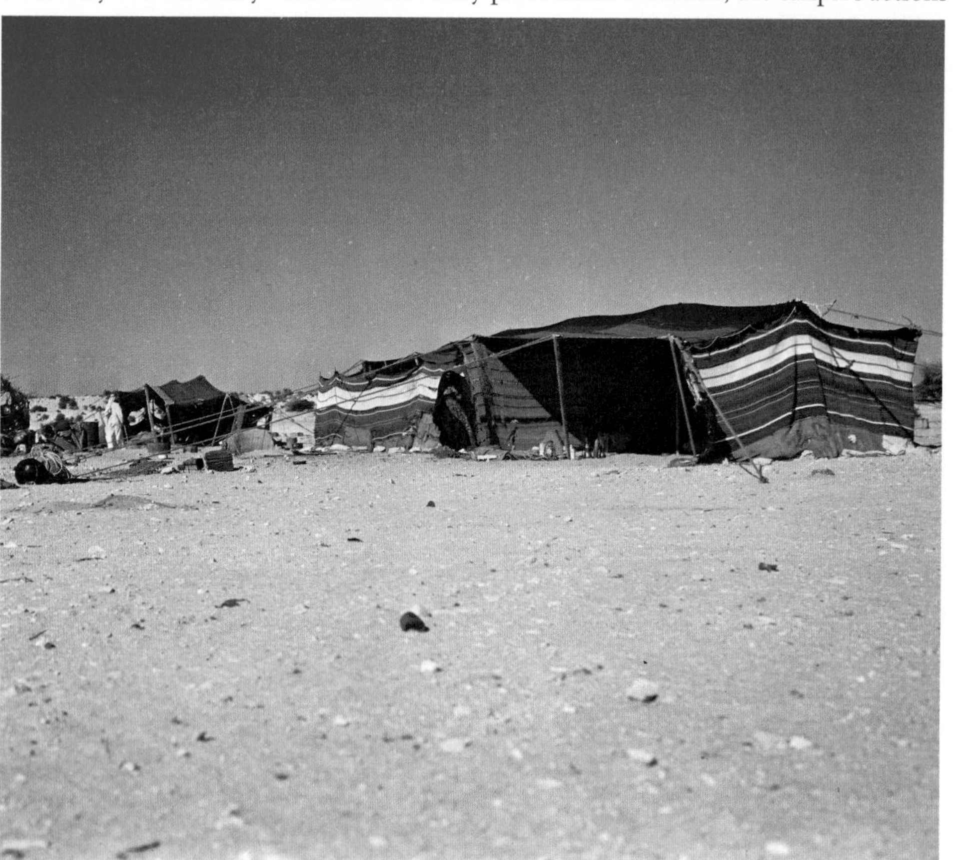

A bedouin encampment in central Qatar on the Persian Gulf. The name "bedouin" comes from the French form of an Arabic word meaning "a dweller in the desert"—and modern bedouin still live a nomadic life much like that of their ancestors in the time of Muhammad.

and claims contradicted his religious obligations, and transformed a sacred office into a purely secular arrangement.

As opposition to the Omayyad dynasty increased, the growing rift culminated in a series of civil wars, beginning with the battle between the supporters of the Caliphs Ali (656–661) and Mu'awiya (661–680).

The Muslims who supported Mu'awiya and the Omayyad dynasty held his predecessors in the caliphate to be the legitimate heirs of Muhammad, and became known as *sunni*. Their opponents considered that Ali, Muhammad's son-in-law, should have become caliph after the prophet's death, and they rejected the authority of the other caliphs. They were called *shii* (a shortened form of the Arabic words meaning "the party of Ali"). The rift between Sunnite and Shiite Muslims became a permanent political and later religious division in the Muslim community.

In the same period, a breakdown of the barrier between the Arab caste and the subject peoples fostered social change. Arab settlement in the garrison cities, towns, and villages caused a drastic transformation of the old bedouin society. The Arabs became landowners, merchants, craftsmen, and peasants, and their originally exclusive settlements were flooded with foreign soldiers, administrators, merchants and workers, and peasants fleeing the hardships of rural life. Many converts to Islam became the clients of the Arab masters. Thus the garrison towns which had been planned for uniformly Arab populations became cosmopolitan capital cities. At the same time Arabs filtered into the countryside, and peoples who had migrated to the towns and adopted Islam often returned to their old homes, bringing with them their newly acquired Arab language, religion, and customs. Slowly in Iraq, where the Arabs were concentrated in cities, and more swiftly in Iran, where they were more often dispersed in village garrisons, the Arabs and their subjects intermixed.

The garrison centers thus initiated far-reaching economic and social changes. Throughout the Middle East, a century of Arab-Muslim rule revived international trade on routes crossing central Asia to China and passing through Iraq to the Persian Gulf. Iraq underwent intensive reclamation and irrigation in districts settled by the Arabs. In Iran, the influx of population, the growth of towns and cities, and the stimulus to agriculture and trade produced unprecedented urbanization and prosperity. On the other hand, in Mesopotamia, Syria, and Egypt, Arab administration brought economic decline. Arabic became the lingua franca of all written communication, and the spoken language of peoples in Iraq and the western provinces. In the east, Persian became the usual spoken language, even of Arabs.

Population movement was stimulated by the growth of new cities and the decline of old ones. New careers developed in teaching, administration, the army, military contracting, international trade, and land speculation. Economic change and social movement caused the decline of old elites and the emergence of new ones. In many provinces the Arab administration favored small landowners at the expense of great estateholders. Arabs became part of the landowning aristocracy, and in Iran the growth of commerce fostered a new urban elite of bankers, merchants, and craftsmen.

Social mobility brought an increase in conversions to Islam. Although there was no mass conversion of Christians, Zoroastrians, or Jews, and although the Arab interest lay in inhibiting conversions in order to maintain tax revenues, Christian bedouins, migrants to the garrison towns, and others, were attracted to Islam both by its religious appeal and by the opportunity that conversion offered for social success. At the middle of the eighth century the mass of Middle Eastern peoples still retained their traditional faiths, but a significant body of converts spearheaded a future society no longer divided between Arab and non-Arab but united in Islam.

# Medieval Arabic Science

Egyptian planispheric astrolabe, made by Abd al-Kharim Mifri, c.1236.

For a period of 500 years the transmission and development of the Western tradition of learning and science lay largely in the hands of the Arabs. This period begins with the establishment around A.D. 700 of Islamic power over much of Europe and Asia and ends with the decline of the Islamic Empire around 1200, which resulted from the growing economic and military strength of Western Europe and the Turkish and Mongol invasions from the Steppes. At its height, the Islamic culture provided a remarkably favorable climate for the compilation and clarification of classical learning, and indeed many of its best scholars regarded their role as just that. As al-Biruni (973–1045) put it: "We ought to confine ourselves to what the Ancients have dealt with, and to perfect what can be perfected." The translation of the major Greek scientific writings into Syriac began in the seventh century, centered in Damascus. By the ninth century Arabic had become the dominant language of learning, and a succession of Abbasid caliphs from Harun Al-Rashid to Al-Mamun encouraged and financed the gathering of Greek works and their translation. The Baghdad school of translation, which Al-Mamun established, eventually became the dominant center. Its doyen was Honain Ibn Ishaq, who served nine caliphs and personally translated almost the whole of the works of Galen, and much of Aristotle and Ptolemy. During this period there was also an active intake of ideas and texts from Indian and Persian sources, and possibly also of Chinese. Certainly, it was a period in which scholars could travel freely over much of two continents. The outcome of this gathering of sources was a set of compilations of classical learning that remained standard text books throughout the civilized world until the seventeenth century.

In the sphere of mathematics, there were two outstanding compilations by the Persian Al-Kwarizmi (c.830)—*Arithmetic* and *Algebra*. His *Arithmetic* was a synthesis of the best of Greek arithmetic with the Indian notation, in which tens, hundreds and thousands are designated by the position of the digit, and it played such an important part in the spreading of this (now universal) notation that it is now normally called "Arabic" notation. His *Algebra*, which is the first work in which that word appears in its modern sense, brought together the Hellenistic and Hindu learning. Although there was little that was original in their mathematics, the Arabs had some success in applying their mathematics to astronomy. Here the outstanding figures were Al-Battani (Albategnius in Latin) and Aboul Wefa of Baghdad, Arzachel of Toledo and Al-Bitrugi of Seville (Alpetragius in Latin). Their observations were more accurate than those of the Greeks, and they played an important part in keeping up the continuous chain of astronomical observations from 3000 B.C. onwards which has been vital to so much astronomy since. All of these scholars published tables of data and used them to make minor corrections to the Ptolemaic system of interpretation. The only really significant correction however—Aboul Wefa's discovery of the "third inequality" in the moon's motion—was forgotten, and had to be rediscovered by Tycho Brahe six centuries later. On balance, the nineteenth-century historian of science, William Whewell, was probably not far wrong in saying that "The Arab astronomer was the scrupulous but unprofitable servant, who kept his talent without apparent danger of loss, but also without prospect of increase." However his contemptuous dismissal of Arab alchemy as a useless mixture of incoherent and confused ideas is less than just. Admittedly, alchemy had a substantial element of mystical nonsense in it, but it also contained the seeds of modern chemistry, and the complexity of the subject matter of chemistry is such that it is difficult to imagine how it could have evolved differently. The earliest alchemical writer of whom we hear is Jabir (Geber in Latin), a romantic figure who was a member of the mystical brotherhood of the Sufis (whose doctrines influenced the Assassin sect) and a friend of caliph Harun Al-Rashid of the *Thousand and One Nights*. Some passages in his *Book of Properties* almost have the flavor of a modern chemical handbook:

> Take a pound of litharge (lead monoxide), powder it well and heat it gently with four pounds of wine vinegar . . . then take a pound of soda and heat it with four pounds of fresh water. Filter the two solutions and then gradually add the solution of soda to that of the litharge. A white substance is formed which settles to the bottom . . .

This is lead hydroxycarbonate (white lead), used for pottery glazing and as paint.

Jabir classified substances into "spirits" (volatile solids such as sulphur, mercury, camphor and ammonium chloride), "metals" (of which he knew seven—gold, silver, lead, tin, copper, iron and perhaps zinc) and "pulverizable substances." It was clear to him, from experiments such as the one just described, that transformation of substances could be induced in the laboratory, and it was therefore perfectly possible (and obviously much to be wished) to transmute base metals into gold, the fundamental doctrine of alchemy. The search for a procedure that would achieve this motivated much of the chemical research during this period, just as a belief in astrology had long motivated attempts to predict astronomical events. In both cases the eventual outcome was scientific progress, though in the short run this was overlaid with superstitions or even plain fraud.

The most distinguished Arab writer on alchemy was Rhazes, whose *Secret of Secrets* includes descriptions of nitric and sulphuric acids, alkali, borax, and alum (all Arabic words), bellows, crucibles, weighing scales, flasks, phials, filters, funnels and kilns. There is also much discussion of the process of distillation. The distillation of alcohol, because of the Koranic prohibition of wine, was not attempted by the Arabs: the earliest recorded preparation of "absolute alcohol" was by Arnold of Villanova at Montpellier in 1300. In spite of his essentially chemical approach, Rhazes believed in the possibility of transmutation. However, later in the tenth century Ibn-Sina (Avicenna in Latin) denied this possibility, and explained all apparently successful transmutations as involving alloys.

Both Rhazes and Avicenna also practiced medicine, and both produced major textbooks. The *Liber Continens* of Rhazes was a vast medical compendium, which included the first adequate description of smallpox and measles. Avicenna's *Canon of Medicine* was more systematic, and became a dominant influence in western Europe, remaining influential well into the seventeenth century.

In the sphere of technology, the Arabs were responsible for improving and passing to the West a number of inventions that probably originally derived from India and China, including the horse-collar, the windmill, mechanical clocks, the magnetic compass, gun-powder and paper. One native Arab invention was the glass lens for magnification and reading, although the idea of mounting such lenses in frames as spectacles appears to have arisen in Eastern Europe later in the thirteenth century. This development effectively doubled the reading life of scholars, and doubtless contributed to the Renaissance revival of learning. It also aroused curiosity concerning refraction, and the *Treasury of Optics* by Ibn Al-Haitham (Alhazen 965–1038) was the first textbook on the subject, on which all medieval optics was based.

Enough has been said about the Arab approach to science to indicate that their contribution lay more in the way they presented scientific ideas than in the ideas themselves, which in large measure originated elsewhere. A most important aspect of this presentation was that they largely avoided the barren conflict between science and religion that hampered the development of science in medieval Christendom. During the twelfth century however a great change came over Islamic thought, due substantially to the influence of Al-Ghazzali (Algazel) of Baghdad, whose book *The Destruction of the Philosophers* denounced scientific study as liable to "lead to loss of belief in the Creator and in the origin of the world." Tolerance gave way to persecution, and in spite of a spirited answer of Ibn Rushid (Averroes 1129–98) in his *Destruction of Algazel's Destruction of the Philosophers*, the intellectual climate of the Arab world became chill. The work of Averroes was burned by royal decree, and generations of succeeding scholars were forced to lead an itinerant life to avoid the attentions of the faithful. It is no accident that during this declining phase of Islamic culture it was the Jews who played an increasing role in preserving and transmitting scientific knowledge—for example Moses ben Maimon (Maimonides of Cordoba 1135–1204). Jewish scholars were also active in the great task of translating the vast legacy of Arabic scholarship into Latin, which was the main intellectual activity of the thirteenth century.

Social change amplified political conflict. In addition to the tensions within the Arab elite and between the caliphate and the Arab masses, non-Arab converts to Islam contested the political and social supremacy of the Arabs. Excluded from equal opportunity in government and the army, the converts now demanded their rightful share of status and power as Muslims. The Omayyad caliphs sought to placate both Arab and non-Arab factions, but their inept and inconsistent policies only alienated both sides. The result was another civil war between 744 and 750. A faction of the Shiite movement called the Abbasids, claiming descent from Abbas, the uncle of Muhammad, assembled a coalition of Arab peasants from Khurasan, soldiers, and clansmen, overthrew Omayyad rule, and brought the new Abbasid dynasty (750–1258) to power. The coup of 750, although stemming from routine grievances, became the focus of the vast social and cultural upheaval already underway in the Middle East. Rebellion would be followed by revolution in the ordering of empire, society, and religion.

## THE ABBASID DYNASTY (750–946)

The Abbasid dynasty came to power with the revolt of Arab peasants and trib factions in Iran. But the Abbasid caliphs evidently realized that Arab caste supremacy could no longer be the political basis of the empire. To resolve the smoldering discord left by the Omayyads, state policy must resolve inter-Arab disputes, relieve the grievances of converts, and accept the new economic and social situation. This the Abbasids did. Under their regime, loyalty to Islam and to the dynasty replaced Arab blood as the basis of elite status. Abbasid policy favored men of economic, social, or political importance, regardless of Arab background and sometimes regardless of whether or not they were Muslims. The new regime was based on a coalition of Middle Eastern elites. While Arabs remained important in the court, in the army,

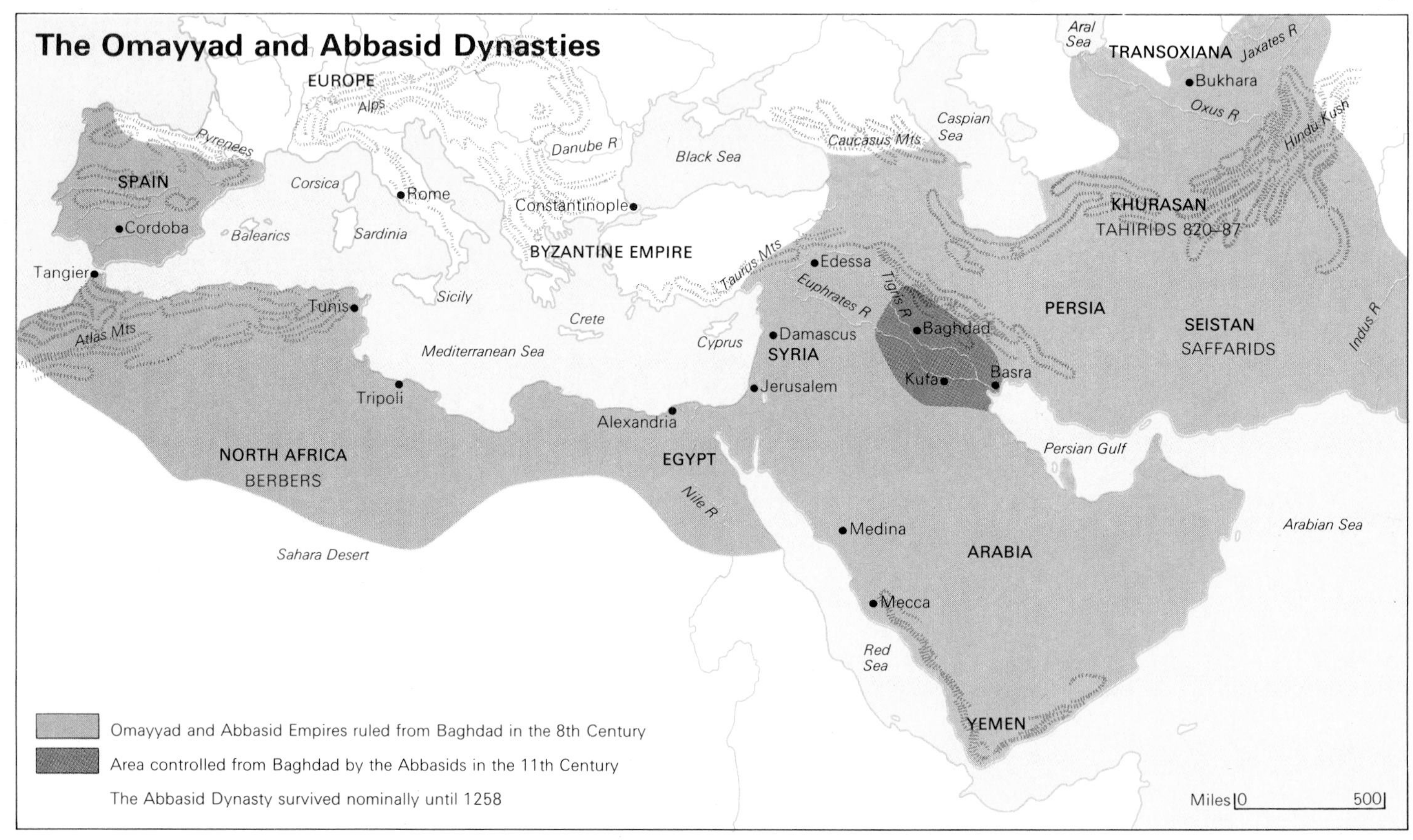

and in judicial and religious life, Persians, central Asians, and Turks were incorporated into the army; Khurasanian Persians and Nestorian Christians from Iraq entered administration; and Shiite merchants and Jewish bankers aided in government finance.

Baghdad, founded in 756, was the Abbasid capital city. Originally developed as a palace and administrative center, it rapidly grew into a city of unprecedented size and cosmopolitan quality. Alongside the caliph and his court were people of many racial and religious backgrounds: soldiers, administrators, merchants, and workers, from Syria and Iran; intellectuals from Basra and Arabia; and peasants from all over Iraq. These people were settled in a metropolitan district of six adjacent cities, with a total population of between 300,000 and 500,000, ten times larger than that of any previous capital in Iraq and representing the sum of the conversions, population movements, and vast economic and social changes wrought by the Arab conquests. Baghdad would supply the political cadres to unify the empire and the cultural genius which would fashion Islamic civilization, thus transforming and uniting the Middle East.

In 613 Muhammad began to preach the message he had received three years earlier in a visitation from the archangel Gabriel, who appeared to him in a cave on the mountain of Hira, near Mecca. But the citizens of Mecca spurned his teaching and in 622, accompanied by his early followers—seen here in a miniature painting—he made the migration to Medina called the *hegira* (departure), an event which the Muslim calendar takes as its starting-point.

## Centralized Government

In many respects Abbasid government followed the organizational precedents of the Omayyads. In its heyday, the period from 750 to the middle of the ninth century, the Abbasid army was a professional force made up of the original Khurasanian Arab supporters of the dynasty and their descendants, who were replaced in the early ninth century by Persian, and then Turkish, slave regiments. The Abbasids had a centralized administration, with new offices to handle correspondence, record keeping, taxation, military pay, and court and pension expenses. In the core provinces of the empire—Iraq, Mesopotamia, western Iran, and Egypt—the central administration maintained a regular bureaucratic organization reaching down to each district and village. In outlying provinces, the caliphate depended upon the loyalty of appointed governors, or upon the submissiveness of local magnates. Despite the strong central bureaucracy, the empire continued to function as a loose coalition of provinces relating in different degrees to the central government. The powers of empire were always relative to provincial power and were checked by the forces of provincial autonomy.

To control and tax provincial communities, the caliphal administration had its own staff of soldiers, police, scribes, surveyors, bookkeepers, tax collectors, and the like; but the actual collection of taxes required the collaboration of local persons, who could furnish indispensable and otherwise unavailable information about local economic conditions, property and water rights, distribution of income, and so on. These headmen, landlords, grain merchants, moneychangers, and other notables, constituted a local elite which mediated between the demands of the state and the resources of the people. Its members negotiated taxes, advanced payments to the authorities, and also made loans to the peasants. Their collaboration with the state was motivated variously by fear of force, by possible financial gain as middlemen, and by the political and social prestige they derived from associating with government authorities. But, in addition, local elites easily identified with the imperial establishment precisely because they originated from the same classes and families. Family and class ties, racial sympathies, and patronage affiliations bound the elites in the center to those in the provinces—sometimes even crossing religious boundaries—and helped to make the empire a working whole. The policy of broad recruitment of elites was not only a solution to the antagonisms generated by Arab caste rule, but also came to be an essential mechanism for the efficient working of imperial government.

Non-Muslims, who still comprised a substantial part of the empire's population, had a recognized place in the imperial order. Christianity, Judaism, and Zoroastrianism were recognized as legitimate faiths and, in their weakened state, tolerated in the Muslim-dominated empire. Non-Muslims were conceded freedom of worship, but they were subject to various legal disabilities, including a poll tax, designed to mark them as socially inferior and to restrict their public acts of worship. Non-Muslims also suffered from sporadic outbursts of persecution by the public authorities and by Muslim mobs. Even so, many non-Muslims were wealthy and powerful —to the envy and resentment of Muslims. In spite of their disabilities, non-Muslims in many ways shared common values and a common style of life with Muslims.

Abbasid administration was not invariably routine and peaceful. Even the best-established administrative procedures involved a tug-of-war between local and central interests and much haggling, even fighting, over taxes. In addition, many areas and peoples refused to submit to imperial control. Bedouins, peasants in distant mountain areas, urban lower classes, some religious minorities, and princelings in remote provinces, persistently opposed caliphal efforts to impose routine controls. Every degree of centralization had to be won by constant struggle.

Baghdad was not only a center of power, but also a center of culture. However diverse in origins, the new elites were unified by loyalty to the caliphate as the head of the Muslim community. The caliphate presided over Muslim learning, sponsored judicial organization, guided worship, and was even an authority on religious doctrine. In addition, Muslims—and many non-Muslims—respected the caliph as the emperor of Middle Eastern peoples, and as God's anointed king who would uphold the natural order of the created world.

### Intellectual Development

Underlying the devotion of Muslims to the caliphate were sympathies based on the growth of Islamic culture. Muhammad had left the Koran and the example of his own life as the basic teachings of Islam, but not until the early eighth century did this kernel of religious inspiration begin to develop into a full-fledged culture and way of life. Then, in the Arab-Muslim society of Arabia and the main garrison towns, interest in the Koran expanded into specialized religious studies. A new elite of learned persons arose, who would become teachers of their people and leaders in communal life. Devout scholars, called the *ulema*, pursued the disciplines of *tafsir*, Koranic commentary; *hadith*, the recollection of the sayings of Muhammad, which provided supplementary guidance on both religious and everyday matters; law, the rules governing ritual, familial, and business relations; theology, rational inquiry into the meaning of religious teachings; and mysticism, the effort to lead a life devoted entirely to god in thought, feeling, and deed. These religious pursuits were supplemented by various secular interests, derived in part from religious sources. Interest in the Koran sparked interest in philology and lexicography. Arabic poetry and history became important to the understanding of the Koran in its original linguistic and historical context. Thus the basically religious nature of early Islamic culture assimilated the cultural tradition of the bedouin past.

The religion which lay at the heart of the larger literary culture stressed faithful practice of all of the precepts set down in Koran, *hadith*, and law. Yet, to Islam, observance of rituals is not enough; practice is the external testing ground for the more important reality of inner spirituality, ethical reform, and devotion exclusively to god. Although knowledge and reason have a part in this inner life, Islam characteristically emphasizes faith and submission of the will to god, making god's command the motive for every thought and action. Islam is a religion of works; but works that must be generated by true faith.

Islamic studies soon confronted the cultural heritage of Iran and Greece. Iranian scribes and merchants diffused Persian political wisdom, history, ideals of morals and manners, and scientific and religious concepts. Some Persian teachings, especially religious dualism, hierarchical conceptions of governmental and personal morals, conflicted with Arab-Muslim views and provoked prolonged controversy. In time, however, Persian values and styles were partly integrated into Islamic culture.

In a similar way, Islam gained through the influence of Hellenistic thought. Converts to Islam, the tolerant courts of the caliphs, and debates between Muslims and Christians, brought Hellenistic ideas into the developing Islamic culture, and Hellenistic science and philosophy began to receive formal attention. Caliphs and courtiers patronized the surviving ancient schools of Jundishapur, Alexandria, and Edessa, which were now active in Baghdad, and Nestorian scholars translated the works of Plato, Aristotle, and other Greek thinkers from Syriac and Greek into Arabic, thus preserving the classical heritage. Later in this account, when Muslim rule in Spain is discussed, it will be seen how this aspect of Muslim culture affected the West.

Muslim interest in Greek culture flourished on two levels. Greek logic and science were considered indispensable elements of secular learning; Greek philosophy and theology helped Muslim scholars to clarify their religious ideas and defend them against Jews, Christians, Zoroastrians, Manicheans, and factional Muslim competitors.

At the same time, Hellenistic philosophic and theological concepts posed grave problems for Muslim thinkers. Greek learning invited questions about the relationship of philosophy to religion, of rational to revealed truth, and of philosopher to prophet. Questions new to Islam, regarding the nature of god and man's free will

From his headquarters at Medina, Muhammad attempted to bring Mecca and the tribes of the area under his control. In 624, at the battle of Badr, 300 soldiers led by Muhammad himself put to flight more than 1,000 Meccans escorting a caravan from Syria. Although Muhammad's forces suffered a setback at Uhud in the following year, when the prophet himself—seen here washing his hands before the battle—was wounded, the Meccans were finally forced to acknowledge Muhammad's authority in 630.

were posed. Although rational philosophy stimulated Islam, it also presented a challenge to a religion based on the supremacy of faith and total submission to god, and established an almost permanent conflict of values and perspectives within the framework of Islam. As a result, Islam, compounded of Koranic religious inspiration, Arabic literary forms, and substantial elements of Persian and Hellenistic thought, became an eclectic, multifaceted culture, rich in intellectual and spiritual possibilities, and bearing within itself its own diversity, its own contradictions, and therefore its own possibilities for further development.

The Abbasid empire which sponsored the new civilization thus represented more than a government; it was itself the sum of a new civilization. As an organized state it represented a Middle Eastern-wide coalition of elites; as an organized society it had created a religious, literary, and philosophic culture compounded of the legacy of several Middle Eastern experiences. State, society, and religion all developed under the aegis of the caliphate, which aspired to an empire with universal jurisdiction and total embrace of the cultural experience of Middle Eastern peoples. But history swiftly disposed of the political empire, leaving only Islam as an enduring legacy for Middle Eastern civilization.

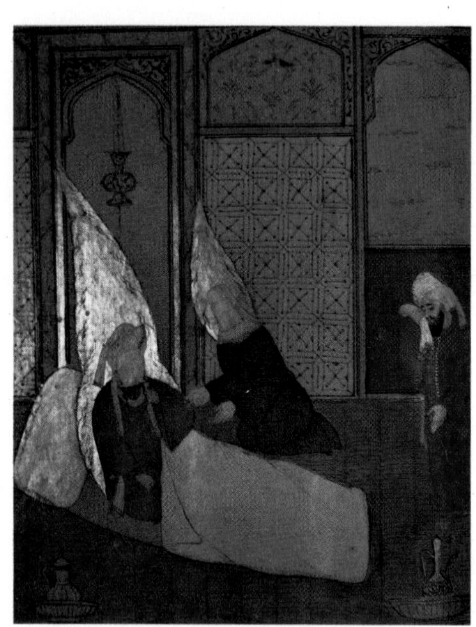

The death of Muhammad. On June 8, 632, three months after making a pilgrimage to Mecca, his new religious capital, Muhammad died in Medina. He had appointed no successor, so Abu Bakr, his father-in-law, was chosen as the first caliph, leader, of the Muslim brotherhood. In spite of opposition to the caliphal authority, the expansion of Islam was rapid: Syria was taken in 633–636; Iraq in 637; Egypt and Mesopotamia in 641; western Iran in 644; Fars in 649; and Khurasan in 654.

### The Abbasid Decline

In the ninth and tenth centuries, the Abbasid empire disintegrated. The first signs of serious trouble go back to the civil war for control of the caliphate between al-Amin (809–813) and al-Ma'mun (813–833), the sons of Caliph Harun al-Rashid. The war, brief but bitter, did irreparable damage to the political and religious fabric of the caliphate. In the succeeding decades, almost every pillar of the empire—religious loyalty, reliable armies, efficient administration, and cooperative provinces—collapsed.

In the wake of the civil war, the victorious Caliph al-Ma'mun attempted to consolidate his position by proclaiming the caliphate to be an authority for religious doctrine; but instead of winning the support of the religious elites with this new policy, al-Ma'mun antagonized them. The *ulema* considered themselves the independent caretakers of Islamic teachings and opposed the excessive interventions of the caliph. Caliphal pretensions also revived a latent dislike for the caliphate's subordination of religious concerns to political ones, and for its supposed corruption, violence, and abuse of power. Thus, in the course of the ninth century, the caliphate lost the direct support of the devout and found its authority gravely weakened.

The civil war had similar effects on military affairs. The old Abbasid armies had supported the defeated al-Amin, and al-Ma'mun was obliged to recruit new armies of Persians, central Asians, and Turkish slave regiments. Instead of loyally serving their masters, the new regiments took charge of the caliphate. They interfered with and exploited the administration, seized provincial governorships, temporarily moved the capital from Baghdad to Samarra, and determined succession to the caliphate. By 870, factional fighting among the various regiments had reduced the central government to virtual chaos.

The new forces had further disastrous repercussions on the general political position of the caliphate. Until al-Ma'mun, the caliphate had recruited military manpower from select groups of its own subjects. But with the increased use of Turkish slaves, the caliphate instead attempted to dominate its subjects with foreign forces who had no attachment to the people. Thus, the effort to centralize and consolidate the military power of the caliphate paradoxically led to the recruitment of forces which alienated the very people upon whom the caliph depended.

Changes in methods of administration also served to weaken the empire. The bureaucracy ceased to serve the interests of the ruler, and instead served only the personal and factional interests of the scribes. In time, the families which had achieved government positions with the rise of the Abbasid dynasty entrenched themselves and their supporters in power, restricted the entry of new talent into the government, and exploited their monopoly of offices for private ends. Government officials embezzled revenues, accepted bribes, and seized provincial estates.

As efficiency and revenue declined, the caliphate could find no effective way to inhibit peculation. No one faction proved better than another. As an expedient, the caliphate began to modify the structure of provincial administration. To raise revenue, large tax concessions, called *iqtā*, were sold to the highest bidders, who were then entitled to collect taxes from the peasants at full rates, but had to pay only a fraction to the treasury. Tax farms, another method of selling tax-collecting privileges to private entrepreneurs, also gained favor as a way of assuring a certain, if reduced, revenue. But the consequences of these expedients were grave. *Iqtā* and tax farms subverted the regular administrative apparatus, and fostered a new class of provincial landlords and notables whose main interest was to deprive the central government of provincial revenues. Thus, the structure of centralized administration was rapidly eaten away.

### The New Elites

Administrative changes entailed a social revolution. The early Abbasid administration relied on the recruitment of provincial notables and elites, but the entrenchment of these began to exclude other provincials from the central government. Within a century, the Baghdad administration was controlled by cliques of professional scribes who no longer had any personal contact with the provinces. Iranians, Egyptians, and Syrians were no longer represented in Baghdad, but local Shiites and Christians, and local merchants and bankers, became increasingly important. The government was becoming isolated in its capital.

At the same time the provincial elites themselves were in decline. A new class of *iqtā* holders, merchants, and tax farmers superseded the old notables. The new elites, who owned large estates, were little disposed, unlike the old elite of middling landlords and village chiefs, to cooperate with the central government. They saw autonomy rather than collaboration as the way to political and financial power. Both in Baghdad and in the provinces, the new elites had interests contrary to the maintenance of a centralized empire. The empire had created the very social forces which would destroy it.

Over a long period, the caliphate saw its provinces break away from central control. In some provinces, war lords, especially Turkish generals, seized power. Governors usurped the caliphal prerogatives, and local dynasties were established in Khurasan by the Tahirids (820–873) and in Egypt by the Tulunids (868–905).

Throughout the ninth century the caliphate strove to restrain the movement toward provincial separation, but from the beginning of the tenth century the movement was beyond control. The Saffarid dynasty which rose in Seistan controlled many of the eastern provinces for a time. Shiite-sponsored rebellions in remote places like Yemen and Tabaristan (modern Mazanderan), in Iraq and Syria, also cost the caliphate substantial portions of its empire. One district after another fell, until the caliph's authority was reduced to Baghdad and its immediate vicinity. Finally, in 946, the Buwayhid brothers, mercenaries from Daylem on the Caspian Sea who in the previous decade had siezed most of western Iran and Iraq, took control of Baghdad and of the caliphate itself. Although the Abbasid dynasty survived until 1258, the empire's political unity had disintegrated. The Abbasid empire was effectively at an end. Its demise amounted to a revolution in Middle Eastern civilization.

Chapter 8

# ISLAM AFTER THE ABBASIDS

## THE POST-ABBASID AGE IN IRAN AND IRAQ

The Abbasid dynasty continued its nominal reign until it was destroyed in 1258 by the Mongols. Iraq and western Iran were dominated until 1055 by the Buwayhid family, which had captured control of the caliphate. Buwayhid rule saw confused struggles for power, and civil wars among the various branches of the ruling family. Meanwhile the government was dominated by undisciplined army regiments composed of Daylamite infantry and Turkish slave cavalry, who competed for power and abused their Persian and Arab subjects. Military dominance meant vast changes in administration, society, and economy. The Buwayhids widely distributed *iqtā* to leading army officers, and also adopted the quasi-feudal practice of granting land to soldiers in lieu of pay. The central bureaucracy was reduced to keeping records of land concessions and services due, while the military gained direct control of local administration and tax collection. Socially, the result was a progressive shift in the balance of power from scribes, officials, and local landowners to an alien force of officers and soldiers. Economic domination of the countryside by the military meant exploitation of the peasants and neglect of irrigation and other rural investments. It led to a rapid decline in the economy of Iraq and Iran, so severe that not until recent times has Iraq begun to recover from the disasters of the late tenth and early eleventh centuries.

Farther east, the Samanid dynasty governed Khurasan and Sogdiana (or Transoxiana) and managed to sustain the Abbasid pattern of government, society, and culture for another half-century. Samanid rule was based on bureaucratic administration and the political support of the landowning nobility. The Samanid capital, Bukhara, became a creative center for the development of Islamic culture.

In 999, in the midst of a cultural renaissance, the Samanid state was defeated by the Turks, and a Turkish government—the Qarakhanid dynasty—was established in Sogdiana. Under Qarakhanid rule, Arabic and Persian Islamic literature was, by a process similar to that encouraged by the Samanids, translated into Turkish and given new life. By the eleventh century, Islam as a religion and culture had become available to virtually all Middle Eastern peoples, regardless of ethnic background.

West of the Oxus, the Ghaznevids, originally vassals of the Samanids in Afghanistan, seized Khurasan. The Ghaznevid regime, founded by Turkish slave officers, was the first post-Abbasid regime in which the army displaced hereditary and legitimate dynasties by selecting its own general as *sultan*, or head of state. Ghaznevid rule, however, was brief: absorbed in Indian adventures and hated in Khurasan for their heavy taxation, the Ghaznevids were easily defeated by new waves of Turkish peoples pushing into Khurasan.

Turkish nomads from central Asia had long been moving westward and were converted to Islam in the late-tenth century. Some of them had established the

A European artist's impression of Saracens on the march. "Saracen," from the Greek word *Sarakenos* (which may in turn derive from the Arabic *sharqui,* an oriental), was the name given by medieval European writers to Arabs in general and especially those who opposed the Crusaders. The first crusade, launched in 1095 by Pope Urban II, resulted in the Christians' capture of Jerusalem in 1099.

Qarakhanid dynasty; others, Ghuzz tribes under the leadership of the Seljuk family, crossed the Oxus in 1029 and by 1040 defeated the Ghaznevids and inherited their empire in eastern Iran. Pushing westward, the Turks defeated the Buwayhids, and occupied western Iran, Iraq, and finally Baghdad in 1055. Another front of the Turkish advance penetrated northern Iran and eastern Anatolia, defeating the Byzantine Empire at the battle of Manzikert (Malazgirt) in 1071. This Turkish victory presaged the eventual displacement of the Greeks of Asia Minor by Turkish peoples. Other Seljuk-related tribes established small principalities in Mesopotamia and Syria, and within fifty years the Seljuks and their nomadic followers had built the largest Middle Eastern empire since the ninth century.

The new empire was large, but fragmented. Dynastic and factional quarrels, tribal insubordination, and the sharing of land among family chieftains soon split the empire into a number of independent segments loosely affiliated by family ties. The Seljuk sultans of Iraq were nominally heads of the empire, but the Seljuk regime, like the Buwayhid, was a confederation of tribes and related princes, each governing his own province. Important Seljuk regimes were established in Anatolia, Iraq, and eastern Iran, with many small Seljukian principalities in Mesopotamia, Syria, and southern Iran.

## Seljuk Rule in the East

In the east, the Seljuks controlled Khurasan until 1156 and Iraq until 1194, until they were overwhelmed by new waves of nomadic invaders. For the Seljuks proved to be only the first of a long series of nomadic peoples invading eastern Iran. Other Ghuzz peoples, Kara-Khitay, Naymans, and finally Mongols, moved across the steppes of central Asia and pressed into Iran. From the mid-twelfth century to the rise of the Safavid dynasty in 1500, the history of Iran is one of invasions, short-lived Mongol

*Above:* An illustration from a thirteenth-century Turkish manuscript showing the great Arabic scholar Maimonides (the Latin name of Musa ibn-Maymum) with other scholars. Maimonides, a Jewish rabbi, was born in Arab-ruled Córdoba, Spain, in 1135. His wide learning—his writings ranged over astronomy, theology philosophy, and medicine—is symbolic of the highly developed culture of Muslim Spain, which brought European scholars who came into contact with it back to a knowledge of the great Greek writers whose work had been preserved in Arabic translations.
*Right:* the tomb of Chingiz Khan at Samarkand.

and Timurid regimes, and economic devastation, culminating in the Mongol invasions of the early thirteenth century.

But in spite of general political instability, the eleventh and twelfth centuries in Iraq and Iran saw the development and consolidation of a number of important institutions inherited from both the Ghaznevids and the Buwayhids.

Although their empire was originally founded by migrating nomadic armies, the Seljuks soon built up professional slave forces to replace their initial supporters. They may have been the first to systematize the training of slave officers, administrators, and courtiers, setting the precedent for the later Egyptian Mameluke and Ottoman palace schools. Following administrative precedents, the Seljuks made the *iqtā* system of land grants and military payments almost universal in Iraq and Iran. But although the Seljuk *iqtā* involved the delegation of authority to collect taxes in lieu of payment for military services, it was not a genuinely feudal system. The Seljuk sultans gave no manorial rights to landlords, nor did they concede their political jurisdiction over the peasants. They did not develop a system of vassalage, contractual obligation, or any feudal substructure. The concept of a single supreme ruler from whom all authority derived remained unshaken, and it was combined with the rudiments of a central bureaucracy to sustain the sultan's claims. Although Seljuk administration involved considerable decentralization of power, it did not amount to a feudal disintegration of organized government.

In the same period, Middle Eastern society as a whole was slowly taking on a new form. The collapse of the Abbasid empire involved the decline of the scribal class and the small and middling landowners and the rise of new slave military forces and large-scale *iqtā* holders. Changing economic conditions had their inevitable effect on the fortunes of all classes.

Ceramic bottle dating from around 1250 bearing a picture of a Mongol horseman. The Mongols of central Asia followed the Seljuks into Iran, which they invaded in the early thirteenth century. Under their leader Chenghiz Khan, who is said to have described himself as "the scourge of God sent to men as a punishment for their sins," the Mongols sacked such cities as Bukhara, Balkh, and Samarkand, and slaughtered their inhabitants.

### The Teachers

Only the Islamic religious elites survived with their prestige and authority intact. Resistance to the abuses of caliphal authority had freed the *ülema* from identifying with a corrupt, oppressive regime, and the collapse of the empire gave them the opportunity for a more active social role. The political and social power vacuum created by the collapse of the empire provided new scope for Islamic missionary activity: in Fars, *sufi* missionaries converted whole peasant communities; in Khurasan various Islamic sects made fresh converts; missionary activity reached even into central Asia. In this era, Islam may have made more converts at the expense of Zoroastrianism and Christianity than it had under Abbasid rule. Islam had finally become the religion of the masses.

The leadership of religious scholars led to new developments in the organization of local communities. Ever since the eighth century, students of law and religion had gathered in groups, or schools of law, each of which developed its own variation of the Shari'ah, the Muslim holy law. In time, the schools of certain scholars acquired popular followings, until most people identified with one or another of the four main Muslim schools—the *Shafi'i*, *Hanafi*, *Maliki*, and *Hanbali*. By the eleventh century, the populace of any given city, town, or large village was affiliated with several of the schools of law or with other Muslim sects. The schools served as forums where the elite might discuss public as well as purely religious matters, and popular allegiance to the schools facilitated the mobilization of opinion and the organized management of public affairs. At the same time, in many areas there were *ayyarun*, youth gangs, which were less amenable to *ulema* leadership and often constituted criminal societies.

Eastern communities under *ulema* leadership achieved a degree of organization essential to the local management of public affairs, but still remained divided into numerous schools, sects, and factions, causing endless competition, hostility, and even violent feuds between the various subcommunities. Nonetheless, an organized and armed populace also had the potential to resist its Buwayhid, Ghaznevid, Seljuk, or other alien military overlords. The resistance of local communities was strengthened because they neither participated in the organized state bureaucracy nor felt any deep loyalty to the reigning princes.

The teachers of Islam had helped to fashion a communal life on a truly Muslim basis. In this period, Islam was fully translated from an elite literary culture, as created in Baghdad, Bukhara, and other capitals, into a religion and culture of the masses.

## Al-Ghazzali and Sufism

A thirteenth-century ceramic plate with an eagle design. This is work of the Seljuk period, which began in the eleventh century when Turkish nomads from central Asia, converted to Islam in the late tenth century, moved into Iran and Iraq and overthrew the Ghaznevid and Buwayhid rulers.

Very little is known about popular Islam, but the most profound religious thinker of the age, Al-Ghazzali (1058–1111), may be taken to represent the synthesis of the broad religious currents which comprised Islamic religious teaching and practice. Al-Ghazzali was a professor in a *madrasa* and a teacher of law who, in his late thirties, questioned his faith in Islam and the value of his teaching. Doubting the truth of what he had always believed, practiced and taught, he studied the teachings of theologians and philosophers and the doctrines of the Shiites, but failed to find a new direction and a new certitude. He abandoned his family, position, and home, and took up the life of a wandering *sufi*, dedicated to knowing god by direct experience. Some ten years later Al-Ghazzali returned to his teaching career, having discovered the true way to live a Muslim life and to interpret the various aspects of Islamic teaching and practice.

Al-Ghazzali and his contemporaries brought together the numerous literary, religious, and philosophic strands of Islam and reconciled them to popular belief and practice, giving equal importance to scripture and *sufi* mysticism. In so doing, they established what have remained the perspectives of orthodox Islam.

The legitimation of Sufism and its incorporation into the core of Islam had enormous implications for the religious life of Muslims. *Sufi* preachers organized brotherhoods which spread throughout the Muslim world. Since that time, for many or most Muslims, affiliation with these brotherhoods, adherence to their teachings, veneration for the *sufi* saints, and participation in *sufi* worship and *sufi* religious exercises have become everyday religious experiences. Alongside the established mosques and prayer rituals, the five pillars of Islam, and other Koranic doctrines, Sufism has become an essential expression of Muslim religiosity.

Thus, in the tenth and eleventh centuries, the teachers of Islam had transformed an elite culture into a mass religion, standardized its teachings, and organized a society dedicated to living according to the revealed will of god as expressed in Muslim *hadith*, law, and theology. Henceforth, doctrine and social life were inextricably identified. What Muhammad had accomplished for Arabians had been reproduced throughout the eastern Islamic world. The Seljuk age saw the creation in the Middle East of the Islamic community as it is today.

The new organization of Muslim local society created a kind of dual regime: on one level, the Seljuk state with its armies and the administrative apparatus which sustained them; on another level, local government by *ulema* notables. The relationship between the state and the *ulema* elites was essentially collaborative, despite many conflicts of interests. The state extended its patronage to the religious elites, confirmed them in positions of authority, appointed them to judicial and administrative offices, and supported the infrastructure of school organization.

In return, the *ulema* lent their support to the Seljuk regime. Local religious leaders arranged for the capitulation of towns in the early phases of the Seljuk migration and later assisted the Seljuk authorities in administration and taxation. They restrained popular hostility to the Seljuks and preached obedience to state authorities as a religious duty. In return for patronage and protection, they lent an alien regime the indispensable aura of legitimacy.

This cooperative relationship, in many ways reminiscent of the Omayyad period, resolved the problem of assimilating nomadic conquerors into a settled society—with one crucial difference. Whereas the Arabs brought their own religion and language and thus profoundly altered the peoples they conquered, the Seljuks were fully assimilated by the settled society and, indeed, helped to assist in the consolidation of that society.

Furthermore, the cooperative relationships between state and religious elites also resolved the disarray which had followed the collapse of the Abbasid empire. From the confused remains of military and administrative precedents, social classes, and religious and cultural teachings, there developed an organized government. society, and religion. Out of the late Abbasid experiments with slave military forces, decentralized administration of the *iqtā* type, politically independent religious elites, and religious and cultural developments—forces which totally disrupted the initial order of the Abbasid empire—came a new balance, a new form of Islamic civilization.

## THE MUSLIMS IN SPAIN

From 711 onward, with the aid of Berber mercenaries, the Arabs had moved into Spain from north Africa. A large part of southern Spain fell beneath their sway; some Christian settlements, like Toledo which retained semi-independence for some 200 years, came to terms with the invaders, while others took on a Muslim identity with a fairly high rate of conversions from Christianity to Islam. However, the earlier period of Arab domination in Andalusia, with its capital at Córdoba, was marked by a general spirit of toleration towards Christian and Jewish communities which, broadly speaking, may be said to have ended only when the Christians on the fringes of the Arab domains began to manifest increasing aggression.

The Madrasa of Sultan Hasan, Cairo, was begun in 1356 and completed in 1363. It is reckoned to be one of the finest examples of Islamic architecture, with a *sahn*, interior courtyard, about 100 feet square surrounded by walls rising to a height of 113 feet. Shown here is the *mihrab*, shrine, set into the *qibla* wall, facing toward Mecca.

Muslim Spain was characterized by a flowering of Islamic culture in literature, philosophy, and architecture (the pointed arch characteristic of European Gothic architecture may have derived directly from Arab example in Spain and in the Holy Land). Christian Europe learned Muslim techniques of agriculture and irrigation and began to cultivate such exotic produce as lemons and sugar. But there was to be a far more important result of contacts between Christian and Muslim in Spain at this time.

The Muslim preservation of the Hellenic heritage has already been noted, and now, through its contact with Islam, the West made what amounted to a rediscovery of the Hellenic culture. European scholars traveled to Spain to translate the Greek classics, particularly the works of Aristotle, from Arabic into Latin.

But the position of Muslim Spain as an intellectual clearing-house between East and West did not endure for long. A branch of the Omayyad family had established a dynasty in Spain in 756, and in 928 its strongest ruler, Abd al-Rahman III (912–961) took the title of caliph and began a campaign to subdue the Christians of León. Although al-Rahman did not succeed, the Muslim position in Spain was not seriously threatened until the beginning of the eleventh century. Then, under a series of weak caliphs, internal strife resulted in the fragmentation of the Muslim domains into a number of petty kingdoms. Despite Muslim successes against Christian attacks in the late eleventh and the twelfth centuries, under the Almoravid and Almohad dynasties from north Africa, the reconquest of Spain by the Christians went slowly forward. It did not reach completion until the fall of Granada, the last Muslim kingdom in Spain, in 1492.

## POST-IMPERIAL DEVELOPMENTS IN THE WEST

North Africa, like Spain, was wrested from the direct control of the Abbasid caliphate. In the later eighth century, three dynasties—Idrisids, Rustumids, and Fatimids—asserted both their independence and their caliphal claims. The Fatimid dynasty was founded by the Ismailiya movement, an offshoot of Shiism, which conquered and ruled Egypt from 969 to 1171. Although the Fatimid regime in north Africa was ousted by bedouins moving westward in the tenth and eleventh centuries, the Fatimids maintained a bureaucratic government in Egypt. Factious slave regiments and religious controversy, however, eventually undermined bureaucratic rule, until the last Fatimid caliph was removed by Saladin in 1171.

No single regime succeeded the Abbasid empire in Syria and Mesopotamia, which fell into virtual anarchy. The Fatimids held southern Syria as far north as Damascus; the Hamdanids, a bedouin regime, occupied the north. The rest of the region was fragmented into tiny bedouin and city-based principalities.

Divided as they were, Syria and Mesopotamia were now exposed to centuries of foreign invasions. Beginning in the early tenth century, the Byzantine empire sought to regain its long-lost Syrian possessions. Encouraged by the presence in Syria of a large Christian minority, the Byzantines launched the first of the crusading movements, occupying Edessa, Aleppo, and Antioch, which they held until 1085. Both the Byzantine and Fatimid spheres of influence, however, were swept away by the Seljuk invasions in the late eleventh century, although the Seljuks only succeeded in replacing the two empires with another host of small principalities, leaving the region more fragmented than ever.

A battle scene from a Persian manuscript of the late sixteenth century, a period which saw the beginning of the reunification of the Arab territories that had originally formed part of the Byzantine empire—including Syria, Egypt, and north Africa—under the Ottomans.

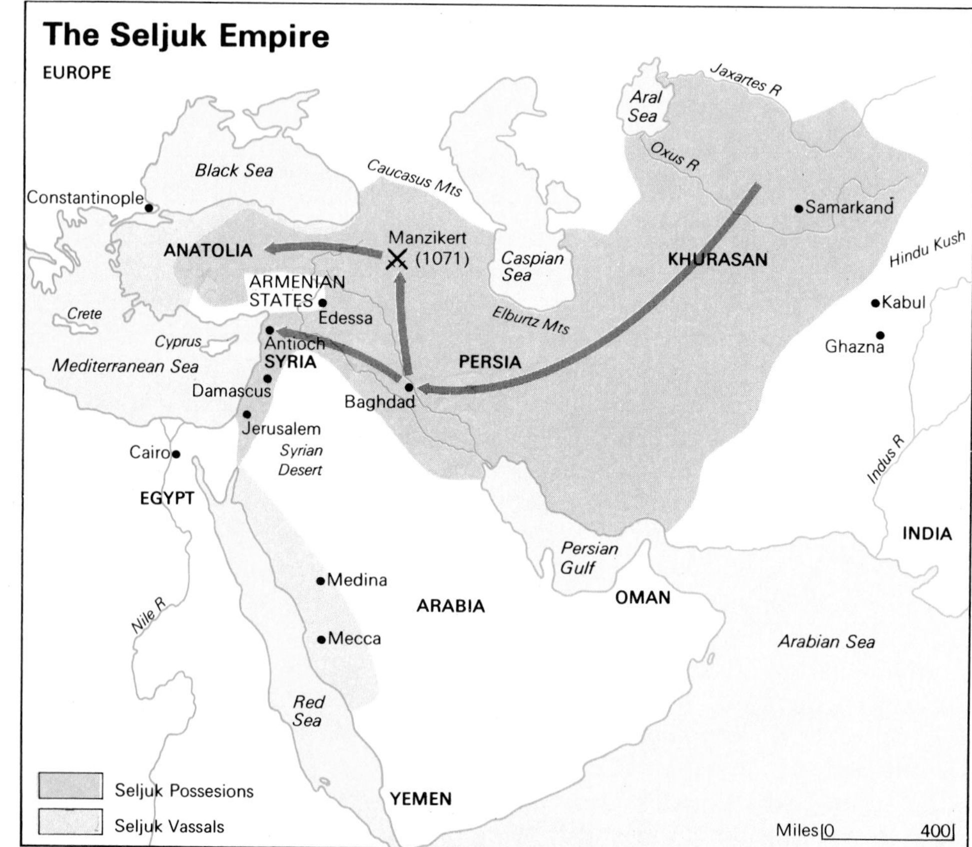

Into this confusion the European crusades were launched. Like a great wave, Christians began to push back the Muslims. Sicily was taken by the Normans. In Spain, the reconquest reached Toledo in 1085. In the Levant, between 1099 and 1109, the crusaders seized Edessa, Antioch, Tripoli, and Jerusalem, and established four small principalities of their own. Although politically fragmented, Syria, with its substantial Christian population and recent Byzantine occupation, scarcely reacted to Christian invasion. Ambitious Muslim princes eventually began to chafe at the disunity of Syria. Saladin, who seized power in Egypt in 1171, finally managed to subdue the Muslim principalities of Syria and Mesopotamia and restore unity to the region. Turning against the crusaders, he defeated them at the battle of the Horns at Hattin in 1187 and at Acre in 1191. But the crusader states, in a reduced form, survived for another century.

The small coastal principalities established in Asia by the crusaders stimulated international trade, but otherwise had little effect on local Muslim society. But an important outcome of the crusades in the Muslim world was the growth of Muslim antagonism to Christians, a contributory cause of the persecution of eastern Christians in the twelfth and thirteenth centuries and the gradual reduction of the substantial Christian populations of Egypt, Mesopotamia, and Syria to the small minorities of today.

The most important development in this period was the reestablishment of a unitary regime and a relatively orderly succession of dynasties. Saladin was succeeded by the Ayyubid dynasty in Egypt and Syria (1192–1250), the Ayyubids by the Mameluke regime (1250–1517), and the Mamelukes by the Ottoman empire. The Ottomans were originally Turkish settlers in western Anatolia who began, as early as 1300, to encroach upon the remaining Byzantine possessions in Asia Minor. In 1354, the Ottomans crossed into Europe to conquer both the Balkan and the Anatolian possessions of the Byzantine empire, a process culminating in the capture of Constantinople in 1453. In 1517, the Ottomans extended their empire to Syria and Egypt, and later to north Africa as well.

In Syria and Egypt, both the Ayyubid and Mameluke regimes were based on slave armies; in fact, the armies themselves chose the Mameluke Sultan. Both used the *iqtā* form of administration, although in Egypt a long tradition of central adminstration permitted relatively close bureaucratic control over *iqtā* distribution. But like their eastern counterparts, these regimes were inherently unstable and suffered from incessant factional strife among the leading slave officers and regiments for the control of the state.

The crystallization of a Muslim communal pattern with *ulema* leadership, organized schools of law, and strong military communities, reproduced the essential political and social pattern pioneered in the east. The specific relationship between regime and society no doubt differed from place to place, but a pattern of collaboration among different elements of society prevailed. Alien slave-based regimes supported the local *ulema* and Muslim orthodoxy, while local religious-based communities gave a qualified allegiance to the state, while trying as best they could to resist exploitation and abuse. In the twelfth, thirteenth, and fourteenth centuries, the Seljuk pattern of state-society relations was reproduced in the west.

Moreover, by the beginning of the sixteenth century the political fragmentation and provincialism of the earlier age yielded to a more orderly pattern. The Ottoman empire reassembled the territories of the Byzantine empire, including Syria, Egypt, and north Africa. Iran, with part of Iraq, was unified under the Safavid dynasty, the first unified Iranian regime since the Sassanian empire. A common culture, seen in two empires, marked Islamic civilization down to the eighteenth century—and its fateful encounter with the west.

An illustration from a French manuscript showing the battle of Roncesvalles, a semi-legendary encounter that took place in 788. In fact, Roncesvalles, in the Pyrenees mountains, was the site of the defeat of the Frankish Emperor Charlemagne's army by Basque mountaineers. In the medieval romance *The Song of Roland*, however, Charlemagne is returning from an expedition against the Arabs in Spain when his rearguard, under the hero Roland, is ambushed by a Muslim army of 400,000 men. Roland and his companions fall gloriously, after fighting a battle to the last man against overwhelming odds.

# Part IV
# Black Africa

**Chapter 9**

# BLACK AFRICA

Thanks to modern news media, there is no lack of information about modern Africa. This is not surprising: the political and social development of a continent about three times the size of Europe, with an area of nearly 12 million square miles and a population well over the 300 million mark, is bound to interest contemporary journalists and writers. But, until recently, historians showed little interest in "black Africa," the larger part of the continent, south of the Sahara desert. Now, this attitude is changing: the growth of schools and universities in Africa since World War II has created a demand for African historical studies and has encouraged scholars—both black and white—to undertake the necessary research. Enough is known already to dispose of the old, popular idea that Africans have no history of their own, other than that dealing with their contact with the white races.

Using radio-carbon dating methods, archaeologists have traced the introduction of agriculture and iron-working during the last millennia B.C. and the first millennium of our era. Linguists have compared the major language groups, to show how they developed and spread out across the continent. The oral traditions of modern African peoples provide information about local political history during the last few centuries. Careful cross-checking and interpretation are needed to distinguish myth and propaganda from historical fact, but the methods are simply those of historians working from documents. Besides, the written sources for African history are far more plentiful than is often supposed. There have long been literate governments in Ethiopia and Muslim west Africa, where some records were preserved. European archives, especially those of Portugal, are rich in material on the coastal regions of Africa since 1500. Then there are the reports of medieval Arab geographers, and a vast literature of travel by European explorers, traders, and missionaries. When all these sources are used, and combined with a knowledge of African geography and sociology, much of the African past can be reconstructed.

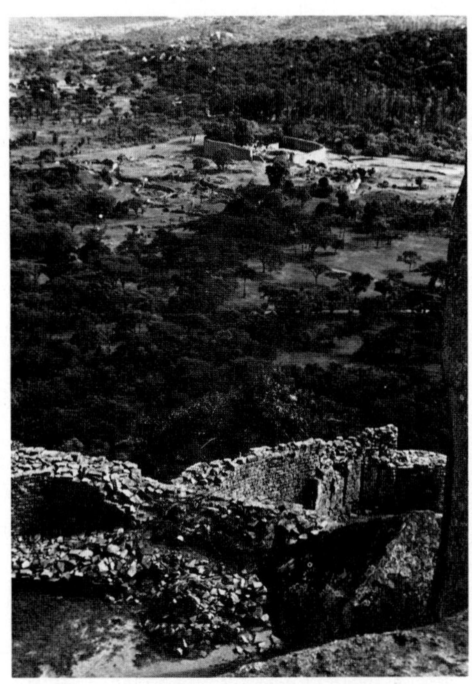

*Above:* View of the Zimbabwe site taken from the hill on which the so-called "acropolis" stands, looking down on the "temple" in the valley below.
*Left:* The entrance to the "temple" enclosure at Zimbabwe. In spite of the theories of early historians, who surmised that Europeans must have had a hand in so advanced a work, the Zimbabwe buildings are of purely African conception and workmanship. It is possible that the complex served as the capital of the god-kings known as Monomotapa, a name given by Europeans in the sixteenth century to both Mutota and Matope, rulers of the Shona people. In 1833, Zimbabwe was sacked by the Nguni people, who used it as a cattle enclosure.

## ENVIRONMENT

The geography of Africa has profoundly influenced the course of African history. In the first place, there were always major obstacles to contact between Africa and the rest of the world. The Sahara, stretching from the Atlantic to the Red Sea, has been a desert for the last 4,000 years or so. It was never a complete barrier—for many centuries, important trade routes crossed it—but, like a great ocean, it severely restricted the movement of people, livestock, and goods. As for the African coastline, it has few natural harbors, and the prevailing winds and currents render much of the coast inaccessible to sailing ships. Also, there are few water-routes to the interior: the greater part of Africa is a vast tableland which slopes quite sharply to the coast, so that even great rivers, such as the Congo or Zambezi, tumble over falls and rapids before reaching the sea.

About 40 percent of all Africa is desert or bush, while about 9 million square miles on both sides of the equator (which divides the continent into two nearly equal halves) is tropical. About another 40 percent of Africa is savanna, ranging from tropical grassland to semi-arid steppe, or forest. Apart from the Sahara, the major desert areas are the Kalahari in the south and the Namib in the southwest. Rain forests, which cover about 8 percent of Africa, cover much of the northern Congo basin and the northern coastal areas of the Gulf of Guinea, in the west. The areas south of the Sahara most suitable for human settlement and cultivation are those where rainfall is most consistent and reaches a total of above twenty-five inches annually: in the west, the Guinea coast and the Niger delta; in the east, the area around the great lakes, particularly Lake Victoria, and the coastal highlands from Mombasa in Kenya to Cape Town in South Africa. Other areas especially suited to settlement and cultivation are found, notably in the highlands of Ethiopia and parts of Angola, Botswana, Cameroon, Ghana, Malawi, Mozambique, Niger, Nigeria, Rhodesia, and Tanzania. Crops of many kinds, from cereals to rubber, are successfully raised in these areas. Areas most suitable for the raising of livestock are found in the south and east, in Kenya, Rhodesia, and South Africa.

Wooden figure of a mother and child produced by the Bakongo people, who live along the lower reaches of the Congo River. The mother and child theme is extremely common in Bakongo art. It is possible that this subject, and the naturalism with which it is executed, stems from the influence of Christian art. The Bakongo received Christian missionaries soon after their first contact with the Portuguese in 1482, and King Manikongo (died c.1545) was baptized a Christian under the name of Affonso I.

The most important constraints on human movement and settlement in Africa are those imposed by tropical soils, climates, and pests. Tropical soils tend to be acid, and thus unfavorable to many crops grown in temperate zones. This meant that in the past many African diets were short of proteins and vitamins (a problem which still exists in some areas), retarding mental and physical development. Soil fertility is also affected by rainfall, which in Africa is often very irregular: a region may suffer from a long drought, and then be deluged by floods of warm water, which wash away valuable chemicals from the soil. Before the introduction of modern medical techniques, the life of men and animals was threatened by insects and parasites which flourish in steady high temperatures, especially in humid atmospheres and stagnant rainwater. Different kinds of mosquito spread malaria and yellow fever. Tsetse-flies infected men, horses, and cattle with sleeping-sickness. Minute snails and worms caused a variety of intestinal diseases, such as dysentery and bilharzia. And when, despite these difficulties, man produced a food crop, it was liable to be destroyed by elephants, baboons, or locusts. Not all these problems have yet been solved.

However, the harshness of the African environment must not be exaggerated. As has already been stated, some regions, such as the volcanic highlands of eastern Africa, are suitable for cultivation; and, in general, the plateaus of the interior are healthier than the humid coastal belts. Travel within the interior has been aided by a number of factors: horses have been bred successfully in Ethiopia, and in west Africa between the Sahara and the rain-forest, and some rivers are navigable for long stretches. There are few areas south of the Sahara where human habitation is physically impossible. All the same, physical conditions have usually made it hard for Africans to produce much more than is needed for basic subsistence. Limited food production, poor diets, and tropical disease, tended to restrict population growth until quite recently; and low population densities served to limit both the incentive and the means for major political or technical change. So the physical features of Africa, together with its relative isolation, help to explain why for so long Africans shared little in the progress made elsewhere by men in mastering nature.

## EARLY FARMING AND IRON-WORKING

Up to about 7,000 years ago, Africa was inhabited mainly by small bands of hunters and gatherers. In north Africa, the "Mediterranean" type, resembling the modern "Caucasian" of western Asia, predominated. Farther south were Negroes, whose features resembled those of most modern black Africans. In northeast Africa, the mingling of Negroes with Caucasians produced a distinctive long-nosed, dark-skinned type. Most of eastern and southern Africa was occupied by lighter-skinned people, whose modern descendants may be found among the Bushmen and Hottentots.

The cultivation of food crops, and the keeping of sheep, goats, and cattle, originated in southwest Asia and can be traced back in north Africa to about 5000 B.C. These practices spread southward during the next 2,000 years, when much of the Sahara was still grassland. By about 3000 B.C., various indigenous food plants, such as guinea rice, millet, and sorghum, had been developed for cultivation in Ethiopia and the woodland regions of modern Sudan and west Africa. Thereafter, the peoples of west Africa began to cultivate the oil palm and African yams, which encouraged them to move south into the rain forests along the west coast. From about 1000 B.C., they began also to occupy the equatorial forests in the Congo basin

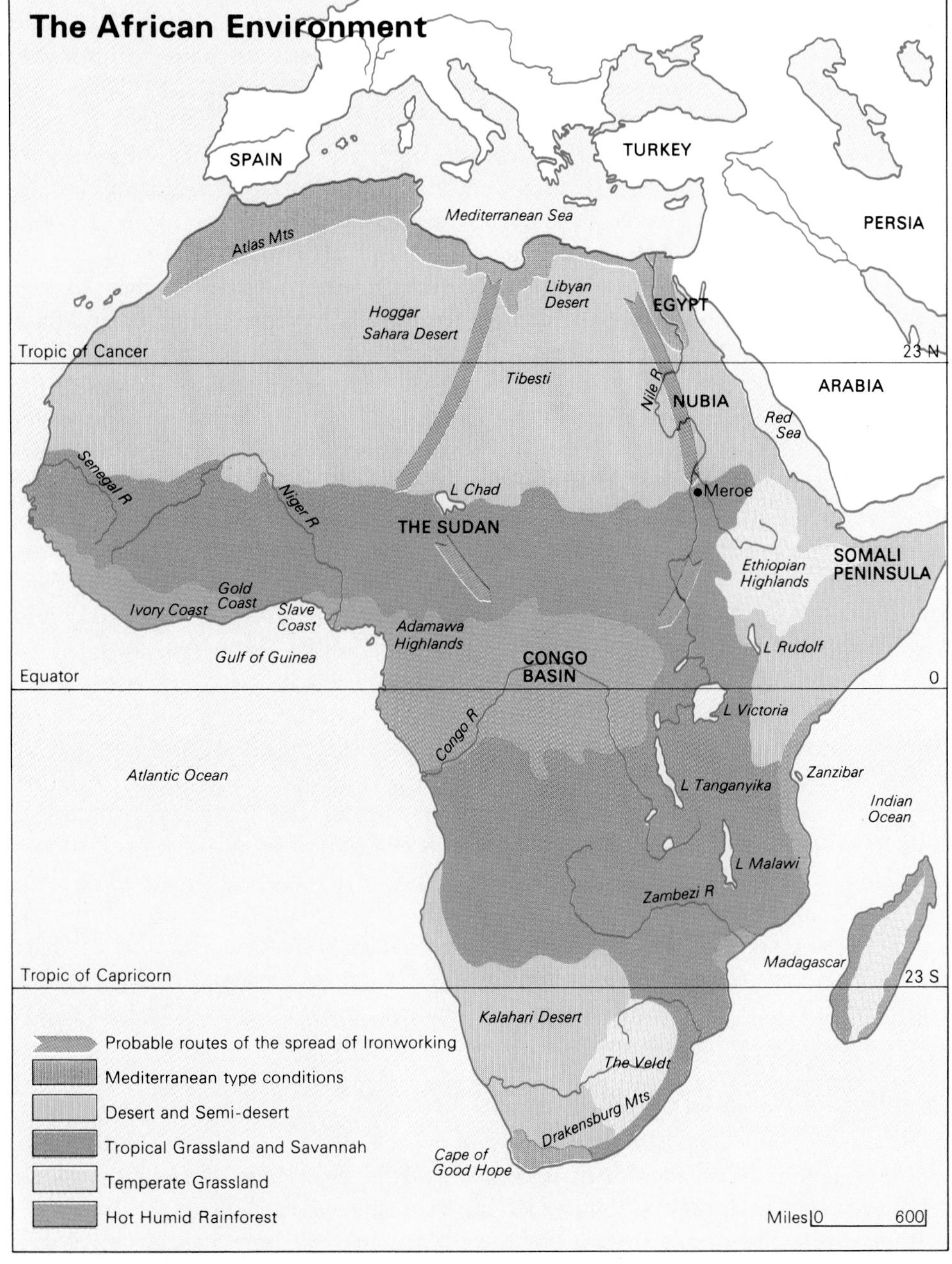

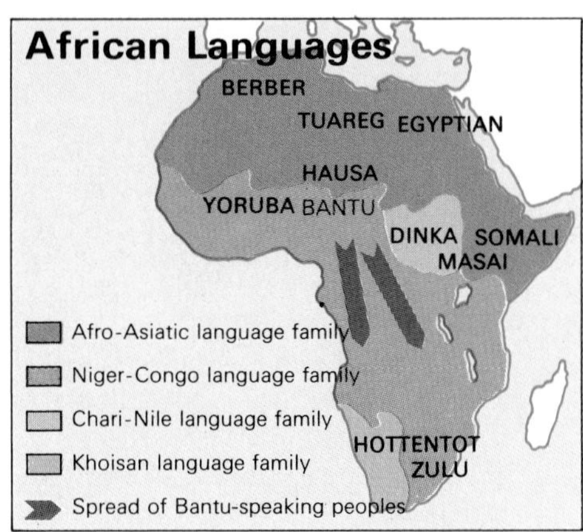


and around Lake Victoria; meanwhile, cattle-keeping cultivators moved down the east African Rift Valley, as far as the crater highlands of northern Tanzania.

The growth of agriculture stimulated human migration: it enabled people to inhabit regions which had not been favorable to hunters and gatherers (although fishing and hunting often continued to be important to farmers). Once a group of cultivators found suitable country, they were likely to stay there until a rise in population forced some of them to move on. And a community which lived for a long time in one area developed cultural habits which made it increasingly different from its neighbors. In this way, a great variety of languages emerged in Africa. The Afro-Asiatic family includes the African Semitic languages, such as Amharic in Ethiopia; the Cushitic languages, such as Somali; and the Chadic languages, such as Hausa in Nigeria. The Chari-Nile family includes the Sudanic languages, and thus the larger Nilotic group in the southern Sudan and east Africa. The Niger-Congo family includes most of the language groups of west Africa south of the Sahara, and also the Bantu group. This last appears to have originated in what is now eastern Nigeria; from there, pioneer Negro cultivators may have spread early forms of Bantu speech southward into the Congo basin.

The early African cultivators were men of the Late Stone Age, although their stone and wooden tools were more refined and specialized than those of the hunter-gatherers. Iron-working was only introduced to Africa in about the seventh century B.C., when it reached Egypt from Assyria. During the next few centuries, the craft spread through north Africa and up the Nile valley, where by about 400 B.C. there was a thriving iron industry at Meroe, in the kingdom of Kush. The earliest traces of iron-working south of the Sahara come from Nok, in central Nigeria, and have been dated to the last few centuries B.C. Thus, it is clear that iron-working in black Africa was ultimately derived from Asia; it may have spread both from Meroe and across the Sahara from north Africa.

The adoption of iron-working was a major technological advance. Furthermore, it was during the early centuries A.D. that new food-crops—bananas, yams, taro—reached Africa from southeast Asia. (They were brought by migrants from Indonesia who colonized Madagascar: this is why the language and physical appearance of the Malagasy people are not at all "African"). Improved food production caused iron-using populations to expand, and the new tools and crops enabled them to occupy what had hitherto been unsuitable country.

The most dramatic population movements took place in the Congo basin, south of the equatorial forest. This region gave rise to a rapid expansion of iron-using farmers, speaking early forms of Bantu languages, into regions still dominated by hunter-gatherers. By about A.D. 500, iron-using cultivators and herdsmen were living in many parts of east Africa; in southern Zambia and Malawi; in Rhodesia; in the northern Transvaal; and as far south as Swaziland. This was clearly a "Bantu explosion," for the styles of the earliest pottery found in these regions are all more or less related, and their distribution corresponds very closely to the distribution of the Bantu languages. Few human bones survive from these sites, but it seems clear that these Bantu pioneers were mainly of Negro stock. They interbred with the original Bushmen or Hottentot-type inhabitants, but the greater numbers of the newcomers meant that their physical features tended to prevail.

### Production and Trade

By A.D. 1000, the foundations had been laid for the cultures of black Africa as they appear today. The spread of iron-working, and the expansion of Bantu-speaking peoples, were the most profound changes in black Africa before the twentieth century. More important migrations took place, and African peoples developed a great variety of social and political institutions. But the underlying technology changed much more slowly. In particular, black Africa generally lacked two devices which have been of great importance in the growth of civilizations elsewhere: the plow and the wheel. With a plow, a man can cultivate much more land than he can with a hoe, which means that he can produce more food. But this is done by using animals, such as horses or oxen, to draw the plow—and in most of Africa the breeding of such animals was prevented by various diseases. This seems to be why plowing was adopted in Ethiopia but nowhere else in black Africa. The lack of suitable draft-animals may also explain why the wheel was not used in black Africa. (Also, population density may have been too low to create an urgent desire for labor-saving devices). Population figures can only be guessed at, but the population of black Africa was probably not much more than 40 million in A.D. 1500—and it may have been less. Whatever the reason, the lack of the plow and the wheel was an enormous handicap. Black Africa made very limited use of animal power, and entirely lacked windmills, watermills, or water-lifting wheels. By and large, production and transport in black Africa relied on human muscles.

Despite this limitation, African peoples made some advances in exploiting the resources of their tropical environment. Lack of good soil, regular rainfall, irrigation, or animal manure meant that intensive agriculture—using the same area year after year—was seldom possible. Instead, many Africans practiced forms of shifting cultivation. Clearings were made in forest or woodland, and staple food crops sown or planted. After two or three years, these plots would be left fallow, to recover their fertility, while new clearings were placed under cultivation. Such systems may at first appear wasteful, but this is to overlook the generally slow rate of population growth in pre-colonial times: cultivable land was rarely under such pressure that it was permanently ruined. Shifting cultivation was usually an intelligent adaptation to local conditions, based on long practical experience. Besides, there were areas where more obviously sophisticated techniques were practiced. In some mountainous regions, such as the foothills of Kilimanjaro, gardens were nourished by irrigation channels, which also served to reduce soil erosion. For the same reason, many east African hillsides were contoured with ridges and terraces.

Whatever the form of agriculture, it was usually necessary for most people to produce their own food, because it was seldom possible for a family to produce very much more than its own requirements. But agriculture was by no means a full-time occupation. Men did the heaviest work, such as bush-clearing; but women usually performed the more time-consuming tasks of sowing, harvesting, and grinding. So there was plenty of time, especially during the annual dry season after the harvest, for people to engage in other kinds of production, and to exchange their products. The ill-informed sometimes suppose that the only trade in pre-colonial Africa was in gold, ivory, and slaves. But these were simply the merchandise which most attracted foreigners. Far more important for ordinary Africans was trade in the things they needed for everyday use, such as salt, ironware, pottery, and cloth.

Sources of abundant, high-quality salt were rare throughout black Africa; as in medieval Europe, salt was often traded over hundreds of miles and commanded a high price. Iron ore was more common, but the quality varied, and African miners lacked the tools and techniques to dig far underground; in any case, the ore had to be taken for smelting to areas with the right sort of wood for making charcoal. Pot-clay was also unevenly distributed, as were the kinds of trees from which bark-cloth was made. A less common source of cloth was cotton, which seems to have first been spun and woven in tropical Africa about 1,000 years ago. Finally, copper, although not strictly a necessity in African Iron Age economies, was valued from

*Top:* Ivory leopards, symbolizing kingly power, made in Benin, Nigeria, in the eighteenth century. Each consists of five large elephant tusks with inset spots, held in place by copper pins, arranged in a formal decorative pattern. Benin remained an independent kingdom until the nineteenth century.
*Above:* Fulani potter at work in Bé, north Cameroon. The Fulani, a northern Hamitic people with origins among the nomadic herdsmen of western Sudan, are Muslims, barred by religious law from making images. They are noted for pottery, leather-work and the production of decorated calabashes.

early times in the shape of bangles and bracelets. The sources of copper were few and far between, but by A.D. 950, and probably a good deal earlier, copper was being mined in the copperbelt region of Zambia and Katanga, and at Palabora in the eastern Transvaal.

The distribution of minerals and other resources shaped the patterns of trade between African communities. Much trade was simple barter at a local level, between different kinds of producers—as when a lakeside or riverside people exchanged pottery and fish for hoes made in wooded hill-country. Some cattle-keeping people, like the Masai in east Africa or the Fulani in west Africa, had to keep on the move in search of pasture so they exchanged cow-hides and milk for iron, salt, or grain from their more settled agricultural neighbors. But trade might also be conducted on a more formal basis, involving greater distances. Chiefs levied tribute, both on their subjects' products and on the imports of traders. This tribute was redistributed at court, according to the needs of different areas. And where goods were exchanged with great quantity and frequency, as in the more populous parts of west Africa, genuine market-places came into being.

The passage of traders between such courts and markets gradually defined regular trade-routes. By the mid-fifteenth century (well before the first Europeans reached the coast), Hausa merchants from northern Nigeria were traveling to Gonja (Salaga), north of the forest in modern Ghana, to buy kola nuts, a delicacy which is still a major item in west African trade. There was no coinage of African origin, but other forms of currency were adopted wherever trade became particularly intense. Copper crosses may have been used as currency in Katanga as early as A.D. 950; standard lengths of copper wire were used a few centuries later on the middle Zambezi. By the fourteenth century, cowrie shells from the Indian Ocean were used as currency in western Sudan.

*Above:* Brass head of an *oni*, a religious chief, of Ife, a federation of small states in southwest Nigeria. The modern Yoruba people stem from the peoples of Ife, which is known to have flourished as far back as A.D. 1000. This head is typical of the naturalistic Ife style which was to influence the figurative art of Benin.
*Right:* An area cleared for slash-and-burn cultivation in northeast Zambia. A clearing is made, staple food crops are grown for two or three years, and the area is then burned over and left to lie fallow while it recovers fertility.

# Tell us what you think...

Students today are taking an active role in determining the curricula and materials that shape their education. Because we want to be sure *Civilization: The Emergence of Man in Society* is meeting student needs and concerns, we would like your opinion of it. We invite you to tell us what you like about the text—as well as where you think improvements can be made. Your opinions will be taken into consideration in the preparation of future editions. Thank you for your help.

Your name ______

City and State ______

School ______

Course title ______

How does this text compare with texts you are currently using in other courses?

☐ Excellent ☐ Good ☐ Average ☐ Poor ☐ Very Poor

Name other texts you consider good and why ______

Do you plan to sell the text back to the bookstore or to keep it for your library? ☐ Sell it ☐ Keep it

Circle the number of each chapter you read because it was covered by your instructor.

Book I Part I Chapters: 1 2 3
Part II Chapters: 4 5 6 7 8 9 10 11

Book II Part I Chapters: 1 2 3 4 5 6 7
Part II Chapters: 8 9 10 11 12 13 14
Part III Chapters: 15 16 17 18

Book III Part I Chapters: 1 2 3 4
Part II Chapters: 5 6 7 8 9 10 11 12 13

Book IV Part I Chapters: 1 2 3
Part II Chapters: 4 5 6
Part III Chapters: 7 8
Part IV Chapter: 9

What chapters did you read which were not assigned by your instructor? (Give chapter numbers.) ______

Please tell us your overall impression of the text.

| | Excellent | Good | Adequate | Poor | Very Poor |
|---|---|---|---|---|---|
| 1. Did you find the text to be logically organized? | | | | | |
| 2. Was it written in a clear and understandable style? | | | | | |
| 3. Did the graphics enhance readability and understanding of topics? | | | | | |
| 4. Did the captions contribute to a further understanding of the material? | | | | | |
| 5. Were difficult concepts well explained? | | | | | |
| 6. Did you find the examples and applications helpful? | | | | | |

Can you cite examples which illustrate any of your above comments? ______

Which chapters did you particularly like and why? (Give chapter numbers.) ______

Which chapters did you dislike and why? ______

After taking this course, are you now interested in taking more courses in this field? ☐ Yes ☐ No

Do you feel that this text had any influence on your decision? ☐ Yes ☐ No

What topics did the instructor discuss that were not covered in the text? ______

General Comments ______

FIRST CLASS
PERMIT NO. 59
DEL MAR, CALIF.

**BUSINESS REPLY MAIL**
No Postage Necessary if Mailed in the United States

Postage will be paid by

**CRM BOOKS**
Del Mar, California 92014

Just fold, staple and mail. No stamp necessary.

## Political Organization

It is often supposed that before colonial rule Africans were organized in "tribes." But it is useless to search for the history of African tribes, because "tribe" is such a vague term. Occasionally, a group of people with a strong sense of cultural or political unity might call themselves "the so-and-so," but many tribal names were conferred upon groups of strangers because they seemed somehow different from the group that thus named them. This is why it is so often impossible to define the difference between one tribe and another. The political history of Africa must be defined instead in terms of the particular units of political organization underlying the ever-changing proliferation of tribal names.

The political systems of pre-colonial Africa were extremely varied, ranging from loose-knit alliances of lineage groups to fully fledged kingdoms and empires. To some extent, these differences were due to variations in environment and economy. The nomadic herdsmen of eastern Africa and the Sudan were organized in relatively small groups of kinsmen, thinly scattered over the large area which they needed for grazing. Such groups might well be linked in such a way that disputes between them could often be settled without fighting, but there was no central authority with power to enforce its decisions. At the same time, other kinds of small-scale political organization were found among agricultural peoples, such as the Ibo-speakers of eastern Nigeria, the Kikuyu of Kenya, or the Plateau Tonga of southern Zambia. And in contrast to such "acephalous," or leaderless, peoples were the great number of societies in Africa centered around kings and chiefs.

It is hard to determine how these more centralized political systems came into being. At one time, it was supposed that they were all ultimately derived from the powerful and elaborate kingship of ancient Egypt, but it is unlikely that enough will ever be known about early African kingdoms to prove this theory true or false.

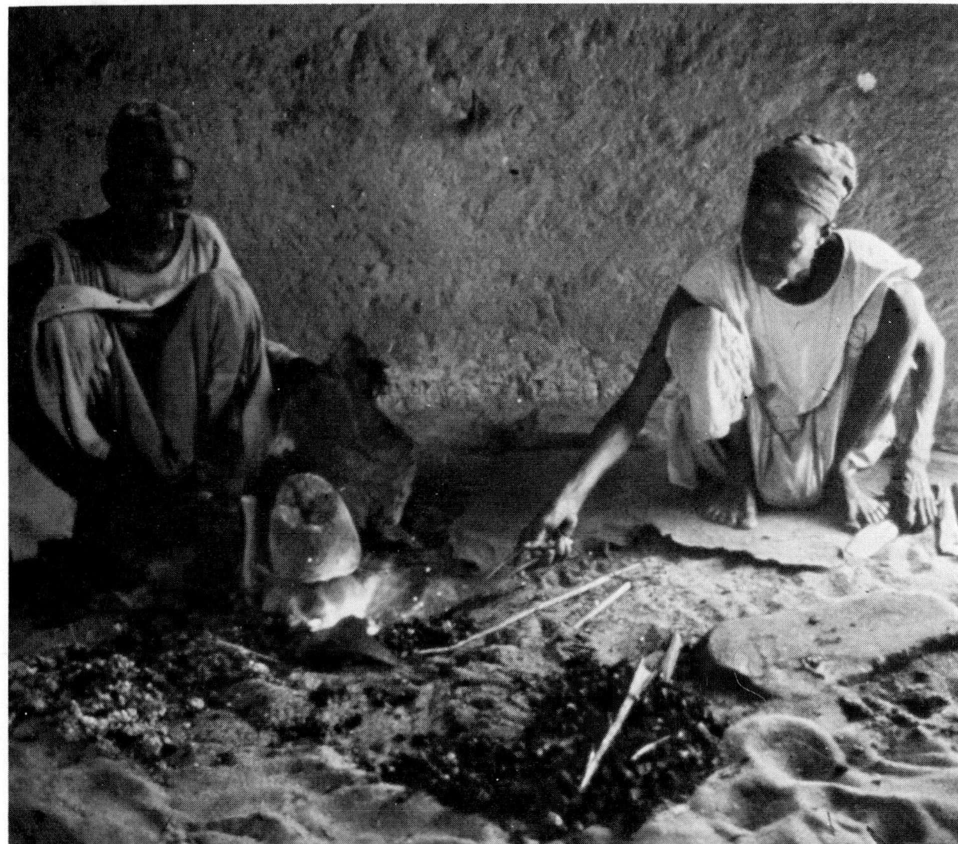

*Above:* Cast bronze head of an *iyoba*, queen-mother, wearing a headdress and collar of coral beads. Probably dating from the sixteenth century, it is typical of the famous bronzes commemorating the rulers of the kingdom of Benin. The art of bronze casting was probably introduced into Benin from Ife around the year 1280.

*Left:* A smith of the Durra people forging a hoe, in Bé, north Cameroon. Iron was already being mined and smelted in west Africa by the third century B.C. This skill may have developed independently in Africa; or come from Egypt and the Sudan; or along the desert trade routes, from Carthage.

In any case, it now seems more important to examine the various local pressures—geographical, economic, cultural—likely to have caused major political change. And there is often no hard-and-fast line dividing kingdoms from "tribes without rulers." Among the latter, there were often religious leaders, rain-makers, and judicial arbitrators whose authority was widely recognized. In certain circumstances, such leaders might gain enough prestige, or enough control over scarce economic resources, to attract a following of kinsmen and dependents; these might then be able to enforce their leader's will. And where, as in Africa, great importance was attached to kinship, the authority of such a leader could well be inherited on his death by junior members of his family. In this way, hereditary chieftainship came into being, and a chiefdom took shape as a chief extended his political authority over particular groups living in particular territories. Military conquest was the most obvious method for such expansion, but it could also be the result of chiefless peoples voluntarily submitting their disputes to a successful chief. And because trade, especially long-distance trade, needs stable political conditions, kingdoms tended to attract foreign merchants and to flourish at the intersection of trade-routes.

A divining bowl for the detection of witches, a product of the Bavenda people of northern Transvaal, South Africa. The bowl is filled with water on which seeds are floated. Their movements, and in particular the various symbols on the rim and the bottom of the bowl on which they come to rest, tell the seer where to seek for evildoers.

It is difficult to trace back the political history of black Africa in any detail for more than a few centuries. But there is at least evidence for the existence of African kingdoms well before A.D. 1000, by which date there were a number of black kings along the southern fringes of the Sahara. The capitals of such states as Takrur, Ghana, or Kanem were sizable towns, sustained by trade across the desert and by the concentration of cultivators along the banks of the Senegal and upper Niger Rivers and in the Chad basin. During the next 500 years, a number of chiefdoms took shape among the Yoruba in southwest Nigeria, and farther east the Benin kingdom was founded among the Edo peoples. Well before 1500, there was a cluster of kingdoms between the great lakes of east Africa: the Kongo kingdom flourished beside the lower reaches of the Congo River; while during the fifteenth century, south of the Zambezi, the Mwenemutapa dynasty briefly held sway over an empire of subordinate kingdoms which extended over much of modern Rhodesia and Mozambique.

Farther north, on the east side of the continent, a line of Christian rulers extended their power over the Ethiopian plateau. The Ethiopian emperors claimed descent from the biblical King Solomon, through the Queen of Sheba (the biblical Sheba is sometimes identified with Ethiopia), but this was no more than a traditional belief. However, in the fourth century the kingdom of Axum, near the Red Sea, was converted to Christianity by missionaries from Alexandria, and the religion spread over parts of Ethiopia. After the seventh century, the Ethiopian border territories, particularly those near the Red Sea, fell under the increasing sway of Islam, and Ethiopia later provided one of the bases from which Islamic ideas, and Muslims in search of trade and slaves, moved farther into Africa.

The internal workings of these African kingdoms, like those of the multitude of smaller chiefdoms, were largely shaped by relations within and between ruling families. This is why so many African kingdoms and empires tended not to survive for very long. Much African history consists of the quarrels of brothers and cousins, uncles and nephews, who all had a more or less equal right to inherit the throne. In case of failure, there was often little to stop the disappointed claimants moving away to set up independent kingdoms of their own. It was only in special conditions that kings were able to counterbalance their "line organization" of territorial, usually hereditary chiefs, with a "staff organization" based on the royal capital, such as a standing army and a team of specialized administrators. To maintain such a staff of royal officials called for a sizeable food surplus, and the possibility of sharing out wealth from trading and raiding.

One of the few examples of such highly centralized government was nineteenth-century Buganda, where the abundance of bananas made food production relatively easy, and there the topography permitted rapid communication, by foot and canoe, throughout an expanding kingdom. Buganda, moreover, was one of the few areas in pre-colonial black Africa (Ethiopia and Dahomey were others) where some land at least was sufficiently productive to be valued for its own sake, so that officials could be rewarded with estates. In most kingdoms, it was control over people (and sometimes cattle) that counted, rather than rights of continuous occupation in one area. For this reason, African kingdoms cannot really be called "feudal"; in any case, it was only in Ethiopia, and parts of west Africa where climatic conditions allowed horse-breeding, that rulers could employ cavalry, so important in European feudalism. At the same time, the generally low degree of centralized power meant that in practice very few African kings could behave like

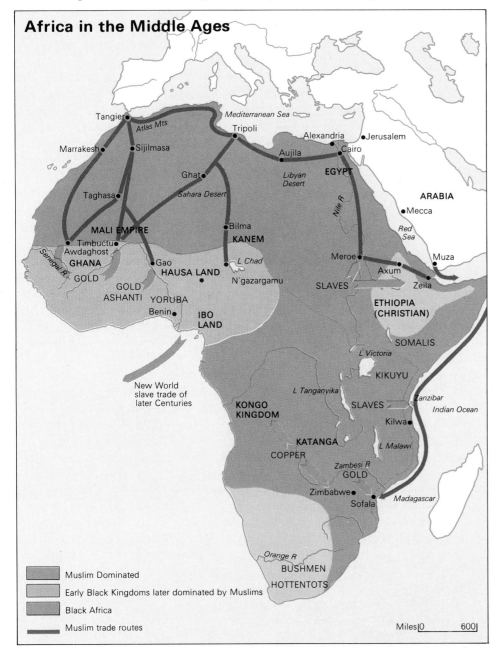

**Africa in the Middle Ages**

Tangier
Atlas Mts
Mediterranean Sea
Tripoli
Alexandria
Jerusalem
Marrakesh
Sijilmasa
Aujila
Cairo
Ghat
Libyan Desert
EGYPT
Taghasa
Sahara Desert
ARABIA
Nile R
Mecca
Bilma
MALI EMPIRE
KANEM
Red Sea
Timbuctu
Awdaghost
GHANA
Senegal R
Gao
L Chad
Meroe
Muza
HAUSA LAND
Axum
GOLD
GOLD
N'gazargamu
SLAVES
Zeila
ASHANTI
YORUBA
Benin
IBO LAND
ETHIOPIA (CHRISTIAN)
SOMALIS
L Victoria
KIKUYU
New World slave trade of later Centuries
L Tanganyika
Zanzibar
KONGO KINGDOM
SLAVES
Indian Ocean
Kilwa
KATANGA
L Malawi
COPPER
Zambesi R
GOLD
Zimbabwe
Sofala
Madagascar
Orange R
BUSHMEN
HOTTENTOTS

Muslim Dominated
Early Black Kingdoms later dominated by Muslims
Black Africa
Muslim trade routes
Miles 0 600

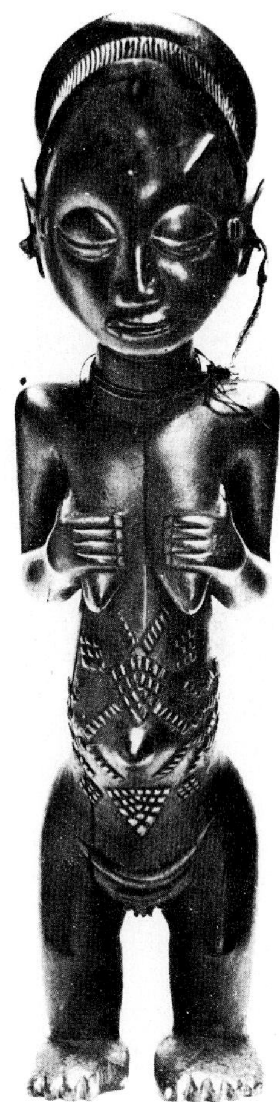

Figure of a female ancestor, work of the Baluba-Hemba people of Congo-Kinshasa. The rounded, flowing style is typical of Baluba art. The carved figures of ancestors have a magical significance: they are thought to appease the dead, who would otherwise torment the dreams of their descendants. This particular figure is eighteen inches high, but smaller figures, carved in ivory or hippopotamus tusk, were made to be carried on the person, either tied to the arm or tucked into the armpit.

despots. They might be greatly feared at court, but their control over outlying chiefdoms was usually limited. There were few genuinely representative councils, but respect for the elders usually ensured that traditional law and custom was observed. In this sense, the "rule of law" was by no means unknown in pre-colonial Africa.

## Culture

The contrast between most African kingdoms and those of medieval Europe is striking in the intellectual and cultural spheres. Writing—which has only been invented in a few times and places, and never in Europe—was introduced to Africa by outsiders, and it spread very slowly until the present century. The reason for this may simply be that black Africans had little use for permanent records. Even where they handled large quantities of goods, they could seldom preserve them for long periods so there was little need to count them exactly. Nor did Africans usually need to record details of land use and inheritance (Christian Ethiopia, once again, was an important exception). The lack of writing was of course an obstacle to learning, whether from literate foreigners or from the experiences of earlier African generations. Black Africa lacked an independent "great tradition" of science and learning: most kings and peoples shared in a common tradition of pre-scientific thought and belief. And as in popular traditions the world over, there was no real idea of *chance:* puzzling situations which more sophisticated peoples might put down to mere coincidence were attributed to some kind of supernatural agent, and diviners ("witch-doctors") decided whether this was an angry ancestor, a nature spirit, or a human witch. There was nothing inherently illogical about such beliefs, which persisted among uneducated Europeans until recent times, but they tended to thwart individual initiative: if a man were too successful—as hunter, farmer, or trader, perhaps—he was liable to be accused of practicing witchcraft, and this could mean a most unpleasant death.

A headrest supported by two figures. The figures may be meant to represent female wrestlers, work of the Baluba-Shankadi people, members of the loose group of Baluba tribes who live in an area extending from Rhodesia to north of Lake Tanganyika. In recent years, experts in African art have succeeded in ascribing works not only to specific tribes, sub-tribes, and villages, but also to individual artists. The work shown here is attributed to an artist known as the Master of the Cascade Coiffures.

Yet even measuring by conventional Western standards, there is much to admire in the cultures of black Africa. Superstition can inspire as well as inhibit artistic achievement, and it can be quite compatible with technological expertise. There is little need here to stress the rhythmic genius of black Africa, whether expressed in singing and dancing or by drums, xylophones, thumb-pianos, bow-harps, and flutes. The oral literature of Africa displays both the skills of the story-teller and the insights of the seer. Much African carving and building is lost forever, for most woodwork soon crumbles away in the tropics, but such artifacts as the wooden masks of the Kuba, or the great thatched palaces of the lake kingdoms in east Africa, bear witness to long traditions of high craftsmanship. In many African villages, housewives can still be seen molding graceful pots by hand with remarkable skill. Sometimes more durable materials were used for building or craft work. In western Nigeria there may have been a continuous tradition linking the terra-cotta heads of the Nok culture, dating from the last few centuries B.C., with the terra-cotta and bronze heads of Ife (A.D. 1000–1200) and the bronze heads and reliefs of Benin (some of which date from as late as the fifteenth century). Among Africa's architectural remains, Ethiopia boasts the rock-hewn churches of Lalibala (thirteenth century) and the very ancient cathedral and monuments of Axum, besides the seventeenth-century palaces of Gondar, which were heavily influenced by Portuguese architecture. In Rhodesia, where numerous granite outcrops enabled early African kings to surround their courts with walls of stone rather than reed and wood, Zimbabwe (probably thirteenth and fourteenth century) provides the most famous example of such dry-stone walling. It is not possible to say with certainty how labor was organized for such a massive enterprise, but the roughly contemporary earthworks at capital sites in western Uganda and Benin show that such tasks were by no means beyond the resources of African rulers.

## AN AFRICAN CIVILIZATION: THE KONGO KINGDOM

This brief account attempts to show how the history of black Africa differs in important ways from that of other parts of the world. But is it possible to speak of a distinct "African civilization," as it is to speak of the civilizations of India or China? Is it possible to point to a "typically African" society? At least, it can be said that the peoples of black Africa had a good deal in common. The limited technology and literacy; the problems of life in the tropics: these prevailed across the continent. The major language groups extended over large regions, within which similar ideas, beliefs, and customs easily spread. These broad cultural resemblances—as among the Mandingo of west Africa, or the Bantu-speaking peoples—partly overrode differences in geography and economic life. Bearing this in mind, a brief examination of the Kongo kingdom, which was situated in the area roughly corresponding with the north of modern Angola will serve to give some impression of what life may have been like in many other African societies.

A bronze figure of a hunter carrying an antelope, found in Benin although not executed in the Benin style. This is the product of a school which a modern art historian has named the "Lower Niger Bronze Industries." The method of casting bronze by the *cire-perdue* (lost wax) process is of considerable antiquity in Nigeria. A figure is molded in wax, with raised ornamentation in wax, on a core of clay and a second layer of clay is applied to cover it. The mold is heated, the melted wax runs out, and molten metal is poured into the space left between the clay layers. When the metal has set, both layers of clay are broken up and the metal cast is polished and finished.

The people of Kongo mostly lived in small villages, each of which comprised a few closely related families together with their domestic slaves (war-captives or lesser criminals). They lived in wattle-framed houses, with walls of palm-matting and roofs of thatch. Their furniture consisted of sleeping mats, a few cooking pots, baskets, and gourds for drinking palm wine. Each homestead had its own granary, in which was stored the annual harvest of millet, the staple crop. Every day, the women ground this into a white flour and stirred it in boiling water to make a stiff porridge, which was eaten with peas or beans and spicy sauces made from palm oil. Meat, whether chicken, fish, or game, was a luxury for most people, but bananas, yams, and pumpkins provided some variation from the usual millet. Clothes were made from skins and cloth woven from raffia palm: ordinary people wore a simple skirt hanging from the waist, but the king and other notables wore finely woven raffia fabrics, beautifully dyed, which European visitors likened to velvet, silk, and brocade. Trade was a major feature of Kongo life. A description of the Kongo kingdom published at Rome in 1591, typical of accounts by missionaries, states that the people of one province sold or bartered

> *... salt, colored cloth from India or Portugal, and the seashells which they use as currency. In exchange they receive palm cloths, ivory, skins of civet-cat, and belts made from palm leaves, which are much prized in these parts. Crystals are found here in abundance, and also various metals. The people mainly seek iron, as they use it to make knives, weapons, axes, and other such useful and necessary tools. By contrast, they regard other metals as of no practical use.*

Each village had a hereditary headman, who had some authority over other heads of families, but serious quarrels and crimes were referred to district judges. These were appointed—and could be dismissed—by the king himself, or by one of the six provincial governors. There were also numerous titled officials with various duties at the royal capital. This was a substantial town, surrounded by a cluster of suburban villages, its total population running into tens of thousands. In the southern quarter there was a large square where public dances and military reviews were held, which the king watched from under the shade of a great fig tree. Nearby was the king's own enclosure, nearly a mile in circumference, with entrances guarded by royal musicians bearing drums and ivory trumpets. The royal palaces were hidden by a labyrinth of palisades. The towns of the provincial governors were built on the same pattern, but on a smaller scale.

The main function of the administrative hierarchy was to collect tribute. This is vividly shown in another Vatican document:

> *The village chiefs have above all to take care to collect from their subjects the taxes which are due to the king, and which they carry to the governor of their province. The governor presents himself twice in each year at the royal capital in order to pay in the tribute, and if the king is satisfied, he replies with the one word* wote, *which means "you have done well." In this case the governor esteems himself highly favored and makes many clappings of his two hands. As a sign of joy he throws himself on the ground, covering his body with the dust. His servants do the same, and then take him on their shoulders, and go through all the city crying his praises. . . . But if the king does not say this word* wote, *he retreats greatly discomfited, and another time he takes care to bring a larger tribute. The tribute is not fixed as to quantity; each brings as much as he can. But if the governor does not do better, the king addresses to him a strong reprimand, and takes away his post. Such a man then becomes as poor as the most miserable of all the blacks. The king does this because he is the absolute lord of all the kingdom: and whenever the desire so takes him, he takes away the offices and the inheritances and the goods of whomever he wills, and there is no one who can say him nay.*

An ivory mask from the royal regalia of Benin. Representations of the heads of European traders are incorporated into the diadem. The Portuguese made contact with African kingdoms on the west coast around the end of the fifteenth century, and soon established a trade in slaves, ivory, gold, and spices. Particularly in Benin, works of art in which Europeans are represented display greater freedom of pose and style than do the traditional portraits of royalty or works of religious significance.

It would seem from all this that the Kongo king was indeed an absolute ruler. But in practice his power was limited by various factors. His only standing army was a bodyguard, mostly recruited from foreigners; if the king wanted to make war, he had to issue a draft order to his able-bodied male subjects, and such a conscript army could not be maintained for long in the field. Besides, the kingdom was extensive, and some provincial capitals were over 100 miles from the king's capital. The appointment of governors was often a result of compromise between the king's wishes and those of certain aristocratic families. There was, in any case, a central council of twelve clan notables. The growth of royal power was also checked by recurrent conflict over succession to the kingship. All descendants of Affonso I (died 1540) were eligible. The new king was selected by a small group of titleholders (including at least two provincial governors). They were likely to choose the man who had most support from the country at large, and this meant that there was constant intrigue and internal warfare: rival factions fought each other on the king's death, or even rebelled against reigning kings. So Kongo, although fairly prosperous by African standards, proved very vulnerable to interference by well-armed Europeans with commercial and political ambitions.

### Africa and the World

This account has concentrated on the "African" factors in African history. But parts of the continent have long been exposed to outside influences. Several ports along the east coast were known to Greek sailors as sources of ivory in the early centuries of the Christian era. The trade of the Indian Ocean rapidly expanded with the rise of Islam, and Muslim traders from Arabia and Persia settled along the African coast. By A.D. 1000, the most valuable export was gold, mined by Africans on the Rhodesian plateau and brought down to Sofala (modern Nova Sofala) in Mozambique. It was this gold trade which helped make possible both the great buildings at Zimbabwe and the Arab palaces on the coast, as at Gedi in Kenya and Kilwa Kisiwani in Tanzania; and all these sites imported Chinese pottery has been found. Moreover, it was the mingling of Arabic-speaking immigrants with black Africans along the coast which gave rise to the Swahili language, although the Swahili-Muslim culture made little impact on the interior until the nineteenth century.

Islam was far more important in west Africa, where the trans-Saharan trade routes long kept open direct links with Muslim centers of learning in north Africa. Throughout the European Middle Ages, the Mediterranean world derived much of its gold from mines near the upper Senegal River and in Ashanti, in modern Ghana, which was carried north across the Sahara. In the powerful Mali empire, as in other black kingdoms of the western Sudan, the religion and law of Islam was adopted.

By the sixteenth century, Europeans had discovered the Americas and had sailed round Africa to the Far East. For the next few centuries, Africa was mainly valued by whites as a source of slaves for plantations in the New World. White traders usually confined themselves to forts along the coast of West Africa, although the Portuguese also established colonies in Angola and Mozambique. Slavery was nothing new to Africa, where criminals and prisoners-of-war were often deprived of ordinary civil rights. But such slaves were still treated as people, and they were often adopted into families. Indeed, they were sometimes given positions of responsibility, such as the leadership of trading caravans or the negotiations of business on their masters' behalf. They could usually own property, and it was possible for a slave to be richer than a free man. Moreover, it was common practice that a slave who ran away from his master and found another need not be returned.

The vicious chattel slavery of the West was quite foreign to Africa, and for many Africans the slave trade was an unmitigated disaster. Quite apart from the misery and death inflicted by white men, the trade provoked much fighting between African peoples far into the interior. The liquor, guns, and cloth brought by the whites were strong temptations, and rulers such as the kings of Dahomey and Benin became extremely rich and powerful by selling slaves. But the only solid gain by ordinary Africans from this phase of European contact was the introduction of new food crops: maize, cassava, and the sweet potato were brought by the Portuguese from the Americas.

# Suggestions for further reading Book 1

Works preceded by an asterisk (*) are known to be available in paperback editions at the time this list was compiled. However, the number of paperback books is increasing constantly and rapidly. Therefore, in the case of works not so designated in the following list, the reader is advised to enquire from his bookstore whether a paperback edition has subsequently been published.


## Part I:

*__Albright, W. F.,__ *From the Stone Age to Christianity* (Baltimore 1967)
*__Childe, V. G.,__ *Social Evolution* (London 1951)
**Cornwall, I. W.,** *Prehistoric Animals and their Hunters* (New York 1969)
**Pilbeam, D.,** *The Evolution of Man* (New York 1970)
*__Powell, T. G. E.,__ *Prehistoric Art* (New York 1966)
*__Redfield, R.,__ *The Primitive World and its Transformations* (Cornell 1957)
**Roe, D.,** *Prehistory* (Berkeley 1970)

## Part II:

*__Aldred, C.,__ *The Egyptians* (New York 1963)
*__Daniel, G. E.,__ *The First Civilizations* (New York 1968)
*__Frankfort, H., et al.,__ *The Intellectual Adventure of Ancient Man* (Chicago 1946)
**Kramer, S. N.,** *The Sumerians: Their History, Culture, and Character* (Chicago 1963)
**Linton, R.,** *The Tree of Culture* (New York 1959)
*__Mellaart, J.,__ *The Earliest Civilizations of the Near East* (New York 1966)
**White, J. W.,** *Everyday Life in Ancient Egypt* (New York 1963)
**Wolff, W.,** *The Origins of Western Art: Egypt, Mesopotamia and the Aegean* (London 1972)

## India

*__Piggott, S.,__ *Prehistoric India* Harmondsworth 1950)
**Rawson, P.,** *Indian Art* (New York 1972)
**Wheeler, M.,** *The Indus Civilization* (Cambridge 1968)
**Wheeler, M.,** *Early India and Pakistan to Ashoka* (London 1959)

## The Minoans and Mycenae

*__Higgins, R.,__ *Minoan and Mycenaean Art* (New York 1967)
**Hood, S.,** *The Minoans* (New York 1971)
*__Hutchinson, R. W.,__ *Prehistoric Crete* (New York 1962)
**Taylour, M.,** *The Mycenaeans* (New York 1964)

## China

*__Creel, H. G.;__ *The Birth of China* (New York 1954)
*__Fairservis, W. A.,__ *The Origins of Oriental Civilization* (New York 1959)
*__Watson, W.,__ *Early Civilization in China* (New York 1966)

## America

*__Coe, M. D.,__ *Mexico* (New York 1962)
**Jennings, J. D.,** *Prehistory of Northern America* (New York 1968)
*__Mason, J. A.,__ *Ancient Civilizations of Peru* (New York 1969)
*__Wormington, H. M.,__ *Ancient Man in North America* (Denver 1957)

## The Middle East

*__Albright, W. F.,__ *The Archaeology of Palestine* (New York 1960)
*__de Burgh, W. G.,__ *The Legacy of the Ancient World* (New York 1960)
**Finegan, J.,** *Light from the Ancient Past* (Princeton 1959)
*__Frankfort, H.,__ *The Art and Architecture of the Ancient Orient* (New York 1971)
*__Gurney, O. R.,__ *The Hittites* (New York 1961)
*__Harden, D.,__ *The Phoenicians* (London 1962)
*__Roux, G.,__ *Ancient Iraq* (New York 1964)
**Saggs, H. W. F.,** *Everyday Life in Babylonia and Assyria* (New York 1965)

## Science

*__Bernal, J. D.,__ *Science in History, I* (Cambridge, Mass. 1954)
*Westermanns Atlas zur Weltgeschichte, I* (Braunschweig 1956)

# Suggestions for further reading Book 2


## General Accounts:

GREECE

**Andrewes, A.**, *The Greeks* (London 1967)

***Bowra, C. M.**, *The Greek Experience* (New York 1957)

***Finley, M. I.**, *The Ancient Greeks* (New York 1963)

***Kitto, H. D. F.**, *The Greeks* (New York 1957)

***Livingstone, R., ed.**, *The Legacy of Greece* (Oxford 1921)

***Rostovtzeff, M. I.**, *Greece* (Oxford 1963)

**Starr, C. G.**, *The Origins of Greek Civilization* (New York 1961)

***Tarn, W. W., and Griffith, G. T.**, *Hellenistic Civilization* (New York 1952)

**Toynbee, A. J.**, *Hellenism: The History of a Civilization* (Oxford 1959)

ROME

***Baldson, J. P. V. D., ed.**, *Roman Civilization* (New York 1970)

***Barrow, R. H.**, *The Romans* (New York 1949)

**Fowler, W. W.**, *Rome* (Oxford 1967)

***Grant, M.**, *The World of Rome* (New York 1966)

**Macdonald, A. H.**, *Republican Rome* (New York 1966)

***Rostovtzeff, M. I.**, *Rome* (Oxford 1960)

***Scullard, H. H., and van der Heyden, A. A. M.**, *A Shorter Atlas of the Classical World* (New York 1962)

***Brown, P.**, *The World of Late Antiquity* (New York 1971)

**Jones, A. H. M.**, *The Later Roman Empire, 284–602* (London 1964)

***Lot, F.**, *The End of the Ancient World and the Beginnings of the Middle Ages* (New York 1966)

## Special Studies

GREECE

***Andrewes, A.**, *The Greek Tyrants* (London 1966)

***Boardman, J.**, *Greek Art* (New York 1964)

***Bowra, C. M.**, *Ancien Greek Literature* (Oxford 1960)

***Clagett, M.**, *Greek Science in Antiquity* (New York 1963)

**Glotz, G.**, *The Greek City and its Institutions* (New York 1965)

**Rostovtzeff, M. I.**, *A Social and Economic History of the Hellenistic World* (Oxford 1941)

***Seltman, C.**, *Women in Antiquity* (London 1956)

***Tarn, W. W.**, *Alexander the Great* (New York 1956)

ROME

***Carcopino, J.**, *Daily Life in Ancient Rome* (New York 1971)

***Charlesworth, M. P.**, *The Roman Empire* (Oxford 1968)

***Duff, J. W.**, *A Literary History of Rome* (New York 1960)

**Ferguson, J.**, *Religions of the Roman Empire* (Cornell 1970)

**Gibbon, E.**, *The History of the Decline and Fall of the Roman Empire* (abridged by D. M. Low, New York 1960)

**Rostovtzeff, M. I.**, *A Social and Economic History of the Roman Empire* (Oxford 1957)

***Scullard, H. H.**, *A History of the Roman World from 753 to 146 B.C.* (New York 1969)

***Scullard, H. H.**, *From the Gracchi to Nero: A History of Rome from 133 B.C. to A.D. 68* (New York 1970)

**Toynbee, J. M. C.**, *The Art of the Romans* (New York 1965)

## Historical Fiction:

***Bryher, W. E.**, *The Coin of Carthage* (New York 1963)

***Graves, R.**, *I, Claudius* (London 1939)

***Graves, R.**, *Claudius the God* (London 1940)

***Renault, M.**, *The Last of the Wine* (New York 1963) (set in Athens during the Peloponnesian War)

***Shakespeare, W.**, *Julius Caesar; Antony and Cleopatra; Coriolanus*

***Yourcenar, M.**, *Hadrian's Memoirs* (New York 1963)

# Suggestions for further reading Book 3

## General Accounts:

### EARLY MIDDLE AGES

*__Moss, H. St. L. B.,__ *The Birth of the Middle Ages, 395–814* (Oxford 1964)

*__Wallace-Hadrill, J. M.,__ *The Barbarian West: The Early Middle Ages A.D. 400–1000* (New York 1961)

### CENTRAL MIDDLE AGES

**Brooke, C.,** *Europe in the Central Middle Ages* (New York 1964)

**Davis, R. H. C.,** *A History of Medieval Europe* (London 1957)

*__Hay, D.,__ *The Medieval Centuries* (New York 1964)

*__Southern, R.,__ *The Making of the Middle Ages* (New York 1953)

### LATE MIDDLE AGES

*__Hay, D.,__ *Europe in the Fourteenth and Fifteenth Centuries* (New York 1967)

*__Heer, F.,__ *The Medieval World* (New York 1970)

*__Huizinga, J.,__ *The Waning of the Middle Ages* (New York 1924)

### ECONOMIC AND SOCIAL HISTORY

**Ferguson, W. K.,** *Europe in Transition 1300–1520* (Boston 1965)

*__Hodgett, G. A. J.,__ *A Social and Economic History of Medieval Europe* (London 1972)

*__Latouche, R.,__ *The Birth of Western Economy* (New York 1967)

*__Pirenne, H.,__ *An Economic and Social History of Medieval Europe* (New York 1956)

*__Bloch, M.,__ *Feudal Society* (Chicago 1968)

*__Brooke, C.,__ *The Structure of Medieval Society* (New York 1971)

*__Power, E.,__ *Medieval People* (Garden City 1955)

*__McEvedy, C.,__ *Atlas of Medieval History* (New York 1961)

## Special Studies:

### BYZANTIUM

*__Diehl, C.,__ *Byzantium: Greatness and Decline* (Rutgers 1967)

**Obolensky, D.,** *The Byzantine Commonwealth and Eastern Europe 500–1493* (New York 1971)

### THE FRANKS

*__Lasko, P.,__ *The Kingdom of the Franks* (New York 1971)

**Bullough, D.,** *The Age of Charlemagne* (New York 1966)

*__Pirenne, H.,__ *Mohammed and Charlemagne* (New York 1955)

### THE CHURCH

*__Bainton, R. H.,__ *The Medieval Church* (New York 1964)

*__Barraclough, G.,__ *The Medieval Papacy* (New York 1968)

### WAR

*__Runciman, S.,__ *A History of the Crusades* (New York 1951–4)

*__Perroy, E.,__ *The Hundred Years' War* (London 1951)

### THOUGHT

*__Laistner, M. L. W.,__ *Thought and Letters in Western Europe A.D. 500–900* (Cornell 1957)

*__Brooke, C.,__ *The Twelfth Century Renaissance* (New York 1970)

*__Copleston, F. C.,__ *Medieval Philosophy* (New York 1967)

*__Knowles, D.,__ *The Evolution of Medieval Thought* (London 1962)

*__Wieruszowski, H.,__ *The Medieval University* (New York 1966)

*__White, L.,__ *Medieval Technology and Social Change* (Oxford 1962)

### ART

*__Talbot Rice, D.,__ *Byzantine Art* (New York 1968)

*__Beckwith, J.,__ *Early Medieval Art* (New York 1964)

*__Gimpel, J.,__ *The Cathedral Builders* (New York 1961)

*__Martindale, A.,__ *Gothic Art* (New York 1967)

## Historical Fiction:

*__Graves, R.,__ *Count Belisarius* (New York 1968) (the story of the sixth-century Byzantine general)

*__Muntz, H.,__ *The Golden Warrior* (New York 1949) (set against the background of the Norman conquest of England)

*__Bryher, W. E.,__ *The Fourteenth of October* (New York 1951) (another novel of the Conquest)

*__Oldenbourg, Z.,__ *The World is Not Enough* (New York 1967) (a panorama of twelfth-century Europe)

*__Waddell, H.,__ *Peter Abelard* (New York 1959)

*__Chaucer, G.,__ *The Canterbury Tales*

*__Shaw, G. B.,__ *St. Joan* (New York 1951)

*__Scott, W.,__ *Quentin Durward* (set in fifteenth-century France)

*__Hugo, V.,__ *The Hunchback of Notre Dame*

*__Reade, C.,__ *The Cloister and the Hearth* (a classic tale of fifteenth-century Europe)

*__Tey, J.,__ *The Daughter of Time* (New York 1970) (a fascinating rehabilitation of the reputation of Richard III of England)

# Suggestions for further reading Book 4


## Part I: India

### GENERAL

**Basham, A. L.,** *The Wonder that was India* (New York 1963)
**Garratt, G. T., ed.,** *The Legacy of India* (Oxford 1937)
***Rawlinson, H. G.,** *India: A Short Cultural History* (New York 1952)
**Smith, V.,** *History of India* (Oxford 1958)
***Spear, T. P.,** *A History of India* (New York 1965)
***Thapar, R.,** *A History of India* (New York 1969)

### RELIGION, LITERATURE AND ART

***Conze, E.,** *Buddhist Thought in India* (Ann Arbor 1967)
***Zaehner, R. C.,** *Hinduism* (London 1966)
***Alphonso-Karkala, J. B., ed.,** *Anthology of Indian Literature* (New York 1971)
***Rowland, B.,** *The Art and Architecture of India* (New York 1953)

## Part II: China and Japan

### CHINA

**Carrington Goodrich, L.,** *A Short History of the Chinese People* (New York 1959)
***Dawson, R., ed.,** *The Legacy of China* (Oxford 1972)
**Fitzgerald, C. P.,** *China: A Short Cultural History* (London 1965)
**Latourette, K. S.,** *The Chinese: Their History and Culture* (New York 1964)
***Creel, H. G.,** *Chinese Thought from Confucius to Mao Tse-tung* (Chicago 1953)
**Wright, A. F.,** *Buddhism in Chinese History* (Stanford 1959)
***Swann, P. C.,** *Art of China, Korea and Japan* (New York 1963)

### JAPAN

**Boxer, C. R.,** *The Christian Century of Japan* (Berkeley 1967)
**Sansom, G.,** *Japan: A Short Cultural History* (New York 1962)
**Sansom, G.,** *The Western World and Japan* (New York 1950)
**de Bary, W. T., ed.,** *Sources of Japanese Tradition* (New York 1958)
***Munsterberg, H.,** *The Arts of Japan* (Rutland 1957)

## Part III: Islam

**Arnold, T. W.,** *The Caliphate* (New York 1966)
**Arnold, T. W., and Guillaume, A., eds.,** *The Legacy of Islam* (Oxford 1931)
**Belyaev, E. A.,** *Arabs, Islam and the Arab Caliphate* (New York 1969)
***Lewis, B.,** *The Arabs in History* (New York 1966)
***Gabrieli, F.,** *Muhammad and the Conquests of Islam* (New York 1968)
***von Grunebaum, G.,** *Medieval Islam* (Chicago 1953)
**Southern, R.,** *Western Views of Islam in the Middle Ages* (Harvard 1962)
***Watt, W. M.,** *Muhammad: Prophet and Statesman* (Oxford 1961)

### ART AND LITERATURE

***Kritzeck, J.,** *Anthology of Islamic Literature* (New York 1964)
***Talbot Rice, D.,** *Islamic Art* (London 1965)

## Part IV: Africa

**Davidson, B.,** *The Africans* (London 1969)
***Davidson, B.,** *The African Past: Chronicles from Antiquity to Modern Times* (New York 1966)
**Fage, J. D.,** *A History of West Africa* (Cambridge 1969)
***Marsh, Z., and Kingsnorth, G. W.,** *An Introduction to the History of East Africa* (Cambridge 1965)
***Oliver, R., and Fage, J. D.,** *A Short History of Africa* (New York 1966)
***Seligman, C. G.,** *Races of Africa* (Oxford 1966)
**Trimingham, J. S.,** *The Influence of Islam upon Africa* (New York 1968)
***Willett, F.,** *African Art* (London 1971)
**Fage, J. D.,** *Atlas of African History* (New York 1968)

# Picture Acknowledgments

### Volume I Book 1

p. 8 Copyright by the California Institute of Technology & the Carnegie Institution of Washington. Photograph courtesy of the Hale Observatories; 9 Picturepoint Ltd; 10 *top* Chicago University Press/ Weidenfeld & Nicolson Ltd; 10 *btm* Weidenfeld & Nicolson Ltd; 11 Helmut Albrecht/Bruce Coleman Ltd; 13 Newberry Library Chicago; 17 Picturepoint Ltd; 18 Picturepoint Ltd; 19 CRM; 20 Dr F. Stoedtner; 21 *top* Jane Burton/Bruce Coleman Ltd; 21 *btm* E. G. Neal/Bruce Coleman Ltd; 22 Masood Quarisky/Bruce Coleman Ltd; 23 British Museum (Natural History); 24 British Museum (Natural History); 26 Erich Lessing—Magnum Photos from the John Hillelson Agency; 30 Michael Holford Library; 32 *top & btm* Sonia Cole/Weidenfeld & Nicolson Ltd; 33 Joseph Muench; 34 Picturepoint Ltd; 35 Dr F. Stoedtner; 37 Hamlyn Group Picture Library; 40 Michael Holford Library; 43 Picturepoint Ltd; 44 C. M. Dixon; 45 Hirmer Fotoarchiv: Courtesy M. Andre Parrot; 46 *left* Michael Holford Library; 46 *right* Michael Holford Library; 47 *left* Michael Holford Library; 47 *right* Michael Holford Library; 51 Mansell Collection; 52 Roger Wood/Picturepoint Ltd; 53 Michael Holford Library; 54 *top & btm* Roger Wood/Picturepoint Ltd; 55 National Aeronautics & Space Administration; 57 *top & btm* Roger Wood/Picturepoint Ltd; 58 *top & btm* Roger Wood/Picturepoint Ltd; 59 Picturepoint Ltd; 60 Josephne Powell/ Weidenfeld & Nicolson Ltd; 62 Michael Holford Library; 64 Courtesy of Sir Mortimer Wheeler/Weidenfeld & Nicolson Ltd; 66 Picturepoint Ltd; 67 Picturepoint Ltd; 68 *top & btm* Hannibal, Greece; 69 Hirmer Fotoarchiv; 70 *top* Picturepoint Ltd; 70 *btm* Erich Lessing-Magnum Photos from the John Hillelson Agency; 71 Picturepoint Ltd; 72 Freer Gallery of Art, Washington D.C. 74 *left* CRM; 74 *right* Black Star London; 75 *top* British Museum; 75 *center & btm* John Freeman/British Museum; 76 Michael Holford Library; 77 British-China Friendship Association; 78 Irmgard Groth; 79 C. A. Burland; 80 Museo Nacional de Antropologia & Historia, Mexico City: Collection Saenz; 81 Irmgard Groth: Collection Saenz; 82 Museo Nacional de Antropologia & Historia Mexico City: Collection Saenz; 83 Museo Nacional de Antropologia & Historia, Mexico City; 84 *top* C. A. Burland; 84 *center* Staatliche Museum für Volkerkunde, Munich; 84 *right* Cia. Mexicana Aerofoto S.A.; 86 Roger Wood/Picturepoint Ltd; 88 *top* Picturepoint Ltd; 88 *btm* Picturepoint Ltd; 90 *top* Roger Wood/ Picturepoint Ltd; 90 *btm* C. M. Dixon; 92 BPC Picture Library; 93 Picturepoint Ltd; 94 *top* Michael Holford Library; 94 *btm* Scala; 95 *top* Michael Holford Library; 95 *btm* C. M. Dixon; 96 *top and btm* Picturepoint Ltd; 97 Giraudon; 98 Bisonte; 99 M. A. Snelgrove; 100 *top* Michael Holford Library; 100 *btm* Science Museum London; 101 *top* M. A. Snelgrove; 101 *btm* Science Museum London; 102 Aerofilms Ltd; 106 *top* C. M. Dixon; 106 *btm* Roger Wood/Picturepoint Ltd; 107 *top & btm* C. M. Dixon

### Volume I Book 2

p. 114 BPC Picture Library; 115 Mansell Collection; 116 Michael Holford Library; 117 *top* Louvre; 117 *btm* C. M. Dixon; 119 C. M. Dixon; 120 Michael Holford Library; 121 C. M. Dixon; 122 C. M. Dixon; 123 *top & btm* Michael Holford Library; 124 Staatliche Antikensammlungen, Munich; 125 Bisonte; 127 Josephine Powell; 128 C. M. Dixon; 129

C. M. Dixon; 130 C. M. Dixon; 131 *top* M. A. Snelgrove; 131 *btm* C. M. Dixon; 132 Michael Holford Library; 133 Scala; 134 Michael Holford Library; 135 Mansell Collection; 136 C. M. Dixon; 137 *top* Mansell Collection; 137 *btm* M. A. Snelgrove; 138 *top left* Mansell Collection; 138 *top right* C. M. Dixon; 138 *center* Mansell Collection; 138 *btm* C. M. Dixon; 139 *top* Mansell Collection; 139 *btm* Picturepoint Ltd; 140 *top* Michael Holford Library; 140 *btm* BPC Picture Library; 141 Michael Holford Library; 142 *top* C. M. Dixon; 142 *btm* Mansell Collection; 143 Scala; 144 *center & top left* Picturepoint Ltd; 144 *top right* C. M. Dixon; 144 *btm left* Scala; 144 *btm right* C. M. Dixon; 145 *top, btm left & right* C. M. Dixon; 146 Picturepoint Ltd; 147 BPC Picture Library; 148 Scala; 150 Staatliche Museen, Berlin; 151 C. M. Dixon; 152 Snark International; 153 BPC Picture Library; 154 Michael Holford Library; 157 Michael Holford Library; 159 Bodleian Library: BPC Picture Library; 161 BPC Picture Library; 162 Scala; 163 Bodleian Library; 164 Mansell Collection; 165 Mansell Collection; 166 Bodleian Library; 167 Mansell Collection; 168 Bodleian Library; 169 Mansell Collection; 172 Erich Lessing-Magnum Photos from the John Hillelson Agency; 176 Hamlyn Group Picture Library; 177 Scala; 179 Michael Holford Library; 180 Erich Lessing-Magnum Photos from the John Hillelson Agency; 184 Michael Holford Library; 186 Bisonte; 188 Bisonte; 189 Erich Lessing-Magnum Photos from the John Hillelson Agency; 190 Erich Lessing-Magnum Photos from the John Hillelson Agency; 191 C. M. Dixon; 192 Bisonte; 193 M. A. Snelgrove; 194 Mansell Collection; 195 *left* Bisonte; 195 *right* Michael Holford Library; 196 Mansell Collection; 197 Bisonte; 199 Michael Holford Library; 200 Bisonte; 202 M. A. Snelgrove; 203 M. A. Snelgrove; 204 Bisonte; 206 M. A. Snelgrove; 207 Crown Copyright: Newcastle Museum of Antiquities: Weidenfeld & Nicholson; 208 *top* Bisonte; 208 *btm* Michael Holford Library; 209 Bisonte; 212 Erich Lessing-Magnum Photos from the John Hillelson Agency; 214 M. A. Snelgrove; 215 Scala; 216 Bisonte; 217 Anderson-Giraudon; 218 Scala; 221 Scala; 222 Scala; 223 BPC Picture Library; 224 Erich Lessing-Magnum Photos from the John Hillelson Agency; 226 Bisonte; 227 Scala; 228 Erich Lessing-Magnum Photos from the John Hillelson Agency; 230 Erich Lessing-Magnum Photos from the John Hillelson Agency; 231 C. M. Dixon; 233 Scala; 234 Erich Lessing-Magnum Photos from the John Hillelson Agency; 237 Erich Lessing-Magnum Photos from the John Hillelson Agency; 239 Michael Holford Library; 242 Erich Lessing-Magnum Photos from the John Hillelson Agency; 243 Michael Holford Library; 245 Bildarchiv Foto Marburg/BPC Picture Library; 246 Bildarchiv Foto Marburg; 248 Mansell Collection; 251 Michael Holford Library; 252 Mansell Collection; 254 *top* Michael Holford Library; 253 Mansell Collection; 254 *btm* Bisonte; 255 Erich Lessing-Magnum Photos from the John Hillelson Agency; 256 M. A. Snelgrove; 258 M. A. Snelgrove; 259 Mansell Collection; 260 Michael Holford Library; 261 M. A. Snelgrove; 262 M. A. Snelgrove; 263 *top & btm* M. A. Snelgrove; 264 M. A. Snelgrove; 265 M. A. Snelgrove; 266 Bisonte; 268 Mansell Collection; 269 *top & btm* Mansell Collection; 270 Mansell Collection; 271 Mansell Collection; 273 Michael Holford Library

**Volume I Book 3**

p. 280 Sonia Halliday Photographs; 282 *left* Louvre; 282 *right* Hirmer fotoarchiv; 283 *top & btm* Scala; 284 Scala; 285 *top & btm* Sonia Halliday Photographs; 288 Mansell Collection; 289 *center* Cabinet des Medailles, Paris; 289 *btm left* Sonia Halliday Photographs; 290 Scala; 291 Scala; 292 Scala; 293 British Museum; 294 Scala; 295 Scala; 296 Scala; 297 Bisonte; 298 Scala; 299 Mansell Collection; 300 Scala; 301 Scala; 304 Michael Holford Library; 305 Bisonte; 306 M. A. Snelgrove; 307 *top* Erich Lessing-Magnum Photos from the John Hillelson Agency; 307 *btm* M. A. Snelgrove; 309 Scala; 310 Michael Holford Library; 312 Michael Holford Library; 313 Museum of National Antiquities, Stockholm; 314 Museum of National Antiquities, Stockholm; 315 Michael Holford Library; 316 M. A. Snelgrove; 317 M. A. Snelgrove; 319 M. A. Snelgrove; 320 Scala; 328 M. A. Snelgrove; 329 M. A. Snelgrove; 330 Centre de Documentation du Monde Oriental, Geneva; 331 M. A. Snelgrove; 332 BPC Picture Library; 333 *top left* Snark International; 333 *btm* left Snark International; 333 *right* Mansell Collection; 334 M. A. Snelgrove; 335 M. A. Snelgrove; 336 M. A. Snelgrove; 337 BPC Picture Library; 339 Erich Lessing-Magnum Photos from the John Hillelson Agency; 340 M. A. Snelgrove; 341 *top* Bodleian Library; 341 *btm* BPC Picture Library; 344 M. A. Snelgrove; 345 M. A. Snelgrove; 346 Erich Lessing-Magnum Photos from the John Hillelson Agency; 347 Fitzwilliam Museum, Cambridge/BPC Picture Library; 348 M. A. Snelgrove; 353 Istituto Aerografico, Venice; 354 Erich Lessing-Magnum Photos from the John Hillelson Agency; 356 Dr F. Stoedtner; 357 Dr F. Stoedtner; 358 Giraudon; 359 Mansell Collection; 360 Bisonte; 361 Mansell Collection; 362 Mansell Collection; 363 Bodleian

Library; 364 M. A. Snelgrove; 365 BPC Picture Library; 366 Mansell Collection; 368 By courtesy of the "Wellcome Trustees"/BPC Picture Library; 370 Bodleian Library; 371 *top & btm* Bodleian Library; 372 London Museum; 373 Mary Evans Picture Library; 374 M. A. Snelgrove; 378 M. A. Snelgrove; 380 M. A. Snelgrove; 382 BPC Picture Library; 383 British Museum/BPC Picture Library; 384 M. A. Snelgrove; 385 Bisonte; 387 *top & btm* Bisonte; 389 BPC Picture Library; 390 Sonia Halliday Photographs; 391 Sonia Halliday Photographs; 392 Sonia Halliday Photographs; 393 Sonia Halliday Photographs; 394 M. A. Snelgrove; 395 Bodleian Library; 396 Bisonte; 397 Bisonte; 398 Mansell Collection; 399 Facetti; 400 Bodleian Library; 401 *top* Mansell Collection; 401 *btm* Bodleian Library; 402 Mansell Collection; 404 Bisonte; 405 Mansell Collection; 406 Colorphoto Hinz; 407 Bisonte; 408 *left* Facetti; 409 *btm* Bodleian Library; 410 Facetti; 411 Bisonte; 412 National Gallery, London; 413 Scala; 414 Scala; 415 National Gallery of Art, London; 416 *left* Mansell Collection; 416 *right* Scala; 417 *left, top right, center right* Scala; 418 Picturepoint Ltd; 419 National Gallery, London

**Volume 1 Book 4**

p. 426 Marilyn Silverstone-Magnum Photos from the John Hillelson Agency; 427 Michael Holford Library; 430 William MacQuitty; 431 *btm left* William MacQuitty; 431 *right* British Museum; 434 Spectrum Colour Library; 435 William MacQuitty; 436 Michael Holford Library; 438 Michael Holford Library; 439 Maharaja Manvinder Shah of Tehri Garhwal; 440 *top & btm* Camera Press Ltd; 441 Michael Holford Library; 442 Michael Holford Library; 443 BPC Picture Library; 444 Camera Press Ltd; 445 *btm left* William MacQuitty; 445 *right* Camera Press Ltd; 446 Barnaby's Picture Library; 447 Spectrum Colour Library; 448 Spectrum Colour Library; 449 *top & btm* Michael Holford Library; 450 Michael Holford Library; 454 Michael Holford Library; 455 Michael Holford Library; 457 Michael Holford Library; 458 *top* William MacQuitty; 458 *center* Barnaby's Picture Library; 459 Camera Press Ltd; 461 William MacQuitty; 466 Michael Holford Library; 467 W. Jenner/E. P. Wilkinson; 468 Michael Holford Library; 469 *top* Mary Evans Picture Library; 469 *btm* W. Jenner/E. P. Wilkinson; 471 Emil Schulthess/Black Star (N.Y.)/Transworld Feature Syndicate Inc.; 472 Emil Schulthess/Black Star (N.Y.)/Transworld Feature Syndicate Inc.; 473 W. Jenner/E. P. Wilkinson; 474 W. Jenner/E. P. Wilkinson; 476 Bisonte; 477 W. Jenner/E. P. Wilkinson; 479 W. Jenner/E. P. Wilkinson; 480 W. Jenner/E. P. Wilkinson; 481 Mansell Collection; 482 Mansell Collection; 483 Mansell Collection; 484 Wellcome Historical Medical Museum and Library/BPC Picture Library; 485 A. Horton; 488 W. Jenner/E. P. Wilkinson; 489 Freer Gallery of Art, Washington D.C.; 490 Bisonte; 491 Dr F. Stoedtner; 492 *top & btm* Victoria and Albert Museum, London; 494 Barnaby's Picture Library; 495 Michael Holford Library; 496 Michael Holford Library; 497 Michael Holford Library; 499 Michael Holford Library; 500 Spectrum Colour Library; 501 *top & btm* Barnaby's Picture Library; 502 Michael Holford Library; 503 *top* Barnaby's Picture Library; 503 *center* Spectrum Colour Library; 504 *top & btm* Spectrum Colour Library; 505 William MacQuitty; 508 Sonia Halliday Photographs; 509 Sonia Halliday Photographs; 511 Barnaby's Picture Library; 512 Barnaby's Picture Library; 513 Sonia Halliday Photographs; 514 Spectrum Picture Library; 516 Michael Holford Library; 519 Sonia Halliday Photographs; 521 Sonia Halliday Photographs; 522 Sonia Halliday Photographs; 524 Michael Holford Library; 526 *top & btm* Bisonte; 527 Bisonte; 528 Bisonte; 529 Michael Holford Library; 530 Giraudon; 531 Bisonte; 534 A. D. Roberts; 535 A. D. Roberts; 536 Royal Scottish Museum; 539 *top* British Museum; 539 *btm* A. D. Roberts; 540 *left* C. A. Burland; 540 *btm right* A. D. Roberts; 541 *btm left* N. David; 541 *right* British Museum; 542 British Museum; 543 British Museum; 544 British Museum; 545 British Museum; 546 C. A. Burland.

# Index

## A



## B

# H

# N



# O



# P

Walter L. Meagher *Project Director*

**Civilizations Book Team**

Adrian Brink *Editorial Director*
Germano Facetti *Design Director*
Mandy Merck *Associate Editor*
Brian Mayers and Associates,
Henning Boehlke, Eugene Fleury *Design and Cartography*
Fred Eden *Map Editor*
Edith Hathaway *Picture Coordinator*
Noel Wright *Time Lines*

# Z